Schuyler Colfax

BEYOND
THE
MISSISSIPPI
SAN FRANCISCO
NEW YORK
ALBERT D. RICHARDSON.

BEYOND THE MISSISSIPPI:

FROM THE GREAT RIVER TO THE GREAT OCEAN.

LIFE AND ADVENTURE

ON THE

PRAIRIES, MOUNTAINS, AND PACIFIC COAST.

WITH MORE THAN TWO HUNDRED ILLUSTRATIONS, FROM PHOTOGRAPHS AND ORIGINAL SKETCHES, OF THE PRAIRIES, DESERTS, MOUNTAINS, RIVERS, MINES, CITIES, INDIANS, TRAPPERS, PIONEERS, AND GREAT NATURAL CURIOSITIES OF THE NEW STATES AND TERRITORIES.

NEW EDITION.

WRITTEN DOWN TO SUMMER OF 1869.

BY

ALBERT D. RICHARDSON,

AUTHOR OF 'FIELD, DUNGEON AND ESCAPE,' AND 'PERSONAL HISTORY OF ULYSSES S. GRANT.'

(Issued by subscription only, and not for sale in the book-stores. Residents of any State in the Union desiring a copy should address the Publishers, and an agent will call upon them.)

HARTFORD, CONN.,
AMERICAN PUBLISHING COMPANY.
R. W. BLISS & CO, NEWARK, N. J. AND TOLEDO, OHIO.
F. G. GILMAN & COMPANY, CHICAGO, ILL.
NETTLETON & CO., CINCINNATI, O.
H. H. BANCROFT & COMPANY, SAN FRANCISCO, CAL.

Printed by Wiley, Waterman & Eaton, Hartford, Conn.

Electrotyped by R. H. Hobbs, Hartford, Conn.

Behind the squaw's light birch canoe,
  The steamer rocks and raves;
And city lots are staked for sale
  Above old Indian graves.

I hear the tread of pioneers
  Of nations yet to be—
The first low wash of waves where soon
  Shall roll a human sea.

The rudiments of Empire here
  Are plastic yet and warm;
The chaos of a mighty world
  Is rounding into form.

WHITTIER.

How canst thou walk in these streets, who hast trod the green turf of the prairies?
How canst thou breathe in this air who hast breathed the sweet air of the mountains?

LONGFELLOW.

PREFATORY.

Twenty years ago, half our continent was an unknown land, and the Rocky Mountains were our Pillars of Hercules. Five years hence, the Orient will be our next-door neighbor. We shall hold the world's granary, the world's treasury, the world's highway. But we shall have no Far West, no border, no Civilization, in line of battle, pressing back hostile savages, and conquering hostile Nature.

I have sought to picture a fleeting phase of our national life; not omitting its grotesque, lawless features; not concealing my admiration for the adventurous pioneers who have founded great States from the Mississippi to the Pacific, and made a new geography for the American Union.

It is discreditable to Americans—peculiarly so to those with means and leisure for traveling abroad—that they know little of this geography; little of the greatness, richness and beauty of our national inheritance.

In exhaustlessness and variety of resources, no other country on the globe equals ours beyond the Mississippi. In grand natural curiosities and wonders, all other countries combined fall far below it.

Its mines, forests and prairies await the capitalist. Its dusky races, earth-monuments and ancient cities importune tne antiquarian. Its cataracts, canyons and crests woo the painter. Its mountains, minerals and stupendous vegetable productions challenge the naturalist. Its air invites the invalid, healing the system wounded by ruder climates. Its society welcomes the immigrant, offering high interest upon his investment of money, brains or skill; and if need be, generous obliviousness of errors past—a clean page to begin anew the record of his life.

The themes are fruitful. The Pacific Railroad hastens toward completion. We seem on the threshold of a destiny higher and better than any nation has yet fulfilled. And the great West is to rule us.

The field is very large. In crossing it here and there, I have only lingered at some noteworthy points. Future writers will study and depict it, State by State, more minutely and more worthily.

NEW YORK, May, 1867.

POSTSCRIPT.

In view of the unexpectedly large and continuing demand for this work, a revised edition is issued, with a corrected map, a copious alphabetical index, and fifty pages of new reading matter, bringing it forward to the date of the completion of our first railroad across the continent.

NEW YORK, June 1869.

ILLUSTRATIONS.

ARTISTS' NAMES IN SMALL CAPITALS; ENGRAVERS' IN ITALICS.

CONTENTS.

CHAPTER I.

CHAPTER II.

CHAPTER III.

CHAPTER IV.

CHAPTER V.

CHAPTER VI.

CHAPTER XIII.

CHAPTER XIV.

CHAPTER XV.

CHAPTER XVI.

CHAPTER XVII.

CHAPTER XVIII.

CHAPTER XIX.

CHAPTER XX.

CHAPTER XXI.

CHAPTER XXII.

CHAPTER XXIII.

CHAPTER XXIV.

CHAPTER XXV.

CHAPTER XXVI.

CHAPTER XXVII.

CHAPTER XXVIII.

CHAPTER XXIX.

CHAPTER XXX.

CHAPTER XXXI.

CHAPTER XXXII.

CHAPTER XXXIII.

CHAPTER XXXIV.

CHAPTER XXXV.

CHAPTER XXXVI.

CHAPTER XXXVII.

CHAPTER XXXVIII.

CHAPTER XXXIX.

CHAPTER XL.

CHAPTER XLI.

BEYOND THE MISSISSIPPI.

ON the 28th of May, 1857, I left St. Louis, whirling westward by the Pacific Railroad of Missouri. It was begun in 1850 when there were but seven thousand miles of railway on the American continent. Now there are thirty-seven thousand miles.

Slavery had greatly retarded this richest State of our whole Union. Illinois, building the longest railway in the world and reaching every hamlet with the locomotive, was far in advance of her. Chicago, stretching out iron arms in every direction, was fast gaining upon St. Louis. But Missouri already felt the free atmosphere of her great metropolis and the surrounding States. She had plunged heavily in debt to inaugurate a generous railway system, guaranteeing bonds of the companies to the amount of many millions of dollars. Several of these roads, in default of payment, were afterward forfeited to the Commonwealth, and sold to new corporations at a heavy loss. But they developed the unequaled resources of Missouri, and were the entering wedge—the first deadly blow at her relic of barbarism.

We looked up at tall fantastic turrets crowning high limestone walls, and down into deep valleys of luxuriant oaks, elms, maples, black-walnuts, sycamores, and cottonwoods, with network of parasitic vines. In August the landscape is black with enormous clusters of elder-berries from which skillful housewives make a pleasant, domestic wine. Now, among dead, ghostly, standing trunks of girdled trees, thriving corn and tobacco concealed the rich, jet-black soil. Autumn corn-stalks often rise high above the log farm-houses, and completely hide them,—

'A mighty *maize*, but not without a plan.'

At the few very modern villages, we heard native depot-masters report 'Right smart o' sickness down the crick,' and little darkies warn each other, 'Get out of the way, the train has done started.'

Hermann, a German settlement upon our route, was then producing more native wine than any other point west of Ohio. Now, California far exceeds it. Wherever the sharp bluffs of Missouri slope to the southward, they are specially adapted to vine-growing; and the State is believed to embrace ten million acres upon which the grape will thrive—double the area of all the vineyards of France. The capacity of the Ohio valley also, is practically illimitable. Already the mellow lines of Longfellow are not merely the poet's fancy, but literal truth,—

'For richest and best
Is the wine of the West,
That grows by the Beautiful River.'

The next generation will see the choicest wines of the world made in California, Ohio and Missouri. They will be exported to every foreign land. Americans will give them to their children, and use them freely in their households as our farmers do milk, or the Germans their Rhenish wines. Men will have stimulants. No nation, civilized or savage ever existed without them. And wherever our native wines are introduced they diminish the consumption of whisky and brandy, and promote health and temperance. 'They who drink beer think beer,' but Catawba and Muscatel neither muddle the brain nor fire the passions.

Our train dashed up and down heavy grades, darted around curves and shot through tunnels, to the tune of Festus:

> 'By Chaos! this is gallant sport—
> A league at every breath;
> Methinks if I ever have to die,
> I'll ride this rate to death.'

The locomotive seemed rolling straight to the Pacific; but the fullness of time was not yet come, and it made a weary halt at Jefferson, one hundred and twenty-five miles west of the Mississippi. In the crowded intervening years, the iron horse has taken many a long leap, over prairie, across desert, and through canyon, until now he snuffs the salt air of the western ocean.

At Jefferson—dreariest and dismalest of State capitals—I took steamer up 'the great yellow river of the Massorites,' as La Hontan named it two centuries ago. Later travelers called it 'the Messourie.' It is still dense as then with the crumbling prairies which it cuts away to deposit along the lower Mississippi, or add to the new land at its mouth, rising from the gulf, as rose the primeval earth from the face of the deep.

John Randolph exaggerated in declaring that the Ohio was frozen over one-half the year and dry the other half. But Benton told almost the exact truth when he described the Missouri as a little too thick to swim in, and not quite thick enough to walk on. By daylight the broad current is unpoetic and repulsive—a stream of liquid brick-dust or flowing mud, studded with dead tree-trunks, broken by bars and islands of dreary sand, and inclosed by crumbling shores of naked soil. Its water will deposit a sediment an eighth of an inch thick upon the bottom of a tumbler in five minutes. Though at first unpalatable and medicinal, one soon finds it a pleasant, healthful beverage. I have seen errant Missourians so partial to it, as to urge that the pure waters of the Rocky Mountains were unfit to drink because of their clearness!

One of our eastern passengers, pouring out half a pitcher-full for ablution, was utterly disgusted with its color in the white porcelain basin.

'Here waiter,' he exclaimed, 'bring me *clean* water; somebody has washed in this.'

Its aspect quite justifies the Indian appellation of 'strong water,' and possibly accounts for the tendency of whites to the manner born, to weaken it with whisky. A novice fancies bathing in it must sadly soil any one not very dirty to begin with; but it proves soft and cleansing.

Only in the day's full glare is the stream revolting. Morning twilight, while the east is silvery, late evening when the west is blood-red, and moonlit night, all mellow and idealize it. Then every twig and leaf is penciled sharply upon clear sky, the turbid waters sheeny and sprinkled with stars; and the environing woods dreamy and tender. Often they are exquisitely tinted; and the night pictures of the despised Missouri, rival in beauty those of the familiar Hudson, and the far, stupendous Columbia.

The lofty ranges of Montana hem the chafing torrent into a narrow chasm, but through these prairies of Kansas, Nebraska, and Missouri, its valley is often ten miles wide. In its long-ago stalwart youth, the great river filled this gorge with a mighty flood. Now, old and shrunken, it zigzags across from hill to hill. Never having a high bank upon both sides at once, it will be difficult to bridge for future railways.

We found most of the banks low, wooded, miasmatic bottom-lands, dotted by a very few log-houses. Nature has been little disturbed by man. It is one vast wilderness with a tree blazed here and there. The soil consists of sand deposits, those of a single year often a foot thick. It has no cohesiveness, and is cut by the water like sawdust. The shifting channel sometimes moves forty or fifty yards in a single week. Hundreds of huge trees lately undermined, and still in full leaf, lie in the water, clinging to the shore by one or two claw-like roots. When these give way, the trees float until the roots grasp and firmly imbed themselves in the sandy bottom. Then the sharp stems, often entirely under water, form snags, the special horror of Missouri navigation. Always pointing down stream, they are dangerous only to vessels moving against the current. Thousands rise above the surface, frequently so thick that a boat can hardly find room for passing. Floating logs are caught upon these upright posts; the water pours over them in little cascades till they collect waifs and form a great tangled heap of drift-wood to be swept away by the first freshet. The *fatal* snags are hidden under water. When a steamer at full headway strikes one it often pierces her to the vitals. A few weeks after our passage, the Tropic, a first-class boat, moving ten miles an hour, ran upon one of these death-dealing spears. It penetrated her hull, pierced through the deck, pantry, and two state-rooms, and came out at the hurricane roof, breaking

A SNAGGED STEAMER.

the main pipe, deluging the cabin with hot steam, killing an engineer and leaving the wretched ship impaled like a fly upon a needle. No sagacity nor experience is proof against these unseen weapons, and one does not wonder at the wrinkled faces and premature gray hairs of pilots and captains. Even boats appear to share their terror. I could distinctly feel our steamer thrill with disgust when she ran upon a sand-bar, and shudder with horror at every snag grating against her keel.

Navigating the Missouri, at low water, is like putting a steamer upon dry land, and sending a boy ahead with a sprinkling pot.

Our boat rubbed and scraped upon sand-bars, and they stopped us abruptly a dozen times a day. From the extreme bow on the lower deck a man sounds with line and plummet. Every minute or two, he reports in drawling sing-song, 'Four and a h-a-l-f,' 'F-i-v-e feet,' 'Quarter less t-w-a-i-n,' (a quarter fathom less than two fathoms,) 'M-a-r-k twain,' 'N-o bottom,' until the pilot rings his bell and the danger is past.

Compared with ocean vessels, these river steamers seem light and fragile as pasteboard, and if they take fire, they burn like tinder. But many run fifteen miles an hour with the current, carry enormous loads, and often pay for themselves in a single year. Still their hey-day is over. The conquering railway robs them of nearly all passengers, and much freight. Gone forever the era of universal racing, with all its attendant excitements;—its pet steamers, high wagers, and fierce rivalry!

A good share of American human nature was exhibited by the old lady, who took passage, for the first time, on a steamboat, with several barrels of lard from her Kentucky plantation for the New Orleans market. Familiar with horrible legends of explosion, collision, midnight conflagration, she was tremblingly alive to the dangers of her position. She had extorted a solemn promise from the captain that there should be no racing, which relieved her pressing anxiety. But on the second day, a rival boat came in sight, and kept gaining upon them. Their speed was increased, but still, nearer and nearer came the rival until side by side the noble steamers wrestled for victory. Quivering in every tense nerve and strong muscle with the life and will and power that man had given them, they shot madly down the stream.

The passengers crowded the deck. Every pound of steam was put on. The old lady's nerves began to thrill with the general excitement. Life was sweet and lard precious, but what was death to being beaten?

'Captain,' she implored, '*can't* we go faster?'

'Not by burning wood,' was the reply; 'we might with oil.'

At that moment the prow of the other steamer darted a few feet ahead. This was too much.

'Captain,' she shrieked, 'if you let that boat pass us, I'll never travel with you again. Knock open my lard barrels and fire up with *them!*'

Upon this strange old river a boat stops wherever she likes, extemporizing a wharf by running out a staging to the bank for landing passengers and freight. After dark, we tied up to a tree in front of a wood-pile, where a shingle, nailed to a stake, was labelled 'Fore Dollars a cord.' By glaring torches we saw the well-drilled negro deck-hands follow each other briskly up the staging, out among the huge trees, and come back in endless procession, bending under enormous burdens of cottonwood. Almost as soon as our clerk could pay the owner, who mysteriously appeared from some hidden log-house in the forest, four cords were loaded, and we moved on. These dwellers in the wilderness, whose whole income is derived from selling wood to steamers, abound along the shores.

Thus we journey up against the strong current, which drains a continent, forming a great natural highway, for four thousand miles, from the gates of the Rocky Mountains to the southern gulf. This is the annual migration. Every spring hundreds of thousands of our countrymen go westward, as inevitably as wild geese fly south on the approach of winter. We are indeed 'A bivouac rather than a nation, a grand army moving from Atlantic to Pacific, and pitching tents by the way.' It is not from accident, or American restlessness, but Law fixed, inexorable as that compelling water to its level, or the magnet to its pole.

In all ages and countries, how uniform the course of civilization toward the setting sun—that Mecca which needs the memory of no prophet to draw thither its living pilgrims—that 'land beyond the river,' where Greek poet and American Indian, alike place the abode of their dead! From the dim confines of Egypt and China, has the spirit of Progress, like the fabled one of Jewish legend doomed to no respite from his wanderings, marched on—by Greece, Rome, and Western Europe, across the Atlantic, through Jamestown harbor, over Plymouth Rock—on, on, toward the serene Pacific. Ere long through the Golden Gate of San Francisco, it will go out by the islands of the sea to that dreamy Orient where it was born. And then—what?

On our crowded steamer every state-room is filled, and nightly the cabin floor is covered with sleepers upon mattresses. One can not promenade without endangering some unfortunate slumberer, and calling forth expostulations, or curses, according to his ruling temperament. Forward, near the clerk's office, is a convocation of restless passengers around a little table. Upon it a gambler with hang-dog face, wearing a white hat with broad band of black crape, has arrayed two or three gold and silver watches, with money, penknives, ear-rings, breast-pins, and other cheap articles, each in one of the little numbered squares of an oil cloth.

'Gentlemen,' he begins, 'you can throw the dice for fifty cents. For every figure you turn up there is a corresponding figure on the cloth, and you draw whatever rests upon it. There are no blanks. You may get this superb gold chronometer watch worth one hundred and forty dollars, or this magnificent English lever, which cost fifty dollars at wholesale, or this elegant silver goblet, cheap at ten dollars. You are certain to get *some* article worth twice your money.'

A backwoods Missouri boy in white wool hat and corduroys produces half a dollar, and with nervous hand throws the dice.

'All right, sir—two, five, fourteen. Fourteen draws these splendid gold ear-rings, worth three dollars and a half,' (actual value about one dime.) 'Try again, sir? Very well; here is your change. Luck again. Eight wins you this ten-dollar bead purse. Once more? Wait a minute; *this* gentleman's turn first. Sixteen. *You* have won that splendid enamel-cased ivory-handled bowie. You'll try another? Certainly. Twenty-one. By Jove! you have the silver goblet. At this rate you'll break me in two hours; but I won't back out—not one of the backing-out kind. What will I give you for the knife and goblet? Five dollars. Take it, do you? Here's your money. Who will be the next lucky man? Keep the game lively, gentlemen.'

The gentlemen do keep it lively. That re-purchase was a master-stroke. It brings down the half dollars like rain, and the gambler reaps a rich harvest. The secret is, that the three or four really valuable articles are upon figures which the dice never exhibit, and on the others there is a profit of three or four hundred per cent. The victims are as profound philosophers as those who proposed to buy all the tickets in a lottery, and thus be sure of the prizes! They have failed to learn the great principle of commerce, that goods do not sell for less than cost.

At the same moment the dim lights shine upon a serious group holding a prayer-meeting at the other end of the cabin, and we hear the faint, subdued tones of hymn, exhortation, and prayer. Was there a Missouri steamer pictured in the prophetic soul of old Daniel Defoe when he wrote,—

'Wherever God erects a house of prayer,
The devil always builds a chapel there;
And 'twill be found upon examination,
The latter has the largest congregation?'

Our passengers exhibit life in every phase. Here are young men and young married couples from eastern and middle States, seeking fairer opportunities and broader fields of effort in the ample, generous West. Here is the youthful Missourian with slouched hat, whose red flannel shirt is decorated with black anchors and glaring scarlet braid; the sallow, nervous merchant with his summer stock of goods; the well-to-do planter, tall and portly, with large, brunette wife, and two or three white-eyed coal-headed young Topseys—all returning from trips to St. Louis. Mingling with them are the young missionary in solemn black, and white cravat; the irrepressible agent of a new Kansas town proving incontestably by statistics and diagrams that his will become the largest city west of New York; the eager-eyed speculator bound for the land sales, with wonderful stories of his uncle who became a millionaire from Chicago investments, or his wife's cousin who made forty thousand dollars in six months upon Michigan pine-lands; the enthusiastic German whose blue eyes sparkle as they catch the gleam of a golden future, or grow tender in the subduing moonlight, as he talks of his boyhood's home on the Rhine. So our boat moves on, bearing its measure of hope and joy and sorrow—a *little* world, but holding in nice proportion all the elements of the great world without. Ruled by the same sweet love, and the same restless ambition—by memory whose tender sorrow no future can turn into gladness, and hope, the light of whose eager eyes no darkened past can quench.

We reached Kansas City, Missouri, in two days from St. Louis, and thought it excellent time. Once afterward, in low water, I was nine days making the journey. The cars now accomplish it in fourteen hours.

Kansas City perching on a high bluff commanding a fine view of the river for miles below, was a very important point—in a neck-and-neck race with Leavenworth and St. Joseph for the rich prize of the great commercial metropolis of the far West. In front of the town the broad bouldered landing sloping down to the water's edge presented a confused picture of immense piles of freight, horse, ox, and mule teams receiving merchandise from the steamers, scores of immigrant wagons, and a busy crowd of whites, Indians, half-breeds, negroes and Mexicans.

There were solid brick houses and low frame shanties along the levee, and scattered unfinished buildings on the hill above, where 'the Grade' was being cut fifteen or twenty feet deep, through abrupt bluffs. Carts and horses wallowed in the mud of these deep excavations; and the houses stood trembling on the verge as if in fear of tumbling over. Drinking saloons abounded, and every thing wore the accidental, transition look of new settlements.

'THE GRADE' IN KANSAS CITY.

But there was much stir and vitality, and the population, numbering two thousand, had unbounded, unquestioning faith that here was *the* City of the Future. A mile and a half from the river building lots one hundred feet by fifty were selling at from three hundred to seven hundred dollars. Lots three blocks from the landing commanded one thousand dollars, and a single warehouse on the levee rented for four thousand dollars per annum.

The proprietor of the local newspaper was an old editorial associate of mine. Four years earlier we had been connected with the Cincinnati Daily *Unionist.* The Kansas-Nebraska Act was then pending in Congress. With strong anti-slavery convictions, my co-laborer wrote pungent editorials against it; and headed the daily telegrams recording its progress, 'Latest from Washington: The Nebraska Infamy.' Now, his paper was emphatically 'border ruffian.'

He received me with cordiality, after the manner of the country instantly inviting me into the nearest saloon and, What would I drink? To my suggestion of lemonade, he replied with a glance at the rough crowd about us,

'That will never do in *this* country. Say whisky.'

Then we took a quiet evening stroll beside the strong, noiseless river, which shone and sparkled in the moonlight. He not only declared that denouncing the pro-slavery aggressions, would have ruined him pecuniarily; but seemed at heart thoroughly in sympathy with the community where he had cast his fortunes. Upon the organization of Kansas and Nebraska, societies for organized emigration sprang up in the North. Under their auspices many settlers, going in a body, obtained passage at lower rates. In a few cases, the fare of needy emigrants was paid by these societies. The South attempted similar movements, but with indifferent success, only 'Buford's men' from Georgia, and one or two other bands going in large parties. In the North, after the troubles began, there was a rage for armed emigration. Even churches and Sunday schools, took up collections for it, and the Quakers of Pennsylvania and Indiana found their peace doctrines yielding to their anti-slavery sentiments, and contributed money to buy Sharpe's rifles for emigrants. Whittier's lines, written at this period, were very expressive of northern sentiment:

'We cross the prairie as of old
 The pilgrims crossed the sea,
To make the West as they the East
 The household of the free.

We go to rear a wall of men
 On Freedom's southern line,
And plant beside the cotton-tree
 The rugged northern pine.

Upbearing like the ark of old
The bible in our van,
We go to test the truth of God,
Against the fraud of man.'

My friend thought the aid societies of New England war upon *the* institution of Missouri, and full justification for the hordes which had poured into Kansas, overawed the ballot-box and taken possession of the Territorial legislature. I asked if there was any doubt about the border ruffian incursions.

'O, no,' he replied, 'I have seen thousands of armed Missourians cross the Kansas river two miles from here to vote at an election, and return home the next day.'

He could not comprehend that the New Englander—who came as an actual settler to spend his life, and establish a home for his children—had a right to vote, whether helped by an aid society or not: while the Missourian, crossing the border for a day to put in his ballot by force and then returning to his home in another State was a criminal invader, striking at the foundation of free government.

I spoke of the wrong of slavery: of the fact that it was fighting all the agencies of modern civilization which must inevitably conquer it sooner or later. He replied:

'O yes; I thought so once: I was just as fanatical as you are. But I have learned better. It is a mere question of political economy. Kansas, like Missouri is adapted to hemp and tobacco, which can be raised only by slave labor. The negro is far better off here than in the so-called freedom of the North. These Missourians, too, are in dead earnest; they will fight and be killed to the last man, rather than let Kansas become a free State. And you know the whole South is behind them.'

Months afterward, when as a citizen of Kansas, I tried to help in her struggle for freedom, my friend rebuked me with great bitterness. But time at last makes all things even: he learned his error, became an eloquent advocate of emancipation, and springing to arms in our great civil war, shed his blood for freedom and the Union. Missouri, redeemed, regenerated, disenthralled, recognized his talents and services, and while I write he is one of her representatives in the Congress of the United States.

CHAPTER II.

After a single night in Kansas City, a morning walk of two miles up the south bank of the Missouri, over the richest black soil, shaded by stately sycamores, brought me to the Kansas or Kaw River.

'Kansas,' signifying 'smoky,' is the name of a degraded and nearly extinct Indian tribe. Lewis, and Clark, and all other early explorers, spelled it as pronounced, with a 'z.' It was first familiarized to American ears by the bill of Senator Douglas, repealing the Missouri Compromise—that little fire which kindled so vast a conflagration. Then many official documents and newspapers followed the early orthography, and to this day a few journals spell it 'Kanzas;' but the later mode is irrevocably established. At its mouth the river is three or four hundred yards wide. Its waters would be called muddy, east of the Alleghanies; but by contrast with the turbid Missouri they are pure and transparent. Crossing in a skiff I stood upon the soil of Kansas, already classic, and baptized in blood, a battle-ground of warring ideas.

I landed on the tented field, not of sanguinary strife, but of the city of Wyandotte. This prophetic Babylon was four months old, with a population of four hundred. Its beautiful site on a gentle, symmetric eminence, overlooks low wooded bottom-lands of Missouri on the east, Kansas City on the south, and the Missouri river for miles below. A few pleasant white warehouses and residences, and unpainted plank shanties were erected. Many more were going up; and meanwhile waiting settlers dwelt under heaven's canopy or in snowy tents. Everywhere busy workmen were plying ax, hammer, and saw; and the voice of the artisan was heard in the land. The settlers were merry over the attempt of 'Governor Robinson and a few other lunatics' to found a new town called Quindaro among the rocks and hills three miles above. The spot they had selected was utterly impracticable; they might as well have sought to build a city upon the Natural Bridge of Virginia, or the Palisades of the Hudson. This information was imparted to me with great zeal and emphasis immediately upon my arrival, and repeated at frequent intervals, during a stay of two hours.

Wyandotte shares of ten building lots were selling at eighteen hundred dollars. In founding a city, a few speculators become corporated, by special act of the legislature, as a town company. Then, if the land is already open for preëmption, they survey and stake out three hundred and twenty acres—the quantity which Government allows set apart for a town-site—at one dollar and a quarter per acre. But the large ideas of the West will never be satisfied with such a pent-up Utica. So they engage settlers each to preëmpt one of the adjacent quarter-sections, (one hundred and sixty acres.) The settler can only do this by swearing that it is for his homestead, for his own exclusive use and benefit; that he has not contracted, directly nor indirectly, to sell any portion of it. The invariable alacrity with which he commits this bit of perjury, is a marvel to strangers not yet free from eastern prejudices. When his title is perfected, he deeds his land to the corporation, and receives his money as per agreement. Thus the company secures from five hundred to a thousand acres, cutting it into building lots usually twenty-five by one hundred and twenty-five feet. Ordinarily ten lots are embodied in a 'share,' which runs in this form:

NEW BABYLON COMPANY.

No. 514. New Babylon, April 1, 1857.

This is to certify that ——— ——— is the owner of ten lots, viz:—Lot 6 in Block 19; 1 in Block 30; 20 in Block 45; 7 in Block 68; 23 in Block 104; 3 in Block 147; 14 in Block 170; 24 in Block 189; 12 in Block 241; and 17 in Block 252, in the City of New Babylon, Territory of Kansas, as officially surveyed, platted and recorded.

THOS. MUGGINS, *President.*
JOSEPH SNOOKS, *Secretary.*

(Transferable by assignment on the back of this certificate.)

If the town succeeds, the original proprietors grow rich. If it fails, having risked little, they lose little. The site I now visited was purchased directly from the Wyandottes, one of the three or four Indian tribes who own their lands in fee-simple.

Strolling on up the river, over an excellent road, I was in a richly wooded region, dotted with neat log-houses and well tilled farms, inclosed by substantial Virginia fences six or seven feet high. This tract, six miles square, is the reservation of the Wyandottes. Here the surviving members of that once dominating tribe have permanently settled. They sustain churches and free schools, speak English, intermarry with the whites, and embrace civilization more readily than any other branch of their race.

Two hundred years ago, the great Wyandotte nation dwelt on the shore of Lake Erie. There is a legend of a far-famed beauty in the tribe, who attracted many lovers, but none could move her obdurate heart. At last a stalwart chief laid siege to her affections. Scores of scalps hung from his belt, and he bore the scars of many a hard-fought battle. Though neither young nor fair, he had a face

'That glow'd
Celestial, rosy-red, love's proper hue.'

Before this ardent woer the dusky beauty relented; but she would accept him only upon solemn promise to do a deed which she was to name, after he should assume the obligation. It was rash; but red human nature is like white human nature, and when was lover known to hesitate? He took the vow. Then she made her demand. He must bring her the scalp of a Seneca chief, his friend and the ally of his nation. Entreaties and remonstrances were in vain, her hate was stronger than her pity.

It was hard, but the old brave had sworn by his great medicine, and, like young Melnotte, he kept his oath. He brought the coveted scalp to this modern Herodias; but the wanton murder inaugurated a bloody war which outlasted the seige of Troy. It continued for more than thirty years, greatly reduced the Wyandottes, and almost exterminated the Senecas.

Why are the banks of the Sandusky, less classic than the shores of the Hellespont? Why are Senecas and Wyandottes forgotten, and Greeks and Trojans immortal? The war of the former was three times longer, greater, more romantic. But the Homer was wanting to sing its epic.

> 'Vain was the chief's, the sage's pride;
> They had no poet, and they died.'

Three miles above Wyandotte, I reached Quindaro, also on the Indian reservation. It was in dense woods, among great ledges, sharp hills, and yawning ravines—the roughest site for a town which it hath entered into the heart of man to conceive. But here was absolutely certain to spring up the St. Louis of the Missouri river. The proprietors proved this to me incontestably by maps and statistics; by geography that never blunders and figures which can not lie.

Quindaro founded upon a rock would stand unmoved when the floods should come and the winds blow. The wildest lashings of the Missouri, could never disturb its rocky serenity. But Wyandotte was built upon the sand: its shore was constantly changing, and, as every body knew, the great bar in front made it impossible to land a steamer except at very high water. It was midsummer madness to build a town *there.* Lieutenant Governor Roberts and the other founders knew this, and only wanted to make money out of immigrants unacquainted with the vagaries of the great river. Quindaro would have five thousand people within two years; and—as I was a newspaper correspondent on delightful terms of familiarity with the public ear, and *as* I could serve them by writing the truth, the simple uncolored truth—a few choice lots could be secured for me at very low figures! They would double in value within three months.

Shares were offering at one thousand dollars, and soon after a single lot changed hands for one thousand five hundred dollars.

The New England founders were very much in earnest. They had built a three-story frame hotel, the largest in the Territory, and a steam saw-mill with an engine of one hundred and twenty horse power. Substantial edifices of stone and wood were rising. The main thoroughfare, Kansas avenue, at right-angles with the river, was being excavated into a formidable bluff, with the wild expectation of cutting through it. Ultimately, the work was abandoned and the street stopped midway in the hill against a rock and a bank of gravel.

'Quindaro,' was an intelligent Delaware Indian woman, wife of a white man, whom the town projectors had employed to purchase the land for them from the Wyandottes. She conducted the negotiation so skillfully, that her name was perpetuated in the new city. It signifies a bundle of sticks—strength in union.

In this town, four months old, was printed a creditable weekly newspaper, called the *Chin-do-wan*—(pilot, or leader.) Its proprietors were capable and hopeful: but after that experiment they retired from journalism. One left editing for agriculture, and is now a thriving Indiana farmer. The other exchanged types for theology, and is a prominent clergyman of Cincinnati.

A few days later, I took the stage for Lawrence, thirty-five miles in the interior. The route was through the reservation of the Delawares, containing two hundred and fifty thousand acres, with no white settlers except one Baptist missionary, the Rev. John G. Pratt. For fifteen miles we rode through dense hilly forests, with occasional Indian farms. Then we struck the rich billowy prairie—indeed a 'beautiful meadow,' as the Indian word signifies,—

> 'Stretching in airy undulations far away,
> As if the ocean in his gentlest swell
> Stood still, with all his rounded billows
> Fixed and motionless forever.'

Bryant describes with exactness the rolling prairie. It *is* like a swelling sea over which a magician's wand has stretched, transforming it instantly, and holding it in bondage evermore. Glancing over thousands of acres covered with tall grass, and dotted with groves, it appears the perfect counterfeit of cultivated field and orchard. One can hardly persuade himself that he is not scouring a long-settled country, whose inhabitants have suddenly disappeared, taking with them houses and barns, and leaving only their rich pasture and hay-fields. Not a habitation is seen; for the Kansas Indians build their log-houses only in the woods which here skirt the low creeks.

Wagon roads, revealing the jet-black soil, intersect the deep green of graceful slopes, where waves tall prairie grass with wild flowers of blue, purple, and yellow. Sometimes over hundreds of acres these blossoms predominate, making the earth blue or yellow instead of green. In spring bloom the flowers of modest, delicate hues; those of deep, gorgeous color flame in late summer and early autumn. Nature revels in beauty for beauty's sake alone. Before her simple children of the forest she sits in robes of state, outvying the purple and gold of Solomon. Slowly the myriad years come and go—upon her solitary places tender spring-time and glorious summer drop down their gifts from overflowing coffers, though only the steps of bounding deer, and the voices of singing birds break upon the lonely air.

The sky is of wonderful clearness. Narrow belts and fringes of forest mark the winding streams. In the distance rise conical isolated mounds wrapt in the softest of veils—a dim and dreamy haze. Upon our beaten road are immigrants with their household goods and household gods packed in long white covered ox wagons, teams hauling freight from the river, speculators working their way upon refractory mules, half-breed girls with heavy eye-lashes and copper-brown cheeks, jogging steadily along upon horseback, Indian boys mounted on black ponies, their hair decorated with feathers and their tattered garments streaming in the breeze as they dash by us, yelping 'How?'—the universal 'How-d'ye do?' of their race,—and footmen with cane upon the shoulder and carpet sack suspended from it, who look up wearily and ask 'How much further to Lawrence?'

We dined at a log-house on Wolf creek, kept by a 'civilized' Delaware family. In our presence the squaw thrust her hand into the boiler upon the stove, and with stout bony fingers took out the corned beef which was to serve for our repast. It was a trying spectacle; but no worse than one may sometimes see when led by fatal curiosity into the kitchen of a first-class hotel, where the fingers of perspiring cooks intrude officiously in the places where forks ought to go. In real, as in mimic life, he who would enjoy the play must not peep behind the curtain.

Our meal would not have tempted epicurean souls who hold a successful salad the highest triumph of human intellect; but it was sauced with hunger, and eaten heartily.

We continued upon the rich prairie. Here the once powerful and warlike Delawares, dwindled to a few hundreds, after a long retreat before the fateful army of civilization had made their last stand, and were waiting certain extinction.

We crossed the old bed, now dry and grass-grown, where the Kansas river flowed within the memory of living Indians. A few miles further, after half an hour's ride through dense heavy timber, over a jet-black soil of incalculable richness, we reached its present channel. The Charon who ferried our coach over, had a rope stretched across the stream, connected by pulleys with another

A PART OF LAWRENCE, KANSAS, IN 1857.

rope extending from stem to stern of his long flat-boat. By turning the head of his craft in the right direction he forced the currant to propel it to and fro—a bit of Yankee ingenuity which brought little work and many dollars. It was trustworthy as steam power, and cheap as air. It was like harnessing the forces of nature into a gig. Sneer not at its unknown inventor, unless thou too canst 'draw out leviathan with a hook, or his nose with a cord which thou lettest down.'

We landed in Lawrence, the pioneer settlement. One night in 1849, when this was unknown Indian territory, a party of overland emigrants for California chanced to camp near the Kansas river. One, Charles Robinson of Massachusetts, was deeply impressed with the beauty of the spot. The next morning the emigrants pressed on. They made scores of camps thereafter, on prairie slopes, in green valleys, among mountain glens, and by singing streams. They had the pleasure and peril, the suffering and adventure of all that Early Migration—that modern crusade whose unwritten history matches every marvel recorded in literature, from the Arabian Nights to the Book of Martyrs.

When the goal was reached, Robinson took part in the most stirring scenes of California. Among other experiences he was shot in a Sacramento riot arising from a conflict about real estate titles. The ball passed through his body, entering the stomach and coming out at his back; but he seemed bullet-proof and soon recovered. Speculators had laid out a city, and held property at high figures. But it was upon Government land to which they had no perfected title. So other settlers 'squatted' upon the lots, built houses, and claimed ownership; hence the Sacramento war. The courts sustained the speculators, and Robinson was imprisoned as a ringleader in the riots. But the squatters, who were largely in the majority, elected him to the legislature while he was still in bonds: so the governor pardoned him out, and he left his cell among the law-breakers, to take his seat as one of the law-makers.

Robinson returned to his New England home: but that shirt of Nessus, the restlessness born of border life, made him one of the earliest emigrants to Kansas. Through all the years, that green prairie by the softly-flowing river, had been photographed in his memory. Thither he led his company of pioneers, and there they founded the first town in Kansas.

Five miles south ran the little Waukarusa. Pleased with the name, they gave it to their nascent city. Their first *Herald of Freedom*—for a newspaper is mother's milk to an infant town—bears date 'Waukarusa, Kansas Territory, October 21, 1854.'

But the settlers soon learned this unromantic legend of the origin and significance of the name:—Many moons ago, before white men ever saw these prairies, there was a great freshet. While the waters were rising, an Indian girl on horseback came to the stream and began fording it. Her steed went in deeper and deeper, until as she sat upon him she was half immersed. Surprised and affrighted she ejaculated 'Wau-ka-ru-sa!' (hip-deep.) She finally crossed in safety, but after the invariable custom of the savages, they commemorated her adventure by re-naming both her and the stream, 'Waukarusa.' On reflection, the settlers decided not to perpetuate the story, and changed the name of their town to Lawrence, in honor of one of its most generous patrons, Amos Lawrence of Boston.

'WAU-KA-RU-SA.'

It had two weekly newspapers, a Congregational and a Unitarian church, five or six religious societies, and a large school-room, well furnished, through Boston liberality. On Massachusetts street were the ruins of the Free State Hotel, and for one-third of a mile on both sides, rows of frame trading-houses, with three or four brick and stone buildings, interspersed with a few pioneer log-cabins. On the elegantly lithographed map of the town the other streets were systematic and regular. But actually their buildings were too few and far between to indicate the thoroughfares at all. The eye only saw a smooth expanse of prairie dotted with a few plain frame dwellings. Lots were selling at from two hundred to two thousand dollars each, while wretched shanties, which could not have cost one hundred dollars, commanded eight dollars per month.

Lawrence was already historic. Here, in 1854, the vedettes and scouts and advance guard of Freedom in the great conflict, stimulated by the organization of Kansas and Nebraska, pitched their tents. Here, in 1855, armed Missourians took possession of the polls, and, later, placed the town in a state of siege; and men were killed on both sides. Here, in 1856, after a Lecompton grand jury had indicted as a nuisance the Free State Hotel, (a curiosity in legal proceedings,) and the citizens had given up their arms under promises of protection to person and property, the invaders blew up the hotel, burned the house of Governor Charles Robinson, destroyed two printing offices, and plundered stores and dwellings. Then blazed the flames of civil war.

Now they were extinguished, or only smoldering. The hotel ruins and two mud forts remained relics of those stirring times. Yet no halo of romance clothed the miry streets and rude scattered buildings. All was prosaic and commonplace, from the soiled floors and little dingy sleeping-rooms of the public houses, to the horse traders and town-lot speculators along the thoroughfares.

MUD FORT.

But at sunset climbing Mount Oread, still crowned by Lane's old stone fort, I viewed an evening picture of surpassing beauty. The site of Lawrence would have charmed Gibbon's irreverent monarch who declared that the Almighty never could have seen the kingdom of Naples, or he would have placed the Garden of Eden there. Nature made this for a city. It is flanked by terraced hills for suburban dwellings, commanding pleasant views of the town below. On the north glides the dark Kansas, with deep forest beyond. Toward the south, smooth prairie affords amplest room for expansion. From the rude hill-top fort, while day died and twilight faded, my eyes lingered upon the enchanting landscape,

> 'Till clomb above the eastern bar,
> The hornéd moon and one bright star.'

CHAPTER III.

FROM Lawrence, I took stage for Topeka, thirty miles further up the Kansas river. We passed a log-house, the home of Colonel Titus, a notorious Pro-slavery leader. One morning he offered a reward of five hundred dollars for the head of Samuel Walker, captain of a Free State company. According to an old East Indian officer, 'Hunting the tiger, gentlemen, is capital sport; but sometimes the tiger turns to hunt you, and then it isn't so funny.' This was precisely the experience of Titus. That very day with a party of followers, he was surrounded and besieged by Walker's men in his little dwelling. Its logs were bullet-proof; but through the cracks between them whizzed and whirled and screamed leaden missiles from the Sharpe's rifles of the assailants, who lay in the tall prairie grass. The Border Ruffians vigorously returned the fire; but every flash from the house was answered by a dozen from the prairie, and many a half-ounce ball came tearing in, wounding a man or plowing up the floor.

Titus received one of these ugly visitors in his own arm, and before night a white flag floated from the beleaguered cabin. The attacking party ceased firing, and approached. One by one, the inmates came out and gave up their arms. Titus did not appear, and it was feared he had escaped. But at last he was dragged forth from a closet. His boots and coat had been thrown off, and his shirt sleeve was red with blood. Running up to Walker, and clinging to his garments, he entreated,

'For God's sake, captain, don't let them kill me! Remember that I have a wife and children. For God's sake, save my life!'

Knocking down one of his own men, who attempted to shoot

CAPTURE OF COLONEL TITUS.

the crest-fallen fire-eater, Walker conducted the prisoner to head-quarters. The feeling was bitter; many Free State settlers had been murdered, and Titus was one of their most unscrupulous oppressors. A 'drum-head' council was instantly held to decide his fate. Daniel S. Dickinson used to say: 'If there be any thing beyond the fore-knowledge of God, it is the verdict of a petit jury.' His remark applies equally to a council of war. According to the proverb it never fights; but it may do any thing else under heaven. This decided to kill Titus on the spot. But more humane suggestions prevailed; the wounded prisoner was taken to Lawrence, kindly nursed, and liberated on the first lull in hostilities.

Topeka is an Indian word signifying 'potatoes.' Satirists translated it 'small potatoes,'—an interpretation which the Topeka philologists indignantly rejected. Here the Free Soil settlers had established the capital of their future State. I found it a hamlet of fifteen or twenty houses scattered over a green prairie, quite as beautiful as the site of Lawrence.

Kansas politics were curiously involved. There was a fierce struggle, and two conflicting governments. After a conflict which convulsed the country from Maine to Texas, the Congressional law organizing the Territories of Kansas and Nebraska was enacted in May, 1854. It abrogated the Missouri Compromise, but declared its purpose neither to establish nor prohibit slavery—only to leave the question to the actual settlers. The North regarded this as opening to servitude a region solemnly consecrated to freedom. In some communities bells were tolled, and the national flag lowered to half-mast. The South, especially Missouri, received it joyfully, convinced that it would make Kansas a slave State. Thus, in a moment, the great contest which had been growing for thirty years, was transferred from halls of Congress and eastern rostrums, to the soil of the new Territory.

At the first election armed Missourians overawed the polls in nearly every precinct, and chose a legislature composed of non-resident slaveholders. Bloodshed soon followed. A. H. Reeder of Pennsylvania, the first Territorial governor appointed by President Pierce, refused to ratify all the proceedings of these spurious legislators, and was removed from office upon a frivolous pretext. His successor, Wilson Shannon, of Ohio, was a mere tool of the Border Ruffians. So were most of the other Federal appointees. Some were notorious criminals, who should have been in penitentiaries, instead of representing the power and dignity of law and the National Government. When a murderer, sentenced to death in western Missouri, escaped from jail, a witty Ohio editor warned the sheriff to catch him at once, or the president would appoint him to some important office in Kansas.

Missourians, in the main honest, but ignorant, were inflamed by Atchison, the Stringfellows, and other demagogues, into the belief that abolitionists meant to establish a free State beside them, and 'steal' their negroes. Come what might, peace or war, they were bent on planting their pet institution in the new soil.

The members of the alien legislature left their Missouri homes to enact the farce of framing laws for Kansas. They made it an offense punishable with death to harbor or assist runaway slaves and rendered any man, woman, or child, circulating anti-slavery publications, or denying the right to hold slaves in the Territory, liable to imprisonment for five years. 'In Asia there are no questions—only affirmations;' and these profound Solons sought to transfer that oriental despotism to the far west. They required every voter to swear support to the odious Fugitive Slave Law. Then they enacted in mass the ponderous statutes of Missouri, filling a large octavo volume of eight or nine hundred pages. In too hot haste even for their clerks to change the proper names in these laws, they prefaced them by a general act declaring that wherever the words 'State of Missouri' occurred, all courts should construe them to mean 'Territory of Kansas.' The outrageous despotism of this unexampled legislation was only eclipsed by its ludicrousness.

The Missourians proposed, but the Kansans disposed. Only a few had been assisted to come by emigrant aid societies of Connecticut and Massachusetts, but an overwhelming majority of all were Free State men. They would pay no taxes, vote at no elections, recognize no officers originating with the Territorial legislature. They scoffed at its 'bogus laws,' and except in Leavenworth, Lecompton, Atchison, and Kickapoo—Pro-slavery settlements—utterly refused to acknowledge them, and would not suffer even a constable to serve a civil process under them. Occasionally United States troops were called out to enforce the statutes. Though the soldiers were insignificant in numbers, the people would not fight them, for they represented the National Government, however sadly its authority was abused. But they resisted the Missourians and Pro-slavery settlers in repeated skirmishes; and during this guerrilla warfare several wanton murders were committed.

The Free Soilers, in a delegate convention at Topeka, had formed a State constitution, ratified it by popular vote, elected Charles Robinson governor, with a full board of State officers, chosen a legislature, and applied for admission into the Union. Thus far Congress had refused to receive them as a State. But they kept this machinery of the Topeka government in constant readiness for use. Some advocated putting it in force at once; but the measure was revolutionary, and most preferred to wait until their oppressions should become intolerable. James Buchanan was president, and they shrank from an unequal contest with the National Government, likely in the excited feeling North and South, to light the flames of civil war throughout the Union.

I found in the contest two noteworthy features: (1.) Practically, it was hardly a contest at all. Despite the tremendous odds in its favor, there was no reasonable probability that slavery would take deep root. In the entire Territory, there were not a hundred bondmen, and all of them could have escaped during a single night, without much difficulty. Not fear of the institution, but knowledge that the ballot-box was violated, and force substituted for law, exasperated the settlers. (2.) The Free State men warred not against slavery in the abstract, only slavery in Kansas. Hundreds were Missourians or northern democrats—in deadly terror of being termed 'abolitionists,'—frightened at the mere mention of that mysterious specter, 'negro equality,'—but opposed to fraud, and believing unpaid labor prejudicial to the interests of their forming State. As yet comparatively few were anti-slavery men, either from sympathy or conviction. In adopting the Topeka constitution, an overwhelming majority had decided that negroes should not be permitted to live in Kansas.

Buchanan's administration was bitterly hostile to the Free State movement. Robert J. Walker, the newly appointed governor had just arrived from Washington. His eight-column inaugural, discoursed very learnedly and unintelligibly about 'isothermal lines' and prospective railways from side to side and end to end of the Territory, to be endowed by enormous land-grants from Congress. Upon the only question of living interest it was silent: but Walker was understood to acknowledge the validity of the 'bogus' laws, and to sustain the attempt about being made to collect the taxes under them. The people were as inflexibly opposed to these taxes, as were their New England ancestors to the duty on tea, or their Old England ancestors to the ship money of King Charles.

A Free State convention at Topeka, on the ninth of June, enabled me to study the celebrities. It was held in the open air, and attended by five hundred people. Their intelligence and culture surprised me. Delegates in blue woolen shirts, slouched hats, and rough boots, with bronzed faces, and unkempt beards, discussed freshly-sprung questions with rare fluency and grace. The standard of speaking was higher than I had ever found it in Congress, legislature, or national convention.

There was Robinson, the Free State governor, who had been held a prisoner, for months, by the Pro-slavery authorities,—tall, sinewy and bald, cold, argumentative and logical,—a walking embodiment of serene common sense, the brake and balance-wheel of his party.

There was Lane, uncouth and unscrupulous, zealous without convictions, pungent, fiery, magnetic, his keen, eager eye steadfastly fixed on the Senate of the United States,—contorting his thin, wiry form, and uttering bitterest denunciations in deep, husky gutturals. He was once lieutenant-governor of Indiana. Afterward, while representative in Congress from the same State, he voted for the Kansas-and-Nebraska bill. A dead politician at home, he came to Kansas to help make it a slave State. But *his* bread never fell on the buttered side; he was soon an Anti-slavery leader and major general of Free State forces in the field. If common report was not a common liar, his domestic life was shameless. The Border Ruffians declared that he was heartily in sympathy with them until the first 'bogus' legislature refused to grant him a divorce. He finally obtained the decree in court, but was afterward re-married to his divorced wife, and lived with her until his death. In pecuniary matters, his unscrupulousness was proverbial. Again and again, I heard tales like this: One day Lane said to a Lawrence merchant,

'I want five hundred dollars this morning. I have the money on deposit in the Ohio Life and Trust Company bank; but it will consume two weeks to write and get a remittance. Will you cash my sight-draft?'

There was no telegraph in those days, and eastern exchange was always in demand. The trader cashed the draft; and in due time it came back from the Cincinnati bank, endorsed—'Don't know the man; he never had any funds with us.' Lane declared it a mistake, but years after, he had never repaid the merchant.

Lane was an anomaly of our civilization. No other country could have produced him; our own never saw his parallel. With but narrow education, very little reading, and utterly uncouth manners, he was as truly a born orator as Clay, or Prentiss, or Wendell Phillips. No other American has lived in our generation who could sway masses and legislatures as Lane swayed these men of the prairies. In early days, without much fondness for fighting, he obtained extravagant military reputation, which extended to the remotest cabins of Missouri and Arkansas. Again and again, through those inaccessible regions, two hundred miles from railway and telegraph, have I been asked by settlers before the evening fire:

'Do you know that man Lane, up in Kansas? I reckon he must be a powerful fighter!'

A seemingly transparent demagogue, sooner or later betraying every cause and every friend, he invariably claimed to embody some great principle, and made the sincere, the honest, and the earnest, his enthusiastic supporters. In spite of his notorious personal character, he was twice elected to the United States Senate. For years he controlled the politics of Kansas; even when penniless carrying his measures against the influence, labor, and money of his united enemies. His personal magnetism was wonderful, and he manipulated men like wax.

Like John Wilkes, he had a sinister face, plain to ugliness; like him, too, he could talk away his face in twenty minutes. Defying every recognized rule of rhetoric and oratory, at will he made men roar with laughter, or melt into tears, or clinch their teeth in passion. In war times the Free State soldiers, half-starved, ragged and foot-sore, often grew weary of fighting the Missourians, and the power and patronage of the United States Government, and declared that they would go home to their suffering families and neglected cornfields, and leave the great question to settle itself. Then Lane would mount the nearest barrel or dry-goods box, make a ten-minute speech, and conclude amid a shower of cheers for free Kansas, the Topeka government and 'Jim Lane,' with his hearers, begging him to lead them against the enemy.

Repeatedly the United States marshal from Lecompton with an armed posse at his heels galloped into Lawrence with a warrant for Lane's arrest. But the Lawrence people were miracles of heroic reticence. The first person asked would perhaps reply that he 'never heard of any such man.' Another would report him 'gone down South.' A third saw him an hour ago, but thought he was now over upon the reservation. Then a young man with revolver at his side would step up and demand gravely:

'Hallo marshal, looking for Jim Lane?'

'Yes: where is he.'

'Just left town. I saw him start for Iowa ten minutes ago with a twelve-pounder under his arm.'

Amid the derisive laughter which followed, the angry officer and his posse would ride homeward. Before they were fairly out of sight, Lane would come strolling leisurely up Massachusetts street, wearing the old black bear-skin overcoat, which enveloped him winter and summer, and asking if anybody had heard a gentleman from Lecompton inquiring for him!

He was a man of rare physical endurance. Once when the routes through Missouri to Kansas were blockaded, he started from Nebraska on horseback, accompanied by twelve men, all anxious to reach Lawrence at the earliest possible hour, as their counsel and their rifles were alike needed. They rode hard, day and night, exchanging their horses for fresh ones with friendly settlers, and stopping only for meals. After they entered Kansas a cold, violent storm came on, but they did not halt. One by one they broke down, utterly exhausted, and took shelter until they could recruit. Seven miles from Lawrence, Samuel Walker, Lane's only remaining companion and a man of iron constitution, reached home so completely prostrated that he thought he could have gone little further had his life depended upon it. But Lane pressed on, reached the city alone, and after three or four hours' rest was attending to his ordinary business.

Now, with intense earnestness, talking through every pore of his skin, he warned the authorities not to attempt collecting the taxes or enforcing the bogus code. Though quiet on the surface, Kansas was a smoldering volcano. Those who would open the crater should beware lest its hot lava make many a Herculaneum and Pompeii even within the borders of Missouri. By promising donations of public land for future railways, Governor Walker would bribe them to fall down and worship their relentless enemies. Once upon a time another personage took the Saviour of men upon a high mountain, and offered him all the kingdoms of the earth—whole townships of rolling prairie, section upon section of the best bottom-land—when, as we all knew, the old scoundrel never owned a single foot of it!

There was Phillips, resident *Tribune* correspondent—of Scotch birth, restless-eyed, agile as a deer, able to out-travel any horse in the Territory, an invaluable scout, calm, with suppressed earnestness, integrity personified—whose terse, compact words exploded from his lips like percussion-caps, while hearers stood with heads bent forward and ears strained lest they lose a single sentence. Years afterward in the great struggle of which this was prelude and epitome, he did gallant service at the head of a brigade fighting for the Union.

There was Conway—slender, boyish in face, red-haired, of Baltimore birth and South Carolina education, yet the warmest Abolitionist of all,—a man of books, a student of Emerson, now at twenty-eight a judge of the supreme court under the Topeka constitution,—a speaker of flowing rhetoric and sonorous periods. In those early days when I believed slavery through the South would ultimately die a natural death, he said:

'You are wrong. It is a thing of violence, and can only go out in violence, with blood and the clash of arms.'

Yet in 1862, when representing Kansas in the national Congress, he alone among republicans openly advocated the recognition of the Southern Confederacy, and the abandonment of the war, as the shortest way to abolition. The Kansas legislature passed a unanimous vote of condemnation; and at the next election his constituents left him at home. There is a legend that when Andrew Jackson was president, complaint was made of the drunkenness of an army officer, to which he replied:

'Sir, the colonel's gallant conduct in the war of 1812 justifies him in keeping drunk during the rest of his life, if he sees fit!'

Upon the same principle Conway's faithful and efficient services in the early days might excuse all later aberrations.

There was Leonhardt, a Hungarian refugee, with splendid frame, noble head, and soul-full eye,—a born orator, speaking English like his mother-tongue,—with flowing, brown beard, a voice like Niagara, and a heart like Vesuvius. At the latest tidings he was a soldier in our war for the Union. Whither he has since gone I know not; but storms are his native element, and he is somewhere an actor in the world's tumult.

There was Daniel Foster, a new-comer, a Unitarian clergyman, full of fire and earnestness, believing in an anti-slavery church and an anti-slavery God. *He* sleeps in the valley of the James, where he led his Massachusetts company when a rebel bullet pierced his brain.

There was Dwight Thacher, editor of the *Lawrence Republican*, a young man eloquent from the State of New York. After enumerating the successive Kansas executives who had sided against the Free State majority, he added:

'And next comes Governor Walker'—

A voice in the crowd interrupted:

'Here he *does* come and no mistake;' and an open carriage containing the governor, his secretaries, and two ladies, returning from a drive, halted within a few feet of the speaker. In no wise disconcerted—for Kansas governors were never held in awe, and seldom in respect—Thacher continued, and the representative of Buchanan heard sentiments which he regarded as revolutionary.

The same evening a crowd gathered at Garvey's Hotel and clamored for a speech from Walker. Small in stature, with a squeaking voice, and without that mysterious something which we call Presence, the new governor did not impress them as a gun of heavy metal. When he spoke in 'the big bow wow strain' of wielding the power of the nation, he seemed

> 'A painted Jove,
> With idle thunder in his lifted hand.'

But he spoke plausibly and fairly, pledging his honor to resist any incursions or interference with the rights of the settlers. On the tax question he was profoundly silent. And here I may explain how this was finally settled. Missouri papers and democratic journals both in the Territory and throughout the North, urged the collection of the taxes, even by the strong arm of the National Government. But the people were inflexible. In Lawrence when the assessor asked one man for a list of his property, a mob began to gather, and he departed abruptly. Upon his arrival in Topeka he heard a party of young men step into an adjacent store and inquire:

'Can you lend us a rope?'

'For what purpose?'

'There is a bogus assessor in town, and we are going to hang him.'

The officer absconded again in what Choate used to call 'terrific and tumultuous haste,' fully convinced that the post of safety, was a private station. No further tax efforts were made.

During a lovely June night I returned from Topeka to Lawrence on foot, in company with Samuel Walker, the captor of Titus. He beguiled the hours with tales of the early troubles. The Border Ruffians burned his house and barn, and destroyed his growing crops. Hunted like a wild beast, he had several narrow escapes. Repeatedly, while his pursuers were close at hand, he hid in a field of tall corn, and he thought it the safest ambush in the world. For weeks he only entered his dwelling by stealth. Once, going in suddenly, he found seven of the enemy waiting for him. Fortunately they did not know him, and even his children, six or seven years old, had been educated by constant peril to such caution that they made no sign of recognition. It was raining, and he addressed his wife as a stranger:

'I am on my way to Lecompton, madam, and called to borrow an overcoat. Can you lend me one?'

'I have one here,' she replied; 'but it belongs to my husband, who will be at home in a day or two, and may want it.'

'Oh, well; I shall return in the morning and will leave it. Good day, madam.'

So he escaped, but feeling as he phrased it, 'pretty streaked' until once more out of sight. Brave, modest and true, Walker inspired warmest affection. The Free State men afterward elected him sheriff of Douglas County, and in the war of the Rebellion, he was colonel of a Kansas regiment.

Once more in Lawrence, I saw how debts were collected in the absence of law. A mechanic had sold a street-sprinkler for which the purchaser, though profuse in promises, had never paid. One morning the creditor and two friends, armed with revolvers, met the debtor on the street and made a final demand. The money was not forthcoming, so they unharnessed his horse and drew the cart back to the shop of the original owner. The water-man swore and threatened lustily, but finding a majority both in numbers and weapons against him, finally yielded to inexorable destiny. It was a writ of replevin on first principles.

Ordinarily, disputed accounts were left to referees. Much business was done on credit; but obligations were met with great promptness. If laws for the collection of debts were everywhere abolished, would it not be better for all honest men? Gambling obligations—the only ones which cannot be enforced by law—are the only debts always promptly paid.

Lawrence was distinctively a Yankee town. The 'melodious twang' of New England sounded on all the streets. In Lecompton and Atchison were heard 'whar,' 'thar,' and 'reckon;' in Lawrence 'neow,' 'idear,' and 'guess.' During the early troubles, when it was difficult to approach Kansas save through Missouri, the Border Ruffians placed a guard at the chief ferry, and compelled every emigrant who attempted to cross to say 'cow.' If the unfailing 'keow' of the Yankee betrayed him, he was turned back again.

Three thousand years ago the Children of Israel had a test precisely similar. The Gileadites held the passage of the Jordan, and whenever a fugitive sought to cross asked him:

'Art thou an Ephraimite?' If he replied, 'Nay,' they commanded him to say 'shibboleth,'—an ear of corn. If he rendered it 'sibboleth,' they knew he was of the tribe of Ephraim, unable to give the sound '*sh*' and killed him on the spot. 'And thus,' according to the book of Judges, 'there fell forty and two thousand.'

Dialect is undisguisable. It is asserted that eighty years ago the county of every member of the British Parliament might be known by his speech. Five hundred years ago, the gentle Dante counted one hundred distinct dialects on the little Italian peninsula. And in the judgment hall the Jews said to the terrified apostle:—'Surely thou art a Galilean, for thy speech bewrayeth thee.'

I reached Quindaro again, in season to attend a public meeting. There were always public meetings. The people were the victims of oratory. Almost nightly a hand-bell would gather together from fifty to two hundred citizens, who would elect a president and secretary, call upon two or three fluent speakers to harangue them, pass resolutions and then adjourn, to await the record of their proceedings in the next issue of the *Chin-do-wan.*

This was a temperance meeting. Quindaro was distinctively a temperance town. Lots had been deeded with the express stipulation that they should not be occupied by liquor sellers. Still several low groggeries, fountains of bad habits and worse whisky had arisen to fright the isle from its propriety. All the leading women joined in a petition to the men 'to take speedy and efficient measures for casting out the vile demon.'

The meeting accordingly selected three of its members to appoint a vigilance committee of twenty, to cast out the vile demon. It was organized forthwith, and sallied out at daylight the next morning. The first saloon was kept by a herculean German who, refusing to give up his keys, retreated behind his bar, pointing two enormous self-cocking six-shooters at the invaders, and swore he would blow out the brains of the first man molesting him or his whisky. Several of the visitors also drew revolvers, but the German's eye was wicked, and they hesitated.

Their leader, a lithe, young man, armed only with a whalebone cane, had served in Lane's army and smelt gunpowder. Turning to his companions, he said quietly:

'Kill him, boys, if he shoots me.'

Then he sprang over the bar and wrested both revolvers from the plucky but overpowered Teuton. But suddenly the German's wife, awakened by the noise, rushed from her bed-room to the scene of conflict, dragging a clothes-line which had caught her foot, and which was about the only thing in the line of clothes adorning her person. She flung hard words, broken English, and all other loose articles she could lay hands upon, at her unceremonious callers. But they unlocked a closet, rolled out and emptied

A PROHIBITORY LAW.

two casks of whisky, and one of brandy. Two other saloons were similarly visited and purged. The Irish keeper of one vowed by all the saints that he had 'not a drap of the crathur,' and none was discovered in his house; but a mound of fresh earth, just outside suggested dark suspicions; and from it was exhumed a barrel of whisky, which was soon spilled, to his sore discomfiture. Neither ale nor beer was destroyed; and just after sunrise the committee separated for breakfast. A few weeks later, I encountered most of them at a champagne supper in the very hotel where they had organized, and from whose front steps some had addressed the temperance meeting which gave them authority.

'Strange all this difference should be,
'Twixt tweedle-dum and tweedle-dee.'

CHAPTER IV.

My next trip was to Leavenworth, then, as now, the largest town in Kansas. It was two years and a half old, with a population of four thousand. Fort Leavenworth—two miles above, occupying one of the most beautiful sites on the Missouri—gave it life and stimulated its growth.

Steamers were discharging freight at the levee, new buildings were springing up, all was activity. As yet brick and stone were little used, and timber was a serious want. The chief native species are black-walnut, oak and cottonwood. The latter, which resembles the New England forest-poplar, but is even softer, cutting almost like cork, was largely used as a make-shift. When put in green and left unpainted, it warps wonderfully, making the house twist about like a corkscrew. Pine from Minnesota and western New York was largely in demand at one hundred dollars per thousand. None grows nearer than the Rocky Mountains, six hundred miles to the west.

Building lots, twenty-five feet by one hundred and twenty-five, upon the river landing, were valued at ten thousand dollars. Three or four blocks back, they sold for two thousand, and on the hills half a mile away, for twelve hundred. Prices were fast rising, money plentiful, and everybody speculating. One lot, which cost eight dollars six months before, had just sold for twenty-two hundred dollars. Eleven thousand dollars was now offered for eleven lots purchased for fifty-five dollars a year and a half earlier. Suburban lands three miles from the river, bought during the previous winter for one hundred dollars per acre, were now divided into building lots which commanded from one hundred to two hundred dollars each. Hotels were crowded with strangers, eager to invest. Almost any one could borrow gold without security or even a written promise to pay; and the faith was universal that to morrow should be as this day and yet more abundant.

I left Leavenworth on foot. Back of the young, crude, life-full city, the prairie exhibited rapid settlements. Ten miles out, I supped with a family of intelligent Missourians, who had lived here for eighteen months. Half of their quarter-section was fenced and in corn. The claim was not yet preëmpted; they must pay the Government one dollar twenty-five cents per acre before receiving a perfect title, yet they had refused four thousand dollars for it.

The day had been hot as the one in which Sidney Smith declared himself compelled to take off his flesh, and sit in his bones. But the evening air was cool and fragrant, and the night brought its blessing of peace. I could feel and almost *hear* the brooding stillness that rested upon the wide-spread prairies. At nine o'clock, meeting a lank settler upon a little mule, I asked the distance to Judge Young's, whither I had been directed for lodgings; for on the frontier every farmer has accommodations for man and beast, and welcomes guests, who bring him the latest news from the outside world. The rider, long and ludicrous in the dim starlight, replied:

'Two miles; but I reckon you won't get to stop thar. The Judge is away, and his family is sick. But thar's a place just over yon ravine—Hayes's—whar I think they'll keep you.'

'What kind of people are they?'

'Well,' (hesitatingly,) 'they'll treat you well, and give you good accommodations. A heap of travelers stops thar.'

He rode beside me toward the house. My further inquiries about the family he evaded, replying only that they were from Missouri. We reached the dwelling to be greeted by two ferocious dogs. For ten minutes we shouted and rapped, meeting with no response. There were sounds within, but the door was secured. At last said my despairing guide:

'We mought as well give it up. My place is over here three-quarters of a mile. We're poorly fixed for strangers, but it's good enough for us all the time; so I reckon you can stand it a single night. Come, and you're welcome. The fact is,' he continued, as I walked beside his horse, 'Charley Hayes, who lives in that house, is supposed to be the murderer of Buffum.* I am deputy sheriff, and have had to arrest him twice in the night. They knew my voice, and probably thought I was after him again. Perhaps he has been up to some new devilment, and expects me. They are my neighbors, and I avoided answering your question, because I didn't want to say any thing fornenst them. Beside, they would have treated you well, and they keep strangers almost every night.'

We were now on my guide's farm, which he declared 'bully land.' He lariated his mule upon the prairie to graze; (tied him to a stake by a long rope or lariat.) Then with a pull at his hospitable whisky flask, we entered his one-story log-cabin by a door which compelled us to bend low. Striking a light he illuminated the single room of the dwelling. It had a huge fireplace, and was neatly 'chinked' and 'daubed;' (the cracks between the logs filled with bits of wood and plastered with mud.) His wife and baby occupied one bed, his father and brother, both long and lank like himself, the other, while a second brother of equal dimensions, with two white-headed children, rested upon a mattress on the floor.

Picking up his youthful soundly-slumbering scions as if they had been sticks of wood, he deposited them beside their mother, and called forth his brother from the feathery deep. Standing upright in a single garment, that bewildered Kansan filled the mathematical definition of a line: length without breadth or thickness. The mattress was re-arranged, and lying between these prairie twins, I soon felt with Solomon that the sleep of a laboring man is sweet.

An hour after daylight I awoke, to find the family all up and grouped around the old patriarch, who was in the act of cocking my revolver, which I had left on the mantle before going to bed. There was a certain unpleasantness in its sharp click; for the house stood alone on the prairie, and this was Kansas, from which almost daily for two years I had been wont to read some tale of blood in the damp newspaper over my morning coffee. But mine host was merely scrutinizing the weapon to learn how it worked.

---

* A Free State settler wantonly killed two years before.

After the whisky flask went round, we breakfasted on strong coffee, fried bacon and corn-dodgers—little oblong loaves of corn-bread, baked in the ashes, which only attain perfection in Kentucky. These were the genuine articles, and prepared me for the assurance that my entertainers were Kentuckians.

'In fact,' they added, 'we are Pro-slavery men—Border Ruffians.'

What could I reply, save that I was a Yankee Abolitionist? They supposed Kansas was bound to be a free State, but hoped bloodshed was over, and that all future contests would be decided by the ballot-box. When I took out my purse, they insisted that they did not invite strangers to their house and receive money from them; and after mutual good wishes, we parted.

Five miles beyond, on the Missouri, I reached Sumner, barely a month old. The first landing from the river here, was made in the summer of 1855. The Border Ruffians tarred and feathered the Reverend Pardee Butler, and then placed him upon a raft to float down the Missouri. The facetious scoundrels ran up a flag from the craft with these inscriptions:

'Eastern Emigrant Aid Express.'

'Agent for the Underground Railroad.'

'The way they are served in Kansas.'

'For Boston.'

'Cargo insured; unavoidable Dangers of the Missourians and the Missouri River excepted.'

'Let future emissaries from the North beware. Our Hemp Crop is sufficient for all such scoundrels.'

Mr. Butler, thankful to escape even thus from his enemies, finally effected a debarkation in the silent, unbroken forest, where Sumner now stands.

I found the town with few houses completed, but many in progress. Its aspect was promising, and its shares sold for one hundred dollars. Six weeks later they had doubled in value. Three years later, they were without money and without price—and would not command ten dollars a dozen.

Three miles further up the river, I came to Atchison—the most violent Pro-slavery settlement in Kansas. It was named for the chief Border Ruffian leader, David R. Atchison, of Missouri, who had fallen from his high estate, as president of the national Senate, and acting vice-president of the republic, to organize and lead armed and criminal invasions into the new Territory.

Recently, General* S. C. Pomeroy, and other Free State men, had bought heavy interests and settled here, but they were subjected to perils and indignities. When three or four wanted to converse with me upon political subjects, they carefully locked the doors of the little law office where we sat, and we talked in whispers, like guilty conspirators. That evening I dined at the house of the stanchest of them all. Specially obnoxious to the enemy, he had been dogged, insulted and threatened; and his young wife was fearful for his safety at the approaching elections. With pathetic glances at their sleeping child, she implored him to return to their Ohio home. But that mild, determined man had come to stay; and stay he did, and is yet a leading citizen of Kansas.

Atchison wore the dull, thriftless air of Pro-slavery towns; for Border Ruffians still haunted it: but property was already high, and the new settlers had given it a fresh impetus.

Doniphan, five miles farther up, named from another invading Missouri leader, was also a Pro-slavery settlement. But General Lane and other Free Soilers were now joint owners. Fifteen hundred acres were laid out in building lots, and held a population of three hundred. Shares were selling at five hundred dollars.

This was the limit of my journeyings up the river; but in Doniphan I heard much of Geary City, a few miles above, where shares had advanced from two hundred and fifty to four hundred dollars within a week; and of Elwood, still beyond, which exhibited similar marvels.

The Missouri flows along the eastern border of Kansas for one hundred and twenty-five miles. On its bank fourteen 'cities'

---

* When on his way to Kansas, he was accompanied by a friend, also from Massachusetts, familiar with the western fondness for titles, who said: 'Pomeroy, a man on the frontier, without a handle to his name, is nobody. Now what shall we call you? You were once a member of the Massachusetts *General* Court, (legislature.) That title sounds well, and you must have it.' The new-comer was accordingly introduced as 'General' Pomeroy, and never lost the prefix afterward.

were begun. In each property was enormously high; and the inhabitants firmly believed it destined to be the St. Louis of the far West.

When Themistocles at a feast was asked to play upon a musical instrument, he replied: 'I cannot fiddle; but I know how to make a small town a great city.' Every Kansan thought himself a Themistocles. Nearly all transactions were cash, and money was plentiful, though commanding from three to five per cent. a month. Shares often doubled in price in two or three weeks. Servant girls speculated in town lots. From enormous buff envelopes men would take scores of certificates elegantly printed in colors, representing property in various towns, and propose to sell thousands of dollars worth, certain to quadruple in value within a few months! If you declined to purchase, they might ask to borrow six shillings to pay their washerwoman, or twelve dollars for a week's board. Three days later, meeting you again, they would cancel the debt from pockets burdened with twenty-dollar gold pieces, and offer you five hundred or a thousand dollars for a few days, if it would be the slightest accommodation.

This pantomime of actual life began with beggars clothed in rags. But the genie of real estate speculation touched them with his wand, and lo! the tatters were gone, and they stood clothed in purple, adorned with jewels, and weighed down with gold. Young men who never before owned fifty dollars at once, a few weeks after reaching Kansas possessed full pockets, with town shares by the score; and talked of thousands as if they had been rocked in golden cradles and fed with the famous Miss Kilmansegg's golden spoon. On a smaller scale was repeated the story of that Minnesota wood-sawyer who accumulated half a million in half a year.

On paper, all these towns were magnificent. Their superbly lithographed maps adorned the walls of every place of resort. The stranger studying one of these, fancied the New Babylon surpassed only by its namesake of old. Its great parks, opera-houses, churches, universities, railway depots and steamboat landings made New York and St. Louis insignificant in comparison. But if the new-comer had the unusual wisdom to visit the prophetic city before purchasing lots, he learned the difference

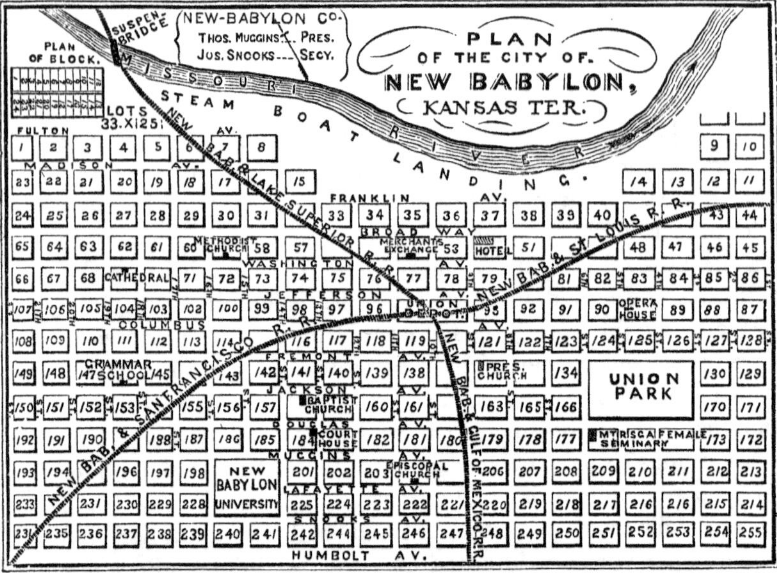

THE CITY OF NEW BABYLON ON PAPER.

between fact and fancy. The town might be composed of twenty buildings; or it might not contain a single human habitation. In most cases, however, he would find one or two rough cabins, with perhaps a tent and an Indian canoe on the river in front of the 'levee.' Any thing was marketable. Shares in interior towns of one or two shanties, sold readily for a hundred dollars. Wags proposed an act of Congress reserving some land for farming purposes before the whole Territory should be divided into city lots. Towns enough were started for a State containing four millions of people.

It was not a swindle, but a mania. The speculators were quite as insane as the rest,—

'Themselves deceiving and themselves deceived.'

Any one of them could have turned his property into cash at enormous profits. But all thought the inflation would continue; and I do not remember a single person who sold out, except to make new investments.

Much eastern capital was sunk in these paper cities. When the collapse came it was like the crushing of an egg-shell. Again the genie waved his wand, and presto! the spangles and gold disappeared, and the princes of an hour were beggars again. The shares had no more market value than town lots in the moon. Cities died, inhabitants deserted, houses were torn down.

THE CITY OF NEW BABYLON IN FACT.

The reaction caused little actual suffering; for in the elastic new countries, men's fortunes, as the Chinese proverb avers of women's hearts, stand a great deal of breaking. But the speculation-fever unsettled the mind, bred extravagant habits and contempt for the slow accumulations of legitimate business.

Of the fourteen river 'cities,' Leavenworth, Wyandotte, and Atchison alone survive. He who died o' Wednesday is no more lifeless than the other moths of cities which flitted for a noonday hour. In degree, this is the history of all new States. Here at least, involuntary man is as profuse as voluntary Nature, whose fruit-tree smiles in a thousand blossoms for every maturing germ. Inscrutable influences of climate and geography determine the centers of population, and the track of empire. Man can no more choose the focus of emigration's converging rays, than he can by taking thought add one cubit to his stature. The dense western settlements of that unknown race which melted away before the Indians, and of which no vestiges remain but stupendous earthworks, were identical with our own—near Cincinnati and St. Louis, in the Ohio, Scioto, Muskingum, and Miami valleys, and along the great lakes. Four-fifths of all civilized nations past and present, have lived within the world-encircling belt between the thirtieth and fiftieth parallels of north latitude. Our own day shows a line of great cities—Baltimore, Cincinnati, St. Louis, Chicago, Omaha, Leavenworth, Salt Lake, Virginia Nevada, and San Francisco—extending, almost as directly as the bird flies, across the broad continent. Here run the grooves of commerce, the routes of travel, the pathway of empire.

Before the railway era, one studying the map, soil and climate of the United States, would have selected the mouth of the Mississippi, its junction with the Ohio, and its junction with the Missouri, for the three principal cities of our great valley. But with water communication only, and in spite of the strenuous efforts of man, they sprang elsewhere. Such results arise not from mistakes nor contingencies. They are controlled by immutable laws, far beyond mortal ken. Nature keeps her own counsel. She shuts down upon her secrets of state the iron pressure of mysterious years; and Death and Life, who wait with potent arms to do her will, turn to the eager questioner lips of marble.

Leavenworth had two deciding advantages over all competitors: 1. It was near a military post. Ordinarily, this settles the question. Cincinnati, St. Louis, Chicago, Detroit, San Francisco, all had similar rivalries; but each was beside a garrisoned fort, receiving its protection, and—far more important—its heavy trade. 2. Leavenworth obtained 'the start.' Emigrants to new countries, who would cast their fortunes in the metropolis which is to come, must make no drafts on the future. Let them turn deaf ears to plausible theorists with elaborate maps, who prove geographically, climatically and statistically, that the great city *must* spring up in some new locality; but go to the largest town and wait until some rival surpasses it. In nine cases out of ten, they will find no occasion to move.

Walking back from Doniphan down the river on the Missouri side, I saw two illustrations of the rapidity with which the stream shifts its course. Like the Nile, the lower Mississippi in countless ages has raised its bed above the surrounding country and with every break in the banks swept over thousands of acres. From the deck of a steamer, passengers look *down* upon houses and farms. Its mud-deposits have enriched the lands along its whole course, and formed a vast tract at its mouth. This wealth of soil is chiefly gathered by the Missouri. I passed one farm from which, within a few months, the heavy current had cut away twenty or thirty acres, and undermined out-buildings until they were taken down, to save the lumber from floating away. The house, lately in the midst of a corn-field, was now tenantless, and on the very verge of the water.

A MOVING ACCIDENT BY FLOOD AND FIELD.

Weston, Missouri, was once a leading and thriving town. Now the erratic stream had made deposits in front, until large buildings formerly on the bank, were one-third of a mile inland. At St. Joseph, forty miles above, and upon underlying quick-sands, the river was fast cutting *into* the city. Several acres had disappeared in a single year. Brick warehouses on the levee were now deserted, and their outer walls falling. A family in the lower part of the town were at dinner, when the ground beneath them began to tremble. At first they thought it an earthquake, but it proved a water-quake. They fled to a safe distance, and saw house, garden and an acre of land, slide into the encroaching element. One might contract to sell lots here and deliver them in St. Louis! It was a flight of fancy to call such property *real* estate.

At St. Joseph, the river originally flowed in front of First street. Now it ran along Fourth, and the intervening land had disappeared. A non-resident who purchased levee lots soon after the city was laid out, returned in 1858, to look after them. He supposed them somewhere in the bed of the stream, but had the curiosity to ascertain by survey. They proved to be on the other side of the river, in Elwood, Kansas!

A new town was begun on the Nebraska bank of the Missouri, where the stream forms the dividing line between Nebraska and Iowa. Buildings rose, lots rose likewise, and the warm imaginations of proprietors saw, in the smiling distance, a great city. Alas for human expectations! It was at the extreme point of an ox-bow curve; and during a freshet, the perverse Missouri took a new path, straightened its crooked channel, and left the great commercial city of Nebraska, standing in Iowa, five miles off—as uncertain about its own identity as the heroine of the nursery legend who wondered 'if I be I!' It was a curious disregard of State rights, a rare form of involuntary annexation, a novel freak of manifest destiny!

CHAPTER V.

I VISITED Leavenworth again on the 29th of June, believing the municipal election of that day could not pass without armed collision. Nor did it. Late at night when our steamer landed, watch-fires blazed on the levee, drinking saloons were crowded, excited men bearing guns and revolvers were gathered in little knots, or walking to and fro. A friend whom I met pacing the sidewalk with a Sharpe's rifle upon his shoulder, explained the cause.

Most of the Pro-slavery men, satisfied that their rule was over, refrained from voting. The entire Free State ticket was elected by a vote of three hundred and eighty-five to seventy. James T. Lyle, the city recorder, was a young Georgian who during the early troubles assisted in tarring and feathering and shaving the head of Phillips, a Free Soiler afterward wantonly killed in Leavenworth. He was also present at the atrocious murder of Captain E. P. Brown, who was literally chopped to pieces with hatchets, at Easton, Kansas, in January, 1856, and his bleeding corpse flung before his young wife, who was made a maniac by the horrible tragedy.

At the polls on the day of my arrival, a Border Ruffian ballot was offered to a German. He tore it to tatters, asking:

'Do you suppose I would vote that d—d Pro-slavery ticket?'

This instantly provoked an affray in which all the bystanders took part; and upon both sides several revolvers were fired. William Haller, a young Ohioan whose property had once been burned by Pro-slavery men, urged the German to stand his ground. Lyle turned upon Haller, asking:

'What is it to you?' and raised a knife. But before he could strike, Haller stabbed him to the heart, and he fell dead.

Haller was arrested, and strongly guarded by the police; but they were intensely Pro-slavery, and Lyle's friends were arming and threatening to lynch the prisoner. So the Free State men with rifles and revolvers were on duty to protect their comrade and *watch the officers.* The Pro-slavery party was also gathering and bearing weapons.

Through the long night streets resounded with tramping feet, and five hundred men were under arms, in drinking saloons, at street corners, in front of the guarded building in which Haller was confined, and around the little office where rested the white, fixed face and rigid form of Lyle. But no further outbreak occurred. The next morning a preliminary investigation was held before a relic of Border Ruffian rule, who had risen from a livery stable to the justice's bench. It was in the unfinished stone court-house, with unhewn walls, rough benches and a single table. The cigars of the lawyers darkened this temple of justice, and the magistrate heard the testimony while reading a newspaper. Many witnesses were examined, and, as in all affrays, persons who looked on from the same point at the same moment, swore to exactly opposite statements. Once an attorney for the defense took his cigar from his mouth, and behind a huge puff of smoke, objected to certain testimony on the other side as inadmissible. The justice gravely replied:

'The court sustains the objection and rules that the question cannot be asked *at this stage of the game.*'

The inference was, that 'the court' played poker. Haller was held for trial. Application for his admission to bail was argued before Judge Lecompte, chief justice of the supreme court of the Territory. His decisions had been so uniformly and flagrantly partisan, that he was nicknamed 'Jeffries Lecompte.' Under the 'bogus code' framed by his own party, all degrees of homicide were bailable; and Lecompte had released notorious criminals charged with the murder of Free State men, upon their giving bonds for appearance at trial.

But this was his own ox which had been gored. In summing up the testimony, he called Lyle's bowie 'a small knife which he did not purpose to use offensively,' though witnesses had sworn that it was from eight to twelve inches long, and that deceased had raised it to strike when he received the mortal wound. He refused to admit Haller to bail, ordering him to Fort Leavenworth for safe keeping. The prisoner was taken from the court-room in the custody of six United States soldiers, amid the flashing eyes and suppressed breathing of the Free State lookers-on, who despite their reverence for the Federal uniform, wanted only a leader to have rescued him by force. (At Lawrence one morning the following winter, I encountered several mud-stained men who during the previous night had escorted Haller from the fort, whence he escaped by bribing the guards. He reached Ohio safely, and six months later resumed his residence in Leavenworth, where he was never again disturbed.)

Leavenworth was the scene of frequent violence. On a July evening upon the river bank, a stranger named James Stephens, was murdered, and his body robbed of one hundred and eight dollars. Quarles and Bays, two of his friends residing in the city, testified before the coroner's jury that they were walking with him, when robbers attacked the party and murdered him, while they ran for their lives. But 'conscience is a thousand witnesses;' their statements were so contradictory and improbable, that the jury returned a verdict charging *them* with the murder, and they were at once taken into custody. Then Quarles made a full confession.

Hitherto, every homicide in Kansas had resulted from the slavery controversy. According to historians, the remorseless Marats and Robespierres of the French Revolution, who shed blood like water, did not take a piece of money or a watch from their butchered victims. They even guillotined their own wretched agents detected in plundering. They would have life, not gold. So the Kansas conflict had witnessed no mercenary element in all its atrocious crimes. But here was a cold-blooded murder for money. Free State and Pro-slavery men, alike hopeless of the laws, meant to punish it.

Two thousand people gathered at the jail. Judge Lecompte addressed the mob, deprecating violence, and asserting that all who engaged in it would be liable to indictment for murder. This was answered with the howls: 'Indict and be d—d!' Lecompte attempted to go on but he only elicited hoots, and at last ominous suggestions about making an example of *him* for permitting and aiding criminals to escape; so he wisely withdrew. Then another speaker sprang upon a box and commanded the peace, announcing himself as the United States marshal for Kansas. Instantly arose a storm of cries:

'Down with him!' 'He's the greatest scoundrel in the Territory.' 'Let's hang *him!*'

The officer's voice grew husky, and his face bloodless; and he too, disappeared in the crowd.

The mob picked up the city marshal and police as if they had been children; carried them a few yards, and there held them; battered down the iron door of the jail with a stick of timber; dragged forth Quarles, and hung him from a cottonwood tree overlooking the city. For a moment the poor wretch clutched the rope above his head, lifting himself up; but a heavy ruffian caught him by the feet, his grasp gave way,and he never struggled again.

Two hours later the crowd again surrounded the jail and demanded Bays. In vain the Free State mayor and other leading citizens sought to restrain them. The prisoner's wife, a vigorous young Irish woman fought like a tiger; but they took her away as gently as possible, again used the battering ram, brought out the criminal, and ran with him to the gibbet. He refused to confess; held his own hands behind him to be tied; and cast on the crowd a half-scornful, half-triumphant expression, while he was swung off from the limb. To what base uses may come the stuff of which martyrs are made!

Meanwhile, Woods, an alleged counterfeiter, and Knighten, a weak young man, who like poor dog Tray had fallen into bad company, were arrested as accomplices and confined in the mayor's office. Blood inflames a mob like a wild beast; the appetite grows by what it feeds on. On Sunday night, twenty-four hours after the executions, six hundred persons collected in the street and began to clamor for Woods, with shouts of: 'Hang him!' 'hang him.' But this was not so easy. The mayor's office in the second story of a high frame building, was only approachable by an outside flight of rickety stairs. At the foot stood four determined guards, with drawn revolvers. If the crowd overpowered them and made a rush, the stairs would certainly give way, and precipitate the ministers of vengeance into a yawning cellar, twenty feet below.

While calmer citizens were expostulating, and urging that the prisoner should have a trial, the shouting mob surged like a heavy-swelling sea. One young man sprang upon a brick pile and displayed a rope. Then went up tremendous cries,—

'Woods!' 'Woods!' 'Bring him out!' 'Hang him!'

But now another, mounting the brick pile, harangued them

'With throat of brass and adamantine lungs.'

He approved yesterday's proceedings; but now let us impanel a jury of twelve leading citizens, and try these prisoners.

'All right!' 'Go ahead.' 'We'll give you just twenty minutes for doing it.'

Eleven residents answered to their names, and went up the stairs; but there was difficulty in finding the twelfth; and one or two whose names were called, declined to serve.

'Send along any man,' suggested the volunteer marshal; 'send the man with the rope.'

Enthusiastic cheers followed. The crowd bore their champion to the foot of the stairs, where, with American respect for the jury-box, he left his rope behind before ascending.

The open sesame of 'the Press,' admitted me to the trial room, whose windows were raised that the crowd outside might see the prisoner. Woods was a Kentuckian, fifty years old, who had been spending the day in making a will, leaving eight thousand dollars of property to his two daughters in Tennessee. Knighten was a thin-witted boy whom the criminals had taken into their confidences. But he only knew from the statements of Quarles and Bays, that Woods was their confederate in circulating counterfeit bank-notes. Woods was closely interrogated, but denied every thing.

The crowd now grew impatient, fired with the usual fondness of mobs for hanging a man first and trying him afterward. Shouts of 'Time up!' 'We have waited long enough!' 'Hang them both any how!' rent the air.

The scene was exciting. A single dim candle lighted the room, showing the anxious, troubled faces of jurors, grouped around the prisoners, in momentary expectation that the bloodthirsty outsiders would rush in. The questioning ceased, and the suppressed painful breathing of every man present was heard. Knighten grew pale as death, and great drops of sweat stood upon his forehead. Woods, huge, brawny and hardened, sat erect, waiting his fate. He spoke doggedly:

'Well, gentlemen, *you can't hang me but once!*'

'YOU CAN'T HANG ME BUT ONCE!'

Despite this bravado, his facial muscles twitched, and as all confirmed lovers of tobacco use it more freely under strong excitement, he tore off great shreds of Virginia leaf, and his craunching jaws rose and fell with the haste of desperation. Outside, it was light as day, and the full moon of that Sabbath night illumined a moving sea of fierce, upturned faces—a dense, surging mass of clamoring uncontrolable men. Lady Wortley, surprised at the costly dress of our working people, declared that a mob in the United States, is a mob in broadcloth; but this was a mob in shirt-sleeves. A few wore coats, carelessly thrown open, revealing leathern belts, where glittered the silver mounting of bowie knife, or the polished steel of revolver.

From the windows the jurors begged more time, which was reluctantly granted. With two or three repetitions of this scene, the trial lasted till midnight. Then they reported to the assembly, that after rigid investigation, they had only elicited a few facts throwing suspicion upon Woods and Knighten, but nothing that would *convict* them of murder or other crime in any court of justice. To which the crowd responded by calling for 'the man with the rope.' Their champion strong at hanging, but weak at speech-making, appeared in the window, was cheered, and confirmed the statement of his associates. Then the mayor, in a temperate address, urged that the law should take its course; and the quieted mob at last dispersed. The prisoners were committed for trial; and after the usual mode of Kansas justice, bribed their keeper and escaped from jail before the expiration of two weeks.

While I was in Leavenworth, one hundred recanting Mormons arrived from Utah, and sought homes in Kansas. These families, bringing all their earthly possessions by ox-teams, had been sixty days on the long road from Salt Lake. They represented the tyranny of the Mormon church as unendurable, and the practical workings of polygamy as repulsive and disgusting. Violent threats were made to prevent their escape; and they believed that only their numbers saved them from violence at the hands of the remaining Saints.

In July one hundred thousand acres of public lands were sold at Osawkee, Jefferson county. Theoretically to the highest bidder; actually each quarter-section to its occupant at its appraised value: from one dollar and fifty cents, to four dollars and fifty cents per acre. The 'settler,' who lived fifty or a hundred miles away, had built a cabin or driven a stake upon his claim, and could therefore swear that he was a bona fide resident! The constructive squatters respected each others' rights and protected their own. The first man who ventured to bid against one of them was instantly shot down; so there was no further competition.

Many sold their newly-acquired lands to speculators at double the cost within an hour after bidding them off. But hundreds borrowed money at five per cent. a month, and invested it here. I knew a Tennesseean who loaned funds at this rate to forty-five young men, taking the Government title to each tract in his own name, but giving a bond to deed it back to the actual purchaser upon the payment of principal and interest. Two years later, he told me that he still held every one, as not a single note had been paid.

Money abounded and times were flush. One evening I borrowed one hundred and fifty dollars from a total stranger, to aid in purchasing a quarter-section; for I had not escaped the universal mania. When I offered a mortgage as security, he replied:

'It would be some trouble to have the papers drawn, and cost us five or ten dollars. Just send me the money by express within two or three weeks.'

David's covetousness for the wife of Uriah, was no stronger than the lust of the frontier Yankee for territory. Town shares and quarter-sections passed as currently as bank-notes or gold dollars. It was history repeating itself; for according to Parton, in the early days of Tennessee, people in trading used to say: 'I will give you a three-twenty,' or 'I will take a six-forty.' Six hundred and forty acres near the present city of Nashville, once sold for three axes and two cow-bells. 'The circulating medium of Europe is gold, of Africa, men, of Asia, women, and of America, land.'

Two thousand people attended the sales at Osawkee. In this interior town of a dozen houses, a huge hotel had been erected; every building was crowded, and hundreds of strangers lived in tents, or slept on the grass in the open air. Streets were filled with blinding dust, and heated like furnaces by the July sun; gambling and drinking booths stood upon every corner: reeking odors poisoned the air, and a new Coleridge might have sung of this mushroom Cologne:

'In Colin, a town of monks and bones,
And pavements fanged with murderous stones,
And rags, and hags, and hideous wenches,
I counted five and seventy stenches.'

The public temper was very inflammable and kindled like gunpowder from the faintest spark. The Pro-slavery party claimed to be distinctively 'Law-and-order men,' but their courts of justice were the most dangerous places in the whole Territory. Scores of murders had been committed, but no one had ever been punished for any crime against a Free State citizen.

At Tecumseh, Boynton, an inoffensive Free Soiler, surrounded by Pro-slavery neighbors who were trying to drive him from his claim, brought suit against one Adams, who had thrice attempted to shoot him. The United States commissioner merely held *both*

LAW-AND-ORDER MEN.

parties to five-hundred-dollar bonds to keep the peace. During the investigation Newsom, Territorial prosecuting attorney elected by the bogus legislature, denounced Boynton as a d—d liar.

After the court adjourned, Boynton asked an explanation, when the official repeated the epithet, and struck him upon the head with a bowie knife, cutting a gash three inches long. This fired even the man of peace, and he responded with his clinched fist, which sent Newsom reeling through an open door into an adjoining office. The bystanders, including Adams, upon whose bond to keep the peace the ink had not yet dried, drew their revolvers; but Boynton flying the court-room, escaped their bullets and found refuge in Lawrence.

The previous spring's immigration, almost exclusively from the North, had given the Free Soilers large numerical ascendency. Now they began to stand boldly upon their rights and defy Missouri. Their July Territorial convention passed a quiet, but significant resolution:

Whereas, preparations are being made in Missouri to control the coming Kansas elections;—

Resolved, That this convention appoints and authorizes General James H. Lane, to organize the people in the several districts, to protect the ballot-boxes.

After this quasi declaration of war there were no further invasions.

Osawkee was a Pro-slavery town. One day during the land sales, Governor Walker, Secretary Stanton of Tennessee, and other 'National Democrats,' made political speeches. When they had finished, the Free Soilers present called out one of their own number, Charles Foster of Osawatomie. In a fiery address he urged that under the rule of the same National Democracy which was now willing to bring Kansas into the Union even as a free State, their property had been destroyed, their homes invaded, and their soil drenched with innocent blood.

Some of his hearers hissed! others shouted: 'Knock him down!' 'Out with him!'

Instantly twenty cocked revolvers were displayed by his friends around the stand, and he was permitted to go on.

Frequently while riding in the vicinity of Osawkee, I encountered the original owners of the soil, jogging along on horseback, sometimes sober and reticent, but often whisky-inspired and uproarious. The squaws usually rode in couples, with papooses strapped on their backs, and older children astride before and behind them. Nearly all the Kansas Indians lived in log-cabins, and made some pretenses to civilization; so they were less migratory than their race in general. But sometimes they sought fresh fields and pastures new, or were joined by immigrants and visitors from Texas and the Cherokee nation. These bedouins of the prairie invariably carried their lodges with them, the buffalo robes rolled and strapped to poles, attached to the ponies like wagon shafts at one end, and dragging upon the ground at the other. Papooses were suspended between the poles, and seemed to enjoy journeying by this rudimental 'one hoss shay.'

INDIANS TRAVELING.

My stay in Osawkee, was cut short by a fresh excitement. The Lawrence people, without authority from the bogus laws, had formed a municipal organization, electing a mayor, alderman, and other city officers. It was a movement common in new countries, and chiefly designed to impose and collect taxes for removing offal, grading streets, and protecting the public health. But Governor Walker, great in his new-fledged dignity, thought it part of a universal plan for organizing the nascent State, and putting the Topeka government in force. He held it treason and grim-visaged war. In a flaming proclamation he declared:

'A rebellion so iniquitous, and necessarily involving such awful consequences, has never before disgraced any age or country!'

He marched three hundred Federal soldiers from Fort Leavenworth upon Lawrence; and it was even thought that the little city would be a second time destroyed for the crime of Free State sentiments.

At this perturbed and expectant moment, late one Saturday night, a breathless messenger reached Osawkee. He asserted, with minutest particulars, that he was just from Lawrence, which Walker's troops had begun to bombard, and that he left the city wrapped in flames. What did I in the North when I should serve my employer in the South? With several friends I started for the new seat of war, thirty miles away, expecting to find the town in ashes.

After a hard night's ride, we came in sight of it, just as the sun was rising. It was very unlike smoldering ruins. Not a gun had been fired, a building disturbed, or a man arrested. There stood the city in the light of that Sabbath morning, calm and peaceful as any hamlet in the world. A mile west, on the prairie, gleamed white tents of the encamped soldiers, with sentinels pacing to and fro; and that was the sole foundation for the story. Our messenger had somewhere heard the rumor which he repeated as a fact of his own observation. To me it was a valuable lesson. Again, and again, during the great civil war, that experience saved me from being misled. All army correspondents learned sooner or later that strong excitements breed rumors as great swamps breed mosquitoes; that most human testimony is utterly untrustworthy; that one can believe only the evidence of his own senses, and those persons in whose truthfulness he places absolute confidence. Every day, in courts of justice, honest and intelligent sworn witnesses contradict each others' statements in the most positive manner. In a company of a dozen, it is an interesting experiment to whisper the details of some simple bit of news in fifty words to one's next neighbor. Thus let it pass around the circle; then request the last recipient to repeat it; and the innocent little morsel that was sent forth on its tour, will scarcely retain an infinitesimal part of its identity.

Governor Walker's blunder was more fatal than a crime. There was nobody to arrest, for no overt act had been committed; and there was nobody to fight, for nobody had taken up arms. The Kansas people who held Federal governors their natural enemies, enjoyed the rupture amazingly. According to Emerson's test, they were the best orators, for they could call the most nicknames. The two or three feeble Border Ruffian papers yet surviving, made faint and doubtful essays in favor of their weak champion. The Free State journals flushed with new-born strength, abounded in droll chronicles of 'the siege of Lawrence,' and the great 'isothermal war.' Wags issued solemn burlesque proclamations declaring it high treason, punishable with death, to grade streets or remove dead cats from the gutters. In a public meeting, the people resolved to receive no communication from the governor, unless made through their newly elected mayor. Walker had sown dragons' teeth, and he reaped armed men. Half a dozen communities, which had never thought of it before, (one embracing the very land upon which the troops were encamped,) immediately imitated Lawrence, and elected municipal officers. A committee from one of these towns consulted the governor upon their movement. He replied:

'Go on gentlemen—if you wish to fight the entire army of the United States.'

The entire army of the United States is strong, but not strong enough to defend a man against ridicule. Destiny in the form of the Lawrence Yankees was too much for his excellency. Tired of an unequal contest which had made him the laughing-stock alike of the Territory and the entire North, he imitated the historic Charles who,

'With twenty thousand men,
Marched up a hill, and then—marched down again.

CHAPTER VI.

In August I became a squatter, and made 'a claim.' This is the frontier term for the one hundred and sixty acres which the real or constructive settler 'improves' and claims for his future home. Only after preëmption and a perfect title from the Government, is it called his farm.

With several companions whose eyes were dazzled by visions of landed proprietorship, I started from Quindaro on a tour through the unsettled county of Johnson, one of the fairest and richest regions of Kansas. In the belt of deep woods eight or ten miles wide along the Missouri, the summer tints were of wonderful beauty and variety. Purple wild plums of delicate flavor, half the size of apples, abounded; from tree and bush hung vines heavy with ripening grapes, not larger than peas, but plump, palatable, and much used in cooking; wild cherries and crab apples grew in profusion; and the thickets bent under heavy loads of elder-berries, of which a bushel could be gathered in a few minutes. They lack pungency, but in the absence of other fruits frontier housewives convert them into tasteless preserves and insipid pies.

Crossing the Kansas, we reached the prairies and left the woods behind. Here and there were scattered trees along the far-apart streams; but they were like angel visits. This lack of timber was the most serious drawback of pioneers; yet the farmer would far better settle where he must go twenty-five miles for house and fence lumber and firewood, than where he must clear away forests to make room for his corn and grass fields. The latter is the work of one or two generations; but in this rich Kansas soil the locust grows like Jonah's gourd, and the cottonwood attains a trunk-diameter of five or six inches in six years. Its feathery seed floats on the wind and takes root in plowed fields miles away from the mother tree.

Toward evening we passed several parties of immigrants, chiefly from Missouri. Come to this encampment, and see how

A FAMILY ENCAMPMENT.

kindly frontier families take to a roving life. The long, heavy wagon, its roof covered with white cotton cloth, stands a few yards from the road. It is packed with provisions and household utensils; and two or three pots and kettles are suspended from the hind axle. The tired oxen graze upon the neighboring prairie. The white-haired children are playing hard by—five or six in number, for these new countries are marvelously prolific. The husband is milking the patient cows, the wife is preparing a supper of griddle-cakes bacon and coffee in the open air, at the camp stove, the hens are cackling socially from their coop, while the old family dog wags his tail approvingly, but watches with solicitous care the baby creeping about the wagon.

When crossing the great deserts to Utah or California they toil wearily along from twelve to twenty miles per day. The long-bearded, shaggy drivers, tanned to the hue of Arapahoes, look like animated pillars of earth, and seem under the perpetual sentence: 'Dust thou art and unto dust shalt thou return.' Each keeps his trusty rifle or shot-gun within grasp; and at night the wagons are parked in a circle, and the cattle driven into the extemporized yard which they inclose, as a protection against Indian surprises. Eternal vigilance is the price of travel. The children of the immigrants revel in dirt and novelty, but their mothers cast eager longing eyes toward their new homes. There is profound truth in the remark that 'plains-travel and frontier life are peculiarly severe upon women and oxen.'

We found the prairies robed in emerald green, and lit up with the gorgeous flowers of late summer. The wealth of the soil appeared inexhaustible. Where the spring streams had cut into it for thirty feet, the ravines displayed rich alluvium, black as jet, down to the bottom. It seemed as if no soundings could penetrate beneath it. It is like those rich bottom-lands along the Muskingum and Miami rivers of Ohio, which without the application of any fertilizing substance, have produced corn every season for half a century, and still yield fifty or sixty bushels to the acre. The grass was a miniature forest. In some of the wet lowlands it rose above our heads and completely hid us from each other, when a few yards apart, though we were mounted on tall steeds.

There is a curious logical connection between civilization and rain. All along the frontier, Indians declare that the white man brings rain with him. Thirty years ago, Missourians living on the opposite bank of the river thought the soil of Kansas good for nothing on account of its rainless climate. Since the young State was settled, it has suffered only twice from dry seasons, and of late good crops and increasing rains have dispelled all apprehensions.

Now, however, we found the weather intensely hot, and the high prairies parched with drowth. Hour after hour we journeyed under the scorching sun, discovering neither shade nor water. Several of my comrades suffered intensely from thirst.

Their tongues became swollen, and their lips cracked, until the blood ran from them. At last we espied in the distance a feeble willow, sure indication of moisture. Spurring thither our jaded horses, we found a pool of stagnant water. The surface was covered with green scum, and as I lay down to drink, a sluggish lizzard crawled in from the bank. But necessity knows no scruples, and the famishing never criticise. Every mouthful of that jelly-like fluid was flavored with fever-and-ague; yet my long draught was the sweetest I had ever tasted.

We found hundreds of claims already taken, chiefly by Missourians, who had visited them once, and made 'improvements' —inclosing a little square with four logs or rails laid upon the ground. Yet in riding twenty-five miles we saw but one occupied dwelling. We were truly on the outer verge of civilization.

We selected and staked our quarter-sections, and after returning to Quindaro, sent out boards and had a cabin erected upon each. But a few weeks later when we went back to look at our 'dwellings,' some enterprising scoundrel had carried away every one of them! He did not leave a single board, rafter, or splinter. Notwithstanding the forty dollars which his cupidity cost me, I have profound respect for that shrewd speculator who not only obtained so much valuable lumber for nothing, but found it already delivered thirty miles in the interior, when the expenses of hauling were enormous. It must have enabled him to build a palatial mansion; but my experience was a ludicrous satire upon the ancient legal fiction that every man's house is his castle.

From such a school must have graduated the ——th Kansas Infantry which acquired rare reputation for plundering during the great rebellion. A number of Kansas regiments marching through Missouri, revenged themselves upon their old enemies; but this had unapproachable genius for plunder, which the camp stories used to illustrate with genuine American exaggeration. One of them ran thus: In an Arkansas campaign a general officer found the entire ——th grouped around a saw-mill and weeping like Niobes.

'Why, boys,' he asked, 'what is the matter?'

Matter enough!' sobbed one enterprising volunteer. 'Thus

far we have never left any thing behind us; but we can't possibly steal this saw-mill!'

In August I attended the trial of Governor Charles Robinson at Lecompton. The Border Ruffian capital, in a rough little hollow, was composed of few dwelling-houses, many land-offices, and multitudinous whisky saloons. Free State friends pointed out to me the building where they were confined as prisoners during the early troubles. In close, filthy quarters, and covered with vermin, they spent many weeks, not only cheerfully, but often in a state of absolute hilarity. It seemed incredible; for I had not then learned how much contentment depends upon temperament, and how little upon the externals of life. Years later, I noted the same fact in rebel prisons. The feelings of men in those dens of misery, shut out from all the comforts of life, and with suffering and death constantly before their eyes, did not differ materially from their feelings after they were restored to liberty. Indeed, a friend declares in all sincerity that the two years he spent in their scenes of horror were the most cheerful of his life. Doubtless, love for the cause in which he suffered, and unshaken faith in its triumph, account for some of his fortitude.

The world owes much to her prisons. They have been storehouses in whose safe keeping ripened seeds which have borne a plentiful harvest. How often have they given back blessings to the hand of tyranny, and lavished upon ungrateful ears music, which the following generations caught up to bear along in triumph! Chambers of royalty, they have held enthroned our sages and singers. There sat Socrates and Bacon, Raleigh and More and Tasso. There Marco Polo recorded his strange, romantic story. There brilliant, tireless Defoe edited his semi-weekly *Review*, forerunner of the modern newspaper. There Cervantes commemorated the immortal Quixote. There John Bunyan opened that well of living water,

> 'Whose drops
> Of cool refreshment drained by fevered lips,
> May give a shock of pleasure to the soul,
> More exquisite than when nectarean juice
> Renews the life of happiest hours.'

The United States district court at Lecompton was held in a rude apartment, furnished with three tables, two chairs, and half-a-dozen planks for seats, resting upon blocks, stones, and boxes. Judge Cato was an avowed disunionist of the South Carolina school. Tall and thin, with closely-shaven face, and overgrown moustache, he wore the ermine carelessly, studied the *Charleston Mercury* intently through his heavy gold spectacles, and gave only an occasional glance at the business before him. Wier, the district attorney, stout, florid, and red-whiskered, sat on a table with his feet elevated upon the stove. The lookers-on exhibited every variety of dress and physiognomy. Robinson was charged with usurpation of office. He admitted his election as governor under the Topeka State constitution, his issuing messages to the State legislature, approval of its enactments, and other gubernatorial functions. But the witnesses swore that this action was only preparatory; that it had never been the intention to put the government in force, until Kansas should become a State in the Federal Union. This was not quite true. Nearly all the Free State men *had* designed to set the Topeka government in motion and support it by force of arms, whenever the Border Ruffian Territorial authorities should drive them to the wall.

The judge was overbearing and violent; but Robinson's counsel, confident that the Pro-slavery rule was nearly ended, faced him boldly, objected to some of the jurors as vagabonds and notorious partisans, and took exceptions to nearly all his rulings. Even the prosecuting attorney, from long habit repeatedly spoke of the prisoner as '*Governor*' Robinson, though always quickly changing it to 'Doctor' Robinson.

In summing up, the court charged the jury that if they found Robinson had assumed to be governor of the State of Kansas, (which then existed only in name and not at all in law or in fact,) they must find him guilty as charged by the indictment, of usurping the office of governor of the *Territory* of Kansas!

After two hours absence the jurors re-appeared and asked that the case might be re-opened, and one witness re-examined, as they had forgotten his testimony! Even Cato refused to do this; and soon after they returned a verdict of Not Guilty. Thus ended the last treason trial in Kansas.

THE TRIAL OF GOVERNOR ROBINSON FOR TREASON, IN AUGUST, 1857.

A few days later, a Territorial Free State convention was held at Grasshopper Falls. Going thither with two friends, I journeyed for hours on the Delaware Indian reservation, fifteen miles by forty. Its richness and beauty showed Kansas a country worth struggling for. There are many old lake beds, basins scooped out of the prairie. Around their shores runs a well defined stratum of limestone, like an artificial wall; and for miles a similar line girdles the isolated hills, suggesting that they were islands before the waters were gathered into one place and dry land appeared. But geologists decide that these seemingly ancient water-marks are only limestone strata which lie evenly in all the bluffs.

Our road was an obscure track in the prairie grass. We journeyed on and on until dark, and then for hours afterward, finding no traces of human life. Late in the night we met four Indians on horseback, of whom we inquired the distance to Oskaloosa. They replied in pure English, that they knew no such town; certainly it was not in that vicinity; the nearest white settlement was ten miles distant upon the Kaw river.

In spite of the Indian fondness for romance, their seeming intelligence and honesty convinced us that we had mistaken the way. So we lariated our mules to graze, and slept soundly upon our blankets on the ground, with the soft grass for a pillow, and the gemmed sky for a roof.

In the morning we woke to find hair and beards dripping with dew; but cold and rheumatic twinges are strangers to that pure summer air. Fifteen minutes after starting again, we were in sight of Oskaloosa. We had not wandered from our road, but the noble savage, true to the instincts of his race, had been fabricating falsehoods out of whole cloth.

We breakfasted at Hickory Point, a little group of buildings besieged and captured by Free State men in 1856, after several had been killed on both sides. One log house still displayed huge apertures where the shells had torn through its thick walls. Our landlord of this morning commanded the Pro-slavery garrison during the skirmish; and still bears the scar where a rifle ball struck him as he was taking a drink. This fire in the rear spilled his whisky, and gave him an ugly wound. Yet he lived, not to fight another day, but to regale us with an excellent meal. He seemed chatty, courteous and honest.

The convention was large and earnest. It elicited exciting discussions upon voting at the fall elections. Hitherto, after being repeatedly overpowered by Missouri invasions, the Free Soilers had absented themselves from the polls, believing that the Border Ruffians, who held all the machinery of government, would cer-

A FIRE IN THE REAR.

tainly defeat them by force or fraud. Now the Free State men held an immense numerical majority. But to vote on the day and in the manner prescribed by the illegal and invading legislature seemed to give a kind of recognition to the bogus laws. Advices from Washington had just assured them of President Buchanan's design 'with the help of God,' to enforce those statutes. *They* were fully determined to resist them to the last. The apportionment too was notoriously unfair. The old Pro-slavery counties were given an enormous excess of representation, while a Free State section of twenty counties comprising almost half the population of the Territory, was entitled to only three out of fifty-two members of the legislature.

But Governor Walker had promised that the test oath should not be enforced, and that he would insure them a fair election. Many, distrusting him, earnestly opposed voting. Others advocated it as a stratagem: to beat the enemy at his own game; to get possession of the Territorial government, at all hazards. Their counsels prevailed; it was decided to vote. Lane declared:

'The Territorial legislature belongs to us, and we are going to have it—by the ballot if we can, by the rifle if we must. If we elect only one member we intend to make him a good working majority.'

The fall canvass was exciting. Pro-slavery men confidently asserted that they should triumph—which meant either invasion or fraud. The Free Soilers organized and went armed to the polls.

In Quindaro, when the voting was over and before the general result was known, public feeling was painfully wrought up. It was like the choking anxiety in a court-room, after an absorbing trial, while prisoner and foreman stand up face to face, and all wait breathless for the verdict. First came a report that the Territory was so closely divided, that Leavenworth, the most populous county and electing eleven members, would decide the character of the legislature. At the heels of this followed another rumor, that through gross frauds and hundreds of illegal votes at the little precinct of Kickapoo, Leavenworth county had elected the Pro-slavery ticket; and that Governor Walker had given certificates to the candidates fraudulently chosen, thus retaining the government in Border Ruffian hands for two years more.

In the midst of the indignation this caused, his excellency paid Quindaro a visit. Within half an hour after his arrival, a gray-haired citizen, who, until then, had always borne the reputation of a Conservative, took me aside, and said with flashing eyes:

'We shall never get our rights peaceably. Walker persuaded us to vote with fair promises; and now he has betrayed us. Here he is; let us make an example of him, and teach old Buchanan that we are in earnest. The boys are all ready.'

'Ready for what?'

'Ready to take him out of the hotel, and hang him upon that tree!' was the startling reply.

My fiery friend finally acquiesced in the suggestion that we should wait to verify the reports. The event proved that Walker *had* given certificates to the fraudulently-chosen delegation. But there was a large Free State majority in the legislature, which turned out the spurious members during the first week of its session. And thus the Territorial government passed into the hands of the bona fide settlers.

But the end was not yet. During the previous summer a Proslavery convention to form a State constitution had been held at Lecompton. The act of the bogus legislature authorizing it disqualified all but registered voters from participating in the election of delegates. In half the counties no registry was made; in others the Free State men were not registered, and they staid away from the polls. They would have dispersed the convention by force of arms but for Governor Walker's emphatic assurances that he would oppose any constitution it formed, unless submitted to a vote of the people, and that President Buchanan had solemnly promised him to take the same course. So they quietly ignored the gathering, intending to repudiate its offspring at the polls.

But the convention did not submit to the people for ratification the constitution which it made. Buchanan, infamously violating his plighted faith, urged Congress to admit Kansas as a slave State under this fraudulent instrument adopted by a minority of the voters in less than half the counties of the Territory. He even used the patronage of his high office to induce senators and representatives to join in the outrage. Governor Walker kept his pledges, and Buchanan remorselessly dismissed him. Senator Douglas, too, broke away from his life-long political associates, and stood firm against this outrage upon the rights of the settlers, declaring that if it was persisted in they ought to resist, even to fighting the Government of the United States. Thus began that rupture in the democratic party which resulted in the election of Abraham Lincoln and the southern rebellion; and thus the Lecompton convention has a national and historic interest.

In Kansas the attempt to thrust it upon the people kindled hot resentment. Several assassinations ensued, and in south-eastern counties along the Missouri border frequent and bloody skirmishes occurred. At Territorial conventions all the delegates, in writing, pledged their lives their fortunes and their sacred honor to resist the usurpation, even by force of arms. Ordinarily the Free Soilers were divided into cliques and factions, but this pressure compacted them into concord and forgetfulness of old feuds.

The legislature held an extra session, passed, over the governor's veto, an act for organizing and enrolling the entire population capable of bearing arms, and elected a military board, consisting of one major-general, (Lane,) eight brigadiers, and adjutant, inspector, quartermaster, commissary and surgeon-general. I knew no more of military matters than of Sanskrit; but the greatness thrust upon me converted me into assistant adjutant-general and secretary of the board.

That body meant business; but its paraphernalia was not gorgeous. Indeed it looked a good deal like the Arizona legislature, which used to meet in a log-cabin with a dirt floor. Our sessions were held in a Lawrence hall over the 'Commercial' restaurant. The members lived in widely separated portions of the Territory. Chilled with long winter rides, they would enter, in slouched hats, top boots and blue army overcoats with enormous capes; crowd around the stove, and canvass the latest news or rumor of disturbance. No inferior rank was tolerated; every man was a general. At the appointed hour Lane, ex-officio president, would rap on the table and command in his hoarse gutturals:

'The board will come to order.'

Then he pulled at the bell-rope until a waiter appeared.

'John, bring us one, two, three, four,' (counting the members present,) 'fourteen hot whisky punches and a box of cigars. Ah! John, *fifteen* hot whiskies. General Walker, you are just in time. General Richardson, you will read the minutes of the last meeting.'

The completion of the reading found the board warmed externally and internally for the transaction of business. Under its auspices organization and enrolment progressed rapidly. The Territorial governor, (Denver,) issued a proclamation against it; but proclamations were cheap and plenty, and his was unheeded. There were frequent rumors that he was about to promote its leading members to the honors of martyrdom by arresting them; but, once begun, he could hardly have stopped without arresting the whole population of Kansas. So he confined his warfare to paper bullets of the brain.

CHAPTER VII.

The winter of 1857–8 was a stirring one for a Kansas newspaper correspondent. Every week was alive with excitement—an alarm to-day, an outbreak to-morrow; and the point of interest shifting so constantly kept one flying back and forth like a shuttlecock to meet it. I took long prairie rides, sometimes remaining all night in the saddle. The nights were most lovely; often so bright that even in the woods, and when there was no snow upon the ground, I could easily read the finest type of a daily newspaper.

Sometimes the fast-falling snow would obliterate the prairie roads, and clouds darken the sky. More than once I wandered bewildered until daylight, and then found myself miles out of the proper course. The wind always blows: it chills the whole frame, and at times is so violent that in riding against it, one is in danger of being swept out of the saddle. I frequently saw men so chilled that after walking awhile to warm themselves, they had to be lifted upon their horses.

Some of the night rides were easy and agreeable—peaceful hours passed in the soothing society of nature; and hours, too, of rest, for while the horse walks, or even trots slowly, the practised rider often sleeps, until the stopping or changing gait of his steed awakens him. There is no appreciable danger of falling, unless the horse stumbles or the saddle turns. Mexicans and Indians easily sit on horseback when so drunk that they cannot stand upon the ground.

In equestrianism men have an easy, natural and safe position. If women were to adopt it instead of their present tiresome and perilous mode of riding, the gain in health, comfort and security would be very great.

At the end of these nocturnal journeys I often reached home with bloodshot eyes, and every shred of skin shaven from my lips by the wind as if by a razor. But one or two days always restored me: for nature pardons every hygienic sin in him who loves her free, health-giving atmosphere. Hardships which would prove fatal in cities, are easily endured upon prairie or mountain.

A COMFORTABLE SLUMBER.

On a dark December evening I left Lawrence for Quindaro. Fifteen miles out on the lonely road, the clouds gathered themselves into an unbroken dome of black; and the darkness grew so dense that I could hardly see my open hand two inches before my eyes. Then the rain poured in torrents. Fortunately I was in a little strip of forest, where my horse could not leave the track without running against the trees. In this extremity I joyfully detected lights, shining through the chinks of a log-cabin. Riding up and pushing open the door, I was greeted with the clamor of half a dozen noisy dogs. It was the only dwelling within ten miles; and its interior conveyed a certain suggestion of comfort. I asked:

'Can I find lodgings here to-night?'

There were three Indians upon stools around the rude supper table. The oldest and most stolid grunted an affirmative, beckoned me in, and sent one of his companions to care for my horse.

Throwing off my dripping overcoat, I stretched myself before the log fire, which from the great hearth lighted up the whole cabin. It was a single room, ten or twelve feet square. The

A NIGHT IN THE CABIN OF FOUR MILES, PAGE 91.

three men, dressed in coats and pantaloons, had long coarse black hair, sinister eyes, and brooding, suspicious countenances. A stout squaw, cheery and open-faced, who wore zinc ear-rings as large as silver dollars, sat humbly waiting for the nobler sex to finish their repast. Crouching beside her was a girl of eight years also wearing the metallic ear-rings.

Before I had completed this inventory, a vigorous squall drew my attention to a distant corner. There, from a swinging hammock, an Indian papoose of American descent screeched so lustily that his dusky mother seized him, dandled him on her knee, and soothed him with the sweetest baby-talk of the Delaware tongue. He looked like an infant mummy. He was on his back, bandaged so tightly to a board that he could only scream, roll his head and wink; but he performed all these functions at once with miraculous vehemence. His lips were at last silenced by application to 'the maternal fount;' and then he was set up against the wall like a fire-shovel, to inspect the company.

Supper over, the little girl filled and lighted an earthern pipe with reed stem a foot long. Smoking a few whiffs she handed it to her mother. That stolid matron finished it; and we all sat staring silently into the fire. The girl, true to her sex, found courage to scrutinize my gold sleeve-buttons, watch and chain, and every other glittering article she could find about me, greeting each with some fresh ejaculation of delight. Then she kissed the papoose, and crept to her straw nest in another corner. Mine host knew a few English words and I asked him:

'What is your name?'

'Umph. Four Miles.'

'And his?'

'Umph. Fall Leaf.'

'And the little girl's?'

'O-kee-au-kee. No English.'

And Four Miles was again overcome by one of his brilliant flashes of silence.

At bed-time, as I unbuckled my revolver, he glanced inquiringly toward it, took it with nervous care, turned it over and over, stared solemnly into the barrels, and then returned it.

'Umph. Good. How much?'

'Twenty dollars.'

And with another grunt, Four Miles relapsed into speechlessness.

My bed was of plank, well covered with blankets. Through the whole night I had a dreamy consciousness of shivering; and when daylight appeared I noticed the absence of a log in the cabin wall beside me, which left an aperture sufficiently large to admit either a man or enough cold air to cover him. A generous style of ventilation for which I was not adequately grateful.

Upon the stone hearth blazed a bright log fire, and around it were grouped the family, all with colds in the head, and all in fearful contiguity to the open cooking utensils. I forced down a few morsels of breakfast; but it was a signal triumph of mind over matter. My horse was brought to the door, and I asked:

'How much?'

'Umph—two dollars.'

Which I paid and departed, while the noble savage grunted a friendly adieu.

A few weeks later while driving to Lawrence, with my wife and child, and the wife and child of a friend, another sudden and violent storm compelled us all to spend a night in the same cabin. The ladies relished the novelty of the experience but when breakfast appeared, no entreaties could induce them to taste it. After we reached our journey's end, they began a vigorous scrutiny of the children's heads, which, judging from their ejaculations of horror, was not altogether barren of results.

Four Miles received his name because he once ran four miles without stopping.

Another Delaware taken captive in war, escaped and made a long journey back to his own village, eating nothing on the way but a little loaf of corn bread. He was immediately re-christened 'Journey-cake.' Several of his descendants yet survive and bear that family name, though the white settlers corrupt it into Johnny-cake.

Years ago, in battle with the whites, a Delaware youth was made prisoner. One day he took up a plank from the floor of his guard-house, descended to the ground, and crept out in the long grass, eluding the sentinel. Finally, having a fair start, he rose up to run. One soldier fired at him without effect, and then shouted to his comrades:

'Catch him!'

But he was nimble-footed and made good his escape. He lived to become head chief of the Delawares, who gave to him and his children the appellation, 'Ketch'm' or 'Ketchum,' which ever afterward they bore. In 1857, overtaken by the pale Pursuer whom no swift foot outruns, he gave up the race, and went to dwell in the happy hunting grounds.

Each of the eight Indian tribes in Kansas lived upon a 'reservation.' The very word bears a sad suggestion of the retreating and dwindling of their fading race. These reservations were always excellent lands; consequently the Indians were driven away whenever the white settlers coveted them.

The tract of the Delawares, embracing some of the richest portions of the Territory, was forty miles by twelve. This desert of barbarism contained one oasis of civilization—the generous dwellings and school-house of the Baptist mission. In the early days, prairie travelers would ride hard to spend the night in that pleasant and homelike retreat. Rev. John G. Pratt, who conducted the mission, had resided here among the Indians for twenty years. The little pupils of his school illustrated the mysterious bleaching process of the frontier, by exhibiting faces of every shade from aboriginal brown to Saxon white. The teachers averred that they equaled white children in intelligence; but it was almost impossible to teach them cleanliness and truthfulness. In many branches they were apathetic and stolid, but music roused them wonderfully, and it was pleasant to see their eyes sparkle while they sang with animation and zeal. Among the names on the school register were 'Fall Leaf,' 'Black Stump,' 'Beaver,' 'Bullet,' and the like, interspersed with Jones, Brown and Robinson. One Delaware was called 'Best Quality,' and another 'White Stone.' How these primitive names recall the long roll in English history: 'Ethelred the Unready,' 'Flambeau the Firebrand,' 'Rufus the Red,' 'Richard of the Lion Heart,' and 'Edward the Longshanks!' How they suggest the more familiar American appellations, 'Old Hickory,' 'Old Bullion,' 'Rough and Ready,' 'Martin the Fox,' 'Old Public Functionary,' 'the Pathfinder,' 'Little Giant,' and 'Father Abraham!'

The Delawares were once the leading tribe on our continent, so eminent for their valor and wisdom that more humble Indians styled them 'the Grandfathers.' They dominated other nations, and treated with William Penn where Philadelphia now stands. For several years the Baptist mission has been supported by Government. The school contains ninety pupils. Under the influence of peace and education, the Delawares have increased from eight hundred to one thousand two hundred during Mr. Pratt's residence among them. Now the railway surrounds them. A few will remain and become citizens; the rest migrate to the Cherokee country, south of Kansas.

Evening once overtook me at one of their cabins ten miles from the nearest white settlement. Rain was falling fast and the road was a quagmire. Of a youthful Missourian who stood in front of the dwelling I asked:

'How far is it to Sacoxie's?'

Sacoxie was an old chief whose house was popular among travelers. A pert young squaw standing beside the Missourian, with a knowing grunt held up all the fingers of her right hand and one of the left, while he replied:

'Six miles; and awful roads. But you can get good accommodations here. *I* stop here.'

'How long have you lived among the Indians?'

'Three years.'

'Do you like it?'

'Yes,—not exactly: but you know a fellow likes best where he can do best.'

'Have you married into the tribe?'

'No—not particularly. I just stay here.'

'The Delawares are not very strict about marriage?'

'No, they are sort of promiscuous; when a fellow likes a squaw he just gives her old man a present—sometimes a pony, sometimes four or five dollars in money—and takes the girl. They live together as long as they like, and then separate, or trade off with some other couple. The children go with the mother; and the more children the better, because every person in the tribe gets one hundred and sixty dollars a year from the United States Government.'

'Have many white men married Delaware women?'

'Only eight in all.'

'But half-breed children seem numerous?'

'O yes, stranger; there are a good many whites traveling through here!'

I found the good accommodations of the cabin to consist of a single room with earth floor, which could only be entered through a filthy hen-house. Upon one of the beds sat a stolid squaw in a bright red calico frock, nursing a little papoose, who greeted me with an infantile whoop. Three more tawny children were playing in the mud; four scurvy dogs lying in corners, and a dozen chickens pervading the apartment. It contained three bunks, a table, four or five chairs, a rifle, a broken looking-glass, various kitchen utensils, and an enormous fire-place in which I could stand upright. Mine host was a burly, reticent savage. Our entire conversation was as follows:

HE.—Umph. How?

I.—How? Wet weather.

HE.—Umph. Much wet.

My supper was of fat pork, corn bread and strong coffee. My couch of straw was deluged with rain and pre-occupied by bed-bugs. Early in the morning I indulged in a repetition of the evening bill of fare, disbursed the required 'six bits,' (seventy-five cents,) and bade a glad adieu to my aboriginal entertainers. I never learned their name, but could very feelingly have dubbed them 'Good Accommodations.'

The Shawnees like the Delawares were once a warlike nation. They still cherish a legend that their ancestors crossed the sea; and they are the only tribe who have any such tradition of a foreign origin. Their reservation was in Johnson county. They occupied good houses, and in civilization were second only to the Wyandottes. By the organic law of Kansas, Indians who had 'adopted the customs of the white man' were allowed to vote. *All* had adopted one frontier custom: that of drinking whisky. But only the Shawnees and Wyandottes were permitted to use the elective franchise.

One Shawnee was called 'Blue Jacket,' and another 'Silver Heels;' while a young Wyandotte belle rejoiced in the name of 'Mud-eater.'

Spending a night at the house of Charles Fish, a Shawnee chief, I encountered several of his tribe who had come from Texas to claim two hundred acres of land each, which had just been secured to them by a treaty with the United States. One was a dumpy old brave, with pumpkin face and so many ornaments dangling from his dusky ears, that they sent forth the enticing music of sleigh-bells. Another, a fantastic youth, had a kerchief of bright red encircling his forehead like a band of flame. He wore deer-skin moccasins, with gay fringes, a calico hunting shirt also trimmed with fiery red, and cloth leggings which left his hips bare to the winter winds. Some of the squaws were very dark, others nearly white; and all by glaring kerchief or shawl betrayed the barbarian fondness for bright colors. I often encountered these women on the prairie with bright-eyed papooses firmly bound to their backs peeping over their shoulders, and one or two older children sitting before them; while wooden pails, chairs and other heavy burdens weighed down the unfortunate steed. The men rode beside them carrying nothing but their whisky bottles, out of respect to the Indian principle of leaving work to women.

The reservation of the Pottawatomies was thirty miles square. No white man could settle upon it unless he first married into the tribe. In 1846 the Pottawatomies numbered five thousand. In 1858 they had become reduced to two thousand seven hundred, and were diminishing at the rate of five per cent. a year. Their dead are buried with their guns, saddles, 'medicines,' food, and tobacco beside them. Sometimes a favorite horse is killed and interred with his master. The medicine-men or prophets conduct the funeral service, which consists of a prayer to the Great Father in this strain:

'We are sorry to part with our brother who was a daring brave and a good Indian, and whose lodge contained many scalps of his enemies. But we have yielded to Thy will, and we commit him to Thy care. We have outfitted him, as Thou seest, for his long journey; and now we desire Thee to lead him to the fair land beyond the setting sun, where game is always plentiful, and bad Indians and white men never come.'

A stake at the head of the grave is carved into a rough effigy of the 'medicine' of the deceased, and is marked with a notch for each scalp he had taken, if he did not find this brief life all too short for successful indulgence in that favorite pastime of his tomahawking race.

Some bodies are buried in sitting posture; and others are placed on the boughs of trees, where they remain until from decomposition the bones fall to the ground. The Pottawatomies observe many fast days, with wild fantastic dances and music. One band in the tribe claims lineal descent from the Children of Israel.

INDIAN BURIAL.

Kansas towns perpetuate many Indian names. Osawattomie, the home of old John Brown, was formed from the Osage and Pottawatomie rivers at whose junction it is built. Oskaloosa was named in joint honor of Oska, an old chief, and Loosa his squaw. Osawkee signifies 'the yellow leaf.' Hiawatha in Brown county commemorates Longfellow's hero. Kinnekuck is a corruption of Ke-an-ne-kuck, (the foremost man,) a great Kickapoo prophet. 'White Cloud' was a brave chief among the Iowas, and the city of White Cloud is built on his old hunting ground. Waubonsee is from Wau-bon-sie, (the dawn of day,) the name given to a Pottawatomie leader who attacked an enemy just at daybreak.

There is a legend of an old brave within the present limits of Wisconsin whose squaw annually presented him with a girl. Women are of little repute among the Indians, and the heart of the chieftain longed for a son and heir. But the squaw had all the obstinacy of her sex; and every twelvemonth the appearance of the inevitable girl filled him with despondency and chagrin. On one of these sad occasions the unhappy brave visited a little grocery, for settlers were already encroaching upon his domain. He was plunged in profoundest gloom, and refused to drink or talk.

A white loafer, knowing his disappointment, congratulated him upon the new arrow added to his domestic quiver. With a look of unutterable disgust, he ejaculated 'She-boy-'gin!' (she-boy again!) strode from the house, and never again returned to the scene of his broken hopes. And when a flourishing town sprang up around the little grocery, it was named by common consent Sheboygan.

'I cannot tell how the truth may be;
I say the tale as 'twas told to me.'

CHAPTER VIII.

EXCITEMENT now ran high. Force was almost the only law. Civil war seemed ready to blaze forth again at any moment. The fierce strife had lasted for three years, and the end was not yet. According to Daniel Webster, our fathers fought seven years for a preamble; a later writer declares that the people of Kansas battled four years to veto an act of Congress. Every newspaper, North and South, teemed with Kansas reports, received by telegraph and mail, from exchanges or resident correspondents. According to a popular story, a country subscriber stepped into the *Tribune* counting-room, desiring to purchase a back number.

'Which edition?' asked the clerk.

'The Weekly.'

'Do you know the date?'

'Not exactly,—about a year ago.'

'How can you identify it?'

'Well, it contained *something about Kansas!*'

As that description applied to every issue of the *Tribune* for the last three years, the countryman went away empty-handed.

This winter Buchanan appointed James W. Denver governor, superseding Robert J. Walker, who had refused to become a party to the bad faith of the administration. Denver was an Ohioan by birth, and had been a California pioneer, once representing the latter State in Congress. In 1852 he killed in a duel Edward Gilbert, editor of the *Alta California* and member of the Congressional delegation.

Denver came to Kansas as a national democrat, and entered upon his new duties on the twenty-second of December, 1857. His first official experience was novel. A year before, the

Territorial authorities had seized one hundred and fifty muskets and carbines from a Free State emigrant train, and they were now stored at Lecompton in the basement of the governor's office.

Sixty citizens of Lawrence, under Colonel Eldridge, called upon Denver the morning after he reached Lecompton, and demanded that the arms be given up. Denver declined, on the ground that he had no authority, and that the Free State men wanted them to overawe the ballot-box at the approaching election of January fourth. Eldridge offered to give any required security that the guns should be used for no such purpose. His excellency still refusing, Eldridge remarked:

'Governor, those guns are private property; taking them from us was an outrage; keeping them there has been an outrage. We have come here fully armed, and we are going to have them!'

This was a final argument, and proved effective. The arms were carried triumphantly to Lawrence. In Delaware City a hundred United States muskets were stored in the office of a physician. At midnight the doctor was roused by a messenger who implored him to visit a dying man several miles distant. He saddled his horse and rode to see his suppositious patient, but no dying man was found. When he returned the arms were gone. Delaware was a Pro-slavery town, and this ruse was adopted by Free State men from another settlement to obtain the guns without bloodshed. In January, a party of Free Soilers from Leavenworth, visited Kickapoo, and captured a brass twelve-pounder belonging to the Kickapoo Rangers. Harnessing six horses to the gun, they adorned it with flags, and brought it home, bearing the label, 'Election returns from Kickapoo.' This inscription was the key to much bitter feeling. At two provisional elections under the Lecompton constitution the most glaring frauds had been practised. The figures from a few precincts will illustrate:

Precinct.	Legal Voters.	Votes Returned.
Oxford,	100	1288
Delaware Crossing,	35	535
Kickapoo,	100	1057
Shawnee,	163	729

Of seven thousand votes polled for the Lecompton constitution in December, less than two thousand were legal. In Kickapoo the voters formed a ring which enclosed the polls and a whisky saloon. As it slowly revolved, one man deposited his ballot, while another on the opposite side of the circle, improved the halt by taking a drink. Many voted half a dozen times under ficticious names; the judges conniving at the fraud. The poll-books returned Henry Ward Beecher, James Buchanan, Horace Greeley, William H. Seward, and Edwin Forest, duly sworn to as amongst the voters! The returns from one precinct of Johnson county contained more than a thousand names copied *alphabetically* from an old Cincinnati business directory.

VOTING IN KICKAPOO.

The legislature, now under Free State control, passed a law submitting the Lecompton constitution to a vote of the people on the fourth of January. The same day was set apart by the Pro-slavery authorities for electing State officers under it, to be ready to serve the moment Congress should ratify it and change the Territory into a State.

There was much discussion among the Free Soilers as to whether they should vote for these State officers, that in the possible contingency of Congress admitting Kansas into the Union, under the Lecompton constitution, the power might still remain in their hands. A Territorial convention of three hundred delegates met in Lawrence and discussed the question for two days. One party favored voting to get possession of the government. The other opposed it on the grounds that all the Free Soil settlers had steadily repudiated the Lecompton constitution as illegal and fraudulent; that to vote under it would recognize its validity; and that all the election judges, being Pro-slavery, they would surely be defeated by false returns.

This warm debate continued hour after hour. The convention was nearly equally divided, but the trembling scale was suddenly turned. Lane was in the field near Fort Scott, where of late there had been much bloodshed. At midnight, on the last day of the convention, while the flaring candles in the unfinished church where it was held, lit up hundreds of anxious unwearied faces, messengers arrived in hot haste from the camp and were instantly called upon the stand. They stated that Lane's men were intrenched ready to resist the Border Ruffians and, if the Territorial authorities attempted to make them lay down their arms before their enemies were dispersed, they would fight the United States troops. This startling report was received with tremendous applause; and the convention decided not to vote. But the next morning the blood of the members had somewhat cooled, and prudence prevailed over impulse.

When the fourth of January came they *did* vote. And despite some glaring frauds, Free Soilers were elected to every office under the Lecompton constitution. These newly-chosen officers, from governor down, united in a memorial to Congress, protesting against the admission of the State under that fraudulent instrument—perhaps the only instance on record of Americans petitioning themselves out of office. The people of Kansas, also, repudiated it at the polls by a majority of about eleven thousand; (the entire vote of the Territory was thirteen thousand,) but the Pro-slavery men had refused to participate in *this* election.

J. T. Henderson, late editor of the Leavenworth *Journal*, had been secretary of the convention forming the Lecompton constitution. Now he was charged with tampering with the returns from Delaware Crossing, by inserting '5' before '35,' and thus increasing the Pro-slavery vote five hundred. Several Lawrence officers, with a volunteer posse, overtook and stopped a stage coach in which he was escaping eastward, near Westport, Missouri. As they had no legal authority in that State, Henderson drew his revolver and threatened resistance. But Providence favored the strongest battalions, and they brought him a prisoner to Lawrence. The evidence against him was not altogether convincing, and after a few days' confinement he escaped.

Nine years later Colonel William A. Phillips met the former fugitive on Pennsylvania Avenue in Washington. As they shook hands, the ex-*Tribune*-correspondent remarked:

'When I last saw you, you were clerk of the Lecompton convention.'

'Yes,' replied Henderson; 'but do you see that leg?'

Phillips glanced at the shortened limb, maimed by a rebel bullet, and answered:

'I have nothing more to say; your apology is ample!'

In this respect Henderson stood not alone. Hundreds of men who took part with the Border Ruffians during the Kansas troubles, brought forth fruits meet for repentance by fighting in the Union armies during our great war.

The legislature appointed a commission to investigate the election frauds. To do this understandingly the members needed the poll-books and returns. L. A. McLean, chief clerk of John Calhoun, (president of the Lecompton convention,) was brought before them and swore that the returns were not in Kansas—that he had sent them to Calhoun in Missouri. This was believed to be false; and a search-warrant was placed in the hands of Sheriff Samuel Walker. Armed with this document, and with a posse of eight men, Walker visited McLean's office in Lecompton.

'Search wherever you like,' said McLean; 'you will find nothing. I sent the returns into Missouri a week ago.

'We shall see,' persisted Walker: 'Boys, just pitch into that woodpile outside the door.'

McLean's cheek blanched as he answered:

'I forbid it, until I can call a lawyer to examine this warrant.'

'Call your lawyer responded the sheriff; 'but, meanwhile to save time, we will go on with the search.'

Under the wood-pile, buried in the earth, was discovered a box bearing McLean's name, and labeled 'candles.' Within it were the election returns, and they aided materially in ferreting out the frauds. McLean escaped punishment by flight, but the 'candle-box' achieved a notoriety that never candle-box won before; and its contents were so luminous that they prevented Congress from carrying out Buchanan's recommendation to admit Kansas under the Lecompton constitution.

A year later, after the strife was ended, I was present at a Free State jubilee, in Atchison county, which closed its ceremonies by burying the Lecompton constitution in a candle-box, under a wood-pile. But the Kansans will hardly re-enact the farce annually for two hundred years, as the English repeat the drama of Guy Fawkes upon each anniversary.

This winter, for the first time, the legislature was composed of Free State men. They proved faithful politically but not pecuniarily. They laid out a town twenty miles south of Lawrence, calling it Minneola; passed a charter enabling the company to hold two thousand acres of land; and then enacted a law making Minneola the Territorial capital. The members owned the town, and by making it the seat of government hoped to make their fortunes likewise.

The people emphatically disapproved of the project. The bogus legislature had located the capital at Lecompton in precisely the same way; and the Free State men had always denounced *that* proceeding as a shameless fraud.

The journalists in Lawrence held a secret evening meeting to consider the movement. The entire Free State press of the Territory and nearly all leading journals of the East were represented. An informal vote showed that every one present was hostile to the Minneola project. A consultation followed as to the most effective method of breaking it up. The men of the quill agreed to expose its true character; arranged a line of attack; studied the most vulnerable points of the scheme, and determined to keep their own counsel. A large amount of Minneola stock had been set aside for members of the press. A representative offered to present me with a share, but I declined it on the ground that I was opposed to the whole movement. He assured me that its acceptance would involve no pledge either direct or implied; and I received an elaborate certificate which in flaming colors and imposing typography declared me the owner of 'eight lots in the town of Minneola, the capital of Kansas Territory, said lots not being subject to taxation by the Minneola company.' As I received the document he remarked:

'We are going to make a great thing out of the town; in six months this share will be worth five hundred dollars. You don't believe it? How much do you owe me on our last account?'

'A hundred and fifteen dollars.'

'Well, assign this certificate over to me and I will give you a receipt in full.'

I declined the offer; bidding my interlocutor not to be over sanguine but to wait for developments. In a few days the newspapers began to be heard from. Minneola was assailed with unsparing ridicule and execration. The company not knowing whence they originated had to fight in the dark. They made a spirited contest, however; built great hotels and legislative halls in the embryo city; plausibly defended their conduct, and fancied that hostilities would soon abate. But they did not; and the schemers were nearly all ruined politically and pecuniarily. The thirty-nine representatives and their chief clerk received the appellation of the 'Forty Thieves.' The governor refused to recognize the law. Subsequent constitutional conventions and legislatures did the same, and the enterprise ended in total failure. Three or four of the company sold out during the first excitement and pocketed a handsome profit. But the next year I gladly disposed of my share for fifteen dollars; and at present Minneola consists of several excellent farms.

How history repeats itself even in petty details! In 1795 the Georgia legislature passed a law selling forty million acres of public lands for five hundred thousand dollars. The event proved that the members with one solitary exception were interested in the purchase: every one receiving money or land for his vote. The next legislature, chosen solely on that issue, declared the law null and void; ordered it to be expunged from the records and burned by the common hangman. Nearly every grand jury in the State presented the statute as a robbery and a fraud. In Congress years later, strenuous efforts were made to re-imburse the companies which had since purchased the lands, on the ground that they were innocent third parties. The postmaster-general of the United States who had bought a large interest, was at the head of one of these organizations; but the effort was defeated by a majority in the House, headed by John Randolph, who opposed the scheme in some of his most bitter speeches.

During this session of the Kansas legislature, General Lane whom President Buchanan had denounced by proclamation as 'a dangerous and turbulent military leader,' sold a piece of land, and came in possession of some money. Lucre was a novelty to the grim chieftain, and made him uncomfortable. So he issued cards informing his 'dear five hundred friends' that General Lane would 'receive' that evening at the representative hall.

Eight o'clock found the room densely crowded. Hail storms of oysters were followed by showers of champagne. On that far frontier these unwonted luxuries ripened into their legitimate American fruits—enthusiastic toasts and endless speeches. No ladies were present, and at last the hilarity became very boisterous. At its greatest hight Lane leaped upon a table, and in stentorian tones which penetrated that whole pandemonium, announced that Judge Arny had just arrived from Washington and would address the meeting. (Enthusiastic and tumultuous applause.) The expectant orator, a well-known citizen who bore the formidable initials 'W. F. M.,' was profanely entitled 'Alphabetical Arny.' He was a harmless gentleman, with a genius for getting his name into print, and a hallucination that he was a candidate for the United States Senate. Ordinarily public meetings voted him tedious, but the Lecompton constitution was pending; railways and telegraphs were as yet unknown, and there was deep anxiety to hear the latest news from Washington.

Arny came forward intensely gratified at his enthusiastic reception. Just as he uttered 'Fellow Citizens,' an inebriate auditor within three feet of him shouted in unearthly tones: 'Arny!'

Again he essayed to speak, and again that voice thundered '*Arny!*'

Meanwhile the audience had attained the perfection of confusion. Some lay upon the floor; some were stretched upon tables; others lounged over the backs of chairs, and were hurling champagne bottles at each other's heads.

At last through Lane's persuasion comparative order was restored. Arny was *full* of a very eloquent speech which probably he had been rehearsing all the way from Washington. Unfortunately it was hardly adapted to the occasion, for he commenced very solemnly:

MY FELLOW CITIZENS: After spending many months among other and different surroundings, *it does my heart good to look once more upon a scene like this!*'

'A SCENE LIKE THIS!'

The assembly had just intelligence enough left to appreciate the absurdity of such an exordium. Shouts upon shouts of laughter followed, bursting forth afresh whenever the speaker attempted to go on. At last he indignantly retired; and his sonorous oration remains unfinished to this day.

On the eve of adjournment the legislature passed the following, with only two or three dissenting voices:

RESOLVED by the Legislative Assembly of the Territory of Kansas:—

That we do hereby for the last time solemnly protest against the admission of Kansas into the Union under the Lecompton constitution.

That we hurl back with scorn the libelous charge contained in the message of the president of the United States, to the effect that the freemen of Kansas are a lawless people.

That relying upon the justice of our cause, we do hereby in behalf of the people we represent, solemnly pledge to each other and to our friends in Congress and in the States our lives, our fortunes, and our sacred honor to resist the Lecompton constitution and government *by force of arms, if necessary.*

That in this perilous hour of our history, we appeal to the civilized world for the rectitude of our position, and call upon the friends of freedom everywhere to array themselves against this last act of oppression in the Kansas drama.

That the governor be requested immediately to transmit certified copies of these resolutions to the president, the speaker of the House of Representatives, the president of the Senate, and our Territorial delegate in the Congress of the United States.

Though a Buchanan democrat, Denver proved more fair and just than any previous governor of Kansas. During the rebellion he was a brigadier-general in the Union service; and the thriving metropolis of Colorado still perpetuates his name.

One of the last deeds of the legislature was a statute authorizing a new constitutional convention which in due time formed the Leavenworth constitution. There were now four goverments, all claiming authority: the Territorial; and the three State governments under the Topeka, the Lecompton, and the Leavenworth constitutions—all awaiting ratification by Congress.

Infant constitutions are proverbially weak, and none of these three State governments ever gained vitality. Ultimately, Kansas came into the Union under a fourth constitution, framed at Wyandotte. But all these governors, beside three or four beheaded executives of the Territory were called by their titles. Governors were as plenty as blackberries and quite as cheap. Almost every prominent citizen held office in one of the conflicting organizations, and some in all of them. All public positions were sought for with eagerness. As they brought neither power, honor, nor emolument, their value was hardly appreciable, unless to remind some new Burke what shadows we are and what shadows we pursue.

CHAPTER IX.

In May I went on a tour through Johnson county, from which during recent disturbances, several Pro-slavery settlers had been driven into Missouri. Reports as to the origin and character of the difficulties were as conflicting as the stories of the notorious liar described to Dr. Franklin. 'A very pleasant fellow' said his eulogist, 'although you must not believe more than half he says.'

'Exactly,' replied the philosopher; 'but *which* half?'

On my route was the abortive little village of Turpinville, which irreverent settlers called 'Turpentine.' It consisted of three or four wretched shanties with little trade except in whisky by the glass. But recently a town company had been formed, the named changed to Johnson City, and a magnificent plan printed, with streets, avenues, and public buildings in imposing array. One day a wistful young immigrant, carpet-sack in hand, approaching the shanties, asked a farmer by the roadside,

'Can you direct me to Johnson City?'

'O, yes! there it is.'

'Where?' inquired the stranger, whose eye slowly and blankly swept the horizon.

'*There;* right before you!'

With long-drawn sigh the young man went away sorrowful, for he had *not* great possessions. He had made a small investment in the town upon the assurance that it contained thirty-three houses with thirty more in progress, property rising and prospects bright. He paid less for his knowledge than most victims, and thereafter listened not to the voice of the charmer, charm he never so wisely.

Just before my trip a marauding Free State band visited a settler at midnight and inquired his politics. Supposing them to be

Missourians he declared himself Pro-slavery. They took his horse and departed. Afterward learning that he was a Free Soiler, they tied the animal to a tree, where he found it with a note pinned to the bridle, containing the wholesome injunction never to tell a lie at ninety days, when he could tell the truth for cash! Another unfortunate fellow, just arrived was stopped by an armed band who demanded his opinions. He answered:

'I am a Free State man.'

His interlocutors, being Missourians, robbed him of his watch and money and departed. Before noon he encountered another company who made the same inquiry, but he promptly replied:

'I am Pro-slavery.'

This time the marauders, who loudly professed to be Free State men, took his horse and departed. Just at night while journeying on foot, he was met by a third party who asked the old question. The bewildered traveler replied:

'OLD KAINTUCK.'

'What are *your* politics? It makes no difference to me: I agree with you perfectly!'

He was not further molested.

In a field beside my road two men were planting corn. Near them, hands in pockets, lounged a third, tall and gaunt, eyes bloodshot, nose red, hair long and matted, beard ragged, and one cheek distended by a great roll of tobacco. He inquired gruffly:

''Whar are yer from, stranger?'

'Ohio. Where are you from?'

'Old Kaintuck. I reckon thar'll be a smart fight right soon; and like to know whar every man hails from.'

'Did the fight begin the other night at your neighbor's who was robbed and warned out of the country?'

'No sir; them fellers was just a pack of d—d thieves. They did'nt care any thing about politics—only wanted old Evans's money.'

'Did they molest you?'

'Nary time. They knew better. I have got twelve Mississippi rifles, seven bowie knives, and six revolvers up in my house. Six of us stops thar, and if they come near us we will kill every mother's son of them, by —! I have got ten niggers in old Kaintuck; did'nt dar bring them here; will sell them next year, and hire poor white men. If they won't let me have black servants, I will have white ones, by —!'

I afterward learned that the marauders did visit this Bombastes Furioso only a few nights before, and he proved the meekest of non-resistants, begging them to spare his life, and a little of his whisky.

I found Olathe, the county seat, under military guard; and public sentiment throughout the county universal against the robbers, who under political pretexts, were plundering promiscuously. Before many weeks the citizens effectually suppressed them.

Returning, I took the Lawrence road, and at nine in the evening sought lodging in a little white cottage, to find it occupied by a brawny Indian. He answered my greeting:

'Umph! what um want?'

'Want to stop over night. Where?'

His long, bony finger pointed down the road, and he muttered:

'Um—good woman—big house.'

'How far?'

'Um—mile—two mile—half!'

The next building was a log-house. After I had tapped several times upon its door an anxious voice from within asked:

'Who's thar?'

'A stranger. Can you keep me to-night?'

'Are you alone?'

'All alone.'

A pair of eyes peered through the crack to reconnoiter; then a whole head was visible, and the door slowly opened.

'ABOUT FULL HERE.'

'Come in stranger. Sorry to keep you waiting, but thar's so many gangs prowling the country that we have to be cautious at night.'

The only room of the little cabin contained three beds, all filled with slumberers. Despairingly asked I: Could they accommodate me for the night? The prairie patriarch, whose unkempt head loomed up like a bundle of hay above his long night-shirt, replied:

'I wish I mought, but the fact is, stranger, *we are about full here!* However, thar's the Widow C——, half a mile from here, who always keeps travelers.'

To the Widow C——'s I rode, and tapped on the door. A masculine voice promptly replied:

'Halloa! who is it!'

'A traveler: can you lodge me?'

'I reckon,' was the terse reply.

Eureka! I had found it. I was placed in the old house hard

by, where I slept refreshingly in one bed, while a hen with a brood of chickens occupied another.

Breakfast proved the widow a model of cookery, and her conversation a marvel of loquacity. Then I went on my way rejoicing, riding toward Lawrence in the society of a drunken Indian, who by the slipping of his saddle-girth was three times thrown head-foremost on the ground while his horse was at full gallop, and yet did not break his worthless neck.

On Thursday, June third, I was in the office of the Lawrence *Herald of Freedom*, when a boy came in with the report:

'There has just been a fight up town.'

'This was such an every-day affair that I did not look up from my writing. A moment afterward another messenger entered and said:

'There's a man killed.'

Even this excited little attention in those times of violence. But suddenly a voice was heard from the street:

'Jim Lane has killed Gaius Jenkins, and a mob has gathered around his house to hang him.'

There was no more indifference; the unarmed ran for revolvers; and we all hastened to Lane's house half a mile away. Around it were two or three hundred excited men, a few proposing to lynch Lane, but the majority declaring that he should be tried by due course of law. Among the former was the notorious ex-Sheriff Jones, who had led the Border Ruffian horde in sacking Lawrence two years earlier. During the comparative quiet which now prevailed, he frequently visited the city. In the midst of his loud talk, sheriff Samuel Walker quietly remarked:

'Look here, Jones; be careful how you recommend hanging. These people are a good deal excited already, and if they hang anybody, will be very likely to begin with *you!*'

The visitor instantly apologized for his intrusion into Lawrence affairs, and took the first stage for Lecompton.

I found General Lane upon a bed in his house, crippled by a pistol shot in the knee, and surrounded by his wife and children, all in tears.

At the residence of Jenkins only a few yards away, lay the bloody corpse of the husband and father, while the air rung with shrieks from the widow and the fatherless.

Sheriff Walker at once took Lane into custody, and the excitement soon subsided.

Lane and Jenkins both lived upon a contested 'claim' worth from ten to fifteen thousand dollars. Each insisted that he was the rightful owner, and for months the title had been in litigation at Washington. Jenkins, brave and impetuous, was widely known, having held a colonel's position in the Free State army, and been one of the famous treason prisoners in 1856. He seemed to believe that if he could drive Lane from the premises, it would improve his prospect of gaining the suit. He therefore made many threats, and at last stimulated by Lane's political rivals and enemies, proceeded to violence.

For months Lane had remained in undisputed possession of the house he occupied. Within its inclosure was a well from which the family of Jenkins obtained water. As the quarrel progressed, Lane ordered Jenkins off the premises. Jenkins persisted, cut down the fence, and forced open the cover of the well. Lane mended both breaches, and messages of defiance passed between the parties. Jenkins with three armed companions again cut down the fence, and started toward the well. Lane, gun in hand, standing near his house, warned them off, but they continued to approach menacingly. Then he fired, killing Jenkins instantly. The Jenkins party answered with two or three revolver shots, one of which entered Lane's knee.

Though justifiable by no code of sound morals, Lane did exactly what two out of three frontier settlers would have done under the circumstances. The case was fully investigated by a board of magistrates, who unanimously discharged him; and the grand jury refused to find a bill against him.

For months afterward he took no part in public affairs. He rejoined the Methodist church from which he had long been suspended, and he seldom appeared in public. But the people pardoned the homicide, and when Kansas was admitted to the Union, elected him to represent them in the Senate of the United States. For six years he remained in that high office; but as I write these pages, intelligence comes of his death by his own hand. Following Andrew Johnson's defection from the republican party which elected him, Lane had received unmistakable evidences of the indignant disapproval of his constituents. It was believed too, that he feared developments about to be made, proving him in league with a band of Kansas cormorants who were despoiling the public treasury through Indian contracts. For some weeks he showed signs of insanity and at last, near Leavenworth, fired the shot which proved fatal in a few days. Poor Lane! Under all his monstrous defects must have been some goodness, or he had never so gained and held the attachment of pure, earnest men. Through many dark years he stood true to the Free State cause and he organized the first regiment of negro troops in our great war. His life was very turbulent; now he sleeps in peace among the green prairies of the young State he struggled so long to mold.

The Kansas river, six hundred miles in length, was at first believed navigable from its mouth to Lawrence through the year, and to Fort Riley during the winter months. But it proved adapted only to that traditional steamer which could run wherever there was a heavy dew. In 1857 a small boat drawing but fourteen inches was advertised to ply semi-weekly between Kansas City and Lawrence. Her first trip occupied ten days; her second, five months. She spent the entire summer among the sand-bars.

NAVIGATION OF THE KANSAS RIVER.

During the excessive drowth, a huge cat-fish, (identical in appearance with the New England horned pout, which in its native streams seldom reaches the weight of one pound,) came swimming down the river. Just opposite Lecompton, the luckless voyager struck a sand-bar on which he landed high and dry. He was captured by hand, and found to weigh one hundred and seventeen pounds. There was one afterward caught in the Missouri, weighing one hundred and sixty pounds. But the former demonstrated that the Kansas is not navigable for catfish in low water. In 1858 however, there was an unprecedented freshet, and a little steamer drawing eighteen inches, plied upon the river with comparative success. During the same season, a party of fifteen men went safely down the great rivers from St. Joseph, Missouri, to New Orleans in a rough flat-boat, propelled by side wheels driven by cranks; and another party floated from Omaha to Leavenworth in a skiff.

Eastern people know nothing of mud. In Leavenworth, on the river bank where pedestrians were wallowing and drays plowing through the mire, which dropped in streams from the wheels and horses' feet, I saw a daintily dressed lady and gentleman attempting to walk the plank from a steamboat to the land. It proved as perilous as Mohammed's single hair over the bottomless gulf, which formed the bridge to Paradise. When half way to the shore they both slipped off and fell four or five feet into the mud-jelly and there rolled over. Each arose a pillar of mud, a modern edition of Lot's wife. They were a shade darker than the Missouri itself which early explorers called 'the Yellow River' as habitually as Roman poets sung of the yellow Tiber. Old Pactolus, where sluice-mining doubtless originated, was fabled to run itself in golden sands. Were the Missouri's discoloring element of the same material, it would be as priceless as those molten streams which pour from the furnaces in our public mints.

The 19th of May is memorable for the most revolting deed in the blood-stained history of Kansas. It was done upon the bank of the Marais des Cygnes (marsh of the swans) river, sixty miles southeast of Lawrence, and three west of the Missouri line. There eleven quiet unoffending citizens, who had never participated in the troubles, were dragged from their farms and workshops and shot down in cold blood—five of them cruelly murdered for the crime of holding Free State sentiments. The butchers were seventeen Missourians and eight Kansans, led by two wretches, Charles Hamilton and —— Brockett. They found nearly all their victims unprepared and unresisting. But one settler named

THE MARAIS DES CYGNES MASSACRE, KANSAS, MAY 19, 1858. Page 117.

Snyder successfully repelled them. Hamilton and six of his band rode up to the blacksmith shop in which Snyder was working and shouted:

'Hallo, there!'

Snyder, who had acquired considerable repute for fearlessness, stepped out of doors to find himself confronted by seven armed men.

'*Now*, by G—, sir,' exclaimed Hamilton, 'you are my prisoner!'

Snyder, if unlike the historic Pickens of South Carolina, born insensible to fear, was at least difficult to intimidate. He replied:

'Not yet!'

Then springing back into the shop he seized a shot gun, and ordered his boy of seventeen to run to the house after *his* gun. The dwelling was several rods distant, up a steep bank, entirely open to the fire of the ruffians. The son replied:

'Why, father, they will kill me.'

'Don't be afraid; I'll protect you.'

The young Vulcan started on a brisk run.

'Stop!' commanded Hamilton, 'or we'll shoot you down in your tracks.'

'Go on!' thundered the father, with his gun pointing at them; 'I'll kill the first man who takes aim at you.'

Snyder was so prompt that not one of the band raised his rifle till the boy had reached the house; then Hamilton suddenly fired at Snyder but overshot. The dauntless blacksmith immediately replied with his gun but Hamilton dropped unharmed behind his horse, though the animal fell dead.

Snyder flew back into the shop, reloaded and fired, wounding one of the assailants, who now began to retreat; then he also ran for the house. Several shots were fired after him and one took effect in his hip. He dropped behind the fence and reloaded, while the ruffians, supposing him disabled, once more approached. He unexpectedly rose up and again fired among them.

By this time the boy came out with his gun, and both father and son took shelter in a little grove near by and continued to fire briskly. Like all men who despise their lives they proved masters of the situation, and the baffled and exasperated murderers retired to join their companions.

The eleven captives already collected were taken into a deep ravine and formed into a line a few yards in front of the horsemen. Hamilton briefly gave the commands:

'Present arms. Fire.'

Twenty-five rifles and revolvers answered. Every prisoner fell. Four were killed and all but one of the rest wounded. The murderers slowly galloped away but in a few moments three returning kicked and rolled over the bodies to see if they were dead. As one appeared only slightly wounded, one of the miscreants placed his revolver to his ear and fired remarking:

'I have always found *this* a certain shot.'

The ruffians then departed leaving five men dead, and six lying beside them in extremest terror. Of the killed all were estimable citizens and all but one married. One of the survivors was not wounded but shrewdly fell with the rest, and thus escaped.

The massacre, unparalleled upon American soil, sent a shudder of horror through the North. A few partisans sought to palliate it on the ground that Pro-slavery settlers also had been brutally murdered; but Hamilton and his men bearing the brand of Cain, became fugitives and vagabonds upon the earth. Whittier's muse, never silent when freedom was wounded, sent forth the strain:

LE MARAIS DU CYGNE.

A blush as of roses
  Where rose never grew;—
Great drops on the bunch-grass,
  But not of the dew;—
A taint in the sweet air
  For wild bees to shun—
A stain that shall never
  Bleach out in the sun

From the hearths of their cabins,
  The fields of their corn,
Unwarned and unweaponed,
  The victims were torn,
By the whirlwind of murder
  Swooped up and swept on
To the low, reedy fen-lands,
  The Marsh of the Swan.

With a vain plea for mercy,
  No stout knee was crooked;
In the mouths of the rifles
  Right manly they looked.
How paled the May sunshine,
  Green Marais du Cygne,
When the death-smoke blew over
  Thy lonely ravine!

In the homes of their rearing,
  Yet warm with their lives,
Ye wait the dead only,
  Poor children and wives!
Put out the red forge-fire,
  The smith shall not come;
Unyoke the brown oxen,
  The plowman lies dumb.

Strong man of the prairies,
  Mourn bitter and wild!
Wail, desolate woman!
  Weep, fatherless child!
But the grain of God springs up
  From ashes beneath,
And the crown of his harvest
  Is life out of death.

On the lintels of Kansas
  That blood shall not dry;
Henceforth the Bad Angel
  Shall harmless go by.
Henceforth to the sunset,
  Unchecked on her way,
Shall Liberty follow
  The march of the day.

CHAPTER X.

THE Marais des Cygnes massacre re-lighted the flames of civil war in Linn, Lykins, (now Miami,) and Bourbon, all southeastern counties of Kansas, bordering upon Missouri. In Linn, James Montgomery, a Free State guerrilla leader with many adherents, drove out every obnoxious Pro-slavery settler. Several times he crossed the line into Bourbon, and attacked Fort Scott, the county seat. This Border Ruffian stronghold (Bourbon had not yet been reclaimed to Free State rule) contained the United States land office and was defended by Federal troops. Twice the soldiers endeavored to arrest Montgomery; but he sturdily resisted and put them to flight. All along the border there was no safety for life or property except in the strong arm of violence; and at the distance of fifty miles it was difficult to determine whether Montgomery's men were defending their hearths and making legitimate reprisals or shedding blood wantonly.

Governor Denver and one of his aids on behalf of the Pro-slavery party, accompanied by Governor Robinson, Judge John W. Wright and other prominent Free State citizens, made a tour through the disturbed regions endeavoring to promote peace. With Lewis N. Tappan, Edmund Babb, and other correspondents, I accompanied these peace commissioners.

June 9.—Left Lawrence in a drenching rain, riding over a great expanse of green, smiling with countless flowers. Little mounds, five or six inches high, abound, thrown up by the gopher in digging his hole. The rosin-weed or compass-plant is also plentiful, its leaves always pointing north and south. Both the mounds and the plant are unfailing indications of rich soil.

Beyond the Waukarusa we found one solitary 'black-jack' (oak.)

In Missouri there is a flourishing town named Lone Jack from a tree of this species whose pleasant shade and a cool spring at its roots, made it a favorite camping-place for early travelers.

At night we sought refuge from a thunder storm in the hospitable log house of Ottawa Jones, a Pottawatomie half-breed, educated and bearing no appearance of Indian extraction. His white wife was a native of Maine. Both had been adopted into the Ottawa tribe, and he was a chief of the band. For his Free State sympathies the Border Ruffians had burned his house, whose blackened ruins were standing a few yards from the present dwelling.

June 10.—Still raining. With difficulty we crossed the large stream, in Missouri called the Osage, and in Kansas the Marais des Cygnes. The former is from a tribe of Indians along the bank, —the latter was given by early French explorers. Passed beds of the wild onion many acres in extent. 'Chicago' is an Indian name for this plant. Stopped to ask about roads at a white farm house where we found water a foot deep on the dirt floor, and two forlorn bachelors who assured us that they were compelled to tie down their cooking stove to keep it from floating off; and that they slept very comfortably at night sailing about the room upon a raft!

In Franklin county we halted at Ohio City, containing four or five houses. In old England only cathedral towns are cities; in New England only incorporated towns; but in the ambitious West any thing is a city from a board-pile upward.

Ohio City boasted a hotel where we spent the night, as effectually bound by the water as was Victor Hugo's pioneer steamer Durande by the the rocks upon which it perched high and dry. We could not go forward, for the creeks were impassable; we could not turn back for the Marais des Cygnes, swollen since we crossed, was no longer fordable. So we spent the evening drying before the tavern fire, while our landlord gave his loquacity free course to run and be glorified,—

> 'And skilled in legendary lore,
> The lingering hours beguiled.'

From him we learned that, a few days before, a constable with four assistants attempted to take a yoke of oxen and a wagon from a neighboring farmer on an execution. The man offered no resistance, but his wife first gave the officer a 'piece of her mind,' and then drove the entire posse from the premises with a Colt's revolver. It was one woman against the Territory of Kansas, and that woman triumphed.

June 11.—Still raining. While fording the first creek Governor Robinson's whiffletree broke, and the horses sprang to the shore leaving his vehicle in the middle of the stream, The governor leaped into the current and bore Judge Wright upon his back to the bank amid shouts of laughter from the other carriages. After all the jests about Kansas governors seldom being teetotalers, and getting into hot water oftener than cold, and the executive supporting the judiciary, had been duly delivered, and the fracture repaired with ropes, we continued on to Osawattomie where we halted for the night.

THE EXECUTIVE SUPPORTING THE JUDICIARY.

In 1856, after a gallant defense by old John Brown and thirty men, this town was burned to the ground by three hundred Missourians; but it had sprung up again, and now contained a hundred houses. Brown was now absent from the Territory, but we heard many legends of the old hero and his seven sons, all of whom handled their Sharpe's rifles with fearlessness and accuracy, and constituted quite a little army.

A Pro-slavery resident was popularly known as 'Bogus Williams' to distinguish him from a Free State namesake who did *not* recognize the bogus laws. The Osawattomites would have appreciated the confusion of the French critic who described William Shakespeare as 'the divine Williams!' Before our arrival some of Montgomery's men had robbed Williams the spurious, and warned him to leave the Territory. But Montgomery, learning that their victim was a peaceful citizen who had no affiliation with murderers like Hamilton and Brockett, restored the property and charged his followers to molest no man whose acts were not obnoxious, for opinion's sake.

Of course the arrival of our party was the signal for a meeting. The expectant citizens gathered in front of the hotel and demanded speeches. The two governors and Judge Wright gratified them, indulging in some denunciations of lawlessness in general and of Montgomery in particular.

This was warring upon the Douglas in his native highlands. Charles Foster, a resident next called out, defended the partisan leader and was vociferously applauded.

Our landlady—from Ohio,—admitted us to her confidences to the extent of assuring us that her husband had been a democrat; but the burning of the town by the Border Ruffians, had singed his pockets, and transformed him into a radical abolitionist. For her own part she declared herself 'a Montgomery man,' and expressed the mild hope that Governor Denver might be drowned if he should attempt to harm that popular chieftain.

June 12.—While we were constructing a raft of planks and skiffs for crossing the swollen Pottawatomie, Pat Devlin, a young Irishman, in the apparent costume of a model artiste, holding his clothing and Sharpe's rifle high above his head, swam his fine gray horse across the stream. Then he re-dressed, gave a vigorous whoop and galloped out of sight.

Wm. Hairgrove, a Georgian fifty-eight years of age returning homeward, has accompanied us from Lawrence. He carries in his breast four bullets received from Hamilton's party in the Marais des Cygnes massacre. His beard is long and grizzly, for he has not shaved since the day of the tragedy, and swears that he never will until all the criminals are under the sod.

Hamilton who led the cut-throats is also a Georgian, and Hairgrove once aided in electing his father to the legislature of that State.

Most of the farmers along our road, are working in the fields with their rifles near them and scouts posted on the roads. They all defend Montgomery.

At night in a drenching rain we reached Moneka. While I was drying my dripping garments before the kitchen fire, a little girl of five or six years with eyes like sunbeams, and a shower of golden ringlets, was playing beside me. She was soon won to a seat on my knee and began to prattle freely of her play-things, her playfellows, and the other treasures of childhood.

Would I take her to ride in my buggy?

Yes, if she would go home with me.

'O, I can't; I can't leave my ma.'

'Why not?'

'Because she is alone—all alone.'

'Where is your father?'

'My pa's dead. The Missourians killed him.'

'Why did they kill him?'

'Because they were bad men and *he* wasn't a Missourian. They came to our house and took him away, and shot him dead. Was'nt that too bad? I can't go home with you, because I'm afraid the Missourians will come and get my ma. You don't think they'll kill *her*, too, do you?'

The little prattler was indeed the child of one of the butchered citizens. Her mother had taken temporary refuge in the hotel. She was a modest, pleasing young woman, and told her sad story very artlessly:

'My husband was sitting in the house with me, when we saw the murderers coming. I begged him to go away where they could not find him; for after the threats which had been made, I feared they would kill him. But he was very firm, and would not go. He had done nothing he said, that he should sneak off and hide like a dog; if he was to die, he would stay and die like a man. * * * We were poor, but we were living very happily together on our claim. When I felt lonely, I used to take my work out and remain with my husband in the field. Now the world is all dark, and I have nobody to go to for sympathy or advice.'

June 13.—Found all the settlers justifying the 'Jayhawkers,' a name universally applied to Montgomery's men, from the celerity of their movements and their habit of suddenly pouncing upon an enemy. Nearly all the citizens under arms, to defend their homes and if possible ferret out and punish the Marais des Cygnes murderers. They were commanded by R. B. Mitchell, then a conservative member of the Kansas legislature; afterward a major general in the Union army. Their search was unsuccessful; for the cut-throats had fled to Arizona and the Indian country.

Of course in the eye of the law Montgomery was a criminal and a freebooter. At breakfast this morning I asked Mitchell,

'Will Montgomery show himself now the governor is here?'

'No; he is too wary for that.'

But just as we were starting, the famed leader accompanied by only two men rode up and halted within a few feet of our carriage. Here he was at last—the guerrilla chieftain, whose name was in every man's mouth throughout Kansas and the neighboring States. He was about forty years old, lightly built, with thin Roman nose, light blue eyes and straight hair, then parting in the middle, which gave him a certain resemblance to John C. Fremont. The people greeted him with cheers, and one citizen remarked to our party:

JAMES MONTGOMERY.

'Now you can judge of the estimation in which we hold Montgomery. Even the conservative Free State men, who censured him before the massacre, now regard him as their protector and champion. Were any attempt made to arrest him, the entire population of the county would resist it.

When we started on, Montgomery rode beside our carriage for several miles, talking modestly but freely in a voice as low and musical as that for which Alexander Pope was termed 'the little nightingale.' He was a native of Kentucky, where he had been a school-teacher and an exhorter in the Methodist church. He was a peculiarly entertaining conversationalist and seemed more familiar with the geology of Kansas than any other man I had met. To our questions about his own exploits, he replied diffidently that he had been compelled to organize a guerilla company to protect himself and his neighbors. He continued:

'Now a guerrilla company, to be effective, must be self-sustaining—must subsist on the enemy. Therefore we feed ourselves at Pro-slavery larders and our horses at Pro-slavery corn-cribs.'

To our queries about his residence, he answered:

'I live with my wife and five children, in a very good log house. I did'nt erect it myself; a gentleman from Missouri built it; but soon after, he was unexpectedly compelled to leave the country, and so I have taken possession until he returns.'

Which meant that he had driven out some Pro-slavery citizen and occupied his dwelling. It was safe to presume that the former occupant would never come back.

His daring was beyond question and no one doubted his purity from mercenary motives. He was that most formidable of characters: a praying fighter. He held daily religious worship in his family and was reported very amiable and just in private life. Quiet, modest and silver-tongued, he was indeed

> 'The mildest-mannered man
> That ever scuttled ship or cut a throat.'

But his eye had the uneasy glare peculiar to hunted men, and his hollow laugh aroused the constant and unpleasant suggestion of a mind diseased.

Beside him rode Pat Devlin, the young Irishman who crossed the creek yesterday in such breathless haste. He had heard a report that Governor Denver was about to arrest Montgomery and hastened on to give him warning. Devlin was one of his followers, actuated partly by hatred of the Border Ruffians, partly by native recklessness. In a future chapter we shall see how this pitcher which went often to the well was at last broken.

During the day we were stopped by scouts again and again. We arrived at Lebanon where Governor Denver addressed the people, urging them to settle all future difficulties through the ballot-box and courts. He left instantly after speaking and then

Montgomery, called out by the meeting, promised that *he* would make no trouble if the courts were purified and the laws justly administered.

Finding the Marmaton dangerous to ford, we left our horses and vehicles on the north bank and crossed in a skiff to Fort Scott, the county seat of Bourbon. This was originally a military post to guard the Missouri frontier, but the Government recently abandoned it and sold the buildings to private parties. Now it is the most important town in southern Kansas. The old barracks with their ample windows, deep porticoes, fronting the public square, and stately shade trees, give it an air of age and comfort, very unusual upon the frontier.

We find all business suspended on account of the troubles. In this most violent Pro-slavery settlement, even the courts of justice have long been controlled by criminals and desperadoes who have used them to gratify political revenge, and frequently called out United States troops to enforce their processes. Here Brockett and several of the other Marais des Cygnes murderers resided, until their last atrocious deed compelled them to fly from the Territory.

Montgomery lives twenty miles distant. For months the Border Ruffian authorities have held processes for his arrest and frequently called out a large force of Federal dragoons to arrest him. But only a few nights ago he attacked the town, riddled the principal buildings with rifle-balls, and attempted to burn them. But a violent rain set in extinguishing the flames, and the little band withdrew unmolested, though their assault was made within fifty yards of an encampment of three hundred United States troops, supported by a section of artillery.

Several months ago, the county prosecuting attorney mounted upon a showy white horse, led a posse for Montgomery's arrest. The guerrilla leader, not only routed the party, but like a new Thomas á Becket, captured the officer's steed and has been riding it ever since. Indeed he was mounted upon it yesterday while accompanying our party. Later the county sheriff with a large force likewise went out to arrest the great guerrilla, the officer riding a fine spotted mule. Montgomery's rifles easily dispersed this second party. The sheriff was glad to find his way back on foot; and the partisan captain presented the captured mule to one of his lieutenants, who still retains it as a trophy.

This afternoon, a peace convention of three hundred was held on the public square. Governor Denver, Governor Robinson and Judge Wright addressed it from the hotel piazza, urging honest men of both parties to unite hereafter in putting down violence and sustaining the legal administration of justice. They were followed by Epaphroditus Ransom, a tall, herculean, gray-haired ex-governor of Michigan, who under appointment of President Buchanan now holds a lucrative position in the United States land office here. Ransom began moderately, but soon plunged into a violent Pro-slavery address. Among other intemperate statements, he declared that Free State men had originated the difficulties and committed all the outrages. Judge Wright of our party, as old as Ransom and quite as hot-blooded, instantly sprang up in front of the speaker and exclaimed:

'It is false, sir, totally false!'

Ransom retorted by giving him the lie; and for a few seconds the two aged men faced each other defiantly.

From the speakers' stand, I glanced down upon the assemblage. Instinctively, as by the law of gravitation, the auditors fell apart into two bodies, separated only by a space of eight or ten feet. For an instant, there was breathless silence, then the air was rent with the shouts:

'It's true!' 'It's false!' 'It's a d—d lie!'

A few raised their rifles, and shot guns. The rest drew revolvers from their belts, and on every side was heard the sharp click, click, click of the cocking weapons.

The speakers' platform, containing thirty or forty persons of both parties, presented a similar scene. Revolvers were drawn, threats exchanged, and Governor Robinson, the mildest of conservatives, stood close behind Ransom with clinched fists ready to hurl him down the steps the moment hostilities should begin. All this occurred almost in the twinkling of an eye; and a bloody fight seemed inevitable. But just at this moment Governor Denver who was in the hotel parlor conversing with a party of ladies, heard the tumult, rushed out, sprang between Ransom and Wright and commanded the peace.

A PEACE CONVENTION AT FORT SCOTT, KANSAS, PAGE 128.

'Fellow citizens,' said he, 'is *this* the way to reconciliation? How can order be restored if all these old sores are to be re-opened.' Both these gentlemen are my seniors but I must censure them. They should not let passion run away with reason. We came to promote harmony; let us have no more of these disgraceful scenes.'

This restored quiet; there were apologies and conciliatory speeches and then the meeting adjourned.

June 15.—Governor Denver has removed the obnoxious county officers, and appointed good unpartisan citizens to fill their places.

To-day both parties signed a written agreement hereafter to avoid intemperate language, obey the laws and discountenance violence. Both seem thoroughly weary of the reign of disorder.

June 16.—Left Fort Scott this morning, going north within two or three miles of the Missouri line. The country is dotted with conical mounds from fifty to a hundred feet high. Nearly all the houses are deserted. At one cabin I found a young Scotch couple surrounded by evidences of their national industry and thrift. Nearly all their neighbors had been frightened away. The girlish wife had come alone from the far Highlands, across the sea and over the land, to fulfill her plighted troth; for her lover emigrated five years before her.

The next occupied house had but one apartment, and contained only an old German who had apparently forgotten his own language and never learned any other. Sitting upon a box he was bathing a sore knee from a tin cup. Our colloquy was brief:

'A warm day, sir.'

'Ya, saer varm.'

'Do you live here all alone?'

'Ya, mein herr.'

'Where is your family.

'Ah, mein vife dead. Mein sons go off, get claims.'

'Are you not afraid of the Missourians?'

'Oh!' (shrugging his shoulders,) 'Misshourian bad man—kill Free-shlave man. I shtop door—fasten,' (pointing to the door-bar,) 'let him nicht in. If he come, den,' (showing his double-barreled gun,) 'I shoot!'

'Good! Now father Gambrinus have you any cool water?'

'Vater? Oh, ya.'

And the ancient Teuton deliberately emptied his cup, filled it from a bucket and offered us a draught! We adjourned our thirst to the next brook, and bade him good morning.

Beyond, two sentinels armed with Sharpe's rifles, stopped us, but learning that we were friends, took us to the Free State camp of twenty-five men whose scouts were out for miles north and south, guarding the Missouri line. We crossed the Marais des Cygnes and spent the night at 'Trading Post,' a little cluster of houses, two miles from the nineteenth-of-May tragedy.

June 17.—This morning we visited the scene of the massacre, finding nearly all houses in the vicinity deserted. Our old friend, Mr. Hairgrove, one of the fortunate who escaped with wounds, showed us the several dwellings from which the victims were taken and the dark ravine where the foul murder was committed. We also visited the rough little shop where the blacksmith, Snyder, made such gallant resistance. In the afternoon, a meeting of several hundred settlers was addressed by Denver, Robinson, Wright and Montgomery. Denver appointed new township officers and both parties signed a pledge similar to that given at Fort Scott. Montgomery promised, if the agreement now made were kept, to lay down his arms, and devote himself to his cattle and corn-fields. His remarks were manly and eloquent. He said:

'I have accepted the olive branch. To-day I come from home without my rifle—the first time for months. I have been charged with foulest crimes; but you all know my acts. I have done nothing under a bushel. If any man asserts that I have disturbed one peaceable citizen, I deny the charge and defy the proof. If any assert that I have abused or insulted a woman, I deny the charge and defy the proof. I have said I never would be tried at Fort Scott, and I never will. No Free State man could hope for justice there. But I trust we are now to have honest courts in our own county. If so, I pledge my honor to answer promptly any indictment. I will obey every legal process; stand my trial and abide the issue.'

We returned to Lawrence, and for a few months there was quiet in southeastern Kansas. Montgomery became a peaceful citizen. In 1862, I met him again—serving as colonel of a Kansas regiment in the Union army. His eye had become healthy, and he had lost his hollow jarring laugh.

CHAPTER XI.

I 'ASSISTED' at a rural celebration of the Fourth of July in the village of Monrovia, Atchison county. The adjacent settlers came thronging in on horseback, on foot, and in heavy ox-wagons, sitting upon rush-bottomed chairs. One family even rode triumphantly on a stone drag,—a broad plank dragged over the ground by two horses.

Speeches were made in the open air, and the young people entertained themselves by dancing most perseveringly from Friday night until Sunday morning.

In the midst of the assembly sat an elderly matron in decorous black, patiently listening and smoking a cigar. While traveling in Missouri, I have seen a mother and her little girl of ten years, smoking their pipes over the breakfast they were cooking. Once, stopping to spend the night with an intelligent young squatter from Tennessee, I found his wife a lovely blonde with liquid eyes and long drooping lashes; but alas! after serving tea, she drew from one of the smoky nooks of the chimney an old black pipe, and sat down to enjoy an evening whiff.

During this summer and fall, fever and ague visited almost every farm-house. The disease is inevitable wherever a rich soil is broken for the first time, loading the air with miasma. Fruit and fresh vegetables are good preventives; quinine the invariable remedy. With ordinary care blondes may avoid it, but brunettes, being of more bilious temperament, rarely escape. Before attacking it gives forewarning in blinding headaches and nauseous mouths. The ounce of prevention is cheap, the pound of cure costly; for if lodged in the system it clings tenaciously. An old settler in the Wabash valley of Indiana once told me that he had suffered from it every season for twenty-seven years. Still he not only clung to his cot but thought the valley he loved, a very Eden. Nearly all western States cherish legends of remote villages where the church bells are rung every day at noon for the people to take their quinine. But though the traveler is often told that chills and fever abound in the next settlement, he never finds a section which the inhabitants admit to be an 'ague country.'

Kansas has no swamps and little bottomland. But most of the early settlers (Missourians) regarded this disease as a necessary evil. I remember a matron from Kentucky, pale and wan from years of its enervating and dispiriting attacks, who said:

'I have been chilling now for two months and I never seen a well day in Kansas. A freestone country is never so healthy as a limestone country, anyhow.'

The invalid favored me with this oracular utterance late in the evening while indulging in a hearty supper of hot corn bread and molasses, fat pork and strong coffee!

In Kansas one heard the slang and provincialisms of every section of the country, beside some indigenous to the soil. The importations were chiefly from Missouri, which had furnished more than half the entire population. Most readers have heard Ohioans spoken of as 'Buckeyes,' (from the buckeye tree,) Illinoians as 'Suckers,' Indianians as 'Hoosiers,' and Michiganders as 'Wolverines.' Early Californians christened as 'Pukes' the immigrants from Missouri, declaring that they had been vomited forth from that prolific State. And however shocking to ears polite, the appellation has adhered to them ever since. Missourians transplanted into Kansas many of their pet home-phrases. One morning at breakfast a squatter host of mine remarked:

'*These* molasses is sweeter than any maple molasses I ever seen.'

This unique use of the national saccharine only in the plural, not uncommon through the Southwest, originated in Pennsylvania. I heard another Missourian reply to inquiries touching his health:

'I had the shakes last week, but now I have *got shut* of them.'

A third, asked concerning his crop of corn, responded:

'Yes, I raised a power of it. I have fed a heap to my cattle and got a right smart chance left.'

Still another with the prevalent contempt for small estates, told me with great merriment about a traveler from Ohio who had only thirty acres of land, and actually called *that* a farm! It was the one memorable jest in that Missourian's experience, and I am confident he never mentions it to this day without roars of laughter.

'Tolerable' is forced into universal service. Once in Missouri I asked a fellow traveler:

'Is it a good road from here to St. Joseph?'

'Tolerable good, sir.'

It proved intolerably bad. Just afterward meeting a teamster, I changed the form of the question, thus:

'A bad road from here to St. Joseph, is it not?'

'Tolerable bad, stranger.'

Next encountering a little darkey with staring white eyes, I inquired:

'Is it a straight road from here to St. Joseph?'

'Tolerable straight massa,' replied young Ebony, displaying from ear to ear a row of ivory. The same evening, at a country inn, I heard a wayfarer ask:

'Can I get to stay with you to-night.

'I reckon,' answered Boniface, 'though we are right smart crowded.' And before our evening fire he spoke of a swelling upon his knee as 'a rising.'

A school girl in Kansas asked her playmates from Missouri,—

'Will you go a berrying with me?'

'A *burying!* Why who's dead?'

'Nobody: I mean, to gather blackberries.'

Rural Missourians never carried burdens, but always 'packed' or 'toted' them. Among other provincialisms through the Southwest, the use of 'crapped' (a corruption of cropped,) is sometimes droll and startling. General Marcy tells of an Arkansan who, pointing to a little man with a huge wife, inquired:

'Cap, don't you reckon that that thar little man has a bit *over crapped* his self?'

The use of 'beef' as the singular of 'beeves,' obsolete through the East, is common—the western farmer usually saying, 'I have just sold a beef.'

The New Englander shouts to a distant friend:

'Hallo——a, John!' The southerner or westerner cries:

O-o-o-o, John!'

Immigrants from the East were very merry at the expense of their Missouri neighbors. In a street discussion a lounger was defending as correct, the rural southern phrases,—'We 'uns' and 'You 'uns.' One of the bystanders asked him:

'Are you a grammarian?'

'Which?' was his bewildered inquiry.

'Are you a grammarian?'

'Why, no, I'm a Missourian!'

It was a distinction *with* a difference. But the fun is not all on one side. I remember an old Missourian who was brought in contact with many eastern men by the establishment of a new stage line through his neighborhood. Said he:

'I've lived on the frontier all my life. I know English and the sign-language, and have picked up a smattering of French, Spanish, Choctaw, and Delaware; but one language I *can't* understand, and that is this infernal New York language!'

One frequently heard the senseless phrase: 'Not by a dog-on-d sight,' or 'I wanted to go dog-on-d badly'—meaning 'a great sight' and 'very badly.' From Minnesota had been imported the mysterious term 'scull-duggery,' used to signify political or other trickery. One often heard, even from educated men remarks like this:

Do you see Smith and Brown whispering there in the corner? They are up to some scull-duggery.'

Another and more significant barbarism is 'the dead wood,'—from the game of 'ten-pins,' in which a fallen pin sometimes lies in front of the standing ones so that the first ball striking it will sweep the alley. 'I have the dead wood on him' was used familiarly, meaning: 'I have him in my power.' 'I have him *corraled*,' originating in New Mexico and California from the Spanish *corral* or cattle-yard, bore exactly the same signification. 'Scooped' was an importation from Wall Street. 'I am badly scooped' meant: 'I am used up' or 'defeated.' 'Bursted' sometimes appeared even in print as the past tense of 'burst.'

In his instructive Notes on the English Language, George P.

Marsh observes: 'In no part of America do the natives confuse their v's and w's after the manner of the Weller family.' But he will find native Pennsylvanians who say 'werry' and 'wulgar.' Even some graduates of leading universities habitually use 'oncet' and 'twicet.' Still our country has fewer provincialisms than any other, and the railways on their march of improvement are rapidly sweeping those away.

In August Kansas was stirred by two new excitements. One was the reported discovery of abundant pearls on the Verdigris river, near the uninhabited southern border. The settlers rushed from all directions to pick up handfuls of such a tempting crop; for human nature will not stay to dig potatoes and gather pumpkins when it is promised pearls. But these treasures proved to be worth about five dollars a bushel—solely for the magnesia they contained.

Simultaneously with this came a gold fever, caused by the return of several adventurers from the mountains. From earliest explorations by white men, the vast region of sand and alkali, sage-brush, greasewood and cactus, extending from western Kansas to the Sierra Nevadas, and from the British Possessions to northern Mexico, was called the 'Great American Desert.' Its boundless wastes, often sweeping for hundreds of miles in dreary sand-hills and plains destitute of water, trees and grass, were peculiarly repulsive and believed to be utterly unproductive. But the Rocky Mountains, crossing this whole tract from north to south, in a series of ranges sometimes a thousand miles in width, were more alluring. Their deep solemn forests of pine and fir, their flashing streams and lovely vistas of greensward inclosed by vast walls of rock with snow-covered summits were a pleasant relief to the eye wearied by desert wastes. There were early traditions of gold and other treasures. A book published in Cincinnati fifty years ago, says:

'These mountains are supposed to contain minerals, precious stones and gold and silver ore. It is but late that they have taken the name Rocky Mountains; by all the old travelers they are called the Shining Mountains * from an infinite number of crys-

---

* Idaho signifies 'the shining mountains,'—a fitting name; for some of its peaks glitter in the sunlight with unequaled brilliancy.

tal stones of an amazing size, with which they are covered, and which, when the sun shines full upon them, sparkle so as to be seen at a great distance. The same early travelers gave it as their opinion that in future these mountains would be found to contain more riches than those of Indostan and Malabar, or the golden coast of Guinea, or the mines of Peru.'

These surmises excited little notice, for the 'early travelers' believed every mountain an El Dorado and every stream a Pactolus. The first statement which appeared worthy of serious attention was made by Colonel William Gilpin of the United States army. This gentleman, a zealous student of the natural sciences, crossed the continent with a party of Oregon explorers, and again with his command during the Mexican war. In 1849, in an address at Independence, Missouri, as the result of all his observations, he asserted the abundant existence of gold, silver, and precious stones throughout the Rocky Mountains. But his hearers voted him an enthusiast; and for ten years longer the only white inhabitants of the remote mountains continued to be trappers and traders.

The first organized attempt to prospect the mountains for gold was made by a party of Cherokee Indians, in 1857; but they were driven back by hostile savages. General Marcy relates that in May 1858, a teamster of his expedition returning from New Mexico to Utah, washed grains of gold from the sandy bed of Cherry Creek, where Denver now stands. In the spring of that year a party set out from Georgia to seek gold in these mountains, and at the same time several young men from Kansas stimulated by the sight of a rich nugget which a Delaware Indian declared he had found there, started for the same region.

In August they returned, ragged and shaggy, but reporting that they had found rich deposits near the base of Pike's Peak. They told extravagant stories; but when asked to show specimens of the precious metal one would produce from the bottom of his pocket a little quill containing a few shining grains. All the gold they brought home would not have paid a week's board for the party.

But their reports were corroborated by rumors from other sources and strengthened by 'the well-known proclivity of lumps to increase in size the further they roll.' Gold—talismanic word! —stirred the hearts of the mercurial population of the frontier. Several hundred persons immediately started for Pike's Peak—

among them a persevering printer, who with precisely ten cents in his pocket trundled his complete outfit of clothing, provisions and mining tools in a wheelbarrow, seven hundred miles—from Kansas City to the base of the mountains! Thus began the first migration to the Rocky Mountain gold region.

RETURNED PIKE'S PEAKERS.

Rattlesnakes were one unpleasant feature of Kansas life. While camping out, one sometimes found them unpleasantly near him in the morning. In houses whose floors were laid with green lumber, which in seasoning left broad openings, the inmates were occasionally startled to see one of these reptiles peer up through a crack, and stare about the room. I knew one delicate lady from Connecticut, who on blackberrying expeditions in the woods, frequently killed huge rattlesnakes three or four feet in length. I think the western species is less poisonous than those of the East; for old settlers from Missouri and Illinois hold them in little terror. When bitten they drink from a pint to a quart of raw whisky, which is believed to neutralize the virus, and reputed an unfailing remedy. The rattle of the snake has a peculiarly hollow, death-like sound; but he never springs without this warning, and he can only strike half the length of his body.

During this fall many residents were preëmpting their claims. The law contemplates a homestead of one hundred and sixty acres at a nominal price for each actual settler and no one else;

but land is plenty and everybody preëmpts. A young merchant, lawyer, or speculator, rides into the interior, to the unoccupied public lands, pays some settler five dollars to show him the vacant 'claims,' and selects one upon which he places four little poles around a hollow square upon the ground, as children commence a cob-house. Then he files a notice in the land-office that he has laid the foundation of a house upon this claim and begun a settlement for actual residence. He does not see the land again until ready to 'prove up,' which he may do after thirty days. Then he revisits his claim, possibly erects a house of rough slabs, costing from ten to twenty dollars, eats one meal and sleeps for a single night under its roof. More frequently, however, his improvements consist solely of a foundation of four logs. He goes to the land-office with a witness, and certifies under oath his desire to preëmpt the north-west quarter of section twenty-four, township ten, range thirteen, (or whatever the tract may be,) for his 'own exclusive use and benefit.' The witness also swears that the preëmptor settled upon the land at the time stated, and erected 'a habitable dwelling,' in which he still resides. Sometimes he is interrogated closely; but he can reply under oath to as many questions as the officer can ask; so the preëmptor 'locates' a land-warrant upon the claim—*i. e.*, leaves one in payment

A MORNING CALLER.

A HABITABLE DWELLING.

for it, as warrants can always be bought for less than one dollar twenty-five cents per acre, which must be given for Government lands when paid for in money. In return, he receives a preliminary title or 'duplicate' in the following form:

(Preëmption Act of Sept. 4, 1841.)

MILITARY BOUNTY LAND ACT OF MARCH 3, 1855.

No. 3614.

Register's Office, Kickapoo, K. T., March 3, 1859.

Military Land Warrant No. 77,298 in the name of Mary Wilkins, has this day been located by John Smith upon the Northwest quarter of Section Twenty-three, in Township Six, South of range Nineteen, subject to any preëmption claim which may be filed for said land within forty days from this date.

Contents of tract located, }
160 acres.

J. W. WHITFELD, *Register.*
By THOS. P. BEACH.

After the lapse of a few months, required for reporting the preëmption to the General Land-office at Washington, upon the surrender of his duplicate he obtains a final title or 'patent' from the Government, inscribed on parchment, and running in this wise:

THE UNITED STATES OF AMERICA.

To all to whom these presents shall come, Greeting·—

Whereas, in pursuance of the Act of Congress approved March 3, 1855, entitled 'An Act in addition to certain Acts granting Bounty Land to certain Officers, and Soldiers, who have been engaged in the Military Service of the United States' there has been deposited in the General Land Office, Warrant No. 77,298 for one hundred and sixty acres, in favor of Mary Wilkins, widow of Willis Wilkins, Private, Captain Kenshaw's Company, Tennessee Militia, War 1812, with evidence that the same has been duly located upon the Northwest quarter of Section Twenty-three, in Township Six, south of range Nineteen, in the District of lands subject to sale at Kickapoo, Kansas Territory, containing one hundred and sixty acres according to the Official Plat of the survey of the said land returned to the General Land Office, by the Surveyor General—the said Warrant having been assigned by the said Mary Wilkins to Santford M. White, and by him to JOHN SMITH, in whose favor said tract has been located: Now know ye that there is therefore granted by the United States, unto the said JOHN SMITH, as assignee as aforesaid, and to his heirs, the tract of land above described, to have and to hold the said tract of land, with the appurtenances thereof, unto the said JOHN SMITH, as assignee as aforesaid, and to his heirs and assigns forever.

In testimony whereof, I, James Buchanan, President of the United States of America, have caused these Letters to be made Patent, and the Seal of the General Land Office to be hereunto affixed.

Given under my hand at the City of Washington, the Tenth day of September, in the Year of our Lord One Thousand Eight Hundred and Sixty, and of the Independence of the United States the Eighty-fifth.

By the President,

Seal of the General Land Office.

JAMES BUCHANAN.

By J. B. LEONARD, *Secretary.*

J. W. GRANGER, *Recorder of the General Land Office.*

Recorded Vol. 412, page 221.

In three cases out of four, after 'proving up,' the preëmptor never visits his land again unless for the purpose of selling it. Says the Spanish proverb, 'Oaths are words, and words are wind.' Thus this unequivocal perjury is regarded upon the frontier. The general feeling is that it wrongs no one, and that the settlers have a right to the land.

Hundreds of men whose families are still in the East find witnesses to testify that their wives and children are residing upon the land. I have known men to preëmpt who had never been within twenty miles of their claims, facile witnesses swearing with the utmost indifference that they were residing upon them.

A HOUSE 'TWELVE BY FOURTEEN.'

The preëmptors must state under oath that they have made no agreement direct or indirect for selling any part of the land. But in numberless instances these statements are falsehoods, connived at by the officers.

In most land-offices a man cannot preëmpt unless he has a house at least twelve feet square. I have known a witness to swear that the house in question was 'twelve by fourteen,' when actually the only building upon the claim was one whittled out with a penknife, twelve *inches* by fourteen.

Some offices require that the house must have a glass window. While traveling in the interior, I stopped at a little slab cabin, where I noticed a window-sash without lights hanging upon a nail. As I had seen similar frames in other cabins, I asked the owner what it was for.

'To preëmpt with,' was the reply.

'How?'

'Why, don't you understand? To enable my witness to swear that there is *a window in my house!*'

Sometimes the same cabin is moved from claim to claim, until half a dozen different persons have preëmpted with it. In Nebraska a little frame house, like a country daguerrean car, was built for this purpose *on wheels*, and drawn by oxen. It enabled the preëmptor to swear that he had a bona fide residence upon his claim. It was let at five dollars a day, and scores of claims were proved up and preëmpted with it. The discovery of any such malpractice and perjury would invalidate the title. But I never knew of an instance where the preëmptor was deprived of his land after once receiving his title.

A BONA FIDE RESIDENCE.

No woman can preëmpt unless she is a widow or the 'head of a family.' But sometimes an ambitious maiden who wishes to secure one hundred and sixty acres of land, *borrows* a child, signs papers of adoption, swears that she is the head of a family, and preëmpts her claim; then annuls the papers and returns her temporary offspring to its parents with an appropriate gift.

During an August excursion I was impressed for the hundredth time with the surpassing beauty of a night in Kansas. Upon a soft background of pure sky, trees and foliage lay penciled with wonderful distinctness; the silent river was broken up into restless little waves that tossed hither and thither gleams of moonlight; and profoundest quiet rested upon wood and water, broken now and then by the cry of a whippowil or the far-off tinkle of cow-bells upon the prairie.

Kansas life had novel social features. A prisoner in Atchison county was held to bail for appearance at court on some minor criminal charge. Any one's bond would have been taken; but he resolutely refused to give bail. There was no jail wherein to confine him. There was no money in the treasury to hire a guard. The deputy-sheriff was obliged to take him into his personal custody; and the prisoner, improving his first opportunity, leisurely walked away.

William Arthur, a resident of Sumner, one day crossed the river in a skiff, with his wife and children. Near the Missouri shore was a long sand-bar, which the boat could not pass. Arthur secured it and left his family in it, remarking that he would swim the narrow arm of the stream, transact his business, and return in a few minutes. He was an excellent swimmer; so his wife offerred no opposition, and he plunged in. For a few yards he swam rapidly and easily; but suddenly he threw up his arms and sank, his hat floating away. In a few seconds he rose to the surface, struggled wildly, then sank again, and was seen no more. The cries of the distracted woman brought several men in skiffs, who searched for two days but without success;—in the strong Missouri current bodies are seldom found near the place of drowning.

Arthur and his wife had sometimes quarreled, but the grief of the *widow* was very poignant. I shall never forget the shrieks and groans of the poor woman during the days and nights immediately after her bereavement. But Time the great healer calmed her; the estate was finally settled and the little property secured to herself and the children.

She afterward learnt that her husband sank *intentionally*, swam several rods under water, came up behind a log and breathed for a moment, then continued, still under water, to the shore, and gained the bank unperceived. There the ingenious scoundrel amused himself for a while by watching the search made for his corpse, then procured a hat and spent the night at the house of a confidential friend; traveled across Missouri and Illinois to Indiana, and there under an assumed name married again! When his wife heard this, she started in pursuit of her old husband and his new partner in a spirit illustrative of Congreve's aphorism:

'Hell hath no fury like a woman scorned.'

I never learned the result, but there must have been a 'wreck of matter' when she caught them.

About the same time the invalid wife of a Territorial officer was sent to New Orleans for her health. Her husband received several letters from her dated and postmarked at the Crescent City. But one day in St. Louis, while awaiting dinner in the reading-room of the Planters' House, he glanced at a weekly newspaper published in an obscure Indiana town. Suddenly his attention was arrested by an advertisement notifying him that his wife had applied for a divorce and that the case would be tried the following day. The truth flashed upon the thunderstruck husband. While sending her letters to New Orleans for mailing, his wife had resided in Indiana long enough to claim a residence under the peculiar divorce laws of that State. As the statute required, she had notified him by publication; relying upon the trivial circulation of the paper as a safeguard against its reaching him. Though one of the best laid schemes, it went 'a-gley.' Her distracted lord rushed upon a train of cars just leaving for the East, chartered a special locomotive from an Indiana junction to the county seat, and entered the court-room while the case was pending, just in time to prevent judgment against him by default. He found his wife under the protection of another prominent Kansas politician, who had been for some weeks ostensibly in New York. Proceedings were stopped, the trio returned home, and husband and wife resumed their old relations.

During night rides in winter, I often saw prairie fires blazing along the horizon. Though never dangerous to men or animals, as depicted in our school-geographies, they are always startling and grand. The sky is pierced with tall pyramids of flame, or covered with writhing, leaping, lurid serpents, or transformed into a broad ocean lit up by a blazing sunset. Now a whole avalanche of fire slides off into the prairie, and then opening its great, devouring jaws closes in upon the deadened grass.

One of my December trips was to St. Joseph. Crossing the Missouri my road led along rich bottomlands, from three to eight miles wide, densely wooded with noble trees, and prolific of fever and ague. Like the high Kansas prairies, which sometimes yield one hundred and twenty-five bushels to the acre, this damp jet-black soil produces corn in incredible abundance. If political economists are right, and the happiness of a people is in exact proportion to their rapidity of increase, Missouri must be the very home of the blessed; for at every cabin tow-headed boys and girls spring up and grow like weeds. They can hardly be more plentiful along the Nile, where it is said to cost only three dollars apiece to rear children to maturity.

Leaving this narrow valley, I entered the garden of Missouri. Instead of log-cabins plastered with mud, appeared generous frame and brick dwellings surrounded by natural parks of oak and elm. On all sides were fields of corn wheat and hemp. The latter requires rich soil; a Missouri proverb asserts that land which will raise hemp will produce any other crop. Here in fields of a hundred acres the hemp, already cut, was rotting upon the ground, or standing in stacks like wheat sheaves. The slaves were fat and comfortable-looking, but few in number; for recent mechanical improvements in cutting and breaking hemp were rapidly taking the place of manual labor—silent colporteurs spreading the gospel of freedom. Twenty years before, the farmers preëmpted their land at one dollar and twenty-five cents per acre; now it was held at thirty and forty dollars. The settlers had grown rich by selling their products for the heavy overland-trade. This commerce built up successively Jefferson City, Booneville, Independence, Kansas City, Westport, Weston, St. Joseph, Leavenworth, Atchison and Omaha, as each in turn became the chief out fitting point for the emigration to California, Oregon, Colorado, Montana, and Idaho.

St. Joseph now contained five thousand inhabitants, was built mainly of brick, and pleasantly shaded. But wise ones prophesied that it could never be a great city, as it stood on the east side of the river, while all important commercial towns on the frontier spring up on the western banks. On the way homeward, I encountered an Indiana family en-route for Kansas, in a covered wagon drawn by two horses. They had not slept under a roof for two months. The ground was covered with snow, and the mercury below zero; but the wife and little children all declared that they slept comfortably in their vehicle in the open air.

Reaching the Missouri again, I found the ice running so heavily, that it was impossible to cross. Two days passed before the winter bridge became firm enough for footmen and horses.

This autumn certain rash friends in Sumner had nominated me for the legislature. Upon election morning one of my Pro-slavery neighbors, an ex-Missourian, addressed me at the polls with great earnestness:

'Mr. R—, I heard your speech the other night, and I liked your sentiments. But I am told that after I came away you avowed yourself a black republican. I had concluded to vote for you, but I cannot vote for a black republican. Did you say it?'

'No. I know no political distinctions now except Free State and Pro-slavery. But I did say that whenever the Territory became a State, and the issue should arise between republicanism and democracy, I should be a republican.'

'Well!' (very earnestly,) you didn't say *black* republican, did you?'

'No, sir.'

'Then I shall vote for you, for I liked your speech; but I'll be d—d if I ever vote for a black republican!'

Several democrats labored long and patiently to convince him that the obnoxious adjective was inseparable from the inoffensive noun. He heard them patiently, but then replied:

'Gentlemen, I don't think Mr. R— is that kind of a man. He don't act like it, he don't look like it, he don't talk like it; and I am bound to vote for him.'

And vote for me he did, to their great disgust.

CHAPTER XII.

The Territorial legislature of this winter was a more reputable body than that of the previous year. Still one of the representatives, originally from Indiana, in recording himself a physician transcribed very promptly the letters 'P-h-i-s-i'—then hesitated a moment, and at last, turning to a bystander asked in all seriousness:

'Do you spell physician 'tion,' or 'sion?'

This parliamentary body had the genuine frontier fondness for rollicking humor. One day a jovial lobby member from Coffey county, whom for convenience I will call Jones, was discovered attempting to kiss a chamber-maid at his hotel. This was a good pretext for sport. So, late that night a burlesque court was organized. A Hoosier judge, named Baker, irrepressibly funny, presided. Mr. Larzalere the speaker of the House of Representatives, was appointed to the high dignity of constable. An indictment was framed against Jones, charging him with the offense already mentioned, as committed 'in defiance of the form of statute for such cases made and provided, and against the peace and dignity of the Territory of Kansas.'

The constable found him in bed; but he was unceremoniously dragged forth, and after a hasty toilet, brought into the court-room. A jury was impaneled with some difficulty, many persons being challenged on the most novel grounds. Territorial Secretary Walsh, for example, was excused from serving, on the allegation of bad moral character. Two members of the House were appointed, one to prosecute, and the other to defend the suit. It being well understood that all fines there assessed were payable in oysters, the witnesses, instead of being sworn to tell the truth the whole truth and nothing but the truth, were reminded that they stood before an august tribunal in the great Mississippi valley; and warned to stand on their dignity, and give the testimony which, in their judgment, would *produce the most oysters* for the court!

The proof, though utterly contradictory, was held conclusive, the court ruling that names and dates were immaterial, and that hearsay testimony was circumstantial evidence. The case was made out in the most minute manner, even to exhibiting the bald head of Jones, from which the young woman was alleged to have plucked the hair in self-defense! The prosecuting attorney—John W. Wright, who had been for twenty years a district judge in Indiana—attempted to break down a witness for defense named Warren, by asking impertinent questions, when Warren retorted by giving such testimony as implicated Wright himself in the assault, and he was promptly taken into custody as an accessory to the crime. R. B. Mitchell, counsel for defense, upon hinting that the court was partial, was fined two cans of oysters for contempt.

The case was argued. The court, in charging the jury, instructed them peremptorily to bring in a verdict of guilty. The prosecutor suggesting some further instructions in regard to the amount of the fine, the judge rebuked him sharply, assuring him that the court understood herself perfectly! Jones was of course found guilty. The judge, after a touching appeal to his feelings, fined him twelve cans of oysters and two baskets of champagne; assured him that it being a court of original and exclusive jurisdiction, there could be no appeal from its decisions, and ordered him into custody until the fine and costs should be paid. He, entering fully into the spirit of the occasion, did not demur; and within half an hour, court, jury, spectators and the prisoner, sat down to the repast. Toasts, songs and speeches followed, and the festivities were prolonged until the total expense to Jones of attempting to kiss the pretty chamber-maid, footed up to about a hundred dollars.

The legislature passed scores of divorce bills. Practically, any one asking for a divorce, could obtain it; and in every case both parties were authorized to marry again. One lady (whose husband had separated from her in Boston because like the mightiest Julius he would have a wife above suspicion,) now residing temporarily in Kansas, sent in a petition to be released from her bonds. The chairman of the House committee on marriage and divorce—

a confirmed old bachelor—reported with grim satire, that the wrongs she had suffered appealed to the humanity of every member present; and recommended that her prayer be granted. A bill was at once reported: the rules were suspended and in four or five hours it passed both branches, was signed by the governor and became a law.

One wag in the House, introduced a bill declaring marriage abolished in Kansas, and free love established in its place. A second moved that the legislative bachelors proceed to ballot for the 'widows' who had been divorced. A third in an earnest speech declared that divorce bills were now passed so hastily as to render it unsafe for a married man to seek his domestic couch at night, lest he should wake up in the morning to find himself violating a commandment. I received a letter from a citizen of Massachusetts asking whether his wife, who was spending the winter in Lawrence, passed by her maiden or wedded name, and whether she had applied for divorce. Upon examining the statutes, I learned that she had been divorced for more than six months.

The divorce laws of all our new States and Territories are practically very liberal; seldom compelling men or women to remain in marriage bonds which they wish severed, save in cases where the motive for gaining freedom is obviously mercenary. It is a striking illustration of the differing customs of different sections, that while in South Carolina, and also in New Mexico where the doctrines of the Roman church rule, no one can obtain a divorce for any cause, yet in Utah even the probate courts have full power with or without public notice to divorce any person demanding it, with or without cause.

This Kansas legislature abrogated by a single act, the multitudinous and barbarous laws passed by the legislature of Missouri invaders, and until now in nominal force. The repeal caused general rejoicing; and in a bonfire of tar barrels at Lawrence, the huge volume of bogus statutes was burned amid joyful shouts and huzzas. Another copy was sent to the governor of Missouri, with a statement that the people of Kansas had no further use for it.

The legislature also passed an 'amnesty act,' directing that all persons charged with crimes arising from political disturbances in several counties named, should be set at liberty, and be exempt from further trial for deeds of the past. This compromise measure was designed to put a stop to the endless feuds, and to start

THE END OF THE 'BOGUS LAWS.'

anew, with a clean record under an agreement from Free State and Pro-slavery men, to discountenance all further violence. But on the day after the adjournment of the legislative assembly, the quiet city was stirred by an excitement, sudden and fierce as a Texas norther. It was caused by the arrival from Bourbon county, of fifteen Free State prisoners, handcuffed and strongly guarded. The officer in charge was reported to be Hamilton, the Marais des Cygnes murderer. As the party entered town, the news passed through the streets like a gust of wind over a field of ripe wheat. The citizens, without organization or leader, rushed forth to rescue the prisoners. They bore them triumphantly to a blacksmith shop, and cut off their irons.

The shaggy, wild-looking guard, half intoxicated, and wholly frightened, attempted to fly, but were pursued by a madly-shouting crowd. Successively each was caught, dragged from the saddle, and deprived of horse, gun, and revolver, with the speed of lightning. Then the eager cry rang out:

Hamilton! 'Where's Hamilton?'

A horseman suddenly struck spur and galloped away. The excited crowd saw him, and pursued.

'There he goes!' was the shout, followed by the flash of twenty rifles and revolvers. But the bullets passed harmless, and he was out of range.

Afterward it appeared that the horseman was not *the* Hamilton and did not belong to the posse; but was a quiet citizen who chanced to ride into town with it. He learned precisely what's in a name,

WHAT'S IN A NAME?

and narrowly escaped death because an acquaintance had been overheard to call him 'Hamilton.'

The guns taken from the posse were United States arms. The captors retained them; to the victors belonged the spoils.

Fighting and speech-making were the two essentials of a Kansas excitement. Now that one was over the other followed. The crowd, swollen to a thousand people, gathered in front of the Eldridge House and called for the Territorial governor, Samuel Medary. He was an old Ohio journalist and politician who had succeeded Denver. Thus far he had been popular, and he was now received with cheers. He commenced by condemning the violent proceedings; and insisted that the captured guns should be given up. Many of these guns were visible in the crowd, but Medary's demand was received with universal shouts of 'No, no, no.'

The angry governor reiterated that the arms were Territorial property and should be surrendered if it took twelve months and the United States army to accomplish it. Sidney Smith's friend who had once voyaged to the polar regions, and ever afterward bored everybody about them, one day met a literary acquaintance upon the street. The great reviewer, hurried and impatient, submitted to be button-holed until he heard the stereotyped beginning:

'When I was at the North Pole'—and then irascibly broke away, ejaculating:

'Oh, d—n the North Pole!'

Shocked and appalled, the poor explorer walked on until he met the immortal wit, who proved a patient listener to the story of his wrongs, and after its rehearsal remarked solemnly:

'It was just like ——; he is the most irreverent man I ever knew. Why I have heard him speak disrespectfully of the equator!'

The Kansans were equally reckless; they had no mite of respect even for the equator. The governor's threat caused shouts of derisive laughter, with sarcastic suggestions that his excellency should take the guns at once! Medary saw that he was on dangerous ground, and after a few general patriotic remarks, retired from the rostrum.

Then there was a spontaneous call for Lane. That old war horse emerged from the crowd, threw off the black shaggy bearskin overcoat which he invariably wore, mounted a wagon and spoke for half an hour, drawing a shout of laughter or a round of applause with almost every sentence. Lane was distinctively a vessel of wrath. He had long hated Medary politically, and owed him a personal grudge, because in an official communication the governor had addressed him as 'Mr.' instead of 'General.' The grim adventurer now wreaked his revenge in a most fierce and withering excoriation. He seemed to have studied Medary's entire biography and recited an appalling catalogue of his political crimes for the last twenty years; first in Ohio, and afterward as Territorial governor of Minnesota where he was charged with conniving at gross election frauds in the remote Pembina regions.

Medary was in his hotel, within ear-shot, while Lane thus paid up old scores and left a large margin for the future. Then speeches were made by other leading Free State men, and the meeting adjourned. The guns were never given up.

It was reported that Medary, by direction of President Buchanan, had offered a reward of two hundred and fifty dollars for the capture of old John Brown. Brown retorted by offering a reward of two hundred and fifty dollars for Buchanan's head. He said he would have proposed it for Medary's head if he had not feared that some of his men would actually take it!

Brown was now residing in Kansas. I never met him though I heard much of him from followers, friends and enemies. He seldom participated in public meetings, always declaring himself ready when any fighting was to be done, but adding that there was too much talking, and too little shooting. The Free State men knew his unbounded bravery and perfect integrity, but regarded him as partially insane; and there were well-grounded reports that he had approved of some dreadful reprisals in the form of killing unarmed Pro-slavery settlers.

During this winter Dr. John Doy of Lawrence was conducting thirteen negro fugitives across the Territory toward Iowa. A party of Missourians, without legal process, captured him in Kansas, fifty miles from the State line, and by force carried him to St. Joseph, where he was tried on the charge of enticing away slaves—a felony punishable with death.

The kidnapping of Doy caused much excitement in Kansas, and the legislature voted a thousand dollars to secure legal counsel for him. I attended the trial in St. Joseph. One of the counsel for the State, Colonel Doniphan, of Border Ruffian renown, said in addressing the jury:

'If we allow our negroes to be stolen with impunity, our fair-skinned daughters must be reduced to the contemptible drudgery of the kitchen!'

Ex-governor Shannon of Kansas, another of the counsel, with great gravity, and without the least intention of satire, announced that he had learned during a long residence near the border of Virginia, that slaves *would* sometimes run away of their own volition!

The indictment charged the offense as committed in Platte county, Missouri, though the prosecution was unable to prove that Doy had ever been within thirty miles of that State till he was kidnapped. On the first trial the jury failed to agree. At the next term of the court the prisoner was convicted, and sentenced to the penitentiary. But one dark night old John Brown and a party of followers crossed the Missouri, broke open the jail, rescued Doy, and carried him safely back into Kansas—beating the kidnappers at their own game.

Old settlers of Kansas preserve many traditions of John Brown's shrewdness, daring and religious enthusiasm. At Osawattomie, in 1856, when Henry Clay Pate with his Missouri soldiers attempted to capture Brown, the old Spartan captured *him* and his entire command. On another occasion he escaped unperceived from a house which his pursuers beseiged and guarded for three more days and nights, supposing him still there and not daring to enter. Again and again he captured officials who had been sent in pursuit of him. He so inspired his followers with his own religious enthusiasm, that they deemed themselves under the direct protection of the Almighty, and seemed absolutely fearless of death. Hundreds of runaway slaves were led by that little band through the perils of Kansas, to the freedom and safety of Iowa; and in camp every morning their captain read a chapter in the bible and knelt down in prayer before starting on their day's march.

In December, 1857, I spent eight days upon a little steamer ascending the Missouri to Kansas. The tedious hours were pleasantly abbreviated by a pair of bright eyes from Connecticut, owned by a maiden bound on a music-teaching mission to Missouri. 'That teaching was a very clever subterfuge' said everybody, 'she was really an Abolition emissary in pursuit of a Border Ruffian husband.' Miss Fanny was indignant; but she met such badinage with all the denials in her vocabulary. Finally, one dreary evening we left the little pilgrim on the muddy shores of her new world; and desolate but undaunted she went on her way.

In March 1859, in the cabin of a steamer near St. Joseph, I encountered a little lady making laudable pretenses of matronly dignity. It was the Miss Fanny of our memory—the Madam Fanny of our prophecies, accompanied by the Border Ruffian of her fancy as well as ours. Like many other mortals, her intentions were good, but destiny was too strong for her.

Early in the spring of 1859 the Hannibal and St. Joseph railroad was completed across the State of Missouri, placing Kansas in direct communication with the eastern States. With the railroad came the telegraph; and we were no longer isolated from the world.

How marvelous are the changes of half a century—changes witnessed by some who read these lines! Go back with me forty years to one of our Atlantic cities, and imagine that Mr. Smith of Boston finds it necessary to take a trip to what has since become known as Kansas. Smith looks forward to the journey as a most solemn affair. For weeks the feminine members of his household are employed upon his wardrobe; it will hardly do to start with less than a year's outfit. Intelligence of his proposed trip creates a great sensation, and everybody looks upon him as a daring fellow.

The hour of departure draws near. What solemnity pervades his domestic circle! Finally, having completed his preparations, settled up his business, and made his will, Smith bids his weeping family a long farewell, and starts on his perilous journey. What untold dangers are before him! Hardships by land, sea, canal and river—in stage coaches, in sloops, in canal boats, on horseback, and in batteaux propelled by human power against the strong current of the mad Missouri. If no hostile Indian steals his scalp, he reaches Kansas after a journey of three months. He remains

AN ABOLITION EMISSARY. Page 154.

but seven days—a short respite after so long travel—and then turns his face eastward. Perhaps at St. Louis, three weeks later, he finds awaiting him a missive from home—a letter which has been seventy or eighty days on the way.

After seven months' absence and many hardships, he is overjoyed to reach home; for the journey has taught him that 'the world has a million roosts for a man but only one nest.' He is received as one risen from the dead. For the rest of his life Smith is a hero; he is lionized by everybody, regarded as one of the seven wonders of the world and pointed out to strangers on the street as a living man, who has actually been four hundred miles beyond the great Mississippi into the howling wilderness.

Contrast that period with the present. Now, Mr. Brown of Boston, reflects on a Saturday night while walking home from his counting-room, that he is a little worn down by close attention to business, remembers that he has a few investments which need looking after and concludes to take 'a run' out to Kansas. So on Monday morning he gives a few directions about his business, packs half a dozen clean shirts, a Railway Guide and an *Atlantic Monthly* into his carpet-sack, says 'Good-by' to Mrs. Brown and the little Browns, and steps into the railway carriage.

For the next three days he lives at the rate of twenty-five miles an hour. At night he retires to his couch in the sleeping-car, almost as luxurious and secluded as his own apartment at home. If an old traveler and familiar with the route, he spends the hours of darkness in unbroken slumbers, all unmindful of city and village, forest and prairie, that whisk by in panoramic beauty. In the morning he wakes two or three hundred miles further on, to find awaiting him his boots freshly polished by the porter, and convenient bathing and dressing saloons in which to make his toilet.

On Thursday morning he breakfasts in Kansas. He too, remains seven days and meanwhile receives daily telegrams announcing that all is well at home. Finally, on the second Thursday morning, he takes a return train. If he is fortunate enough to retain his head—for locomotives are quite as dangerous as Indians—he reaches home on Saturday evening after an absence of two weeks. He finds tea awaiting him, smoking hot on the table; for on the way he telegraphed that he should arrive by the six o'clock train. His journey attracts no attention. Ordinary acquaintances have not missed him. A few friends as they meet him on the street, remark:

'Hallo, Brown! haven't seen you for a few days. Been in the country?' And he replies:

'Yes, just taken a little trip out to Kansas.'

In three days the locomotive has borne him sixteen hundred miles in its iron arms. In a period absolutely imperceptible, the telegraph has flashed to him messages from the loved ones at home along its sensitive nerves. Such the triumphs of forty years. The Florentine philosopher was right—'Still it moves!'

CHAPTER XIII.

Thus far there were no trustworthy reports of gold in paying quantities among the Rocky Mountains. But every newspaper on the Missouri river expressed absolute confidence that rich mines existed; and demonstrated irresistibly that the town wherein said newspaper was published was nearer the mines than any other, and therefore *the* place for emigrants to purchase cattle, wagons, provisions and mining tools.

In the early spring of 1859, there was a grand stampede for the mountains. The hitherto solitary plains suddenly became densely peopled. A line of daily coaches was put on from Leavenworth to Denver, via. the new Republican route, costing three hundred thousand dollars before the first vehicle started, and involving a running expense of eight hundred dollars per day. Stations from 'One' upward were established from ten to twenty-five miles apart, over prairie and desert. A thousand mules and a hundred stages were scattered along the route. The fare from Leavenworth to the mountains was one hundred dollars; way tariff twenty-five cents per mile.

But most emigrants went by private conveyances. Every great thoroughfare was white with wagons, and by night the smoke of ten thousand camp-fires curled to the astonished clouds. Some emigrants drew their entire supplies in handcarts, to which they had harnessed *themselves;* others bore them packed upon their backs—each a domestic Atlas, with his little world upon his shoulders.

Some who started too early had hands and feet frozen. Others consumed all their provisions before one-third of the journey was accomplished, and were fed for weeks by those more bountifully supplied. Thousands took an unexplored route, up the Smoky

Hill river, where grass and water proved wofully scarce and fearful suffering prevailed. The road was lined with cooking-stoves, clothing and mining tools, thrown away to lighten the loads. In the absence of grass, many emigrants were compelled to feed flour to their exhausted cattle. Some wandered off upon the desert, in the hope of finding a shorter route and nearly perished from hunger. A few died from starvation; and one emigrant from Missouri actually subsisted for several days upon the body of his deceased brother, and when found was a raving maniac.

THE DEAD BROTHER.

The rush to the mines was now succeeded by a panic quite as contagious. Reports that the exhibited gold had come from California and not from the mountains, turned back thousands of emigrants—some before they had gone fifty miles from the river and others when they were within twenty-five of the alleged gold region. Still many pressed forward, and large parties of undismayed adventurers continued to start daily. The country had known nothing like it since the great California excitement ten years before, when thirty thousand emigrants crossed the plains. It was an uncontrollable eruption—a great river of human life rolling toward the setting sun—at once a triumph and a prophesy.

On the twenty-first of May, the first return coach from the mountains reached Leavenworth. It brought only three thousand five hundred dollars in gold dust; but there was an enthusiastic celebration with sonorous speeches and sanguine predictions. The arriving vehicle was richly decorated, and bore the high-sounding motto:

'The gold mountains of Kansas send greetings to her commercial metropolis.'

Another coach which went out to escort it into the city was correspondingly labeled:

'Leavenworth hears the echo from her mineral mountains and sends it on the wings of lightning to a listening world.'

May 25.—I left Leavenworth by the overland mail carriage built in Concord, New Hampshire, known as the Concord wagon. In a dozen localities its manufacture is imitated with more or less success but never equaled. The little capital of the Granite State alone has the art of making a vehicle which like the one-hoss shay, 'don't break down, but only wears out.' It is covered with duck or canvas, the driver sitting in front, at a slight elevation above the passengers. Bearing no weight upon the roof, it is less top-heavy than the old-fashioned stage-coach for mud-holes and mountain-sides, where to preserve the center of gravity becomes, with Falstaff's instinct, 'a great matter.' Like human travelers on life's highway, it goes best under a heavy load. Empty, it jolts and pitches like a ship in a raging sea; filled with passengers and balanced by a proper distribution of baggage in the 'boot' behind, and under the driver's feet before, its motion is easy and elastic. Excelling every other in durability and strength, this hack is used all over our continent and throughout South America.

Two coaches, each drawn by four mules, leave Leavenworth daily and make the entire trip together, for protection in case of danger from Indians. A crowd gathered in front of the Planters' House to see our equipages start. Amid confused ejaculations of 'Good-by, old boy.' 'Write as soon as you get there.' 'Better have your hair cut, so that the Arapahoes can't scalp you.' 'Tell John to send me an ounce of dust.' 'Be sure and give Smith that letter from his wife.' 'Do write the facts about the gold,' the whips cracked and the two stages rolled merrily away.

Beyond Easton and Hickory Point we passed hundreds of freight and emigrant wagons stalled in the mud. William H. Russell the chief freighter of the plains, owns many of them. Last year he employed twenty-five thousand oxen and two thousand wagons, chiefly in transporting supplies for our army in Utah. He stipulates that any one of his teamsters who whips cattle unmercifully or utters an oath, shall forfeit his wages. Of course the precaution proves ineffective, for there is a logical connection between mud-holes and profanity.

Before night we entered the Pottawatomie Indian reservation, where prairie wolves, prairie hens and rabbits abound. Spent the night at Silver Lake, (Station Four,) with a half-breed family. Playing upon the floor were two dusky children both, as we were informed, born like Richard with teeth; and in the mother's arms reposed an infant three months old, whose jaws already displayed similar ornaments.

At midnight arrived two return coaches from the mines. The passengers encountered the Missourian, with whose horrible story we were already familiar. He showed them the severed head of his brother, and declared that he found the brains a delicious morsel. Days' travel sixty-eight miles.

May 26.—This morning rode in a driving rain over the prairies. Passed St. Mary's Catholic Mission—a pleasant, home-like group of log-houses, and a little frame church, bearing aloft the cross—among shade and fruit trees, in a picturesque valley. The mission has been in operation twelve years. In the school-room we saw sixty Indian boys at their lessons.

Rock Creek was swollen to a torrent, which compelled us to spend the afternoon and night at the city of Louisville—a city of three houses. Its hotel affords the inevitable fat pork, hot biscuits and muddy coffee. The landlady is a half-breed; and her two daughters with oval faces, olive complexions and bright black eyes the only pretty Indian girls I have ever seen.

Scores of emigrants are encamping along the stream. One having caught a turtle as large as a peck measure, invited us to partake of a savory soup, which we imbibed from tin cups, sitting on a log.

Two returning coaches filled with passengers were detained on the opposite side of the stream through the night. One enterprising traveler attempted to reach our side in a skiff; but was overturned and gained the bank by swimming. Day's travel twenty-eight miles.

May 27.—At daylight the creek had fallen so that our mules crossed without swimming. Some of the countless emigrants on the road have cows yoked with oxen, serving as motive power by day and giving milk at night. We passed one two-wheeled cart drawn by a horse in the shafts, with a yoke of oxen before him. Beyond the three houses which compose the town of Pittsburg, we crossed the Big Blue river and reached Manhattan—a flourishing Yankee settlement of two or three hundred people in a smooth and beautiful valley. It is overlooked by a conical mound two hundred and fifty feet high, commanding a fine view of the rich, well timbered soil along the Kansas and the Blue.

Thus far I had been the solitary passenger. But at Manhattan Horace Greeley after a tour through the interior to gratify the clamorous settlers with speeches, joined me for the rest of the journey. His overland trip attracted much attention. A farmer asked me if Horace Greeley had failed in business, and was going to Pike's Peak to dig gold! Another inquired if he was about to start a newspaper in Manhattan. And as we were leaving one station an Indian girl said to a new-comer:

'Horace Greeley in his old white coat is sitting in that coach!'

Twenty miles beyond, after passing three large farms based on 'a horizontal rather than a perpendicular agriculture,' we reached Fort Riley, one of our most beautiful military posts, and in the geographical center of our national possessions. All the buildings are two stories high, of light limestone resembling marble.

Just beyond, we crossed the Republican river, which rising near the Rocky Mountains, winds eastward for six hundred miles and here unites with the Smoky Hill Fork to form the Kansas. The dim, conical, smoky hills from which the chief tributary is named are visible on the horizon though a hundred miles distant. Timber abounds near the fort; a cottonwood tree nine feet in diameter, was recently cut here. We stopped for the night at Junction City, (Station Seven,) the frontier post-office and settlement of Kansas.

The editor of its weekly newspaper, an old Californian, spoke with great enthusiasm of the Golden State. Mr. Greeley replied:

'I have heard some hundreds of returned Californians use the same expressions; but one thing I cannot understand. If you liked California so well why didn't you stay there?'

'Because I was a d—d fool!' replied the roving journalist.

In the evening by invitation of the citizens, Mr. Greeley addressed an attentive audience in the unfinished stone church. Theme, 'Republicanism.' Day's travel forty miles.

May 28.—At a creek-crossing, a little tent beside our road is labeled 'grocery' in enormous letters. With keen appetites we awake the melancholy merchant who in green spectacles is sleeping soundly between two whisky barrels.

GROCERY.

'Have you any crackers?'

'Nary cracker.'

'Any bread?'

'Any *what?*'

'Bread.'

'No *Sir*,' (indignantly,) 'I don't keep a bakery.'

'Any ham?'

'No.'

'Any figs?'

'No.'

'Well what *have* you?'

'Why I have sardines, pickled oysters, smoking tobacco, and stranger, I have got some of the best whisky you ever seen since you was born!'

The narrow valleys of the streams are still rich; but the upland soil grows thin and sandy. At one fertile valley-farm we saw herds of fat cattle and a corn-field of a hundred acres, in addition to the common frontier spectacle of a tow-headed mother, with nine tow-headed children.

Left behind were the last outposts of civilization; now

'Away, away, from the dwellings of men
To the wild deer's haunt, and the buffalo's glen.'

Dined at Chapman's creek, in a station of poles covered with sail cloth, but where the host superior to daily drenchings, gave us an admirable meal upon a snowy table-cloth.

Timber disappearing; only straggling fringes remain along the creek, with an occasional solitary tree on the prairie indicating the whereabouts of water.

Began journeying now among the buffalo grass, two inches high, thick, wiry, nutritious and little injured by frost or drowth. Prairies spangled with wild onions, and antelopes bounding over the slopes.

Met thirty Cheyenne Indians on a begging and stealing expedition, who asked for whisky and tobacco. Nearly all bore certificates of good character from white men; but one solemn old brave complacently presented me the following testimonial which some wag had given him:

'This Indian is a drunkard, a liar and a notorious old thief; look out for him!'

Stopped for the night at Station Nine, consisting of two tents. In the evening wrote newspaper letters in the coach by a lantern. As the air was damp and chill with rain and the vehicle shaken with wind, I fancy the *Tribune* printers will find Mr. Greeley's manuscript even less legible than usual. At ten o'clock composed ourselves to sleep in the carriage to the music of howling wolves and heavy thunder.—Day's travel sixty-eight miles.

May 29.—Wild roses, wormwood of various species, thistles, narrow-leafed dock and many other new plants and flowers, some of rare beauty, appear along our road. Crossed Hurricane Creek, named from a furious tornado two weeks ago, which overturned heavy freight wagons, blew a light buggy into fragments, tore open boxes and scattered dry-goods for several miles, and rolled cooking-stoves forty or fifty yards.

The distant slopes are dotted with the antelope, the best living illustration of the poetry of motion. Miles away, when his earth-colored body is quite indistinguishable, one sees his white tail flut-

To be set up but not so in title
Try so.

The True Bases of Reconstruction.

About to leave for some weeks' sojourn in the West, whence I cannot so readily and constantly confer with the general public, I wish to leave my contribution to the general mass of suggestion and criticism touching the true bases of National restoration and concord so plainly set forth that it cannot be misquoted nor misapprehended.

That I have long held the main foundations of a genuine enduring settlement of our disturbed and unhinged National structure to be Universal Amnesty and Impartial Suffrage must be tolerably well known. I only apprehend that versions to be said that I commend them

FAC SIMILE OF HORACE GREELEY'S MANUSCRIPT. (FROM A TRIBUNE EDITORIAL, 1866.)

tering in the breeze like a shred of linen—a perpetual flag of truce to human enemies. Here he ventures near us, but on the older roads, rifles and shot-guns have made him shy and difficult to approach. Old hunters are wont to stick a ramrod in the earth with a handkerchief flying from it, and then conceal themselves among the grass or sand-hills. The antelope, lured by a curiosity fatal as mother Eve's, circles nearer and nearer, until he falls by the cruel bullet. From a close view his liquid eyes suggest infinite pathos and more than human tenderness. He is easily domesticated, and naturally tame.

The antelope and the buffalo are antipodes. One is incarnate grace; the other clumsiness itself. The antelope gallops airily over the hills, with an elasticity surpassing the fleetest race-horse. The buffalo is heavy and awkward; and the male, with huge head and enormous shaggy neck from which the hair hangs to the ground, canters lumberingly along like a mastodon suddenly awakened and uncertain of his native element.

Dined at Station Ten sitting upon billets of wood, carpet-sacks, and nail-kegs, while the meal was served upon a box. It consisted of fresh buffalo meat, which tastes like ordinary beef though of coarser fiber, and sometimes with a strong, unpleasant flavor. When cut from calves or young cows it is tender and toothsome.

Hundreds of deep buffalo trails cross our road; and through the whole afternoon the prairies for miles and miles away, quite black with the huge animals, look like bushes covered with ripe whortleberries, or like wood-land afar off. The cows are about the size of our domestic cattle. The bulls are twice as large, and roll in the sand and wallow in mud-holes like hogs. While great droves are feeding in the valleys they keep sentinels on the ridges, ready to give notice of the approach of danger. Running herds produce clouds of dust, and shake the earth like thunder. The calves are kept in the center of the drove for protection against men and wolves.

A huge tree beside our road is completely covered with names of emigrants and dates and messages for their friends behind: an ingenious and very public post-office.

Six weeks ago not a track had been made upon this route.

Now it resembles a long-used turnpike. We meet many returning emigrants, who declare the mines a humbug; but pass hundreds of undismayed gold-seekers still pressing on.

One Ohio wagon bears the inscription, 'Root Hog or die.' A returning passenger states that further on he encountered a philosophical emigrant whose wagon was labeled, 'Pike's Peak or Bust.' One after another the traveler's cattle died, till only one cow and an ox were left. During a luckless night these either strayed away or were stolen by Indians. The next day my informant found this prairie Micawber sitting upon his wagon-tongue smoking his pipe and waiting for something to turn up. But under the first inscription he had penciled with charcoal: '*Busted, by thunder!*'

'BUSTED, BY THUNDER!'

Spent the night at Station Eleven, occupied by two men who gave us bread and buffalo meat like granite.—Day's travel, fifty-six miles.

May 30.—Large gray wolves abound near our road. They often kill old or wounded buffaloes, and sometimes open graves and devour human bodies. Upon this newly-opened thoroughfare through the heart of the buffalo country the animals are very tame. Tens of thousands are feeding beside the track, and they often cross it five or six yards before us, compelling the driver to stop, lest they should stampede the mules. The mule never becomes reconciled to buffalo or Indian, and if stampeded, the most rheumatic animal will dash off at incredible speed. In some instances they have run fifty miles before they could be stopped.

One serene old bull approaches within twenty rods of us and the driver waits while I fire at him again and again with Sharpe's rifle. He continues to approach, only greeting each ball that strikes him with a nervous movement and switch of the tail, as a sensitive horse would respond to a fly. As he is facing me I am unable to hit him back of the fore-leg; and forward of that, the buffalo is not vulnerable. After I have fired four or five times he turns and limps slowly away into a ravine. Afterward I fire at several others with the same brilliant success. Mr. G. urges me to continue, on the ground that it amuses me and does not hurt the buffalo; but is quite too uncertain of his own marksmanship to try the rifle.

These animals add inconceivably to the poetry and life of the plains. 'Geographers and road-makers by instinct, the best routes across the continent have been established upon their beaten trails. They once roamed over the entire Pacific slope and thence eastward to Lake Champlain. The last buffalo east of the Mississippi was killed in 1832. According to Fremont, up to 1836 one traveling between the Rocky Mountains and the Missouri never lost sight of them. They have now greatly diminished, as more than half a million are killed annually—often from wantonness or curiosity. Every emigrant is ambitious to shoot a buffalo; and whitened skulls perforated by bullets, make the road a Golgotha. But even now, some authorities believe that they outnumber all the domestic cattle of the United States.

To the prairie Indian they are useful and indispensable as the camel to the Arab, or the reindeer to the Laplander. Their flesh supplies him with food during the entire year. Their hides clothe his person, protect his lodge from winter storms, and afford him an article of barter with the traders. Their hoofs furnish him with glue, for manifold purposes; and in these treeless wastes their excrement is an admirable substitute for firewood. Their strong necks and their tough foreheads, which will flatten a rifle ball like a wall of stone, constitute a formidable battering-ram, almost justifying the belief that if a buffalo had taken the place of the unfortunate bull which attempted to butt the locomotive off the track, he would have met a happier fate than that brave but indiscreet animal. A blow from the head of a calf two months old, is sufficient to prostrate an athletic man.

R. B. Fuller, superintendent of this division of the stage route, while riding in a desert-valley encountered several thousand of these wild cattle; and his mule with characteristic perversity, refused to budge an inch, but stood broad-wise to the approaching herd. Under the horns of the first buffalo the steed dropped dead upon the spot, almost without a single kick. His rider, stunned by the shock, fortunately fell close beside the mule, and so escaped being trampled to death. In a few seconds, recovering his consciousness, he saw that several of the ponderous brutes had already leaped over him; and drawing his revolver he fired six shots in rapid succession. The reports and smoke broke the herd into two columns; and in a few minutes with saddle and bridle upon his shoulder he was walking briskly toward the road, vowing that he would never, never, never ride a mule again.

A NARROW ESCAPE FROM THE BUFFALOES. Page 168

CHAPTER XIV.

MAY 30.—(Continued)—At Station Twelve where we dined, the carcasses of seven buffaloes were half submerged in the creek. Yesterday a herd of three thousand crossed the stream, leaping down the steep banks. A few broke their necks by the fall; others were trampled to death by those pressing on from behind.

This afternoon our coach was stopped at a creek-crossing by a mired wagon which blocked the road. Several Ohio emigrants with their weary cattle were endeavoring to extricate it. Mr. G. assisted them in their efforts to lift the wheels from out the Slough of Despond. While they paused a moment one inquired of the stranger his business. He replied that he was connected with a New York daily journal.

'What journal?'

'The *Tribune!*'

'Ah! that's old Greeley's paper, isn't it?'

'Yes sir.'

Just then another of the party who had been absent, returned and recognizing the ablest editor and the most influential American of our generation laboring at the wheel, said to his comrades:

'Gentlemen, this is Mr. Greeley of New York.'

The curious interrogator was dumb with amazement and chagrin.

Nearly every train we pass contains some emigrant who stops the coach and remarks:

'Mr. G. my name is ——. I heard you lecture fourteen years ago.'

And the veteran journalist invariably replies:

'O, yes! How are my old friends A. and B. and C.?' naming half-a-score of citizens in the region—whether of Maine or

Minnesota—from which the stranger hails. But to-day on the outskirts of a crowd a stolid-looking gold-seeker asked me earnestly:

HORACE GREELEY.

'Stranger, is that *John* Greeley those fellows talk so much about?'

'No—Horace.'

'Horace—Horace Greeley—who is he?'

'Editor of the *Tribune*.'

'Which?'

'Editor of the New York *Tribune*.'

'What's *that*?'

I enlightened my interlocutor, who seemed to feel that he had gained valuable information, and explained that he was 'born and raised' in Missouri.

After being mired in the same creek for two hours, our own vehicle was drawn out by the oxen of friendly emigrants. Spent the night at Station Thirteen. Day's travel, fifty-six miles.

May 31.—Though still plentiful, the buffaloes are diminishing. Mr. G. believes them nearly identical with the buffaloes he has seen on the Campania in Italy, though considerably larger. But the authorities call the American animal the bison, to distinguish him from the Asiatic buffalo. The former was never seen by Europeans till Cortez and his followers found two or three in the zoölogical gardens of Montezuma.

When Lewis and Clark ascended the Missouri, half a century ago, a herd of these animals crossing at one point choked the stream for a mile, compelling the explorers to wait till they had passed. Their report hesitatingly asserts that they 'thought' they saw twenty thousand at once; but I am confident we looked upon forty thousand from one stand-point, and that in all we have seen half a million. For several days we have never been out of sight of them except when our coach was in some deep ravine.

To-day we have been among prairie-dog towns, passing one more than a mile long. Some of their settlements are said to be twenty miles in length, containing a larger population than any metropolis on the globe. The little animal is a trifle larger than the gray squirrel, subsists on grass and has none of the characteristics of the dog but his yelp, which is like that of a young puppy. Small owls perch upon the mound beside his hole; but there are no signs of the traditional rattlesnake said to be an unwelcome joint occupant of his subterranean city, whose labyrinthine passages honeycomb the ground. The hillock of earth extracted from each hole, is ten or twelve inches high and two feet in width. Upon this stands the prairie-dog, erect on his hind legs. His house is his castle. His own picket and scout, he maintains a sharp lookout for his foreign enemy the wolf, and has an occasional domestic feud with his persistent co-tenants, the rattlesnake and the owl.

The most honest of real estate dealers, he acts upon the great truth that inhabitants are indispensable to a city, and never offers lots in paper towns to unsuspecting victims. There is no deceit in that honest jovial face. Vegetarian diet has not made him an ascetic; he takes the world like a philosopher and a gentleman; frolics merrily with his fellows in the warm sunlight, and as you approach, scampers home. There from his own roof he gazes quizzically at you, shaking his fat sides with laughter; and as you reach forth your hand to take him, he turns a graceful summersault, gives a series of hearty cachinnations, and affording a dissolving view of his tail, dives into his underground domicile. This evening we supped on his flesh, and found it very palatable, resembling that of the squirrel.

We spend the night at Station Fifteen, kept by an ex-Cincinnati lawyer, who with his wife, formerly an actress at the Bowery Theater, is now cooking meals and making beds for stage passengers on the great desert three hundred miles beyond civilization. The mimic stage presents few sharper contrasts. Our road, following the valley of the Republican river, is here two thousand three hundred feet above sea-level. At midnight arrives a return coach bringing a fair delicate Indiana boy who ran away last spring, froze his feet en route for the mines, and after many hardships is now glad to return to home and school. Day's travel fifty-six miles.

June 1.—Like Dombey and Son the Indiana boy proved 'a daughter after all!' She was dressed in male costume with a slouching hat which she wore at table to conceal her features. She talked little, but in walking from the tent to the coach her gait betrayed her. She is twenty years old; appears intelligent and well educated; professes to be returning to her parents in Indiana after spending three months in the mines; but gives no reason for her dangerous and unwomanly freak.

Dined at Station Sixteen, kept by a Vermont boy who has roamed over twenty-seven States of the Union. Near it was encamped a party of Arapahoes, with thirty or forty children playing upon the grass. Those under four or five years were entirely naked. The older boys wore breech-clouts of buffalo skin, and the girls were wrapped in robes or blankets. All were muscular and well developed. Old trappers assert that they never saw an Indian idiotic or naturally deformed. Only in the centers of civilization, the bee-hives of the human race, are the helpless little ones thus smitten. Herbert Spencer describes the British laws as 'those twenty thousand statutes which every Englishman is supposed to know and which no Englishman does know.' Relentless nature is like the State. She presumes every man to know her laws; she pardons none for his ignorance; she inflexibly punishes every disobedience. Nay, severer still, she visits the sins of the fathers upon the children to the third and fourth generation.

Indian women, accustomed to hard labor in the open air, never compel a traveling party to stop more than three or four hours on the birth of a child. If left behind they overtake the expedition the same evening or the next day, with the little new-comer strapped on the maternal back. They ride astride like men.

The boys of this company were very expert with the bow, easily hitting a silver half-dollar at sixty or seventy yards. All were inveterate beggars, asking by signs for food and drink. Their camp consisted of twenty conical lodges twelve or fifteen feet high—buffalo robes with the fur inside, stretched around a circle of poles. These dwellings ten or twelve feet in diameter, with a hole at the top for the escape of smoke, are warm in winter and cool in summer. The Sibley tent used in our army is modeled upon them.

In front of each the shield and quiver of the brave rested upon a pole or tripod. The shields, worn upon the left arm, are covered with antelope skin or buffalo hide stuffed with hair, and will usually ward off any rifle ball which does not strike them perpendicularly. The bows have great force, sometimes throwing an arrow quite through the body of a buffalo.

Several squaws who were making moccasins fringed with beads offered me a pair for a cup of 'sooker,' (sugar.) Others were eating soup with their fingers from a kettle, while naked children on the ground were gnawing tough buffalo meat. A dozen muscular half-naked braves lying in the sun shook hands with me, declaring themselves 'Good Indians.' But only yesterday they threatened to kill and scalp a station-keeper unless he should leave their country.

Descending an abrupt hill, our mules, terrified by meeting three savages, broke a line, ran down a precipitous bank, upsetting the coach which was hurled upon the ground with a tremendous crash, and galloped away with the fore-wheels. I sprang out in time to escape being overturned. From a mass of cushions, carpet-sacks and blankets soon emerged my companion, his head rising above the side of the vehicle like that of an advertising boy from his frame of pasteboard. Blood was flowing profusely from cuts in his cheek, arm and leg; but his face was serene and benignant as a May morning. He was soon rescued from his cage, and taken to Station Seventeen, a few yards beyond, where the good woman dressed his galling wounds.

From their village near by many Cheyennes pressed around our baggage which was scattered upon the ground. They are instinctive thieves, and we watched them with drawn revolvers until it was carried to the station. There were three chiefs in the party: 'Little Bear,' 'Antelope,' and 'Black Wolf.' Two had cut-throat faces; their features, as often occurs among savages of every race, reminding one strongly of wild beasts. But Black Wolf looked good-humored and honest. Complacently joining me in a cigar he assured me by signs and the few English words in his vocabulary, that he was going to shoot 'heap of buffaloes.' Then pointing toward the west and digging in the ground with his fingers he ejaculated: 'Money! money!' to indicate his knowledge of the gold discoveries. An old brave of at least ninety now hobbled up, telling me in dumb show that he was aged, almost blind and

A CHANGE OF BASE.

should soon sleep in the ground, and—would I give him a little tobacco?

In the evening Black Wolf took me through his village. The warriors wore long hair dressed in cues, and lengthened by a strand of buffalo hair until it reached the ground. Ornaments of tin and silver jingled from their ears. The cheeks and foreheads of squaws were painted bright vermilion. At nightfall the women brought in the ponies and picketed them among the lodges, that they might not be unprepared for a midnight alarm. In profoundest peace, the Indians maintain all the system and precaution of an army in time of war. As usual we sleep in the coach which, vibrating in the strong prairie wind, rocks like a cradle. Day's travel forty-nine miles.

June 2.—Mr. Greeley awoke so stiff and sore that he could not move a muscle without suffering; but we continued on by the sandy valley of the Republican, destitute of tree and shrub and barren as Sahara. Spent the night at Station Nineteen. Day's travel sixty-four miles.

June 3.—Encountered several Indian villages moving; their ponies drawing the lodge-poles, beside carrying heavy loads upon their backs. The life of these Indians is simply a bivouac, never a settlement. The savages found on our Atlantic coast by pioneer settlers, lived in permanent villages, cultivated corn, were without horses, hunted on foot and seldom wandered far from home. But these prairie Bedouins all travel on horseback, taking their effects with them. At half an hour's notice they gather up their wives, children and all other earthly possessions and start on a journey of hundreds of miles. Reaching their destination, they are entirely domesticated in another half-hour. They do not till the ground, but live exclusively on fresh meat, which they eat in enormous quantities. This arid desert is one of the healthiest regions in the world, and its pure air a wonderful appetizer. The regular allowance of the American Fur Company for each employee was eight pounds of buffalo meat daily.

As usual passed hundreds of emigrants. The latest coach from Denver brings fine specimens of gold dust, and reports new rich discoveries, to the great elation of all the pilgrims. At Station Twenty-one where we spent the night, we first encountered fresh fish upon our table. Here the enormous cat-fish of Missouri and Kansas has dwindled to the little horned-pout of New England, lost its strong taste and regained its legitimate flavor. Day's travel fifty-nine miles.

June 4.—We still follow the Republican which at one point, sinks abruptly into the earth, running under ground for twenty miles and then gushing up again. We saw one thirsty emigrant digging in the dry bed for water. At the depth of four or five feet he found it; but it argues a lively imagination to speak of such a sand plain as a river. These subterranean passages are as common among the streams of our deserts as in the far Orient.

After riding twenty-five miles without seeing a drop of water, at Station Twenty-two we crossed the Smoky Hill route which from a point far south of ours, abruptly turns northward across the Republican to the Platte. Emigrants who have come by the

THE REPUBLICAN RIVER.

Smoky Hill tell us they have suffered intensely, one traveling seventy-five miles without water. Some burned their wagons, killed their famishing cattle and continued on foot.

We are still on the desert with its soil white with alkali, its stunted shrubs, withered grass, and brackish waters often poisonous to both cattle and men. Day's travel forty-eight miles.

June 5.—At daylight Pike's Peak more than a hundred miles away, appeared dim and hazy on the horizon and we began to feel the inspiring breath of the mountains. Most emigrants were encamping out of respect for the Sabbath, and the sore feet of their cattle, which they carefully bandaged.

At our dining station, Twenty-five, I met several old Kansas acquaintances, so dust-covered and sunburnt that for several minutes I did not know them. That would be a keen-eyed mother who could recognize her own son at a glance under the dirt and disguise of plains-travel. Toward evening, Pike's Peak loomed up grandly in the southwest, wrapt in its ghostly mantle of snow and streaked by deep-cut gorges shining in the rays of a blazing sunset—

'The seal of God
Upon the close of day.'

In the northwest Long's Peak was sharply defined against a mass of ominous black clouds which rising slowly left behind them a scattered trail, dark and wild as the locks of the storm-god.

What solemn influences descend to us from these mountain summits! Year after year, upon their echoless heads has rested the finger of Silence. Around their feet are wrapped the dark pine forests. Rigid and unimpressible, yielding neither to summer's gentle ministry nor winter's despotic strength, to the soft touch of caressing winds and light-dropping showers, nor the fierce assault of warring blasts, they stand stately and undisturbed.

But now human voices made musical the solitudes. The unaccustomed air responded in glad echoes, and before us smiled a bright little valley, dotted with white tents and gleaming with many camp fires.

Supping at Station Twenty-six we made a comfortable bed in the coach, and rolling on at the rate of seven miles an hour, slept quietly through the night.

June 6.—Woke at five, still in motion, and obtained a glorious view of the mountains, their hoary peaks covered with snow and their base, thirty miles across the valley into which we were descending, seeming not more than two miles away.

At last we struck the old trail from Santa Fe to Salt Lake, rode a mile along the dry bed of Cherry Creek, and at eight this eleventh morning reached Denver City. Day-and-night's travel one hundred and thirty miles. During our journey from Leavenworth we have doubtless passed ten thousand emigrants.

—Making governments and building towns are the natural employments of the migratory Yankee. He takes to them as instinctively as a young duck to water. Congregate a hundred Americans anywhere beyond the settlements, and they immediately lay out a city, frame a State constitution and apply for admission into the Union, while twenty-five of them become candidates for the United States Senate.

True to this instinct, the people of this unfledged community, nominally in Kansas but practically as far from government and civilization as central Africa, were already making a State constitution; and months before, they had laid out Denver City.

It was a most forlorn and desolate-looking metropolis. If my memory is faithful, there were five women in the whole gold region; and the appearance of a bonnet in the street was the signal for the entire population to rush to the cabin doors and gaze upon its wearer as at any other natural curiosity. The men who gathered about our coach on its arrival were attired in slouched hats, tattered woolen shirts, buckskin pantaloons and moccasins; and had knives and revolvers suspended from their belts.

We took lodgings at the Denver House. True to the national instinct, the occupants of its great drinking and gambling saloon demanded a speech. On one side the tipplers at the bar silently sipped their grog; on the other the gamblers respectfully suspended the shuffling of cards and the counting of money from their huge piles of coin, while Mr. Greeley standing between them, made a strong anti-drinking and anti-gambling address, which was received with perfect good humor.

Thus far no gold had been discovered within sixty miles of Pike's Peak; but the first reports located the diggings near that mountain, and 'Pike's Peak'—one of those happy alliterations which stick like burs in the public memory—was now the general name for this whole region.

The first extravagant statements had all been based upon supposition. Prospectors found 'the color'—infinitesimal quantities of the shining dust—and nothing more, chiefly in the bed of the Platte. The mountains had not been searched to any extent. So little confidence was felt in the mines, that in Denver, picks commanded only ten or fifteen cents apiece, and town lots and log houses were bartered for revolvers, or sold for ten or twenty dollars. Of the few men engaged in mining, not half-a-dozen were realizing one dollar per day.

But on the sixth of May—just one month before our arrival—John H. Gregory, an old Georgia miner, struck rich deposits of gold in the mountains among the head-waters of Clear creek; and from that discovery dates the history of Pike's Peak as an ascertained gold region.

CHAPTER XV.

On the morning after reaching Denver we started for the Gregory Diggings, forty miles to the northwest. Along the bank of the Platte which bounds the town on the north, immigrant wagons extended for a quarter of a mile, waiting to be ferried across for two dollars and fifty cents each. The boat was propelled by the current, and its daily receipts were from two to three hundred dollars.

Immediately beyond, stretched a succession of low sandy hills, entirely destitute of trees, and with thin ashen grass, dreary enough to eyes familiar with the rich green prairies of Kansas and Missouri. But we passed several ranches where idle cattle and horses, whose owners were in the diggings, were kept and guarded by the month at from one to two dollars per head. By day they grazed on the desert and really fattened upon its unpromising diet. At night they were *corraled*—driven into enclosures—to prevent them from stampeding and protect them against the cattle-thieves, which infest all our frontier regions until exterminated or frightened away by the sudden, decisive administration of lynch law.

From Denver to the foot of the range seemed only a stone's throw, but we found it fifteen miles. The only well-defined spur is Table Mountain; which rises five or six hundred feet from the valley, with symmetric stone walls. It looked down upon two little tents, then the only dwellings for miles; but in the intervening years it has seen a thriving and promising manufacturing town spring up under the broad mountain-shadow.

At its base we found Clear creek, greatly swollen so we left the coach, saddled our mules and rode them through the stream amid a crowd of emigrants who sent up three hearty cheers for Horace Greeley. The road was swarming with travelers. In the

CLIMBING INTO THE MOUNTAINS.

distance they were clambering right up a hill as abrupt as the roof of a cottage.

It seemed incredible that any animal less agile than a mountain goat could reach the summit; yet this road only five weeks old, was beaten like a turnpike; and far above us toiled men mules and cattle pigmies upon Alps. Wagons carrying less than half a ton were drawn up by twenty oxen, while those descending dragged huge trees in full branch and leaf behind them, as brakes.

We all dismounted to ascend except Mr. Greeley, still so lame that his overtaxed mule was compelled to carry him. The astonished brute yielded to destiny and climbed vigorously, experiencing painfully the climax of Ossa upon Pelion.

GREGORY GOLD DIGGINGS, COLORADO, MAY, 1859. Page 181.

In an hour and a half we reached the summit. Far below, on the top of Table Mountain gleamed a little lake. At the foot of the long hill were the pigmies again; and beyond, the valley of the Platte with its dark timber and shining water. Before us mountain lay piled upon mountain; some grassy, others gaunt and bare. From most rose the pine, spruce and hemlock in perfect cones, interspersed with quivering aspens; while brilliant flowers clothed the desolate rocks with beauty.

Our road led us past the new-made grave of a young immigrant, one of many victims to the careless use of fire-arms. Up and down the steep mountain sides, across swift-running, ice-cold streams, over jagged rocks and through deep canyons overshadowed by sullen walls, we wound our toilsome way. An eager crowd kept pace with us; some walking, others with ox-wagons pack-horses or mules, and all pressing toward the mines.

At night we turned our patient animals out to graze, and encamped under a sloping roof of fir and pine boughs. Our cook elect kindled a blazing fire, by which we sat listening to the conflicting reports of the sanguine or disheartened gold seekers; those going forward led by buoyant hope, and those coming back bringing dearly-bought experience.

Wrapt in our blankets upon the hard ground, we gazed through fir boughs at the far-off stars, until the deep soothing music of the pine, the Eolian harp of the forest, mingled with our dreams.

The next morning we started early, and descending a steep hill reached at last the Gregory Diggings. The valley presented a confused and constantly-shifting picture, made up of men, tents, wagons, oxen and mules. The first miner we encountered was digging a hole like a grave beside a little rivulet, but reported to us that he had not yet 'struck the color.'

Along the rocky gulch for five miles were scattered log cabins, tents and camps covered with boards sawn by hand or with pine boughs. At the grocery tents, meat was selling at fifty cents per pound; and beside the stream women were washing clothes at three dollars per dozen.

After breakfasting in the open air, we went from camp to camp talking with miners, and studying their operations. They found no gold in the stream-beds; but were washing out the 'rotten quartz' which they gathered from narrow crevices in the granite on hill-sides. Gregory, Green Russell and the other old Georgia miners, very expert in detecting lodes, found abundant employment in 'prospecting' for new-comers at one hundred dollars per day. In our presence one miner washed two dollars and fifty cents from a pan-full of dirt, and told us that another pan had just yielded him seventeen dollars and eighty-seven cents.

Some twenty sluices were in operation. In gulch or placer-mining the dirt is shoveled into a long wooden sluice or trough, through which a stream of water pours, washing away the earth and leaving the heavy gold dust at the bottom. These sluices were of lumber, which was cut with hand-saws and commanded three hundred dollars per thousand. There was much speculation in claims; some had sold as high as six thousand dollars, cash.

Most of the miners were exultant and hopeful; but a few, utterly discouraged, were about to return to the States. There were five thousand people in the Gregory Diggings, and hundreds more were pouring in daily.

Mr. Greeley, Henry Villard of the Cincinnati *Commercial* and myself, spent two days in examining the gulches and conversing with the workmen engaged in running sluices. Most of the companies reported to us that they were operating successfully. Then we joined in a detailed report, naming the members of each company and their former places of residence in 'the States,' (that any who desired might learn their reputation for truthfulness,) and adding their statements as to the number of men they were employing and the average yield of their sluices per day. We endeavored to give the shadows as well as the lights of the picture, recounting the hardships and perils of the long journey, and the bitter disappointment experienced by the unsuccessful many; and earnestly warning the public against another general and ill-advised rush to the mines. Little time is required to learn the great truth, that digging gold is about the hardest way on earth to obtain it; that in this as in other pursuits great success is very rare. The report was widely copied throughout the country as the first specific, disinterested and trustworthy account of the newly-discovered placers.

Mr. Greeley's presence afforded too good opportunity for speech-hearing, to be overlooked by his errant countrymen. That evening fifteen hundred people assembled, forming the first mass meeting ever held in the Rocky Mountains. It was a motley gathering in the open air, of men with long unkempt locks, shaggy beards, faces reduced by the sun to the color of a new brick, and bowie knives and revolvers hanging from their belts. They gathered in all the freedom of the frontier. Some were reclining upon the ground, some sitting upon stumps and the half-finished walls of new log buildings, and others perched upon the friendly limbs of neighboring trees. The presiding officer occupied a log instead of a chair; and one of the speakers was clad in a full suit of buckskin with long fantastic fringes. The meeting, in a grove of stately pines, was called to order as the light of the dying sun was falling upon the gashed and rugged peaks like a benediction.

Mr. G., received with enthusiastic cheers, spoke hopefully of the mines, though he thought they would not equal those of California; advocated the forming of a new State without the troublesome preliminary form of a Territory; and urged his hearers to avoid drinking and gaming, and live as the parents, wives and children left at home would desire. It was one purpose of his trip to do every thing in his power toward hastening the Pacific railroad, which ought to have been built long before.

After three final cheers for the editor, the probate judge of the county, was called up and made glowing predictions of a new Commonwealth, the real Keystone State of the Union, to spring here like Minerva from the brain of Jove. (This voluble speaker did not remain to witness the fulfillment of his prophecy, but emigrated to Montana; and after being warned from that Territory by the vigilance committee for suspicious relations with a gang of murderers, took up his residence in Nevada.) When he had concluded, the assembled citizens were kind enough to call for me and to applaud with due enthusiasm my brief invocation to the American eagle, and apotheosis of the great Pacific railway of the future. Then the meeting adjourned, with cheers which made the old mountains ring. It must have astonished the wild elk and grizzly bears which until a month before had held undisputed sway.

In a little tent ambitiously labeled the 'Mountain City Hotel, six of us spent the night on the ground,

"Snug
As a bug
In a rug,'

lying so close that none of us could turn over separately.

The next day as we descended from the mountains Mr. G. was so lame that he could barely hobble. One of his companions was badly bruised, being thrown from his steed and dragged over sharp rocks by the stirrup. Another, pitched from his mule by a broken girth and alighting on the top of his head upon a rock, naturally complained of seeing stars and declared himself the victim of misplaced confidence. A third half submerged by his stumbling animal while crossing Clear Creek, and quite cured of his belief in hydropathy, was wrung out and dried before an immigrant's fire. After supping and lodging with some friendly travelers, we reached Denver at seven in the morning, prepared to play 'the Serious Family' to the satisfaction of the most critical.

MISPLACED CONFIDENCE.

The excitement of the journey over, Mr. G's. wounded limb which had enjoyed no rest since the capsizing of the coach, grew excessively painful and confining. The Denver House with its ceaseless noise and gambling, proved unfavorable to literary pursuits; so according to the custom of the country we 'jumped a cabin:'—selected the best empty one we could find, moved in our effects, and took possession.

'Imagination fondly stoops to trace,
The parlor splendors of that festive place.'

It was twelve feet square, of hewn pine logs new and smooth, the cracks within chinked with wood and outside plastered with mud. A great fire-place of sticks and dried soil occupied one corner. A single chair of elders fresh from the forest, with the bark still on, a little table of the same material, and the rare luxury of a mattress resting upon slats laid across from one log to another, constituted the furniture. The roof was of baked mud upon a layer of split logs and grass; the floor of hard, smooth earth. No window invited adventurous burglars, and the solitary door which swung upon wooden hinges, opened to the touch of no key but a pen-knife. We extemporized a shelf from which a few curiously assorted books looked down with a bewildered air, carpeted the ground with coffee-sacks—and did we not take our ease in our inn?

A few days later, the owner of the cabin came down from the mines and looked in upon us quite unexpectedly; but observing that the nine points of the law were in our favor, he apologized humbly for his intrusion, (most obsequious and marvelous of landlords!) begged us to make ourselves entirely at home, and then withdrew, to jump the best vacant cabin *he* could find, until the departure of his non-paying tenants. We design exhibiting him at the next world's fair as the best specimen of the Polite Gentleman on the terrestrial globe.

There was little business; money was in great demand and loaned on collateral security at twenty-five per cent. a month.

The experience of every mining region demonstrates that salt pork is the most nutritive and stimulating diet for miners, whose labor is the most exhausting in the whole world. All plains travelers also use it, on the theory of the shrewd philosopher, that no other substance contains 'so much board in so little compass.' As agriculture was not begun, vegetables were unattainable for love or money. Late in the season however, a few enormous watermelons appeared in market, selling at two or three dollars apiece. The chief meat was antelope, always abundant at four cents per pound. Though more tasteless than the flesh of the deer, it is pleasant and nutritive.

Denver society was a strange medley. There were Americans from every quarter of the Union, Mexicans, Indians, half-breeds, trappers, speculators, gamblers, desperadoes, broken-down politicians and honest men. Almost every day was enlivened by its little shooting match. While the great gaming saloon was crowded with people, drunken ruffians sometimes fired five or six shots from their revolvers, frightening everybody pell-mell out of the room, but seldom wounding any one. One day I heard the bar-keeper politely ask a man lying upon a bench to remove. The recumbent replied to the request with his revolver. Indeed firing at this bar-tender was a common amusement among the guests. At first he bore it laughingly, but one day a shot grazed his ear, whereupon, remarking that there was such a thing as carrying a joke too far and that *this* was 'about played out,' he buckled on two revolvers and swore he would kill the next man who took aim at him. He was not troubled afterward.

Gaming was universal. Denver and Auraria, (now West Denver,) contained about one thousand people, with three hundred buildings, nearly all of hewn pine logs. One third were unfinished and roofless, having been erected the previous winter for speculative purposes. There were very few glass windows or doors and but two or three board floors. The nearest saw-mill was forty miles away, and the occupants of the cabins lived upon the native earth, hard, smooth and clean-swept. One lady, by sewing together corn-sacks for a carpet and covering her log walls with sheets and table cloths, gave to her mansion an appearance of rare luxury. Chairs were glories yet to come. Stools tables and pole-bedsteads were the staple furniture, while rough boxes did duty as bureaus and cupboards. Hearths and fire-places were of adobe, as in Utah California and Mexico. Chimneys were of sticks of wood piled up like children's cob-houses and plastered with mud. A few roofs were covered with shingles split by hand, but most were of logs spread with prairie grass and covered with earth. They turned water well, even during the daily showers of June and July. During the rest of the year rain is unknown.

Between my cabin and the Denver House were a dozen Indian lodges, enlivened by squaws dressing the skins of wild animals or cooking puppies for dinner, naked children playing in the hot

SEVEN VIEWS IN DENVER COLORADO 1859. Page 186

sand and braves lounging on the ground, wearing no clothing except a narrow strip of cloth about the hips.

Hundreds of immigrants passed through daily; their white, unending caravans stretching across the river to the foot of the range. Daily too a great refluent wave rolled in *from* the mountains—dissatisfied miners who sold their superfluous provisions and tools at less than cost and started for California or turned homeward.

The Denver House was a long low one-story edifice, one hundred and thirty feet by thirty-six, with log walls and windows and roof of white sheeting. In its spacious saloon, the whole width of the building, the earth was well sprinkled to keep down dust. The room was always crowded with swarthy men armed and in rough costumes. The bar sold enormous quantities of cigars and liquors. At half a dozen tables the gamblers were always busy, day and evening. One in woolen shirt and jockey cap drove a thriving business at three-card-monte, which netted him about one hundred dollars per day. Standing behind his little table he would select three cards from his pack, show their faces to the crowd, and thus begin:

'Here you are, gentlemen; this ace of hearts is the winning card. Watch it closely. Follow it with your eye as I shuffle. Here it is, and now here, now here and now,' (laying the three on the table with faces down)—'where? If you point it out the first time you win; but if you miss you lose. Here it is you see,' (turning it up;) 'now watch it again,' (shuffling.) 'This ace of hearts gentlemen is the winning card. I take no bets from paupers, cripples or orphan children. The ace of hearts. It is my regular trade, gentlemen—to move my hands quicker than your eyes. I always have two chances to your one. The ace of hearts. If your sight is quick enough, you beat me and I pay; if not, I beat you and take your money. The ace of hearts; who will go me twenty?'

By this time some bystander who has watched the winning card closely is confident that he can point it out. It seems perfectly simple. Beside, he noticed that one corner was slightly turned up; and is it not there face downward with the corner still elevated? Confidently he throws down a twenty-dollar gold piece. The gambler covers it with another. The victim points to the card with a raised corner when lo! it is not the ace of hearts after all. At the last moment the operator dexterously turned down the corner of *that* and turned up the corner of another!

'My friend, you have lost. It is very plain and simple, but you can't always tell. Here you are, gentlemen; the ace, and the ace. Who will go me twenty dollars?'

The last sufferer, from sheer anger, bets again and loses again. After being mulcted of a hundred dollars he goes his way. But there is always a fresh victim ready to take his place.

Sometimes the gambler permits a stranger to win once or twice for the sake of leading him on. Again a bystander familiar with the game wins two or three times in succession; then the sporting orator refuses to take more bets from him. When the game flags, a secret confederate or 'pigeon' in the crowd offers a few wagers and wins, refunding the money when they are alone.

As a class, the gamblers were entertaining in conversation, had curious experiences to relate, evinced great knowledge of human nature, and were specially kind to each other in misfortune. Some were gentlemanly in manners. Like all men who gain money easily, they were open-handed and charitable. I never saw a place where more dollars could be obtained in less time for a helpless woman or orphan than among those gaming tables.

I saw the probate judge of the county lose thirty Denver lots in less than ten minutes, at cards, in this public saloon on Sunday morning; and afterward observed the county sheriff pawning his revolver for twenty dollars to spend in betting at faro There were no women and children; and hence none of that public opinion without which few men can stand alone.

One New Yorker still under thirty-five, had been successively owner of a Lake Erie steamer, captain of a Cape Cod fishing craft, professional gambler in Cuba, real-estate speculator in Leavenworth and stage driver on the great plains. Here he was a successful lawyer. But when last I saw him he had been a cripple for months—the result of an accidental shot from the pistol of his law partner, who had taken a drop too much.

Among the Denver pioneers I found a relative whom I had last met as a New York wholesale merchant, in the glossiest of broadcloth and the most spotless of linen. Now he wore the half-Mexican, half-Indian costume of the country. One of the chief thoroughfares, Blake street, still bears his name.

Denver had its weekly *Rocky Mountain News.* Editor and printers cooked ate and slept in the one room of the log building where articles were written, type set and paper worked off.

There were no public mails. Private enterprise is always far in advance of Government, and the express company brought all letters from the Missouri river—one thousand per day—for twenty-five cents each.

There was no paper money and the smallest coin in circulation was twenty-five cents. The people of the frontier have never taken kindly to coppers. In 1794, when the first barrel of them was introduced in Cincinnati by a merchant, the citizens were disgusted and his brother traders with difficulty restrained from mobbing him. In Kansas three-cent pieces passed for five cents, and in New Mexico eight dimes for one dollar. Says a European writer: 'Money must be very plentiful and people very prosperous, where the smallest coin is five or ten cents.'

The thousand Arapahoes encamped in the heart of the city were ordinarily peaceful, but dangerous when intoxicated. One evening I saw a brawny brave, with a club thwack two of his drunken brethren upon their heads, so lustily that the blows were heard a quarter of a mile away. Then musing for some minutes, he solemnly ejaculated:

'Whisky — bad! Make Indian bad.'

After which bit of wisdom he walked thoughtfully away. In ten minutes however, he returned with a bottle and a silver dollar and begged me to buy whisky for *him.* Like Hosea Bigelow he was 'in favor of the Maine Law, but agin' its enforcement.'

The Arapahoes, always treacherous and bloodthirsty, are now almost extinct from wars and small-pox—that terrible scourge of their race. They are thoroughly migratory. At a moment's notice they

'Fold their tents like the Arabs
And as silently steal away.'

They sometimes devour the entrails of animals; and I have seen squaws and children pluck and eat greedily vermin from their own heads. Chastity is unknown among their women; and nearly all suffer from loathsome diseases. Young girls are sold by their parents to Indians or white men—usually in exchange for one horse; but special beauty or aristocratic lineage sometimes commands four or five.

The savage like Falstaff is a coward on instinct—also treacherous, filthy and cruel. But one chief, the 'Little Raven,' was the nearest approximation I ever met to the Ideal Indian. He had a fine manly form and a human, trustworthy face. To spend an hour in our cabin was his custom always of an afternoon; and, though his entire ignorance of English was only equaled by my utter innocence of Arapahoe, we held pleasant communion together. Our conversations were carried on by signs and the very few words we had in common. The tongue was weak, but the gesticulation eloquent.

Usually by some means we could make each other comprehend; but twice or thrice we became, as actors say, hopelessly 'stuck.' Then my visitor sent for one 'Left Hand,' a linguist; for as Day & Martin the great blacking manufacturers, 'kept a poet,' so the chief of the Arapahoes maintained an interpreter. Left Hand spoke English fluently, having acquired it from traders in boyhood, and soon extricated us from our conversational quagmire. I will report from memory one of our interviews:

Little Raven enters; salutes me with a cordial grunt and a shake of the hand. I place him in the only chair our cabin affords, perching myself upon the table; fill his long pipe with Virginia tobacco, light a cigar on my own account; and then ensues a period of solemn and smoky silence. An occasional remark is ventured about the Utes, the weather, the mines; gradually we become communicative and at last familiar. He studies one of my maps with great curiosity and attention; inquires earnestly for the whereabouts upon it of the great father at Washington; and asks other questions which show how vague stories of the wonders of civilization have thrilled his simple heart, as fabulous tales of the New World thrilled the Spaniards of old. At last he folds the map and interrogates me on personal matters:

Who is my lame companion lying upon the bunk?

I reply that he is a great chief and named the 'Goose Quill,' endeavoring to explain that his realm and authority are purely

A VISIT FROM LITTLE RAVEN.

intellectual, but giving up in despair when the Raven interrupts me to ask how many horses he owns!

Where is my lodge?

I signify that it is by the great waters a hundred sleeps away; at which he gazes in wonder, tinged with that incredulity which civilized persons sometimes manifest for the tales of travelers.

How many squaws and papooses have I?

When I have replied with due humility, he exultantly assures me that *he* is the happy husband of seven squaws and the proud parent of ten papooses. The comparison is odious; he evidently feels his social superiority

How many horses have I?

Sorrowfully I admit that I can lay claim to no solitary piece of horse-flesh. The Raven answers by pointing triumphantly at *his* thirty sleek ponies grazing on the adjacent prairie. As one's wealth and position in Arapahoe eyes depend solely upon the number of his wives and horses, I feel that the Raven is becoming directly personal and inferentially abusive. So I place him in the witness-box, and become questioner myself:

How many revolvers has he?

He shrugs his shoulders—a pantomimic cipher. I produce Colt's new patent which he examines with great curiosity and admiration; handling it cautiously, as if it were an infernal machine, and showing a childish satisfaction not unmingled with terror, as I discharge the five barrels in rapid succession.

How much, he ventures to ask, did it cost?

I mention an almost fabulous sum and his respect for me is visibly augmented. Even the Indian is moved by the almighty dollar—or rather the almighty half-dollar; for that is the only denomination of specie in which he will receive payments. I follow up my advantage:

How many locomotives has he?

A mournful shake of the head is his only response; and while I convey to him crude ideas of the fiery, untiring monster which will carry me further in one sleep (day) than his fleetest horse can bear him in ten, he manifests intense interest, signifying that he has heard of the prodigy before, but never saw him. The impression left upon his mind, that I am the individual owner of several of these monsters, I am careful not to dissipate; and thereafter he treats me with the profound deference due a 'big Injun' and a fit associate of the Arapahoe monarch. And so, the topics of the day exhausted, with another cordial hand-shaking, he takes his departure.

Alas for Little Raven! Immortality did not hedge the king; and a year later he was killed in battle with the Utes.

CHAPTER XVI.

LITTLE RAVEN was not only brave, but devout. One day seeking him in his own village, I discovered that with several other warriors he was shut up in a low lodge, by which two young sentinels kept guard. The weather was intensely hot; the lodge without a single aperture and covered with masses of buffalo robes. Beside it upon a little mound of fresh earth were the skin of a wolf and the horns of a buffalo. Soon eight perspiring, naked braves emerged and threw themselves upon the ground, utterly exhausted. They had been taking a vapor bath, to propitiate their 'medicines.'

That night the entire band including the women paraded the town, pausing before many dwellings and drumming upon a circular piece of buffalo hide stretched over a wooden frame, while they chanted a weird refrain. Early the next morning the braves started on the war path against the Utes; and this ceremony was an invocation to the whites to protect the squaws and children during their absence.

The language of the Arapahoes is harsh and guttural. Dubray, an old trapper who had spent several years among them, spoke it fluently, but thought the tongue of a tribe in New Mexico much more difficult. He said:

'I lived among the Apaches eleven years, and only learned two of their words. I will pronounce them; and if you can repeat either immediately after hearing it, I will give you fifty dollars!'

He uttered them deliberately, but though they were not composed of more than four or five syllables, I was utterly unable to remember them.

Philologists conjecture that the language of manual signs originated in the infancy of the race, before articulate words. Deaf and dumb persons from different quarters of the globe on meeting for the first time, converse readily by signs which seem arbitrary, but which must be founded upon the natural relation between gesture and thought.

There is a dialect of hands arms and features, in common vogue between mountain men and Indians. A trapper meets a dozen savages, all of different tribes, and though no two have ten articulate words in common, they converse for hours in dumb show, comprehending each other perfectly, and often relating incidents which cause uproarious laughter or excite the sterner passions. To a novice, these signs are no more intelligible than so many vagaries of St. Vitus' dance; but, like all mysteries, they are simple and significant—after one comprehends them. The only one I recollect requiring no explanation, is the symbol for Sioux Indians—drawing the finger across the throat, like a knife. It is an apt and epigrammatic delineation of their blood-thirsty character.

The Arapahoes or 'Smellers' are indicated by seizing the nose with the thumb and forefinger; the Comanches or 'Snakes' by waving the hand like the crawling of a reptile; the Cheyennes or 'Cut-arms' by drawing the finger across the arm; the Pawnees or 'Wolves' by placing a forefinger on each side of the forehead pointing like the sharp ears of the wolf; the Crows by clapping the palms of the hands in imitation of flapping wings; women by moving the hand down toward the shoulder to indicate their long flowing tresses; whites by drawing the finger over the forehead in suggestion of the hat.

General Marcy's entertaining work, 'Army Life on the Border,' also states that to ascertain whether strangers at a distance are friends or enemies, some tribes raise the right hand with the palm in front, and slowly move it forward and back. This is a command to halt and will be obeyed if the approaching party be peaceful. Then the right hand is again raised and slowly moved to right and left, as an inquiry: 'Who are you?' The strangers reply by giving the sign of their tribe, or by raising both hands grasped as in friendly greeting, or with the forefingers firmly locked together in emblem of peace. If enemies, they refuse to halt, or place the shut hand against the forehead in sign of hostility.

All Indian languages are so imperfect that even when two members of the same tribe converse, half the intercourse is carried on by signs. Mountain men become so accustomed to this, that when talking in their mother tongue upon the most abstract subjects, their arms and bodies *will* participate in the conversation. Like the Kanackas of the Sandwich Islands they are unable to talk with their hands tied.

Thus the Greeks carry on long dialogues in silence; and the Italians when in fear of being overheard often stop in the middle of a sentence, to finish it in pantomime. It is even related that a great conspiracy on the Mediterranean was organized not only without vocal utterance, but by facial signs without employing the hand at all. How much more expressive than spoken words is a shrug of the shoulders, a scowl, or the turning up of the nose! The supple tongue may deceive; but few can discipline the expression of the face into a persistent falsehood; and no man can tell a lie—an absolute, unmitigated lie—with his eyes. If closely and steadily watched they will reveal the truth, be it love or hate or indifference.

For three weeks after our return from the mountains Mr. Greeley lay prostrate with his lame leg. Indeed the injury was so severe, that a year later he still limped.

But on the twenty-first of June, he continued the then dangerous journey across the continent. In Green river he lost his valise; but it was fished out by an honest emigrant and months later, reached its owner in New York. At Salt Lake he spent several days among the Saints: then pressed on through the present State of Nevada, (containing when he traversed it less than a hundred white inhabitants,) and across the Sierra Nevadas to California. There he was visited with the traditional annoyance of plains travelers—boils which covered his body, compelling him to return home by steamer instead of the Butterfield overland route.

After he left me Denver grew monotonous and I again started for the mountains. At Clear creek under the vast shadow of Table Mountain I found a new town springing up called Golden City. Of course its founders regarded it as an embryo Babylon. Golden City! How smoothly fell the unctuous syllables from the lips. How suggestive of merchant princes and pockets full of rocks. The El Dorado which Pizarro sought was studded with golden palaces and paved with precious stones—'the City of the Gilded King;' but our democratic El Dorado must be the city of the gilded people.

Two miles further, a few rudimentary log huts were named Golden Gate. The hill-road of three weeks before was already abandoned. I entered the mountains by a newly-cut thoroughfare, threading the easy canyon of a tumbling, foamy brook, inclosed by gloomy walls more than a thousand feet in hight.

BURNED TO DEATH.

The narrow pathway resounded with the tread of many feet, some slow and unelastic from weariness and disappointment; others keeping step to the jubilant song, 'I'm bound for the land of gold.' Horses oxen and mules struggled on, heavily loaded with shovels, sacks of flour sugar and meat. Many exhausted animals lay dead or dying along the way.

The trail wound through grassy valleys, among enormous rocks, beside mountains with icy springs gushing from their sides, and up and down rugged hills studded with tall pines and white-stemed aspens.

These cheerful surroundings were succeeded by a dreary black expanse. Fires had raged for two weeks and were still burning. It was impossible to check them, for the ground was half covered with dead fallen trunks, and thickly carpeted with successive layers of pine needles and pitch, which had accumulated for years and were like tinder to the hungry flames. The unendurable heat and suffocating smoke drove me far out of the road. In one ravine the miners had found three charred, blackened corpses. The victims were evidently running for a place of safety when the changing wind blinded them with smoke, and the fiery death overtook them. Their clothing was consumed; their gun-barrels, a case-knife and a quantity of gold dust were the only articles near them. Even their dog had been unable to escape, and his bones lay beside theirs. Several other corpses were discovered the same day; and the number of deaths from the fires was computed more than twenty. Who shall sing in saddest strain of the nameless graves which thicker than mile-stones, dot the old emigrant roads from Missouri to California, and wherever men have sought for gold form great cities of the dead?

On the route I encountered my friend Little Raven with his braves, returning from their expedition. Their buckskin quivers and rifle-cases were as white and their moccasin fringes as gay as ever; but the warriors were sad and taciturn, for the Utes had fled and their war path proved bloodless.

I dined under a tree with several hospitable Arkansans who were feasting upon raw salt pork. Cooking a slice to a crisp on the end of a long stick before the camp fire, I found it palatable; but when I asked for bread, they gave me a stone. I could neither bite break nor cut the solid biscuit; but after soaking in the brook one at last succumbed to my bowie knife.

In the evening I reached the diggings. A single month had changed them greatly. An incredible amount of work had been expended in seeking for gold. The same labor would have converted hundreds of miles of Kansas or Minnesota prairies into one continuous garden. Gregory Gulch now rejoiced in the hum and bustle of a city. Ravines were vocal with the crash of falling pine and hemlock, and the ring of hammer ax pick and spade. The women had increased to more than a hundred. Every mechanical trade and every traffic was pursued. A single 'town' lot had sold for five hundred dollars. When I asked a miner if there was any church, he replied:

'No; but we are going to build one before next Sunday.'

Erecting a temple of worship in a week was in thorough accordance with the prevailing spirit.

Thousands of miners were busy at the sluices, which now numbered several hundred. All reported gold-bearing rock abundant; but as yet there were no mills for crushing the quartz within a thousand miles. The 'pay dirt' was brought from the hill sides to the sluices in coffee sacks, borne upon the shoulders or drawn on rough sleds along smooth freshly-peeled pine trunks—a rudimental inclined-plane railway.

Several miners were each taking out two hundred dollars per day; but not more than one in four was obtaining five dollars. By the established regulations the size of a claim was fifty feet by one hundred; and some were selling at from ten to forty thousand dollars. Generally only a few hundred dollars of the purchase money was paid down; if the claim did not yield the balance it was never liquidated.

Climbing a hill side, I obtained a vivid evening view of the Alpine city. Beyond it a fire was raging upon an isolated peak. The flame swept evenly higher and higher, till at the summit, striking a single dead tree, it ran fiercely up the trunk into a perfect cone of fire, against a background of mountain and cloud.

At my feet the valley was lighted with scores of camp-fires, casting the shadows of tall pines and firs in every direction, and throwing a lurid glare upon the swarthy faces of the miners. Some were cooking in the open air, some taking their evening meal upon tables of pine bark, and others sitting upon logs or reclining upon the ground smoking and talking.

From one camp issued the lively notes of a violin; and from another, 'Home, sweet home' floating forth upon the evening air in a low, plaintive voice, told that the heart of the singer was with dear ones far away.

On Sunday morning, a walk through the diggings revealed nearly all the miners disguised in clean clothing. Some were reading and writing letters, some ministering to the sick, and some enacting the part of Every-man-his-own-washer-woman—rubbing valiantly away at the tub. Several hundred men, in the open air, were attending public religious worship—perhaps the first ever held in the Rocky Mountains. They were roughly clad, displaying weapons at their belts; and represented every section of the Union and almost every nation of the earth. They sat upon logs and stumps, a most attentive congregation, while the clergyman upon a rude log platform, preached from the text: 'Behold, I bring you good tidings of great joy.' It was an impressive spectacle—that motley gathering of gold-seekers among the mountains, a thousand miles from home and civilization, to hear the 'good tidings' forever old and yet forever new.

During the two weeks I spent in the mines the unhealthy diet and miasma arising from the freshly-broken earth, produced much fever. Many a poor fellow weak and listless, on straw bunk in squalid cabin, waited the approach of that grim specter with whom the ancients found prayers and sacrifices alike unavailing. Many with folded arms and rigid faces were consigned by strangers to hill-side graves, with no child's voice to prattle its simple sorrow, no woman's tear to bedew their memory.

We slept upon the ground under fir boughs. The sweetest of all rest is on the bosom of mother earth, watched by sentinel stars, lulled by the sad-hearted pine and falling water.

I found in one camp a party of Kansas acquaintances living upon ham and eggs. The latter were a rare luxury, costing two dollars and fifty cents per dozen. My friends had packed several barrels in Leavenworth, pouring liquid lard around the eggs, which forming a mold enabled them to sustain with admirable composure their wagon-journey of seven hundred miles.

Flour sold at twenty dollars per hundred, and milk at fifty cents a quart. Flapjacks were the substitute for bread. I think enough were made during the season to pave the road from Leavenworth to the mines. At every camp one saw perspiring men bending anxiously over the griddle, or turning the cake by tossing it skillfully in the air. To a looker-on, such masculine feats were decidedly amusing. Four years later, in rebel prisons, I found practical cookery far less entertaining.

Many professional men were hard at work in the diggings. One often heard sunburnt miners while resting upon their spades, discussing Shakspeare, the classics, religion, and political economy.

FLAPJACKS.

The stream beds abounded in mica, which old miners call 'fools' gold.' A shrewd German washed out and secreted an immense quantity, supposing he had discovered a new Golconda. Upon learning that it was not the precious metal he started back in disgust to the Pennsylvania coal mines.

When the melancholy John Phenix occupied the tripod of the San Diego *Herald*, he advertised for a lad to bring water, black his boots and keep the sanctum in order—one by whom obtaining a knowledge of the business would be deemed a sufficient compensation. The caution which he added—'No young woman in disguise need apply '—was needful in a mining country. I encountered in the diggings several women dressed in masculine apparel, and each telling some romantic story of her past life. One averred that she had twice crossed the plains to California with droves of cattle. Some were adventurers; all were of the wretched class against which society shuts its iron doors, bidding them hasten un-cared-for to destruction.

The Utes* killed a number of the miners. William M. Slaughter a Denver pioneer, was out prospecting with two friends, when these savages, after dining with them in apparent friendliness, attacked the party, killing and scalping two. Slaughter

* Or 'Utahs '—an Indian word signifying 'Dwellers among the Mountain Tops.' Those living near the Great Salt Lake were called 'Pah' (or water,) 'Utes,'—corrupted into 'Pi-Utes.' The Utahs were once a powerful nation, though embracing some wretched bands of Diggers who subsisted upon roots, worms and grasshoppers, and were perhaps the lowest of the human race.

though repeatedly shot at, sprang into the bushes, concealed himself two days, and finally escaped.

After spending six weeks in the new gold region, my published impression of the mines was thus summed up:

> 'I have absolute confidence in the permanency extent and richness of these diggings. I believe that the mountain ranges, *from Salt Lake to Mexico*, abound in gold and the secondary metals, and that their yield will be the richest ever known in the world. Yet those who are doing moderately well at home should remember that not more than one man in ten meets with success in any mining country, and that the prairies of Kansas Nebraska and Missouri offer much stronger inducements to settlers than the gold regions.'

I also hazarded the prediction that with proper cultivation the valleys of the Platte and its tributaries within fifty miles of Denver, would produce enough small grains and vegetables to support a population of two hundred thousand. This was scoffed at; and the arid sands did look unpromising. But now the settlers of Colorado have tested the agriculture of their new State, and yearly they raise enough farm produce for their own consumption.

Returning down the mountains I found opportunity to contrast the two classes common to all gold regions. The new-comers going into the mines were sanguine and cheery, climbing with elastic step, and beguiling the way with song and laughter. But the stampeders turning homeward, convinced that gold digging was hard and unremunerative, left their packs and shovels behind, and trudged mechanically with downcast woe-begone faces.

Reaching Denver again, I found the 'jumped cabin' lonely, and the novelties of the city exhausted. So early in July I started eastward. The stage line had been transferred from the Republican to the northern route. For four hundred miles from Denver it followed down the valley of that long tributary of the Missouri, which the Indians call the Nebraska, and French traders named the Platte—both appellations signifying shallow. They are specially fitting; for though the broad stream appears sufficient to float the navies of the world, it averages less than a foot in depth and abounds in treacherous quicksands. Many discouraged miners were attempting to descend in boats, but sooner or later all were skiff-wrecked. One Boston physician lost his boat and entire outfit, and when I saw him had just escaped from the river minus every article of personal property except a single shirt which he 'happened to have about him at the time.'

GOING INTO THE MINES.

The Platte mosquitoes covered our mules with blood, and lacerated me through the thick sleeves of two woolen shirts. Our untiring coach rolled day and night, halting only for meals and changes of teams.

We passed the Cache a la Poudre (Burial of the Powder) creek, named from an old French trapper, who years before interred a quantity of powder to conceal it from the Indians. *Cache* (to hide,) is a very common word throughout the far West for any thing concealed in the ground. In 1848 a shrewd California emigrant, whose cattle died near Fort Laramie, *cached* sundry casks of brandy by the road-side; piled the earth in the form of a grave; erected a head-board and inscribed upon it the name, age, nativity and virtues of a fabulous traveler, representing that he died of cholera. The ruse succeeded admirably; after reaching San Francisco he sold the spirits at a large profit to a person who returned and exhumed them.

At the South Platte Crossing where our road struck the old emigrant trail from the Missouri to Salt Lake, we found several lodges of Sioux Indians, who termed our mail coach the 'paper-wagon,' the little log post-office the 'paper house,' and our driver the 'king of the mules.'

Among thousands of returning emigrants we passed one jovial party with a huge charcoal sketch of an elephant upon their wagon cover, labeled: 'What we saw at Pike's Peak.'

The Platte valley, level as a floor from the Rocky Mountains to the Missouri, is the best natural route for a railway in the world. Though without timber it is well supplied with grass, and it ranges from five to fifteen miles in width.

COMING OUT.

At Fort Kearney, a Federal military post with wooden and adobe barracks, our road left the Platte. Soon the soil grew less sandy and more fertile. After we crossed the Blue rivers, dram-shops and paper cities—advance guards of civilization—began to appear; then occasional farms; then live towns and flourishing settlements. We were in the world again. Coming from rugged mountains and dreary deserts, the first grain field seemed to me the most beautiful of gardens. How little we appreciate the beauty of Indian corn! Few of our poets deign to mention it, though Holmes has a passing tribute:

> 'The green-haired maize, her silken tresses laid
> In soft luxuriance on her harsh brocade.'

A German florist after exhibiting to an American his rarest plants, added:

'Now I will show you the most beautiful of all;' and then conducted the visitor to a stalk of Indian corn. The American replied contemptuously that he had ridden for fifty miles through unbroken fields of that plant; but the German was not far wrong.

We reached Leavenworth in six days and twenty hours from Denver, then the quickest trip ever made.

CHAPTER XVII.

Next I visited the iron region of Missouri, eighty miles south of St. Louis, embracing Pilot Knob, Iron Mountain, and Shepherd's Mountain. These are eastern spurs of the Ozark hills or high table-lands which range from one thousand to one thousand five hundred feet above sea level.

The St. Louis and Iron Mountain railway terminates at Pilot Knob, a conical hill of solid ore six hundred feet high, and covering three hundred and sixty acres. Only two furnaces were in operation, turning out about thirty tons of pig-iron per day. The sides of the mountain are covered with oak hickory and ash saplings. The summit is a mass of enormous bowlders fifty feet high, and upheaved into every conceivable position. Some stand erect, sharply defined pillars. Two, a few feet apart, form a gigantic natural gateway. Another huge slab leaning against a solid wall constitutes a picturesque cave. Though exposed to the atmosphere for centuries, these bowlders contain fifty per cent. of iron. Below the surface, the rock contains sixty per cent.

The miners were digging horizontally into the mountain, drilling, blasting, and prying off great fragments of rock which fell crashing over a little precipice. In the pit below, some were breaking up these fragments with sledge hammers; others loading them into cars which conveyed the ore by an inclined-plane railway to furnaces at the base.

In European mines the clothing of workmen is carefully examined at night, to see that they do not carry away ore. But here, a few hundred blocks as large as a dwelling house would not be missed. The laborers were French, German and Irish.

Five miles further north is *the* Iron Mountain—a slight elevation over which the railway to St. Louis passes. Busy laborers were blasting out and breaking the ore, within a few yards of the

IRON MINERS AT WORK.

track. In 1833, this mountain was 'entered' in the land-office at one dollar and a quarter an acre. Three years later, the entire tract sold for six hundred dollars. Its present value is incalculable; for it is the largest and richest mass of iron yet found upon the globe. Its base covers five hundred acres. The ore, which contains seventy-one per cent. of pure iron, has been penetrated nearly four hundred feet below the surface, with no sign of exhaustion even at that depth.

In reducing, crude blocks one or two feet in diameter are placed upon a foundation of logs, in alternate layers of charcoal and ore, until they form a huge pile. For a month they are exposed to a fire as hot as they can endure without melting. This expels impurities, and leaves the ore brittle and easily broken into lumps three or four inches thick.

It is next hauled to the furnaces and cast into their fiery jaws together with limestone and charcoal in proportions varying with its quality. The furnaces are either 'hot blast' or 'cold blast,' according to the strong currents of hot or cold air pumped into them to supply oxygen, without which the ore would turn to 'cinder,' yielding no iron. The heat is two thousand seven hundred degrees Fahrenheit.

The cinder, separating from the iron, rises to the surface of the molten mass, and is skimmed off. Some of it hardens into a dark mass resembling coke, coarse glass or variegated marble. But when the charges and blasts are properly adjusted, it is white as snow and like the most exquisite moss suddenly petrified.

The ore remains in the furnace some twelve hours. Then from the bottom of the great crucible it pours a red, glowing stream into molds of sand where it hardens into 'pigs.' The workmen guide these dazzling currents of liquid fire into their proper channels with long-handled hoes.

By night the furnace buildings,—with their brick arches, blackened roofs, clouds of smoke, fiery torrents and sooty workmen darting hither and thither, catching lurid gleams on their dark faces,—are grotesquely suggestive of Pandemonium, and contrast sharply with the white villages and the dark wooded hills.

Shepherd's Mountain contains rich ore, but has been little mined. All these iron hills are of volcanic origin. In 1866 the furnaces of Missouri turned out twenty-five thousand tons of domestic iron. The State geologist reports in this vicinity sufficient deposits of ore near the surface to yield one million tons per annum of manufactured iron, for the next two hundred years!

A few miles distant is the solid Granite Knob in the heart of a great limestone region—almost the only granite between the Rocky Mountains and the Alleghanies.

On the fifteenth of August I again started for the far frontier. At Syracuse, one hundred and sixty-eight miles west of St. Louis, and then terminus of the Missouri Pacific Railway, I left the cars for a coach of the Butterfield Mail Company.

Our coach, leaving Syracuse after dark, jolted along for fifty miles during the night, and at sunrise stopped for breakfast in Warsaw, Benton county—a genuine southern town, surrounding a hollow square with court-house in the center; streets gullied by water and overgrown with weeds; frame houses, log houses and stucco houses, with deep porticoes and shade trees; negroes trudging with burdens upon their heads; deserted buildings; tumbling fences and a general tendency to 'the demnition bow wows.' While washing on the hotel porch we asked the host for soap.

LANDLORD, (imperious and tobacco-stained.)—Soap for the gentlemen.

CLERK, (obsequious and flippant.)—Soap for the gentlemen.

PORTER, (white and Celtic.)—Soap for the jintilmin.

WAITER, (white-eyed and Ethiopic.)—Cook, bring soap for de gemmen and be quick about it!

The cross-eyed cook, from Afric's sunny fountain, at last appeared with the longed-for article; but the incident was a shining illustration of the Institution.

We forded the Osage though it is navigable above Warsaw for half the year. The region was hilly and rocky, intersected by many streams and timbered with a dozen varieties of oak; the houses long and low with outside chimneys; corn the principal crop; great numbers of cattle raised chiefly for the California market; and not more than one farmer in ten owning slaves.

After passing some beautiful prairies and enduring another night of uneasy slumber, we woke in Springfield, on the summit of the Ozark Mountains—the leading town of southwestern Missouri. Here was the office for the sale of Government land in that quarter of the State, amounting to three millions of acres. Some of this was subject to entry at twenty-five cents per acre; but settlers had secured the fertile tracts years before, and the residue was rough and sterile.

Springfield had pleasant, vine-trellised dwellings, and two thousand five hundred people. The low straggling hotel with high belfry, was on the rural southern model: dining-room full of flies, with a long paper-covered frame swinging to and fro over the table to keep them from the food; the bill of fare, bacon corn bread and coffee; the rooms ill-furnished, towels missing, pitchers empty, and the bed and table linen seeming to have been dragged through the nearest pond, and dried upon gridirons.

During my stay a half-witted negro was arrested for outraging a lady. In the fierce excitement it aroused, some hot-heads proposed collecting all the slaves from the adjacent farms, and burning them on the public square. Two years earlier, two negroes had been burnt at the stake in Jasper, the second county to the west, for a similar crime, aggravated by the murder of their victim and her family. Now, Springfield would have no burning, declaring it too barbarous. But on the second day a mob broke into the hall where the negro was confined, took him from the officers, who did not attempt resistance, and hooting and yelling ran with him to the outskirts of the village and hung him upon a locust tree. He seemed to die of fright, for he never struggled after he was drawn up over the limb. Leading citizens assured me that for the same offense a white man would have received the same punishment; but how terribly unjust the system which, denying light and education to these poor creatures, still held them to a strict criminal responsibility!

Many immigrants were passing through the town. I was told of eight North Carolinians bound for Arkansas, who stopped a few hours on the public square, and were asked innumerable questions. One communicative fellow replied that they were going to found a town; the pursuit of each person was already marked out, and there were no drones among them.

What was this man to do?

He was to open a store.

And that?

Start a blacksmith's shop.

And the other, standing behind him?

Engage in sheep raising.

So they were nearly all classified, when a decrepid, white-haired octogenarian, venerable enough for old Time himself, was observed sitting in one of the wagons.

'Why, who is that?' asked the eager questioner.

'That's my grandfather.'

'What is *he* going to do? He can't be of any use to your settlement.'

'O yes,' replied the North Carolinian promptly, 'we are taking the old man along to start a graveyard with!'

Missouri with her unequaled resources of timber, coal, iron, lead, stone, and farming lands—with an area larger than New England, a genial climate, central position, and the grandest rivers of the world bounding her on two sides—was now prosperous and flourishing. Two years later I passed over the same route from St. Louis, to find the country blazing with civil war which swept away many fruits of the labor of twenty years. But it extirpated the poison that embittered her springs of life; removed forever the mammoth stumbling-block from her path of progress; cut loose the fetters that bound the young giantess hand and foot.

From Springfield I continued by coach sixty-five miles to the little, dilapidated settlement of Cassville, where I left the coach for the great Lead Region. The village merchant was sitting upon a keg in front of his grocery smoking a pipe.

Could he tell me the distance to Granby?

About thirty-four miles, he reckoned. Was never thar, but had been in sight of the siminary.

Could he furnish me with a horse?

Whar was I from?

Kansas.

Not born thar?

No; in Massachusetts.

Ah! (suspiciously) Did I allow to settle in these parts?

No; only to visit the Lead Region. Could he let me have a horse?

He reckoned not. One of his creturs was at work, another lame, and the third, though a right peert beast, too thin for the journey. But probably Jones, over across the field thar, could.

In consideration of two dollars, Jones furnished a hardy little pony, and I started on my forest ride. It led by a few thriving orchards, corn-fields dotted with blackened stumps, and low log dwellings with looms and spinning wheels on their porches. Beyond the little village of 'Gad-fly' I stopped at one of these farm-houses for a drink of water. An old woman smoking a long pipe and knitting on the porch was ready for a chat.

This was a healthy country, though thar was some chilling;

but then stranger they did'nt mind that much. She was born in Virginny, had lived in Kaintuck; but was never in a free State. She did'nt think much of slavery, but we had the niggers and what could we do with them? They were lazy and thriftless, making a heap of care and bother. But somebody must do the work. The North employed poor whites, who, she reckoned, were no better off than our niggers.

I dined with a young squatter whose lonely cabin was gladdened by five blue-eyed children though his wife was but twenty-five. She was born in this country and thought it a mighty rough one. Last winter she and her old man traveled all through Texas, hard-on-to a thousand miles, and seed more than she would have learned in a life-time at home. Texas was a mighty fine country, but a poor place for stock. They would go back there as soon as they could sell their farm of four hundred acres, mostly unimproved. They offered it at six dollars an acre—cheaper than any other land thereabouts. This year the corn crop was good; but three years before the drowth had destroyed it, not leaving enough for bread. The neighborhood was not much for learning, though just down the crick school tuck up (began) last week, and would continue two months.

In a fertile, flower-covered prairie ten miles wide, an oasis among the hills, I reached Newtonia, a neat village with tasteful buildings, including the 'siminary' of the Cassville trader. Five miles further I found Granby, in the largest and richest lead region of the United States.

All mining districts have a mysterious family resemblance; and this instantly reminded me of the Rocky Mountain gold diggings, though it was difficult to tell what features they had in common. Here on a rough woody tract of six hundred and forty acres, three thousand people were living—two-thirds of them working under ground. The rude village was dotted with log buildings, and like a prairie-dog town, with mounds of red loam gravel and stone thrown up from hundreds of shafts. From a valley near by rose the low heavy chimneys of smelting furnaces.

The hotel landlord told me he was born in old Virginny; came to St. Louis when that city had but three brick houses; had since roved among lead mines of Iowa, Wisconsin, and Illinois, gold diggings of California, pine forests of Oregon and Washington, and Indians of the Rocky Mountains, by whom his brother

GRANBY (MISSOURI) LEAD-MINERS, ABOVE GROUND.

was murdered. He had 'seed a heap of country and of human nature.'

Granby had at least one characteristic feature of mineral regions: it was prolific of drinking saloons, and two deadly affrays occurred during the night.

A mining firm to whom I bore letters, honored the draft upon their hospitality by ensconcing me in their neat cottage, in a picturesque valley a mile from the hamlet, where books newspapers and music afforded pleasant contrast to the dreariness and noise of Granby. Their furnaces had cost forty thousand dollars before they were ready to smelt the first pound of ore; but were now proving remunerative.

The lead is found from ten to seventy-five feet below the surface. From most shafts the ore is raised in buckets by the common windlass and crank; but at a few, horse-power is used.

Arrayed in a miner's suit of corduroys which age had withered and custom staled, I stepped into the descending bucket, and clung to the rope above. The owner of the mine shared the conveyance with me, using one hand and one foot to ward off the rough walls. At the depth of seventy feet we reached the bottom of the shaft, which was blasted through lime and flint rocks.

DOWN THE SHAFT.

Then my conductor bearing a tallow candle, guided me through the labyrinth of passages, at times not more than two feet high, until we reached the miners. Some were quarrying out the metal; others blasting it from 'pockets' in the rock. In one place they were lying flat upon their backs, digging it with picks from the roof of a passage a foot high; in another they were perched up in a gallery, breaking off the blocks and rolling them down. Then the ore was carried by cars upon a wooden railway to the bottom of the shafts, whence it was drawn up into daylight, and hauled to the furnaces.

A few feet above the floor was a stratum of flint, which made a secure roof. Where the excavation did not extend up to it props were set to keep the earth from falling in. The ore is found in seams from six inches to a foot thick. Sometimes there are huge masses nearly pure; again it is mingled with flint rock; and again the vein seems to run out, but re-appears in unexpected directions. One pure block weighing two thousand pounds was taken out. The ore averages eighty per cent. of lead.

Here as everywhere mining was a lottery. Workmen sometimes obtained no reward for many days, and again cleared a hundred and fifty dollars per week. Promising claims proved utterly worthless, and others which were believed exhausted afterward yielded richly. The dark unwholesome mines were half

LEAD MINERS UNDER GROUND.

full of water and often dangerous from foul air. Yet laborers were glad to work in them at one dollar and twenty-five cents per day, boarding themselves.

My conductor, a miner from childhood, had witnessed many fatal accidents, and declared it 'a slave's life;' but was unable to content himself in any other pursuit.

The ore is reduced in 'Scotch ovens' by a heat much less than that required in smelting iron. It is broken into fragments no larger than walnuts, then mingled with lime, and melted upon a fire of charcoal and dry wood. In a stream bright and shining as silver, it falls into the basins. Thence it is ladled into molds where it cools into marketable 'pigs' of eighty pounds. This process extracts sixty-six per cent. of the lead. The refuse matter is then subjected to much greater heat by which ten per cent. more is obtained. The smelting is very trying to health. Smelters received ten dollars per week, laboring five hours a day. The annual product of the region is now (1867) two and a half millions of pounds, and the deposits in that section are believed to underlie an immense tract. Lead mines are less liable to 'run out' than silver or gold; some in the Hartz mountains of Germany have yielded steadily and richly for five hundred years.

Returning to Cassville I journeyed on by the mail coaches, which over mountainous roads accomplished more than a hundred miles every twenty-four hours. Great pride was felt in this 'Overland' line, and an old local mail stage still lumbering over the same track was derisively known as 'the Underland.'

Our first point was Keetsville—a dozen shanties which looked like a funeral procession in honor of Keets, whoever he may have been. The neighbors called the place 'Chicken-Thief.' Another hamlet a few miles to the southward was known as 'Scarce-o'-Grease!' Near most of the farm dwellings were spring-houses where the matrons kept their milk and butter. Cellars were little known through Missouri and Arkansas because reputed damp and unhealthy—justly in a few sections, but unjustly in most.

After crossing the State line we were jolted over the rough Boston Mountains, and obtained a moonlight view of Fayetteville, a pleasant county town with several churches, the United States land-office for northeastern Arkansas, and pleasant dwellings. A rough village beyond is named 'Hog-Eye.' If not euphonious the nomenclature hereabout is at least original. The generous log-house where the passengers breakfasted was kept by a widow, whose wordly condition a local clergyman on board thus described: 'She's got lots of niggers and a heap of truck,' (property.)

All day we were among mountains with farm-houses few and far between; and at evening we looked down upon a pleasant picture. At our feet the village of Van Buren nestled among shade trees; immediately beyond, the shining waters of the Arkansas river wound through a rich green valley; still further, the deep many-hued foliage of the Indian Territory dotted with blue mountain peaks melted into the deeper blue of the sky.

Crossing the stream by a ferry of two-pole power, and riding five miles along its deeply-shaded valley, we reached Fort Smith, in western Arkansas, on the border of the Indian Territory.

CHAPTER XVIII.

FORT SMITH is an abandoned military post, nominally head of navigation on the Arkansas, (Indian: smoky, bow-shaped river,) though steamers ascend to it only half the year. At high water they run one hundred and sixty miles above to Fort Gibson.

The pleasant town now contained three thousand people. Its chief trade was with the neighboring Cherokees and Choctaws. By law, debts contracted by the Indians out of their own Territory could not be collected; but the Fort Smith merchants trusted them freely and were faithfully paid.

Every day scores of Aborigines added picturesqueness to the streets. The men wore gay, fringed frocks instead of coats, and red kerchiefs or turbans for hats; but otherwise dressed like whites. The petticoats and frocks of the women displayed as many colors of the rainbow as their purses would permit.

Though more civilized than any other tribes the males scorned labor. Often one trudged empty-handed up from the ferry, while behind toiled his squaw with heavy keg or other burden upon her shoulders, and one of their negro slaves also unincumbered brought up the rear. He came as interpreter; the negroes all spoke English while many of their Indian masters did not.

According to my voluble landlord there were many slaves about Fort Smith. In winter especially, field hands had a far easier time than their masters. They were well supplied with spending money and went to a frolic almost every night:

'I overseed for three years on a Louisiana cotton plantation. There the niggers have to work right on through the winter, for that's the picking season. They begin at daylight and keep at it till dark; an overseer follows them with a big whip, and you'd think at first that they had a powerful hard time. But no matter how tight they are worked, just let them get together at night with a fiddle, and Lord, how they *will* frolic! Keep it up till morning too, dancing and singing. That's the place for niggers; put them in the South and they are just happy.

'The man I overseed for was a mighty fine master—kind, but right strict. He kept them well clothed, for half of them are too careless to look out for the future. Growing cotton is the most profitable business in the world; the planters don't raise any thing else except a few sweet potatoes, but buy all their provisions. Picking cotton is the great thing. A woman will pick faster than a man, but a child twelve years old will frequently beat them both. It can't be learned—it's a kind of sleight. Those planters think nothing of paying twenty-five hundred dollars for a good picker.'

'Are there many slaves among the Indians, across the river?'

'Yes sir. John Ross governor of the Cherokees has over a hundred; and there's a right smart sprinkling through the whole nation.'

'How are they treated?'

'Badly. The Cherokees and Choctaws don't govern them; in fact, the niggers are masters and do about as they please.'

The negroes of Fort Smith had Methodist and Baptist churches. Like the temples of the whites, these places of worship had no bells; and the Sunday morning congregations were called together by the tooting of a dozen horns—a ludicrous form of the church-going bell.

THE CHURCH-GOING BELL.

Many negroes had bought their freedom, and some had acquired considerable property. Several laundresses and nurses first redeemed themselves, and then their husbands and children. But the Arkansas legislature had passed a stringent law requiring every free negro remaining in the State after January 1860, to be sold as a slave, and have his property confiscated to the county. He was graciously permitted to choose a master, who after paying his appraised value would own him absolutely. In western Arkansas schools are very rare, and many children grow up incredibly ignorant. At the time of my visit several of the State legislators were unable to write their own names.

Outside of the few large towns, the epicurean tourist endures many tribulations. In rich stock-growing regions he finds sweet milk for his tea and coffee a rarity, and for drinking a myth. Butter seldom visits his table, but sometimes confronts him laden with odors never wafted from Araby the Blest. Of strong coffee, sour milk as a beverage, molasses, hot heavy biscuit with saleratus visible to the naked eye, and fat pork floating in gravy, he will find abundance. Pastry may haunt his dreams, but seldom his repasts. Even the inevitable corn-bread though of richest meal, comes in such a questionable shape as to have no temptation for his palate. One waggish old settler told me this story:

'I have been living down here for twenty years. The desk in my office is at the head of a long flight of stairs; and in the haste of business my inkstand is often knocked off and rolled down. For a long time I could get no material that would stand this usage. Glass was out of the question. Stone broke like crockery. The hardest wood soon gave way. Finally a lucky thought struck me. I sent up to one of my neighbours—the widow B.—for a piece of her corn-bread. After ruining several fine tools I succeeded in hollowing it out into an inkstand. That was ten years ago; and, stranger, I've used that inkstand ever since and I reckon it's good for two generations longer!'

Banks were unknown, and gold and silver the only currency. The State contained just forty miles of railroad—from Memphis toward Little Rock. The speed of regular passenger trains by the time-table was seven miles an hour.

A pioneer who settled in Fort Smith when there were only five houses, and before the military post was established, told me stirring tales of the early days. The town was a rendezvous for adventurers and desperadoes. By crossing the Arkansas on the north side, or the Oporto on the west, criminals reached the Indian country beyond the reach of civil process. Deadly affrays were common; and the most trivial quarrels settled by pistol and bowie knife.

During my stay a lad of fourteen became angry with a gentleman who taught a girls' singing school; and while the teacher was surrounded by pupils twice snapped a pistol at him. The caps failing he flung a bowlder which knocked the teacher down senseless and bleeding, among his terrified little singers. The young would-be murderer was held to bail. Two planters quarreled about a real estate trade, and the lie was passed. Two days later one lay in the woods several hours, and while his enemy was passing killed him with a shot gun. *He* was held to bail.

In a drinking saloon a youth of eighteen wantonly murdered a Cherokee Indian. The city council offered two hundred dollars for his capture, and when taken he also was held to bail. For years no one had been punished for homicide. The carrying of concealed weapons was common; and a citizen assured me that he had seen a clergyman in the pulpit on Sunday with the handle of a bowie knife protruding from his pocket.

My chief personal experience at Fort Smith came in the form of a typhoid fever, prostrating me for weeks. In that climate the disease often clings to a patient for five months. Producing a dull stupor with little perceptible pain, it is accompanied by malignant inflammation of the bowels. But nature provides a remedy. The green leaves of the bene plant, maturing at just the right season, after soaking in cold water, produce an agreeable glutinous syrup which rapidly replaces the lining of the intestines carried away by the dangerous disease. This tropical plant, grows in profusion, and is said to be identical with the *Sesamum Orientale.* Who knows but that it was the mysterious 'open sesame' of the Arabian robbers?

I was among strangers and they ministered unto me. Good fortune threw me under the roof of a Maine family who nursed me with patient tenderness. After weary days, I escaped from the sick chamber to breathe again the blessed open air. The stifling cloud upon my brain passed away, and left me like one just awakened from a heavy slumber. In that humid climate I

GOVERNOR WALKER'S RESIDENCE, CHOCTAW NATION, INDIAN TERRITORY. Page 219.

convalesced but slowly, and longed for the inspiring air of the mountains. At last in open rebellion to my physician I parted from the new friends to whom I owed my life, rolling away in the overland stage which by a shaky ferry crossed the Oporto into the Indian Territory.

On the rich bottom-lands, oak, cottonwood, sycamore and pecan were festooned by vines burdened with delicious grapes, and inclosed by dense canebrakes. The small canes are shipped North for pipe stems, the larger ones for fishing rods. Three soft blue mountains melted into the southern horizon.

Fourteen miles out, I left the coach at the residence of Governor Walker, executive of the Choctaw nation. He was educated in Kentucky, intelligent and agreeable; nearly as white as myself, and with no betrayal of Indian origin in speech or features. His wife, a very dusky half-breed, did the honors of his table gracefully. His farm of one hundred acres was all inclosed and under high cultivation. His log house, long low and hospitable with broad portico in front, was surrounded by stately oaks and graceful locusts. Several out-buildings served for kitchen, executive office and negro quarters. Little darkeys were ubiquitous, decorating every niche and perch with nimble cupids in bronze; performing gum-elastic feats unequaled; visible suddenly from behind corners, over fences, through windows, and under one's feet; dropping down from every point of the compass as if scattered by some genie from his overflowing pockets; gathering themselves together with whoop and somersault; displaying rows of ivory, and wooly curls; then miraculously vanishing again.

The Indian Territory contains sixty or seventy thousand inhabitants: Cherokees, Choctaws, Creeks, and Chickasaws. Each tribe resides on a separate tract, and has courts, legislatures, schools, and universities.

Their physicians are great botanists, knowing the virtues of every green thing from the cedar of Lebanon to the hyssop upon the wall. They use a large horn for cupping, exhausting the air from it with the mouth through a little aperture, and piercing the spot with a sharp, neat lance, of ingeniously-ground glass. They are firm believers in the counter-irritant principle, and for every internal inflammation press a burning brand against the body.

The Cherokees lead in civilization. They are largely tinctured with white blood. In their most populous sections one may travel all day without seeing a person of unmixed Indian extraction.

Slavery among them was farcical rather than tragical. The negroes, far more intelligent than their masters, did much as they pleased, owning money, cattle and ponies; and as they made all purchases for the family, often feathering their own nests.

A COUNTER-IRRITANT.

John Ross, head chief of the Cherokees, was a very wealthy land and slave owner. He was nearly white, and had married a lady from Philadelphia.

I was interested in a volume of Choctaw laws, a curious grafting of the forms of civilization upon a stock of barbarism. Each statute began:

'Be it enacted by the Warriors and chiefs in National Council asssembled.'

One was authenticated by the signatures of 'Black Fox, Principal Chief; Path Killer, Secretary.' Another was signed 'Turtle-at-Home, Speaker of Council;' and a third 'Ennautanaueh, Speaker.'

One legislator bore the name of 'Big Rattling Gourd'—appropriate for many a white Solon. Another was called 'The Dark;' I fancy *he* was full-blooded. One act was 'for the relief of Betsey Broom,' doubtless a good housewife—while she was new. Among other names in the volume were: Going Snake, The Hair, Sleeping Rabbit, Spirit, The Bark, Deer-in-Water, Bridge Maker, Woman Killer (unquestionably a dandy,) Walking Stick, Old

Feather, the Turkey, Sour John, The Tough, Flying Buffalo, Spring Frog, Big Head, John Jolly, and Soft-Shell Turtle.

The Creeks are less advanced in civilization. In summer after working part of a day they often seek some cool shallow spot in the river, and lie in the water for hours. Thus old travelers relate that dwellers on the Isle of Ormus were wont to sleep in wooden cisterns immersed in water up to their heads.

They are famous pedestrians, often walking sixty or seventy miles a day. With a little sack of dried meat suspended from his neck, and his pockets filled with cakes of pulverized potatoes and beans, carefully wrapped in husks, the Creek starts on a tour of two or three hundred miles, and leaves the hardiest horse behind.

The Choctaws used to flatten their foreheads artificially. From the extreme of barbarism they have advanced steadily in civilization since 1831, when they removed from Alabama to this region. They are honest faithful and peaceable, owning all lands in common, but permitting any one of their tribe to remain undisturbed on the tract which he cultivates. Most are of unmixed Indian blood, though whites who have married Choctaw wives and been adopted into the tribe, enjoy all the privileges of citizenship save eligibility to the three highest offices. Where the father is of pure white blood and the mother an Indian or half-breed, or *vice versa*, five of the children may be entirely white, with Saxon features, and a sixth will have unmixed Indian lineaments, with a skin dusky as the darkest Comanche or Pueblo.

The Choctaws produce much cotton in their rich valleys. Stock raising is the most lucrative employment. I found oxen selling at fifty dollars per yoke, cows at ten dollars each, and horses at twenty dollars apiece. Calves and colts branded with the owner's mark run at large, require no feeding in winter, and in two or three years are ready for the market. Every citizen's brand is registered in the public records, so that stray animals are easily reclaimed. According to Marco Polo the same system existed among the Tartars in the thirteenth century:

'Every man who owns oxen or other cattle marks them with his seal and then turns them out upon the plains or among the mountains; and whoever finds one straying brings it to him whose mark is upon it.'

The Choctaw language though rude and rudimentary is often poetic. Fingers are 'sons of the hand,' and leaves 'tree-hair.' A river is a 'water-road,' and the moon, 'the night-traveling sun.' Arrows are 'cane-bullets, and bows 'wooden guns.'

In sharp contrast to their white Arkansas neighbors the Choctaws appropriated money freely for the education of their children. At ten large mission boarding schools six hundred pupils were studying. After graduating here promising boys were sent to eastern colleges at the public expense. In a girls' school superintended by a Methodist clergyman, the sixty pupils all slept in a long hall. Sometimes at the dead of night one would strike up a sacred hymn; one by one all the little sleepers would wake and join her, until the building rang with their voices. Next some little copper-hued girl in night-gown would mount a chair for a religious exhortation. Others would follow, till the little devotees with their groans, sobs and shrieks, rivaled a camp meeting.

At other times a single girl would wake and begin some low weird song. One after another all would rouse and join her, the chant swelling until all these little throats roared forth the old war whoop of the Choctaw tribe! The teachers could not prevent these midnight entertainments even by whipping. The girls acquired language readily, were intelligent and in average capacity equaled white children.

The constitution of the Choctaws contained this provision:

> 'The tenure of all offices shall be for some limited period of time, if the person appointed or elected thereto so long *behave well!*'

Elections were by ballot. The legislative debates were in Choctaw but the records in English. Neither atheists nor 'persons not believing in future rewards and punishments' could hold office. Murderers were almost invariably caught, and publicly shot ten days after conviction. The penalty for stealing 'negroes, horses, mules, or jackasses' was 'one hundred lashes well laid on the bare back' for the first offense, and death for the second. Kidnappers were branded with the letter T (thief) on the forehead, and received a hundred lashes, also 'well laid on.' Excessive cruelty to animals was punishable by fine and thirty-nine lashes; treason, by death;

manslaughter by one hundred lashes; grand larceny by one hundred lashes, and the second offense by death; libel, by

'Such number of lashes on the bare back, *well laid on*, as the court in its discretion may adjudge, having regard to the nature and enormity of the offense.'

Obviously this was no place for a roving journalist; and I took the coach going west. It was filled with passengers, including a loquacious Californian who introduced himself as General ——, without stating upon what bloody fields he won the title. Our road led among wooded hills and park-like forests and across rich prairie openings, alive with hundreds of grazing cattle often white as snow. Men women and children of all hues between alabaster and ebony, lounged upon the long porticoes or on the grass under the tall trees. Some Indian girls wore the latest city modes with enormous crinolines. How absolute the sway of that gentle empress whose silent commands from her silken chambers go forth over sea and land, even penetrating the primeval forest and ruling the dusky daughters of an unknown race!

A CHARMED LINE.

Many farmers had superb corn-fields. In early days the untamed Choctaws raised only grain enough for their subsistence. The first night after planting a corn patch, the hunter's wife walked around it, trailing her night-gown upon the ground, thus encircling it with a charmed line which neither voracious worm nor noxious insect could cross. The brave fancied that, Byron-like, the destroyers of his grain venerated a petticoat:

'A garment of a mystical sublimity,
No matter whether russet silk or dimity.'

The second day, we had left the mountains behind and were among beautiful prairies. Boggy Depot capital of the Choctaw nation contained two trading houses and half a dozen dwellings. It is near the country of the Chickasaws who have a separate government. A few years ago their legislature abrogated all existing laws and passed a fresh code. They sent the new manuscript laws into Texas to be printed, without retaining a copy. The messenger lost them while fording a river; and they were never recovered. The courts were in a muddle which would have surprised Stephen Blackpool himself, until a new legislature supplied the deficiency.

Approaching Texas we sang with the jolly German travelers:

'Nut-brown maids and bread that's white,
These shall be our lot to-night;
Maids of white and bread of brown,
Shall greet us in to-morrow's town.'

The Indian Territory, nine time times larger than Massachusetts, is better watered and timbered than Kansas or Illinois; has a delightful climate, a soil unsurpassed in the world, and enormous fields of coal. Adapted to every product from cotton to Indian corn, it is the most beautiful farming country under our flag, and when the railroad shall penetrate it, will leap into the condition of a populous and powerful State.

Before seeing its inhabitants I was skeptical about the possibility of civilizing Indians. But these once cruel and barbarous tribes were now governing themselves, educating their children, protecting life and property far better than adjacent Arkansas and Texas, and rapidly assuming the habits of enlightened man.

At Preston we crossed the Red river into Texas. Light-draught steamers have sometimes ascended to Preston; but the river is really navigable only to Shreveport, Louisiana. Thirty miles above Shreveport begins the great 'Raft'—an immense collection of trees and drift-wood half imbedded in the earth and firmly wedged together. It extends for seventy miles up the channel, sometimes spreading out to a width of thirty miles, and dividing the stream into many branches which do not all reunite for a hundred miles.

CHAPTER XIX.

ONE authority derives 'Texas' from *Teha*, (happy hunting ground) applied by the Aztecs who fled thither after the subjugation of their country by Cortez. According to another tradition it is an Indian word signifying 'friend.'

Before daylight on the first morning we met the California mail, with six smoking horses on a swift run through the drenching rain, and the passengers lustily singing:

'Down upon the Suwanee river.'

Every day thereafter we encountered a stage from San Francisco, always stopping a moment to exchange gossip and newspapers. At midnight one coach-load sent a thrill of horror through our little company by intelligence that Broderick the favorite Free Soil senator from California had fallen in a duel. Judge Terry, Broderick's adversary, was charged with foul play in the selection of weapons of the very finest trigger, with which he had practised for months, while Broderick had never seen them before. Five years later, Terry himself was killed while serving as an officer in the rebel army.

Our first Texan town was Sherman, capital of Grayson county, on a high rolling site, with a population of five hundred. Five hours later we breakfasted at Gainesville, in Cook county, another pleasant village. Beyond stretched undulating prairies with soil as black and rich as that of Kansas—a good stock region though liable to destructive drowths, which ruin grass and sometimes compel the farmers to fatten their cattle on wheat. During the day we passed but five or six farms; and night overtook us on a barren soil among thin groves of low scrubby oaks.

September 28.—At one o'clock, A. M., found the West Trinity river too much swollen for fording. The little station was full; so we slept refreshingly upon corn-husks in the barn, or in the western vernacular, the 'stable.' After breakfast we crossed the stream on foot by a slippery log, while drivers and conductor brought over heavy mail bags and trunks on the same precarious bridge. On the west bank another waiting coach was soon rolling us forward among mesquite groves. The long narrow leaves of this shrub are indeed 'tree-hair.' The slender hanging pods contain beans which both raw and cooked are palatable and nutritious to man. Horses also thrive and fatten upon them. Indians convert them, pods and all, into bread. Mexicans extract sugar and beer from them. Short fine mesquite grass also abounds. Like the buffalo grass it is eagerly devoured by stock, and does not lose its nutriment in winter.

Breakfasted in Jackson county where the Indians were so troublesome that settlers dared not enter their fields to cut their wheat. In one direction the nearest white neighbors were a mile distant; in another five; in another eight, and to the north (toward Kansas,) two hundred and fifty miles. Lumber for doors and floors of the log station had been hauled from the nearest saw-mill, a hundred and fifty miles.

All which I learned from our landlord who nervously paced his porch, ravenously chewing tobacco, and casting uneasy glances at the navy revolver by his side. Three weeks before, he had killed an employee of the stage company in a sudden quarrel, upon the very spot where we now conversed. He was under three thousand dollars bail to appear for trial; but in this lawless region men were seldom convicted of homicide, and never punished. Within a month there had been three other fatal shooting affrays near by; and our driver enjoined us:

'If you want to obtain distinction in *this* country, kill somebody!

At dusk we passed old Fort Belknap, the last outpost of civilization. Thence to the Rio Grande stretches a lonely desert for six hundred miles. Our horses were now exchanged for little Mexican mules. Four stout men were required to hold them while the driver mounted to his seat. Once loosed, after kicking, plunging and rearing, they ran wildly for two miles upon the road. They can never be fully tamed. When first used, the drivers lash the coach to a tree before harnessing them. When ready for starting, the ropes are cut and they sometimes run for a dozen miles. But on this smooth prairie they do not often overturn a coach.

Fording the Brazos, we passed a wretched log-cabin whose squatter, a frontier Monte Christo, had a hundred-acre cornfield, which here represented fabulous wealth.

We were soon on the plains, where Indians claim exclusive domain, and every traveler is a moving arsenal. We met a train

A MEXICAN CART.

of Mexican carts loaded with corn for the mail stations. A rude, primitive invention is this vehicular ox-killer, which must have come in vogue soon after the flood. The enormous wheels are of huge logs, clumsily framed together and loosely revolving upon a rude axle. The frame, of slats covered with hide or canvas, resembles a gigantic hen-coop. No iron is used in its construction; and the lumbering cart creaks and rattles and sways along the road, apparently just about tumbling to pieces. It is drawn by oxen, with a straight strip of wood across their shoulders and strapped to their horns, serving for a yoke. Ropes are substituted for chains and bows. The poor animals are driven with long sharp poles, by dirty Mexicans, blanketed and bare-headed.

All night our coach rolled noiseless over the soft road, while the wind trembling through the mesquite leaves swept after us a ceaseless lullaby.

September 29.—Daylight found us at Phantom Hill, named from the white ghostly chimneys of a burned fort. Beyond were barren hills dotted with mesquite and cactus, and covered with cities of prairie-dogs which often live twenty miles from water. Some conjecture that they dig subterranean wells; others that they live without drinking. In winter they remain torpid, closely shut in their holes, and when they reappear it is an unfailing indication that the weather is about to moderate.

All day upon the silent desert, stopping only to change mules at lonely little stations. Air delicious and exhilarating. In the evening passed Fort Chadbourne, sixteen hundred feet above sea level,—a cluster of long low white barracks garrisoned by one company of infantry. But the Comanches regard our soldiers much as they would a company of children armed with pop-guns and penny whistles.

After dark, finding the Colorado* impassable, we slept in the coach waiting for its waters to subside. The vehicle's roof was like a sieve, and cold pitiless rain deluged us all night.

September 30.—Awoke cold and rheumatic; but holding with Sancho Panza that a fat sorrow is better than a lean, breakfasted heartily upon pork and mesquite beans; and dried our clothes before the fire of the adobe hut-station.

The Colorado, usually an insignificant stream a hundred feet wide but now a fierce torrent, compelled us to spend the day here in the favorite range of the Comanches. These fierce untamed savages roam over an immense region, eating the raw flesh of the buffalo, drinking its warm blood, and plundering Mexicans Indians and whites with judicial impartiality. Arabs and Tartars

* [illegible] stream of the Arkansas, often confounded with the Colorado of Utah and Cali[illegible], and sometimes with the Minnesota Colorado or Red river of the North.

of the desert, they remove their villages (pitching their lodges in regular streets and squares) hundreds of miles at the shortest notice. The men are short and stout, with bright copper faces, and long hair which they ornament with glass beads and silver gewgaws.

On foot slow and awkward, but on horseback graceful, they are the most expert and daring riders in the world. In battle they sweep down upon their enemies with terrific yells, and concealing the whole body, with the exception of one foot, behind their horses, discharge bullets or arrows over and under the animals' necks rapidly and accurately. Each has his favorite war horse which he regards with great affection, and only mounts when going to battle. With small arms they are familiar; but 'gun-carts' or cannons, they hold in superstitious fear, from the effects of one fired among them long ago by a Government expedition which they attacked upon the Missouri. Even the women are daring riders and hunters, lassoing antelope and shooting buffalo. They wear the hair short, tattoo their bodies hideously, have stolid faces, and are ill-shapen and bow-legged. When a Comanche would show special fondness for an Indian or white man he folds him in a pair of dirty arms and rubs a very greasy face against the suffering victim's.

A COMANCHE GREETING.

These modern Spartans are most expert and skillful thieves. An old brave boasted to Marcy that his four sons were the noblest youths in the tribe, and the chief comfort of his age, for they could steal more horses than any of their companions!

They are patient and untiring; sometimes absent upon war expeditions two years, refusing to return until they can bring the spoils of battle. When organizing a war party, the chief decorates a long pole with eagle feathers and a flag, and then in fighting costume chants war songs through his village. He makes many raids upon white settlers, but his favorite victims are Mexicans. Like all barbarians he believes his tribe the most prosperous and powerful on earth; and whenever our Government supplies him with blankets sugar or money, attributes the gifts solely to fear of Comanche prowess. He is terrible in revenge; the slightest injury or affront will have blood. An American writer saw one chief punish the infidelity of his wife by placing the muzzle of his gun over her crossed feet and firing a bullet through them both.

After death the warrior is buried on some high hill in sitting posture, with face to the east, his choicest buffalo robe about him and the rest of his wardrobe deposited by his side. His relatives mourn by lacerating themselves with knives or cropping their hair; and if he was killed in disastrous battle, by clipping the tails and manes of their horses and mules.

On vast deserts the Comanches convey intelligence hundreds of miles in a few hours. By day, green pine, fir, or hemlock boughs piled upon burning wood produce a heavy black smoke which is seen far away; and at night they telegraph by bonfires. Their signals are as well defined and intelligible as those of civilized navies—smokes and fires with stated intervals between, indicating the approach of enemies or calling the roving bands together for any purpose whatever.

They are inveterate smokers, mingling dried sumach leaves with tobacco; and they drink whisky to excess. When needful they easily abstain from food for days together, but afterward eat fresh meat in incredible quantities.

Never tilling the soil, insensible alike to the comforts and wants of civilization, daring, treacherous, and bloodthirsty, they are the destroying angels of our frontier, the mortal terror of weaker Indians and of Mexicans. According to tradition their ancestors came from a far country in the West, where they expect to join them after death.

October 1.—This morning the river had so far subsided that we crossed, though the strong current swept our six little mules several yards down the stream, and compelled them to swim. Beyond, in ancient lake beds, our coach wheels crushed rattlesnakes, lying lazily in the road. They seldom bite except in August, when they are said to be blind and to snap indiscriminately at every living thing. Hogs do not fear them but kill and eat voraciously. Their flesh is a favorite dish with old plainsmen.

Dined at the North Concho. Our spirited little landlady, reared in eastern Texas, gave us a description of an attack made by a hundred and twenty Comanches three weeks before. A stock-tender, her husband and herself shut themselves in the house, and with their rifles kept the assailants at a respectful distance. The savages drove away all their mules and cattle, and a dozen of their iron-pointed feather-tipped arrows were still sticking in the cottonwood logs. That very morning a party of Comanches had pursued the station-keeper when within two miles of his dwelling. One of their arrows passed through his hat, but his fleet horse saved him. He laughed heartily at this morning amusement, but his little wife was only angry, declaring vehemently that they would not be driven out of the country by worthless Red-skins.

A MORNING AMUSEMENT.

Many species of cactus beside our road. One, the soap plant, has a large fibrous root said to possess saponaceous properties, and the Mexicans are reputed to use it in washing their persons and clothing; but generally they cherish strong antipathy to *all* soap. Most of them would be improved by spending half an hour under a pump-spout, with a vigorous man at the handle. Scores of spotted antelopes in sight. The wolves are said to chase them in a circle, thus enabling a fresh pursuer to take the place of the weary one every time they pass the starting point. Fleetness falls a victim to cunning, and the poor antelope soon furnishes a feast for the hungry pack.

At dark, with fresh strong team and additional rifles and revolvers on board, we entered upon that old terror of immigrants, the Great Staked Plain. In the cold dreary night this barren table land stretched afar—an utter sand-waste with a few shrubs of cactus and grease-wood. A few weeks before, travelers had narrowly escaped death from thirst. At one stage-station during four-fifths of the year, water for the mules was hauled in casks twenty-two miles. But now the ground was saturated. Again and again during the dark night our conductor left the stage with his lantern, searching for the track, which neither driver nor mules could see many yards ahead; there was danger of wandering off into the wilderness.

October 2.—Daylight found us on a shoreless ocean of desolation. Excepting the faint mail road,

'Nor dint of hoof nor print of foot
Lay in the wild and arid soil;
No sign of travel, none of toil—
The very air was mute.'

The ancient Mexicans marked a route with stakes over this vast desert, and hence its name. It is four hundred miles long by two hundred in width, and two thousand eight hundred feet above sea level. Among its gypsum deposits are large sheets of 'the pure transparent selenite which' according to Hitchcock 'the ancients used for windows. It has the curious property of enabling a person within the house to see all that passes abroad, while those without cannot see what is passing within. Nero employed it in his palace.'

We journeyed for eighty miles across a corner of the desert, passing two or three mail stations, the most desolate and lonely of all human habitations. Then through a winding canyon we descended into the broad valley of Pecos river and halted at a station of adobe. Thence I traveled eight hundred miles before I again saw a wooden building.

Crossing the swollen river in a skiff we took another waiting coach and soon struck the old trail of the Comanches to the City of Mexico. Eight beaten paths side by side indicated the frequency of their bloody raids into northern Mexico, for cattle horses and children. They once kidnapped a daughter of the governor-general of Chihuahua, tatooed her and furnished her with an Indian husband. When discovered by her father she was the mother of several children, and refused to leave the tribe. Single warriors possess two hundred stolen Mexican horses.

Among these barren sands we suddenly saw on the horizon a lake of clear blue water fringed with wooded shores; but while we

THE MIRAGE.

gazed in wonder it vanished. This wonderful mirage was a lovely miracle; but it sometimes proves a terrible mockery to lonely American emigrants perishing from thirst; and it bitterly betrayed the French army in Egypt.

Beyond Camp Stockton—a military post of three or four edifices with pearly misty mountains in the background—we reached the well-trodden mail road from San Antonio to El Paso.

October 3.—After an intensely cold night breakfasted on delicious venison, at a mountain station where last winter the supply gave out, and the inmates subsisted for twelve days wholly upon corn, ground in a coffee-mill.

Sunrise overtook us in Limpia Canyon whose rocky walls, a thousand feet high, have been sculptured by water into fantastic figures. Some are isolated, others in bass-relief. Great pagan idols show worshippers in flowing garments kneeling before them. Beside these stands a sentinel with hands in pockets, wistfully eying an enormous cask, as if waiting for his matutinal dram. Around the cask a sharp-nosed wolf is cautiously peeping, while beyond tapestry incloses the group in graceful folds.

The striking, beautiful gorge soon widens into a secluded valley, where the Apaches often stole the stock of the San Antonio mails. Once they killed the driver and took mail bags and all. At their next camping ground they opened one sack and discovered several illustrated papers. They had never seen an engraving; and a new world was revealed to them. Lying upon the ground with the pictures spread before them, these overgrown children were absorbed in wonder and delight. But suddenly the comedy was changed to tragedy. A squad of cavalry approaching unperceived dashed in among them, killing fourteen and routing the rest. The Apaches believed the papers had revealed their whereabout; and still supposing that pictures can talk they avoid them with superstitious dread.

INDIANS SURPRISED AND DEFEATED IN LIMPIA CANYON. PAGE 234.

CHAPTER XX.

PASSING a little Mexican house with roof and chimney of adobe, walls of upright poles and gables of cotton cloth, we reached Fort Davis, four thousand two hundred feet above sea level, named in honor of Jefferson Davis while he was secretary of war. The site is of unequaled beauty: surrounded by tall conical mountains and fronting upon a fair valley. The buildings are of dark stone with straw-thatched roofs; and noble trees shade the grounds.

Twenty miles beyond we crossed the highest ridge between St. Louis and El Paso. The California general was still on board, and an army colonel now joined us. At the first station, the little stage mules were so wild that they could only be caught in the stable yard by lassoing them. When we started they proved altogether unmanageable. In the headlong race, while the coach was poised on two wheels, I sprang out. The vehicle barely avoided capsizing; and after a circuit of a mile, the driver brought his riotous steeds around again and stopped for me to re-enter.

'My friend,' observed the colonel, 'you are fortunate to escape a broken neck.' 'Whatever happens, always stick to the coach.'

'And,' added the general, '*never* jump out over a wheel!'

Scarcely had these golden axioms been uttered, when the spirits of our mules again effervesced. The coach was transformed into a pitching schooner, which the bounding billows of prairie tossed and rolled and threatened to wreck. I kept in the vehicle; but both my military companions jumped headlong over a hind-wheel to the sure and firm-set earth. After that climax, equilibrium was restored; but the colonel picked up with a sprained ancle, and the general, with a severely bruised foot, both seemed in doubt whether to laugh or fight, when their own wise counsel was repeated to them.

The country was dreary enough to recall the traveler's experience among the barren hills of Virginia. In a specially forbidding region, he passed a tumble-down log-hut with old hats stuffed in the windows. At one aperture appeared a face surmounted by a shock of hair and half-hidden in an ambush of wrinkles.

'I say, stranger!' shouted its owner; 'I'm not so poor as you think. I don't own *all* this land about here!'

Our natural mountain road was equal to the best turnpike. Among the many species of cactus, one low, turnip-shaped plant holds in its rough thorny skin a watery pulp, which quenches the thirst of man and beast. Another common variety, the spanish bayonet, is here ten feet high, its upright stem crowned with long sharp spurs like bayonets, so firm that it is said they will pierce through the body of a man.

THE SPANISH BAYONET.

October 4.—At daylight we reached the Rio Grande and looked across it upon Mexican territory. Three dirty blanketed barefoot men smoking cigarettes, shivered over the fire on the river bank, where two Mexican women cooked our breakfast of frijoles.

At Fort Quitman, whose white-washed adobe buildings look like marble, we left the colonel, so lame that his Irish servant lifted him from the coach like a baby. The general while asleep had lost his hat overboard, for the second time within forty-eight hours. Unable to purchase a new one he wrapt his head in a fiery red comforter, like a sanguinary and turbaned Turk.

We continued up the sandy valley of the Rio Grande, from five to forty miles wide, and bounded on the west by a notched line of mountains. We passed Mexican villages, where bright-eyed, dusky-faced, half-naked children were playing about the streets, and through open doors women were visible in very simple dress or undress, reclining upon matresses, gossiping and smoking cigarettes. Toward evening we were among ranches, herds of cattle, and great corn-fields. There are no fences; but all cattle are watched by herders from planting-time until November. Water is conveyed from the river through ditches to every portion of the farms. In this sandy soil and rainless climate, no crop can be raised without irrigation.

Passing the pleasant, shaded Mexican hamlet of Socorro, with quaint old churches and low houses of adobe, and Ysletta, a Pueblo Indian settlement with its tall white cathedral, we reached El Paso at eight in the evening, having traveled ninety miles since dawn, and two hundred and twenty-six during the last thirty-four hours.

El Paso, twelve hundred miles from St. Louis and from San Francisco, was the half-way point on the great Overland route. This was the first rapid line across the continent. John Butterfield and his associates were paid six hundred thousand sand dollars a year for carrying tri-weekly mails between St. Louis and San Francisco. Ruling influences in Congress and the White House compelled them to adopt a far southern route through the Indian Territory, Texas and Arizona; while a branch line from Memphis also joined the main stem at Fort Smith, Arkansas. The coaches ran day and night, ordinarily going from St. Louis to San Francisco in twenty-one days, though the law allowed twenty-five. It was the longest stage route in the world.

To establish this line three thousand miles across mountains, deserts, dangerous rivers and the territory of hostile Indians, was a gigantic enterprise. The stages ran by a time-table, and with so much regularity that during twelve months there had not been a single failure to deliver the mail on schedule time. Every day for two winter months, near the middle of the long route, the coaches from St. Louis met those from San Francisco within three hundred yards of the same spot. The through fare was a hundred and fifty dollars, exclusive of meals, which cost from forty cents to one dollar. The line continued in operation till the war broke out in 1861, when the Texans and Arkansans seized most of the mules and coaches. It was then removed to the central route. The Wells-Fargo company, composed of the same stockholders, now carry mails and passengers from the western termini of the Kansas and Nebraska railways, via Denver Salt Lake and Nevada, to California.

The early settlers upon Massachusetts bay, after exploring the country for twenty miles 'out West,' reported the fact with triumphant surprise, and boasted that the soil was tillable for that entire distance. Most adults remember when Buffalo was spoken of as 'out West.' How rapidly the application of that familiar phrase has since moved toward the setting sun! Now, on this remotest frontier, I heard a merchant speak of sending goods 'out West.'

'And pray,' I asked, 'where may *that* be?'

'O,' he replied carelessly, 'about a hundred miles over into Mexico.'*

The Texan town of El Paso had four hundred inhabitants, chiefly Mexicans. Its business men were Americans, but Spanish was the prevailing language. All the features were Mexican: low, flat, adobe buildings, shading cottonwoods under which dusky, smoking women and swarthy children sold fruit, vegetables, and bread; habitual gambling universal, from the boy's game of pitching *quartillas* (three cent coins) to the great saloons where huge piles of silver dollars were staked at monte. In this little village, a hundred thousand dollars often changed hands in a single night through the potent agencies of monte and poker. There were only two or three American ladies; and most of the whites kept Mexican mistresses. All goods were brought on wagons from the Gulf of Mexico, and sold at an advance of three or four hundred per cent. on eastern prices.

From hills overlooking the town, the eye takes in a charming picture—a far-stretching valley, enriched with orchards, vineyards and corn-fields, through which the river traces a shining pathway. Across it appear the flat roofs and cathedral towers of the old Mexican El Paso; still further, dim misty mountains melt into the blue sky.

---

* A native word, signifying the home or seat of Mextilli, the Aztec god of war.

Western Texas has a poor soil and is very thinly settled. El Paso county is three hundred miles long, and from eighty to two hundred miles in width.

The vocabulary of slang was large and novel. When two friends shook hands the invariable salutation was the Indian 'How?' 'Outfit,' (always familiar on the verge of regions where the traveler must carry every thing he needs on the journey,) might mean one's clothing, his watch, his horse, or even his mistress. One's 'ranch' was his dwelling, office, bed-chamber, or trading-house. To 'go under,' or 'go up,' was to die. To 'jump a man' was to attack or kill him. A 'greaser' was a Mexican—originating in the filthy, greasy appearance of the natives.

Slavery was only nominal in western Texas, as negroes could easily cross the Rio Grande into Mexico, where the natives sheltered them. But here, as throughout old and New Mexico, peon labor was universal. Natives of the lower classes, ignorant and thriftless, were always ready to contract a debt and agree to work it out, receiving from three to ten dollars a month and clothing themselves. As no one else would supply him with goods this placed the peon at his master's mercy, and compelled him to pay most exorbitant prices. But he seemed to like it; and cases where one liquidated his debts and became free were very rare. Just before my arrival, a peon by years of labor had earned his freedom; but in less than a week he bought an eighty-dollar silk dress for his wife, contracting a debt which would make him a slave for life.

The American residents believed in the inalienable right of the white man to bully the inferior race. At Messilla all public records and legal proceedings were in Spanish. A Kentuckian was brought before the alcalde or magistrate for assault and battery. The native judge, with shaggy beard uncombed hair and dirty face, appeared on the bench in a soiled calico shirt and buckskin sandals. He knew no English. Sternly motioning the Kentuckian to rise he ordered the sheriff to ask the prisoner whether he spoke Spanish.

'Nary Spanish.'

'Then,' said the alcalde, 'he must hire an interpreter.'

The delinquent, shifting his tobacco quid to the other cheek, replied:

'Ask him whether this court is sitting in Mexico or the United States?'

STREET SCENES IN EL PASO, OLD MEXICO.

'In the United States!' responded the angry official.

'Then tell him that I understand the United States language, and if he don't I'll see him d——d before I hire an interpreter for *him*.'

The enraged alcalde fined the Kentuckian twenty-five dollars for contempt. The prisoner in return commended the court to the infernal regions, and drawing his revolver strode away, anathematizing any country where Greasers presumed to administer justice to white men!

Hundreds of many-colored sheep and goats graze the valleys and hill-sides. The shepherd dogs which guard them are sometimes left in sole charge for hours. They keep the flocks compact, driving all stragglers back upon the herd, and never leaving their posts.

Immediately west of the Texan El Paso runs the Rio Grande, dividing our possessions from old Mexico. On its west bank is the Mexican city, El Paso Del Norte, thus named by the Spaniards from the pass through the mountains at this point. Coming from the south they called it 'the North Pass.' Long afterward our own pioneers from the east named a mountain-crossing on the Salt Lake road 'the South Pass.' Consequently the latter is a thousand miles further north than the former, to the sore perplexity of travelers and geographers.

The Mexican El Paso contains twelve thousand people, and extends up and down the river for miles. Next to St. Augustine Florida, it is the oldest European settlement on our continent. As essentially un-American as India or China, it is a quaint old city of gardens and corn-fields, orchards and vineyards, shaded by green cottonwoods, with a net-work of ditches crossing the streets spanned by rickety log bridges. A city of swarthy, diminutive, sinister-faced men, and dusky women who permit only their lustrous eyes to be seen in public. Of narrow, crowded thoroughfares through which Mexican carts creak and rumble, half-naked boys and indolent men bear water-kegs suspended from poles between them, women balance huge jars upon their heads, and little donkeys stagger under enormous loads of corn-stalks. Of ancient adobe houses with wooden doors and window shutters, quaintly carved but without a pane of glass; and of a crumbling cathedral erected before the Pilgrims landed on Plymouth rock.

The Mexican is pre-eminently social. If an American enters the saloon where he is drinking, with endless bows he insists that the new-comer shall taste from his glass. If another Mexican enters, he even takes the cigar from his mouth and hands it to his friend, who after a few whiffs passes it to a neighbor. Thus it goes around the company before returning to the owner's lips.

His idea of heaven seems to be a maze of long-robed priests, gorgeous paintings and wax candles; a blessed asylum where cigarettes, wine and brandy never fail, where there is no work, much gossip, and a fandango every night.

By 'the gift of Nature,' he is a wine connoisseur, a dancer, and a walking cigar manufactory. While earnestly talking, he produces a square bit of corn-husk or paper from one pocket, a box of fine-cut tobacco from another, and rolls up and lights a cigar without once looking at it.

The large and delicious El Paso grape grows abundantly. For a few pennies one is allowed to enter any vineyard and eat his fill. The wine though a little heavy is rich and unctuous. I do not covet my Mexican neighbor's house nor his wife, his man-servant nor his maid-servant, his ox nor his ass; but I confess to twinges of envy that he can enjoy throughout the year the glowing vintage of El Paso.

The first evening's duty was to attend a fandango. When we entered, the dancing had begun. Several Texan whites, all armed, were present. One while dancing dropped his enormous revolver and bowie knife—a display which excited no attention. There were black spirits and white, red spirits and gray. The faces of dancers and spectators in the low basement, lighted by tallow candles, made up a medley of hues from dark Indian to fairest

A MEXICAN FANDANGO.

Saxon. On the platform at one end, three musicians without coats were hard at work. All entered into the amusement with enthusiasm; and participants and lookers on of both sexes were smoking. When a woman rose to dance she handed her cigarette to a neighbor to smoke until she returned. A demented old hag whose hideous face would have made her fortune as Meg Merrilies or the chief of Macbeth's witches, was raving about the room wearing no clothing except a chemise. The women were coarse-featured and homely, but their voices low and pleasing as they chattered in liquid Spanish. Many had beautiful, luminous eyes, and all a grace of motion rarely seen in their English or American sisters.

At ten o'clock we left the lively fandango for a ball of 'the first society'—a few families who claim that their pure Castilian blood has never mingled with that of the native Indians. They were not wont to associate with Americans, but to-night a few Texans were invited.

I found this patrician *baile* in an ancient family mansion, built around a hollow court after the old Moorish mode, for protection against attack. The servants recognizing my companion opened the great barred gate, and conducted us through the court to a spacious well-lighted saloon. Its earth floor was covered with plain hemp matting. There were no chairs, but stationary benches against the walls.

The dancing had already begun, but it was listless; and like most aristocratic affairs this proved heavy and stupid. Among the thirty or forty guests I saw no Indian features. The ladies were no darker than our own brunettes. Some had faces regular and almost classic; but not one showed intelligence and vivacity. Their movements were languid and graceful. Wine was frequently passed, each lady taking a dainty sip and then replacing the glass upon the waiter for twenty or thirty others to drink from. Only a few were smoking.

The next morning (Sunday) the market on the great plaza was crowded and the stores open, for this is the grand gala and business day of the week. A harsh, cracked bell from the old cathedral summoned the people to worship. The shaky tower of the crumbling edifice had contained a bell brought from Spain, nearly as ancient as the building itself. A few months before my visit an old friend, Edward E. Cross, surreptitiously pocketed the tongue and carried it to 'the States' as a curiosity. The natives so resented this sacrilege that Cross's life would not have been safe for a moment among them. He had been an editor in Cincinnati, and a rover through every State in the Union; and was now publishing a newspaper in the wilds of Arizona. Afterward he commanded a regiment of Mexicans under Juarez until our great rebellion. Then he became colonel of the fifth New Hampshire infantry; participated in almost every battle of the glorious Army of the Potomac, and was wounded again and again. At last, in 1864, he received the fatal shot and yielded his life for his country.

The old cathedral was in the form of a cross. The congregation numbered five thousand, more than half women. The men looked like cut-throats, but were the most devout worshippers I ever saw. All the women wore the rebozo or broad scarf, covering the entire face except the luminous, brilliant eyes. The services were conducted by an unctuous, sensuous-looking priest, who seemed in no haste to join the church triumphant.

There was an irrepressible conflict between the Mexicans and their Texan neighbors. Peons would escape into Texas, and slaves into Mexico; and both found sympathy and refuge. Several armed Texans had lately attempted to carry back an alleged fugitive after the alcalde had tried the case and declared the negro free. There was a good deal of random shooting on both sides; but the Texans were finally captured and heavily fined.

CHAPTER XXI.

LEAVING the trans-continental route I turned northward from El Paso, taking the weekly mail coach for Santa Fe:—three hundred and fifty miles; forty dollars exclusive of meals.

Our old-fashioned stage was drawn by six mules, with a seventh led beside them for emergencies, and an eighth ridden by a young Mexican armed with a 'black-snake' whip, whose pistol-like crack and keen stroke terrified if it did not hasten the lazy little animals.

Our road was up the sandy valley of the Rio Grande, barren of vegetation but prolific of lizards and frequented by the deadly tarantula, resembling an enormous black spider.

Soon entering New Mexico, we saw no habitation for twenty miles until we reached our adobe dinner station. A little Mexican village hard by had just been ravaged by the Apaches, who entered in broad daylight, stealing every horse and mule they could find, and unresisted by the terrified natives.

At Fort Fillmore—a collection of pleasant Government barracks—a slave woman black as Erebus took passage, journeying alone from Virginia to a new owner in Santa Fe.

Passing frequent villages, at midnight we entered upon the *Jornanda del Muerto*, (journey of the dead man.) This desert ninety miles long, contains no water except a single spring several miles from the road. Many travelers have perished from thirst, and upon the ground bleach the bones of scores of animals. But two days before us the mail party discovered two corpses by the road-side. We journeyed all night, and in the morning while we halted for men to breakfast and mules to graze, a horseman came into our camp nearly famished, as he had thirsted for twenty-four hours. Our keg of fresh water strapped behind the coach revived him and he went on rejoicing. Good riders have often crossed the tract without water accomplishing the journey in a day and night, and not taking food, as that always aggravates thirst.

'JOURNEY OF THE DEAD MAN.'

Our conductor, a Virginian who had lived for thirteen years in this region, was an express-rider across the desert for eight years before the establishment of the mail. He had repeatedly crossed in twelve hours, when in fear of the Apaches, who murder and rob upon its dreary road. He ran that gantlet of death one day in each week for eight hundred dollars per annum.

'Some people,' he gossiped, 'sneer at running from Indians; but *I* always found my heels my best weapons. Thar was one Apache band led by old chief Mangus, that came near getting me. They chased me a heap of times, and I thought oncet or twicet that I was gone under, sure. They were commonly in companies of a dozen to forty; but one day I met old Mangus alone. He was mighty glad to see me then, and powerful friendly; but I had my six-shooter cocked in his face before he know'd it. 'It's no use to play good,' says I; 'you've been after me too many times. Now you d—d old scoundrel, I've got *you*, and I'm bound to take your har!' How the old fellow did beg! Finally he pawned me his honor that if I'd let him off I should never be troubled again; and he kept his word. I rode here for years afterward, and often met his men, but nary one ever molested me.'

Mexican women he thought the kindest in the world. Many an American owed his life to them. They were fond of white men, which made the Greasers jealous and dangerous.

'Are the men treacherous?'

'*I* never had any trouble with them; but stranger, I always watch a Greaser, and at night I never let one travel behind me. It's the safe way, if you don't want to get stabbed or shot in the back.'

All day without meeting a human being, we rode among dreary wastes with clumps of Spanish bayonet, grease-wood, faint tufts of grass, and solitary delicate flowers variegating the ashen landscape, and the wonderful mirage painting the far horizon. At night, the desert left behind, we lodged at a ranch where the face of the landlord, (an Indiana rover with a Mexican wife,) so revealed his Hoosier origin that he who ran might read.

MEXICAN GRIST-MILL.

The next morning we started by starlight. Day broke upon fleecy clouds drifting up from the valleys and half hiding the rugged peaks in floating draperies. Beside our road many a rough wooden cross marks the spot of some violent death. Passing travelers each add a stone to the pile at its foot, aiding to form a rude monument.

At our dining station native women were re-plastering the adobe house with fresh mud, using their hands for trowels; but stopped to prepare our repast. Here I first saw the genuine Mexican grist-mill. It is locally known as the *mitata*, is propelled by one-woman power, and has been in use from remotest antiquity. One of our dusky entertainers crushed corn for *tortillas*, (griddle cakes) in this rude stone morter; then another pounded coffee in it; then a third pounded, mixed, and baked red peppers and buffalo meat, for the chief staple of our meal.

'Unless your stomach be strong do not eat cockroaches.' Disregarding this wise African proverb I tasted a morsel of the fiery dish. It was like red-hot iron! The natives are extravagantly fond of it. Red peppers, in general use even before the Spanish conquest, are still raised in enormous quantities. The year's supply spread out to dry upon the flat roof of each Mexican dwelling, would suffice for five hundred Americans. The pepper enters into every article of food, and is Nature's preventive of some malignant fevers common to tropical countries.

The next day we found many settlements. Each town, with its plaza, old Catholic church, narrow streets, and naked children is like every other. At every ranch sheep and goats graze the hills. Women and girls are husking corn beside every house, spreading the yellow ears upon the roof to dry. The stalk is so sweet that babies suck it like sugar.

At noon while our coach halted, a hospitable widow sent a servant with a lunch of goats' milk cheeses for the hungry passengers. We spent the night in Peralta, at the house of a wealthy native farmer.

Would Senor have supper?

Had they any tea?

'Si, Senor.'

'Any eggs?'

'Si, Senor.'

'Any mutton?'

'Si, Senor.'

Then Senor *would* have supper, if those articles could be prepared without onions or red peppers. It proved a savory repast.

The house, better furnished than most here, had only two rude chairs. Mattresses served for seats by day and beds by night. The smooth, whitewashed walls were hung with crucifixes, and saints in lithograph.

Our swarthy landlord was busy with his peons gathering corn, for November was close at hand. His young wife, pretty, intelligent and vivacious, went soberly about the rooms with a huge bunch of keys dangling by her side. She was the only comely Mexican woman I ever saw; and her little girl of two years had a face and figure which would have driven a sculptor mad with despair. The youthful matron, to enlarge my little vocabulary of Spanish, patiently repeated the names of objects about her house and court. Any dullard would acquire Castilian under such a teacher. She spoke no English. Some idea of New Mexico socially may be gathered from the statement made to me before leaving El Paso, that this lady was the only woman reputed chaste on the entire route to Santa Fe, three hundred and fifty miles through the most populous portion of the Territory.

We passed Albuquerque, (population, three thousand,) one of the richest and pleasantest towns, with a Spanish cathedral and other buildings more than two hundred years old. While we were halting, an enormous pile of patent office reports and other public documents sent hither by a member of Congress, at the public expense, was sold at auction for thirty-seven-and-a-half cents. The shrewd purchaser, an illiterate Mexican, declared that he wanted them for fire-wood. It showed one of the many beauties of the franking privilege.

A disgusted immigrant from Pike's Peak also arrived with nine yokes of oxen, vowing that he wished himself back on the rich Nebraska prairies, that he would not exchange his cattle for all the land between Fort Kearney and Albuquerque, but would push on till he found a country fit for white men, whether it took him to the Gulf of Mexico or to the bottomless pit.

On the road beyond, farmers were treading out their wheat with horses and oxen precisely as did the children of Israel three thousand years ago. Others were cutting corn with a rude hoe-like instrument, threshing wheat upon the ground with long, clumsy poles and mowing grass *with sickles.* The ruder and older the implements the better they suit the Mexican. His farming tools show no improvement upon those of his Aztec forefathers. His plow is only a crooked stick. Merchants endeavored to introduce iron plows but could not persuade the natives to adopt them. Threshing machines also were brought from the Missouri, but the ignorant farmers who hire ground, paying the rent with a portion of the crop, believed them a diabolical invention for cheating them out of their share of wheat!

After spending a night at Algondes we turned eastward from the Rio Grande. A lonely, mountain journey of a few hours brought us into Santa Fe.

All New Mexican settlements look venerable. The adobe buildings with grated windows and low carved doors all suggest:

> 'The events
> Of old and wondrous times,
> Which dim tradition interruptedly teaches.'

Titles to estates, two hundred years old, are still preserved in the public archives, and in Taos there is a dwelling of Indian origin

A MEXICAN FARM-HOUSE.

which tradition declares was built three centuries ago. In the narrow, crooked streets one looks instinctively for the haughty Spaniard, in complete steel, striking terror to the hearts of the natives.

Santa Fe de San Francisco, (the city of the holy faith of St. Francis,) was begun in the fifteenth century. Its founders were of that wonderful Order whose unflagging zeal and perfect organization almost achieved the conquest of the world. Traces of old Jesuit missions abound throughout California, Arizona, New Mexico, old Mexico, and Central America. These vast regions were converted to the Roman faith by patient life-long labors of the Society of Jesus, not by the furious zeal of Cortez and his fellow robbers who hurled the native idols down the steps of their temples, to replace them with the cross. New Mexico, thoroughly Roman Catholic, contains only one Protestant church and one Protestant school.

Santa Fe, the political and business metropolis, now boasted four thousand inhabitants, of whom three or four hundred were Americans. On the sunny side of the plaza sat dirty boys, shriveled, blanketed old men and hideous women vending *tortillas*, bread, mutton, onions, tomatoes, red peppers and candy. The buildings were all adobe save the unfinished capitol and the penitentiary—both of stone—and one frame edifice. None except the cathedral and a smaller church were more than one story high.

Santa Fe, the highest town of any importance in the United States, nestles among the mountains seven thousand feet above sea level. The overlooking peaks are white with snow. One summer all the ice in the city was bought by a hotel keeper, who refused to sell at any price to a rival house. This was ruin. Cold water and hard butter might be dispensed with, but no hotel could live here without sherry cobblers among its possibilities. In a moment of inspiration the landlord sent a train of donkeys twenty miles into the mountains. They came back loaded with huge blocks of ice; the cobbler trade revived and prosperity returned to the Napoleonic host.

As in every Spanish American country the natives are inveterate gamblers. Soon after he learns to walk, the child risks his first penny; and the gray haired man tottering into the grave, stakes his only coat or his last dollar. Americans too plunge into games of chance with their national recklessness. Though times were now dull, the city contained fifty American 'sporting men,' as professional gamblers are politely termed. At the Santa Fe hotel I often saw three monte banks in a single room in operation from daylight until midnight. They were attended by a motley crowd of Indians, Mexicans and whites, darkening the saloon with tobacco smoke. The deep silence was broken only by the jingle of coins and the suppressed breath of players. Enormous piles

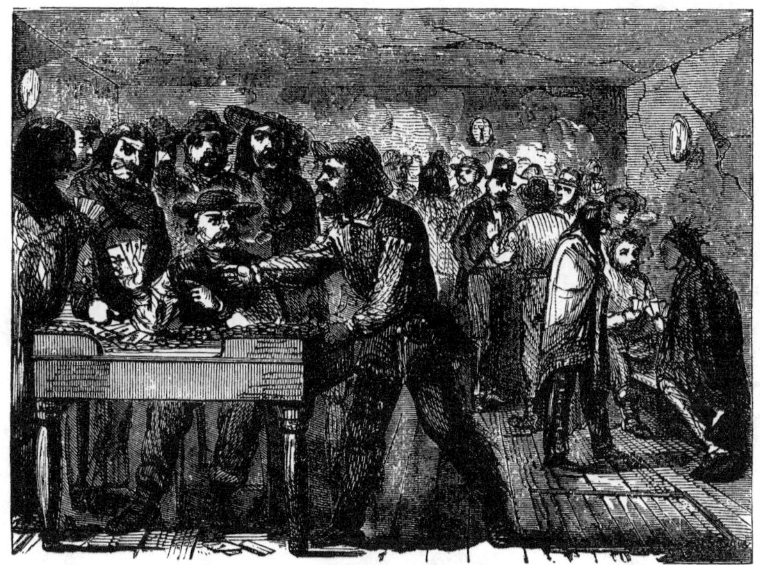

GAMBLING IN SANTA FE.

of silver weighed down the tables, and frequently ten thousand dollars changed hands in ten minutes.

Business men would publicly lose or win a thousand dollars with the greatest nonchalance. One evening I saw a clerk with only five dollars sit down to the game. In a few hours he had won a thousand, but before morning he was penniless. A young surveyor after winning twelve hundred dollars, left the table, saying:

'When you have a good thing, keep it.'

During the previous winter, an American had enjoyed a rare 'run of luck.' Knowing nothing about the game, (and if it was honestly conducted no skill nor experience could have aided him,) he began betting at monte. The bank always began the evening with a capital of a thousand dollars. For a month he staked against it, breaking it every night, and then found himself the possessor of thirty thousand dollars. Now, his fortune had changed; every evening he lost heavily, and doubtless he soon gained his old safe stand-point of beggary.

The Santa Fe cathedral is a huge 'adobe' with effigies of the Saviour and the Virgin, and lurid paintings of the sufferings on Calvary, decorating its walls. The Sunday congregation was chiefly women. Unlike the worshippers at El Paso many had adopted the European fashions, and appeared in shawls and bonnets. Many too had pleasing features, and all displayed the sparkling eyes of their race. Immediately after the services, at the church-yard gate, most of the masculines lighted their cigars.

The old men of Mexican towns look older than any others in the world. According to a local proverb, the region is so healthy that its aged inhabitants never die, but dry up and are blown away! Gaunt, attenuated, wrinkled and blanketed, their youthful hose a world too wide for their shrunk shanks, they totter about like re-vivified Egyptian mummies, or those uneasy ghosts which,

> 'In the most high and palmy state of Rome,
> A little ere the mightiest Julius fell,
> Did squeak and gibber in the Roman streets.'

In the establishment of William J. Howard, a Santa Fe jeweler, I found a long necklace of the first joints of human fingers, collected by the Utes from Apaches killed in war; and another horrid trophy in the form of an Indian scalp with coarse black hair two feet long. Among the living wonders were cat-fish with well defined *legs*, curious lizards, horned frogs and a venerable owl which subsisted upon live mice, swallowing them whole. There were Aztec battle axes of marble, Comanche pipes of slate, necklaces of bear claws, drinking cups and cooking utensils of Aztec and Apache pottery, bows and arrows, spears, shields, curious petrifactions of wood, and specimens of native lead, copper, silver, amethyst, alabaster, quicksilver and gold—the last very fine and beautiful. New Mexico abounds in mineral treasures; and before it was Americanized the Mexicans dug gold from its mountains to the amount of three hundred thousand dollars per year. Now most Americans are engaged in trading; but ere long a mining excitement will cause immigrants to pour in and revolutionize the country socially and politically.

Some silver mining is done, but the general feeling is expressed by the Mexican proverb that only three classes of men work silver mines: those who have other people's money to spend, those who have more money than they know what to do with, and, fools.

Mr. Howard collected his curiosities during a visit to the Zunians a branch of the Pueblo Indians among the mountains, far from any white settlers or Mexicans. Among them he found four *white* Indians with blue eyes and flaxen hair. Tradition asserts that a few families of the tribe have always been of this complexion. The other Zunians make these whites perform all the manual labor, refusing to associate or intermarry with them. I have already related how the mixed Choctaws render pure whites ineligible to their highest offices. And I remember a Kansas Delaware half-breed, so indignant because three or four mulatto boys were admitted to the only accessible school, that he permitted his eight children to grow up in ignorance. Though some of our fantastic tricks before high heaven may make the angels weep, our prejudices against color must make them smile.

All groceries and other supplies for New Mexico were hauled from the Missouri. New York to Kansas City (railroads) fourteen hundred miles; freights one and a half cents per pound. Kansas City to Santa Fe (wagon roads) eight hundred and forty miles; ten cents per pound. Moral: the Pacific Railway.

Dancing, a passion with the ancient Aztecs and mingling in all their religious exercises, continues the staple amusement of their mixed descendants. There were three or four fandangoes in Santa Fe every night, the Mexicans always participating with wonderful zest.

There were only one or two American ladies in the Territory; though the number has since increased. Many native women were mistresses of the white residents by the consent, even the desire, of their degraded husbands. Chastity is practically unknown among them, but they possess all the other distinctive virtues of their sex. These poor creatures, utterly devoid of personal purity, willing to give or suffer any thing to obtain jewelry and silks, are uniformly tender and self sacrificing, ready to divide their last crust with the hungry, and deny themselves every comfort to nurse the sick and minister to the wretched.

Is there some drop of Bedouin blood even in the blue veins of civilized man? In 1855, Sir George Gore an Irish nobleman with an annual income of two hundred thousand dollars, buried himself in the Rocky Mountains to spend two years in hunting, fishing and periling his scalp among the Indians. The few white residents of this Territory find strange fascination in its isolation, lawlessness and danger. Whenever I asked if they did not find it lonely, they indignantly replied that no temptation could induce them to return to their former homes. An old trader, Colonel Ceran St. Vrain, after accumulating an ample fortune, went to New York city with the determination of spending his days. But he found life there insupportable, and soon returned to New Mexico vowing he would never leave it again.

Here, as in Arizona and Idaho, the Indians are always troublesome. A year before my visit, William J. Rose, with twenty families a costly stock of goods and three hundred and fifty cattle, started for California. The Mojaves captured the goods stock and wagons, and killed several of the emigrants. One youth, shot from his horse, was lying half insensible with an arrow sticking in his head, when a savage approached with a bloody knife. The boy had made up his mind to die, but scalping was more than he bargained for. Terror inspired him with such new vigor that he leaped upon his horse and the faithful animal bore him out of danger. Rose lost every dollar of his property, but in this novel region however far down one sank in the deep, deep sea of pecuniary ruin, he soon rose again. Now, Rose was the flourishing landlord of the Santa Fe hotel, with an income of a thousand dollars per week.

CHAPTER XXII.

I DESIGNED returning from Santa Fe by the weekly mail direct to Kansas City, eight hundred and forty miles. But the Kiowa Indians after blockading the route for a month, had captured the two last eastward coaches, stolen the stock and left thirteen passengers, including two women, killed and scalped by the roadside. The indignation of the people at the failure of Government to protect immigrants and freighters, found vent in maledictions in bastard Spanish and broken English.

My own line of march was cut off. Eastward the Kansas City route might remain closed for months. I could retrace my steps south to El Paso, and return by the Butterfield Line; but with that, familiarity had bred contempt. Northward, toward Pike's Peak, were no carriage roads, but the lonely trail promised novelty and adventure.

While I was pondering upon ways and means, a 'sporting man introduced himself as a stray New York printer and journalist, and inquired if he could serve me. I wanted to reach Taos; and as good luck would have it, he desired to send thither a pony which he had borrowed from a Taos Indian. Gladly accepting the proffer, I sold all my luggage except one blanket and a few indispensables which could be pressed into saddle bags.

At the hotel supper-table I noticed a stout middle-aged man, with straight brown hair, mild eye and kindly face. He wore a suit of gray, and looked like an Illinois farmer; but when he took off his hat the face and head indicated character. My printer-gambler friend nodded to the new-comer, and I asked:

'Who is he?'

'Kit Carson, the mountaineer.'

Carson was about returning home to Taos, and at ten the next morning we galloped away together. He was reputed the most daring and reckless of riders. I had not mounted a horse for months and was still weak and reduced in flesh. But we flew over the rocks through canyons and across ditches until my blood tingled to the finger-tips. Kit's special delight was to dash down steep hills at full gallop. This new experience made me shudder. But he was far heavier than I and his American horse nearly twice as tall as my little steed. Moreover Indian ponies rarely stumble, so the odds were largely in my favor. Our road was nearly all hills; and after three or four trials I began to enjoy it and to forget the Spanish proverb: 'A running horse is an open sepulcher.' On foot Carson looks stout and ungraceful. He avers that much riding with the short stirrups of the border has made him bow-legged; but he sits a horse splendidly and rides with rare grace and skill.

KIT CARSON.

He declares that the happiest years of his life were spent as a mountain trapper. Like all men in constant peril and excitements, the trappers found strange fascination in their dangerous career, though the rifles and arrows of bloodthirsty savages made it a constant race with death. They adopted the dress and habits of the Aborigines, buying one or more squaws to lighten their labors and 'rear their dusky race.' Kit gave me a striking illustration of the healthfulness of mountain air and out-door life:

'Our ordinary fare consisted of fresh beaver and buffalo-meat, without any salt, bread, or vegetables. Once or twice a year, when supplies arrived from the States, we had flour and coffee for one or two meals, though they cost one dollar a pint. During the winter, visiting our traps twice a day, we were often compelled to break the ice, and wade in the water up to our waists. Notwithstanding these hardships sickness was absolutely unknown among us. I lived ten years in the mountains, with from one to three hundred trappers, and I cannot remember that a single one of them died from disease.'

In that golden age of the trappers, beaver-skins commanded eight dollars a pound, and every stream and canyon was rich in game. Now, beavers and otters were almost extinct, and the few remaining trappers, like true conservatives, sighed for the 'good old times.'

With something of the modesty of true greatness Carson never spoke of his own exploits except in reply to my questions. Then he described some exciting battles, including the story of four trappers in a mountain stronghold who kept a hundred and fifty Blackfeet at bay for half a day, and finally defeated them. He said that as a boy he was daring and reckless; but now when traveling he exercised great vigilance, having seen many of his comrades killed by Indians through their own carelessness. Once he was in the Snake Indian country, with five companions. One night a party of wily Sioux, completely disguised in wolf-skins, and tapping buffalo bones together to imitate the snapping of wolves' teeth, stole into their camp so adroitly that they never suspected their visitors to be human until they rose up with a yell and began to shoot. All the whites were killed except Carson.

The flesh of a wild horse he deemed better than any other meat. A young mule furnished excellent steaks, but meat from an old one was tough, strong-flavored, and unpalatable. The most sorrowful meal he ever took was when necessity compelled him to kill and eat a faithful horse which had borne him many hundred miles. He loved Fremont and spoke enthusiastically of the pleasant years they spent together.

Our road led over barren plains and among snow-streaked mountains; but passed some rich valley-farms, with speckled ripening corn and plump wheat.

Turning our horses out to graze, we lunched upon bread and dried buffalo meat, and smoked our mid-day cigars upon the grassy bank of a clear stream, in the Canada (pronounced 'can-*ya*-tha,') a battle-ground of the Mexican war. Here General Sterling Price, with four hundred Americans, defeated two thousand Mexicans. Histories describe the charge of his soldiers up the steep hill-side as bloody and gallant, adding in confirmation that the Americans lost *one* man!

Starting again we struck the Rio Grande, here an insignificant stream in a narrow valley. At four, P. M., the sun had disappeared; so we halted at a spacious adobe whose swarthy owner received us in great dirt and dignity. We performed our ablutions in the little acequia or irrigating canal; supped on mutton, *frijoles* and eggs and slept on floor-mattresses with yellow-haired saints and a pink-faced virgin staring down from the walls.

Breakfasting at daylight before our host was up, we left a quarter-eagle upon his table and started on. The hospitable Mexican entertains all travelers, but never demands payment; leaving that question wholly to his guest.

We galloped through El Ambudo, (the funnel,) in 1847 scene of another sanguinary battle, in which two hundred Americans under a raking fire dislodged five hundred of their foes, and had but one man killed! That is our version; but like the lion in the fable the Mexicans had no painter.

We entered a dark cold canyon, its frowning walls crowned with odorous pine and hemlock. The mountain scenery grew so wild that I lingered behind my companion to enjoy it. In a lonely dell I was stopped by two brawny Indians, who imperiously demanded whisky and tobacco, and manifested an unpleasing interest in my saddle-bags. A handful of smoking tobacco failing to satisfy them, I drew my revolver and sternly motioned them away. They instantly obeyed; but had they known how poor a marksman I was they would have laughed in my face. Next I encountered a party of Apaches moving their village, with children and household utensils in baskets suspended from the dragging lodge-poles.

At two, P. M., sore in every joint, from the ride of eighty miles, equal to one hundred and twenty upon level roads, I reached Taos, and was soon housed under Carson's roof.

Taos, (named from an Indian tribe now extinct,) beside the narrow, flashing Taos river which gushes from the mountains a few miles above, has two thousand five hundred inhabitants. It is the third city of New Mexico, Santa Fe being the first and Albuquerque the second. With irrigation its valley produces bountiful crops of wheat which is chiefly converted into whisky, known throughout the far West as 'Taos lightning.' The native women are the most comely in the Territory.

Here at the age of fifty Kit Carson had settled to crown a youth of labor with an age of ease. His wife was an intelligent Spanish lady, and his home was brightened by four or five children. He

MEXICAN CARRIAGES.

had accumulated a handsome competence and was now Government agent for the Ute Indians with a salary of one thousand dollars per year. Owning a large farm with many horses and mules, he designed thenceforward to avoid horseback riding and travel only in carriages,— a plan which he doubtless carried out as far as practicable in a country destitute of wagon roads.

He is by birth a Kentuckian, of excellent abilities but narrow education. Reading with difficulty, and writing little beyond his own name, he speaks fluently English, French, Spanish, and several Indian tongues, all acquired orally. As if figuring fancifully in romances numerous and yellow-covered were not misfortune enough, he is also the victim of a biographer. His romantic life is set forth in a large octavo volume, from data furnished by himself to a persistent author. He confessed to me—most modest of heroes—that he had looked into the book here and there but had never read it!

He is a gentleman by instinct; upright, pure, and simple-hearted, beloved alike by Indians, Mexicans, and Americans. When serving as scout and guiding Fremont on his explorations he held a lieutenant's commission in our army. After several years of civil life he was made a brigadier general of volunteers during the war for the Union, and he now commands a fort in New Mexico.

The narrow streets of Taos, like those of Santa Fe and El Paso; are usually crowded with 'Mexican carriages.' The burro, or donkey, little larger than a Newfoundland dog, serves for mule, ox, horse, cart, and barouche. He staggers like a runaway haystack under huge loads of grass, straw, husks, and corn-stalks. He brings from the mountains enormous piles of pine and cedar for fuel. He transports trunks, sacks of coffee, kegs, and even barrels of whisky. Often he carries burdens quite as heavy as himself. Women and children jog soberly along upon the patient little beast. They use neither saddle nor bridle but guide him by a club, mercilessly thwacking his thick skull. While making a call or visiting a trading house they leave him alone for hours. They 'hitch' him by throwing a blanket over his head which blindfolds him and prevents his stirring an inch. The duties of the burro are as varied, exacting, and little appreciated as those of a country clergyman or a metropolitan editor. He ought to take the place of the eagle on the national device of the Mexican republic.

HITCHING A DONKEY.

The American residents claimed that the instinctive hostility of the natives, who formed a majority upon all juries, rendered it impossible to punish any Mexican through the courts, for the grossest outrages upon 'white men.' This was their excuse for wearing revolvers and knives and wreaking private revenge for every real or fancied injury. Homicides even among themselves were common; and in that marvelously healthful climate there was some foundation for the current proverb that Yankees never died except from revolver shots, hard drinking, or a personal vice still more repulsive.

I heard a hopeful American youth of seventeen, who with drawn bowie knife had wantonly attacked a native at a fandango, bitterly regret that he was not able to 'cut the Greaser in two' before they were separated. And a burly Mexican, in a frenzy of anger, cut off the ears of his wife! For a timid gentleman of quiet habits the society was not alluring!

Our Government acquired this extensive Territory almost without bloodshed during the Mexican war. A year after its annexation, in a general rebellion which began at Taos, Mexicans and Indians massacred Governor William Bent, every other United States civil officer whether of Mexican or American birth, and most of the white private citizens. Carson was absent from home, but the savages who took every thing from his house even stole all the clothing from his wife's person except her chemise. They scalped their victims and burned out the eyes of one, a lawyer from Ohio, before life was extinct. Friendly native women had given frequent warnings, and some escaped the massacre by flight. The national authority was soon restored and eighteen of the murderers were hanged.

The old Aztec priests had the confessional, granted absolution and taught the people to dramatize scenes in the lives of their gods. These customs were easily assimilated to the new faith. During Holy week, in all large towns, churches and altars are richly adorned, priests appear in gorgeous robes, and figures of the Saviour and the virgin, as large as life, are exhibited.

The European 'mysteries' of the middle ages originated with returned pilgrims from the Holy Land, who, in public streets, leaning upon well-worn staffs, and wearing cloaks and chaplets picturesquely decorated with shells and images, recited poems describing the consecrated spots they had visited, interwoven with traditions, simple and extravagant, of Christ and the apostles. In time pious citizens erected stages for these performances. One of the quaint dramas represented the beloved apostle cast into a caldron of boiling oil. Another exhibited the eleven drawing lots with straws for a successor to the apostate Judas. Some began with the creation and ended with the last judgment—at least a comprehensive plan. Even the Almighty was personated; and anecdotes are preserved of one curate who came near expiring on the cross, and another, who while playing Judas and hanging upon a tree narrowly escaped suffocation through the slipping of his rope. The New Mexican devotees closely imitate their medieval prototypes, enacting the trial of Christ, the ghastly death, the watching of the body by Pontius Pilate, (!) and other incidents real, fanciful, and grotesque in the first great tragedy of the Christian religion.

The Aztec priests fasted and did cruel penance, scourging and piercing themselves with thorns until blood streamed from their wounds. The *Penitentes*, a secret society of the most ignorant Catholics including many criminals, still reproduce these horrors. They spend Easter week in a secluded lodge or ranch, dragging stones, crucifixes, and other heavy burdens, cutting their flesh with swords, and tearing it with cactus thorns. On Thursday and Friday, wearing only drawers, they are led blindfolded through the streets, lashing themselves with a tough weed until blood flows freely, sometimes to the infliction of fatal injuries. These tortures end in the cathedral, where they represent the darkness and chaos which they believe followed the crucifixion. After again lashing their bodies pitilessly, they remain in total darkness for an hour, groaning, shrieking, and hurling sticks and stones. This week of penance they deem ample atonement for all their sins of the year.

The priests (Irish and French, with a few natives) are often very ignorant. Nearly all live openly with mistresses, whose children bear the mother's name, though their paternity is neither concealed nor denied. The priests' marriage fees range from ten to one hundred dollars. Among the poor, burial costs from one dollar to one hundred, according to the distance of the grave from the altar. The wealthy are sometimes charged a thousand dollars for interment in sacred earth.

The personal names of these devout Catholics startle Protestant ears. I encountered one dirty, cut-throat looking Mexican bearing the appelation *Juan de Dios*—'John of God;' and received an invitation to a *baile* at the house of Don *Jesus Vigil.* Jesus (pronounced *He*-soos) is very common; one native near Taos is called *Jesus Christo.*

PENITENTES LASHING THEMSELVES.

Degenerate descendants of that strange race, whose 'gorgeous semi-civilization' was once the world's wonder, modern Mexicans are treacherous, effeminate, cowardly and superstitious, almost meriting John Randolph's bitter invective: 'a blanketed nation of thieves and harlots.'

Conceded to the southern Propagandists, New Mexico kept the word of promise to the ear and broke it to the hope. With the most barbarous and rigid slave code in the entire Union, (shrewdly enacted by native legislators to secure favor from Buchanan's administration) the slaves within her borders numbered less than twenty. Peon labor was cheaper, and the Mexican *would* treat the African as an equal. A disgusted Southron complained to me:

'Before a nigger has been here a month he knows more than his master.'

Pueblo (Spanish: 'a village') is the name applied to a scattered race of half-civilized Indians who live in towns and claim to be unmixed descendants of the ancient Aztecs. They never intermarry with whites, and their women (almost the solitary exception to Indian tribes in general) are reputed inflexibly chaste. Each of their twenty villages is independent, with a democratic government. The largest nestles at the foot of the mountains two miles from Taos. The huge adobe buildings which look like fortresses, are of five or six stories, each smaller than the one beneath, and forming a terrace, till one little chamber crowns the whole. There are no doors on the ground floor, but inmates ascend to the roof of the first story by a ladder—drawing it up at night, for security against intruders—and enter by a trap-door. They formerly kept sentinels upon the house-top, but in these piping times of peace the custom is discarded. Each dwelling contains many families.

One evening I saw a muscular Pueblo native in no clothing except a breech cloth, standing upon his roof apparently engaged in worship. Noticing me, he discontinued his orisons, and with pantomimic eloquence attempted to sell, first a plate of *frijoles* then a string of peppers, then some enormous squashes. Failing in all these he crowned his commercial attempts by pointing at the pony I bestrode and uttering his only English word:

'Swap?'

My negative was the last grain of sand, and he turned despairingly away. Hard by stood the old church with crumbling walls, which one thousand five hundred insurgent Mexicans and Pueblos occupied as a fort after the massacres of 1847. The attacking Americans, numbering four hundred, were led by Kit Carson and Colonel St. Vrain. After skirmishing for an entire day the rebels retreated. The hindmost fifty were killed almost to a man, by a Government force lying in ambush near their road.

Though these anomalous Indians are professed Catholics, some vaguely worship a great Father who lives where the sun rises, and a great Mother whose home is where it sets. A few who adhere to the Aztec faith, cherish a tradition that Montezuma established this Taos village, taught them to build pueblos, and kindled sacred fires for their priests to guard. That he also founded the pueblo at Pecos, where he planted a tree, predicting that after his disappearance there would be no rain, and a foreign race would subjugate them. But he commanded them to keep the sacred fires burning until the fall of the tree, when white men from the east would overwhelm their oppressors, rain would again increase and he would soon reëstablish his kingdom. They aver that the tree fell just as the triumphant Americans entered Santa Fe in 1846.

For years the Indians of that pueblo had been decreasing; and just then an old man the last in the long line of priesthood died at his post, and the holy fire was extinguished.

THE TAOS PUEBLO.

The country indicates that in former ages rain was much more abundant than now; and the Pueblos point triumphantly to the fact that it has increased since the advent of the whites. In the mountains they still burn the hallowed flames, and anxiously await the return of Montezuma. In some pueblos a sentinel regularly climbs to the house-top at sunrise and looks toward the east for his coming.

Like the men of Mars Hill they believe in 'the unknown God,' whose name is too holy to be spoken. They hold sacred all animals living in or near water, which in their rainless climate is the choicest of blessings.

They have a tradition that at the flood a few faithful Zunians gathered upon a mountain top, and waited long but in vain for the waters to subside. At last, a youth of royal blood and a beautiful virgin, decorated with feathers, were let down from the cliff as a propitiatory offering to the angry Deity. The waters soon fell, and youth and maiden were transformed into statues of stone, still pointed out to the credulous among the Zuni mountains.

A hundred miles southeast of Santa Fe are extensive saline lakes supplying the entire Territory with salt. Near them the ruins of a city contain the remains of an aqueduct twelve miles long, walls of churches, Castilian coats of arms and deep pits in the earth. It was probably a Spanish silver mining town destroyed in 1680, when the natives killed or drove out all the invaders. The ruins of several walled towns reveal pottery and other articles similar to those found in the city of Mexico. Ruins in Navajoe county include the remains of enormous houses, of imposing architecture. In some, explorers have counted the traces of one hundred and sixty distinct rooms upon the ground floor. The fallen beams and rafters were hewn with dull axes apparently of stone.

Nearly three hundred years ago, Spanish missionaries found in New Mexico half-civilized Indians who raised cotton, manufactured cloth, and lived in towns with regular streets squares and dwellings like those of the present Pueblos.

Dr. J. S. Newberry of the United States army, found remarkable ruins of old pueblos on the San Juan river, then in New Mexico now in the southwest corner of Colorado. One of these deserted human bee-hives was inclosed by sandstone walls five hundred feet long, twelve inches thick and thirty feet high, and as true and smooth as the walls of the Astor House. The marks on the few timbers still preserved, and implements found in the vicinity, indicate that logs and rocks were split and hewn with tools of hard stone. The huge edifice, six stories high, was divided into small rooms, very evenly and beautifully plastered with gypsum.

The San Juan valley contains many of these ruins which have been deserted from three hundred to five hundred years. Once it swarmed with the busy life of half a million of people, now it has no human being. Dr. Newberry inquired the reason of this from an old and intelligent Pueblo chief, who replied that at the invasion by Cortez, Montezuma made such heavy drafts upon the able-bodied men of the province as to leave old men, women and children unable to defend themselves from the surrounding Utes, Apaches and Navajoes, and compeled the entire population to emigrate southward. This theory is supported by the fact that the most ancient pueblos, which were built in mountain fastnesses easily defensible against numbers and valor, are still inhabited, while those in the open country are deserted.

Hundreds of acres of large cedars, all dead from drowth, and the circumstance that no water is found within miles of many of these ruined cities, prove that the country was once far less dry than now. The elevation of the land for a few feet through some geological agency or the depression of the surface of the Gulf of California, would have been sufficient to produce the change.

The approach of winter forbade me to linger among the strange scenery, inhabitants, antiquities and traditions of this most interesting and least known of all our Territories. Three times larger than New England, it is all mountainous. Even the narrow valleys of the streams are tillable only with irrigation. It has no navigable rivers. Though the Rio Grande is two thousand miles long, vessels ascend only two hundred miles above its mouth.

Of the inhabitants, eighty thousand are Mexicans, two thousand Americans, ten thousand civilized Indians, and about fifty thousand fierce savages who roam the mountain ranges. Twice or thrice New Mexico has suffered from the frontier epidemic of constitution-making; but until new gold discoveries bring in thousands of immigrants to develop its rich and varied mineral resources, and revolutionize its industries and social life, it will not and should not be admitted to the Union as a sovereign State.

CHAPTER XXIII.

From Taos to Denver, three hundred miles due north, a lonely mountain trail led through the range of the murderous Utes. I lingered, hoping to find companions for the journey, but as winter was at hand no one was starting northward. Miners were daily arriving *from* Denver to pass the cold months in Mexico. Some declared the trail as safe as Broadway. Others pronounced the journey madness, and its inevitable price a lost scalp. As the Fort Smith fever had left my crown bare, taking this would be no easy matter. But I felt like the Scotchman about his head, that while 'nae much of a' scalp it would be 'a sair loss' to me. A third class of immigrants had no apprehensions about the savages, but laid great stress upon the danger of perishing among mountain snows.

Despairingly I appealed to Kit Carson as final authority. He replied with a smile that the road, always perilous to a stranger unfamiliar with Indian warfare, was more so toward winter than during the warm months. Just now too there was some possible danger from the Utes. Still if I deemed the trip necessary he had little doubt that I could make it successfully.

I bought a thin, iron-gray pony, two years and a half old, so Liliputian that satirical friends advised me to start upon a rocking horse instead. Even Carson was skeptical of the little brute's capacity. My own confidence was serene, based upon long experience with the hardy creatures, during which I had never known one to die from overwork or any other cause. The entire cost of pony, saddle, bridle, spurs and lariat was thirty-six dollars.

I. On the twenty-fifth of October, with Liliput almost buried under rider, heavy blanket and plethoric saddle-bags, I bade adieu to kind friends in Taos, and galloped away toward the latest El Dorado. Carson obligingly accompanied me for an hour. Pointing at an isolated mountain, a dozen miles away he said;

'Your general course is directly toward that butte.'

'Shall I reach it to night?'

'Hardly! I see you have not learned to estimate distances in this clear atmosphere. Next time we meet, remember to tell me how long you were in getting to it.'

Soon he turned homeward and I was sorry to lose sight of his kind, trust-inspiring face.

After a solitary mountain ride of twenty-eight miles I dismounted at Beaubean's trading-post, beside a rushing transparent little stream bearing the name Colorado, so frequent in Spanish nomenclature. Beaubean was a Frenchman whom long intercourse with this mixed population had converted into a bewildered polyglot. With profuse bows and in a medley of French, German, Spanish, English, and Indian, he begged me to pardon his poor lodgings and his fare so unfit to set before a gentleman. As a sequel to this preamble he gave me a supper of mutton and eggs, the best meal I had eaten in New Mexico, served upon snowy linen, in a pleasant room. Then through the long evening I lounged in a luxurious arm-chair, reading before my cheerful fire with many glances through the skeleton window at tall snow-crowned mountains, with yawning black canyons between.

The dirt floor was smooth and hard. The mud walls, dressed with a trowel and whitewashed, could hardly be distinguished from the finest plastering. They were hung with pictures of saints, and crucifixes, curiously intermingled with views of horse races and cock fights. The mattress upon the floor, covered with fine blankets of whitest wool, was quite luxurious. That afternoon in a wretched hovel across the narrow street, a little child had fallen into the fire and been burned to death. Now shrieks and moans rending the air, showed that in one dusky bosom under all its rags and wretchedness the mother-heart was beating.

II. Soon after sunrise I rode on among scattered ranches with valley-fields of corn and wheat. Irrigation makes the parched, sandy soil wonderfully productive. In most wheat-growing States a yield of fifteen fold from the seed is an excellent crop. But this seeming desert often produces fifty fold and sometimes a hundred fold. It is not adapted to Indian corn on account of the cold nights. In winter farmers do not feed stock; the cattle subsist upon a wild sage so tall that it is seldom hidden by the snow.

Crossing the Costilla (rib) river I dined at the trading-house of Mr. Posthoff, a German resident of gentlemanly manners and liberal culture, with whom I spent an agreeable afternoon and night.

Near by was a Mexican grist-mill—not the human variety already depicted but yet almost as primitive. It is simply a horizontal water-wheel connected by an upright shaft with the millstone one story above. The stone, revolving no faster than the wheel, grinds but slowly, and having no bolting apparatus turns out very coarse flour. There are a few improved steam mills in the Territory. Day's travel twenty-one miles.

III. My morning route over the desert abounded in wild sage, cactus, and great herds of antelopes. At noon as usual I broiled a bit of pork upon a long stick by my little camp-fire, and made tea in my drinking cup. Liliput found excellent grazing on the banks of the Culebra (snake) creek. The afternoon ride was delightful—among grand old mountains with ever shifting colors, water worn sides and whitened crests—a

'Lapse into the glad release
Of Nature's own, exceeding peace.'

At last from a hill-top, I had a dim shadow-like view of Fort Garland far below, its adobe walls dotting the fair valley of a creek fringed with cottonwoods, and the Stars and Stripes floating over it. Late in the cold evening I reached it, after a day's journey of thirty-three miles.

The post-sutler Mr. Francisco was far-famed for his hospitality. Around his cheerful fire I found several gentlemen who brought the latest word of old comrades and new mines in the gold region. One told me that of seven intimate friends who resided in Santa Fe fourteen years before, he was now the only survivor. All the rest had been killed by Indians or in drunken affrays.

IV. This morning I reached the mountain which Carson had pointed out to me from Taos, the distance having proved three days' journey, or more than a hundred miles. Here my course turned eastward through the Sangre de Christo (blood of Christ) canyon, leading from the waters of the Rio Grande to those of the Arkansas. Its tall upright walls are worn by streams pouring down their sides, and streaked with elk paths.

The trail crossed the little creek a dozen times in a single mile, and soon left it to follow another stream. Liliput climbed the steady ascent but slowly, for at that great altitude the atmosphere is thin, makes breathing difficult, and compels both bipeds and quadrupeds to pause frequently.

As night approached the air grew nipping and eager. I had trusted to luck for a camping place, and was nearly a day's travel from human habitation. But just before sundown I overtook two young adventurers with an ox team and a load of wheat. Despite their rough attire and sun-browned faces, the moment they spoke, they betrayed Yankee origin and they proved to be natives of Medfield, Massachusetts. Gladly I accepted their hearty invitation to lodge with them.

We climbed wearily a long sharp hill and stood upon the summit of a high divide. Behind us, within pistol shot, were streams running into the Rio Grande del Norte, which rises among the eternal snows of the Rocky Mountains and continues its sinuous course to the tropical waters of the gulf. Before us were springs which feed the Arkansas; and far to the east over hill and dale, forest and desert, we could discern its wooded valley sixty miles away.

The scenery was inspiring, but the cold and approaching darkness were not. Descending a long terraced hill, we halted for the night. The wayworn animals were turned loose to graze; supper was cooked and eaten by a log fire; after a long chat, our couch was extemporized in the open air by spreading a blanket upon the frozen ground, and we huddled close under a buffalo robe, without even a tree overhead.

The scene recalled Captain John Smith and his men out on their Indian scout in mid-winter. 'The night was cold and dismal; but,' says the stanch old leader, 'we drank our gill of rum each, and having thanked God, slept soundly, though surrounded by manifold dangers.'

As the guest, my new companions had placed me in the middle where the temperature was endurable; though whether sleeping or waking I had a dim consciousness of cold. *They* found it intolerable, and often arose to warm themselves by the fire.

V. Soon after sunrise I bade them adieu and was again on the road. The first creek I crossed, though running water, was frozen so hard that it bore pony and rider, and gave me new appreciation of the intense cold of the night.

Thus far I had not forgotten the alleged danger of this solitary journey, and had plumed myself a little upon facing it. But now I met a miner from Pike's Peak coming *on foot* over the same route and bearing upon his shoulders his blankets, provisions, frying-pan, ax and rifle. Our brief exchange of greetings showed that he regarded the journey as a mere pleasure excursion and it made me a little ashamed of myself.

MY RUEFUL MEXICAN HOST.

Through the day,, the mountain scenery was varied and picturesque. After nightfall I reached Maxwell's ranch on the Greenhorn river. Ever since starting, I had anticipated here an agreeable and luxurious resting place. Maxwell had thousands of sheep and cattle, and his dwelling (the only one within sixty miles) was eagerly looked forward to by every traveler. To my sore disappointment I found that only the day previous he had removed his cattle and men to a distant ranch, leaving no soul here save one villainous-looking Mexican. This unprepossessing host wore a tattered hat, woolen shirt, buckskin breeches and moccasins; and his black matted hair shaded a face which would have hanged him before any intelligent jury. But he was the very pink of courtesy offering hospitality in bastard Spanish with unceasing genuflections of welcome—

> 'Washing his hands with invisible soap,
> In imperceptible water'—

clearly the *only* soap and water with which his person was familiar.

I tied Liliput in a ruinous out-building and gladdened his faithful heart with corn. The dwelling had a rough dirt-floor and was pierced with holes in lieu of doors and windows. Through great gaps in the roof I saw the deep blue sky and the twinkling stars. But a cheerful blaze glowed in the spacious fire-place, and mine host of the rueful countenance prepared a capital supper of broiled venison, biscuit, and coffee. Obsequiously declining my invitation to join me at the meal, and vowing that he would ne'er consent, he not only consented but did ample justice to his own cooking.

Spreading my blankets in one corner and directing him to make his bed in another, I lay down with one hand ostentatiously resting upon the revolver under my pillow. My clothing had become ludicrously ragged. I had carefully concealed my watch; and marvelous indeed must have been the cupidity which that wardrobe, steed, or equipments could excite. But I had been told again and again that an ignorant Mexican would kill a man any day for ten dollars; and if this peon was not a cut-throat his face would have justified a suit against Nature for libel. Studying it drowsily by the flickering light of the log fire I fell asleep.

VI. Gibbon records that during the reign of a bloody tyrant a young Persian nobleman was wont to say:

'I never leave the sultan's presence without first ascertaining whether my head still rests upon my shoulders.'

Waking at three o'clock I instinctively imitated his example. But the jugular veins still continued perfect and the Mexican slept soundly under his sheep skin, until aroused to cook breakfast and feed Liliput for a hard day's journey.

Overwhelming me with thanks for a pecuniary acknowledgment of his hospitality, he uttered a vehement '*Adios, Senor;*' and I was on the road while the stars were yet shining.

Upon a mountainous desert I crossed the imaginary line which then bounded New Mexico on the north. Later, when Colorado Territory was organized it took a slice from the northern border, and also included portions of Kansas, Nebraska, and Utah.

Before noon I descended into the broad rich valley of the Arkansas. Here the stream is a hundred yards wide, shaded with a narrow belt of tall cottonwoods, and its banks covered with waving grass. The river was like an old friend. I had journeyed sixteen hundred miles since leaving it at Fort Smith, eight hundred miles nearer the Mississippi, many weeks before.

Turning out Liliput for a grassy feast, I dined with the conductor of a Mexican flour train for Denver, a Maine Yankee who for twenty years had been roaming over the world by sea and land. Soon after, I struck the Fontaine qui Bouille creek, and followed up its bank during the whole afternoon.

Spent the night at a pleasant ranch kept by an intelligent American family. It was homelike once more to be under a civilized roof and to encounter, for the first time during a journey of a thousand miles, women who spoke English. One of the ladies had been my neighbor in Kansas; but long roving had disguised me so effectually that for the first half hour she failed to recognize me. Day's travel forty-four miles.

VII. Journeyed up the Fontaine qui Bouille directly toward Pike's Peak, which, with its dark, wooded sides, and irregular turreted summit, towers far above all adjacent mountains.

Plump antelopes abounded, so tame that when I stopped my pony a long herd of one hundred and twenty-seven in single file crossed the path before me, within a stone's throw. Some were beautifully spotted and all exquisitely graceful.

Just before dark in the gigantic shadow of Pike's Peak, I reached a little sign-board labeled in bold capitals 'COLORADO AVENUE.' I had not seen a human being since morning, and the idea of a city in these solitudes savored of the ludicrous; but there it stood, unmistakable evidence of civilization and speculation.

A mile beyond, passing around an intervening hill, I reached Colorado City, founded a few weeks before, and containing fifteen or twenty log-cabins. In front of one stood an old Kansas friend, who came inquiringly forward and at last penetrating my panoply of dirt and rags gave me heartiest greeting. Day's travel thirty-five miles.

VIII. A morning visit to the curious Fontaine qui Bouille, (fountains which boil,) two miles from Colorado City, at the head of the creek I had followed up since leaving the Arkansas. The three fountains, bubbling up from the ground and not boiling with heat, are very strongly impregnated with soda. One, whose basin is three feet in diameter, seems to rise from the midst of a great rock which it has incrusted with soda to the thickness of several inches. A column of water nearly as large as the body of a man gushes up with great force. The supplying channel must be far under ground; for between this and one of the other fountains runs a fresh water creek twenty feet below their level.

FIRST VIEW OF COLORADO CITY.

The Indians regard these springs with awe and reverence. They believe that an angel or rather a spirit troubles the waters and causes the bubbling by breathing in them. Before going on war expeditions the Arapahoes formerly threw beads and knives into the fountain, and hung the adjacent trees with deer-skins and quivers as propitiatory offerings to the invisible deity. The Coloradoans mixed their flour in this water without adding soda or saleratus, and it made the lightest and best of bread. Mingled with tartaric acid and lemon-juice, the water foams like champagne, and is more palatable than that from any artificial soda fountain.

It is said to possess rare medicinal qualites. The railroad will make the springs a popular summer resort. The vicinity combines more objects of interest and grandeur than any other spot on the continent: Pike's Peak, the great South Park, the Garden of the Gods and the Fontaine qui Bouille.

Pressing onward toward Denver, I found still another old Kansas friend lunching upon the prairie under the shade of his wagon. After he identified me, we broke bread together and then fought our battles o'er again.

In the afternoon I crossed the high divide between the shining waters of the Arkansas and those of the Platte—an ascent so gentle that with the exception of two or three short hills, it is hardly perceptible. At night I came to a road-side fire beside an ample tent whose solitary sleeper rubbing his eyes, cordially offered me lodgings; for hospitality is preeminently a frontier virtue, and every stranger is tendered food and shelter. My host was of a hunting party, and his two companions were seeking their stray horses. I turned Liliput—now foot-sore from his long journey—out to graze; and, thanks to the kindness of Colorado friends, who had stuffed my pockets with venison, was able to prepare an ample supper by the roaring fire. Then stretching upon the ground with saddle for a pillow, slept soundly after a day's journey of fifty miles.

THE FONTAINE QUI BOUILLE.

IX. At sunrise I was again upon the road. Soon after, from the summit of a hill I could see Denver distinctly, though it was more than twenty miles distant. A lady upon a spirited horse overtook me and accompanied me into the city. From visiting a sister at a saw-mill in the deep pineries she was returning home, a morning ride of twenty-five miles. Ruddy cheeks and a symmetrical form had rewarded her fondness for this health-inspiring exercise.

Descending easy hills over a sand soil we reached the Platte valley, for miles trenched and gullied by miners, some still hard at work, and realizing five dollars per day to the man.

Passing many rude shanties for the sale of whisky and tobacco, along the well-trodden road, soon after noon we galloped into Denver. Here ended my mountain journey, the most enjoyable trip I had ever made. It removed the last vestiges of my Fort Smith illness. The whole desert and mountain region from the British Possessions to New Mexico, and westward to the Pacific, is one of the healthiest in the world. Rains fall only from July to September; the air is so dry that fresh meat cut in strips in summer, and quarters in winter, and hung up, will cure without smoking or salting, so that it may be carried to any part of the globe. In such an air lung and throat complaints have no chance. I have known persons supposed to be hopelessly consumptive, and only able to travel lying upon feather beds in ox wagons, who after crossing the plains and sleeping in the open air, enjoyed for years a comfortable degree of health. Recent experience shows the folly of sending consumptive patients to the tropics. Dry regions, as far as possible from the salt water, and an invigorating air, are precisely what is needed. Probably the most favorable climate on all our continent is the interior of California, and the next, Minnesota. Nebraska, Kansas and the Indian Territory are also excellent, as indeed is every State between the Mississippi and the Pacific.

Along the entire route I had now followed—in Missouri, Arkansas, the Indian Territory, Texas, and even New Mexico—occurred frequent battles or skirmishes a few years later, during the great rebellion. How vast was the war, which along the wide track between the Susquehanna and the Gulf of Mexico, swept from the Atlantic seaboard to the base of the Rocky mountains!

Dismounting in Denver I encountered my old comrade Lewis N. Tappan, who supplemented his cordial greeting with the remark:

'I have met a good many rough-looking customers on the plains and among the mountains, but *you* eclipse them all, and would tempt any 'old clo's' man to carry you off bodily.'

I had long been beyond the reach of mails and eagerly asked the news. He replied:

'Old John Brown has just attempted to excite a slave insurrection at Harper's Ferry; several of his followers are killed, and he is in jail awaiting trial. Our friends fear that his mad movement will defeat the republican ticket in the fall elections.'

THE AUTHOR ARRIVES IN DENVER.

I certainly shared in the fear. 'Heroism is very homely work in the doing,' and immortal deeds look prosaic and foolhardy to the mole-eyed worldly wisdom of to-day.

Denver had developed wonderfully during the four months of my absence. Frame and brick edifices were displacing mud-roofed log-cabins. Two theaters were in full blast; and at first glance I could recognize only two buildings. When I left there was no uncoined gold in circulation; now it was the only currency—incontestable evidence that the mines were a fact. Upon every counter stood little scales, and whenever one made a purchase, whether to the amount of ten cents or a thousand dollars, he produced a buckskin pouch of gold dust and poured out the amount for weighing.

The population was improving, for more families had settled here, but gambling and dissipation were still universal. Nearly all liquors were 'doctored' and excited far more recklessness and malignity than pure whisky or brandy would have done.

The waggish superintendent of the overland mail caught an intoxicated emigrant riding away one of his mules; but instead of having him lynched, boarded the offender gratuitously for a day or two and turned him scot free, on the ground that the whisky sold in Denver would make any man steal.

'Praise the bridge which carries you safely over.' In spite of Kit Carson's incredulity, Liliput had brought me three hundred miles in seven and-a-half days' travel. He reached Denver with tender feet, galled back and a spot on each flank as large as my hand, made raw by the spur; for his many virtues were tempered by the vice of laziness. Still I disposed of steed and equipments at a sum which réduced the cost of the trip to precisely thirteen dollars. Liliput, placed in a ranch soon grew fat, and the next spring sold for a hundred and twenty-five dollars.

On the tenth of November I left Denver by express for Leavenworth. We started in warm weather, when coats were superfluous in the middle of the day; but twenty-four hours out, the thermometer suddenly dropped to two degrees below zero. Our conductor froze his face, our driver his ears, and during the night even mules were frozen upon the prairie. We rode until one o'clock, A. M., suffering much but constantly bestirring ourselves to guard against the last deadly stupor. At last we were relieved by reaching a station, where, with as many other wayfarers as could be packed into the little building, we slept until daylight.

The weather soon moderated, and on the sixteenth of November, after having journeyed twenty-five hundred miles in stages and on horseback since the seventeenth of August, I once more reached the metropolis of Kansas.

CHAPTER XXIV.

In May, 1860, with my friend Thomas W. Knox, I returned to the border. First we made a pedestrian tour of two hundred miles through the interior of Kansas. In this initial experience of pioneer life, my comrade learned how truly 'the stomach is the great laboratory of disaffection whether in camp or capital.' The first evening, foot-sore and wayworn, we began to think of lodgings for the night. A neat little log-house, with well and orchard in front, and several improved farming implements beside it, allured us.

'This settler,' said I oracularly, 'is a gentleman of taste. These indications, to an old traveler, give unfailing promise of wholesome fare, agreeable society, and excellent accommodations. Here will we spend the night, and go forth on the morrow, refreshed, rejuvenated, and at peace with all the world.'

The squatter, a Missourian of the Methodist persuasion, whose great prairie of face was fringed with a dense, untrimmed forest of hair, received us kindly, and 'reckoned' he might accommodate us, could we put up with his indifferent fare. Here was modesty, the sure precursor of good things to come. The inevitable tow-headed children greeted us with their pleasant infant familiarities. The hostess, young and not uncomely, but of that unmistakably coarse fiber which a diet of pork and hominy imparts, retired to the kitchen to prepare supper. Time dragged, for the prairies had given us voracious appetites; but the long delay suggested proportionately splendid results. Just as the clock struck nine we crossed our legs under the festive cottonwood.

Alas, for human hopes! The coffee was like a pool of yellow

soap suds. The conglomerate substance by courtesy called butter was rank and smelled to heaven. The ham was strong enough to perform the labors of Hercules. The English language affords no vituperative epithet which can do justice to the corn bread. Despairingly, we called for sweet milk. Doubtless it *had* been sweet at some previous stage, but the period was far remote. Not a dish was palatable; the trail of the serpent was over them all.

In utter disappointment we left the table, sat for a while in ominous silence, and went to bed, a morose and melancholy pair. But our sufferings had only begun. The couch was in the possession of insectile inhabitants, who resented our invasion of their premises, in the most aggressive and bloodthirsty manner. The reader shall be spared the bristling terrors of that memorable night. It combined the horrors of a prize-fight with being buried alive.

In the morning we assisted at the farce of breakfast, disbursed nine shillings for what by a hideous satire was called our 'entertainment,' and departed with unspoken maledictions upon our host. Of all the Kansas frauds which had come within my knowledge, he was the most glaring and aggravated.

Fifteen miles beyond, we dined at Franklin, where the tavern walls still contained scores of bullets received during its siege and capture in 1856. A friend, one of the attacking Free State men, while lying in the grass and firing his rifle spoke to a comrade immediately beside him. There was no answer. Putting out his hand in the darkness it struck a motionless head, the hair dripping with warm blood. His companion lying within two feet had uttered no sound when he received the death-wound, which was ghastly and gaping, for the spiral motion of the modern rifle bullet makes its aperture three times as large as the ball itself.

Near Grasshopper Falls one fine farm of six hundred acres and another of nine hundred showed us that the wilderness was already being subdued. At Holton we stopped to chat with an old pro-slavery settler whose cheek was enormously distended from a rifle shot, the result of an attempt by himself and several companions to break up a republican convention.

At the lonely log-cabin where we spent the night, in the winter of 1857–8, old John Brown with twelve fugitive slaves whom he was conducting to Canada had waited four days for the creek to fall. Stephens and Whipple were his only white companions. Six men from Lecompton came prowling suspiciously about, when Stephens went out and asked:

PORTRAIT OF JOHN BROWN.

'What are you looking for?'

'Six fugitive slaves.'

'Well gentlemen we have not got *your* negroes, but we have twelve others up at the house. Come and see them.'

This invitation was accompanied by the click of his cocking rifle. The Lecomptonites were armed to the teeth, but five wheeled their horses and fled while the sixth at whom the rifle was pointed tremblingly remained. Stephens made him dismount, give up his arms and follow him to the dwelling:

'Mr. Brown, this man came here hunting negroes; do what you please with him.'

After searching him for concealed weapons Brown took a rope from his pocket, tied the prisoner's hands and feet, and then requested him to take a seat. He kept him confined four days reasoning with him about slavery and the wickedness of negro hunting. When set at liberty the discomfited foe seemed thoroughly converted, and manifested genuine regard for the wonderful old man.

Here came the United States marshal with a posse of thirty, to arrest Brown's party. The three dauntless pilots waited at the windows with leveled rifles to receive them, and Stephens called out cheerfully:

'Come on gentlemen; *we* are ready whenever you are.'

Their proverbial daring was terrible as an army with banners. The negro hunters were fully persuaded that dwellings, out-buildings, and hay lofts swarmed with fighting men. So they left without firing a gun; and when the creek fell the negroes continued on unmolested toward the North Star. All which our host related by his evening fireside. At breakfast he devoutly asked a blessing upon the meal, and a few minutes later coolly remarked:

'I should not be sorry to see the troubles break out again. I know of a few scoundrels who have harrassed Free State men beyond all endurance, and who ought to be killed. But of course we don't want to shoot them unless they give us due provocation.'

When we parted he said:

'Keep this road north for two miles, and then take the one leading eastward.'

This alone would have revealed the Yankee. Missourians never gave the point of compass but only directed the traveler to 'Follow up the crick for two miles and then cross over to the next crick.' In the belts of timber along streams they invariably settled, while northerners made their homes upon high open prairie. The 'crick' lands were prolific of fever-and-ague and democratic voters.

The Missourians were accustomed to letting their swine run at

Albany N Y, 28th April, 1857.

My Dear Sir

The Worcester Gun Factory cannot supply me with Revolvers in *time*; but the Mass, Arms, Co; (whose Revolvers I have used; & which are much the same as Colts) offer to let me have what I need being 200 for $1300, Thirteen Hundred Dollars.

*   *   *   *   *   *

He did *not want* the thing to be made public. Now if Rev T Parker, & other good people at Boston, would make up that amount; I might *at least* be *well armed*. Please write Watson My best wishes to yourself and Family. Very Respectfully Your Friend

John Brown

large. In Brown county we found one intensely disgusted, because the voters of his township had decided that the animals must be shut up to save fencing-in the grain and potatoes. He complained:

'I don't mind so much getting along without negroes; but next year I will move out of this d—d Yankee neighborhood where a man is compelled to shut up his hogs.'

The death of John Brown on a Virginia gibbet had already canonized him. Almost every Free State settler gave some reminiscences of the stanch old martyr. Among his enthusiastic followers was young Kagi, very modest and quiet, a correspondent of the New York *Evening Post.* He had criticised a United States district judge of Buchanan's appointment. Soon after, when he chanced to enter the temple of justice, the court adjourned, and several official desperadoes attacked him with revolvers. Like most quiet men, when excited he proved an ugly customer. He answered their shots with great promptness, giving the judge a wound so serious that it made him helpless for months. When his revolver barrels were emptied, Kagi jumped out of a window and escaped unharmed. He finally fell pierced by scores of bullets, on the bridge at Harper's Ferry.

Nominally, slavery still existed. In Atchison county I found some old southern neighbors greatly exercised over the loss of their chattels. One African, up to the night of his flight, expressed many fears that the Abolitionists might catch and kill him! The incredible depravity of another, a favorite house-maid was thus set forth by her owner:

'Why the ungrateful hussy! Only the week before she ran away I offered her herself for twelve hundred dollars, with the privilege of paying by installments too!'

'Mary Ann,' added the really kind-hearted mistress, 'was raised like one of the family. I took care of her when she was a baby, and always dressed and treated her well. Many and many a time she attended me when I was sick, lifting and moving me as though I was a child. She was a good girl, and I never counted the money before giving her my purse to buy any thing. Poor thing! I reckon she has hard masters now. Perhaps they have dashed her brains out already. I know she would not have left me of her own accord; the Abolitionists must have stolen her.'

In Atchison county, the republican party had nominated John J. Ingalls, a young gentleman from Massachusetts, for the Wyandotte constitutional convention. At a democratic meeting John W. Stringfellow, forgetful that Border Ruffian days were over, spoke of the Yankee with traditional contempt:

Who knew any thing about this young man? How old was he? How long had he lived in the Territory?

The next evening, with Stringfellow sitting prominently beside him, Ingalls repaid the debt with usurious interest. He had been charged with two heinous crimes: short residence in Kansas, and personal obscurity. He could not deny the first, but only urged that it was an offense of which most citizens had once been guilty, and one which time usually cured. He added:

'The allegation of obscurity is yet more aggravated and fearful. Mr. President, most men are obscure once in a lifetime. Some always remain in that obscurity. Others emerge from it to *an infamous notoriety* compared with which obscurity were the kindest gift that charity could bestow!'

This extinguishing retort elicited roars of applause, and shouts of 'Stringfellow,' 'Stringfellow,' which finally drove him discomfited from the stage. Ingalls was triumphantly elected.

On the nineteenth of May, Knox and myself left Atchison in the two-horse wagon of a pioneer, who had contracted to board us on the way and deliver us in Denver for forty dollars each. The swift mail coach was the aristocratic mode; the horse wagon the respectable; and the ox-wagon, known as the 'ox telegraph' or 'prairie-schooner,' the plebian. Oxen traveled about fifteen miles per day; horses twenty to thirty; footmen twenty-five.

As we passed through Kennekuck an emigrant, who had left Atchison without satisfying his creditors, suddenly discovered the sheriff at his heels. Putting spurs to his horse he dashed off at a swift run while the officer pursued. The fugitive dropped overcoat and blanket, but Gilpin-like did not stop for trifles. At last, barely one length ahead, his panting horse crossed the line into the next county. Here, fearless of the sheriff, he turned around, begged that officer to accept his lost blanket as a faint token of regard, and present his love to inquiring friends at home! Scattered among the honest folk migrating to the mountains were adventurers like those facetious scoundrels in the convict colony at New South Wales, who proclaimed themselves:

> 'True patriots all; for be it understood,
> We left our country for our country's good!'

At Ash Point one of the little groceries springing up like mushrooms bore the sign: 'BUTTE, REGGS, FLOWER AND MELE.' There were long droves of cattle for California whose drivers expected to be six months on the way, and thousands of weary oxen coming in from Salt Lake whose thinly clad bones made the buzzards look wistfully. In Marshall county at the crossing of the Big Blue, the clearest stream in Kansas, we passed Marysville founded by Colonel Frank Marshall, a Border Ruffian, of some notoriety. He had a passion for the name of Mary, and called the embryo city in honor of his wife. It had fifty houses and was famed for whisky and shooting affrays. The grand jury had indicted a dozen inhabitants for horse racing, and the criminals were in great glee because the district judge by whom they must be tried had also been a judge at the race in question!

'DO THEY MISS ME AT HOME?'

Beyond Fort Kearney a sudden night-storm blew down our Sibley tent. To replace it was impossible; no man could stand against the bleak desert wind. So we shivered through the long hours till daylight found us half covered with sand, which had permeated all our clothing. At midnight a drove of stampeding cattle came rushing toward us. Frightened by the heap of canvas they divided and ran by without trampling upon us.

We often encamped with old friends, and beguiled the evening hours with reading or whist or the music of violin and flute. By day the road was lively. Many emigrant women rode saddle horses, though most were in ox-wagons. All seemed to enjoy the trip, though each invariably apologized for her untidy looks. We saw one bloomer who weighed two hundred and fifty pounds driving oxen while her husband slept soundly in their wagon. Another leviathan from New Hampshire would have satisfied the great Julius; for he weighed three hundred and fifty, he was fat, he was sleek-headed and he slept o' nights.

There were many fresh graves, and upon one secluded island of the Platte were found the bloody remains of a little girl with broken skull. It was difficult to surmise the motive for the murder of the poor child.

One wagon drawn by six cows bore the charcoal label: 'FAMILY EXPRESS; MILK FOR SALE.' Many displayed the sign: 'OLD BOURBON WHISKY SOLD HERE!' Among other quaint inscription were:—

'I am off for the Peak; are you?'
'Good bye friends; I am bound to try the Peak.'
'The eleventh commandment: Mind your own business.'
'Ho for California.'
'Oregon or death!'

We cooked our own meals of coffee, biscuit and pork, upon the open prairie with buffalo chips for fuel. In our evening camp an ex-clergyman might be seen devoting himself to the supper, a Boston steel engraver and an old California miner greasing the wagon, while a Missouri railway contractor and an Ohio lawyer watched the grazing mules.

At last we felt the invigorating breath of the pines, and saw the shining crests of the Mother Mountains. On the tenth of June, twenty-three days out, we reached Denver. Here Knox and myself spent the summer as correspondents, also editing the Golden City Weekly *Mountaineer*, by way of recreation.

Denver was uncomfortably crowded; so we built a little frame house in the midst of a prairie-dog-town, commanding a superb view of the mountain scenery, probably more grand than that looked upon from any other town in the world.

Colorado Territory was not yet organized. The whole gold

region, nominally within the limits of Kansas, but separated from all her farming population by the vast desert, contained no law, no courts, no authorities. There had been two or three abortive constitutional conventions, and delegates sent to Washington in the vain attempt to secure a Territorial organization. One of these would-be Congressmen was a brilliant example of the vernacular of his native Kentucky. In an earnest public discussion he thus appealed to his auditors:

'Why gentlemen, are you awar whar you are?'

Many wished the nascent State named Pike's Peak—quite as convenient an appellation as Rhode Island. But in due time it was called Colorado, after the great river thus named by Spanish explorers from the red earth along its banks.

Our pioneers enforce order and the right of the majority to rule, instinctively—as water runs down hill. Lord Brougham said that all the bloodshed and rebellions of Great Britain, had been simply to establish the principle that every question of life, liberty or property must be submitted to twelve unbiased men. Our own frontiers recognize this right. Establish a thousand American settlers in the Himalayas, and in one month they would have all needful laws in operation, with life and property quite as well protected as in the city of New York.

The Denver people were a law unto themselves. Whenever a grave crime had been committed, an informal court was organized, some leading citizen placed upon the bench, and a jury made up of substantial merchants and mechanics. The prisoner was tried, allowed counsel, and if guilty sentenced to be hanged within one or two days.

These courts were as alert as the pioneer circuit judge in the early days of Iowa. His honor, accompanied by sheriff and clerk, meeting a horse-thief on a public road, held his court upon the spot, tried and convicted the criminal, and sent him to the penitentiary for five years.

The week after our arrival, a murderer was thus condemed and executed. A few days later, another was tried. The jury found him guilty. The judge asked the prisoner if he had any reason to offer why sentence of death should not be passed upon him. He replied:

'I have nothing to say.'

Then the judge submitted the question to the four or five hundred spectators:

'Gentlemen, you who believe this verdict is just will say Aye.'

The answer was an overwhelming roar of affirmatives.

'Contrary-minded will say No.'

One solitary negative came up from the crowd. With immovable serenity, the prisoner heard the question of his life or death submitted to the assembly, like a resolution or a point of order. He was sentenced to die on the following morning; and remanded to the custody of the volunteer officers. But that night he eluded the guards and decamped, stealing a wagon and a pair of mules to facilitate his traveling. He was never caught; but the indignant people came very near hanging the officers on bare suspicion that they connived at his escape.

AN ARMED NEUTRALITY.

In June an Arapahoe war party went out for wool and came back shorn. After destroying a defenseless village of Ute women and children, they were quietly smoking their pipes in camp, when

Ute warriors swooped down upon them, killed six and wounded thirty more. In New Mexico, twenty-one Arapahoes started in pursuit of the same ugly enemies. While they were supping in camp the Utes suddenly closed in upon them, killing and scalping every one. Two weeks later a party of whites discovered the ghastly corpses with morsels of meat still between their lips.

A desperado named James Gordon, killed a harmless German and then fled eastward. He took refuge in Fort Lupton, a ranch a few miles north of Denver. A party of pursuers had surrounded the fort, when Gordon rode out upon a fleet horse and dashed away. A shower of bullets whizzed about him, but he made good his escape. Officers appointed by a meeting of citizens, tracked the murderer seventeen hundred miles, and captured him in southern Kansas near the Indian Territory. They took him to Leavenworth where the United States district court at once set him at liberty, on a writ of habeas corpus. The large German population of Leavenworth gathered in a determined mob, and three times had a rope around Gordon's neck. But his pursuers and the Leavenworth officers resisted the bloodthirsty assailants. Every shred of clothing was torn from the poor wretch, and he begged the guards to give him up or kill him at once. At last, after an express agreement that he should be returned to the mountains for trial, the mob dispersed. Middaugh, the leading officer from Denver took him back to that city in irons.

Gordon was only twenty-three, and when sober, intelligent and well-behaved. But while intoxicated he had already killed three or four men. He had been specially kind to his aged father and mother. He was tried and convicted in a citizens' court; guarded for a week by armed sentinels against rescue from his friends, and finally executed. No court in the world could have acted with more fairness and firmness. All the expenses of the three-thousand-mile pursuit were defrayed by voluntary contributions.

As in all new mining regions there was an irrepressible conflict between the industrious sterling citizens, and the desperadoes, strengthened by their sympathizers of wealth and position, who formed the connecting link between villainy and respectability. The *Rocky Mountain News* offended the scoundrels by some comments upon a wanton murder. While the editor, William M.

Byers, sat in his office conversing with three pacific strangers from the East, four gamblers rushed in with cocked revolvers and abusive epithets, dragged Byers to a drinking saloon where, only through the strategy of a friend, was he saved from death. After his escape, the enraged gamblers rode back to the *News* office and fired several bullets into it.

The establishment was always in a state of armed neutrality. Printers and editors were moving arsenals, with revolvers at their belts and shot-guns standing beside their cases and desks. The typos returned the fire, killing one of the assailants. By this time half a dozen armed citizens reached the scene and chased the flying gamblers through the streets. One of the latter named Steele, galloping along Blake street, met Thomas W. Pollock whose horse was also upon a full run. Neither checked his speed. Both fired at the same instant. Pollock was unhurt; Steele fell dead with a charge of buckshot in his brain. Another of the gamblers was captured and barely escaped hanging. By a close vote in a popular assembly, he was permitted to leave the country.

The pure air of plains and mountains gives the system unexampled power of resistance to disease and wounds. In July, United States troops at Bent's trading-post, two hundred miles southeast of Denver, captured a number of Kiowa Indians. Afterward ordered eastward, they left the prisoners in Bent's charge, but the wily savages soon escaped. Then Bent dispatched Mark Ralfe, a young Frenchman, down the Arkansas to inform the commanding officer. After Ralfe had ridden forty miles, the Kiowas fell upon him, shooting him in three places, and stabbing him in four. Believing him dead, they took his scalp with a dull knife, leaving no hair whatever except a little lock above each ear. After they had gone he recovered consciousness, and with no nourishment except water, walked back to the fort. In a few months he was well again.

In Colorado City, Pat Devlin crowned his career (see page 126,) by an affray in which he received six heavy slugs in vital organs, yet survived almost three weeks.

How delicate yet marvelous the human organism, which a rap upon the temple or a prick from a needle may destroy, and which yet survives wounds that would kill a buffalo or a grizzly bear!

CHAPTER XXV.

Novel phases of life were exhibited in Denver during this second summer of its settlement. Let reader play the visitor and author the cicerone.

Weeks ago you left the locomotive on the Missouri. The weary journey since has taught you how the railway condenses life. After starting by horse-power, two hundred miles out you left the last farming settlement. Another hundred miles, and you struck the Platte, following it to a point eighty miles from Denver, where you took the great 'cut-off' across the barren, alkaline desert—the unkindest cut-off of all. You have felt the wild pleasure of buffalo hunting, shaken a rattlesnake from your blanket at night, dived into the occult mysteries of cooking, to bring forth biscuits and flapjacks, frolicked among prairie dogs, hob-nobbed with Indians, been drenched by rain-storms, and hungered and thirsted after the newspapers of civilization.

After six hundred miles of naked prairie and monotonous desert, the resinous odor of the pine greeted your nostrils and the distant mountains towered grandly before your charmed and astonished eyes. Last night you again saw the shining Platte, and this morning you rose upon the outskirts of Denver before the sun. But your journey was not yet ended; for this city with its additions embraces five thousand acres of building lots. Blake street is as lively as Broadway. But Saint Charles street, with no devices except the surveyors' stakes and no inhabitants save prairie dogs, is as desolate and uninviting as the Sahara.

The first city you struck was a city of the dead. Denver is but two years old, yet graves are thick in its new cemetery on the bare hill; and of their inmates a large majority met violent deaths. You descended a gentle slope among a few log-cabins and scattered board houses; and now you stand upon our threshold, looking as if you had not loved the world nor the world you—ragged but rejoicing, dilapidated but not downcast. Half an hour for ablutions and toilet.

In New York, our one-story house, fourteen feet by twenty with eight feet of shed for a kitchen, would be an indifferent stable; here it is a palace. Walls of rough upright boards, with cracks battened to keep out rain and dust; chief external features: a square, clapboarded front, three doors, three windows, and a stove-pipe protruding from the kitchen-roof. It cost three hundred dollars, and has 'all the modern improvements' of this longitude—kitchen and cellar. We occupy a better house than any of our neighbors, and what more could human nature ask? The interior boasts neither partition, ceiling nor plastering. Here is a decrepit desk which once did duty in a Cincinnati editorial room and afterward in a Kansas cottage. The one shelf contains the only two 'Unabridged' dic-

OUR HOUSE IN DENVER.

tionaries in the gold region, and a dozen works of travel. A bed on the floor with snowy sheets, two chairs, three stools, one bench, one table, two revolvers, one musket, one bowie-knife and three or four trunks and carpet sacks, make up the inventory of household goods.

During our chat the Ethiopian Sam, caterer, steward and factotum, announces breakfast. Two years ago Sam was a barber in Lecompton. When Samuel Medary, eighth Kansas governor within three years, had taken his initial shave, he proposed to pay by the month. Sam's witty answer went on a newspaper tour from Maine to Oregon:

'If you please, mass'r, I prefer to have you pay by de shave; dese new gub'ners goes away so mighty sudden!'

He is still the slave of Judge Elmore of Kansas. For the last three years he has hired his time at thirty dollars per month; and now the judge has permitted him to come to Pike's Peak, upon his agreement to pay twelve hundred dollars for himself as soon as he can accumulate the money. He reads fluently and writes a little; concocts miraculous sherry cobblers, and is a man of brains. In that cabin a hundred yards away are templed his household gods. His wife, now standing in the door, was formerly a slave of the Rev. 'Tom Johnson,' of the Kansas Shawnee Mission; but from her earnings as a laundress saved and paid six hundred dollars in hard cash for her freedom. In her arms you see a little image of God cut in ebony, with astonishing white eyes, which all the matrons hereabout declare the 'cunningest' of babies.

Our breakfast party is composed of half a dozen rovers who, kept at home, would have famished for travel and excitement—young men to whom 'magnificent distances appear beautiful and the possibilities of infinite far-off-ness delicious.' One used to keep a hotel in Sacramento; another, a smooth-faced boy, has made two voyages up the Mediterranean; the third has done business in Boston, New York, Australia, California, Missouri and Kansas; the fourth, typo and editor, has worked upon newspapers in Chicago, California, Australia, New Zealand, and Peru; the fifth was recently principal of a New Hampshire academy; and the sixth, for ten years a journalistic shuttlecock, has taken notes among eastern newspaper offices, Kansas wars, Nebraska buffaloes,

Missouri iron and lead mines, Arkansas fevers, Choctaw cotton plantations, Texas northers, Mexican fandangoes, and Rocky Mountain Indians.

Here is the morning newspaper, damp from the press, in season for our ultimate cups of coffee. It is about one-third as large as the *Tribune*, delivered by the carrier at fifty cents per week, and edited by an Englishman who cherishes deep-seated malignity against the letter 'h,' and fears neither God, man nor Lindley Murray. With only four thousand people, Denver has three daily newspapers.

Here comes the milk-man, in whose fluid the aqueous largely preponderates over the lacteal; and he is closely followed by the ice-man, and the vender of vegetables. After all we are not so far out of the world; it is only five hundred miles to the nearest telegraph station.

Now we will stroll down and see the lions. Buckling on our revolvers? Most certainly. It may shock you who have always lived in a state of utter civilization, but no journalist who means to tell the truth is wise to step into these streets without some display of fire-arms, unless partial to having his nose pulled or being made a target.

Here is rising a frame Catholic church. Who can travel beyond the far-reaching arms of the Roman power, even in the decadence? A walk of a third of a mile, past lumber yards and scattered nebulous frames daily developing into neat cottages, brings us to Larimer street. One square to the right is the Broadwell House, a large wooden structure, where you can obtain tolerable accommodations at Astor House prices. To the left a labyrinth of buildings including the new brick church, trading houses and dens of vice—temples to God, Mammon and Satan, side by side.

Here is the City Drug-store of brick, which would look well in St Louis or Chicago; within, you may buy the latest newspapers, ten days old, for twenty cents. Ten thousand eastern journals arrive in Denver weekly.

Looking down F street for five blocks we see the shining Platte, its green banks sprinkled with immigrant tents and Indian lodges. Beyond rise the abrupt many-colored mountains. Handsome blocks are everywhere springing up, interspersed with smaller wooden buildings and log-cabins, relics of the remote antiquity of a twelvemonth ago. Bricks are the cheapest material, costing only six dollars prr thousand, while lumber commands five dollars per hundred. A corner lot, twenty-five feet by one hundred, has just sold for twelve hundred dollars.

We stroll down G street past the banking-house , assay office and mint of Clark, Gruber and Company.* Within one sees pouches and bags of shining dust, and glittering nuggets. The firm issue their own gold coins of two and-a-half, five, ten and twenty dollars. They form the chief currency of the town, though much crude dust circulates in the mountains.

Below the corner of Blake street, is the huge frame two-story express office, with low, long, one-story wing, running up nearly one square upon G. In it are the two windows of the express postal department, and from them stretches a long file of anxious inquirers each patiently awaiting his turn to be served with letters. Near by is the office of Hinckley's express which forwards mail matter from Denver to twenty thousand miners in the mountains. On the corner, a hundred people are gazing at the Concord coach of the Central Overland and Pike's Peak Express Company, about

WAITING FOR LETTERS.

* Since converted into the United States Branch Mint.

to start for the Missiouri river. (Tri-weekly; six hundred and fifty-two miles; seventy-five dollars, exclusive of board; six days.) Every seat is filled, and every passenger known or vouched for, as this is the one day of the week upon which an express messenger is on board with forty or fifty thousand dollars in gold dust.

A motley crowd waits to witness the departure. Here is a well-formed elderly man, with a devil-may-care expression, but a face full of character and of wonderful perceptive faculties; long black hair, complexion like a Mexican, and eyes like an Indian. It is James P. Beckwourth the half-breed, so long a chief among the Crow tribe, and the most famous Indian fighter of this generation. His body is scarred from wounds received

> 'In worst extremes, and on the perilous edge
> Of battle, when it raged.'

But he is the very pink of courtesy, and specially devoted to a comely young wife whom he invariably dignifies with the title of 'Lady Beckwourth.'

That symmetrical dark man of thirty, a swarthy Adonis of the plains, has been a Kansas Border Ruffian, a Nicaraguan fillibuster, a prisoner among the Mexicans, wearing a chain and working upon roads for more than a year, a surveyor on the Panama railroad, and a wanderer through the world at large.

Here is the sanguine owner of a new quartz mill in the mountains, which he is persuaded will make him a millionaire. His interlocutor has just sold *his* quartz mill for half its cost, and is returning to the States declaring the gold region a humbug.

When I first met that elderly gentleman, he was a wealthy Pennsylvania banker, in broadcloth and fine linen, who had narrowly escaped being made governor of the Keystone State. When I next saw him he was arrayed in buckskin and corduroys, in a Pike's Peak cabin, cooking flapjacks for his own breakfast. He is now a candidate for Congress.

The tall thin-faced person with mutton-chop whiskers is the famous 'wheelbarrow man,' who trundled his entire outfit across the plains bringing just ten cents in his pocket. Now he also is an aspirant for Congressional honors.

Then there are broken down eastern merchants again facing life manfully, mechanics, speculators, loafers, blanketed Arapahoes and repulsive squaws each with a coal-eyed papoose peeping over her shoulder, and three or four naked young Red-skins at her heels.

The passengers receive the ultimate hand-shakings and final valedictions; the coach rolls away on its long journey.

Now we walk down Blake street. A busy scene, a mingled maze of various life. Liquor stores and saloons at almost every

INDIAN VILLAGE IN DENVER, IN 1860.

door. In the groceries, rich yellow pumpkins, potatoes, beets; turnips, cucumbers, and melons. Here you see a beet weighing thirteen pounds, a turnip weighing fourteen, and a cabbage twenty-three. Strangers offer you investments in mining-claims and building lots; there is speculation in those eyes which they do glare with.

A few yards from this busy street, you may visit the village of the Arapahoes, where barbarism thus far maintains its ground against the advance of (nominal) civilization. But ere long it must be crowded out. In general the Arapahoes are poorer, more filthy, more wretched than most other tribes of the plains; but when prepared for the war-path the braves are sometimes picturesque; and the squaws are at least rich in the number of their children playing about the lodges.

In Denver Hall, where the gamblers are busy, that tall Italian in solemn black, smoking a huge meerschaum, claims to be a count. He formerly resided on the upper Mississippi, which he left to the great bereavement of his creditors. He is now a speculator; last year he was a barber, and his wife a laundress. One morning he entered the room of the editor of the *Tribune*, in this very building, with a basket upon his arm.

COUNT.—I have brought your washing home, Mr. G—; ten pieces.

EDITOR (looking up abstractedly from a half-written letter.)—Yes. How much will it be?

COUNT.—Two dollars and a half sir.

EDITOR (with slightly-elevated eyebrows.)—And you shaved me yesterday beside. How much will that be?

COUNT.—One dollar sir.

EDITOR (with deliberation and solemnity.)—Is that *all* I owe you?

COUNT (cheerfully.)—Yes sir.

With an air of relief the bill was paid; and the count departed gaily, while the editor dryly observed that he would hardly be compelled to leave *this* country surreptitiously, from inability to pay his creditors.

Once more in the street, you notice that knot of idlers in front of the saloon, drawn thither by a drunken brawl. One belligerent produces a weapon. How suddenly half the lookers-on disappear around the corner, while the remaining half instantly draw their revolvers! The disturbance is quelled without bloodshed; but you feel like the epigrammatic sailor who had promised to describe manners and customs wherever he traveled. After being shipwrecked in Patagonia, he reported thus: 'The people here *have* no manners, and their customs are disgusting.'

Still there is a pure, pleasant, social life for those who know where to find it. On the street you observe many ladies dressed tastefully and even elegantly.

The stages have come in from the mountains, crowded with dusty passengers, and bringing the express messengers with their packages of letters and gold dust for the States. The shadows begin to lengthen, and we stroll homeward.

Tea over, we recline upon the greensward before our door. Prairie squirrels look up inquiringly, as they play at our very feet, and blackbirds walk about in confident security, with grateful memories of daily crumbs from our table.

But look up, beyond the city, the tufts of trees and the green prairie! Eighty miles to the south, Pike's Peak, like an old castle, 'majestic, though in ruin,' lies dim and dreamy against the sky. Seventy miles to the north stands Long's Peak, distinct, rugged and corrugated, its feet wreathed in pine, and its head crested with snow. A dark, irregular, variegated wall, at the verge of the sensible horizon, sweeps grandly between; and beyond, on either end, merges into the debatable ground between earth and sky.

It reveals every hue, from the dark, rich purple of the nearest hills, to the unsullied white of the Snowy Range; every form, from the long, flat summit of Table Mountain, to that perfect cone, waiting to impale the dying sun. Gaze on it daily for months and you shall never find the same picture, but always an endless variety, a perpetual delight.

Here, at the door of our rude cabin, Nature spreads before us such a panorama as never feasted the eye of monarch in his palace. Last night that furthest mountain was arrayed in a fiery glory too dazzling to look upon. Now it is robed in the pale, unearthly light of another world. Does it seem that you could ever reach it by mortal means, or clothed in mortal body? You can only think of the Celestial City, as it burst upon the vision of the pilgrim Christian; or those Sabbath evening pictures of heaven opening to earth, received in childhood at your mother's knee.

The sun goes down, but the cold air assails you in vain. Still you lie upon the sward in silence, that "perfectest herald of joy,' until the last fold of Night's curtain has fallen and shut out the miracle. How the glories of painter and poet, earthly ambitions, human life itself, dwarf before it! In wonder, humility and thankfulness you remember the work of the Great Artist.

A ROCKY MOUNTAIN SCENE. FROM A PAINTING BY ALBERT BIERSTADT. Page 302

CHAPTER XXVI.

In September the Government commissioner held a conference with the Arapahoes, Cheyennes, and Comanches at Bent's Fort. The leading chiefs were 'Little Raven,' 'Storm,' 'Big Mouth,' 'Left Hand,' 'White Antelope,' 'Black Kettle,' 'Old Woman,' 'Black Bird,' and 'Strong Arm.' In studying Indian names and customs one is constantly reminded of the striking resemblance between all savage nations, ancient and modern, in their nomenclature, mode of subsistence, and utensils of peace and war. The Phenicians who first visited Great Britain found the islanders staining their faces and bodies with colored earths and juices of plants, wearing no clothing but skins, living in huts of straw and mud, subsisting upon their cattle, planting no corn, doing no manual labor, and each tribe commanded by its own chief.

The commissioner distributed medal likenesses of Buchanan then occupying the presidential chair, and of Douglas and Lincoln rival candidates for it. The warriors received them with infinite pride. Little Raven having lost his Buchanan offered ten horses for the recovery of the priceless treasure!

The Arapahoes illustrated their civilization by bringing in a Pawnee scalp and holding a war dance over it through the whole night. The trophy was nearly destitute of hair, and therefore of comparatively little worth; all tribes holding it a mark of cowardice to shave the head, leaving no scalp-lock for an enemy.

After receiving blankets, shirts, trousers, knives, camp-kettles, tobacco and provisions, the Indians, grotesquely painted, and decked with quills, buffalo heads, bear claws, and elk teeth, gratified the whites with another war dance, accompanied by the usual demoniac yells, whoops and dervish-like contortions.

In September two miners who had entered the diggings in May without a penny, returned to Denver with twenty-seven thousand dollars in gulch gold. I met another, an old acquaintance, who had spent two seasons in hard work without paying his board, but still remained hopefully venturing in the great lottery. Frequently of two equally promising claims, side by side, one would yield thousands of dollars, while the other proved utterly worthless.

Transporting treasure to the Missouri involved the great risk of robbery; hence the express charges were very high. Often passengers eluded them by concealing gold bars to the value of thirty or forty thousand dollars upon their persons. When fairly on the plains they would transfer the heavy burden to their carpet sacks. The express company vainly endeavored to prevent this violation of their rules. During the rebellion they induced the Atchison military commandant to hold one passenger's baggage on his arrival, until he paid express charges upon his bullion. The logic of bayonets was so irresistible that he submitted to the gross outrage.

The absence of government inaugurated original modes of collecting debts. Possession being nine points of the law, it was only necessary for the revolver to establish the tenth. But a Denver dentist, wearied with vain attempts to obtain payment for a set of artificial teeth furnished to a feminine customer, fell back upon strategy. Calling upon the gentle debtor he suavely inquired how the plate was working, and asked permission to examine it. When it was handed to him he coolly pocketed it and walked away. This brought the money very promptly; for is not mastication as essential to dining as dining to existence?

'We may live without poetry, music, and art;
We may live without conscience, and live without heart;
We may live without friends, we may live without books;
But civilized man cannot live without cooks.
He may live without books—what is knowledge but grieving?
He may live without hope—what is hope but deceiving?
He may live without love—what is passion but pining?
But where is the man that can live without dining?'

One day an immigrant wagon on Blake street contained a young cinnamon bear with eyes like glowing coals and teeth like a razor. A loafer of inquiring mind asked carelessly:

'He won't bite will he?'

At the same moment he stroked caressingly the nose of the whelp. Young bruin responded by seizing the hand between his teeth. With air-piercing shrieks and oaths the victim snatched away the bleeding member, the flesh hanging in shreds from all the fingers. The bear, two months old, weighed three hundred pounds. His mother, just killed, weighed eleven hundred.

Almost every week witnessed gross outrages from desperadoes crazed by the poisonous whisky retailed at every bar. Frequently one drew his revolver upon some peaceful citizen, compelling him to fall upon his knees, submit to every vile epithet and beg piteously for his life. The ruffians who did this seemed for the time utterly insane. But fully half the citizens wore six-shooters, and however helpless for the moment would have resented the indignity afterward by killing its perpetrator at sight. And however crazed the desperado might be he never thus insulted a dangerous man! 'The ass knows in whose face he brays.'

It was a fascinating country for a journalist. Over his devoted head daily and nightly hung the sword of Damocles. An indignant aspirant for Congress meeting the editor of the Denver *Herald* in the street spat in his face. Mr. Byers of the *News*, whose establishment after the first murderous assault was a well stocked armory, had his office fired and his dwelling burned, but by taking a bold stand verified the proverb that threatened men live long.

The Denver people, tired of improvising a vigilance committee after every outrage, organized a city government and elected a full board of officers. The desperadoes—like most scoundrels, great sticklers for legality—refused to recognize its validity. The correspondent of the St. Louis *Democrat* excited the ire of one of Buchanan's shining appointees, the Denver postmaster, who was also chief justice of the embryo Commonwealth, under a movement for a State government. One evening this functionary lured the journalist into the post-office; then closing the doors, with a cocked revolver at the head of the luckless scribe, he compelled him to write and sign a statement that he knew his published allegations to be false and slanderous when he made them.

Under that influence which knows no law, the correspondent made this voluntary retraction. But the people took the matter in hand and after a fierce struggle, the postmaster, who was a man of wealth, and sustained by all the leading desperadoes, as his only mode of escape from the gibbet, succumbed to the city government, and gave bonds to keep the peace. In the great war he turned up a quartermaster in the rebel service.

A VOLUNTARY RETRACTION.

Denver already boasted the Apollo Theater, neither ceiled nor plastered, illuminated by twelve candles, and containing rough benches for three hundred and fifty people. As it was the upper-story of a popular drinking saloon, clinking glasses, rattling billiard balls, and uproarious songs interfered with the performances. The price of admission was one dollar; receipts about three hundred dollars per night.

One evening I saw the leading characters of La Tour de Nesle performed not much worse than at our ordinary metropolitan theaters. But the auditors were the real attraction. The entrance fee was a very moderate price for the amusement they afforded. Gaultier agonizingly asked concerning his murdered relative:

'Where, O where is my brother?'

A sepulchral voice from the midst of the house, answered:

'*I* am thy brother!'

The spectators supposed it a part of the play, but discovering that the response came from a favorite candidate for Congress greeted it with cheer after cheer.

Queen Marguerite with due horror gave the exclamation:

'Then I am lost indeed!'

A miner, directly in front of the stage, responded emphatically:

'You bet.'

The tragic death of Marigny, elicited from another spectator:

'Well old fellow, so *you* are gone up too.'

And at the tragic close Gaultier, Marguerite and Buridan were greeted with:

'Bound to have a big funeral, aren't you?'

Among the spectators were several ladies, and despite the boisterousness of the house there was no gross coarseness and no profanity.

I took several summer trips to view the mines and natural curiosities. Within ten miles of the original Gregory Diggings, were now twenty thousand settlers. Some gold seekers were realizing a hundred dollars per day; but not one-third were paying expenses. Two or three quartz mills were just going into operation. Forty or fifty Mexican arastras each with two men and one mule or horse, were turning out about twenty-five dollars a day. The arastra is the most primitive invention for crushing quartz. The fragments of rock are spread upon a circular inclosed stone bed, on which a mule walks led by one arm of an upright shaft, as in the old fashioned cider-mill, and dragging after him heavy rocks which grind out the quartz.

THE ARASTRA.

Mining nomenclature is always curious. The name of one gulch, 'Tarry-all,' explains itself. Two rich lodes were called 'Bob-tail' and 'Shirt-tail.'

Prospectors found three blackened corpses in a district of burnt pines, and named the spot 'Dead Man's Gulch.' 'Negro Gulch,' very rich, was discovered by two African citizens of American descent. Another ravine had been prospected by three parties who all denounced it as a humbug, when a fourth company found in it a rich lode; and it was known thereafter as 'Humbug Gulch.'

I met an old Boston merchant running a quartz mill successfully, and an ex-banker, a Presbyterian deacon from eastern Kansas, selling pies and retailing whisky on Sunday.

For stealing a pair of blankets, a lad was sentenced by the local vigilance committe to a hundred lashes. The sympathetic castigator laid them on very lightly, and at the close, the boy asked:

'Is that all? Why I have been whipped worse at school.'

An indignant bystander immediately proposed to give him twenty-five more. The precocious youth replied:

'No, gentlemen, you can't do *that*. It's against the law to punish a man twice for the same offense.

With the Hinckley express messenger crossing the Platte river at Denver, I turned to the southwest toward Tarryall and Breckinridge. In that clear atmosphere men upon the road five miles away could be seen with great distinctness. Before us were the eternal mountains, pearly, ashen, or snow-white; shrouded in dark masses of pine, brightened with yellowing cottonwoods.

At the foot of the range we passed Bradford, a city of one local habitation and a name. Near it, huge granite rocks resemble an enormous quadruped, and an immense human head.

Passing the unfailing toll-gate, we zigzagged for two miles up a sharp hill. Then we were in the heart of hills, rock-ribbed and ancient as the sun; among tumbling brooks, yellowing aspens and forests of somber pines and bluish green firs, straight as arrows, their tops smooth and symmetric as grain in a wheat field.

Passing saw-mills, shingle factories and log houses, we met hundreds of shaggy miners trudging down, to winter in the valley.

Spending the night at the ranch of a gigantic Kentuckian, early morning found us riding again in the crisp air among Titanic rocks, tall pines and white-stemmed aspens. Six times during the day we crossed the Platte, here less than twenty feet wide. Overworked oxen lay dying among road-side stumps. Toward evening among the tall peaks, we found pleasant grassy valleys where ice had formed nightly since the first of July.

We supped upon savory mountain sheep at a lonely ranch, where the host instructed my companion to bring from Denver a can of Goshen butter for his table, and a hoop-skirt for his young wife. We left him banking his log house up to the eaves to keep out the cold, already biting, although it was early in October.

From the summit of a hill we looked into the great South Park spreading out at our feet. The three parks, North, Middle and South, in the very heart of the Rocky Mountains are impressive natural features. This one is a smooth prairie of crescent shape, forty miles by fifteen, which has been dropped down among these mountain fastnesses to be imprisoned forever by their barriers of rock. Two little lakes gleamed in the green expanse of velvet, which alternated with pale ashen herbage, spotted with clusters of dead brown weeds. On every side the prairie sloped up gently toward the deepening pines of the foot-hills.

A faint line of road wound across the smooth floor. Scattered log ranches with hay-stacks, grazing cattle, snowy tents, and columns of smoke from the camp-fires of travelers, formed quiet pastoral scenes among long vistas of pine-fringed verdure. The waning sun flooded the delicious picture with yellow light.

Descending into the park we found white bleaching buffalo bones along the level road. The thick matted grass is nutritious during the entire winter, and the soil rich though whitened with alkali. One enterprising settler had planted a little tract; but as the park is almost eight thousand feet above the sea with frosts every month in the year, its chief value is for grazing. It abounds in delicate petrifactions of pine-splinters and branches.

Crossing several little affluents of the Platte through an icy atmosphere streaked with warm currents like the breath of a furnace, we reached Tarryall, eighty miles from Denver.

The next morning we breakfasted sumptuously upon mountain trout, larger, whiter and more bony than the trout of the East. Their color is dull brown with specks of red; but just over the dividing ridge in waters running westward, the spots become black. Old trappers when lost among the mountains drop a line in the first stream, and learn from the specks of these Alpine trout whether the waters run to the Atlantic or to the Pacific.

Tarryall contained two or three hundred log houses, now mainly deserted for the winter. The diggings revealed tunnels extending far into the hills and the surface everywhere gashed and trenched. They yielded gold of peculiarly fine quality.

To the east, immediately across the park, towered Pike's Peak. Though grand from every point, the view here is less impressive than that obtained from the opposite side, on the road from Denver to Colorado City. There, forty miles from the foot of the mountain, the best distant picture is gained.

PIKE'S PEAK, FROM FORTY MILES NORTHEAST.

Tarryall is upon the tributaries of the Platte. Breckinridge lies fifteen miles to the west over the water-shed. For half the distance I found the ascent steady and gentle. Beyond, galloping up a short hill I stood upon the ridge-pole of the American continent, then the dividing line between Kansas and Utah. Just before me gushed a spring whose waters feed the Colorado of the Pacific. Just behind, were ice-fringed rivulets flowing to the Atlantic.

My road crossed the summit through a gap between snow-topped mountains two thousand feet high. Below me both on the east and on the west were spread vast troughs and trenches of spruce-pine forest. Descending the westward slope I found the pines of deeper green, perhaps from their northern exposure.

Breckinridge, with sixty or seventy log houses, rested in the eternal shadow of tall peaks containing snow-drifts fifty feet deep, which the oldest trappers and Indians had never known to melt entirely away. Still, turnips, beets, and lettuce were produced in the little valley during the short summers. I found hay selling at from five to ten cents per pound. Breckinridge, French's, Georgia, and neighboring gulches had yielded gold abundantly.

My most memorable summer excursion was made with three friends, from Denver to the summit of Pike's Peak. Before starting we heard appalling reports about the difficulties of the ascent. Many attempting it had failed to reach the crest. One robust gentleman became delirious from the light atmosphere and fatigue. Another who had climbed Orizaba, when five hundred feet below the top of Pike's Peak was so utterly exhausted that he returned without going further. But these failures together with some ridicule and many gloomy prophecies only made the ladies of our party the more anxious to undertake the journey.

SCENE IN THE MONUMENT REGION.

As we rode out from Denver, eighty miles southward the Peak, dim and grand, lifted its wrinkled brow from the horizon. The first evening found us in the curious Monument Region. Here among pleasant groves of little pines are scattered upright shafts and masses of crumbling granite and limestone, curiously worn and sculptured by wind and water. They extend for thirty miles; some crowning hills like great temples built by human hands. One is called Table Rock, another Castle Rock, a third Signal Hill, from signal fires which Indians used to kindle upon it.

Capitol Rock, upon a little eminence, assumes the form of a strong fortress, with frowning walls and arched gateway. Further south, on Monument creek, the pillars and statues rise to the hight of fifteen or twenty feet, in differing colors and fantastic shapes. Pagan idols, cardinals and friars, picturesque little cottages, Siamese twins, and almost numberless images of the palpable and familiar may be detected among them. But most have the form of monumental stones. Standing thickly over hundreds of acres, in the midst of the pines, they make the spectator fancy himself in Greenwood, Mount Auburn, Spring Grove, or some other great American cemetery.

Two miles from Colorado City they culminate in huge walls known as the Gateway to the Garden of the Gods. Enormous portals of red rock rise almost perpendicularly for three hundred feet with tenacious cedars clinging to their sides. On the summit, where no human foot has trodden, eagles build their nests.

Through this natural gateway we passed into a large inclosure walled in by mountains on every side—indeed a garden for the gods. One vast rock has a cave eight feet by sixty and about seventy in hight. Its walls are smooth and seamless.

We entered by the only aperture, barely large enough for an adult to crawl through. Within we struck a light to view the weird picture. For an hour the singers of our party made the walls echo with the strains of sacred music, always most impressive in underground chambers.

After we emerged, Pike's Peak rose clear and distinct, with two little spots of snow near the summit, and a faint line like a trail or foot-path down the side from the crest to the base.

GATEWAY TO GARDEN OF THE GODS.

The picturesque hills around us abounded in game. A few days before an enthusiastic sportsman wounded a juvenile grizzly, when the mother bear appeared uninvited, compelling him to climb a tree so suddenly that he dropped his gun, and was imprisoned in the branches for several hours. At last friends came to his rescue and drove bruin away.

We spent the night at Colorado City then containing a hundred log houses.

CHAPTER XXVII.

The distance from Colorado to the summit of Pike's Peak, as the bird flies, is five miles; by the nearest practicable route about fifteen. A Colorado gentleman who had once made the trip became our guide, philosopher, and comrade.

Early in the morning escorted by a party of friends we rode to the Fontaine qui Bouille, stopping for copious draughts of that invigorating water. A mile further the canyonbecame impracticable for vehicles; so the carriage turned back and we began our pedestrian journey,

> On and up, where Nature's heart
> Beats strong amid the hills.'

Like Denver and Golden City our starting-point was higher above sea-level than the *summit* of Mount Washington.

Six athletic miners, ranch-men and carpenters who chanced to be going up that morning, led the caravan. Our own party of five, in single file, brought up the rear. We were each provided with a stout cane and a drinking cup. The ladies were in bloomer costume, with broad-rimmed hats, and light satchels suspended from their belts. The unhappy trio of men, in thick boots and heavy woolen shirts, without coats or waistcoats, carried revolvers, knives and hatchets, and bent under their heavy packs of provisions and blankets. My own weighed twenty-seven pounds; and I thought it fully twenty-seven hundred before the wearying journey was ended.

The steep narrow canyon, un-marked by any trail, abounded in smooth precipitous rocks, impassable for any quadruped less agile than a mountain goat. Along the bottom of the gorge, a brook leaped and plashed over the rocks in a stream of silver. The overlooking hills were thickly studded with shrubs of oak and

CLIMBING PIKE'S PEAK.

tall trees of pine, spruce and fir. Wild cherries, hops and clustering purple berries grew in profusion. The valley abounds in gems of beauty—'pocket editions of poetry in velvet and gold.' We made our noon camp at one of these which would cause the heart of an artist to sing for joy. The brook, first appearing in view under a natural stone bridge above us, comes tumbling down in a cascade of snow-white foam, torn into sparkling fringes by the jutting rocks, and is lost among the huge bowlders at our feet. An irregular mass of granite rises upon one side more than a hundred feet; and on either bank, the singing waters are shaded by tall pines and blue-tipped firs. Between and beyond their dark branches, a gray, cone-shaped hill, bare of tree or shrub, stands in the background against a wonderfully blue and pellucid sky. I never felt the utter poverty of descriptive language until I gazed upon that matchless picture.

A lively shower soon recalled us to the practical, when it was discovered that our whisky through defective corking had escaped from the bottles. It might prove a serious loss in case of great exhaustion; but after boiling our tin cups of tea by a fire of branches, we started on.

The afternoon climb was still along the canyon, sinking knee-deep into the gravelly hill, clutching desperately at friendly bushes to keep from falling backward, and toiling upon hands and knees over wet slippery rocks.

At four o'clock, cold, foot-sore and weary, we encamped where our advance party had already halted. Supper was prepared and eaten before a glorious fire of tree trunks. Then, for two hours, the deep woods resounded with laughter and song. But long before midnight we all slept, watched by the sentinel stars 'which haste not, nor rest not, but shine on forever.'

On the second morning we made hasty toilets with the brook for a mirror, and consumed our fried pork, biscuit and cups of tea while sitting upon logs. We continued through two rugged canyons, with a smooth, grassy valley between.

Many of the mountains are streaked with broad bare tracks, left by land-slides. Vast masses of disintegrating granite are piled upon each other in dreary wastes. One huge stone chair overlooks a little kingdom of mountain and valley; but the Titan who sat upon it was long ago dethroned in one of Nature's terrible convulsions, which uprooted hills and scattered gigantic bowlders like pebbles.

The burdens already hung like millstones about our necks. I began to comprehend the emotions of a pack mule; and to wonder whether a man who would carry twenty-seven pounds of blankets up Pike's Peak, did not belong to the long-eared species himself.

A cold rain set in; and at noon, drenched and shivering, we encamped under a shelving rock. We kindled a fire and dined upon a rabbit, which had surrendered unconditionally to a revolver.

The only true philosophy of getting wet is to get soaked. Moist clothing brings a hesitating discomfort; but in feeling that every thread is drenched, there is a desperate satisfaction. So we went into the driving rain and feasted for an hour upon ripe raspberries, which grew so abundantly that one could satisfy his appetite without moving. Then we returned to camp thoroughly saturated, and throughout the afternoon made sorry essays at reading and whist playing.

Early in the evening our robust Colorado friends, who had gone a mile beyond us, passed by on their return, having given up the trip as too severe.

We gathered an ample supply of wood. The dead pines, often six inches in diameter and thirty feet high, were easily overturned, their brittle roots snapping like pipe-stems. As the fire was our only solace, we piled on logs until the red flames leaped high and chased the thick darkness away.

Four of us huddled under the rock, while the fifth, as the least of two evils, sat grimly in the open air, wrapped in his blanket and brooding upon destiny. The rain became very violent, and the natural roof, sloping unfortunately in the wrong direction, showered the water upon us in melancholy profusion.

After many dismal jests about our dreary situation, one by one my co-tenants dropped asleep. My own latest recollection of that Procrustean bed was at eleven o'clock, when I was wooing the drowsy god, with my legs in a mud puddle, a sharp rock piercing my ribs, and a stream of water pouring down my back.

At midnight my friends arose—for the air had grown very chill—and sought our great log fire. After enjoying for a few minutes the comfort of its red flames—a comfort mitigated by the pelting rain—wrapping myself again in a wet blanket, and creeping as far as possible under the rock, I soon slept soundly. At daylight, when I awoke, they were still out in the driving rain, sitting before the flames in gloomy contemplation, like Marius amid the ruins.

On the third morning we breakfasted morosely, sore and stiff in every joint. Less than half the journey was accomplished, and

UNDER THE SHELVING ROCK.

we had but one day's provisions remaining. One of the ladies had worn through the soles of her shoes in several places, and both were wet, chilled and exhausted; but they would not for a moment entertain the idea of turning back.

By seven o'clock we are again climbing the slippery rocks.

21

The rain ceases; the breaking clouds once more turn forth their silver linings,

> 'And genial Morn appears,
> Like pensive Beauty, smiling through her tears.'

Behind, at our feet, stretches an ocean of pure white cloud with mountain summits dotting its vast surface in islands of purple and emerald. Before, towers the stupendous peak.

In the genial sunlight we begin to feel the comfort of dry clothing, for the first time in twenty-four hours, and press cheerily on. The hills, swept for miles and miles by vast conflagrations, are black, and bristling with tall dead trunks of pine and fir, like the multitude of masts in a great harbor. The valleys are shaded by graceful aspens, whose leaves quiver in the still air; and carpeted by luxuriant grass, rising to our chins and variegated with flowers of pink and white, blue and purple. Fallen tree-trunks abound, held by their broken limbs three or four feet above the ground. Climbing over them is very laborious, and tears to shreds the meager skirts of the ladies. The bloomer costume is better than full drapery; but for this trip women should don trousers.

After five hours of climbing slippery rocks, we dine luxuriously in a raspberry patch, drinking tea from our cups and water from a spring.

Thus far our journey has been only among foot-hills. Now we reach the base of the Peak itself, and climb wearily up the rocky canyon which extends from base to summit. The thin air makes breathing very difficult.

At five o'clock we encamped, utterly exhausted. With wild eyes and flushed faces, which excited fears of fever and delirium, the ladies fell asleep the instant we stopped; and one of the masculines also sank upon the ground. Two of us started for water down to the stream-bed ten yards distant, but found it dry as Sahara. So we limped down the gorge for half a mile, and in more than an hour reached camp again, each bearing two cups. My companion had barely strength to articulate that he would only repeat the walk to save his dearest friend from dying; I succeeded in gasping out an injunction to take precious care of the costly fluid, and we lay down utterly exhausted.

But the strong tea, as usual, revived us all; and we started on just as the clouds broke, revealing the mountains and vast green prairies far behind us—a dream of beauty.

Two of the party suddenly yielded to illness, accompanied by vomiting fits; and reaching the verge of vegetation we camped for the night. As we rolled ourselves in blankets upon the ground beside our roaring fire, another shower drenched us, and then turned to hail. At nine o'clock our guide reaped the harvest of his exposure and fatigue in a distressing rheumatism, which drove him from his earth-bed and held him writhing in pain during the night, but disappeared with daylight's return.

On the fourth morning ice was lying thick about our camp. All the party wore a lean and hungry look; but our scanty larder allowed to each only a little biscuit, a bit of meat as large as a silver dollar, and ample draughts of tea. At five o'clock we left our packs behind and resumed the march.

In climbing Mount Washington, the vegetation grades down regularly from tall pines to stunted cedar shrubs with trunks five or six inches thick, and branches not more than three feet high, running along the ground like grape-vines. Pike's Peak affords a sharp contrast. We started in a dense forest of pines and firs; but vegetation ceases so abruptly that in ten minutes we stood upon the open, barren mountain side, with no green thing about us except a few flowers, and beds of velvety grass among the rocks.

The remainder of the ascent is very abrupt. We followed the line which in the distance had appeared like a path, but now proved a gaping gorge a mile in width.

The summit seemed very near; but we toiled on and on for hours, up the sharp hight. The thin air made it impossible to go more than a hundred feet without pausing for breath; but amid the grand scenery we forgot our fatigue and remembered our weariness no more. The ladies, imbued with new life, could only find expression in singing the old hymn:

'This is the way I long have sought,
And mourned because I found it not.'

Tufts of wool indicated the haunts of the mountain sheep—

an animal of unequaled agility. He leaps incredible distances down the rocks, and is even reputed to strike upon his broad horns which receive the most violent concussion without injury.

The sky assumed a deeper and richer blue; and the fields of snow and ice began to enlarge. Even here, hundreds of tulip-shaped blossoms of faint yellow mingled with purple, opened their meek eyes beside the freshly-fallen snow! It was worth all our toil to see the cheek of June, with its purple flush, nestle among the silver locks of December.

Finally the last flower and blade of grass were left behind, and only rocks and snow ahead. It became difficult to avoid falling asleep during our brief pauses.

Just below the top we turned southward to look down a tremendous chasm known as the 'Crater.' It is half a mile wide, nearly circular, inclosed by abrupt walls of rock, and fully twelve hundred feet deep. Creeping to the verge of the dizzy hight, while our comrades clung to us with desperate clasp to save us from tumbling over, we dislodged huge rocks into the abyss. Down they leaped, bounding from ledge to ledge, striking sparks and scattering showers of fire, with great crash and roar that came rolling up to us like peals of thunder, long after they were out of sight.

One overhanging rock affords to the spectator, lying flat upon his face, an excellent view of the yawning gulf, though its uncomfortable trembling disquiets his nerves. At last, just before noon, passing two banks of snow which have lain un-melted for years, perhaps for centuries, we stood on the highest point of Pike's Peak, thirteen thousand four hundred feet above sea-level. The ladies of our party—one a native of Boston, the other of Derry, N. H.—were the first of their sex who ever set foot upon the summit.

Pike's Peak was named in honor of General Zebulon M. Pike, a gallant young officer, who discovered and ascended it in 1806 while at the head of an exploring expedition sent by Jefferson's administration. A few years later, before he had reached the prime of life, he fell in defense of his country's flag, at the battle of Toronto.

The summit embraces about fifty acres. It is oblong, and nearly level, composed wholly of angular slabs and blocks of coarse disintegrating granite. We found fresh snow several inches deep in the interstices, but the August sun had melted it all from the surface.

We were fortunate in having a clear day which gave us the view in its full sublimity. Eastward for a hundred miles, our eyes

ON THE SUMMIT.

wandered over dim, dreamy prairies, spotted by dark shadows of the clouds, and the deeper green of the pineries; intersected by faint, gray lines of road, and emerald threads of timber along the streams; and banded on the far horizon with a girdle of gold.

At our feet, below the now insignificant mountains up which we had toiled, stood Colorádo, a confused city of Liliputs; but with the aid of glasses we could distinctly see its buildings and our own carriage, with a man standing near it.

Further south swept the green timbers of the Fontaine qui Bouille, the Arkansas and the Huerfano; and then rose the blue Spanish Peaks of New Mexico a hundred miles distant. Eight or ten miles away, two little gems of lakes were set among the rugged mountains, holding shadows of the rocks and pines in their transparent waters. Far beyond, a group of tiny lakelets, 'eyes of the landscape,' glittered and sparkled in their dark surroundings like a cluster of stars.

Toward the north we could trace the timbers of the Platte for seventy miles, almost to Denver.

To the west, the South Park, and other amphitheaters of rich floral beauty—gardens amid the utter desolation of the mountains—were spread thousands of feet below us; and beyond, peak upon peak, until the pure white wall of the Snowy Range rose to the infinite blue of the sky.

North, south and west swept one vast wilderness of mountains, of diverse forms and mingling colors, with clouds of fleecy white sailing airily among their scarred and wrinkled summits.

We looked upon four Territories of the Union—Kansas, Nebraska, Utah and New Mexico; and viewed regions watered by four great rivers of the continent—the Platte, Arkansas, Rio Grande and Colorado, tributaries respectively of the Missouri, the Mississippi, the Gulf of Mexico and the Gulf of California.

Upon the north side of the Peak, a colossal plowshare seems to have been driven fiercely down from the summit to the base, its gaping furrow visible seventy miles away, and deep enough in itself to bury a mountain of considerable pretension. Such enormous chasms must the armies of the Almighty have left in heaven when, to overwhelm Lucifer and his companions,

> 'From their foundations loosening to and fro,
> They plucked the seated hills with all their load,
> Rocks, waters, woods, and by the shaggy tops
> Uplifting, bore them in their hands.'

At the gorge's head, some enterprising fellow had posted a railway handbill, which with finger pointing directly down the gulf, asserted in glaring capitals: 'Shortest and best Route to the East.'

It seemed impossible to grow weary of the wonderful picture; but my companions, though wrapped in heavy blankets, were shivering with the cold. So we iced and drank a bottle of champagne which a Colorado friend had thrust into one of the packs; and then like more ambitious tourists, placed a record in the empty bottle, which was carefully re-corked and buried under a pile of stones.

We spent a few minutes in the school-boy pastime of snow-balling. Then, after two hours upon the summit, we reluctantly commenced the descent; for living without eating was becoming a critical experiment.

Our guide, weakened by the hard journey, missed his foothold, falling upon a jagged rock. Fortunately the metallic case of his spy-glass saved him from a fractured rib; and after lying upon the rocks for a few minutes, he came limping down with the rest.

In descending, the rarity of the atmosphere did not retard us, but we found climbing down quite as exhausting as climbing up; and a raspberry diet is not invigorating. At five o'clock we reached the last night's camp, glad to break our twelve hours' fast with ample cups of tea and homeopathic fragments of bread and meat.

After a brief halt we hastened on down the ledges and over the tree-trunks. When we sat upon a log for a little rest, one of the ladies appeared utterly exhausted. We asked if we should not camp until morning that she might recruit? She could not articulate a single word; but shook her head with indignant vigor. Again pressing on, an hour later we kindled a fire, went to bed or rather to blanket, and were instantly asleep.

On the fifth morning when we awoke, only that expressive colloqualism which the fire companies have added to the vernacular could describe our condition. We were 'played out.' We swallowed our last provisions—a morsel of meat and a table-spoonful of crumbs each. The unfailing tea measureably restored us; but in our exigency we would gladly have exchanged it for the cup which cheers and does inebriate.

We descended by a new route over hill-sides crossed and re-crossed by tracks of the grizzly bear, and through canyons surprising us constantly with a new wealth of beauty which we were hardly in condition to appreciate.

After journeying five or six hours, we experienced, not the gnawings of hunger, but that irresistible faintness which the Irishman so exactly described as 'a sense of goneness.' Endeavors to talk and think of other matters were fruitless; the 'odorous ghosts of well remembered dinners' *would* stalk unbidden through the halls of memory; and in vain we sought to

> 'Cloy the hungry edge of appetite
> By bare imagination of a feast.'

At noon we halted by the cascade which had so enchanted us on our first day's march, and slept for an hour under the shading pines. Then we shouldered our packs for the last time, and hobbled on down the canyon.

At four o'clock our guide, who was a few yards in advance, suddenly came upon our waiting carriage. Now that the strain was over the nerves of the ladies instantly relaxed. One received the intelligence with a shower of tears, the other with hysteric laughter. In a moment we were surrounded by Colorado City friends who, alarmed at our protracted absence, were out in several parties armed with stimulants and provisions, searching for us among the foot-hills.

Two hours later we reached the town. My companions with haggard cheeks and blood-shot eyes seemed but shadowy suggestions of their former selves. Each of the ladies had lost just eight pounds of flesh in less than five days. One, whose shoes were cut through by sharp rocks early on the journey, had been walking for three days with portions of her bare foot striking upon the stones, gravel and snow.

We were soon clothed and in our right minds, and eating heartily. No lasting inconvenience was experienced from the trip, except the most ravenous and uncompromising hunger, which continued at intervals for the next two weeks. If 'he is well paid who is well satisfied' the journey was far the most remunerative any of us had ever taken.

On the sixth of November I left Denver for 'the States.' Our two coaches each contained six passengers, including successful explorers and miners, a prospector from Georgia, a banker from Atchison, a French-and-Indian trader from Leavenworth, and a lady whose husband had recently died in Denver, and who with two fatherless children was returning to her New York home. Ten days before, she was lying dangerously ill with typhoid fever, her face deathly pale and a flush, purple as ripe grapes, on each cheek. At starting she was still an invalid, and the ride of the first day and night left her hardly able to sit up. But in the inspiring, pure air of the plains she rallied, gained an enormous appetite; and before the end of the trying six days and nights her cheeks again wore the bloom of health. Another passenger seventy years old was also an invalid. For the first two days extreme weakness compelled him to have meals brought to the coach. But he too gained wonderful strength before reaching the river.

During the previous summer a pony express had been established from the Missouri to the Pacific. It was splendidly run, sometimes carrying letters from Atchison to Sacramento (about two thousand miles) in eight days. Once these modern Centaurs conveyed dispatches from St. Joseph to Denver (six hundred and twenty-five miles) in two days and twenty-one hours. The last ten miles was accomplished in thirty-one minutes.

'LINCOLN IS ELECTED.'

The posts were twenty-five miles apart, and the steeds small, fleet, hardy Indian horses. The rider kept his pony on the full run, and when he reached a new station—whatever the hour of day or night—another messenger, ready mounted and waiting, took the little mail-sack, struck spurs into his steed, and was off like the wind.

Is there any thing new under the sun? Marco Polo relates that in the thirteenth century the great Khan of Tartary and China had post-stations '*twenty-five miles apart*,' and stations for foot carriers three miles apart, on the chief routes through his dominions. Says that fascinating writer:

'His messengers sometimes ride three hundred miles in one day and night. They gallop at full speed from one station to the next, where they find two other horses fresh and ready harnessed; and continue on with the same rapidity. They stop not an instant day nor night and are thus enabled to bring news in so short a period.'

But the pony express was new on our continent; and was such a forerunner of the great railway that it excited quite an enthusiasm. The St. Joseph *Democrat* thus discoursed of it:

'Take down your map and trace his foot-prints from St. Joseph on the Missouri to San Francisco on the Golden Horn—from the last locomotive to the first steamship—two thousand miles—more than half across our boundless continent. Through Kansas, through Nebraska, by Fort Kearney, along the Platte, by Fort Laramie, past the Buttes, over the Rocky Mountains, through canyons, along the steep defiles—Utah, Fort Bridger, Salt Lake City—he witches Brigham with his swift ponyship. Through valleys, along grassy slopes, into the snow, into the sand, faster than Thor's Thialfi: away they go! rider and horse, did you see them? They are in California, leaping over its golden hills, treading its busy streets. The courser has unrolled the great American panorama, and allowed us to glance at the future home of a hundred millions of people. He has put a girdle round the earth in forty minutes. Verily his riding is like the riding of the son of Nimshi, for he rideth furiously. Take out your watch. We are eight days from New York, eighteen days from London. The race *is* to the swift.'

One November midnight, upon the plains, the little pony dashed by us on a full run.

'What's the news?' shouted our driver.

'Lincoln elected! New York gives him fifty thousand majority!' came back the cry through the darkness.

It woke up all our republicans who sent forth cheer upon cheer, while the democrats were sure that it must be a hoax.

When we reached St. Joseph there was some excitement; and Jeff Thompson, ex-mayor of the city, had issued a flaming proclamation urging the people to resist the 'northern minions.' Afterward as a guerrilla captain in southern Missouri and Arkansas he found ample opportunity for all the fighting he wanted.

St. Joseph, already containing ten thousand people, though in a slave State had given twice as many votes for Lincoln as for Breckinridge; and more than forty thousand copies of 'Helper's Impending Crisis' had been disposed of by its leading book-seller.

Now the Crisis was indeed impending; and for several years my western wanderings were interrupted.

CHAPTER XXVIII.

There is a permanent westerly current in our social and political atmosphere like that which carries westward all material atoms after they rise to a certain hight. In 1865 I found myself again borne along upon it. The mail companies had proffered to the Hon. Schuyler Colfax, speaker of the national House of Representatives, special coaches for crossing the continent, and unusual facilities for studying the vast and varied interests of the West, yet in their infancy. He invited Mr. William Bross of the *Chicago Tribune*, lieutenant-governor of Illinois, and myself, to join him in the long journey to the Pacific by land and back again by water.

We met at Atchison Kansas, then the western terminus of the railroad. A few days before, Indians had captured a coach coming in from Denver, and killed two passengers. The morning after our arrival another stage reached Atchison, having engaged in a running musketry fight for several miles. Two of the passengers were ladies whom I had formerly known in Colorado. Five years' residence on the frontier had made them so familiar with the horrors which captured women suffer among savages, that they peremptorily instructed their younger brother to shoot them in the coach, rather than permit them to be made prisoners. But after the danger was over, they regarded it with that curious pleasure which the contemplation of perils past always affords.

Our prospects were not alluring; but the telegraph diminished the risk, and we were promised an escort when needed. Beside, our coach was to take out Gen. P. E. Conner, commandant of that military district—a sort of hostage for the safety of the rest, as *Punch* suggested that the president or a director of a railway fruitful of fatal accidents, be compelled to ride upon the locomotive of each passenger train.

Sixteen years before, Conner started from Fort Leavenworth for Mexico, a private soldier. Now he had visited the fort a second time, wearing the star of brigadier general, and in charge of the entire region for twelve hundred miles between the Missouri and Salt Lake.

On the twenty-second of May we left Atchison. I wonder if the Almighty ever made a more beautiful country than Kansas! The eye revels in this wide expanse of softest green. Gemmed with innumerable flowers, and darkened by long lines of forest, the prairies are a joy forever.

At Big Sandy, one hundred and forty miles out, we entered upon the track of the Indian depredations of August, 1864. For three hundred miles west of the Sandy, every house and barn along the road was burned, eighty settlers murdered, and all the stock stolen.

Four cavalry-men accompanied us. We found no women or children at the ranches; but a few soldiers on duty at each mail station. At one was an ingenious mimic cannon—a piece of stove-pipe mounted upon old cart-wheels. This 'light artillery' had frightened the Indians as effectually as the rebel wooden guns, at Manassas in 1862, appalled the commander of the Army of the Potomac.

LIGHT ARTILLERY.

Near Kearney a fierce, sudden tornado overturned emigrant wagons, threw up vast sheets of water from the Platte, and blew several teamsters into and across the shallow stream. We were hardly able to appreciate its ludicrousness, for we had barely leaped to the ground when great hail-stones pelted us like a hot musketry fire. As we cowered to the ground our horses reared and ran, dragging by their bits for a hundred yards the men who attempted to hold them. Near us a terrified mule, having thrown his rider, stood with perpendicular ears, expanded nostrils, and braced legs, facing the tornado, a very concentration of mulish obstinacy. He seemed to declare that a hundred tornadoes and a thousand men should never persuade him to budge an inch. George K. Otis, superintendent of the mail line, who accompanied us, nodding toward the animal, in a little lull of the blasts asked:

'Did you ever see a more perfect picture of whoa (woe?')

I had always wondered before who originated the conundrum which likens the roof of a house to a lame dog, 'because it is a slope up' (slow pup;) but now I knew. Only one man in the world could have been the father of that lingual monstrosity. Otis *fecit!*

A PICTURE OF WHOA.

The station-keeper at Kearney told us that six thousand wagons, each carrying from two thousand to eight thousand pounds of freight, had passed within the last six weeks, nine hundred of them within three days. On the road from the Missouri to New Mexico, for six months of the same year, a toll-bridge keeper made a record of the teams passing, with this result:—

Number of men, ...	5,197
Number of animals, ...	45,350
Pounds of freight, ...	26,123,400

For the same period the commissary at Fort Leavenworth sent Government supplies westward to the various plains and mountain posts:

Pounds of freight, ...	33,000,000
Mules employed, ...	140,000
Horses employed, ...	3,000

A single Salt Lake merchant paid one hundred and fifty thousand dollars for hauling his year's supply of goods from the Missouri.

These items give some faint idea of the commerce of the plains. Government expenditures alone for hauling freights and for Indian wars during the last twenty years, would have built a first-class, double-track railway from the Mississippi to the Pacific.

Ten years ago, adventurous overland travelers crossing the continent, were sometimes compelled to journey three or four hundred miles without seeing a human habitation save Indian wigwams. Now, leaving the cars in eastern Kansas or Nebraska, one passes a settler's dwelling in every eight miles, until he gains the slow-climbing Pacific locomotive, toiling up the western walls of the Sierra Nevadas.

We passed much heavy quartz machinery, including a boiler drawn by sixteen oxen. The ranches forty or fifty miles apart where passengers take meals, are termed 'home stations;' those where the coach only stops to exchange teams, 'swing stations.' By a droll conceit, the drivers call the pebbles which they gather in these treeless regions, to fling at their lazy mules, 'stone whip-lashes.'

The daily coaches, each carrying several passengers and about half a ton of mail, now made the trip from Atchison and Omaha to the Placerville railway in California (Shinkle Springs station) in less than three weeks.

We met the California papers daily in the coaches coming east, and were permitted to read the dispatches for the Associated Press, at telegraph stations. The breakfast of ham, biscuits, and coffee, on the great desert, was the more palatable, when the New York bulletins of the same morning were spread upon the board —literally the board—in the hurried handwriting of the operator, who caught and transfixed them flying on the lightning's wing to San Francisco.

'To the weary, wayworn emigrant, journeying with slow teams through these dreary wastes, the mail coach coming in sight imparts new life. It is the connecting link between the desert and the world. To him it represents home, government, civilization, Saratoga, Bunker Hill, the American Flag, and the Fourth of

July!' Emigrants and ranch-men besieged us for papers. One night, when we rolled up to a lonely station, miles from any other human habitation, the stock-tender, ragged, shaggy, sunburnt and unkempt, put his lantern up to our coach window and implored:

'Gentlemen, can you spare me a newspaper? I have not seen one for a week and can't endure it much longer. I will give a dollar for any newspaper in the United States not more than ten days old.'

He was a representative American. No other nation so subsists upon the daily journals as our own.

In the summer of 1864, Ben Holladay, proprietor of the overland stage line, rode by special coach from Folsom California, to Atchison Kansas, (almost two thousand miles,) in twelve days and two hours. It cost him twenty thousand dollars in wear and tear of stock and vehicles.

That was a trip worth the taking!—a history of the last generation—a prophecy of the coming Pacific railroad, the grandest material enterprise of all time. The very thought of it is inspiring. Whirling over the Sierra Nevadas, along the perilous edge of many a dizzy precipice—spinning through the all-enveloping dust of the Great Basin, with its endless alkaline wastes—rattling along frowning canyons of the Rocky Mountains—shooting across the sands of the measureless desert, and then rolling merrily over the gentle swells of the flower-spangled prairie! Night and day, through storm and sunshine, shivering in bitter frost, panting in tropical heat, shrinking under pelting hail, cowering in the lightning's fiery track—across the continent, from the serene ocean to the turbid river!

Many years ago, F. X. Aubrey galloped from Santa Fe New Mexico, to Independence Missouri, eight hundred and forty miles, in less than seven days. He changed horses three or four times, and won his wager of one thousand dollars; but at the end of the journey he was so stiff that he had to be lifted from the saddle.

The soldiers who accompanied us and guarded the stations were all rebel prisoners or deserters who had taken the oath of allegiance and enlisted in the United States service. They styled themselves 'galvanized' Yankees; were faithful prompt and well-disciplined.

As we reached one station our driver enjoined the waiting hostlers:

'*Gents*, we are four hours behind and want to make up the time. We must change these teams in three minutes by the watch.'

At the last telegraph office before the end of our journey, the operator said to Mr. Colfax and his party:

'The Denver people are making preparations to give *you fellows* a grand reception.'

In four days and a half from Atchison we reached Denver. Scourged by war and fire and blood, the city has grown up through great tribulation. Repeatedly, hostile Indians have cut off communication with the States for months at a time.

The early settlers erected excellent brick and frame buildings on the dry bed of Cherry creek; and for two or three years it remained quite innocent of water. But at midnight, on the nineteenth of May, 1864, without any warning, a great storm on the plains changed the creek from a sand-bed to a deluge. An immense torrent came plunging down, sweeping away every building like gossamer Not a vestige remained. Not a relic was ever found even of the six printing presses of the *News* office, or the great iron safe which contained the archives of the city. Several lives were lost. The next morning the creek-bed was again dry; but real estate there, in great demand before, has not since possessed any marketable value.

For two or three early seasons the crops in the valleys were utterly destroyed by grasshoppers. These plagues of the frontier seem to visit all new States. Again and again they passed through Utah like hungry armies, eating every green thing. At last enormous flocks of birds came upon their track and devoured the grasshoppers themselves, which never afterward troubled the Mormons. The Saints thought the deliverance a special interposition of Providence on behalf of their prophet and the Lord's chosen people. Colorado had no Brigham; but this year the grasshoppers were harmless, and we found the valley abounding in flourishing ranches—the universal term for farms. Ranch, or domestic productions, from their superior freshness, are greatly preferred to those brought from the States. A Coloradoan at one of the New York hotels, finding a bad egg at breakfast, said to the waiter:

'Take away these confounded States eggs, and bring me some *ranch* eggs!'

Colorado agriculture was already successful and there were some grain fields of five and six hundred acres. The next year (1866) careful computation showed that seventy thousand acres were planted; and home crops supplied the population of the Territory with every farm product except corn.

In some departments of business high prices still prevailed. Six or seven daily newspapers were published. Subscription price of the dailies: twenty-five dollars per annum, or seventy-five cents per week by carrier; weeklies, eight dollars per annum. Single copies, twenty-five cents. Advertisements, two dollars per square of ten lines, for each insertion.

At my last visit, five years before, Civilization had barely extended to these wilds the tips of her gracious fingers. Now Denver boasted a population of five thousand, and many imposing buildings. The hotel bills-of-fare did not differ materially from those in New York or Chicago. Single building lots had commanded twelve thousand dollars. One firm had sold half a million dollars worth of goods in eight months.

With fresh memories of the log-cabins, plank tables, tin cups and plates, and fatal whisky of 1859, I did not readily recover from my surprise on seeing libraries and pictures, rich carpets and pianos, silver and wine—on meeting families with the habits, dress and surroundings of the older States. Keenly we enjoyed the pleasant hospitalities of society among the quickened intelligences and warmed hearts of the frontier. Western emigration makes men larger and riper, more liberal and more fraternal.

The mountain view from the city impressed me as more grand and beautiful than ever. Bayard Taylor knows 'no *external* picture of the Alps, which can be placed beside it;' and in average hight the Alps are surpassed by the Rocky Mountains.

On the way to the mines we crossed Clear creek, which tearing down from the range will afford excellent water-power when the manufacturer's bit shall be placed in its foaming mouth. We entered the mountains at Golden Gate, by the first stage-coach which had ever penetrated to the old Gregory Diggings. Thousands of acres, which at my first visit had been covered with stately pines, were now utterly bare. The wood had been consumed for fuel in Denver, and by the mountain quartz mills.

After climbing for hours, reaching the summit of a high ridge

DENVER ARCHITECTURE.

we gazed back upon Denver, nestling down in the valley a city of pigmies and play-houses, and upon the undulating, sea-green plains, spreading out in a limitless ocean. Then we looked forward to the Snowy Range, its rich purple streaked with dazzling white, and one of its peaks draped in soft transparent haze.

With profound truth and suggestiveness, Holmes asks if all the tongues of the world can tell how thrushes sing and lilacs smell! The one lesson of this mountain scenery is the utter poverty of language. Not even the wonderful delineations of Bierstadt and Church convey more than a hint of its beauty and grandeur.

The most exquisite combinations and contrasts of color intermingle. Over vast fire-swept expanses, blackened armless trunks of trees stand weird and ghastly; while beyond rise ridges of smooth greensward, or peaks and walls of rugged rock. Through the valleys, little streams lashed into snowy whiteness foam down stony beds, their grassy banks fragrant with the breath of honey-suckle and violet, sweet with the meek bluebell, dark with the purple larkspur, or bright with the flaming glory of the sunflower.

Winding up North Clear creek we began to pass great quartz mills. Near the old Gregory Diggings we reached the mining settlements of Black Hawk and Central, which thread the narrow valley for three miles, in quaint, crooked, contracted streets—like those of a Swiss hamlet—shut in on both sides by steep, bare mountains. Wood and granite quartz mills, old log-cabins of '59, shops, stables, school-houses, drinking-saloons, handsome brick blocks, newspaper and express offices, side by side crowd each other in the tortuous thoroughfares, while the creek, muddy and turbid from washing out the quartz, tumbles among them. Picturesque cream-colored and stone-colored cottages perch in little niches of rugged hills; and a neat Gothic church overlooks the whole.

Lodes real and supposititious have been staked and worked all over the mountains. During 1864 the fees of the recorder of one mining district, amounted to twenty thousand dollars above office expenses. Lodes are traced by the outcroppings or 'blossom,' a faint line of decaying quartz along the surface. The number of feet along the 'lead' which a claim may embrace, is decided by the miners, and varies greatly in different States.

Most of the inhabitants were engaged in legitimate business; but as in all gold regions there were many loafers, chiefly divided into two classes. Of the lower, locally known as 'bummers,' it was said that when two citizens approached a bar, and one asked his friend—not *if* he would drink, for that is superfluous west of the Missouri, but—*what* he would drink, seventeen immediately stepped up and remarked that *they* would take sugar in theirs! The more respectable class, speculating in claims or mining stocks, talked volubly about the rights of the working people, and of themselves as 'honest miners.'

During our visit there was a hot excitement, very characteristic of a gold country, over a contested claim. A suit was pending between two rival companies, and the chief justice of the Territory granted an injunction restricting one from further work upon their shaft, but permitting Fitz John Porter of army memory, who represented the other, to go on with *his* shaft. Angry at this seemingly unjust discrimination, the hostile company placed an injunction upon Porter, quite as effective and considerably more offensive. There was a draught from one excavation into the other; so they built a fire upon their own premises and Porter found a column of smoke from burning sulphur rising through his shaft, which made it impossible to enter it. An attachment was placed upon his opponents for this curious contempt of court; but they kept up the smoke. Both parties were bitter and armed with shot-guns. The whole community was divided into adherents of one side or the other, and the contest involved much political feeling. With the usual frontier mildness, threats of killing were freely made; but the affair was finally adjusted without bloodshed.

AN HONEST MINER.

The history of Colorado illustrates the uncertainties of mining. Gold-bearing quartz opened very richly; and during the first wild excitement, nearly twenty millions of dollars of eastern capital were invested. One company sold six hundred thousand dollars worth of stock at par for cash, over the counter of its New York office in a single day; and at the close of business hours was compelled to call in the police to clear the room of eager purchasers. 'Children cried for it.' Thus quartz mills with an aggregate of two thousand stamps were sent out, and mines opened. But at a certain depth the character of the veins changed. The gold was associated with pyrites of iron, and could not be separated by any known process. From that day to this Colorado mining has been practically suspended, but the gold is there;

intelligent experimenting is constantly going forward, and sooner or later American ingenuity will surmount the obstacles.

Despite this drawback, Colorado though developed during our great civil war, has produced more treasure than any other State except California. Much of our native gold is used in jewelry and other manufactures, and the following official exhibit shows only that deposited in our Government mints from 1804 to July, 1866:

California,	$584,559.251 23
Colorado,	12,401,374 20
Idaho,	10,771,837 30
North Carolina,	9,278,627 67
Oregon,	8,182,544 36
Montana,	7,272,456 01
Georgia,	6,971,681 50
Virginia,	1,570,182 82
South Carolina,	1,353,663 98
Other sources,	9,785,037 34
Total,	652,146,656 41

This is exclusive of silver, of which all our gold regions yield considerably; and Nevada, Oregon and Idaho turn out almost twenty millions yearly. Most of the yield of the southern States was prior to 1858, though since the great war the product has revived in North Carolina, Georgia and Virginia.

The Colorado mining regions are seven thousand feet above the sea, in regions subject to frequent frosts. Still the mountain-guarded valleys produce excellent vegetables. The auriferous quartz contains from nine to twenty per cent. of copper, which ought to pay all expenses of extracting the gold.

The Rocky Mountain beds of coal, from ten to twelve inches thick, are among the largest in the world; and there are indications of the same material in large quantities all the way from Kansas to the range. Iron is abundant and foundries are already at work. Considerable wool is produced, and large manufactories are going up. Valuable oil wells have been discovered; one is opened seventy-five feet, and yields twenty barrels per day. Now (1867,) Colorado contains thirty thousand inhabitants, and its property is appraised for home taxation at fifteen millions of dollars—all developed since 1859!

CHAPTER XXIX.

BEYOND Denver, the road had been practically closed for several weeks by Indian hostilities. We encountered few emigrants or freighters save in large parties traveling together for protection. At nightfall their wagons were drawn close together, with the tongue of each under the bed of the next, making two elliptical lines which no assault can easily break. Within this extemporized fortification, all the animals are driven, the last gap is closed up; and the emigrant sleeps secure from the Noble Savage, who never moves upon the enemy's works.

More than one Coloradoan, indignant at the failure of the authorities to guard settlements and roads, had remarked in our hearing:

'I wish the Indians might catch the Colfax party; for that would stimulate the Government to protect us.'

We were hardly public-spirited enough to echo the prayer. The Indians did not catch us; but a hundred miles west of Denver the troubles grew so serious that we waited for trustworthy information from the front, remaining one day at Virginia Dale station, in a lovely little valley imprisoned by towering mountains. One of their precipitous walls is known as the Lover's Leap. The legend runs that an emigrant, whose mistress had abandoned him and married another, threw himself from it and was dashed to pieces, in full view of the woman for whom he had flung away his life. The Secession founder of the station, not daring to call it Virginia Davis in honor of Mrs. Jefferson Davis, found solace in the name, Virginia Dale.

A hundred miles beyond, the savages had driven off the horses and mules from three stations. Two emigrants were found dead upon the road—one scalped, the other with throat cut from ear to ear, and thirteen arrows in his body. One of these, with the iron point still bloody, was shown to us. The varieties of arrows indicated that the attack was made by a mixed party and not by one tribe.

On a June day, cold as November, at the crossing of the North

INDIAN ATTACK AT NORTH PLATTE CROSSING.

Platte river, we stood gazing at a party of recusant Mormons returning to the States, when running horses, reports of guns and loud yells announced an Indian attack. The wagons of the emigrants, with the women and children, were at the water's edge. Beyond them in a little valley, were grazing their weary horses and mules, well guarded by the men. The Indians came over a hill, in a sharp dash upon the animals, hoping to stampede and secure them. The soldiers of our escort rushed to the ferry-boat to participate in the fray; but I reconciled myself to the decrees of Providence, content to smell the battle afar off—indeed with a secret wish that I were too far off to smell it at all. The river was a safe barrier between the savages and ourselves; for the waters were high, and a coach, horses, mail and all, which had gone to the bottom a week before, was still buried in its depths.

The sturdy emigrants uprose from their concealment among the horses, and fired a volley at their assailants with such coolness and precision that the savages fled yelling over the hills, and were out of sight again in a twinkling.

While our mules were changed that evening, at a station fifteen miles beyond, we chatted for ten minutes with guards and hostlers. Twelve hours afterward, the Indians swept down, killing every occupant except two soldiers, who, wounded, made their escape.

Many of the desert stations are substantial stone buildings, with loop-holes in the walls, with shining rifles and well polished revolvers hanging ready to be grasped at any moment. Some of the women are comely and lady-like, adapting themselves with grace and heroism to the rude labors of cooking meals for passengers, and the horrible, ever-present peril of capture.

At one station, by a lurid candle we saw the red-hot brand of the stage company, pressed on the flanks of the shrinking mules. They had just been purchased to replace those taken by the Indians. The next day they too were stolen. This happened again and again during the summer.

Our road traversed portions of Colorado, Dacotah, Montana and Utah, over endless wastes; and among the Black Hills, Wind River, Uintah and Wasatch ranges and offshoots of the Rocky Mountains. We saw clear trout-haunted brooks and little lakes; lofty peaks; terrible wastes white with alkali; dreary ashen hills of bare drab earth, the parched ground deeply gashed and gullied, the faint streams bitter and poisonous, blinding dust filling the air; and no atom of vegetable life except the sage-brush and the cactus. This is indeed the desert—the very abomination of desolation.

One of our escort, with cavalry rifle at four hundred yards, brought down an antelope with great branching horns, which he flourished wickedly about our soldier, who boldly seized them and then cut his throat. Strapping the fallen chieftain to our coach, we contributed him to the larder of the next station-keeper. Surly gray wolves gazed fixedly at us, until Governor Bross fired at them with his shot-gun; then galloped lazily away. We were a sort of traveling arsenal, with two or three weapons to the man. Attacked, we should have been dangerous indeed—at least to each other. That we all escaped with our lives is due only to that overruling Providence which restrains the recklessness of overland tourists, and sets at naught the aims of amateur sportsmen.

One night a huge grizzly struck an attitude directly before our coach, and refused to stir an inch. An old trapper had lately shown me the scars on his thigh, where, years before, one seized and shook him as a dog shakes a rabbit, and told me of another bear, near Salt Lake, who killed five hunters before he was dispatched. With these fresh memories, we did not attempt either to wheedle or frighten Bruin, but e'en turned out of the road, and left him peacefully studying astronomy. As Artemus Ward observes of the man who insulted him: 'He was larger than we, and we forgave him.'

AN OUTSIDE PASSENGER.

We traversed Bridger's Pass, nine thousand feet above sea-level. There is a story of a California emigrant who, a hundred miles back, sold his wagon to a ranch-keeper, on the assurance that it was just three inches too wide to go through Bridger's Pass!

Here the waters of the Atlantic are divided from those of the Pacific; but there is no gorge or canyon—only a vast desert so nearly level that one can not tell when he crosses the summit.

Two nights later, just as the great moon rose from behind eastern mountains, we reached the Church Butte.

> 'If thou wouldst view fair Melrose aright,
> Go visit it by the pale moonlight.'

The butte is a strange irregular pile of bare gray earth, half a mile in circumference, hundreds of feet high. Crowned with masses of red sandstone, worn by the pitiless elements into all manner of fantastic forms, the mystic moonlight transforms it into a vast ruined cathedral with crumbling walls, quaint turrets and niches holding sculptured figures. There too we can trace a huge fallen sphinx with face downward, a long colonnade with half its noble pillars broken, great human heads, owls, eagles, centaurs, and two enormous lions couchant overlooking and guarding the whole.

Fort Bridger, eight thousand feet above the sea, with gurgling rills threading its green parade ground and supplying its neat log barracks, is one of our most beautiful frontier posts. It was formerly a great rendezvous for traders and trappers. The traders lived with their families in secure forts, buying furs of the trappers and buffalo robes of the Indians. They professed to give St. Louis prices; but paid in coffee and sugar at two dollars per cup, calico at two dollars per yard and whisky and tobacco at corresponding rates. A cup of sugar was the ordinary payment for a buffalo robe.

A few of the trappers still survive, walking cyclopedias of narrow escapes and exciting adventures—living volumes of travel, incident and romance. Buffalo-hunts, hand-to-hand conflicts with grizzly bears, long wanderings when lost among the mountains, without food or shelter, miraculous endurance of hardships and wounds, and deadly fights with Indians, form the staple of their legendary lore. Sometimes a vein of quaint, unexpected humor runs through their stirring naratives.

While waiting breakfast at Fort Bridger, in the gray of this June morning, our party sat around the fire of the great sutler-store of Judge Carter, who combines the functions of merchant and magistrate, listening to the tales of Jack Robinson, a trapper of forty years experience. He supplemented his history of hair-breadth 'scapes with the remark:

'But the most singular thing I ever did was to make a hundred and fifty Blackfoot Indians run.'

'How was that?' we asked.

'It was one year when the red devils were very hostile, and lifted the hair of every white man they could catch. Riding a swift horse, I suddenly came upon a party of them. I turned and ran and *they all ran after me;* but they didn't catch old Jack.'

From Fort Bridger in the fall of 1857, Colonel Marcy with a hundred men started through the mountains for Fort Massachusetts, New Mexico, to bring provisions for the Government expedition against Utah. They lost most of their animals, and were frequently compelled to break the track by crawling through the snow. After suffering untold hardships they at last reached their destination. American pioneer history has nothing more gallant than their energy and endurance.

We found the long warehouse of the post-sutler crowded with goods. His trade was said to net him seventy-five thousand dollars a year. We did ample justice to his hospitable breakfast, and listened wonderingly while his pretty daughters and their governess evoked music from their piano. The instrument answered spiritedly to their touch, manifesting neither loneliness nor debility after its journey of two thousand five hundred miles from New York, one-half the way in an ox-wagon.

When we pressed on, the day was charming. Coming from a desert dreary as Sahara, we began to view mountains that rival Switzerland, and skies of Italian beauty. The air was soft and warm; flowers abounded, and mosquitoes buzzed about us, though patches of snow were on all sides. From the ridges we looked over an immense area of green valleys gay with flowers, bright with silver streams; and mountains of every hue, dotted with dark cedars, streaked with snow, and lost in dim, fleecy clouds. Once we stopped the coach, and in a little aspen thicket where the snow was fifteen feet deep, had a rough-and-tumble snow-balling frolic. But of this diversion man wants but little here below, nor wants that little long. So with well-pelted faces, stinging ears and aching hands, we came back over the greensward, among the mosquitoes, roses, sunflowers, violets, daisies, and forget-me-nots, to the dusty road.

We dined with a Mormon elder, whose young wife rarely gave us a glimpse of her black eyes. The driver assured us that she was his *fifth*—that her four predecessors all ran away from him. From his cheerful good humor I think the husband classed them among blessings which brightened when they took their flight.

That evening we passed through Echo Canyon, twenty miles in length, a wonderful gorge in the mountains, where snows often slide down and overwhelm travelers. As we crossed its flashing stream, and rattled over crazy log bridges, the scene grew wilder and wilder. On the left, steep, grassy, snow-crowned slopes; on the right, an abrupt wall of red conglomerate rock, with lateral canyons breaking it, with the somber mouths of dark caves opening into it, with swallows' nests plastered to its crags, and those 'dewy masons of the eaves' twittering about them. Here the Mormons fortified on the approach of Johnston's army in 1857. Their rifle-pits in the valley, and their little stone houses with loop-holes, on the very top of the dizzy bluff, are still visible. Higher and higher towers the wall on our right, until smooth as if dressed with the hammer, true as if lined by the plummet, it rises two thousand feet. To see Echo Canyon is worth a journey across the Atlantic.

SNOW-BALLING IN JUNE.

Emigration Canyon, the first route through the Wasatch mountains opened by the Mormons, is equally famous and almost equally grand. It begins six miles southeast of Salt Lake City, and abounds in wildest and most beautiful scenery.

On the fifth morning from Denver, we breakfasted with a Mormon bishop, who boasts three wives, *all of them sisters.*

Up one terrible hill, down on its opposite side, through a canyon—and then at our feet was a great basin, walled in by snow-streaked mountains, with blue lakes set like gems in its soft green, and a shining stream lying across it like a ribbon. In the midst of this happy valley, a picture of oriental beauty, we saw the neat houses, the quaint public buildings, the deep shade-trees, the broad streets and flashing rivulets of the City of Great Salt Lake.

EMIGRATION CANYON, NEAR SALT LAKE CITY.

Though several miles distant, we detected small objects in the town with perfect clearness. From a hill on the west, twenty-two miles away, I have twice distinctly seen the dwellings and trees of Salt Lake City. And trustworthy persons aver that, on clear days, the buildings of Fort Boise, Idaho, are seen with the naked eye, from War Eagle mountain, fifty-five miles, as the bird flies!

Mr. Colfax was met by a band of music, and a cavalry escort which conducted him into Camp Douglas, where he paid his respects to the commandant and was greeted with the speaker's salute of fifteen guns. Then approaching the city, weary, sun-browned and dust-begrimed, he found the (Mormon) common council and citizens awaiting him on a bare hill. Of course there were speeches. W. H. Hooper, delegate to Congress, bade the party welcome to their mountain home, to note the beautiful city, the hundred villages, the two hundred mills and the thousands of farms they had established in this remote region. Here in the early days had they unfurled the Stars and Stripes from Ensign Peak; here had they mourned the loss of our beloved President; here had they reaped the benefits of Schuyler Colfax's life-long fidelity to frontier interests; here had they once welcomed Horace Greeley, always a true friend of the Territory and an honored member of that profession which directs public opinion.

Mr. Colfax the while, stood in the blazing sun, his head covered by a white handkerchief, his face wearing the resigned expression of a blessed martyr. At the close, he responded in one of those pointed speeches which, without a moment's preparation, flow from him as water gushes from a spring. A fervid eulogy upon Abraham Lincoln; a warm commendation of the boys in blue who won our battles; a brilliant picture of our country's future, in whose prosperity and honor Utah would share, if faithful to the constitution, devoted to the Union and obedient to the laws.

Remarks and hand-shakings ended, we drove through the city, very quiet on this Sunday morning, to one of the many tepid springs which abound in the Territory. A mile west of town the Sulphur Spring, as large as a man's thigh, gushes from a hill-side. The water is so hot (one hundred and two degrees) that one shrinks from its first touch, but soon finds it delightful. After ten minutes of plunging and swimming, he comes out cleansed from head to foot; every muscle relaxed, every nerve pervaded by delicious languor. It is claimed that the water possesses rare curative virtues for rheumatism.

Two miles further is the Hot Spring, spouting in a column larger than the body of a man, and hot enough to boil an egg. Among the ancients, its sulphurous smell and great clouds of mist and steam, would have declared it a mouth of Tartarus. Beside

GREAT SALT LAKE CITY, UTAH, 1867. Page 347.

it is a lovely little lake, fringed by green poplars, with a background of purple mountains, bearing aloft soft coronets of cloud.

From these springs we rode back, in a glorious atmosphere, under skies of wonderful blue. Behind us were the Great Salt Lake, and the greater mountains.

On our right was the shining Jordan, to the Mormons better than Abana and Pharpar or all the other waters of Damascus. Beyond the river a strip of valley; then lofty mountain slopes, sea-green at the base, dark slate toward the summits.

Before us was the city, with its flashing streams, its low, adobe houses with trellised verandas; its green gardens, and shade-trees of locust, aspen, poplar, maple, walnut, elder and cottonwood; its bustling marts of trade, and cloistered retreats for the offices of a strange religion. Miles beyond stretched the green valley, its blue, shimmering lakes bounded at last by a wall of mountain.

And on our left still towered the range, gashed with great yawning crevices that would swallow New York and its environs—its solid base green and gray, its summits white with eternal snow. Side by side, blending into one matchless picture, were summer and winter, Italy and Switzerland, the dreamy Orient and the restless Occident.

That afternoon and the following Sunday we attended Mormon religious service. The people are erecting an enormous temple of granite which will seat ten thousand people and will be one of the finest church edifices in the United States. As yet it has not made much progress. The Saints worship in a frame building during the winter months, and in summer at the Bowery—a great arbor with seats of rough pine boards, and a low, flat roof of withered branches, supported by upright poles. For the warm season it is far pleasanter than any building; a good substitute for the groves which were God's first temples.

During our stay of eight days we were most hospitably entreated by Mormon authorities and citizens, always kind to strangers and anxious to eradicate any unfavorable impressions of their faith and practices. They entertained us in their houses—a hospitality rarely extended to Gentiles. They showed us the varied industries which have originated in the wise determination of their leaders to make them a self-sustaining people.

One turned us loose among his delicious strawberries and juicy cherries. Apricots, peaches, plums, pears, and apples were all ripening upon his trees. Beside them, just beyond his inclosure, the dreary sage-brush was growing on the dry, sandy soil; and four years before his garden was an unbroken desert like the rest. In his house caterpillers were making silk. The linen of his coat and pantaloons was woven in his own dwelling from his own flax; and his under-clothing was manufactured in a factory of Brigham Young's from cotton grown in the southern counties.

BRIGHAM PREACHING TO HIS CONGREGATION.

On the second Sunday, at the Bowery, the congregation numbered fully five thousand. In accordance with the desire expressed by Mr. Colfax, Brigham preached. He appeared upon the platform in solemn black. He claimed that the Mormons believe implicitly every word of the bible; said that God created Adam 'by the only process known to nature—just as men now create children;' cited history to prove that polygamy had been sanctioned both by Martin Luther and the Church of England; and declared that an English husband dissatisfied with his wife could even now lead her to the public market and sell her!

His sermon was shallow and disjointed. A Mormon elder assured us that it was the weakest he ever heard from 'the president.' But it had one ebullition of naturalness. He said:

'The Latter-day Saints are the happiest people in the world—the most industrious, the most peaceable among themselves. At least they would be, but for a few miserable, stinking lawyers on Whisky street, who for five dollars will prove that black is white!'

That evening in the telegraph office, Mr. Colfax had a pleasant chat with his friend Fred. MacCrellish who chanced to be in the San Francisco office eight hundred miles to the west. The next morning Governor Bross conversed familiarly for half an hour with a member of his family who was in the Chicago office fifteen hundred miles to the east!

Up to this time Brigham Young had never called upon strangers, whether public men or private citizens, until they had first shown their respect for his position as president of the Mormon church, by calling upon him. But Mr. Colfax as a Government official declined to violate the etiquette of the civilized world by making the initial visit. So Brigham, Heber Kimball, and eight other church leaders spent two hours with the speaker and his party at our hotel.

In the long, rambling conversation which followed, Brigham observed that he had dealt largely with Indians and whites, Mormons and Gentiles, and if any man could show that he had wronged him he would restore it fourfold, invited any of us who might be 'religiously inclined' to address his Saints on Sunday; and declared that every dollar of gold taken out in the United States had cost one hundred dollars. It caused murders, anarchy, vigilance committees and idleness. If the Mormons were to enact the lawless scenes common to all gold countries, Government troops would be sent to subdue them. He referred to the prosperity of his people as miraculous, and pointedly and bitterly repeated: 'We cannot be annihilated.'

The next day we returned his visit, at a little building between his two chief residences, the Lion house and Bee-hive house. The former receives its name from a lion couchant over its front door; the latter from a bee-hive (the chosen device of the Saints,) upon its dome. The porter at the lodge, a sentry box beside the gate in the strong inclosing wall, had a revolver hanging beside him; but permitted us to pass, as we were accompanied by a leading Mormon. 'President' Young, with several dignitaries of the church, received us in his large, airy office, with high walls, maps, photographs of prominent Latter-day Saints, a lithographic copy of Bierstadt's Sunlight and Shadow, scales for weighing gold-dust, account books, desks and arm chairs.

At first the conversation was heavy and formal, though Brigham gave us a good deal of information about farming. Nothing is raised without irrigation; but water makes the soil very productive. Corn is more uncertain than small grains; but sixty bushels to the acre are a fair yield, and ninety have been produced. He once raised ninety-three and a half bushels of wheat to the acre; ninety bushels of oats are not uncommon. Many farmers leave their cattle out in winter; but they often die from cold. Coal and iron abound, but iron is not yet successfully smelted.

A lively general discussion upon polygamy ensued. Brigham defended it with skill, historically and scripturally, though admitting that even in Utah male and female births are about equal, and a little staggered when asked if *that* indicated that one man should have a dozen wives! They had adopted 'plurality' (as the Saints invariably term polygamy) only in accordance with a special revelation from God. Their morality justified it. They had not a house of prostitution nor four illegitimate children in the Territory. How did we expect it to be done away with?

Mr. Colfax suggested that he might yet receive another special revelation—to stop it!

Brigham and his supporters earnestly insisted that it was a part of their religion with which Government had no right to interfere; and were indignant at our suggestion that though hanging witches, burning widows and sacrificing human beings to idols had all been practiced as 'parts of religions' they would not be tolerated by modern law and civilization. It was the freest and frankest discussion ever held in the office of Brigham Young.

Our stay in Salt Lake lasted only eight days. But three months later I returned to Utah alone, and spent five weeks among the Saints. The notes in the succeeding chapter are from observations during both visits.

CHAPTER XXX.

SALT LAKE is the city of the future—the natural metropolis of all Utah and portions of Nevada, Idaho, Montana, and Colorado. It contains nearly twenty thousand people, and bids fair to continue the largest city between St. Louis and San Francisco. The overland telegraph connects it with the Atlantic and the Pacific; mail-coaches ply daily to Nebraska and Kansas on the east, California on the west, Montana on the north, Idaho and Columbia river on the northwest, and the Pah Ranagar silver region four hundred miles to the southwest. The hotel is usually crowded with guests; and the streets, one hundred and twenty-eight feet wide and watered by little rills on each side, are thronged with the wagons of immigrants and farmers, with women and children, Saints and sinners, miners and Indians. Some of the trading-houses do an immense business. A single merchant has sold more than a million dollars worth of goods per annum.

There are two daily newspapers: the *Vedette*, representing the Gentile population; and the *Telegraph*, in the interest of the Mormons. The weekly *Deseret News*, almost as old as the city, is the organ of the church. In a Territorial population of nearly one hundred thousand, all are Mormons except a few hundred, who reside chiefly in Salt Lake City.

Camp Douglas is beautifully located on a high plateau, two miles from the city which its artillery commands. This garrisoned post of the United States army has been a potent restraint upon the despotic power of the Mormon church, as it affords protection to all men and women who abandon that faith. Many recanting Saints, chiefly wives dissatisfied with polygamy, have here sought the shelter of the national flag, and been sent from the Territory under military escort.

There is now a flourishing Gentile church and Sunday-school in the city, liberally supported by dissenters of every denomination who, like all small minorities, are very compact, and remain united by the common bond of antipathy to Mormon rule. Even Jews, who are quite numerous, contribute to this church; and in excited moments talk earnestly about 'us Shentiles.' In this strange community all the brethren are Saints, all the outsiders are sinners, and all the Jews are Gentiles!

Joseph Smith founder of the Mormon hierarchy, was a native of Vermont, who claimed that the book of Mormon, the bible of the Latter-day Saints, buried in the earth, was pointed out to him by the angel Moroni; that, digging it up, he found it written upon metallic plates in mysterious characters, which a special revelation from God enabled him to translate. Claiming to be the production of several writers, it is about as large as the Old Testament, of which it is a weak, incoherent and vapid imitation. Several hundred of its verses are stolen with very slight alterations from the New Testament, which according to Mormon chronology was written hundreds of years later than their own inspired volume. Singularly enough, it contains many denunciations of polygamy; but consistency is a jewel rarely found in the casket of the Latter-day Saints. Smith possessed great force of character and business sagacity, and was said to have accumulated a fortune of some millions of dollars.

BRIGHAM YOUNG.

Brigham Young, who succeeded Joseph Smith in the 'first presidency' of the church, was also born in Vermont. He is six feet high, portly, weighing about two hundred, in his sixty-sixth year, and wonderfully well-preserved. His face resembles that of the late Thomas H. Benton, though with a suggestion of grossness about the puffed cheeks and huge neck which Old Bullion never gave. His cheek is fresh and unwrinkled; his step agile and elastic; his curling, auburn hair and whiskers untinged with gray. Is he a new Ponce de Leon, who has found in polygamy the fountain of perpetual youth?

He has grayish-blue, secretive eyes, eagle nose, and mouth that shuts like a vice, indicating tremendous firmness. He uses neither tea nor coffee, spirits nor tobacco. With an affable and dignified manner he manifests the unmistakable egotism of one having authority. In little ebullitions of earnestness he speaks right at people, using his dexter forefinger with emphasis, to point a moral. He treats the brethren with warmth, throwing his arm caressingly about them and asking carefully after the wives and babies.

Provincialisms of his Vermont boyhood and his western manhood still cling to him. He says 'leetle,' 'beyend' and 'disremember.' An irrepressible conflict between his nominatives and verbs, crops out in expressions like 'they was.'

He has observed much, thought much, and mingled much with practical men; but seems unfamiliar with the usages of cultivated society. Yet those who hold him a cheap charlatan are wilder if possible than the Saints who receive him as an angel of light, or those Gentiles who denounce him as a goblin damned. A striking embodiment of the One-man Power, he holds a hundred thousand people in the hollow of his hand. Gathered from every nation, always poor, usually ignorant, sometimes vicious, he has molded them into an industrious, productive, honest and homogeneous community. As a class they have doubtless improved their condition by settling in Utah. Owning the most desirable property at home and well-husbanded investments in England, he is one of the millionares of the United States. He is universally popular among the Saints and rules them with utmost ease. He is a man of brains, who would have achieved great success in any walk of life. Many believe him an imposter and an atheist. But I fancy he is that combination so frequent in history, half-deceiver and half-fanatic.

He has great knowledge of human nature and rare business capacity, and is reputed kind-hearted and just in his commercial dealings. All Mormons are required to pay one-tenth of their incomes annually to the church; and, so far as a Gentile can see, Brigham is the church and the church is Brigham.

His inclosure of ten acres in the very heart of the city is surrounded by a wall, eleven feet high, of bowlders laid in mortar. It contains his two chief dwellings, the Lion House and the Bee-hive House. In them reside most of his wives, though a few favorite

BRIGHAM'S RESIDENCES, LION HOUSE AND BEE-HIVE HOUSE.

ones occupy separate dwellings outside. The inclosure contains various other buildings for his domestic and business purposes, and ample, well-kept gardens abounding in flowers and fruits.

Babies seem indigenous to Salt Lake. Their abundance through all the streets causes wonder till one remembers that they are the only product of the soil which does not require irrigation.

By Brigham's invitation I spent an hour in his school. Its register bore the names of thirty-four pupils; three, Brigham's grandchildren; all the rest his own sons and daughters. There were twenty-eight present, from four to seventeen years old, on the whole looking brighter and more intelligent than the children of any other school I ever visited.

With three of the prophet's daughters I had some conversation.

Their language is good, and their manners graceful. One has a classic face; and another is so pretty that half the young men of the church are in love with her. Afterward, I visited the ward schools of the city. There, the foreheads are narrow and the average intelligence low. Tuition costs from four to ten dollars a quarter. *There are no free schools in Utah.*

Though Brigham has buried eight sons and two daughters, he has fifty surviving children and several grandchildren. His wives number about thirty; he increases the list by one or two additions yearly. The first and eldest is matronly and well-looking; all the later ones I saw are exceedingly plain and unattractive. Among the present generation of Mormons, the men are far more intelligent and cultivated than the women.

The Gentiles relate many stories at the expense of the leading patriarch of the Saints. He is the grand supreme court of all his people; to him they carry their troubles for relief, and their disagreements for adjustment. It is said that one day a woman went to Brigham for counsel touching some alleged oppression by an officer of the church. Brigham, like a true politician, assumed to know her; but when it became necessary to record her case, hesitated and said:

'Let me see, sister—I forget your name.'

'My name!' was the indignant reply; 'why, I am your wife!'

'When did I marry you?'

The woman informed the 'president,' who referred to an account book in his desk, and then said:

'Well, I believe you are right. I *knew* your face was familiar!'

The Saints are fraternal. There are no misters or esquires among them. Every body is Brother A, or Sister B.

Twenty miles from the city is the Great Salt Lake, containing seven islands, all of rugged mountains. Though four fresh rivers flow in, it has no visible outlet, and is bitterly salt. At lowest stage, three gallons of its fluid produce one of clear fine salt. Its specific gravity is said to be greater than that of any other known body of water except the Dead Sea. According to Marcy, one hundred parts of Salt Lake water contain, after evaporation, twenty-two and one-half per cent. solid matter; one hundred parts of Dead Sea water, twenty-four and one-half per cent. The Dead

Sea is thirteen hundred feet below the Mediterranean; Salt Lake forty-two hundred feet above the ocean. Both receive fresh water Jordans. Both are so buoyant that one finds it difficult to wade in them, floats with ease, and could hardly drown save by strangulation. Neither has any known outlet. The Dead Sea is said to contain one species of fish. Salt Lake is believed to hold no animal life. The Dead Sea is forty miles by ten; Salt Lake, forty by one hundred and twenty.

We had a delightful swim in the lake, though the least quantity of its stinging water in nose, eyes or mouth made us very uncomfortable. When we came out we were incrusted with salt from head to foot, and compelled to wash it off with fresh water.

Then we took a sail in a little sloop, which we all found enjoyable except Mr. Colfax, who suffered greatly from sea-sickness. Lake Utah, thirty miles distant, is a clear, shining, mountain-environed body of fresh water, twenty miles by thirty. The silvery Jordan has its origin here, and hence flows across the beautiful valley into Salt Lake.

I frequently attended worship at the Bowery. The congregation usually numbered three or four thousand, and women largely predominated. They were neatly but very plainly dressed; kid gloves were few, silks and satins far between. Hoops abounded in all their amplitude. At first, the preachers denounced them bitterly from the pulpit; but, as usual, feminine persistency triumphed, and crinoline proved more potent than the thunderbolts of the church.

Brigham is the favorite speaker, though he does not preach more than once a month. His sermons are insequential and illiterate. Heber C. Kimball first vice-president, second only to Brigham in authority, and the father of fifty children, is very voluble in the pulpit, always profane and frequently obscene in his harangues. Indeed, many sermons from Brigham, Heber and others of that ilk are utterly indecent, though some speakers are entirely decorous.

From the Sunday desk preachers frequently speak of the crops, and best modes of irrigation; exhort the brethren to be honest and devout; and advise them whether to sell their wheat forthwith or hold it for an advance. They also read a list of letters for the remote settlements, some, four hundred miles away, that they may be sent by private hand to their destination. The singing, with no instrumental accompaniment except a melodeon, is admirable.

Every Sunday, sacrament is administered to the entire assembly, bread being distributed upon metallic plates, and water, instead of wine, from porcelain pitchers. Infants at the breast are all permitted to quaff the water freely. The poor babies are thirsty enough; but it detracts a little from the solemnity of the ceremony.

'WHY, I AM YOUR WIFE!'

My chief interest was in the faces of the congregation. Few of the women are comely; but very few of the countenances impress one as vicious. Nearly all are plain—many extremely so. As we might expect in humble people gathered from every nation, they bear the indelible impress of poverty, hard labor and stinted living. In those faces is little breadth, thought or self-reliant reasoning, but much narrowness, grave sincerity and unreflecting earnestness.

The ordinary sermons are homilies on industry and frugality—praises of polygamy, recital of God's peculiar protection to the Mormon church, and bitter denunciation of the Government and people of the United States. With the exception of the political tone and the inevitable labored defense of polygamy, many of the discourses are such as one hears in an average New England orthodox church. Indeed, plurality of wives is the only distinctive feature of their faith and practice. Mormonism is polygamy and polygamy is Mormonism.

The Saints' theater is *the* grand wonder of Salt Lake City. It was built by Brigham while the town was yet almost a thousand miles from the steamboat or the railway; and it cost a quarter of a million of dollars. Its walls are of brick and rough stone, covered with stucco. It will seat eighteen hundred persons; and is the largest building of the kind west of New York, except the Chicago opera house. The proscenium is sixty feet deep. In the middle of the parquet is an armed rocking-chair, which Brigham sometimes occupies, though his usual place is one of the two private boxes. It is open three nights in the week, when the parquet is filled by the families of the leading polygamists. The Gentiles sit in the dress circle and galleries. The scenery, painted in Salt Lake City, and the costumes, all made there from goods purchased in the eastern States, are exquisite. The wardrobe is very large and rich, varied enough for the entire standard and minor drama, from the sables of Hamlet to the drapery of the ballet girl. With two exceptions, the company are all amateurs—Mormons, who perform gratuitously, and with whom it is a labor of love and piety. Playing in 'Box and Cox' or 'Richard the Third' is a novel way of increasing one's chances of heaven; but Brigham is the church, and they do unquestioningly whatever the church requires.

By day the performers are engaged in their regular pursuits, as clerks or mechanics; and they rehearse only in the evening. Dramatic entertainments have ever been a leading feature of the Mormon faith; and these actors play exceedingly well. In scenery and dressing also, only three or four metropolitan theaters in the United States equal this in the heart of the American desert. The performers are never stagy. Whatever they lack in art they make up in freshness and freedom from the mannerisms, especially the stilted and unnatural readings, of old actors. When a young lady of high dramatic talent presented herself to the veteran Wallack, he gave her a favorable engagement on the express condition that she should not take a single lesson in elocution.

During the season of my second visit, the receipts of Brigham's theater averaged eight hundred dollars per night; and one evening they reached thirteen hundred dollars. Mrs. Julia Dean Cooper was filling a long star engagement at two hundred dollars per night. At first she found the audiences, or as Gail Hamilton would call them, the vidiences, curiously fresh and inexperienced. When she played in 'East Lynne'—that terrible satire on the hardness and injustice of narrow but conscientious men—the lookers-on were moved to sobs; and tears even streamed from the eyes of Brigham, who sat in his private box. But Lady Isabel is perhaps the most pathetic character in the whole range of the legitimate or sensational drama. It is difficult for an old stager to see it well represented, without making what Sam Weller calls 'a water cart of hisself.' 'Camille' produced still greater sensation. During the last scene the audience was

'Like Niobe, all tears.'

One old lady left her seat, passed through the private entrance and rushed upon the stage with a glass of water for the dying girl. Another declared in a voice audible throughout the house:

'It is a shame for President Young to let that poor lady play when she has such a terrible cough!'

Brigham shows unequaled sagacity in strengthening the church and putting money in his purse, by the same operation. He says:

'The people must have amusement; human nature demands it. If healthy and harmless diversions are not attainable, they will seek those which are vicious and degrading.'

Therefore he built this Thespian temple, which spiritually refreshes all the Saints of Utah, and increases his personal income fifty thousand dollars annually.

The Salt Lake valley is walled in by green mountains from four to ten thousand feet high, and of every hue, from the deep, blackish-green of the pines on the foot-hills, to the dazzling white of the snow upon the summits. Many of these peaks, intersected by narrow canyons, are torn and furrowed to their very hearts, and sometimes cleft asunder from head to foot.

Utah, the name of an Indian tribe, signifies 'those who dwell on the mountains.' The Mormons, almost a mile above the sea, in view of some of the finest scenery in the world, are indeed dwellers among the mountain-tops.

The great basin, six hundred miles by three hundred, extending from the Rocky Mountains to the Sierra Nevadas, seems to have been a vast inland sea. Strictly speaking it is a series of basins, of which the one containing Salt Lake is the longest—all dotted and inclosed by isolated peaks and irregular ranges. The immediate valley in which Salt Lake City lies is much its best portion. With irrigation the soil is very productive. Settlements of the Saints extend hundreds of miles in all directions. Almost every valley in Utah is dotted with little dwellings of adobe, herds of

THE GREAT SALT LAKE.

cattle, flocks of sheep, great stacks of hay and barley, and thriving young orchards.

Probably eight-ninths of the Mormons are of foreign birth. Many are English, while Norway and Sweden are largely represented. They thrive in spite of their heavy, enforced contributions to the church; for the leaders are men of rare sagacity who steadfastly inculcate industry, frugality, temperance and peacefulness.

Not more than one man in four or five is a polygamist. Brigham exhorts them to persevere in the system and defend it with their lives, even against the Government of the United States. The women regard it as a sore trial, to be compensated only by the happiness of eternity. Often two or three sisters have the same husband. Some men are married to a mother and her daughter; others to their own half-sisters. When possible, each wife occupies a separate house or room; but poverty sometimes compels three or four to live in the same apartments. I think they never bring in the mothers-in-law. Even Mormon grace would hardly suffice for that!

The Gentile women recognize and visit only the first wives. I conversed alone with three Mormon ladies on their system. Two were young and unmarried. The first was an active member of the church, and apparently an earnest believer in its doctrines. She spoke of it with great ardor, manifesting the anxiety universal in the entire community for the respect and commendation of strangers. She laid great stress upon the honesty, frugality and hospitality of the people, the kindness and justice of the leaders in all their dealings, and the special favor and protection of the Almighty which their history seemed to imply. But to my remark that I liked every thing I saw except polygamy, she answered ingenuously:

'Well, *I* don't like that, and I don't know of anybody who does!'

The second, though reared in the faith, and nominally one of the Saints, had steadfastly refused all offers of marriage. She regarded the leaders as charlatans, declared she would die rather than wed in a community where plurality of wives was tolerated, and would leave the Territory but for family ties. A few months later she did leave, to become the wife of a Gentile.

The third was the wife of a prominent Saint. I had already formed her acquaintance in public, and now I encountered her accidentally for ten minutes in a Gentile parlor. Again and again had I heard her husband aver that the women not merely acquiesced in polygamy, but often urged their consorts to take additional wives. After some general conversation she asked:

'What is the most noticeable thing you find among us?'

'The peacefulness of the rival wives. The fact that they not only refrain from breaking each others' heads, but generally seem friendly, sometimes even affectionate.'

'That is from strong religious conviction. Nothing else could produce it. I believe our women are better, more patient than any others in the world. Nobody knows the severity of the trials they have to endure.'

'Your people have treated us with the greatest courtesy, and shown us much which excites our sympathy and admiration. They have exhibited little of your home-life; but that little only confirms my previous belief that to give another woman the sacred name of wife, is the greatest crime, the last possible outrage a man can commit against his own wife and the mother of his children.'

The lady replied in painful earnestness, with teeth clinched and every muscle tense:

'Certainly it is! I would rather see my daughter in her shroud than married to a pluralist.'

The first wife deems herself superior to the rest, sometimes refusing to associate or speak with them, or to recognize the legitimacy of their marriage.

'Are you Mr. ——'s only wife?' asked a Gentile of a Mormon lady.

'I am,' was the reply; 'though several other women *call* themselves his wives!'

We were told of one poor fellow with a pair of wives, in a single house containing but two rooms. When he brought home his second spouse, the first indignantly repudiated him and would no longer even speak to him. Soon after, the second wife also refused to serve him further; and the luckless man was sleeping alone upon the floor of his cabin and doing his own cooking, washing and mending, while his consorts were at least agreed in hating him cordially! Like old Weller he had 'done it once too often.'

We dined at the house of a leading Saint, whose two wives present at the board, but only as waiters, were dressed precisely alike and really seemed to regard each other as sisters.

One portly brother has a wife in nearly every village; so that when he makes the annual tour of the Territory with Brigham, he can always stay in his own house and with his own family! Polygamy is at least self-sustaining; the women are expected to support themselves.

Many grave crimes including cold-blooded murders are alleged against the Mormons in past years, and there were two peculiarly atrocious assassinations in Salt Lake City in 1866. The first victim,

Brassfield, had married the second wife of a Saint, and was subjected to several harassing suits in the Mormon courts upon charges of stealing her clothing, (from her husband!) and the like. While walking the streets, *in the custody of an officer*, he was shot down by a concealed assassin, the only instance of the kind in American history. The second, Dr. J. K. Robinson, a Gentile physician of high character practicing in Salt Lake City, had incurred hostility by contesting in the courts the ownership of the Warm Spring against the city government. His property was entirely destroyed by the municipal authorities, and after receiving several anonymous warnings to leave, he was decoyed from his residence at midnight to visit a wounded man. Responding to this call of humanity, he went out into the darkness, and was cruelly murdered near his own threshold. Neither assassin was apprehended, though the pervading eye and far-reaching arm of the church could have secured them without the least difficulty, had Brigham and the other unscrupulous leaders desired to have them found and punished.

In all new countries scarcity of money is the mother of invention. Before gold discoveries in California, hides, the general circulating medium, were called California bank-notes. Wheat and beaver-skins were the early currency of Oregon, tobacco of Virginia, and 'coon-skins of Cincinnati. In the last-named city, after the introduction of specie, silver dollars were cut into fifths or tenths to make change. The former passed as quarters and the latter as halves, the rapacious originators of the scheme retaining the extra twenty per cent. to pay them for cutting the coins! Whether from their wedge-shape, or in satire upon the persons who made them, these pieces were called 'sharp-shins.' They acquired general circulation.

The early settlers of Utah, like those of California, Oregon and Colorado, coined their domestic gold, dug from the mountains, for the purposes of commerce. A few of these primitive pieces are still in existence.

It is now twenty years since the Mormon pioneers—one hundred and thirty-nine men and four women—reached the site of their present capital. Their prophet killed, themselves exiles from Missouri and Illinois, after a weary journey of many months they reached this basin to struggle for existence with the unkindly soil, with Indians and with Mexicans. They claim that they left the Missouri with no definite point of settlement; that on the route Brigham Young saw in a vision a beautiful mountain-guarded valley, which heaven assured him was their future home; that on coming in view of Ensign Peak, the Jordan and the great Salt Lake, he instantly exclaimed: 'Here is the spot!'

Immediately upon arrival they knelt down and thanked God for his guidance and protection. The same day they commenced plowing. An old trader, the only white man within hundreds of miles, declared that he would give a thousand dollars for the first ear of corn they could raise from the parched and barren soil. But there is always a future for settlers who pray and then go to plowing. How this strange beginning carries one back to that other despised band which landed at Plymouth on a dreary December morning!

AN EARLY MORMON COIN.

[G(*real*) S(*alt*) L(*ake*) C(*ity.*) P(*ure*) G(*old*).]

Snowy winters and rainless summers, hostile Indians and all-devouring grasshoppers did not dishearten the Mormons. Like other historic emigrants, they combined strong religious enthusiasm with great wisdom in practical affairs. They learned this new agriculture; established homes; began to have cattle upon a thousand hills; contributed largely from their lean purses to the church, sending missionaries all over the world. The great deluge of California migration furnished a market for their grain and beef. Even Johnston's army, sent out to restrain and if needful to subdue them, purchased their crops and added to their wealth; and when it departed eastward, left wagons and guns, enormous quantities of iron, which proved of priceless value to them.

Nevada and Idaho silver, and California, Colorado and Montana gold have contributed vastly to their prosperity. How can farmers fail to grow rich where flour commands ten dollars per hundred throughout the year? They have made the treeless desert indeed blossom as the rose, and laid the foundations for a rich and prosperous State.

But it is an anomaly in our civilization, that a church more rigid than that of Rome, with a domestic system utterly defying the laws of all enlightened nations in modern times, should exist in the center of our continent, openly nullifying the statutes and authority of the national Government. Yet the problem will soon be solved by natural laws. Polygamy, like that other patriarchial institution which is laid in the tomb of the Capulets, can not exist without isolation.

Thus far Brigham has kept his followers from working the rich mines of silver and gold which the mountains contain. This sagacious policy has preserved his power, and greatly increased the prosperity of his people. But within three years Utah will contain a large mining population, composed exclusively of men. The miners are great iconoclasts; and human nature will triumph.

The majority of the women will no longer accept one undivided half or sixth of a husband—in some cases a very vulgar fraction indeed—when a full unit is attainable. They already show strong proclivities for running away with Gentiles. Many have married Federal soldiers and prove excellent wives and mothers.

'By and by,' said one of our stage drivers, 'I shall take one of these second Mormon wives myself. Only the first marriage is good in law; none of the later ones are worth a cuss.'

The future miners will agree with him. Many will take the superfluous women, to find them faithful, affectionate and honest.

Within three years, too, the screaming of the locomotive will be heard in Salt Lake City. Perchance the splendid Mormon temple now rising may yet be the depot of the great Pacific railroad. Brought in contact with our national civilization, the power of Brigham and his associates will cease forever; and the one repulsive and monstrous feature of their domestic life no longer stain a community whose history contains much to challenge respect and admiration.

CHAPTER XXXI.

From Salt Lake we continued our journey westward by the daily coaches. The stations are ten or twelve miles apart. When the vehicle rolls up, whatever the hour of day or night, the stable is opened, four or six clean glossy horses, in shining harness, are led out and substituted for the dusty panting steeds; and in five or eight minutes the stage whirls on.

During Indian hostilities the coaches are seldom taken off, and drivers and superintendents manifest great daring in carrying the mail through the darkness, over lonely and dangerous desert roads. One night the coach containing no passengers save a woman and child, reached a Nevada station, without any driver. Three miles back, overcome by sleep, he had fallen from the box, and the wheels passed over and killed him.

The Overland Telegraph, which Indians call 'the long tongue,' follows the mail route. We passed Lake Utah, shining among the mountains in quiet beauty; crossed the Jordan, the last stream for four hundred miles, and rolled out upon the treeless, ashen desert, where fine alkaline dust constantly enveloped us in 'a pillar of cloud.'

At one lonely adobe station we encountered my old acquaintance, 'Lo, the poor Indian,' in the form of a ragged sorry-looking Goshoot who had been waiting for two days to see Mr. Colfax. He asked which was the 'great capitan;' then bestowed upon the speaker a long stare of curiosity and seeming approval, for he concluded with a grunt of 'Good!' and the request for a little 'tobac.' This man had been a steadfast friend of the whites; yet during the hostilities two years before, our soldiers killed his wife and children in their own lodge, through a mistake. When speaking of it he threw himself upon the ground, beating his head in the agony of remembrance. I should sympathize more with the general frontier feeling that the Indians ought to be exterminated, had I not known many cases of these lamentable 'mistakes,' to say nothing of gross and premeditated barbarities. I am no believer in the Noble Savage. If he ever existed outside of Cooper's romances, he was long ago extinct. The Indian is cruel, bloodthirsty and treacherous; but he often behaves quite as well as the Pale-face.

Twice each day we met a coach going east. For a moment the panting horses would stop and the two great clouds of dust blend into one:

'What news from the States?'

'Give us some San Francisco papers.'

'Did you have any trouble with the Indians?'

'All set; go on driver.'

The whips crack, and the two cars of the desert go rolling forward. Now it is only the rattle of the coach, but ere long it will be the screech of the locomotive. Here on the astonished plains, New York and California, London and China, will meet to exchange greetings and newspapers, while their respective trains are stopping for breakfast.

Along plains, over hills, and down steep winding canyons our horses leaped at their utmost speed. One route of eight miles we traveled in thirty minutes! I wonder if that was ever beaten in the palmiest days of the stage-coach. We spent only seventy-two hours upon the five hundred and seventy-five miles of desert road between Salt Lake, and Virginia Nevada.

The managers of the line manifest great pride in their enterprise, often running it at a heavy loss for months when passenger travel is cut off. A single stockholder has paid assessments to the amount of twenty-four thousand dollars, to meet his portion of the deficiency for one year. The time will doubtless come when twenty daily stages will run to fill up the unfinished gap in the Pacific railroad.

The expenses of the mail company have been enormous. In 1864, they paid twenty-five cents per pound for all grain used between Salt Lake and Austin. Each horse consumes daily from ten to fifteen pounds of oats or barley. But the next year they stopped purchasing grain of the Mormons and opened a farm upon the desert. They sowed oats and barley upon the freshly-turned

EGAN CANYON AND FIRST QUARTZ MILL.

sod of eight hundred and forty acres. The entire tract yielded thirty bushels to the acre, and one-fourth of it fifty bushels to the acre, saving the company more than fifty thousand dollars.

Upon all our sand wastes, as upon those of Arabia, the introduction of water makes the soil productive. Thus far, irrigation is only from streams, except in portions of California where water is drawn from wells by windmills; but in time, simple and cheap machinery for irrigation from wells will doubtless be introduced. Then the great American Desert will become a thing of the past; and the thousands upon thousands of miles of sage-brush and grease-wood, dwarf-cedar and cactus, sand and alkali, from British Columbia to northern Mexico and from western Kansas to the Sierra Nevadas, will yield barley oats and fruit as profusely as the Mississippi valley produces corn and hay.

Two hundred and fifty miles west of Salt Lake we encountered the first quartz mining of Nevada, at Egan Canyon, a picturesque valley. Only one mill was running. It had but five stamps and was so imperfect as to extract little more than fifty per cent. of the silver. But it paid for itself in the first ninety days, and then returned large dividends to the working owners.

Several new mills have since been erected, and the region promises very richly. Ore is reported as averaging one hundred and six dollars to the ton. Wood costs about three dollars per cord. Grass and water are abundant, and the contiguity to Utah renders food cheap. Few silver mining regions possess so many advantages.

Reaching Austin our vehicle whirled around the last street-corner, ran for several yards poised upon two wheels, while the others were more than a foot from the ground, but righted again; and with this neat finishing stroke ended our ride of four hundred miles, accomplished in fifty-one hours.

Austin is the metropolis of the Reese-river district and the most important mining region of Nevada, except Virginia City. It is built upon innumerable slender, parallel veins of ore, threading a belt of country one mile wide and five in length. This was the *young* portion of Nevada. Virginia City, boasted a hoary antiquity of five years. But only two years and a half had passed since the first pick was struck, the first vein opened, and the first cabin erected in Austin.

The first discovery of silver here was made by Talcott, a pony-express rider, in July, 1862. The usual excitement and rush of immigrants followed. A wandering farmer, establishing a ranch in one of the little valleys, struck a fragment of ore while digging a post-hole. It proved to belong to a rich vein, and he sold his claim for seven thousand dollars. The pioneers often manifest great enterprise, in meeting severe hardships and peril from snow and Indians. In February 1864, an exploring party, under Colonel D. C. Buell, penetrated several hundred miles southward, and traveled five and-a-half days upon the desert without finding water. At last, barely able to stand, they reached a thick, stagnant pool whose putrid water was like nectar to their parched throats, and saved them from a horrible death.

Austin contains about four thousand people. Like most mining towns it straggles for three miles down a deep, crooked canyon. Ashen, treeless hills, rising for several hundred feet on each side of the principal thoroughfare, are excavated like a mammoth prairie-dog town. Hundreds of shafts and ditches, surrounded by piles of reddish earth, show the industry of prospectors in pursuit of ore. Compared with these, the fortifications of McClellan on the Virginia peninsula, and the fifty miles of breastworks which commemorate Halleck's stupendous failure before Corinth, dwarf to mole-hills.

There is truth in the proverb that it requires a gold mine to work a silver mine, and often to find one. Austin is a city 'lying around loose.' Along the narrow valley, huge quartz mills thunder incessantly; and far up the brown hill-sides, little dwellings of stone, brick wood and adobe are curiously niched and scattered.

The town is six thousand feet above the sea, and the air so light that the least physical labor causes great shortness of breath. Persons wearing artificial teeth find it difficult to keep them in the mouth, so slight is the atmospheric pressure. Here we first encountered several features of the Pacific coast:

I. No hotels, in the American sense; only lodging houses with restaurants quite distant and often in another part of the city.

II. A specie currency. All transactions were based on gold and silver, though some 'greenbacks' were in circulation at seventy-five cents on the dollar. Since that time a national bank has gone into operation, and the currency is now paper.

III. Gambling. By day, Austin was quiet—more than half the inhabitants working under ground; but at night it flashed up into life and its brilliantly lighted saloons with open fronts, were filled with motley crowds, absorbed in monte and other forms of play, inseparable from young mining regions. At several monte tables women conducted the game, shuffling the cards and handling great piles of silver coin with the serenity of professional gamblers; while men of all classes fought the tiger with all the ardor excited by that infatuating pursuit.

IV. Celestials. Chinamen from San Francisco, had already penetrated to this remote region, and over the doors of many of the little shanties were signs bearing the announcement so comforting to the bachelor heart, that Chin-Kong or Sam-Sing did washing and ironing at the lowest rates, with no extra charge for sewing on buttons!

V. Universal hostility toward Austrian and French interference in Mexico. Everywhere on our west coast, a war for driving Maximillan out of Mexico would have been intensely popular. To call this border the 'Pacific' coast was a glaring misnomer. It was really the Belligerent coast.

All machinery and supplies came from California, hauled by mules three hundred miles through the Sierras and over the desert at from ten to twelve cents per pound. Lumber cost from one to two hundred dollars per thousand; wood sixteen dollars per cord. Laboring men received from four to five dollars per day; mechanics from eight to ten. The region was turning out two hundred thousand dollars of silver per month. Hundreds of thousands of dollars had been squandered by eastern companies in purchasing worthless mines and erecting mills upon them.

The Austin silver veins are very narrow, containing ores rich but intractable and difficult to reduce. Quartz mills, containing in the aggregate more than a hundred stamps, are now in operation.

Continuing westward from Austin we obtained our first view of the grand Sierras. Sierra, (a saw) is the universal Spanish term for mountains, from their notched, saw-like summits. We have discarded the grand early name Sierra Madre, (mother mountains,) for the more pretentious and less descriptive appellation of Rocky Mountains. The Castilian pioneers also named this tall narrow ridge a hundred miles from the Pacific, Sierra Nevada (mountains white with snow) from the deep drifts that bury them almost half the year. They grew more and more grandly distinct before us until we reached Virginia City the metropolis of Nevada. With its adjuncts, Gold Hill and Silver City, this wonderful young town contains fifteen thousand inhabitants. A mining settlement is usually along the trough of some tortuous ravine; but Virginia perches like a child's city half-way up the side of a mountain. Most new cities consist of frame sheds; but Virginia is chiefly composed of substantial brick blocks.

BIRD'S-EYE VIEW OF VIRGINIA NEVADA, AND MOUNT DAVIDSON.

The region is bare and forbidding, treeless and verdureless, but often breezy as if the old fable w . actualized and all e winds of heaven l t loose together. Ha bound and roll thr gh the streets, while t razy antics of crino reveal that we ar rfully and wonderf ma e.

Here ung up like Jon urd a city upon a h , which cannot be h , a city of costly churches, tasteful school-houses, and imposing hotels; many telegraph wires, many daily coaches, two theaters, three daily newspapers—one nearly as large as the eight-page journals of New York!

Like other young mining communities some of its elements are fast and loud; but like every new State it has also much culture, refinement and social worth. The stupid are not the pioneers of empire. The ignorant and dullard are not the men who bear commerce and civilization across the arid desert and over the frowning mountains. Virginia is more than six thousand feet above the sea. Beside the town rises Mount Davidson to the hight of fifteen hundred feet. One fancies the Genius of Solitude standing for ages on that lonely peak, recording upon its stony tablets untold centuries of silence and desolation. How suddenly he was frightened away by the clang of labor, the hum of trade, and the sound of the church-going bell! But five years past, a desert—to-day, a metropolis! The fables of old Romance grow tame before these grand enchantments born in the nation's restless brain and wrought by its tireless arm.

In the heart of the city and its Gold Hill extension, scores of huge quartz mills pound unceasingly, and their smoke darkens the heavens. One of these—the Gould and Curry —cost upward of six hundred thousand dollars, and contains eighty stamps, reducing one hundred tons of ore daily. It is the largest and finest quartz mill in the world, finished throughout with the nicety and exactness of a music-box.

The streets are thronged; there is a perpetual whirl of business, and the theaters are open every night, including Sundays. During some excitements, mining stocks have commanded incredible prices. A foot in one company has sold for eighteen thousand dollars; but it now rates at less than one-tenth of that sum. Six inches in another company netted its owner two hundred and fifty dollars per month. A speculator, at one time, received twenty-five thousand dollars a month from his mining stocks, but had the judgment to sell before the collapse; for the fluctuations of silver have been precisely like those of petroleum.

Here is the original Washoe. In San Francisco it is still known by that name, and not as Nevada. It received the appellation from the Washoe Indians. I do not know where they gained it; certainly not from any Mahomedan reverence for washing. If cleanliness be next to godliness, they are the least divine of human creatures. A few of these 'oldest inhabitants' still remain, gazing in stolid wonder upon the strange civilization which has pushed them from their stools.

This region was unvisited save by small parties of emigrants, pony-express riders, drivers, stock-tenders and the few passengers by overland mail, until toward the close of 1859. Then Comstock and Penrod, two prospectors in pursuit of gold, discovered a vein of dark ore, and were puzzled to decide upon its character. Specimens sent to San Francisco for assay, turned out to be very rich silver-bearing quartz. A great rush for the new region immediately began, and the Comstock Lode proved the richest vein of silver ever found. It is a mile and a half in length, from eighty to two hundred feet in width, and is already opened downward for nearly seven hundred feet, without giving out. 'Once a silver mine, always a silver mine,' is the favorite theory. It is claimed that they are never exhausted. Some Peruvian lodes are already worked to the depth of seventeen hundred feet.

The Comstock has yielded wonderfully. From twelve hundred feet in length, the Gould and Curry company have taken twelve millions of dollars; and four millions were extracted from one 'pocket.' The mine originally cost the company three thousand dollars.

Upon this Comstock Lode began the silver-mining of the United States—an industry yet in its infancy, but destined to prove one of the most important interests of the nation. It is the sole pursuit of Nevada, which has sprung up on the desert and was admitted to the Union in 1863. During 1865, the Wells-Fargo express carried from Nevada to San Francisco fifteen million dollars in bullion, the year's product of this youngest State, born at the outset of a great civil war.

This silver ore is very easily reduced. That of Austin, Egan Canyon and some districts of Idaho must be roasted in addition. In Utah and Arizona many of the silver ores require smelting. The Austin veins are only from six to twenty inches wide. There one stamp will reduce but half a ton a day; crushing costs eighty dollars per ton, and ore must yield one hundred dollars per ton to pay for working. Here is only the one great Comstock Lode, sometimes eighty feet in breadth; one stamp will crush daily a ton and a quarter, and ores which yield twenty-five dollars are profitable. In California, where fuel, labor and water are cheap, ores which contain six dollars to the ton pay for working, and nine-dollar ores are very lucrative. Hasten the Pacific railroad!

Mines are bought and sold by the foot. A thin slice of beet

inserted in an apple will represent a silver vein, and the apple inclosing it the wall-rock. A 'foot' is twelve inches in length on the vein, including its entire width, whether six inches or sixty feet, and its whole depth down toward the earth's center. How deep silver veins extend is only conjectured. In Mexico and South America some have been worked for three hundred years. Of the hundreds opened in Nevada but few have yet proved remunerative. Many companies after immense expenditure reap only assessments, which in this region are termed 'Irish dividends.'

There are many ingenious inventions. The ore comes from the mines in fragments as large as a man's head. They were formerly broken by hand with sledge-hammers into pieces small enough to go under the stamps. Now a machine with a 'hopper' like a grist-mill seizes them and chews them with its iron teeth to the proper fineness, like bits of cheese. At the Savage we saw a new 'safety cage' for lowering miners and visitors down the shaft. A roof of boiler-iron protects the head against missiles falling from above. In our presence the superintendent loaded one of these cages with a ton of ore, and then, two hundred feet above the bottom of the mine and about as far below the surface, cut the rope. The heavy car fell two or three feet, and then suddenly stopped. Two strong arms of steel darting out horizontally struck into the wall on either side, and held the burden firmly over the dark abyss! It was precisely like a falling man throwing out his hands to grasp the nearest object—a marvelous counterfeit of human instinct.

THE CRUSHED TIMBERS.

The subterranean tunnels and chambers are planked and timbered to prevent them from falling in. Some of the timbers, crushed and half broken by the weight of rock, suggest unpleasant possibilities as one creeps under them. We saw a new machine mortise and frame both ends of a pine joist seven feet long by fourteen inches square, in two minutes and forty five seconds. The proprietors of the Savage assured us that it was saving them eighty dollars per day. These are all the productions of practical working miners. Theorists and savans are held in amusing contempt. The workmen declare that they find the richest ore where the geologists pronounced the existence of silver utterly impossible, and vice versa.

The city stands directly over the Comstock Lode, which is honeycombed with hundreds of subterranean tunnels and chambers, from twenty to six hundred feet below the surface.

Standing upon a little platform and holding by an iron bar overhead, down, down a dark, narrow perpendicular shaft we shot breathless through the dense darkness. In a moment the rush of air ceased, and four hundred feet under ground we stepped into a chamber of the Gould and Curry. Already thirty-five chambers, seven feet in hight, have been opened and timbered one above another; and the 'drifts' and tunnels seem endless. There is doubtless more lumber in the Gould and Curry mine than in the whole city of Virginia above ground.

Sometimes the ore ceases, the wall rocks unite and the vein seems to give out. Then, hundreds of feet below, a long tunnel is run in from the hill-side, and in each case after months of labor and enormous expenditure, the ore has been struck again at a lower level.

We walked for hours through long hollow passages where the blows of the pick rang and echoed, while flaring candles threw their lurid light over perspiring miners and carmen. Our stairway labors ended in climbing a perpendicular ladder one hundred and twenty feet high. Some one kindly suggested that on account of weakness I should lead the party. A few rounds up, my candle went out; and toward the top a sensation of faintness came over me in the thin, close air. Glancing instinctively at the succession of tapers twinkling in the dark chasm beneath, I shuddered to think what a clean sweep of every man from the ladder my fall would produce! But we all mastered the ascent, mounted the cage again, and it bounded up into daylight like a schoolboy's ball.

The Gould and Curry mill is kept running day and night by two sets of workmen. It crushes only the lower grades of ore. All yielding more than one thousand dollars per ton is sent in wagons over the Sierras to the railroad and thence shipped, *via* San Francisco, to Swansea in Wales. Even from Austin, rich ore is hauled four hundred miles and sent abroad for crushing.

Swansea mills guarantee that they will extract all the silver to the full amount of the assay; Virginia mills agree to take out only eighty per cent. On the completion of the Pacific railway, this branch of carrying-trade alone will become immense, unless we acquire the same subtlety to extract *all* the metal which Welsh and German mills have attained. The average Nevada ore yields two dollars of silver to one of gold. The Gould and Curry company have paid nearly a million of dollars in a single year for transportation between Virginia and San Francisco.

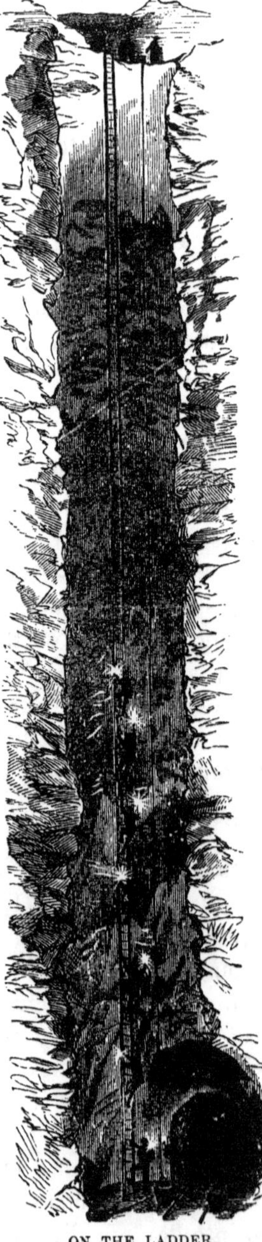
ON THE LADDER.

The profits of many of the richest mines have been consumed in litigation about titles. One company paid its attorneys forty thousand dollars a year for legal services. Another paid the same firm a single fee of a hundred thousand dollars.

I have spoken only of those regions in which mining is carried on extensively. Other sections where development is just beginning are equally rich in valuable ores. The Humboldt region north of Virginia, a large tract south of Austin, and the Pah-Ranagat district near the Colorado river, are said to contain larger and more remunerative mines than have yet been opened; but no single vein has been found equaling the Comstock Lode, which has already yielded more than sixty millions of dollars.

Senator Nye believes that Nevada contains more silver ore than all the rest of the world. Bishop Simpson insists that our silver resources are sufficient to pay off a national debt of twenty billions, present each returned soldier of the Union with a silver musket, and then plate all our war vessels with silver thicker than they are now sheathed with iron. Doubtless both gentlemen are over-sanguine; but the ores of Nevada seem practically inexhaustible; and our silver mining is yet in its infancy. Every dollar spent in developing our quartz lodes enhances the value of every foot of real estate in the Atlantic cities, and every acre of farming land in the Union; and enriches every mercantile, manufacturing and railroad interest. Within fifteen years after the Pacific railroad is completed the silver and gold mines of the United States will be yielding five hundred millions of dollars per annum.

CHAPTER XXXII.

NEVADA abounds in hot springs. A few miles from Virginia, over a tract a mile long following the course of a little brook, sulphur-water boils and throbs under ground, here and there breaking through in jets of hot water and steam. At one point rises from the ground a fountain six or eight feet high, puffing like a high-pressure steamer; wherefore all the waters are known as the 'Steamboat Springs.' Like the great sulphur springs at Salt Lake they possess much curative virtue, and are especially useful in rheumatism.

Hot springs, deserts, alkaline waters, precious metals and precious stones, seem everywhere to have natural affinity for each other. Marco Polo's ancient accounts of wells of petroleum which had caught fire and which the Persians worshipped; of hot springs with swimming baths 'very salutary in cutaneous and other diseases;' of salt and bitter desert waters which 'produce violent purging if a man tastes even a drop;' 'mountains formed entirely of salt;' deep caverns 'cut by those who worked silver mines;' deposits of lapis lazuli, rubies, jasper, chalcedony and asbestos, in Tartary, read like descriptions of our own mining States.

Sixteen miles west of Virginia, Carson City, the pleasant capital of the State, nestles in a green valley at the foot of the Sierras. The city and the neighboring river perpetuate the name of Kit Carson, the trapper and scout.

Carson valley is the largest and richest farming region of Nevada. The State looks so utterly barren and desolate that early settlers believed all its supplies must be drawn from Utah and California. Nothing is raised without irrigation; but experience proves that many of its little valleys have great agricultural capacity, and indicates that the State will one day become self-sustaining. Still its chief interest will be silver mining.

There is some foundation for the satire of a tourist, who insists that the Rocky Mountains, the desert, and the Sierras, must be infinitely rich in minerals because they are worthless for any thing else! Indeed, there seems to be a universal truth in quaint old Wither's observations upon gold:

> 'I've heard those say who travel to the West,
> Whence this beloved metal is encreast,
> That in the places where such minerals be
> Is neither grass, nor herb, nor plant, nor tree.'

In most new mining States rhetorical acrobats, donning blue shirts and buckskin pantaloons, drink bad whisky with the miners and harangue themselves into Congress. These political Micawbers never *will* desert the honest miners, nor stop abusing the Government for disregarding western interests.

Nevada was wiser in the bestowal of her public trusts. Governor H. G. Blaisdel her first executive, was a San Francisco merchant. Through a sudden decline in corn, he failed for seventy-five thousand dollars. Coming to Nevada and beginning life anew, he went into quartz mining; and in ten years returned to San Francisco and paid to his creditors every dollar of the old indebtedness. A practical miner, minutely familiar with the interest of the young State, he filled her highest office with ability and fitness.

William M. Stewart, one of her first United States senators, was also a working miner, and able, in the national councils, to give comprehensive and minute information touching the resources, developments and needs of our mineral States.

At Carson, as usual, Mr. Colfax was welcomed by officials and citizens, with processions, banners and artillery salute. Here as in Virginia, we encountered the messengers and officers of the great Wells-Fargo express company, which transports nearly all the freight and treasure and much of the mail matter of the Pacific coast. Despite the difficulties of building up such an enterprise in a new, sparsely-settled country, it appeared better managed and more popular among all classes than any similar organization in the United States. It was then confined to our west coast, but now it covers the vast region between the Missouri and the Pacific; and with special fitness, Louis McLane who organized and managed it for fifteen years in California, is the president of the enlarged company, whose headquarters have been transferred to New York.

LOUIS MC'LANE,
PRESIDENT WELLS-FARGO EXPRESS.

After some pleasant hours in Carson, we continued westward in charge of Colonel F. A. Bee, of Placerville California, builder of the first trans-continental telegraph.

A delightful evening drive of thirteen miles, up the Sierras, brought us to Tahoe, by far the most beautiful lake in the United States. The air was sweet with the breath of the pines; the eye feasted on deep green valleys, great mountains of rock, and hills studded with evergreens. The peerless little lake lies among the clouds, more than a mile above sea level. It stretches for twenty miles, a shining mirror set round with somber firs and bounded by hazy mountains. In the quiet night we strolled down to the shore and lounged on a pile of lumber, listening to the wind's low moan through the pines, and the wave's soft ripple against the sand. The crescent moon made in the burnished lake a great field of light, narrowing toward us until, in the low swell, it broke into a mass of sparkling silver chains.

The next morning the melody of singing birds awoke me, pouring in through my open window at the Glenbrook House. We breakfasted upon the lake trout, which weigh from one to twenty-five pounds. Then we enjoyed a ride of two hours upon the little steamer 'Governor Blaisdel,' which left the water in our wake a streak of indigo blue. The craft *looks* but little longer than his excellency, who stands nearly six feet six!

Tahoe is probably the highest lake on the globe, navigated by a steamboat. It seems as perfectly transparent as if the water were air. The bottom is seen with distinctness at the depth of nearly a hundred feet. In some portions it has been found more than fifteen hundred feet deep. All around, the irregular trace dividing the sea-green of the shallow waters from the sky-blue of the depths, is as well defined as a chalk-line on a blackboard. The shores abound in shining black sand. A movement, eminently characteristic of the large ideas of the Californians, is on foot, to tunnel the Sierras and supply San Francisco and other large towns with water from Tahoe.

The State line crosses the lake; and we soon passed into California. At the Lake House we parted from the twenty Nevada friends who had accompanied us; and exchanged the steamer for a six-horse stage coach of the Pioneer Line. Whirling along up the smooth, winding, graded road, we were among bare granitic peaks of white, gray and brown, in air pungent with odors of the pine and the slender balsam fir. Many noble pines, one hundred and fifty feet high and straight as arrows, are covered on the north side with rich, yellowish-green moss. Rivulets leap hundreds of feet down the abrupt mountain sides, and, flung off by the jutting rocks, bend in arches of alabaster whiteness. They recall the fine conceit of the Spanish poet that a brook is the laugh of the mountain!

Crossing the summit seven thousand feet above the sea, we looked back upon a grand panorama. Far below us glittered Tahoe, brightest gem in the mountain coronet of those twin queens, the Golden and the Silver State. We saw every variety of form and color, mountain and valley, the deepest green and the purest snow. Then we began to descend. Here, where the turnpike in winter is sometimes obstructed by twenty feet of snow, pass three telegraph wires and eight daily coaches.

The winding road is graded like a railway—the finest of turnpikes for the perfection of staging. In early days the ride was very perilous: along rocky sidling roads, upon the edge of dizzy precipices, where one looked down for a thousand feet upon patches of greensward and silver streams.

When the editor of the *Tribune* crossed in 1859, he was driven by Hank Monk, a famous Jehu who like the son of Nimshi, driveth furiously. An apochryphal story of this ride is current all over the great plains and among the mountains. The editor had a lecture engagement in Placerville, and as the horses climbed slowly up the eastern side he feared he would be too late. Twice he urged the driver forward, but the reticent Monk paid not the slightest heed. Soon, they reached the summit and began to descend. Then cracked the long-idle whip; and the horses at full run, tore along beside precipices where a single stone or mis-step might send them rolling over, in which case the passenger was sure that, upon reaching the bottom, coach, horses and men would

MONTGOMERY STREET, SAN FRANCISCO, JULY 4, 1865.

not be worth twenty-five cents a bushel! Tossed about in the bounding vehicle, he assured the driver that such haste was unnecessary, that half an hour sooner or later would make no material difference.

'Keep your seat, Mr. Greeley,' replied the imperturbable Monk, with a fresh crack of the whip—'keep your seat; I'll get you to Placerville in time!'

Through that overruling Providence which cares for the careless, the journey was accomplished in safety. But the fanciful legend so pleased certain Californians, that they presented Monk with a handsome gold watch, bearing the inscription: 'Keep your seat, Mr. Greeley—I'll get you to Placerville in time.'

One night afterward when Monk's coach was late—for these stages run by time-table—he drove very hard, to the terror of a self-important judicial personage who vainly expostulated again and again; and at last with pompous gravity, thundered:

'I will have you discharged before the week is out. Do you know who I am sir?'

'Oh, yes!' replied Monk, 'perfectly well. But I am going to take this coach into Carson City on time if it kills every one-horse judge in the State of California!'

Now, the broad, winding roads are beautifully smooth, and in summer sprinkled from carts for sixty miles to keep down the all-enveloping dust. The carts are supplied from great wooden water-tanks two or three miles apart.

Down the narrow, winding shelf-road our horses went leaping at a sharp gallop. It is a thrilling ride; for, at many points, a divergence of six inches from the track would send the coach rolling from five hundred to a thousand feet down the mountain, into the foaming stream-bed of some yawning canyon. Here is the ideal of staging. For weeks afterward, one's blood bounds at the memory of its whirl and rush. Twenty-four on the coach, with six horses, galloping down the Sierra Nevadas, along a winding, narrow, dizzy road, at twelve miles an hour! It is swift as Sheridan's Ride and stirring as the Charge of the Six Hundred.

The track was half covered with great California freight wagons. One carries from six to ten tons, and is drawn by ten or twelve mules, each bearing on his saddle four tinkling bells. Very striking was the skill and coolness of our driver, as we rolled on our winding way, among these long teams and ponderous wagons. With perfect confidence and nicest calculation, he whirled us around sharp corners and through gaps between the freighters and the precipice, barely wide enough for our wheels. With him, driving long ago ceased to be an experimental accomplishment, and became one of the exact sciences.

We passed in sight of the peak immortalized by Fremont's bum-

DOWN THE SIERRA NEVADAS, IN 1865. Page 381

ble-bee; and rode along the foot of a granite wall, thirteen hundred feet high, so upright that from the summit one might have dropped an apple upon our heads. We dined at Straw-Berry station, which commemorates, not the fruit but, a pioneer named Berry, who used to sell straw for hay to the early Washoe pilgrims until they gave him the patronymic of 'Old Straw-Berry.'

Among the beauties and wonders which feasted our eyes, was one striking scene. Fifteen hundred feet below us glittered a silver-bright section of the American river. Hills clothed with pines and firs, and green with delicious grass, sloped down to it on all sides with perfect symmetry. It was the rarest little picture in a frame of unrivaled verdure.

Early in the evening we reached Placerville, having ridden seventy-two miles in seven hours, including all stoppages. How little we comprehend life's common beauties and blessings! In 1864 when I escaped from Salisbury, after twenty months spent in rebel prisons, every-day comforts, pure water, untainted air, clean clothing and wholesome food seemed the most extravagant of luxuries. So, after our long ride over mountain and desert, these pleasant valley-homes, with trees, and flowers and festooning vines were wondrously beautiful. The reception to Mr. Colfax seemed to come straight from the heart; and for my own part, like the comedian, never was I treated so well—nor so often.

Placerville, among the western foot-hills of the Sierras, is a pleasant town of three or four thousand inhabitants, which formerly had an immense trade in supplying the mines.

The next morning, a final ride of nine miles landed us at Shinkle Spring beside the enormous freight-depot of the Sacramento Valley and Placerville Railroad. After two thousand miles of stage-coaching, here was the locomotive again! From the bottom of my heart I felt like embracing or, at the very least, apostrophizing it.

In two hours the iron horse took us to Sacramento, the capital of the State. The first gold discoveries were made near Placerville; but almost simultaneously gold was found on the ranch of John A. Sutter, a Swiss gentleman who in 1839 had settled three miles from the present city of Sacramento. When Humboldt visited California in 1803, he predicted that precious metals would be found near the surface. But the first discoveries were made upon Sutter's claim in 1848. The news spread like wild-fire. Settlers poured in and destroyed Sutter's crops, stole his horses and killed his cattle. But their recklessness did not prevent him from exercising great kindness and humanity toward all the sick and suffering; and many a pioneer yet remembers him gratefully. He still resides upon his old claim—a large Mexican grant to which our Government has tardily confirmed his title.

Sacramento is at the head of tide-water on the Sacramento river, one hundred and twenty miles above the mouth. Its history is a chapter of moving accidents. Again and again it was destroyed by conflagration and submerged by freshets; and more than once schooners sailed through the principal streets. A friend assured me that one night, upon returning home in a boat, he found a cow in his drawing-room, and tied her to the hall banister, lest the flood should take her up stairs before morning. Levees now guard the city from overflow, and the grade is being changed to afford sure and permanent protection. The well-shaded city, though intensely hot in summer, is agreeable, and contains much wealth and culture. A cottonwood which had grown to a foot in diameter in seven years from the seed, was pointed out to us. We found one of the proprietors of the leading daily journal an old typo from the *Tribune* office.

The summit-line of the Sierras at the nearest point is seventy-five miles east of the town. But in winter the snow-capped mountains can be seen from the capital stretching two hundred miles from north to south.

After spending a few agreeable hours in Sacramento, we embarked on the steamer Crysopolis, much like the Long Island Sound boats, built in California, elegantly furnished, and two hundred and fifty feet in length. Here we lost sight of the snowy mountains, which had not been out of our view for many hours at once since we first saw them, fifteen hundred miles back, before reaching Denver. At midnight, we were looking out upon the great Pacific, listening to its low voice of infinite lamentation.

On the first day of July ended our journey across the continent. We were in San Francisco in season to witness the celebration of 'the Fourth.' It was very spontaneous and enthusiastic. All the thoroughfares were gay with flags, and Montgomery street, the Broadway of the city, was a deluge of tri-colored waves. An enormous arch was built across it, bearing the names of every State in the Union, and portraits of Washington and Lincoln recognizable a quarter of a mile away. There was a warm controversy about permitting negroes to join in the processsion, which at last resulted in the conclusion that as two hundred thousand of them had fought, and twenty-eight thousand died, in the military service of the republic, they had some vested rights in the national holiday. The prejudice against color, always incredibly strong in all the mining States and Territories, was now perceptibly ameliorating.

Soon after us arrived from New York the new steamer Colorado of the Pacific Mail Line, after a voyage of ninety days around the Horn. The steamers for the smooth Pacific are built so large and fragile, as to render even their single voyage down the Atlantic perilous. In making the trip they stop at a few ports on the east coast of South America, pass through the straits of Magellan with their magnificent scenery, and touch at two or three points on the Pacific side. Thirty excursion passengers came on the Colorado. One, Fred. Billings, a San Francisco pioneer, softened the asperities of the trip by bringing a new milch cow for the benefit of the morning coffee.

At Callao Peru, the party were hungry for home intelligence. They had not heard a word since leaving New York, when Grant was still fighting it out on that line. Mr. Billings asked the first Yankee he met on the plank:

'What is the news from the United States?'

Slowly removing his cigar, the stranger replied with genuine American nonchalance, reciting the stupendous events in a tone as monotonous as if reading a washing-list:

'Richmond is taken; Lee has capitulated; Johnston has surrendered; President Lincoln has been assassinated; and Jeff. Davis has been caught in his wife's petticoats!'

The listener stood speechless at the startling catalogue!

The sharp San Francisco winds from the sea proved unfavorable to a lingering lung-weakness, which clung to me in memory of Castle Thunder and Libby Prison. So I retreated to the interior, spending a few delightful days with friends in Placerville. Evening's quiet was broken only by the drowsy tinkling of cow-bells, and every morning the song of the oriole poured in at my open window. The oleander bloomed upon the porch, and the garden air was fragrant with rose and fuchsia, honeysuckle and heliotrope, nasturtium and sweet verbena. It was only the first week of July; but strawberries, (the second crop—the same vines produce four or

A GROUP OF CELESTIALS.

five times a year,) raspberries, blackberries, cherries, plums, apricots, figs, early peaches, pears, apples and grapes were abundant.

My friend's garden of one acre produced two tons of peaches, thirty barrels of apples, and grapes and berries whose name was legion. One peach was eighteen inches in circumference; and the trees bear in two years from the seed. Irrigation—two square inches of water running constantly—cost him thirty dollars for the season. Only ten years before he began to redeem his garden from the barrenness of a parched hill-side.

This is the rare charm of California: its unequaled capacity for fruit; its kindly soil, hiding the pleasant homes in rich trees, flowers and vines. Its towns and hamlets, quite free from the bare naked aspect common to new countries, look as if they had been settled for two generations. What other region thus combines tropical productions with a temperate climate? Where else grow fig, almond, olive, orange and pomegranate, side by side with pear, plum, peach, apple and cherry?

There are fifty thousand Chinese upon the Pacific coast, scattered through the large towns and mining regions. They are engaged in mining, gardening, horticulture, peddling fruit, fish and vegetables, and as nurses, waiters and cooks. They make nine-tenths of the cigars, do nearly all the laundry business, cultivate several great vineyards, are operatives in the woolen factories, and thousands are day laborers upon the Pacific railroad, swarming among the Sierras like flies upon a honeycomb. Some are heavy merchants, large importers of teas, silks, opium, sugar and rice, noted for correctness and fair-dealing. They settle all money disputes among themselves, never appealing to the courts. They have a novel bankruptcy practice. On the last day of the year, the Chinaman who is unable to meet his obligations pays the largest per centage he can, declaring his inability to do more. On New Year's morning his creditors forgive him, embrace him, and declare him 'free of the books.' Afterward, if able, he cancels the debt, from pride, not obligation.

On the lower coast, they are extensively engaged in fishing, shipping the product of their labors to San Francisco and China. As house-servants they are excellent. Every Celestial in the United States, according to his geographical origin, belongs to one of the six Chinese companies, whose head-quarters are in San Francisco. In sickness and health they exercise a paternal discipline over him. Persons desiring servants, procure them from one of these companies, who warrant them for twelve months; will replace them if they run away or prove unsatisfactory, and insure their conviction in the courts if they are guilty of crime. Filth and petty larcenies are the chief offenses to be charged against them. On the other hand, they are quiet, temperate, ingenious, frugal and industrious. They make sad work of speaking English; add double *e* to words; change *r* to *l* and *v* to *b*. 'Want washee?' asks John Chinaman. 'Washee shirtee bellee goodee. Only two bittee.' In a few large towns they have religious temples. Their chief deity is called 'Josh.' In a violent quarrel between a Chinaman and a Jew, the former wrathfully said:

'Oh, yesee; I knowee you—you killee Melican man's Josh!'

On our soil they take no root; bring few women save prostitutes; import from home their food, of which rice is the chief staple; send home their money; send home even their dead, embalmed, to rest in the family dwellings of their far, twilight land, nursery of the human race, where the Orient joins the Occident.

Industrious and frugal, serene and silent under heavy taxes and frequent kicks, poor John Chinaman puts money in his purse and revels in dirt and degradation. In the mines, gleaning only where the white man has reaped, at the year's end his is the larger 'pile.' When he finds a rich lead, by mysterious but invariable coincidence it belongs to some American—inexorable policeman, who bids Johnny 'Move on.' The divine right of numbers and of race is against him. Perfect in imitation, where female labor is scarce he proves unrivaled at nursing, cooking, washing and ironing. Babies intrusted to him he dandles with so much caution and tenderness, that all the maternal instinct must lurk somewhere: under his long pig-tail, in his yellow face, or moony eyes. My friend had a masculine domestic named Afoy, who scrubbed floors, washed dishes and cooked dinners with grave and deliberate fidelity. He characterized me as the 'Whong-ti,' which he averred to be the pure Celestial for 'Big man—heap big man!' I half suspect that he was a solemn wag and that literally it means: 'Humbug! Heap humbug!'

I went to look at hydraulic mining, near Placerville. 'Coon Hill,' originally a mound of many acres, bearing a settlement of five hundred houses, is almost washed away by the miners. A little, ragged section of earth, one hundred and twenty feet high—its brown dirt-walls broken by a stratum of yellowish marl—is all that remains of the hill, rock-ribbed and ancient as the sun. One workman stands at the top, directing a tiny rill which comes pouring over the edge, cutting the earth into perpendicular slices. The rest are at the bottom. Water is brought down to them through a cast-iron pipe from a neighboring summit. At the crest each stream is two feet square; at the bottom it passes through two pipes of three-inch hose. The condensation and the fall, of more than one hundred feet, give it tremendous force. These slender streams directed against the upright bank three hundred

HYDRAULIC MINING.

yards away, send vast clouds of earth and bowlders flying in all directions, bore into the compact gravel like huge augurs and penetrate narrowest crevices of the rock, soon loosening it and bringing it down in fragments twice as large as flour-barrels.

At the bottom, two laborers in India-rubber coats and leggings stand in water up to the thighs, clearing away the *debris*. The stream carries off the dirt and stones with great rapidity; but they toil with picks and crow-bars to assist the heaviest rocks into the flume. This is a wooden trough three feet in diameter, with sharp descent, where all the waters gather in a boiling, rushing torrent which washes away the earth and bowlders, while the sinking gold is caught by slats on the bottom. Once in the flume, a rock which almost fills it is borne along like a cork. With almost every stroke of the pick the laborers glance up uneasily at the quivering earth-wall, which sometimes tumbles unexpectedly, causing fatal accidents. When it is about to fall unobserved, the pipe-men whose position is farther away, shout: 'Look out!' and the workmen spring back, while great masses of earth and rock come crashing down. They labor in the water twelve hours daily for three dollars, boarding themselves. By day their clothing is never dry; yet they are said to remain healthy though prematurely old.

The force of the water is wonderful. One of these three-inch streams would extinguish a conflagration, dwelling and all, in the briefest period, knocking down a brick building like a child's cob-house. At ten feet from the nozzle it would cut through a man as if he were tissue paper; at forty feet it would crush him to a jelly. The proprietor assured me that with these three little pipes he could cut down and wash away a section of hill twenty feet long, twenty wide and two hundred high, in twelve hours. The water cost him thirty dollars per day. No gold is found for the first hundred feet below the surface, but between that depth and the bed-rock the dirt often proves very rich. Nearly five millions of dollars have been taken out in the vicinity since 1849.

It was a novel scene— the dirty cascade pouring down over the top, slicing the hill as with a knife; the glittering, gauzy streams darting to the earth-wall, raising a cloud of dirt like the smoke from a field-piece, and knocking out huge rocks, to fall and bound like foot-balls; the serene superintendent directing the whole; the men in the water with browned faces, long beards and pipes, glancing up nervously at the Damocles-wall; and the great hill melting to liquid and passing away through a wooden trough! It showed the miraculous power of water in changing the surface of the earth.

CHAPTER XXXIII.

On our west coast, the isothermal line bends abruptly northward. San Francisco, in the latitude of Richmond, has the climate of Savannah. Victoria, on Vancouver Island, far north of Quebec is as warm as New York. In Portland, Oregon, roses grow in open air throughout the year. Walla Walla, in Washington Territory, latitude forty-six degrees north, corresponds in temperature to Washington City, in thirty-nine; Clark's Fork, Idaho, in forty-eight, to St. Joseph, Missouri, in forty; Bitter Root Valley, Montana, in forty-six, to Philadelphia, in forty.

All points on the Pacific slope are as warm as those from six to ten degrees further south on the Atlantic side. This difference is sometimes imputed to the numberless hot springs among the head-waters of the Columbia—indeed, everywhere from the Rocky Mountains to the Pacific. But the more prevalent theory refers it to a current of warm water and air from the Indian ocean, striking the coast at an acute angle, near San Francisco, and thence flowing northward. The Coast Range and Cascade mountains arrest and condense the clouds, causing the winters of western Oregon, in which the sun seldom shines on the evil or on the good, and the rain steadily falls both upon the just and the unjust. Satirical Californians call their northern neighbors 'Web-feet.'

The stage route from Oroville, (railroad terminus seventy miles north of Sacramento,) to Portland, Oregon, is six hundred and forty-two miles long. In summer the trip consumes less than a week. In winter, stage-travelers pay their fares for the privilege of being jolted in mud-wagons, or dislocated on horseback, or mired on foot. Then the trip seems interminable, and there are rumors of passengers who have died of old age upon the road.

But starting on the thirteenth of July we found the summer journey speedy and agreeable. At Grass Valley, in addition to the warm reception accorded him, the programme required Mr. Colfax to kiss a bevy of eight or ten bright-eyed young ladies. He gave the greeting with that zeal and resignation which he brings to all the duties and cares of public life.

Near Marysville we passed the little village of Yuba Dam, the scene of an early California story, which *Harper's Monthly* first made public. It avers that on a quiet Sunday morning a traveler reached the three little houses which comprise the town.

'My friend,' he asked of a citizen, 'what village is this?'

'Yuby Dam.'

The stranger, shocked at such impoliteness and profanity, put spurs to his horse. At the door of the next cabin stood a decent housewife, broom in hand. He repeated the inquiry:

'Madam will you please tell me the name of this village?'

'Yuby Dam.'

Still more scandalized, the interrogator rode on until he met a little boy playing in the street. Here at least he might obtain a proper answer:

'My son, what is this place called?'

'Yuby Dam!'

'Heavens!' exclaimed the astounded stranger as he galloped out of the town. 'What a place is this, where even the women and children swear—and on Sunday too!'

At Chico we encountered General John Bidwell, Congressional representative from northern California. He resided here upon his ranch of twenty-thousand acres long before the country was settled by Americans, and is still one of the most extensive farmers in the United States.

The enormous corn, green meadows, and great fields of stubble with barley stacks and wheat sheaves began to wear the parched, fading look of the rainless months. We passed the grave of a rich citizen, buried upon his own farm, whose monument bears the inscription, written by himself:

'Thomas M. Wright, lived and died an atheist, fearing no hell, hoping for no heaven--a friend and advocate of mental liberty.'

At midnight we passed through the little town of Red Bluffs, Tehama (lowlands), county, head of navigation on the Sacramento river. Here lives the widow of old John Brown, wholly dependent upon her own labor. Her daughters teach in the public schools, while she ministers as nurse and physician among neighboring families, by whom she is greatly loved.

MOUNT SHASTA CALIFORNIA, FROM SHASTA VALLEY.

This sparsely-settled mountain region abounds in tall pines, with long hairy strands of brown Spanish moss pendent from their boughs, and straggling white-oaks festooned with misletoe of vivid green, yellowing as death approaches. This parasite, absorbing the sap of the tree, soon kills it, and then itself perishes.

Eighty miles to the east of our road, Shasta, one of the highest California peaks, northern monarch of the Sierra Nevadas, rears its broken crest fourteen thousand feet above sea-level. Its summit, reached with difficulty, commands a grand, inspiring view. Among its eternal snows gushes a boiling-hot sulphur spring. Shasta is an isolated, extinct volcano—a mountain of dazzling white, beyond green, wooded valleys and the purple hills of the horizon. It is about one thousand feet higher than Pike's Peak and more impressive, because the contrasting vegetation is warmer and richer.

The hills abound in glossy evergreen oaks, whose long branches droop to the ground. The exquisite mountain lily, of bluish white, with stems three or four feet high and blossoms somewhat like those of the peerless water lily, also enriches the landscape.

Yreka, the northern settlement of California, is a mountain town thirty-five hundred feet above the sea. It is the site of considerable placer mining. The city and the gold-diggers are supplied with water by a canal one hundred miles long. The name—pronounced '*Wy*-reka'—is derived from a tribe of Indians. Here a pioneer baker placed over his door the sign: 'Yreka Bakery;' and puzzled strangers were often invited to try the experiment of spelling the two words backward.

Crossing a little stream of the Siskiyou mountains, three hundred miles north of Sacramento, we were in Oregon. From the summit, five thousand five hundred feet above the sea, we saw Pilot Mountain, named by Fremont, and crowned by an enormous granite bowlder, apparently a mile in diameter. Descending, we found a changed vegetation, new wild flowers, and abundance of oak, maple and madrona or mountain laurel. The latter is an evergreen of rarest beauty, sometimes seventy feet high, with vivid, shining leaves and bark which deadens and drops off yearly, leaving smooth stem and branches of delicate pale red.

In general, southern Oregon is little inhabited, and its sterile mountains are densely timbered. But our road threads lovely valleys of tall timothy and golden wheat, among dazzling white farm-houses, their porches and verandas shaded with locusts and willows and flanked by immense barns for the long winters; young orchards heavy with ripening plums and pears, apples and peaches; clear rills which pour down the hill-sides to the settlers' doors; log school-houses, 'Where young Ambition climbs his little ladder, and boyish Genius plumes his half-fledged wings.'

In passing from one to another of these narrow valleys, we cross abrupt wooded mountains and go through placer gold-diggings. The gold mines of the young State have already contributed more than twelve millions of dollars to the treasury of the world. But our richest mineral yields in the Northwest are likely to come from the *silver* of Oregon and Idaho. Treasure to the amount of two million dollars per month sometimes passes down the Columbia from these newly-opened regions. It has been well suggested that, as the entrance to San Francisco bay is called the Golden Gate, the mouth of the Columbia should be named the Silver Gate.

At one dwelling an infant grizzly bear, aged ten weeks and weighing two hundred and fifty pounds, is tied to a stake. Checking him with a cart-whip when *too* playful, the owner frolics fearlessly with young Bruin. When Lola Montez resided in California she also kept a grizzly as a household pet.

At Jacksonville, Jackson county, we learn that a fortunate miner has taken out two hundred and eight dollars within the last twenty-four hours. The placer diggings of the county yield fifty thousand dollars monthly.

At Rocky Point we cross Rogue river upon an excellent toll-bridge. A rival bridge-owner, three miles below, made *his* structure free; and for a time took all the travel. But this original Jacob bought the land on Evans creek, six miles to the eastward and running parallel with the river, at its only fordable point; fenced up the ford and then bridged the creek, charging toll there for *both* streams. Discomfited by the shrewd maneuver, the rival retired from the contest. Some of the noble fir trees are one hundred and fifty feet high and three feet in diameter.

There are many local histories and traditions. For a number of years, Ulysses S. Grant, then a captain in the army, was stationed in Oregon. The pioneers give interesting reminiscences of him. His life was commonplace and unnoticeable. He was a reticent, undemonstrative, unambitious officer, habitually addicted to conviviality. How strange are the vagaries of destiny! How few men find the one place and opportunity for showing their highest capacity! But for the great rebellion, Grant had lived and died only to be remembered as an ordinary, silent, honest, infantry captain, of moderate abilities. But for the national contest about the extension of slavery, Abraham Lincoln had been known only as a country lawyer, with unusual capacity for convincing juries, and telling droll, 'pat' stories.

The Pacific coast is the school from which our best officers graduated. Here Sherman lived for years. Here Jo Hooker, when a captain, constructed a military road over which our coach rolls to-day. It passes Leland post-office, Josephine county, on

Grave creek—all commemorating Josephine Leland, a beautiful girl, who died of fever, and whose body Indians disinterred and mutilated. Seven of the savage criminals were afterward killed and buried near the outraged grave.

Another stream is called 'Jump-off-Jo creek.' During the Indian war of 1854, General Jo Lane was pursued by a red foe in a ride for life; when his men shouting, 'Jump off, Jo!' he obeyed, and was saved.

We pass 'Six-bit ranch,' perpetuating the eccentricity of an old settler. Like Mrs. John Gilpin, though on pleasure he was bent, he had a frugal mind. Just as an Indian was about to be hanged for murder, he mounted the scaffold and dunned the doomed man for six bits (seventy-five cents.)

At the next dining station we found the *Tribune*, *Independent*, and *Atlantic Monthly*, upon our host's parlor table, and of course intelligent, agreeable society in his household.

In Douglas county, self-invited guests, we breakfasted with Jesse Applegate, a thoroughly original and entertaining pioneer—a man of genius, too proud to practice the politician's arts, and therefore in private life. He came here in 1843, and was most influential in shaping the political character of Oregon. He asserts that the *Tribune*, which, before the overland telegraph, circulated here more widely than any other journal, home or distant, saved the State to freedom and to loyalty. Upon his farm and the adjacent ones of his children, embracing three thousand acres, Mr. Applegate sustains one hundred cattle and one thousand sheep. He has sold eight thousand dollars worth of beeves in a single year. His rick contains one hundred and twenty tons of hay, already kept three years for his sheep, through winters so mild as not to require it.

At last we descended from the summit of the Calapooya mountains into the great Wallamet * valley, fifty miles by one hundred—the garden of Oregon, and containing half of its entire population. To one coming from dreary Nevada deserts, or California fields dull and withered in the rainless months,

* Often improperly spelled Willamette. It is an Indian word of the same class with Walla Walla. The 'a' is broad and the accent upon the first syllable.

very delightful are its deep forests, rich meadows and groves of drooping oaks—its pleasant homes, embowered in green—its bright, flowing river darkened with slender pines. Excepting possibly the Indian Territory south of Kansas, it is the richest farming region of the United States; though the fathomless mud and endless rain of the winters are serious drawbacks. The Rogue river valley, though smaller, is nearly as fruitful.

Oregon is prolific in grain, grass, fruit and timber. As in all new countries, the bountifulness of Nature is most strikingly exhibited in human life. Old communities are full, and children comparatively rare. New countries must be peopled, and children abound. About the log houses everywhere on our frontier, from six to a dozen white-headed babies attest the fact. Oregon is specially blest. A Marion county lady at sixty years of age, became the mother of an infant. Another had two children born within ten months.

The former United States law regulating public lands in this State, gave three hundred and twenty acres to an unmarried settler, and six hundred and forty to him who had a wife. As the young Territory had five times more men than women, girls married very young; and some became mothers at thirteen and fourteen.

Salem, the pleasant capital of the State, is a village of two thousand people, on the Wallamet. Here we take a little steamer for Oregon City, where we debark to ride a mile upon a wooden railroad, past broken picturesque falls, with eternal clouds of mist winding across the broad river. The silvery water contrasts impressively with the deep gloom of environing rocks and somber hills. Near the falls is a great brick woolen factory, the fourth in the State.

Below the cascade, a second steamer waits to bear us a few miles further, to Portland, the metropolis of Oregon. Many attempts have been made to found a city at the mouth of the Columbia, which seemed the natural point for a commercial center. But those mysterious laws which determine the sites of cities, vetoed the resolution and established the coming town on the Wallamet, twelve miles above its junction with the Columbia and a hundred and thirty above the Columbia's mouth.

We found Portland a pleasant, straggling, growing city of five thousand people, on the smooth, glassy transparent river, broken just above by a mid-channel island, of vivid, drooping foliage. The town is inclosed on the three land sides by an amphitheater of symmetric hills, covered with tall, dark pines. At the great wharves were river steamboats, sailing vessels from San Francisco, Sandwich Islands, China and the Atlantic coast; and ocean steamers which ply to Vancouver Island and to San Francisco. On the lower business streets, ample brick blocks; above, graceful churches, school-houses and spacious frame dwellings, scattering into an irregular fringe of little cottages and rough cabins far up among hill-side stumps.

PORTLAND OREGON, ON THE FOURTH OF JULY, 1865.

The largest and most enthusiastic concourse of citizens we had seen since leaving New York was waiting to receive Mr. Colfax. The Stars and Stripes everywhere flying; streets filled with busy, intelligent faces; fine horses with light carriages trotting up the macadamized road along the river toward a delightful suburban resort known as the White House. Driving is *the* pastime of the Pacific coast, and horse-flesh its ruling passion.

Portland has a heavy trade, and is full of thrift and enterprise. It was founded in 1845, by two wandering Yankees, Prettigrow from Portland, and Lovejoy from Boston. Each desired to give it the name of his birthplace; and they finally decided the vexed question by tossing up the only coin in their possession—a rusty copper. Heads won; wherefore the metropolis of the North Pacific is Portland, not Boston! Having no great city within seven hundred miles, it is the grand supply-point for Oregon Washington and Idaho. Just before our arrival, a corner lot fifty feet by a hundred, sold for twenty-thousand dollars, gold.

With a party of Portlanders, we made an excursion up the Columbia, starting upon the fine steamer New World. She used to run upon the Hudson; but through debt and ill-luck fell into the clutches of the New York sheriff. Her captain, having secretly provisioned her for a long voyage, seduced that functionary into a little ride down the harbor; carried him beyond his own jurisdiction; and then offered him the option of going ashore or a free passage to California. The outwitted sheriff landed; but the New World continued around the Horn, to the hopeless bereavement of her creditors.

Old geographers called this stream Oregon--'the river of the west;' and the great State still fittingly bears that earlier and better name. The Columbia is six miles wide at its mouth, and one mile wide a hundred miles above.

Clear, blue, glassy, dotted with little islands of greenest foliage, and broken by dangerous rapids which make steamers shake like rocking-chairs, the Columbia is unrivaled upon our continent, in grandeur and magnitude. The Hudson no more compares with it than does the Arkansas with the Hudson.

Beside it rise grand abrupt mountains, deeply wooded with firs, crowned with stupendous rocks, carpeted by yellow moss, girdled with strands of snowy cloud, and streaked with water-falls of perfect whiteness.

Cape Horn is a columnar wall of basaltic stone, at some points seven hundred feet in hight—the Palisades on a larger scale. Over many vast upright rocks little falls take bold leaps, dissolving into spray before reaching the bottom. Where the steep bank of velvet grass and pine-crowned rocks is one-third of a mile high, Horse-tail Fall, softened by delicate mist, hangs like an exquisite strand of snowy hair, broken only once in a descent of three hundred and sixty feet, 'a strip of silver in a fringe of green.' Castle Rock, a solitary basaltic dome surrounded by water and quite isolated from the shore, rises grand and gloomy for eight hundred feet. Tall pines find root among its imperceptible fissures and on its bare summit.

Here we reach the Lower Cascades, impassable for boats, and take a steam railway along the rugged bank for five miles.

Our train passes a little log block house where in 1856 Indians beseiged a party of white men for two days. They were finally routed in a dashing charge by a modest young lieutenant of the United States army, whose name was Phil. Sheridan. At the outbreak of the rebellion he confidentially assured a friend of his determination to win a captain's commission or die in the attempt!

SHERIDAN'S FIRST BATTLE-GROUND, COLUMBIA RIVER, OREGON.

Lincoln thought it would fill the measure of his wildest ambition to be made vice-president! Grant only aspired to the city council of Galena, that he might have a new sidewalk from the depot! Sheridan merely hoped to become captain of a company!

> 'How little do we know of what we are,
> How less, of what we may be!'

After leaving the railway we took the new steamer Onconta, built on the ground, and elegantly furnished. She is two hundred feet long, and cost eighty thousand dollars. Upon her we steamed up the current for five hours, to the flourishing town of Dalles, the third in the State, containing twenty-five hundred inhabitants.

Here are the second impassable rapids, and the second railroad of fourteen miles, built at heavy expense, and accompanied by a telegraph wire. Here for ten miles are the Dalles (flag-stones) of the Columbia, worthy of the prominence given them by Washington Irving, Lewis and Clark, and other early writers, as the most noteworthy feature of all this curious region. The river, above and below so broad and glassy, is here of fathomless depth, compressed into one-tenth its usual limits; and even this narrow stream is broken by scores of dark-brown rocks. Boiling, swelling and hissing, the torrent rushes through its close, tortuous confines, lashing the smooth rocks in foamy passion—a river of eddies and troughs, whirlpools and shooting rockets of water, beating out its life against prison walls. On the bank, immense drifts of sand, white as snow, prove most serious obstructions to the locomotive.

On the flat shore-rocks are the bark lodges of Wascopin Indians; naked children, with stomachs distended like bladders, rolling and running in the sand; filthy, repulsive women, who seem hardly members of the human race, bearing bundles of faggots upon their heads; and men at the water's edge, spearing savory salmon, often weighing twenty-five pounds each. On the south in full view towers Mount Hood, the grandest peak on our continent.

It is believed that the great basin of the Upper Columbia, containing four hundred thousand square miles, was once a vast inland sea, broken only by a few islands which are now mountain peaks. If this theory be true, what resistless floods must have burst through the mountain-wall and rolled on to the mighty ocean!

The railway taking us past the rapids leaves us at Celilo, a village of a dozen dwellings. On the river bank is the largest warehouse in the United States, over eleven hundred feet long, built to receive the heavy Idaho freights.

Here we embark on the Owyhee* another new steamer built above these rapids. It is one hundred and twenty feet long, and cost thirty-two thousand dollars.

After a brief rest upon the steamer, Messrs. Colfax and Bross

---

* So called from one of the richest mining districts of the United States, in Idaho, which originally derived the mellow name from a Sandwich Island.

with the Portland friends who accompanied us, returned to Dalles to address the assembled citizens on public affairs. Mr. Bowles and myself, wearied with the excitement of travel, spent a quiet evening upon the little 'Owyhee' in company with Messrs. Deady and Read of Portland. Just after we had gone to bed, the locomotive whistle announced the return of the company.

A MIDNIGHT RECEPTION TO SPEAKER COLFAX.

As Mr. Colfax, through the entire journey had been greeted with flags and speeches, banquets and brass bands on every conceivable and inconceivable occasion, one of our quartette instantly suggested that he should enjoy the novelty of a reception from his own comrades. Enveloping ourselves in sheets, we stepped into the dimly-lighted cabin and waited for the arriving orators and listeners. They soon came on board, Mr. Colfax, fortunately, at their head. Reaching our end of the saloon, he was a good deal startled by four white, sepulchral figures. Like the Ancient Mariner, almost he dreamed that he had died and was a blessed ghost. Apparently here was a committee of shades about to give him the last reception. One of the airy effigies stepping forward, immediately began a speech of welcome which at first bewildered and surprised the new-comers, but before its close, excited their uproarious laughter. The speaker of the House promptly recovered himself; and the moment it was ended, made a neat and graceful reply, abounding in happy hits at the friends who welcomed him. Mr. Colfax has been the victim of more speeches than any other public man in the nation; but he never assisted at any ceremony so unique and memorable as this midnight reception among the forests of the Columbia.

The next morning the Owyhee steamed on. Thus far we have sailed up a stream with deep forests of pines, firs and cedars—with no branches on the side next to the prevailing winds—covering the hills and cliffs. Here is classic ground here:

> 'The continuous woods,
> Where rolls the Oregon, and hears no sound
> Save its own dashings.'

But Bryant sang of a past era. Now a tide of commerce and immigration pours through this remote solitude; and the surprised traveler finds railway carriages and steamers, with the same luxury and elegance he is wont to enjoy between Boston and New York.

Above the Dalles the woods disappear; the banks are smooth, hills of velvet grass, without leaf or shrub in the whole range of vision. The entire country, watered by the upper Columbia, embracing eastern Oregon, Washington, Idaho, and a portion of Montana, looks a dreary desert; but its grasses are rich and nutritive.

Our trip ended at Wright's Harbor, one hundred and fifty miles above Portland. Steamers run nearly three hundred miles higher to impassable rapids; and even above them a little boat plies on the Snake river, in Idaho. But Umatilla is the head of sure navigation on the Columbia. It might be connected with the head of navigation on the Missouri, by railroad of about six hundred miles. Already a short route from Oregon to Montana has been opened via the Pen d'Oreille lake and river, upon which small steamers are plying.

Here should pass a northern Pacific railroad. The great cereal interests of our Northwest, the copper and iron resources of Lake

Superior, the lumber forests of Minnesota, the incalculably rich gold and silver mines of Montana and Idaho, and the vast lumber, fishing, and mineral interests of Oregon and Washington imperatively require steam communication with both oceans. A northern railway line should be inaugurated without delay.

Two 'little stories' shall close this rambling chapter. A sarcastic resident was rallying one of my traveling companions on his inability to drink buttermilk, declaring that no man can be quite civilized who does not relish that beverage. Mr. B. quietly answered him:

'In my section we give the buttermilk to our pigs!'

At an Oregon farm-house, early one morning, we tapped for admission. The door was opened by a girl of fifteen, of whom our spokesman asked:

'Is your father here?'

'No sir; he is mowing in the field.'

'Very well; we will go out to find him and then return and breakfast with you.'

At this unexpected proposition, which was followed by our names, the damsel opened wide her two astonished eyes; but in a moment recovering herself, cheerfully acquiesced in the arrangement. Two hours later, after the morning meal and a delightful visit, as Mr. Colfax shook hands with her at parting, he said:

'You were a good deal surprised at our inviting ourselves to breakfast, were you not?'

'O, no sir. I was surprised; but not at that.'

'What then?'

'At hearing your name.' (Very earnestly.) 'It is not often that we see a great man in this country!'

CHAPTER XXXIV.

WHEN we acquired Oregon it extended north to British Columbia. But the upper half, through its lumber and fishing interests, and its own outlet to the sea—quite distinct from the farming and mineral regions of the lower—was cut off and made a separate Territory. Its resources prove far richer than they promised. And Russian America, added to our area by that absorption which must ultimately give us the entire continent, will likewise better expectation. American skill and enterprise will develop it; American patriotism should name it. One man is commemorated by an infant State; one other ought to be. We have the Territory of Washington; let us have the Territory of Lincoln.

The first settlers of Oregon crossed the continent through the South Pass, in 1839, nine years before the gold discoveries in California. They were stimulated by the richness and beauty of Wallamet valley, whose fame had penetrated even to Missouri and Ohio; and by our national tendency to go to the farthest place. They were not equal in intelligence to the pioneers of California or of Kansas; but their history affords striking examples of the capacity for self-government among our 'plain people,'—of that ingrained respect for law and order and decisions of the majority, which forms the 'bed-rock' of American stability and greatness.

In early days, the miners of Jacksonville elected an alcalde. A party to a contested claim case, thinking himself wronged, posted this notice: 'Whereas, the alcalde has given an unjust and corrupt decision against me, on Sunday next I shall take an appeal to the supreme court.' Sunday saw a hundred miners convened, from curiosity to learn what the supreme court was. They themselves were that august tribunal! The aggrieved party organized them into a mass meeting; they re-tried the case and rendered a verdict reversing the alcalde's decision. All acquiesced in this assize of original and final jurisdiction.

In that remote region, then as far from civilization as the Nile, the pioneers found themselves surrounded by hostile Indians, with no law for the protection of life and property, and no hope of aid from without. The squatters met the emergency by establishing a provisional government, which ruled Oregon for eight years. Unrecognized by the United States, without any technical legality, they framed a constitution, elected legislators, organized courts, imposed and collected taxes, coined money, carried on war and made peace with the Indians, until 1849, when Congress gave to the precocious sister a Territorial organization. The French have always claimed to be 'the Great Nation;' but I think we may contest the title with them.

A few specimens of the early money, the 'beaver coin,' are still in existence. The little specie brought from the States was inadequate for the business of the young community; and in the absence of money, wheat circulated, a cumbersome legal tender, at one dollar per bushel. In this extremity, dies were prepared by a blacksmith, and the five-dollar coin made of gold dug from the surrounding mountains. It bore the effigy of a beaver, and was worth its face at the United States mints.

At the mouth of the Columbia, Indians still exhibit medals left in 1805 by Lewis and Clark, on their exploring tour. It is claimed that the Spaniards were the original discoverers of the great river. The first American knowledge of it was through Captain Robert Gray of Boston, who entered the mouth of the unknown, beautiful stream in 1792, and named it from his ship, *Columbia Rediviva*, the first keel which had ever cut its waters. He sailed up eighteen miles; and coming down, met Vancouver the British explorer, who had ascended one hundred miles from the mouth to the present town bearing his name.

Then as now, the mouth of the stream was the terror of navigators. Gray was nine days in crossing its dangerous bar. In 1811, the Tonquin, one of John Jacob Astor's fur ships commanded by Captain Thorn, lost eight men endeavoring to pass the bar in boats, to reach the site they had selected for Astoria.

Afterward, at Vancouver Island, the imprudence of Thorn angered a party of Indians who visited the Tonquin to sell furs. In the ensuing fierce conflict, the savages killed every man on board except Lewis the ship's clerk, an Indian interpreter, and five sailors who hid in the cabin. After the Indians had left, the four men escaped to the shore; but were all caught and massacred. Lewis and the interpreter remained on the vessel and wreaked a vengeance worthy of classic ages. They decoyed the Indians back again, and while the deck swarmed with savages, fired the magazine! The ship was blown to atoms; Lewis and more than a hundred natives perished; but the interpreter was thrown into the water unhurt—an almost miraculous escape.

The earliest white settlers were the Hudson Bay Company, and Nathaniel Wyeth's two overland expeditions from Massachusetts in 1832-3. The Indians still call every American 'a Boston,' and all English 'King George's men.'

Fort Vancouver was the British company's post. Every June one of their ships arrived with a year's supply of goods; took away the year's accumulation of wheat to Sitka, selling it to the Russian government for furs; carried the furs to China, and exchanged them for teas and silks; transported these to London; and then bringing another supply of goods around the Horn, again reached Vancouver in June. Thus began the commerce of our western coast which, still in its infancy, whitens every sea.

Pioneers gave glowing accounts of the striking scenery of the Rocky Mountains, the beauty of Columbia river, the grandeur of the Sierra Nevadas and the isolated peaks of the Northwest; but they did not attain wide celebrity until very lately. The warm coloring of Albert Bierstadt found ample room in the rich hues of the Pacific coast, and his bold, free pencil, verge enough in the stupendous mountains of Colorado, Yosemite valley and Oregon. Many brother artists following in his train, have worthily continued the work which he most worthily began. But these regions are so vast and their scenes of wonder and beauty so many, that generations must pass before the American people will have any adequate conception of the great features of their own country.

The resources of Oregon are rich and varied. Its yield of the precious metals is already very heavy. The Santiam gold mines, a few miles from Salem, seem to equal even the rich lodes of Idaho. Abundant deposits of iron are found within fifteen miles of Portland. Some specimens assay sixty per cent. pure metal. Wood and coal are plentiful; and doubtless works will soon be erected for the reduction of the ore. The Pacific coast uses seventy tons of iron daily; but imports it all from the Atlantic coast, save the supply for Vancouver Island which comes from Scotland. There are ten large foundries in San Francisco and one in Portland, which turn out every machine, from apothecaries' mortars of one stamp, to quartz mills of a hundred stamps (the mortar upon a large scale, its huge pestles pounding by steam,) from the hand pump to the first-class locomotive.

ALBERT BIERSTADT.

In addition to iron and gold, the State produces silver, copper, lead and marble; and exports wool, lumber, fish and fruit. Sheep-raising is the most lucrative pursuit. The lumber resources are varied and boundless. Redwood—a species of cedar, often twelve feet in diameter—makes the best boards, which, in seasoning, shrink only lengthwise. The water-power is unsurpassed in the world. The apple grows in profusion. Essentially a northern fruit, its flavor here is far more pungent than in California. Oregon cider is famous on the entire Pacific slope, and much is shipped around the Horn, to New York and Boston. Champagne is a great beverage of the west coast; but Mr. Colfax, a total abstinent from boyhood and an old worker in the temperance cause, would indulge in nothing more ardent than native cider. His long Washington career had not even familiarized him with the taste of wine. One evening in a San Francisco drawing-room, he was conversing earnestly with a gentleman beside him, when our host carefully removed the paper from a bottle of sparkling Moselle and neatly substituted the label: 'Oregon Cider.' Then opening the bottle with considerable display, he poured a full goblet and invited the speaker to partake of his favorite beverage. Mr. Colfax sipped it with evident relish during his colloquy; and at last discovering that it was all gone, asked:

'Mr. M. will you give me another glass of that Oregon cider? Its flavor is excellent.'

Grapes, peaches, plums, nectarines, apricots and strawberries grow in the Oregon valleys. Fruit trees, two years old, are twice as large as in New York and Ohio; and the average yield of wheat to the acre is fifty per cent. greater. Not more than one-tenth of the rich Wallamet valley is yet under cultivation. The best improved lands command eight to sixteen dollars per acre; unimproved, one dollar and twenty cents to five dollars.

One of the earliest newspapers in Oregon was printed from wooden types cut out by hand. The State has now three dailies. The *Oregonian*, the oldest journal, is edited by a gentleman who graduated at the Oregon University. It is full of suggestiveness to remember that a generation has matured on this far-off coast—to find leaders of public opinion born, reared and educated on the soil—to hear young men and women who have resided from infancy in what nine-tenths of our people regard a wilderness, discuss appreciatively and critically Emerson and Herbert Spencer, Thackeray and Tennyson, Whittier and Gail Hamilton.

Some Californians grow satirical upon their 'Web-foot' neighbors, jesting at their lack of enterprise, and averring that the wet climate has made them aquatic. The Oregonians retort that if slow, they are solvent; that it is better to be cautious than to go beyond one's means. Dr. Bellows noted the use of brown sugar in their tea. They pithily replied that their sugar was paid for, and that he could not accuse them, as he did the Californians, of borrowing money at three per cent. a month to buy champagne with!

At one stage station in a beautiful valley, I encountered two girls of sixteen and eighteen, with comely faces and neat attire. I asked one when her parents came to Oregon? She replied that it was before she could remember. What State did they come from? She had forgotten that also, if she ever knew; and her sister was equally ignorant. They probably hailed from Missouri, and were by no means fair specimens of Oregon intelligence.

Leaving Portland, we steamed down the clear Wallamet for

twelve miles; down the blue Columbia for thirty-eight; up the muddy Cowlitz for two; and landed at Monticello in Washington Territory. Thence to Olympia, ninety miles, an open stage-wagon carried us over the worst roads and among the grandest woods in the world. It also demonstrated how fifteen passengers can be transported in a vehicle which holds only nine—viz.: by putting six of them on horseback.

This is the forest primeval; thick with slender fir, pine, hemlock, spruce, cedar and arbor vitæ; the trunks gloved in moss of orange green, and branches tufted with long, swaying, hair-like strands of brown Spanish moss; the ground white, yellow and purple with luxuriant flowers. We passed one or two rough villages; and farm-houses five or ten miles apart, in little grassy openings—islands of prairie in the vast, somber, silent sea of woods. Thousands of firs not more than eighteen inches in diameter at the base, yet rise like masts two hundred and fifty feet. Judge Hewet cut one upon his own farm which measured three hundred and twenty-five feet in length. For miles the telegraph wire is supported by trees alone, and not a pole is seen.

On the second evening we passed through the picturesque little manufacturing hamlet of Tumwater, (falling water,) and half an hour later our wagon ride of two days ended at Olympia.

The Indians of Washington are fish-eating tribes, with little intelligence, though the patient efforts of missionaries—especially Jesuits—have shown them capable of great improvement. They often gather on the shore of the beautiful sound, beside some quiet cove and hard by the dwelling of a pioneer, in their favorite pursuit of gambling. They sit in groups, intently pursuing their *Mamook-to-lo*—literally: 'to make, to bet;' but their general term for gambling of every description.

They have no objection to winning from each other, though they commonly select a champion to play against the representative of some neighboring tribe. Then comes their Derby-day. They often bet every article they possess—money, guns, blankets, and even the shirts upon their backs—when the loser goes sadly home in a state of nature, as wild in woods the noble savage ran. They call the game *sla-hal.* Each player alternately shuffles ten wooden disks. Then his adversary must guess which hand contains the one disk that is specially marked. Naming the right one, he wins a disk; if the wrong one, he loses. The one first gaining the whole ten, wins the game.

Washington Territory with twenty thousand people, has no daily newspaper. Olympia, the seat of government at the most

MOUNT RAINIER, FROM PUGET SOUND.

southern elbow of Puget sound, contains six hundred people in winter, and perhaps half as many in summer. It is a settlement *sui generis*, struggling hard against primeval Nature and Aboriginal man. Thus far the advantage is rather with the forest and the Indian; but Civilization is treading sharply on the heels of Barbarism, and jostling it rudely aside.

It is a quaint village among logs and stumps, and traversed by plank sidewalks erected upon stilts to avoid mud and deluge. The arterial street begins on the level shore of the smooth shining sound, climbs a low muddy hill, and plunges out of sight in the deep pine woods. The capitol is a lonely white frame building, like a warehouse; but we found the national flag floating from it, and from nearly all the little neat cottages which constitute the better dwellings.

Acting-Governor Elwood Evans, with other leading citizens, received Mr. Colfax; and the rude throat of an old field-piece did hoarsely counterfeit the dread thunders of immortal Jove to give him welcome.

Olympia boasts two hotels. Quarters were assigned us at the Pacific, kept by a peculiarly intelligent negro woman. Her husband managed the kitchen; but she superintended the establishment, conducted its finances, and put money in the family purse.

In the evening I strolled through the streets, among Aborigines and whites. From great piles of lumber on the long wharf, I saw four Indian women embark in a light canoe, weighing it down to the water's edge, and paddle away, gliding noiselessly over the unbroken wave which reflected the violet and gold of the twilight skies. At last their weird forms and stolid faces were hidden by the deep shadows of the opposite shore. What can life mean to them? What are their joys and sorrows, their fears, hopes and ambitions?

After dark, nearly the entire population—men, women, children and Indians—were addressed by Messrs. Colfax and Bross. I never realized the magnitude of our Union, until in this remotest wilderness, forty-four hundred miles from home, I found not only the same language, and the same currency; but the same flag, and, vibrating from every extremity of the vast continent, the same hopes, sympathies and undying memories. And when at this strange gathering in the primeval forest I saw many eyes grow wet at mention of our martyred President, and heard every voice thrill in cheers for our redeemed republic, my heart swelled with pride and hope for the swarming, potential America of the future. May its name be omnipotent to the weary and troubled of every zone! May its flag betoken to the nations, Stability and Progress, Liberty and Law, Opportunity for the lowliest, and Justice pure and exact unto all men!

From Olympia we took a steamer upon Puget sound, the loveliest body of water in the western hemisphere. Hundreds of islands dot the shining surface, while its clear depths are almost as transparent as air. Spreading in a great complicated net-work of arms, straits and inlets, it has fourteen hundred miles of navigation, and affords to Washington more harbors than are possessed by any other region of equal area in the world. It is surrounded by a vast wilderness. Indeed Washington is the lumber-man's paradise—not because it is a Future State but from its unequaled forests.

The lumber-trade of Puget sound exceeds a million dollars annually. Every town upon the coast contains immense saw-mills. We glanced through one, upward of three hundred feet long, which turns out over a hundred thousand feet daily. Spars and other ship timbers, superior to those of any foreign country, are furnished to the entire Pacific coast, the Sandwich Islands, Japan, China, Australia, England and France. The Puget sound fir has superseded

——'The tallest pine
Hewn on Norwegian hills to be the mast
Of some great Admiral.'

The fish interests of the sound and its heavy coal trade from Bellingham Bay, added to its lumber resources, make it the most important possession of the North Pacific.

Nearly all day we were in sight of Mount Rainier, triple-pointed and robed in snow. Baker, Adams and St. Helen's are all striking. Shasta is grand, Hood is grander; but from this stand-point, Rainier, whose summit has never been trodden by man, is monarch of all, the Mont Blanc of the Pacific coast.

The author of 'the Seasons' was indignant at the thought that one could write an epic poem who had never seen a mountain. These grand peaks tell at a glance why the ancients placed the abode of the immortal gods on the snow-crowned mountains of Thessaly. Indeed one is fittingly named Olympus.

Our boat touched at Steilacoom, Port Ludlow, Seattle, Port Angelos and Port Gamble. The last-named gave one hundred and thirty-eight votes for Lincoln and not one for McClellan; and during the war contributed more proportionately to the Sanitary Commission than any other town in the Union.

At the north end of Puget sound, we crossed the Straits of Fuca, named from Juan de Fuca, the first white man who ever saw Washington Territory. Though of Greek birth, he was sent in 1792, in charge of a Spanish vessel, to fortify a supposititious strait, lest the English should pass through it, from the Atlantic to the Pacific! The geography of his day was a good deal confused. Northwest America is the home of old romance. Here ingenious scholars place the Atlantis of Bacon. Here that greatest of navigators and explorers—Captain Lemuel Gulliver—discovered the kingdom of Brobdingnag.

We landed at Victoria, Vancouver Island, a little metropolis whose rise and growth are wholly due to the traffic of the Frasier river gold-mines. Originally it was the depot of the Hudson Bay Company.

Now we were under the British flag; but the Stars and Stripes waved in every street, in honor of the speaker. The American residents led by the United States consul 'received' him; and then the mayor and city council presented a welcoming address, inscribed on parchment, conveying national congratulations and personal compliments, and with a very English eye to business, soliciting his influence for relaxation of the navigation laws, which fetter commerce with the United States.

Victoria is well built of brick and stone, with a population of five thousand. It is peopled by English, Americans, Chinese and Indians. Yankees who have resided here but five or six years, have quite lost the cadaverous, eager American physiognomy, and exhibit that full, florid face which is the English type the world over. They look like born Britons. Is it the result of half-and-half, climate, association or accident?

The Indians wear the garb of civilization. Some of their women on the streets even display crinoline, and 'water-falls.' Many have very noticeable features. Seattle, from whom a town on the sound is named, is a stolid old patriarch who claims to remember the visit of Vancouver seventy-five years ago. 'King Freezy' and 'Queen Freezy' are dull and stolid specimens of Aboriginal royalty. 'Lightning,' a savage belle, would create a sensation in a civilized ball-room.

If any one doubts that the world is governed too much, let him study the parliament of this little island, which sits ten months in the year! The fifteen members of the lower house are all elective. Of the seven members composing the upper, three are named by the crown, and four, including the colonial secretary, treasurer and chief justice, are *ex officio* members. In endurance, and doubtless in dignity, the body surpasses the British Parliament and the Congress of the United States.

'LIGHTNING,' AN INDIAN BELLE.

It is characteristic, that while New York with four millions of people, pays her governor four thousand dollars a year, the executive of this island, whose population is only seven thousand, receives fifteen thousand dollars per annum. The English do these things better than we.

Sir James Douglas, the former governor, married an educated half-breed lady, and his children have strong Indian features. In July, in his ample garden bloomed many varieties of rose, dahlia, pink, nasturtium, verbena, California poppy and other delicate flowers, with ripe currants and cherries of capital flavor.

That evening the American residents gave a banquet to Mr. Colfax, attended by one hundred and fifty guests, including the governor and other English officials and citizens. British, French, Irish, and American flags festooned the hall. After three hours of eating the speaking began, and lasted for five mortal hours longer. The etiquette was entirely English, differing somewhat from ours. Her Majesty is never cheered nor the toast in her honor responded to by a speech. The president gives: 'The Queen;' the vice-president replies: 'God bless her!' and her health is drank standing, in silence. When any profession—the bar, for example—is toasted, all its members rise and stand till the responses are ended. Speakers address both ends of the table: 'Mr. President, Mr. Vice-president and Gentlemen.'

Of course the English speeches were conversational—couched in the language of plain, every-day talk—though direct, pointed and sensible. And of course the Americans plunged into the profoundest abyss of rhetoric, and soared to the empyrean of declamation. Once or twice they ran into the ludicrously bombastic; but they amazed and delighted the British auditors—like the rest, a little the better for liquor—who applauded to the echo.

In wine is friendliness if not truth. We had not only the inevitable staple of such occasions, about Shakspeare, and Milton, a common language and a common lineage; but a leading British official even predicted that at some future day the two nations would be one!—a remark which was rapturously cheered.

'Nothing succeeds like success.' There *was* much Southern sympathy on the island; now all are our dear friends, our affectionate cousins, our admiring brethren. Johnny Reb. has proved a bad failure; and Johnny Bull, who began by embracing him, ends with a parting kick.

From Victoria we returned to San Francisco by ocean steamer: seven hundred and forty miles; three days; forty-five dollars. We were usually in sight of land, and passed near the mouth of Columbia river, five miles wide and obstructed by the worst bar in the world. There is not a single good harbor between Victoria and San Francisco.

We threaded St. George's Reef—a series of dangerous rocks near the land; some rising two or three hundred feet, others entirely under water. Here we hoped to meet the Brother Jonathan, with papers from San Francisco only twenty-four hours old. The swell was very high, and our captain's face wrinkled with anxiety until the perilous point was passed. Meanwhile we were discussing the chances for life one would have, shipwrecked in that heavy sea.

We missed the Brother Jonathan; but two hours after we passed the reef she reached it, struck a rock, and in forty-five minutes went to the bottom. Of her passengers and crew only sixteen were saved. One hundred and fifty, with their human hopes and fears, their loves and longings and ambitions, were engulfed in that repository which keeps all its treasures and all its secrets till the sea shall give up its dead. Of the six small boats, five were swamped in launching; one reached the shore, full of passengers. After the ship struck, James Nisbet, editor of the San Francisco *Bulletin*, found time and coolness to write his will.

GOVERNMENT STREET, VICTORIA, VANCOUVER ISLAND.

There must be a best way of launching boats under such circumstances. There must be possible machinery to facilitate it. There must be some way for a man with Nisbet's nerve and calmness to save himself, if he only knew it.

Marine disasters are far more frequent and appalling on our coasts than in any other quarter of the globe. They spring largely from our national recklessness; and illustrate the ever-recurring anomaly, that here, where human nature finds its most generous opportunities, human life is less prized than in any other civilized nation. Our whole system of travel by river and sea is shamefully hazardous. Our best ocean steamers are without boats enough to hold all their passengers, even in smooth waters. And when an inspection is to take place, owners and officers often know it in season to borrow hose, boats, and other needful articles of outfit. The slaughter will never cease till proprietors and managers are held to strict responsibility. Convict and punish them for homicide whenever it occurs through their penuriousness, heedlessness, or neglect of precautions which law and humanity require.

CHAPTER XXXV.

SEE Yosemite and die! I shall not attempt to describe it; the subject is too large and my capacity too small. Here might the author of the 'Divine Comedy,' whose troubled brow and yearning eyes appeal to us through the shadows of five centuries, despairingly repeat: 'I may not paint them all in full, for the long theme so chases me that many times the word comes short of the reality.'

Yosemite should be studied for months; I saw it but five days. Volumes ought to be and will be written about it; I can only group a few hints and impressions.

Yosemite—signifying grizzly-bear—was the name of a tribe of Indians. In 1851 they were hostile. The whites pursuing them into their home and stronghold, discovered this crowning wonder of the world. Finding in one lodge a very aged squaw, they asked how old she was. The Indians replied that when she was a girl these mountains were hills! To appreciate the statement one should see the mountains.

Our party of seventeen—the largest which ever entered the valley—included my companions of the overland trip; and among other friends, Fred. Mac Crellish of the *Alta California*, William Ashburner of the California Geological Survey, Frederick Law Olmsted, and Charles Allen, attorney general of the State of Massachusetts.

On the seventh of August, after four days' hard travel from San Francisco, we galloped out of the pine woods, dismounted, stood upon the rocky precipice of Inspiration Point, and looked down into Yosemite as one from a house-top looks down into his garden, or as he would view the interior of some stupendous roofless cathedral, from the top of one of its towering walls. In the distance.

across the gorge, were snow-streaked mountains. Right under us was the narrow, winding basin of meadow, grove and shining river, shut in by granite walls from two thousand to five thousand feet high—walls with immense turrets of bare rock—walls so upright and perfect that an expert crag-man can climb out of the valley at only three or four points.

Flinging a pebble from the rock upon which we stood, and looking over the brink, I saw it fall more than half a mile before striking. Glancing across the narrow, profound chasm, I surveyed an unbroken, seamless wall of granite, two-thirds of a mile high, and *more* than perpendicular—the top projecting one hundred and fifty feet over the base. Turning toward the upper end of the valley, I beheld a half-dome of rock, one mile high, and on its summit a solitary, gigantic cedar, appearing like the merest twig. Originally a vast granite mountain, it was riven from top to bottom by some ancient convulsion, which cleft asunder the everlasting hills and rent the great globe itself.

GOING INTO YOSEMITE VALLEY.

The measureless, inclosing walls, with these leading towers and many other turrets—gray, brown and white rock, darkly veined from summit to base with streaks and ribbons of falling water—

hills, almost upright, yet studded with tenacious firs and cedars; and the deep-down level floor of grass, with its thread of river and pigmy trees, all burst upon me at once. Nature had lifted her curtain to reveal the vast and the infinite. It elicited no adjectives, no exclamations. With bewildering sense of divine power and human littleness, I could only gaze in silence, till the view strained my brain and pained my eyes, compelling me to turn away and rest from its oppressive magnitude.

Riding for two hours, down, down, among sharp rocks and dizzy zigzags, where the five ladies of our party found it difficult to keep in their saddles, and narrowly escaped pitching over their horses' heads, we were in the valley, entering by the Mariposa trail. The diagram shows its form and features. The length of the valley or cleft is nine miles; its average width three-fourths of a mile. The following dimensions are in feet:

Average width of Merced river,	60
Hight of Yosemite falls. (Upper, 1,600: Rapids, 434; Lower, 600,)	2,634
Width of these falls at upper summit, in August,	15
Hight of Bridal Vail fall,	940
Hight of South Fork fall,	740
Hight of Vernal fall,	330
Hight of Nevada fall,	700
Width of Vernal and Nevada, at summits,	40
Hight of El Capitan rock,	3,900
Hight of Three Brothers rock (three turrets,)	3,437
Hight of North Dome rock,	3,720
Hight of Inspiration Point rock,	3,000
Hight of Cathedral rocks (two turrets,)	3,000
Hight of Sentinel rock,	3,270
Hight of Mount Colfax,	3,400
Hight of Mount Starr King,	4,500
Hight of South Dome rock,	6,000

Riding up the valley for five miles, past Bridal Vail fall, (on the brook entering the Merced from the south, above Inspiration Point,) Cathedral rocks and the Sentinel, we dismounted and established our headquarters at Hutchings'. This is a two-story frame house, with interior walls of 'soft finish,' a local term, in contra-distinction to plastering of 'hard finish' and signifying only curtains of white muslin for partitions. They compel guests who don't wish to give magic-lantern exhibitions to extinguish their candles before disrobing; but afford rarest facilities for general conversation after every one has gone to bed.

Hutchings and his family regaled us on the fat of the land and the fruit of the water—sweet milk and savory trout. In winter the sun rises upon them at one o'clock P. M., and sets two hours later. Then they receive mails and news from the outside world once a week, through adventurous Indians, who cross the dangerous mountain snows, twenty feet deep, to Coulterville or Mariposa.

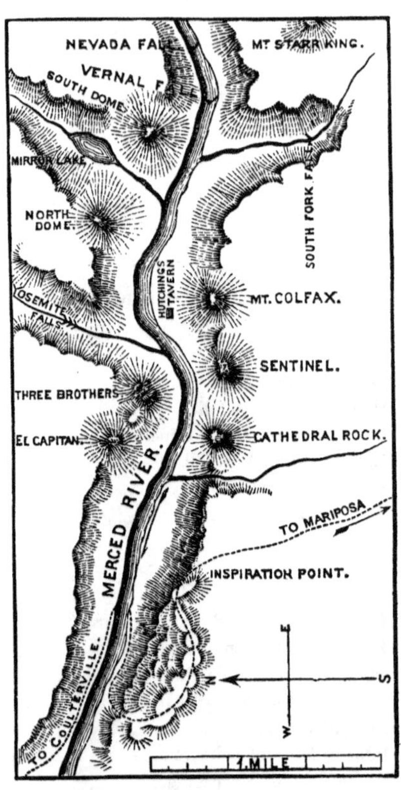

DIAGRAM OF YOSEMITE VALLEY.

Hutchings is landlord and author; his illustrated 'Scenes of Wonder and Curiosity in California' is a creditable and valuable work. A friend, visiting here for the first time, found his wife upon the river-bank, with one hand vigorously turning the crank of a patent washing-machine, and with the other holding the latest *Atlantic Monthly*, absorbed in one of its articles. Only Indian labor is attainable. If eastern ladies who suffer constant martyrdom in respect of 'help,' were compelled to live on the Pacific coast a few months and employ Chinamen and Indians in lieu of servant girls, they would learn who is well off.

In front of Hutchings' runs the Merced, fresh from the Sierras. Delightful and exhilarating, though a little chilly for the swimmer, it is so perfectly transparent as to cheat the eye, and beguile beyond his depth any one attempting to wade it. Crossing it by a rustic log bridge, we are in a smooth, level meadow of tall grass, variegated with myriads of wild flowers, including primroses of yellow and crimson, and a lily-shaped blossom of exquisite purple, known as the Ithuriel spear.

The meadow is fringed with groves of pines and spreading oak, and on one side bounded by the everlasting walls. The pines, like those of Washington Territory, are simply hight, slenderness, symmetry. The delicate tracery of the branch is beautiful beyond description; but the trunk is comparatively small. I procured a photograph of two, wonderfully regular and graceful, and more than two hundred feet high, which dwarfed to a child's block-house a large frame-dwelling at their feet. In the evening, illuminated and softened by the full moon, the beauty of the valley was marvelous. The bright lights of the distant house shone through the deep pines, and the river's low gurgling faintly disturbed the air. At times immense bowlders, breaking from the summits, rolled down thundering, and filling the valley with their loud reverberations.

EL CAPITAN. 3900 FEET HIGH.

The rock mountains are the great feature; indeed *they* are Yosemite. The nine granite walls which range in altitude from three to six thousand feet, are the most striking examples on the globe of the masonry of Nature.

Their dimensions are so vast that they utterly outrun our ordinary standards of comparison. One might as well be told of a wall, upright like the side of a house for ten thousand miles, as for two-thirds of one mile. When we speak of a giant twenty-five feet high, it conveys some definite impression; but to tell of one three thousand feet high, would only bewilder, and convey no meaning whatever. So, at first, these stupendous walls painfully confuse the mind. By degrees, day after day, the sight of them clears it, until, at last, one receives a just impression of their solemn immensity.

Cathedral rocks have two turrets, and look like some Titanic religious pile. Sentinel towers alone, grand and hoary. The South Dome, a mile high, is really a semi-dome. Cleft from top to bottom, one-half of it went on the other side of the chasm and disappeared, when the great mountains were rent in twain. The gigantic North Dome is as round and perfect as the cupola of the national capitol. Three Brothers is a triple-pointed mass of solid granite. All these rocks, and scores of lesser ones which would be noticeable anywhere else in the world, exhibit vegetation. Hardy cedars, thrusting roots into imperceptible crevices of their upright sides —apparently growing out of unbroken stone —have braved a thousand years the battle and the breeze.

El Capitan is grandest of all. No tuft of beard shades or fringes its closely shaven face. No tenacious vine even can fasten its tendrils, to climb that smooth, seamless, stupendous wall. There it will stand, grandeur, massiveness, indestructibility, till the heavens shall pass away with a great noise, and the elements melt with fervent heat. Its Indian name is *Tu-toch-ah-nu-lah.* Both this and the Spanish word signify 'the leader;' but were applied in the sense of the Supreme Being. It ought to be called Mount Abraham Lincoln.

One noble mountain most appropriately commemorates Thomas Starr King. Another, immediately in the rear of Hutchings', our party found nameless, and, excepting only the speaker himself, unanimously voted to christen it Mount Colfax. Whether the name sticks or not, will depend upon future writers. But I am sure it will be perpetual, if adhered to by all tourists and journalists friendly to that orphan printer-boy of not many years ago, whose industry, talents and perfect integrity have won for his early manhood the third place of civil trust and honor in the gift of the American people.

Hutchings' affords a perfect view of Yosemite falls, a mile distant. In April and May, when melting snows swell the stream to a deep torrent, they are grand; but then the valley is half flooded. In late summer their creek shrinks to a skeleton; and they look small because their surroundings are so vast. Niagara itself would dwarf beside the rocks in this valley.

Yet Yosemite is the loftiest water-fall in the world. Think of a cataract, or cascade, of half a mile with only a single break! It is sixteen times higher than Niagara. Twelve Bunker Hill monuments standing upright, one upon another, would barely reach its summit. Ossa upon Pelion becomes a tame and meaningless comparison.

We did not climb to the Rapids and foot of the Upper fall; that is difficult, hazardous and exhausting. Nor did we go to the extreme summit; that requires a circuitous ride of twenty-five miles out of the valley. But we spent much time at the base of the Lower fall, shut in by towering walls of dark granite. The basin abounds in rocks—some as large as a dwelling house—which have tumbled down from the top. Spreading my blankets upon one of these, almost under the fall, I found it a smooth bed, though a little damp from spray; and spent the night there to see the cataract in the varying illuminations and shadows of sunlight, twilight, starlight and moonlight.

Much of the water turns to mist before reaching the bottom; yet looking up from under it the volume seems great. Six hundred feet above, a body of ragged snowy foam with disheveled tresses, rushes over the brink; and comes singing down in slender column, swayed to and fro by the wind like a long strand of lace. For four hundred feet the descent is unruffled; then, striking a broad, inclining rock, like the roof of a house, the water spreads over it—a thin, shining, transparent apron, fringed with delicate gauze—and glides swiftly to the bottom. By moonlight the whole looks like a long white ribbon, hanging against the brown wall, with its lower end widening and unraveled.

Bridal Vail fall, unbroken, much narrower, and softened by a delicate mist which half hides it, is a strip of white fluttering foam, which the wind swings like a silken pendulum. It is spanned by a rainbow; and at some points the thin, glass-like sheet reveals every hue of the wall behind it. Before reaching the end of its long descent, a rill no longer, it is completely transformed to spray—the Niobe of cascades dissolved in tears.

Above Hutchings' the valley breaks into three canyons and the Merced into three forks. North Fork passes through Mirror Lake—the very soul of transparency. It reflects grass, trees, rocks, mountains and sky with such perfect and startling vividness that one cannot believe them images and shadows. He fancies the world turned upside down, and shrinks back from the lake lest he should tumble over the edge into the inverted dome of blue sky.

On the Middle or main Fork is Vernal fall, difficult of access. Leaving our horses three miles from the hotel, we climbed for two weary hours along dizzy shelves and up sharp rocks, where the trail rises one thousand feet to the mile;—pine woods all around us; at our left and far below, the river chafing and roaring in its stony bed. Then we stood at the foot of Vernal fall. Bridal Vail and Yosemite are on little lateral creeks; Vernal is the full, swelling torrent of the Merced. Those creep softly and slowly down, as if in pain and hesitation. This rushes eagerly over gloomy brown rocks; then leaps headlong for more than three hundred feet, roaring like a minature Niagara.

Rainbows of dazzling brightness shine at its base. Others of the party reported many; my own eyes, defective as to colors, beheld only two. But afterward when alone, I saw what to Hebrew prophet had been a vision of heaven, or the visible presence of the Almighty. It was the round rainbow—the complete circle. In the afternoon sun I stood upon a rock a hundred feet from the base of the fall, and nearly on a level with it. There were two brilliant rainbows of usual form—the crescent, the bow proper. But while I looked, the two horns of the inner or lower crescent suddenly lengthened, extending on each side to my feet—an entire circle, perfect as a finger-ring. In two or three seconds it passed away, shrinking to the first dimensions. Ten minutes later it formed again; and again as suddenly disappeared. Every sharp gust of wind showering the spray over me revealed for a moment the round rainbow. Completely drenched I stood for an hour and a half; and saw, fully twenty times, that dazzling circle of violet and gold, on a groundwork of wet dark rock, gay dripping flowers and vivid grass. I never looked upon any other scene in Nature so beautiful and impressive.

VERNAL FALL AND THE ROUND RAINBOW.

Climbing a high rock-wall by crazy wooden ladders, we continued up the canyon for three quarters of a mile to Nevada fall, where the Merced tumbles seven hundred feet, in 'white and swaying mistiness.' Near the bottom it strikes an inclined rock, and spreads upon it in a sheet of floating silver tissue a hundred and thirty feet wide.

Passing over a wide, gaping crack or chasm in this rocky grade, the thin sheet of water breaks into delicate, snowy net-work; then into myriads of shining beads, and finally into long sparkling threads—an exquisite silken fringe to the great white curtain.

These names are peculiarly fitting. Bridal Vail indeed looks like a vail of lace. In summer, when Bridal Vail and Yosemite dwarf, Vernal still pours its ample torrent. And Nevada is always white as a snow-drift.

The Yosemite is hight; the Vernal is volume; the Bridal Vail is softness; but the Nevada is hight, volume and softness combined. South Fork cataract, most inaccessible of all, we did not visit. In spring each fall has twenty times as much water as in summer.

The days we spent in the valley were delightful and memorable. Evenings were devoted to song and merry-making; and the motto of the party was: 'If any man gets up before eight o'clock in the morning, shoot him on the spot.' But by day we wandered where we listed, and viewed the great features of the valley, as all impressive things in nature should be viewed, alone. Most heartily I envied Olmsted, who with his family, with horses, tents and books, remained for several weeks, moving from day to day, and encamping wherever fancy dictated.

On the whole, Yosemite is incomparably the most wonderful feature of our continent. European travelers agree that transatlantic scenery has nothing at all approaching it. Unless the unexplored Himalayas hide some rival, there is no spot, the wide world over, of such varied beauty and measureless grandeur.

Climbing out of the valley, we cast one longing, lingering look behind, from Inspiration Point. Here is the best comprehensive view, not of separate features but of the whole. This vast open cathedral, which would hold fifty millions of worshippers, is true to the ancient imperious maxim of architecture: its mean width about equals the average hight of its walls. Our eyes, now adjusted to its distances and dimensions, were no longer pained by the amazing spectacle. At last we turned away from this sublimest page in all the book of nature. I think few can come from its study without hearts more humble and reverent, lives more worthy and loyal.

Yosemite valley is four thousand feet above sea-level. After climbing out and re-passing Inspiration Point, we still ascend; and then ride for several miles at an altitude of about eight thousand feet. Here, where snow is sometimes twenty feet deep, are meadows of richest grass and brighest flowers.

BED AND BOARD.

The pyramidal, slender pine abounds, frequently two hundred feet high, its trunk and branches gorgeous with yellow moss. So does the exquisite, blue-tipped, silvery fir. This profuse vegetation, with larkspur, daisy, lily, honeysuckle and godola, is at a hight which, in New England would frost-kill tree, flower, grass and twig. Even here are thousands of dwarf oaks and chestnuts rarely four feet high, yet prolific of shriveled nuts. The mountain mahogany also flourishes. Its red berry makes excellent cider; and its acid juice quenches the thirst of men and of grizzly bears.

In 1859, Horace Greeley found upon this lonely summit a stray Yankee, pasturing one hundred and fifty hogs, which he protected at night from the grizzly bears, by building around them a circle of log fires. Long ere this bears have been thinned by pioneer rifles; hogs have made their inevitable journey to the San Francisco slaughter-house; and herdsman perhaps turned to a day laborer in Australian mines, perhaps to a bank president in New York, with parlors at the Fifth Avenue Hotel, and a six-horse equipage in the Central Park.

After coming out of the valley we spent the first night at Clark's, a long low porched log house in the deep woods. Mr. Clark is a hermit and a pioneer of intelligence and kindness, who has turned his back upon civilization, eschewed 'boiled shirts;' and without wife or child, pitched his lonely tent in the wilderness. During winter even he retreats before the Storm-king to Mariposa. Long-bearded and sun-browned, he looks like a modernized Wandering Jew, and talks like a professor of belles-lettres and moral philosophy. He furnished us with bed and board. The ladies occupied straw couches under his roof, filling the house; while their banished lords slept under heaven's canopy. in the lee of a friendly hay-stack, with a blanket for lodgings and a board for a pillow.

The Mariposa Big Trees are six miles from Clark's and thirty from Yosemite valley. We visited them by diverging five miles from our homeward route to San Fancisco. Six hundred of these mammoths are scattered among the noble pines of twelve hundred and eighty acres. Many of the pines are two hundred feet high. Elsewhere *they* would be kings of the forest; but among these hoary giants they become puny, insignificant children. Pigmies on Alps may be pigmies still, but pyramids are not always pyramids in vales.

The Big Trees have been considered redwoods—a species of cedar abounding upon this coast—but the botanists decide otherwise and name them SEQUOIAS. They are the oldest and most stupendous vegetable products existing upon the globe. Already twenty groves have been discovered in California. The Mariposa is largest and finest, though the Calaveras, fifty miles to the northward, is better known.

Of the Mariposa sequoias, two hundred are more than twelve feet in diameter, fifty more than sixteen feet, and six more than thirty feet. The largest, called the Prostrate Monarch, now lying upon the ground leafless and branchless, is believed to have fallen fully one hundred and fifty years ago! Fire has consumed much of the trunk; but enough remains to show that with the bark on it must have been *forty feet* in thickness. Figures give little idea

RIDING THROUGH A TREE-TRUNK.

of such dimensions. Measure up forty feet on a house-wall; then four hundred feet along the ground; and try to picture the diameter and hight of the Prostrate Monarch as it stood a thousand years ago.

The tops of the largest trees are broken off, leaving their average hight about two hundred and fifty feet, though some range between three and four hundred feet. We saw one with a branch—not a fork, but an honest, lateral branch—six feet in diameter, growing from the stem eighty feet above the ground. Into a cavity burned in the side of another standing tree, fifteen of us rode together. Without crowding, we all sat upon our horses in that black, novel chamber, though it occupies less than half the thickness of the immense trunk.

Through a stem lying upon the ground, fire has bored like an auger. Our entire cavalcade, including all the tall men, all the fat men, and all the ample skirts, rode through it from end to end, like a railway train through a tunnel.

One enormous living trunk which parts near the ground into two tall, symmetric, perfect stems, is christened the Faithful Couple. Mr. Clark assured us, in a poetic gush quite unlooked-for from a hermit and a backwoodsman, that they were

'Two souls with but a single thought,
Two hearts that beat as one.'

The faithfulness of this forest Ingomar and Parthenia is like that of some human couples—neither can get away.

The largest standing tree is the Grizzly Giant. Its bark is nearly two feet thick. If it were cut off smoothly, fifty horses could easily stand, or sixteen couples dance, upon the stump. If the trunk were hollowed to a shell, it would hold more freight than a man-of-war or a first-class ocean steamer two hundred and fifty feet long!

One of the Calaveras sequoias was cut down by boring with augers and sawing the spaces between. The work employed five men for twenty-five days. When fully cut off the tree stubbornly continued to stand, only yielding at last to a mammoth wedge and a powerful battering-ram.

The pine cones are cylindrical, and sometimes nearly two feet long. Those of the Big Trees are round, and not larger than apples. Seedlings from them are growing in every country of Europe. They are numerous in English parks, where a mania prevails for coniferous trees. Two hundred are planted in our great Central Park; and many more in the nurseries of western New York. They are thrifty and vigorous: how large they will become is an interesting problem.

There seems to be no convincing or even plausible theory of their origin. I should rather say of their preservation; for they are children of a long-ago climatic era. The age of giants lingers on the entire Pacific coast.

Through California and Oregon stupendous redwoods are everywhere numerous; and on the summit of the Sierras, almost a mile above sea-level, grow sugar pines ten and twelve feet in diameter. Well says Holmes:

> 'In fact, there's nothing that keeps its youth—
> So far as I know—but a tree and truth.'

It was once thought incredible that the yew should live a thousand years. But these monster sequoias are the world's patriarchs. Some botanists date their birth far back of earliest human history; none estimate their age at less than eighteen hundred years. Perchance their youth saw the awkward, thundering mastodon canter over the hills; and the hundred-feet-long reptile, of many legs and mouth like a volcano, crawl sluggishly through torrid swamps. They were living when the father of poets, old, blind and vagabond, sang his immortal song; when the sage of Athens, 'that most Christian heathen,' calmly drank the hemlock; when the carpenter of Judea, from whom the whole world now computes its time, was a man of sorrows and acquainted with grief, despised and rejected of men.

From the groves we continued on horseback to White and Hatch's; thence by carriage to Mariposa, the stage-coach and civilization. Thousands of cattle browse upon the parched grass and wild oats. Their herders, native Yankees, are the most daring of riders—at full speed leaping off and remounting; and throwing the lasso around any leg or horn of wild horse or ox with unerring precision.

One universal feature of California—rainless for half the year—would have driven Don Quixote distracted: windmills at nearly every house drawing water from wells for irrigation.

Traveling time from San Francisco to Yosemite, via Big Trees: four days each way. Preferable route: go by Mariposa and return via Coulterville. Expenses of round trip: about ten dollars per day. Distances via Mariposa:

San Francisco to Stockton, (steamer,)	123 miles.
Stockton to Mariposa, (stage.)	91 miles.
Mariposa to White & Hatch's, (carriage,)	11 miles.
White & Hatch's to Clark's, (horseback,)	14 miles,
Clark's to Yosemite, (horseback,)	26 miles.
San Francisco to Yosemite,	265 miles.

An act of Congress has segregated Yosemite valley and the Mariposa groves of Big Trees, from the general public domain, setting them apart as pleasure grounds for the people of the United States and their heirs and assigns forever. This wise legislation secures to the proper national uses, incomparably the largest and grandest park, and the sublimest natural scenery in the whole world. They are under the care of a commission appointed by the governor of California for their preservation and protection—to render them accessible, keep them free from mutilation, and see that no vandal hand of Art attempts to improve upon the simplicity and grandeur of Nature.

CHAPTER XXXVI.

FROM our out-of-the-world journeyings to Yosemite and the Big Trees, we returned to terrestrial pursuits and Celestial hospitalities. The latter were tendered in the following invitation to each of the four members of our party, printed upon slips of gilt-edged, pink paper, in shape and size like commercial envelopes:

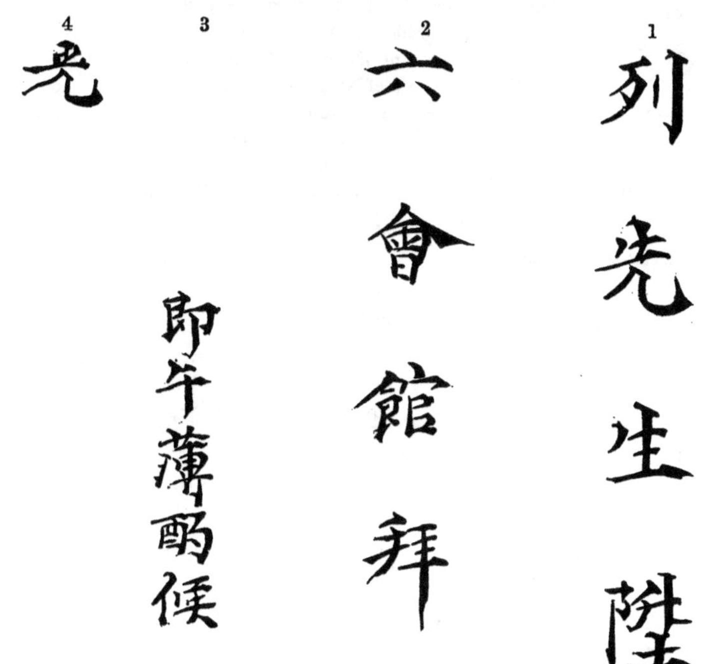
1 列先生陞
2 六會館拜
3 即午薄酌候
4 光

INVITATION TO CHINESE DINNER.

1. (Superscription on envelope.) 'May Mr. —— prosper.'

2. (First enclosure.) 'The keeper of the Luh-hwui saloon presents compliments.' (*Luh-hwui* signifies 'Collecting from all quarters.')

3 and 4. (Second enclosure.) 'This noon a slight repast awaits light.'—('Awaits your presence.') Ordinarily Chinese characters read in column from top to bottom and from right to left. But here, as usual in cases of compliment, the upper, left-hand character for 'light' (used by Chinese custom instead of the pronoun 'you,') is elevated to the top of a new line, as a mark of respect.

In addition to the guests of the evening, thirty-five prominent American gentlemen, and thirty leading Chinese residents received this card:

San Francisco, August 15, 1865.

You are respectfully invited to attend a complimentary dinner, to be given to the Hon. Schuyler Colfax, speaker of the United States House of Representatives; the Hon. Wm. Bross, lieutenant-governor of Illinois; Albert D. Richardson, *New York Tribune*, and Samuel Bowles, *Springfield* (Mass.) *Republican*, by the Six Chinese Companies in California, on Thursday, August 17, at the Hang Heong Restaurant, No. 308 Dupont Street, near Clay, at six P. M. In behalf of

Chui Sing Tong, President of Sam Yap Company.
Khing Fong, President of Yueng Wo Company.
Ting Sang, President of See Yap Company.
Wae Nga, President of Ning Yeong Company.
Chee Shum, President of Hop Wo Company.
Mum Kuae, President of Yan Wo Company.

In a previous chapter I have spoken of the Six Companies, to some one of which every Chinaman in the United States belongs. The six presidents are elective, largely salaried, and of high ability. At the restaurant, they awaited us in rich native dress, with shaved heads and braided cues hanging almost to the ground. Upon our introduction by Mr. Carvalho, the official interpreter—born in China of American parents—they bowed profoundly, and through him tendered assurances of their most distinguished consideration.

The Hang Heong restaurant, of wood, two and-a-half stories high, was imported ready-made from China. The dining saloon is on the second floor. Its walls are hung with Chinese placards giving names and prices of dishes.

Punctual to the hour we took our places at little round tables, each seating nine or ten persons. Mr. Colfax, with the *elite* of our entertainers, occupied the central board. The table on his right, where Providence and Celestial etiquette placed Messrs. Bross, Bowles and myself, was surrounded by several other American gentlemen, and three presidents.

I have sat at good men's feasts, both to the stalled ox without hatred, and the dinner of herbs where love was. I have enjoyed the hospitalities of Mexican haciendas, Arapahoe lodges, Choctaw cabins, negro huts and rebel prisons; but this was a new gastronomic and social experience.

CHINESE DINNER IN SAN FRANCISCO.

The food was all brought on, ready cut, in fine pieces. We ate only with ivory chop-sticks—long, round, polished, and both held in the right hand. After learning the knack, one even takes up rice between them with surprising facility. There were three hundred and twenty-five dishes. Whatever was lacking in quantity was made up in quality, for the choicest cost one dollar per mouthful. Mr. Bowles partook from about a dozen; Mr. Colfax from forty; I suspended somewhere in the seventies; but Gov. Bross religiously tasted every one. Here are a few: bamboo soup, bird's-nest soup, stewed sea-weed, stewed mushrooms, fried fungus, banana fritters, shark fins, shark sinews, reindeer sinews, dried Chinese oysters, pigeons, ducks, chickens, scorpions' eggs, watermelon seeds, fish in scores of varieties, many kinds of cake, and fruits ad infinitum. There were no joints of any kind. Neither butter nor milk is used in cooking.

The Celestials drank champagne and claret as if to the manner born. At every sip, each guest bowed seriatim to every other person at his table. A few dishes were unpalatable; but most were toothsome. The oysters and sharks' fins were especially savory. Bird's nest soup is from a mucilage which certain eastern birds collect for building materials. Under an inviting name it would be popular at the St. Nicholas.

In three hours and-a-half, strong, richly-flavored black tea—the Chinese eschew green because it is artificially colored—was distributed in tiniest cups; and thus ended the first course.

Then three-quarters of an hour for cigarettes, digestion and oriental music, General McDowell and our party occupying a little recess, which contained a divan for opium-smoking, and was labeled: 'For the Guests of Honor.' The instruments were a hollow shell, like a turtle's back, beaten with two sticks; a violin with bow confined between the strings and running like a cross-cut saw; something resembling a viol; and something else like a banjo, the sharp strings struck with a flint instead of the fingers. All were keyed very high, but their shrill music was not unpleasing.

As their rigid etiquette requires, the presidents now retired, after little kindly speeches and replies, duly interpreted. At the second course leading merchants took their places. The three at our table were young, intelligent men, with broad foreheads and quick eyes, who spoke excellent English. Great is Commerce! A knowledge of the Celestial tongue is becoming indispensable even to American merchants; and a newspaper, printed both in Chinese and in English, indicates the mercantile bonds already woven between the two peoples and countries.

Our entertainers had strong individuality; but the lower classes all look alike to American eyes. When one was on trial for murder, several white citizens were ready to swear that they saw him commit the crime; but his counsel placed him among eleven other Chinamen, and not one could select him from the group!

The merchants told us that all Chinese expect ultimately to return home. To my question why they do not bring their wives here, one replied, with great emphasis: 'Wives won't come!' Tea was circulated several times and Chinese wine once, in crockery cups holding about two thimblefuls. It is flavored with roses, intensely strong, and far more intoxicating than brandy. With us it would be termed a cordial.

After this course the merchants made their adieux; and at dessert, others, less prominent, took their places. At the close, one, Toy Chew, made the first English speech ever attempted by a Chinaman on the Pacific coast. With point and fluency he complimented Mr. Colfax; touched upon the wonderful growth of the United States and the warm interest in it felt by all his race.

At midnight ended this novel banquet—the world's oldest civilization striking hands with its youngest. The occasion was curious and memorable. Hereafter, upon every invitation, I shall sup with the Celestials, and say grace with all my heart.

Soon after, I was compelled to bid adieu to my companions. An overland trip is a sort of limited matrimony. One is bound to his comrades for better or for worse; if he select them in haste he will repent at leisure. The Atchisonians warned us in advance that no party ever crossed the continent without quarreling; that for the first week we should ask each other: 'Has any gentleman seen my note-book?' but that thereafter the inquiry would be: 'What d—d scoundrel has stolen my tooth brush?' False prophets they! For fifteen weeks and six thousand miles, we were a happy family, even when every day was Moving-day. The lines had fallen to us in pleasant places. The trip had been full of interest and profit.

For Mr. Colfax it proved one continuous ovation. Now, at its close, he looked back through a long vista of brass bands and banquets, private welcomes and public receptions. It was deserved; for he made it solely to study the great interests of the West, which are national as well as local; and he had always been their liberal and steadfast friend. It must be some compensation for the emptiness and thanklessness of public life, to be thus loved and honored by personal strangers, in the remote, scattered homes of half a continent—to be thus welcomed as an old and dear friend in new communities, thousands of miles from one's birthplace and from all the scenes of his life.

In every position thus far he has achieved signal success; and if his countrymen ever call him to the highest place in their gift, he will fill it with credit to himself and honor to the nation.* In private as in public he steals the heart of every man, woman, and child—by no demagoguery or effort, but by simplicity, naturalness, and overflowing kindness. He is a childless widower of forty-two.

Governor Bross is fifty by the almanac; but in vigor and freshness of feeling, thirty years younger. Like Old Virginia, he never tires. In Illinois campaigns he often makes one hundred speeches;

---

* Three years after the close of this journey Mr. Colfax *was* called, not to the highest, but to the second place in the Government, under circumstances peculiarly gratifying to his friends. In May, 1868, a National Republican convention was held at Chicago. Every State in the Union was represented. For the presidency General Grant was nominated by acclamation. For the vice presidency there were a large number of candidates, including several eminent both for their talents and their services. All usage and probabilities were against a nomination from the West. For eight years the presidential chair had been filled by western men, and now a general from Illinois had been selected to occupy it for four years more. But the moment the delegates began to ballot the tide set inevitably toward the young statesman of Indiana, and in the midst of great enthusiasm he was selected for the second place on the ticket. After a spirited canvass Grant and Colfax were elected in the November following, by a popular majority of more than three hundred thousand. Upon one of the first days of March, 1869, Mr. Colfax resigned the speakership of the House of Representatives, which he had filled for three terms, to assume the duties of the vice presidency. One of his last acts in the speakership exhibited his high qualities as a presiding officer. It was while both branches of Congress were sitting in joint convention, to count the electoral votes for president and vice president. Through the turbulence of General Butler, of Massachusetts, a most disgraceful tumult occurred, stopping the transaction of business and causing a dead lock. The president of the Senate—*ex officio* the presiding officer of the convention—proved utterly unable to quell it; but when the confusion was at its height, a few prompt, decisive words from Speaker Colfax, threatening to place the turbulent members under arrest if they persisted, instantly put an end to the humiliating scene. Soon after his inauguration as vice president Mr. Colfax was married to a lady from Ohio. His new sphere is higher, though more quiet and less exciting than the old; and he bids fair to receive, sooner or later, one promotion more at the hands of his countrymen.

the air of the rostrum is his native element. At San Francisco, a Forty-niner is the pioneer of pioneers—one who came over with William the Conqueror—one of the Conscript Fathers. Said a Californian to me: 'Why, I could have sworn that Governor Bross was a Forty-niner! If he lived here we should send him at once to the United States Senate.' Of eastern birth, Massachusetts education, and long, successful experience in Chicago journalism, he combines keen humor and mellow geniality with ripe judgment and most sterling worth.

The knowledge that Mr. Colfax had been an early and zealous friend, in Congress, of the overland mail, the overland telegraph, the Pacific Railroad, and the development of our great mining interests, caused him to be received everywhere with peculiar warmth. And when it became understood that his journalistic companions had accompanied him only for the purpose of reporting faithfully, and to the best of their ability, upon the scenery, society, and resources of our new States and Territories, the whole party received enthusiastic welcome, and the most liberal facilities for travel, observation, and investigation.

On the second of September the firm was dissolved. The three senior members had withdrawn, seceded, contrabanded. 'When last seen,' they were grouped on a hurricane deck. 'Hip, hip, hurra!' cheered the crowd. 'Boom!' thundered the gun. Groaned the engines, wheezed the steam pipes, creaked the paddle-wheels. Slowly rounded the great steamer from the wharf; deftly she wended out from the forest of masts; then moved like a strong swimmer, past the acres of shipping, past the wonderful city with a history like Aladdin's palace, past Alcatraz, through the Golden Gate—and they were Homeward Bound. So my friends had gone. Simple yet profound is the truth of Enoch Arden: 'Things seen are greater than things heard.' This long and sometimes weary journeying, had added incomparably to their large usefulness; and they returned more intelligent, appreciative and enthusiastic friends of our new States, than they had ever been before.

California politics are an interesting study. United States Senator John Conness, was curiously elected. There was a hot contest, but he was not a candidate. Rivalry was bitter and money used freely. A friend of the leading aspirant was entrapped into offering five thousand dollars for the vote of a legislator, who was none too honest, but in the interest of the other side. It occurred in the private room of the member, who had previously secreted two witnesses in his wardrobe; and they heard the proposition. The legislature, disgusted at the corruption, went outside of all the candidates and elected Conness, who was lying ill at home.

The finest State-house in the Union is building at Sacramento. It is of light sandstone; and agreeable in architecture and situation. A glance at the legislature, in session during one of my visits, was peculiarly entertaining. As in all western assemblies, most of the members were young. There was no prosing. The speaking was spirited and pointed. The faces indicated that the standard of brains was a good deal higher than in most parliamentary bodies.

GOVERNOR BROSS.

Society in the new States has strong distinctive features. It makes the forehead broader and the heart warmer. After a few years' experience, even the most stupid will show

> 'How much the dunce who has been sent to roam
> Excels the dunce who has been kept at home.'

The intelligence of the plainest working men, day laborers, miners, teamsters, is peculiarly noticeable. It is partly due to the sudden ups and downs. I rode on the box with a stage-driver who was working for one hundred dollars per month. Two years before, he owned the entire stage-line, and was worth one hundred thousand dollars. Next year, he may own it again, and the present proprietor be cracking the whip. The man who first found gold in California is now poor. So is the discoverer of the great Comstock silver mine—the richest in the world.

The people are warm and demonstrative. One of them going back to the East is surprised at the general coldness and formality. He fancies that his old friends have never thawed out from the freezing their fathers got on Plymouth rock. California is the culmination of all that is best and pleasantest in frontier life. The people curiously combine shrewdness and enthusiasm. They go fast, have the best, and despise the expense. Parsimony is the Charybdis which they shun with so much terror that a good many go to pieces upon the Scylla of Extravagance. Wo to him who is niggardly, and to the new-comer who puts on airs!

According to Emerson, great cities take the nonsense out of us. So does frontier life. It teaches practical sagacity, rare judgment of men, quick detection of shams, ready weighing of a stranger's capacity, and generous trust in the trustworthy.

ABORIGINAL CALIFORNIANS.

The aboriginal Californians lived upon worms and grasshoppers, and were most wretched and degraded of all barbarians. The world does not contain a more cordial, whole-souled, generous people than the Californians of to-day. Their hearts are as large as their mountains and as warm as their climate. Time will correct faults and supply deficiencies; the next generation ought to see here the best average society in the Union, and therefore in the world.

Already the State cherishes the names of her young heroes—young because the dead can never grow old. Starr King, Broderick and Baker, repose in Lone Mountain cemetery, overlooking the Golden Gate, and the city of their adoption and their love.

In the matter of diet, our first San Francisco experience was amusing. We arrived at midnight; and before two o'clock the next afternoon, in addition to breakfast, we had been beguiled into participating in four 'little lunches.' By this time we began to realize that luncheon is *the* meal of the Pacific coast; that the proper time for it is at any hour of the day or night; and that whenever the stranger is invited to eat 'a bite' or take 'a little luncheon,' it means an elaborate meal, with choice fruits, and often with rare wines.

The new country is prolific of new words and phrases. In conversation, San Francisco is shortened to 'Frisco.' At first it sounded droll enough; but we did in Frisco as the Friscans did, and soon adopted their nomenclature. A 'bilk' is an impostor, from the old Gothic verb 'to bilk.' The noun is common in England, but new, I think, in the United States. To 'slop over,' is to make some foolish mistake, run into wild eccentricity, be ill-balanced. 'That's the way I put it up,' signifies, 'the way I construct or build up my theory.' Sometimes the provincialisms degenerate into slang. 'I don't see it,' (incredulity.) 'You get!' (begone,) 'You bet!' (strong affirmation,) and the rest of that large family, all flourish.

There is a story of a burglar, who at midnight climbed up to a chamber-window, and cautiously opened it. The occupant, chancing to be awake, crept softly to the window, and just as the robber's face appeared, presented the smooth muzzles of two revolvers, with the injunction:

'YOU GET.'

'You get!'

'You bet!' replied the house-breaker, dropping and running. There is no more pithy dialogue on record.

Beyond question the Americans are the wittiest and most humorous people in the world. And on the Pacific coast, one hears, in every-day conversation, more clever sayings and pungent retorts than anywhere else. Shall I record a few to conclude the chapter?

A gentleman who affected great plainness of habit and dress was elected to the United States Senate. One of his neighbors remarked:

'He will instantly have the cobbler put patches on all his new boots, to show that his new position has not made him proud.'

A candidate for another leading office had a very small head and enormous limbs. Said one of his political opponents:

'*He* is certain to be beaten. This State will never elect a man who wears a number-four hat and number-thirteen boots!'

A notorious exaggerator, after describing an impossible tree, said to his auditor:

'I don't wonder that you look incredulous. I would not have believed it myself, if I had not seen it.'

'Well,' replied the dry listener, '*I* don't see it!'

An official surveyor was reputed greedy and avaricious, refusing to survey property, as his duties required, unless the owner would give him an interest in the real estate. Suddenly he was removed from office, when one of his friends declared that his head was taken off because he opposed Senator ——.

'O no,' was the reply; 'that was not the reason.'

'Then why *was* he removed?'

'Because he wanted to be monarch of all he surveyed.'

'YOU BET.'

A senatorial candidate was noted for his slovenly attire. A lady said of him: 'Mr. Blank is really the best man; and I should like to see him elected if the legislature would give him instructions.'

'What instructions?' asked her interlocutor.

'Instructions to put on a clean shirt once a week, and wash his face every morning!'

An ex-governor and ex-senator was a passenger on the wrecked steamer Golden Rule.

'What did you save?' inquired a friend. He replied:

'I saved nothing but my character.'

'Then,' retorted the wag, 'you must have landed at San Francisco with less baggage than any other man who ever came to the Pacific coast!'

CHAPTER XXXVII.

THE general climate of California is equable and balmy, with no snow save in mountain regions; and air so dry that even in Sacramento where the mercury sometimes rises to one hundred and twenty degrees, the heat is less prostrating than that of our eastern summers. The interior is very kind to bronchial and pulmonary complaints.

But San Francisco is a marked exception. The mean temperature of July varies only eight degrees from that of January. Ice is never produced, and thin clothing never worn. Many houses are hidden by luxuriant vines and shrubbery; and throughout the winter, delicate flowers grow in the open air, upon bleakest hills swept by ocean winds. Roses, fuchsias and heliotropes gladden the eye at Christmas and New Year.

Yet San Francisco is one of the very worst climates on the continent for sensitive throats and weak lungs. The incisive winds, commencing at noon and continuing far into night, seem to be the chief cause. I found a fire in my room essential to comfort, on the twentieth of August—often a more severe month than December. The winds are stronger in summer than in winter; but to infirm throats or lungs they are dangerous at all seasons. It is not simply that the air is salt; for many who are robust during ocean voyages cannot endure sea-winds blowing upon the land.

The Golden Gate, the outlet of San Francisco harbor, is a break in the Coast Range mountains. Through its narrow portals rushes a current of air like the blast of a furnace, passing up the valley of the Sacramento to supply the basins west of the Sierra Nevadas. It penetrates every fiber of the body, and cuts into weakened chests and throats like a sharp knife.

But to persons in sound health the city air is pleasant and bracing. Indeed it stimulates like wine. Her climate which makes the blood bound and the nerves tingle, is doubtless responsible for much of the 'fastness' of San Francisco. It brings back the buoyancy of childhood. In the end it must shorten life; for

SAN FRANCISCO FROM THE BAY, IN 1847.

human, like mechanical machinery, cannot increase in speed without increase of friction; the faster it runs the sooner it wears out.

The novelties of the city never cease. One is constantly reminded that twenty years ago here were only sand-hills, with the crumbling cathedral and rude adobe dwellings of a little Spanish post. Every morning he looks out in fresh surprise upon the teeming life of a great metropolis, with stately blocks of brick and stone, railroads, street-cars, gas, markets, exchanges, elegant residences, costly school-houses, imposing churches and generous charities.

More striking still is its magnificent harbor, with miles of steamers and sailing vessels—a harbor which has contained at one time within its anchorage more ships than did ever New York, Liverpool, or London. Our generation has seen no second miracle like the origin and growth of San Francisco.

It is far more cosmopolitan than any other American city except New York. It has four hotels which would be creditable to any metropolis in the world. At these, and along Montgomery street, one sees that curious mingling of faces from every quarter of the globe, which is characteristic of Broadway. Before leaving home, I could remember only one personal acquaintance in California. But on arriving I was surprised to meet scores of familiar countenances—men whom I supposed dead, men whom I fancied still in the East, and men long forgotten. As good Bostonians when they die are said to go to Paris, all other Americans good and bad must go to California.

The heavy earthquake of October, 1865, depressed property for the time, and frightened a few residents into leaving. The falling chimneys and walls did not kill a single person; though some high buildings were cracked from top to bottom, every loose article shaken from tables and mantles, and one fissure, as large as the head of a flour-barrel, left in the earth.

But San Francisco is the inevitable business center for all the interior west of Salt Lake; and for the long coast from Behring's Straits to Patagonia. A brisk trade also is springing up with the Sandwich Islands, Japan and China.

Nature ordained this queen of the Pacific a great metropolis—the second city on the American continent. Burned to the ground six times within eighteen months, her growth was not stopped, nor her prosperity impaired; and if a new earthquake were to shake down every building, not leaving one stone upon another, the town would soon be as large and as vigorous as ever.

I can but barely touch upon the manufacturing, farming, fruit-growing and mining of this wonderful young State.

Manufactures in iron and wool are further advanced than any others. Some cotton cloth is already made; and California, Arizona, Utah, Sandwich Islands and South America will supply the raw staple.

The Mission Woolen Mills, near the old Mision Dolores which John Phœnix immortalized in his unequaled burlesque upon Government railroad surveys, are six years old, with a capital of eight hundred thousand dollars. At first they were a failure, owing to the high prices of labor; but since the introduction of Chinamen, content with one dollar and twenty-five cents per day, (white labor costs about three dollars,) they prove a great success.

There is wide-spread prejudice against the Chinese. In the mines they pay a monthly tax of four dollars per head for the privilege of working, and thereby swell immensely the State

SAN FRANCISCO IN 1849.

revenues; but they are often driven away. Many believe they have no rights which white men are bound to respect; and some leading citizens advocate their total expulsion from our shores. Three hundred dollars is the ideal 'pile' of a laboring Chinaman; and when he has attained it, he is ready to return to his wives and children in the Celestial land for which his heart never ceases to yearn. He has no desire to become an American citizen; he does not settle, he only stays. Is it because he has come eastward, while the irrevocable fiat of Nature requires that emigration shall move only toward the setting sun?

Even the wealthy Chinese merchants expect to return to the home of their nativity. The masses are almost invariably able to read and write their own language. Their imitative capacity is wonderful; they can do whatever they have seen done. They make admirable operatives, working with the exactness of machinery itself; and will yet be largely employed in running quartz-crushers, and in general manufactures.

At the Mission Mills I examined finer, softer, heavier woolen blankets than I ever saw elsewhere. The San Francisco factories have supplied our army with some of its best. All their work is of the highest quality. Throughout the mines of Arizona, Idaho, Nevada and Montana the demand is almost exclusively for California and Oregon woolens, on account of their superiority to those from the Atlantic coast.

I glanced into the Mission church, built by the Spaniards two hundred years ago. It has adobe walls, three feet in thickness, adorned by the cheap paintings and images with which early Jesuit missionaries excited the imaginations of simple natives. In the graveyard beside it lies buried James Casey, murderer of James King of William, editor of the *Bulletin.* This homicide was the immediate cause of the famous vigilance committee of 1856, at whose hands Casey was hanged. An imposing marble monument bears his dying words: 'May God forgive my persecutors!' Why do the most graceless scoundrels, at the point of death, often display so much more piety than anybody else?

Some witty writer defines Photography as 'justice without mercy.' In this art, San Francisco has made enviable progress. It is largely due to the wonderfully clear air. If the ancients, in the childhood of the human race, the world's morning twilight, had such an atmosphere and such an empyrean, no wonder they thought the blue sky the floor of heaven. California photographs are far clearer than the East can produce; and some of the large views of Yosemite, (pronounced Yo-*sem*-i-te,) are beyond comparison the finest sun-pictures ever taken—even excelling the famed photographs of Italy.

The placer mining of California is nearly exhausted. The quartz mining is but just begun. Cheapness of machinery, labor and living, give these lodes great advantages over those of more distant regions. Quartz containing eight or nine dollars of gold to the ton, pays well; while in portions of Nevada, Utah, Montana and Idaho, ore will not justify crushing unless one hundred dollars can be extracted from each ton. The Pacific railway will partially equalize this; but can never do so fully. In general the California quartz-gold is fine and easily worked. Almost half of our mineral product is from this State.

Mining is a lottery; tilling the earth is a certainty, and frugal,

INTERIOR OF MISSION CHURCH.

industrious farmers grow rich. About one-third of all the land is susceptible of culture; and the soil is generally good, though not equal to the Mississippi valley. There is no depth at which it gives out. In most localities, with early sowing and planting, little irrigation is required. In the Sacramento valley and other sections wild oats grow luxuriantly. In the San Jose valley a field produced a hundred bushels of wheat to the acre, and the next year yielded a 'volunteer crop' (without plowing or sowing,) of sixty bushels to the acre.

CALIFORNIA FRUITS AND VEGETABLES. Page 453.

Of the entire agricultural product, barley reaches thirty-nine per cent.—a larger proportion than in any other part of the world;—wheat, thirty-four per cent.; oats, ten; potatoes, ten; and corn only four. Sixty bushels of barley to the acre is not uncommon; and a single acre has produced one hundred and forty-nine bushels. Canning says shrewdly, that nothing is so false as facts, except figures; but this statement is on trustworthy authority.

The root vegetables thrive wonderfully. There have been exhibited at the agricultural fairs, an onion weighing seventy-seven ounces avoirdupois, twenty-two inches in circumference; a turnip, twenty-six pounds; a tomato, twenty-six inches in circumference; cabbage-heads, forty-three to fifty-three pounds; a watermelon, sixty-five pounds; a red beet, one hundred and eighteen pounds, five feet long by one foot in diameter; a squash, two hundred and sixty-five pounds.

Fruit trees are twice as large as in our middle States at the same age. In one year the cherry has grown fourteen feet high; the pear ten feet; and the stem of the peach tree three inches in diameter. One peach tree in a year from the bud grew eight feet high, with a trunk circumference of eight and-a-half inches. A peach twig a foot long, stuck in the ground in 1858, bore fruit the next year. The apple tree bears in the second or third year from the bud; and apples have been exhibited weighing two and-a-half pounds. They lack the sharp, agreeable flavor which New England and Oregon impart. But the enormous peaches, the rich pears, the strawberries and grapes, which grow with incredible profusion, have a peculiarly rich and generous taste that lingers lovingly on the palate.

The California fruits and vegetables for the full-page engraving in this volume, were hastily collected in the Pacific market, San Francisco, on the twenty-eighth of September. They are not unusual specimens; but can be duplicated in all the great fruit markets any morning during six months of the year. The human figure, nearly six feet high, was included in the photograph to show the relative size of the vegetable productions. The two black beets on each side rest upon the floor, and their tops, standing erect, would nearly reach the man's head. They were dug before attaining full growth, and weighed thirty-eight and fifty-nine pounds.

One of the pears exhibited (a Duchess d'Angoulême) weighs thirty ounces; specimens of the same variety weighing seventy ounces have been raised. The apples (Gloria Mundi) weigh from twenty-three to twenty-nine and-a-half ounces. The corn has twenty-four rows of kernels to the ear, with four ears on a stalk. The bunch of grapes (Tokay) weighs eleven pounds. There is a sunflower blossom twenty-four inches across the face; an egg-plant fruit twenty-six inches in circumference; a cabbage fifty-four inches in circumference; quinces weighing thirty ounces each; large radishes and sweet potatoes.

Grapes fresh from the vines are found on California tables from July till December. Fruit at breakfast is one of the most delicious customs of the country. The morning meal begins with grapes, figs, peaches, strawberries, and pears. Of the first, one never tires. I ate grapes statedly at breakfast, luncheon, and dinner, and incidentally at intervals through the day and evening.

In the orchard of Wilson Flint, near Sacramento, I saw hundreds of pear trees, seven years from the graft, bearing sixty pounds of fruit each. Fruits, vegetables, and grain are invariably sold by weight. I noticed a cluster of six pears growing on one twig, almost as close as they could be packed in a fruit dish, and each nearly as large as a man's fist. This was the twenty-sixth of August; and the graft which bore them was put in during the previous April—only four months before. It was the most wonderful sight of my entire journey. Jonah's gourd ceases to be the symbol of miraculous growth.

In the same orchard hundreds of fig trees bent under rich purple fruit. Olives, pomegranates, lemons, and apricots grow in various sections. The State also contains about twenty-five hundred orange trees. When six or eight years old they produce fruit, and continue bearing for half a century. At fourteen years they yield from one thousand to three thousand oranges per tree. They blossom early in spring; the fruit is ripe the next February, and if left on the branches keeps until May.

Bunches of grapes weighing six pounds may be found in almost any market; and a bunch of seventeen pounds was exhibited at one fair. Two hundred varieties are cultivated; the most delicate vines from the Atlantic slope, Europe, Asia, and Africa, flourish in this kindly soil. The fruit-growers begin to export large quantities of raisins and preserved figs. With the completion of the railroad, they expect to supply eastern markets daily with fresh Pacific grapes forwarded in close cars, of dry, even temperature.

The grape crop never fails, and averages double the yield per acre of the vineyards of Ohio, France, and Germany. The Catawba, though smaller than some varieties, excels all others in flavor. The vineyards of the State cover upward of ten thousand acres. The largest, in Sonoma, contains one hundred acres. The wine product is between one and two millions of gallons annually. Many varieties of still and sparkling are produced. Angelica and Muscatel are sweet, still wines—the latter very rich, and with a flavor like Tokay. The port and the hock are sometimes excellent. California champagne, claret, sherry, wine-bitters, and brandies are largely produced. But in general the people themselves prefer imported wines; and often their native varieties taste new, raw, and 'heady.' They are better in New York than in San Francisco. The long sea voyage makes them smoother; and age gives them flavor. Wine making is too young here to be perfect. Manufacturers of experience in Ohio, Missouri, and European vineyards, have not yet learned how to treat the most familiar grapes modified by this climate and soil. But all these difficulties will be overcome; one day this will be a very leading branch of commerce, and the wines of California will excel those of all other countries on the globe.

Among valueless vegetable productions, the cactus impresses strangers, by the beauty of its flowers, its many varieties, and its enormous size. Frequently it grows to the hight of eight feet.

The Wells-Fargo express, which combines the mail, banking, and express business, and has about one hundred offices, pervades every railway, steamboat, and stage route, and every town and mining camp on the Pacific coast. It illustrates the superiority of private enterprise. When its messengers run on the very steamer, or the same railway carriage, with those of the United States mail, three-fourths of the business men intrust it with their letters, which are invariably delivered in advance of the Government consignments. In San Francisco, Mr. Colfax dropped a note into the mail, making an engagement for the next week with a gentleman residing a mile from our hotel. Three days after the appointed time his friend appeared and explained:

'I have but just received your letter. Why didn't you send it by Wells-Fargo?'

CALIFORNIA CACTUS.—FROM A PHOTOGRAPH.

To found and systematize a great enterprise like this, extending over half a continent, new, thinly-settled, with poor means of communication, along routes infested by robbers and Indians, requires more capacity than to 'run' the Government of the United States in ordinary times. I asked the gentleman who has chiefly conducted it:

'What new lessons has your experience taught you?'

His answer pleasantly confirms one's faith in human nature:

'It has taught me to *trust men.*'

The uniform charge for delivering letters is twelve and a-half cents. The company carries them only in stamped envelopes, thus paying a Government tax of three cents on every half-ounce. Yet the post office department constantly endeavors to suppress it. Twenty-five years ago, when postage was twenty-five cents for distances over four hundred miles, and Hall's express carried letters from Boston to New York for five cents, the authorities did their utmost to stop him; but with Daniel Webster for his counsel, he defeated them and hastened the era of cheap postage.

When the operations of the Wells-Fargo company were confined to the Pacific coast and the steamers between San Francisco and New York, it transported twenty-three hundred thousand letters annually. Two and a-quarter millions of writers paid nine and a-half cents extra *not* to have their letters pass through the Circumlocution Office! What stronger proof of the folly of Government's conveying letters? It might with as much propriety sell groceries, convey heavy freights, or deliver washing. Abolish the post office department. Leave this, like other carrying trade, open to private competition, and the mail service of the United States would be performed fifty per cent. cheaper and one hundred per cent. better than it is to-day.

The San Francisco *Alta** *California* and the *Evening Bulletin* print from seven thousand to nine thousand daily, and earn from twenty thousand to forty thousand dollars per annum. Their terms (in specie) are, eighteen dollars per year for the dailies; five dollars for the weeklies; single copies, ten cents. Advertising rates are very high. The *Sacramento Union*, also successful, is one of the very best newspapers on the continent. The *Alta* once cleared eighty thousand dollars in ten months. It is the pioneer journal, the *Californian*, from which it sprang, first appearing in Monterey, on the 15th of August, 1846, immediately after the hoisting of the American flag in northern California. The next year it removed to San Francisco, which then contained less than five hundred inhabitants. Its first issue was about as large as two pages of this book, and was printed upon brown wrapping paper. It was put in type in an old Spanish office; and the fact that there is no W in the Castilian compelled the clumsy manufacture of that letter from two V's. Part of its contents were in Spanish and part in English. The following is a literal copy of an explanatory paragraph from the editor:

'OUR ALPHABET.—Our type is a spanish font picked up here in a cloister, and has no VV's [W's] in it, as there is none in the spanish alphabet. I have sent to the sandvvich Islands for this letter, in the mean time vve must use tvvo V's. Our paper at present is that used for vvrapping segars; in due time vve vvill have something better: our object is to establise a press in California, and this vve shall in all proba-

---

* When American forces captured the country, it was in two divisions—Baja (lower) and Alta (upper) California. After a few years the Americanized portion became known throughout the world simply as California and the adjective was dropped. But the peninsula is still known as 'Lower California.' The word 'California' was first applied by Cortez. He obtained it from Spanish novels of his day, in one of which it was the name of a heroine, and in another, of an imaginary island.

bility be able to accomplish. The absence of my partner for the last three months and my buties as Alcaldd here have dedrived our little paper of some of those attentions vvhich I hope it vvill hereafter receive. VVALTER COLTON.'

I am indebted to Albert S. Evans, of San Francisco, for the sixth issue of the *Californian*, September 19th, 1846, which says:

'California is now lost forever to Mexico; not a shadow of hope can remain that she can recover a foot of the Territory, and we do not believe that one inhabitant in ten, really regrets the result.'

CIRCULAR.—You are hereby advised that war exists between the United States of North America and Mexico, and are cautioned to guard against an attack from Mexican privateers, and all vessels under the Mexican flag.

'The Territory of California has been taken possession of by the forces under my command, and now belongs to the United States, and you will find safe anchorage and protection in the harbor of San Francisco during any season of the year.

'R. F. STOCKTON,

'Commodore and Commander-in-Chief of the Naval Forces of the United States in the Pacific Ocean, and Governor and Commander-in-Chief of the Territory of California.'

The first piece of domestic gold in the United States is said to have been found in Meadow creek, North Carolina, in 1799. Now, our annual product of the precious metals reaches about one hundred and ten millions of dollars annually; from eighty to ninety millions, gold; the residue silver. Eighty-five per cent. of the gross amount is from quartz mining.

In the early days of California, before the establishment of the Government Mint, much gold of private coinage circulated, to meet absolute business wants. Many gold bars, 'slugs,' and five, ten, twenty, and fifty dollar coins were issued in 1849 50. These coinages have now disappeared, and are rare, even as curiosities. The illustration is an exact representation of one of the 'slugs,' issued from the United States assay office in 1850. Having no alloy in its composition, it was very soft, and wasted rapidly by wearing down.

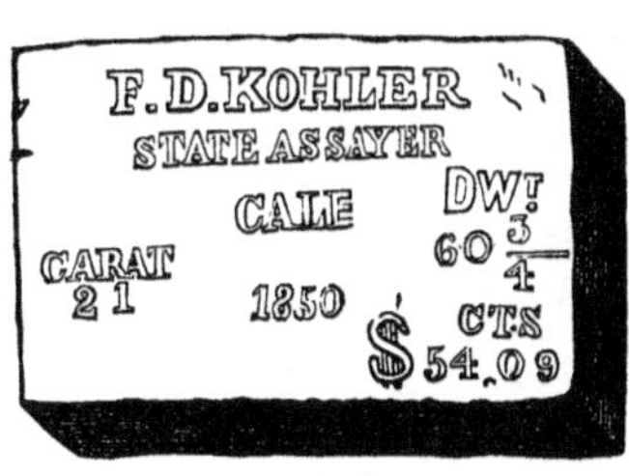

AN EARLY CALIFORNIA COIN.

The United States Branch Mint is one of the most interesting features of San Francisco. The crude metal, received in bars, is melted and mingled, two parts of silver with one of gold; then poured into water, where it cools in fragments like suddenly-cooled lead, or popped corn. It is thus broken into fine pieces, that acids may work upon it more readily—as fire kindles shavings and chips more easily than solid sticks of wood. The nitric acid turns the silver, copper, and lead into liquid; but leaves the gold a dirty brown powder. We saw a rough pile of this, looking as valueless as brick-dust; but worth three hundred thousand dollars. Next, the gold has the water squeezed out by an immense weight; is molded into bars; and rolled into long, thin, narrow strips. From these the round coins are cut, then milled, stamped on both sides, and corrugated—all by machinery. Metallic fingers seize each piece and place it under the stamps, where it is subjected to a pressure of one hundred and sixty tons.

Another machine *counts* the coins, picking out five dollars worth of coppers in one minute, with perfect exactness. Here are scales, too, which will weigh *one four-thousandth of a grain.*

Our coins of precious metal contain nine parts of gold and silver to one of copper. Common salt and zinc are used in hardening the liquid silver and separating it from lead and copper. At night, the employees all leave their working clothing in the mint. When these garments are worn out, they are burned, and the ashes washed, to save the gold. The water in which the workmen wash their hands is also carefully drained off for the same purpose. Through these two sources about fifteen thousand dollars per annum is saved. Practically, there is no loss. In 1864, upon a coinage of twenty-one millions, the deficit was only two thousand dollars, though at the rates allowed by Government for wastage it would have reached seventy thousand.

For the excitement of strangers, the workmen pour a glowing, red-hot stream of melted gold into their hands for a moment, and then empty it out, without receiving a burn. The perspiration protects them, as plumbers thrust their fingers, wet with cold water, into liquid lead, and smelters, into molten iron.

Until the completion of the Pacific railway no man living can comprehend the vastness and variety of our mineral resources between British Columbia and Mexico, and stretching from the eastern wall of the Rocky Mountains to the Pacific.

The road will protect our military interests. Whenever we can transport men and munitions from the Mississippi valley to San Francisco in one week the Monroe Doctrine will enforce itself.

It will revolutionize trade and finance. Travelers in every country will require exchange on New York instead of London. It will give our continent—'its Atlantic front looking upon Europe and its Pacific front looking upon Asia'—the carrying trade of the world. The light, costly silks, teas, and spices of the Orient, rich in barbaric pearl and gold, will seek this route for our markets and for the old world.

It will strengthen us socially. *The* bane of new countries is the absence of the restraining and humanizing influence of women. The oldest States have a surplus of women; the newest suffer for them. With cheap, easy, rapid communication the laws of demand and supply will correct the evil.

It will strengthen us politically. There is infinite pathos in hearing everybody on the Pacific coast, from children to gray-haired men, speak of the East as 'home.' Still, at the outset of the great rebellion, a large party favored a Pacific republic. It was promptly put under foot; and California, debarred from sending her iron, sent her gold to the front. She gave more money proportionately to the great charities of the war than any other State. The Pacific coast contributed to the Sanitary Commission alone almost a million and-a-half of dollars.

Great indeed must be the vitality of the republic when the warm blood from its heart pulsates to these remote extremities; yet we cannot afford to repeat the experiment.

> 'Mountains interposed
> Make enemies of nations who had else,
> Like kindred drops, been mingled into one.'

Do away with isolation; cut through the mountains! This enchanter's wand will make New York acknowledged queen of cities and San Francisco her eldest sister—this magic key will unlock our Golden Gate, and send surging through its rocky portals a world-encircling tide of travel, commerce, and Christian civilization.

CHAPTER XXXVIII.

EX-GOVERNOR LELAND STANFORD, president of the Central Pacific Railroad, and the other gentlemen engaged in building it, were kind enough to organize a pleasant excursion that I might see the progress of their great work. By the Congressional charters, this company constructing the line from Sacramento California eastward, and the Union Pacific working from Omaha Nebraska westward, will each own and run as much road as it can build; so both are engaged in a hard race for Salt Lake.

Each corporation receives in Government bonds sixteen thousand dollars, thirty-two thousand dollars, or forty-eight thousand dollars for every mile of road finished—sixteen thousand where the route is level and grading light; thirty-two thousand among the foot-hills, and forty-eight thousand in the Rocky Mountains and the Sierra Nevadas.

Each company also acquires absolutely thirteen thousand acres of land per mile along its line; and is allowed to issue first mortgage bonds in equal amount to the Government subsidy—the mortgage upon which these company-bonds are based having priority as a lien upon the property of the road over the mortgage given to the Government itself. In addition, the California corporation has a donation of nearly half a million dollars in bonds from San Francisco, and thirty acres of valuable land, in the city limits, from Sacramento. No other enterprise in our country was ever so magnificently endowed. Ultimately the company expect to lay their track to Oakland, just across the bay from San Francisco; at present the western terminus is Sacramento.*

* San Francisco to Salt Lake City by steamer, railway and stage routes: eight hundred and fifty miles. Sacramento to summit of Sierras, by railway route: one hundred and five miles. Summit to Salt Lake City: five hundred and twenty miles.

Ten miles east of Sacramento the track is only one hundred and ninety feet above sea-level; at the crossing of the summit it is seven thousand feet. A peculiarly favorable route, where no elevation is lost after the climbing begins, alone enables it to rise nearly seven thousand feet in ninety-five miles.

The highest grade (one hundred and sixteen feet to the mile) just equals the sharpest ascent on the Baltimore and Ohio road. But it extends only three miles; and no other grade will exceed one hundred and six feet to the mile.

The cars now (1867) run nearly to the summit of the Sierras. At the time of my visit the terminus was Colfax, fifty-five miles east of Sacramento. Thence we took horses for twelve miles. Upon this little section of road four thousand laborers were at work —one-tenth Irish, the rest Chinese. They were a great army laying siege to Nature in her strongest citadel. The rugged mountains looked like stupendous ant-hills. They swarmed with Celestials, shoveling, wheeling, carting, drilling and blasting rocks and earth, while their dull, moony eyes stared out from under immense basket-hats, like umbrellas. At several dining-camps we saw hundreds sitting on the ground, eating soft boiled rice with chop-sticks as fast as terrestrials could with soup-ladles. Irish laborers received thirty dollars per month (gold) and board; Chinese, thirty-one dollars, boarding themselves. After a little experience the latter were quite as efficient and far less troublesome.

LELAND STANFORD.

The Hudson Bay Company in its palmy days was compelled to import laborers from the Sandwich Islands; and without the Chinese the California end of the great national thoroughfare must have been delayed for many years. Twelve thousand are now employed upon it.

Cape Horn is a huge mountain around whose side the track winds upon a little shelf seven hundred feet above valley and stream-bed. At the west end of the road redwood trees are used for ties; in the mountains, spruce and tamarack.

At Gold Run a six-horse coach awaited us. Our day's ride was up a graded winding road, commanding an endless sweep of dense forest and grand mountain, among graceful tamaracks, gigantic pines and pyramidal firs.

Immense barns beside the mountain houses attest the length and severity of the winters. At many points we found the surveyors awaiting our coach to receive their letters and newspapers. The American pioneer can dispense with his dinner, but not with his mental pabulum.

We reached the summit two hours after dark, when its wild, gloomy grandeur is far more impressive than by day. It is boundless mountain piled on mountain—unbroken granite, bare, verdureless, cold and gray.

Through the biting night air we were whirled down the eastern slope for three miles to Donner lake, blue, shining, and sprinkled with stars, while from the wooded hill beyond glared an Indian fire like a great fiendish eyeball. The lake is an exquisite body of water, though less impressive than Tahoe; and the reflections of snowy peak, pine forest, clear sky, and minute twig and leaf in its depths, seem almost miraculous. The illustration, as faithful to nature as artist and engraver can make it, is far less vivid than the original photograph. In that, concealing the boat, figures and trees in the foreground-water, it is almost impossible to decide which side up the picture should be—which are the real hills, snow and forest, and which the reflection.

Donner lake is named from the Donner party of sixty Illinois emigrants, en route for Oregon, snowed in here in 1846. Knowing nothing of the climate, they attempted to cross too late, and were imprisoned by inexorable winter. The logs of one of their cabins; and stumps, twelve feet high, of trees which they cut off at the snow-surface, are still seen. Many ate human flesh; and about forty perished from starvation. Several yet live to tell their horrible story.

We slept at the Lake House; and spent the next day with the surveyors among the precipitious granite ledges, and visiting Lake Angela, a lovely little mountain gem. It was like picnicing at the

North Pole; for snow lined the higher ravines and icicles hung from the water-tanks on the stage-road. Here during the previous

CHINAMEN BUILDING PACIFIC RAILROAD IN THE SIERRA NEVADAS.

winter, two laborers were engulfed by a snow-slide. Seeing it approach they stepped behind a tall rock; but it buried them fifty feet deep. In spring their bodies were found standing upright, with shovels in their hands.

For several miles the track must be roofed to slide off the snow. There will be less than a mile of tunneling, all near the crest. The cost of the most expensive mile of road is estimated at three hundred and fifty thousand dollars. From the summit the line descends to the desert by the valley of the Truckee; and is easy of construction to Salt Lake City. Thus far the work is admirably done, comparing favorably with our best eastern railways.

On the second evening in our tavern parlor, there was a long earnest conference, to determine upon the route near the summit. The candles lighted up a curious picture. The carpet was covered with maps, profiles and diagrams, held down at the edges by candle-sticks to keep them from rolling up. On their knees were president, directors and surveyors, creeping from one map to another, and earnestly discussing the plans of their magnificent enterprise. The ladies of our excursion were grouped around them, silent and intent, assuming liveliest interest in the dry details about tunnels, grades, excavations, 'making hight' and 'getting down.' Outside the night-wind moaned and shrieked, as if the Mountain Spirit resented this invasion of his ancient domain.

SUMMIT-CROSSING OF SIERRA NEVADAS, NEAR DONNER LAKE.

Reluctantly leaving the pleasant party, I accompanied Governor Blaisdel twenty miles over a rough mountain trail, to Lake Tahoe, where, in obedience to a telegram, the little steamer waited to take us to the Glenbrook House. Tahoe forever! Our country has no other lake so beautiful. Its bosom glitters with dazzling diamonds; its depths photograph the most delicate tracery of hill, tree and cloud. Even the shadows of the faint surface-ripples, are clearly penciled upon the bottom, an exquisite, trembling, shining net-work.

Reports of coach robberies and Indian hostilities came from the eastward; so I telegraphed to a Salt Lake friend: 'Are the stage-routes to Montana and Idaho open, and reasonably safe?' He responded: 'Both open, and perfectly safe for passengers going north, who are supposed to have no money.' This described my own condition so exactly that I started by the first coach.

Again I spent several days at Virginia Nevada, that wonderful metropolis of the sage-brush. There as everywhere, mining interests had suffered from wild speculations and reckless expenditures. It was difficult to find a business man in California who had not lost in Washoe stocks. An acquaintance of mine sunk seventy-five thousand dollars in three weeks; but he could afford it and said he counted the lesson cheap. One Virginia company, which spent a hundred thousand dollars in erecting a mill, received all the money back with interest in twelve months. *Their* superintendent realized that mining is business, not gambling; conducted it as men manufacture paper and sell dry goods—not as they speculate in stocks or play monte.

Many new inventions are offered; but the practical miners are ten years ahead of the books and the professors of natural science. The amateur angler comes from the city, with intricate extension-rod, patent fly, water-proof clothing, silver brandy-flask, and all sporting theories in his head, but stands, the entire day, without persuading a single fish; while the unlettered country boy, barefooted, in torn trowsers, with birchen rod, line of twine, and plain hook and worm, secures a splendid string of trout in half an hour. So the chemist experiments in his laboratory and the geologist makes learned reports upon mines; but the men who feed the stamps originate the valuable improvements in machinery, and those who wield the pick find and recognize the real silver lodes.

A resident was pointed out to me, who within five years had paid half a million dollars interest upon borrowed money, and now was not worth a penny! In the mining regions outside of California money on the best security commands from two to six per cent. a month—often compounded monthly! If these rates do not ruin any country, it must be so rich that ruin is impossible to ruin it—just as Scotchmen, according to Dr. Johnson, are so hardy that they cannot be starved.

From Virginia I continued eastward by coach, first having my hair cropped and beard shaven close enough for a votary of the Prize Ring. This lessens the disagreeableness of the alkaline dust which envelops horses and drivers, vehicle and inmates. A ride

REFLECTION IN DONNER LAKE, SIERRA NEVADAS.

in its thick clouds is like a cold bath; one shrinks from it at first; but fairly in, experiences a grim satisfaction.

Among our passengers were several New York gentlemen, bound for Montana, who, deterred by Indian difficulties from coming overland direct, had taken the long isthmus route to San Francisco, and were now going to Bannack via Salt Lake City. A pleasant young fellow on board, just from college, started around the world, but in the steamer lost at gambling the money his careful father had provided; so he too had turned toward Montana, to retrieve his fortunes.

Spending but one day in Austin, I was unable to visit the 'Cortez' mining region on the north, or the 'Twin River,' and 'Silver Peak' on the south. They all promise richly. We entered Utah while the mountains were glorified; and white clouds seemed to rest, not against the dome of the sky, but in front of it, very near us, permitting us to gaze under and far beyond them, into its blue depths. One long bank lay from peak to peak, like a bridge of ice. The ashen ground of the desert was intersected with long slender streaks of light—the sun shining through narrow crevices in the clouds. The sunset was the finest I ever saw; and the twilight a miracle of gold and purple, pink and pearl, all turning at last to sullen lead.

Gladly we reached Salt Lake City, to enjoy baths, New York newspapers, and fresh fruit. Here as in California, delicious grapes and peaches abound. The apples are better flavored than in the Golden State. Almost our entire continent, from the Ohio valley to the Pacific seems adapted to the vine.

During this visit in September and October, I found a good deal of bitterness toward me existing among zealous Mormons, caused by the return of my *Tribune* letters. I had written frankly, but in no unkindly spirit. I *could* say nothing except ill of polygamy; and that excited their indignation. Some of the young Saints too were naturally wroth because I had spoken of the women as homely. At an out-door political meeting one night, they persisted in shouting for me with suspicious zeal and iteration. As I chanced to be visiting a friend a mile away, their vocal exercise was love's labor lost. The next day it was confessed that they had attempted to allure me upon the rostrum for the pleasure of hissing me, and possibly of pelting me. If the young democracy of Salt Lake mean to have a personal quarrel with every traveler who describes the feminine Saints as uncomely, they are not likely to suffer for want of employment.

Porter H. Rockwell, reputed one of the leading Danites or destroying angels of the church, also confused me in his mind with Fitz Hugh Ludlow, who had passed through two years before, and given an unflattering description of him for the *Atlantic Monthly*. Some one told Porter, or he dreamed it, that *I* had characterized him as the murderer of one hundred and fifty men; and he significantly remarked, that if I had said it he believed he would make it one hundred and fifty-one! He finally concluded it a mistake, and contented himself with complaining to me that he had been cruelly slandered by Ludlow, and afterward while in his cups, assuring me that he *would* kill any journalist who should publish falsehoods about him. He is a man of medium size, noticeable for his long black hair, which he wears parted in the middle and hanging upon the shoulders. In general he is said to

THE DONNER PARTY IN 1846.

be hospitable and kind; and his manners mild and courteous. At the time of my visit he was keeping a station on the overland mail route. He is believed to be the person who, years ago, attempted the life of Governor Boggs of Missouri. Boggs had used the State troops to expel the Mormons. One night while sitting in his library in Jefferson City, a rifle ball from the outside wounded him, and he very narrowly escaped death. It was the only attempt to assassinate a public officer which stained American history until the murder of Abraham Lincoln.

THE SALT LAKE POETESS.

(*Mrs. Sarah Carmichael Williamson.*)

Can any good thing come out of Nazareth? Utah, with its utter isolation and iron social and spiritual limitations, would seem the last place in the world for mental development. But the poet once born, no Medusa can strike him dumb. The warblings of a young songstress of Salt Lake City were now beginning to excite attention, from the peculiar and adverse circumstances of their origin. A native of New York, at eight years of age she was carried to Utah, where she had since resided, almost without books, society or other opportunity for culture. She was wholly self-educated; and sustained herself by teaching an infant school. Her father was a rigid Mormon, a day laborer in humblest life. Her 'Funeral of Lincoln,' written in a disloyal community on the very day of receiving telegraphic news of the assassination, pictures vividly the first paralyzing grief which swept over the country:

Every home and hall was shrouded,
  Every thoroughfare was still;
Every brow was darkly clouded,
  Every heart was faint and chill.
O, the inky drop of poison
  In our bitter draught of grief!
O, the sorrow of a nation
  Mourning for its murdered chief!

Strongest arms were closely folded,
  Most impassioned lips at rest;
Scarcely seemed a heaving motion
  In the nation's wounded breast.
Tears were frozen in their sources,
  Blushes burned themselves away;
Language bled through broken heart-threads,
  Lips had nothing left to say.

Yet there was a marble sorrow
  In each still face chiseled deep,
Something more than words could utter,
  Something more than tears could weep.
O, the land he loved will miss him,
  Miss him in its hour of need!
Mourns the nation *for the nation*,
  Till its tear-drops inward bleed.

This bold flight of fancy, all will appreciate who are familiar with the great mountains of Utah, torn and furrowed to the heart, and sometimes cleft asunder from head to foot:

THE ORIGIN OF GOLD.

The Fallen looked on the world and sneered;
'I can guess,' he muttered, 'why God is feared;
For the eyes of mortals are fain to shun
The midnight heaven, that hath no sun.
I will stand on the hight of the hills and wait
Where the Day goes out at the western gate;
And reaching up to its crown will tear
From its plumes of glory the brightest there;
With the stolen ray I will light the sod,
And turn the eyes of the world from God.'

He stood on the hight when the sun went down,
He tore one plume from the Day's bright crown;
The proud beam stooped till he touched its brow,
And the print of his finger is on it now;
And the blush of its anger forevermore
Burns red when it passes the western door!
The broken feather, above him whirled,
In flames of torture around him curled;
And he dashed it down on the snowy hight
In broken masses of quivering light.
Ah, more than terrible was the shock
Where the burning splinters struck wave and rock!

The green earth shuddered, and shrank, and paled;
The wave sprang up and the mountain quailed.
Look on the hills; let the scars they bear
Measure the pain of that hour's despair.

The Fallen watched while the whirlwind fanned
The pulsing splinters that plowed the sand;
Sullen he watched while the hissing waves
Bore them away to the ocean caves;
Sullen he watched while the shining rills
Throbbed through the hearts of the rocky hills.
Loudly he laughed: 'Is the world not mine?
Proudly the links of its chain shall shine,
Lighted with gems shall its dungeon be;
But the pride of its beauty shall kneel to me.'
That splintered light in the earth grew cold,
And the diction of mortals hath called it 'Gold.'

A little volume of the lady's earlier poems, recently published in San Francisco, has been very favorably received. The author, never in sympathy with the Mormon church, surreptitiously left Salt Lake in 1866, and is now the wife of an estimable ex-surgeon of our army, who formed her acquaintance while on duty at Camp Douglas, two miles from the Mormon capital.

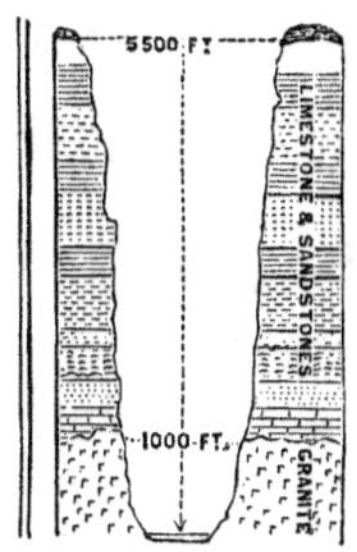

A SECTION OF COLORADO CANYON.

In the Latter-day Saints' metropolis I heard much of the Pah Ranagat (Indian—'water melon,') silver region, three hundred and fifty miles to the southwest, and two hundred miles due south of Austin. It lies in the southeast corner of Nevada, and is now connected with Salt Lake City by a tri-weekly mail coach. Its climate, permitting work through the entire year, is a manifest advantage over the mountain regions of Idaho, Montana, central Nevada and Oregon, where the winters are often very severe. It is so remote that only a few mills are yet in operation; but the veins open very richly, and many believe the district will equal the great Comstock Lode.

Thus far, miners obtain their supplies from neighboring Mormon settlements; but Pah Ranagat promises well for farming purposes, though it lies in the valley of the Colorado of the West, which, according to Horace Greeley, 'offers larger and more favorable

opportunities for successful starvation than any other section of equal area on the surface of the globe—not excepting the Great Sahara!'

The Colorado river rises on the west side of the Rocky Mountains in a thousand sources, from ten thousand to twelve thousand feet above the sea. Its bed is a deep natural trench. It has cut down the high plateau over which it first ran, through the limestone, through the sandstone and far into the granite. Its current, now shallow and insignificant, once filled this vast gorge.

LIG CANYON OF COLORADO RIVER, ARIZONA.

The Big Canyon is above the head of navigation. It crosses three degrees of longitude; by the windings of the river it is three hundred miles long. For this entire distance, the walls rise almost perpendicularly from three thousand to six thousand feet; and the width of the gulf at the top is often less than its depth.

Three hundred years ago, Spanish explorers declared the walls of the canyon *three leagues* high. Only a few Indians, Mexican trappers and American explorers have seen it; but those can find no language extravagant enough to describe its wonderful scenery. The gorge is worn down by water—not torn open by natural convulsions. The top is an even plateau—not mountain peaks as in Yosemite. Our illustration is from the mouth of Diamond river.

According to some authorities Arizona, signifies 'land of the sun.' Less poetic lexicographers assert that it means 'sand-hills.' This Territory, twice as large as the State of New York, is inhabited by about fifty thousand Indians, all fierce and hostile, ten thousand Mexicans and twelve hundred Americans. Its gold and silver resources are very great; but only three or four quartz-mills (in all, running less than fifty stamps,) are in operation. Protecting the miners against the savages is almost impossible.

The Territory is composed of sand wastes, with some green valleys; but enthusiastic residents declare it the best grazing country in the world. It abounds in ruins of ancient cities of stone, usually upon hills now far from water, or near dry stream-beds. Since the establishment of missions by Jesuits—who have the earliest trustworthy records—the Pueblos, to whom these ruins are attributed, have greatly diminished in numbers, and lost many of their early arts, including the curious manufacture of feather cloth.

In addition to Big Canyon, the country contains hundreds of grand mountain scenes. The Cabazin Pass between San Bernadino and La Paz, is famed for noises more unearthly than those which disturbed the thane of Cawdor. They resemble sobs, whoops, and yells of agony. Indian tradition refers them to the perturbed spirits of a savage band once imprisoned and slaughtered there; but prosaic science attributes them to desert winds whistling and moaning through the canyon.

CHAPTER XXXIX.

From Salt Lake City, Virginia capital of Montana, lies four hundred and seventy-five miles north; Boise capital of Idaho, four hundred and fifty miles northwest. The road is like the letter Y; at Bear river, eighty miles out, the main stem forks, the right stroke leading to Montana and the left to Idaho.

I started from the City of the Saints early in October; but already the white plumes of King Winter waved from every neighboring mountain. Most passengers, if provided with feather pillows, slumber quietly and refreshingly night after night, while the vehicle is in motion; and comprehend how the Esquimaux and some other nations sleep from choice in a sitting posture. But for a very few exceptional organizations this night-travel causes 'stage-craziness.' Passengers suffering from it have sometimes fled from the coach to perish in the desert.

For hours along the Great Salt Lake, we viewed its shining mirror, broken by purple mountains of island, and bordered by violet peaks, spotted with white, gauzy clouds. We passed thrifty Mormon villages of dull brown adobe houses, with orchards, and shading cottonwoods, and streets watered by artificial streams; and valley farms with broad fields, great shocks of corn and huge stacks of barley. The Indian warrior indicates the number of scalps he has taken, by the notches on his tomahawk. The Latter-day Saint advertises the number of wives he has secured by the doors to his house. With the poorer settlers rival spouses must occupy the same room; but in well-to-do families each has her own separate little tenement.

Morrisville was built by Mormon followers of Morris, a strange fanatic, who out-Brighamed Brigham. Believing that the world with all its people except themselves was about to be destroyed, he taught them to seize the horses, cattle and grain of their neighbors, as belonging to the chosen of the Lord. It was 'a part of their religion.' But in 1862, the Mormons marched an army against the schismatics, who fought them bravely in a pitched battle. The prophet fell with a bullet in his brain; several of his followers, including women and children were killed, and all the rest driven out. Let Brigham ponder the lesson. 'He who will not be ruled by the rudder must be ruled by the rock.'

At the most lonely farm dwellings multitudes of children, bearing 'shocks of yellow hair like the silken floss of the maize,' attest the presence of the Peculiar Institution in this prolific country. In general though not over-embarrassed with clothing they are hardy, robust, and of excellent physical development.

At Bear river our daylight breakfast is shared by a coach-load of passengers from Montana and another from Idaho, with whom we exchange the latest news. Thence our road winds pleasantly in grassy valleys and across miry little streams; for bridges come only with civilization. We meet many creaking ox-wagons, with dingy covers, bound for 'the States.' From the Missouri river to Utah, Montana or Idaho, a team can make only one round trip per year, as cattle cannot travel on the plains in winter. We see no dwellings except low adobe stations, with huge stacks of winter hay, cut from wild grass of the valleys.

SIX WIVES.

Crossing a low, bare divide, we leave the great basin of Utah behind, and are in Idaho, on waters of the Pacific. After dark, in the twinkling of an eye, whack! goes our coach—over upon one side. We have capsized in a mud-hole; but all escape unharmed. The station-stable hard by has no house, but a little stall for cooking and sleeping, wherein the driver is partitioned off from his mules.

All the next forenoon we ride along the clear Snake. This dim, crooked artery of the great desert's heart, fifteen hundred miles long, must be Butler's original reptile, which

> ———'Wires in and wires out,
> Leaving the reader still in doubt,
> Whether the Snake which made this track
> Was going south or coming back.'

The Indian name, 'Sho-sho-*nee*' or winding stream, is far better than ours. It is the river of desolation. Unrelieved by forests or green banks for nearly the entire length, it is a natural ditch deep in the earth, filled with clear water, and faintly fringed with scattering willows and cottonwoods.

The white man keeping the first ferry has taken a rather comely squaw for the sole mistress of his heart and log-cabin. As we pass, she sits upon the ground sewing moccasins, diversifying her labor by frequent imitations of the first act of mother Eve after her creation, according to Milton's verse—admiring the reflection of her own features in the water.

Passing in view of the Three Tetons (women's breasts) and other exquisite peaks; and toiling over long sand wastes, we cross the divide of the Rocky Mountains from Idaho and the Pacific slope, into Montana among the tributaries of the Missouri.

Down in the deep gulch of Grasshopper creek we reach the city of Bannack, named from a savage tribe. Here, in 1861, began the first settlement of Montana. The diggings often yielded fifty dollars per day to the man; but like most gulch mines, were soon exhausted. In flush times the city had two thousand people. Now it is a dreary succession of straggling, empty log houses, overlooked by a gallows, which has outlived many tenants. Even the county sheriff who built it, like a second Haman was finally hanged upon it, for highway robbery and murder. Rich quartz lodes now opened are giving the town a new lease of life.

Successively crossing Rattlesnake creek, Beaver-head river, named from a rock mountain mentioned by Lewis and Clark, faintly resembling the head of a beaver, and still another tributary of the Missouri bearing the euphonious appellation of the 'Stinking-water,' five days and four nights from Salt Lake City, we reach

Virginia. This young, lively metropolis of Montana, must not be confounded with its Nevada namesake, a thousand miles to the southwest. It was settled in 1862, after Bannack gave out. Now it has about four thousand people. Environed by mountain crests dotted with a few lonely cedars, it lies like a huge serpent, a crooked, irregular strip of low log houses, winding for nine miles down Alder creek. Many of these cabins are deserted. The American miner is a migratory animal, who will always leave five dollars per day for the possibility of twenty, especially when the new diggings are very remote and inaccessible. Alder gulch has yielded millions of dollars; and for its length—thirteen miles—was the richest gold deposit ever found. Now, it is completely cut to pieces; honey-combed with shafts, ridged with ditches, and disemboweled with tunnels. A few miners still wash the gold from the brown earth.

A PROLIFIC COUNTRY.

The heart of the town is within a hundred yards of the diggings. In flush times, streets were thronged; stores choked with a stream of commerce; sidewalks monopolized by auctioneers hoarsely crying horses, oxen, mules, wagons and household goods. Drinking saloons, whose name was legion, were densely crowded. Theaters, which always spring up in mining regions, were closely packed. At hotels, beds were hardly obtainable for love or money. Gaming-tables were musical with clinking coin and shining with yellow gold. Hurdy-gurdy houses, where whisky was sold at fifty cents a drink and champagne at twelve dollars per bottle, were filled with visitors, ranging from judges to blacklegs, in every costume, from broadcloth to buckskin. And all this, in a town less than one year old, in the heart of the Rocky Mountains, a thousand miles from everywhere! For Montana is the remotest Territory of the United States—farthest both from New York and San Francisco, the two cities which will yet contend for the mastery of the world.

Virginia's trade is still heavy, and the business streets always lively. The buildings are of logs, lumber and granite, with the wooden signs of many irrepressible Jews overhanging the plank sidewalks. The currency is gold dust. In small purchases, handling and weighing it involves a waste of about twenty-five per cent. Every morning, little boys with shovels and pans gather up and wash out the sweepings from the stores, and sometimes realize five dollars apiece.

At the leading hotel I found wooden benches serving for chairs. The fare, though with no fruit and few vegetables, was palatable; but the lodgings were open to the objection of that Illinois traveler, who, promised an excellent apartment which Douglas had just left, found two men in each of three beds, and one in the fourth.

'Landlord,' said he, 'this room is good, and I should feel honored to sleep in one so lately occupied by Senator Douglas; but I *will not* sleep with the whole democratic party!'

I visited the theater to see the 'Lady of Lyons.' The admission-fee was one dollar and-a-half. The drop-curtain was of cambric; the stage, as large as a very small bedroom; five tallow candles served for foot-lights; and the orchestra consisted of four performers. Many spectators wore revolvers; but the rough crowd was wholly decorous, in deference to the half-dozen wives and sisters present.

I found the hurdy-gurdy more popular. At one end of the long hall, a well-stocked bar, and a monte bank in full blast; at the other, a platform occupied by three musicians; between, many lookers-on, with cigars and meerschaums. The orchestra leader shouted:

'Take your ladies for the next dance!'

Half-a-dozen swarthy fellows fresh from the diggings, selected partners from the tawdry, bedizened women who stood in waiting. After each dance the miners led their partners to the bar for whisky or champagne; then after a short pause, another dance; and so the sorry revelry continued from nine o'clock until nearly daylight, interrupted only by two fights. For every dance each masculine participant paid one dollar, half going to his partner, and half to the proprietor. This latter functionary, who was dealing monte, with revolver at his belt, assured me that his daily profits averaged one hundred dollars. Publicly, decorum was preserved; and to many miners, who had not seen a feminine face for six months, these poor women represented vaguely something of the tenderness and sacredness of their sex.

The mountain road from Virginia to Helena (one hundred and twenty-five miles northward) is now traversed by the mail coaches from Salt Lake City. It has witnessed some of the best staging in the United States. In 1865, when it was new and little worked, coaches frequently ran the whole distance—equal to one hundred and sixty miles of good roads—during daylight; and sometimes in fourteen hours. The route crosses the main, or Jefferson, Fork of the Missouri, upon a log bridge two hundred feet in length. The river shines along a beautiful valley, between mountains pine-covered and snow-clad.

We pass the log ranches of settlers, with huge hay-stacks, and fields rich in wheat and barley, or overgrown turnips and potatoes. Despite frosts every month in the year, Montana has good agricultural capacity. Small grains, root vegetables, and the hardy fruits produce abundantly. Some irrigation is required. Thus far grasshoppers have injured the crops. Wheat and barley yield twenty to forty bushels per acre; oats thirty to fifty; and potatoes from one hundred to three hundred bushels. All vegetables are excellent and grow to enormous size. It seems far north for

THE HURDY-GURDY HOUSE, VIRGINIA, MONTANA. Page 480.

cereals; but in the British Possessions—still higher latitude—the Hudson Bay Company has raised successfully every product of our northwestern States. Some even believe that the true wheat-growing region of our continent lies north of the Upper Missouri.

On our right, in a deep canyon of rugged mountains, is the junction of the Jefferson, Gallatin and Madison, whose blended waters form the 'Great Muddy.' In Minnesota, a little wooden bridge spans the Mississippi. Here, one can fling a pebble across the Missouri. Still higher, among mountain springs, a soldier of the Lewis and Clark expedition, which had spent a year ascending from St. Louis, thanked God that he was able to stand astride of the largest river in the world!

VIRGINIA CITY, MONTANA.

We enter White-tailed-deer Canyon, twenty miles long, with grand and startling views, ever shifting, like scenes in a theater. Immense granite bowlders, some as large as a railway-car, lie upon and against each other, in all positions, as if the gods had hurled vast rocks in deadly battle. Some walls of the gorge are gray stone; others clothed in firs and pines of dark green and purplish brown sprinkled with yellow cottonwoods. Looking back through the canyon's mouth, we see snowy mountains glorified by the dying sun, like battlements of a celestial city. Through the opposite gateway, some peaks are obscured by slabs of sullen leaden clouds, bridging the gulfs between them; others are robed in drapery white as milk and soft as down.

Whirling along slippery banks and sideling roads, and at Dustan's station passing a spring ten inches in diameter which gushes boiling-hot from the hill-side, we reach Helena. This city is the legitimate successor of Virginia, as is Virginia of Bannack. It has now outgrown the anxious stage, which comes to all new settlements, and in which every arriving stranger is instantly asked:

'Well sir, how do you like our town?'

Helena is about three years old, with a population of four thousand. Its two principal streets are in the form of a cross. At my visit it did not boast a hotel. Now it has several, with pleasant residences, ample business blocks, and a thriving trade.

It is the supply point for the rich placer mines of the Blackfoot country and other northern gulches. I have never been in any other region where gold dust in the hands of working miners circulated freely in so large quantities. Several nuggets, worth from two to four thousand dollars have been taken out. The value of the one shown in our illustration is two thousand and seventy-five dollars. The relative proportions of the nugget and the hand have been carefully preserved from the photograph.

Single claims have produced one thousand dollars per day. These are very unusual cases; but Montana is the richest placer mining region ever discovered in the United States. Thus far its quartz veins promise to average better than those of any other section. As yet, they are little developed; and the season of 1867 opens with less than one hundred and fifty stamps in operation, owing to the remoteness and inaccessibility of the country.

About one-fifth of the supplies come overland from California and Oregon; one-fifth overland from Kansas and Nebraska; and three-fifths up the Missiouri from St. Louis to Fort Benton. This is the nominal head of navigation, twenty miles below the Great Falls; one hundred and forty miles from Helena, and two hundred and sixty-five from Virginia. But ascending to this point is possible only during a few summer weeks, for very light-draft steamers. Many boats are compelled to stop below. Freights from St. Louis cost from eight to fifteen cents per pound; passage, two hundred dollars. Steamers are from thirty to seventy days on the way.

Virginia is five thousand feet above sea-level; Helena forty-two hundred; Fort Benton twenty-six hundred. The Missouri at Benton is insignificant, giving no hint of the grand system of streams flowing to the southern gulf, two hundred rivers in one, which afford fifty thousand miles of steamboat navigation. In the fall, thousands of returning miners float down the Missouri from near Helena (passing around the Great Falls by a portage of ten miles) in fleets of Mackinaw flat-boats—accomplishing the distance to Omaha in about thirty days.

Communication with the head waters of the Columbia is easy, the navigation of Pen d'Oreille lake and river greatly reducing the wagon travel. Much immigration comes from the west coast.

Fort Union, four hundred miles below Benton, is near the mouth of the Yellowstone. This old trading post is well known among trappers and merchants of the early days. It stands on the bank of the clear Missouri, a stockaded fort with two towers; the United States flag flying; Indian lodges in the rear; little cottonwood groves in ravines on either side; and light *batteaux* upon the shining stream in front. I am indebted to Major Culbertson, an old Indian trader, for an interesting view of the fort in its palmy days, painted upon bed-ticking, by an unskilled employé of the American Fur Company, with such brushes and colors as he could obtain in the wilderness.

TWO-THOUSAND-DOLLAR NUGGET

On my return from Helena to Virginia the weather was intensely cold, with deep snow obstructing the precipitous roads and transforming the pine boughs into exquisite white coral. Upon one bleak mountain in a polar air, we met another coach bearing eleven shivering passengers, and were compelled to exchange horses with it. We found the cold intolerable; but the cheery drivers merely remarked that this was 'lightning.'

The driver is invariably a character; always intelligent, often entertaining and witty, never any respecter of persons. There is a story of one, with a clergyman upon the box beside him, who swore long and loud at his balking horses.

'My friend,' expostulated the preacher, 'don't swear so. Remember Job; he was severely tried, but never lost his patience.'

'Job—Job?' pondered Jehu. 'What line did *he* drive for?'

Once, with the governor of a Territory, I spent a night at a lonely desert station. His excellency craved permission to sleep on the driver's bunk.

'Certainly,' was the unabashed reply, 'if you haven't any graybacks about you!'

Night overtook us at a log station with the inevitable bar, gold-scales, and great fireplace. Against the wall hung a native potato weighing three and a-half pounds. Why *will* so many call this American vegetable the 'Irish potato?' We slept soundly in our buffalo robes upon the plank floor. Two of our passengers never lost sight of their heavy valises; they were bringing down forty thousand dollars in gold dust from the mines.

The next morning we were upon a sideling mountain road, coated with ice buried under two feet of light snow. Our six horses were upon a full run, to take the coach over before it should slide down the hill. Suddenly one wheel struck a hidden rock. The vehicle narrowly escaped capsizing; and I did not escape being pitched from the driver's box. The blankets and robes enveloping me, fortunately slipped off without entanglement; and I was projected fully twenty-five feet through the air, describing a section of a circle. As John Phœnix used to say, that was the only 'description' of the affair I should ever have been able to give, but for a friendly snow-bank cushioning the broad flat rock upon which I alighted head foremost. The driver seemed to enjoy the joke until ten minutes later, when a similar rock upon *his* side sent him flying against the brake-handle, where he hung, like Mohammed's coffin, until he found his lost legs and abandoned seat. Some fatal accidents occur in winter upon these unworked roads.

Montana had but one newspaper—the Virginia weekly *Post.* It was about half the size of the *Tribune.* Subscription price: seven and-a-half dollars per annum, specie; single copies, fifty cents. When the publishers received their year's supply of printing paper in May, the freight from St. Louis cost them but fifteen or twenty cents a pound. But more than once they were compelled to get it by express at one dollar and ninety cents (gold) per pound. Obtaining a specimen book from a Philadelphia type foundry cost them sixty dollars. Some of their job work, in colors, was excellent. Before the mails began, a New York semi-weekly journal cost its subscriber one dollar per copy, for express charges from Salt Lake alone.

A MAN OF NERVE.

The Territory had only four post-offices. In summer the tri-weekly mail brought letters from New York in twenty-five days. During winter snows the time might reach two or three months.

The climate is peculiarly healthy. This reminiscence of the early days was given me from a pioneer, vouched for as worthy of credence:—A trapper had his leg badly shattered by a bullet, in a drunken row. Amputation was necessary; but no surgeon within hundreds of miles. He whetted one edge of his hunting knife to its utmost sharpness; filed the other into a saw; and with his own hand cut the flesh, sawed the bone, and seared the veins with a red-hot iron. He still lives in California, walking upon a wooden leg!

Miners' phrases are original and pithy. The 'color' is their name for finest particles of gold in the earth. One remarked of a man tried in various positions and found utterly worthless:

'I have panned him out, clear down to the bed rock; but I can't even raise the color.'

Montana is eight hundred miles from east to west, by nearly three hundred from north to south. It is well named, being mountainous throughout. It contains five large basins—four on the Atlantic slope, one on the Pacific—and numberless smaller valleys. While snow is deep upon the mountains, cattle grow fat among the green bunch-grass of the valleys, a thousand feet lower.

'My father's empire,' said Cyrus to Xenophon, 'is so large that men perish with cold at one end, while they suffocate with heat at the other.' But here, one may find greenest herbage and deep snow less than a mile apart. Sometimes the drifts half cover even the hardy grass of the valleys. Then cattle still subsist upon the protruding tops. Horses and antelopes paw up the snow, to find their hidden food. When it is too deep, they live upon bark of the cottonwood. Thus Cæsar reminds Antony:

'Yea, like the stag when snow the pasture sheets,
The barks of trees thou browsed'st.'

The Territory is occupied by Indians of various tribes. The dialect of the Snakes is talked by them, and more or less by nearly all savages between western Kansas and the Pacific slope. Here are their literal renderings of a few common words:—Deaf—*no ear-holes;* awkward—*no hands;* thunder—*the clouds crying;* Sunday—*the big day;* one hundred—*the hands ten times;* rice—*ant-eggs* (these, roasted, are a favorite diet;) wagon—*wooden horse;* Gallatin river—*the swift river;* Snake river—*the sage-brush river;* Great Salt Lake—*the bad water;* turtle dove—*the rattlesnake's brother.* The last-named is from their tradition that whenever the dove is mocked or its mate killed, it tells the rattlesnake, who follows and bites the offending Indian.

Montana, now containing twenty-five thousand people, will soon apply for admission to the Union. Thus far, nominally it has been ruled through a Territorial legislature elected by the people, and governor and judges appointed by the President. Actually, the power has vested in the 'Vigilantes,' a secret tribunal of citizens, organized before civil laws were framed, when robberies and cold-blooded murders were of daily occurrence. The highwaymen were called 'road agents,' from their assumed authority over the stage roads and stage companies, transcending that of the superintendents themselves. Coaches and private conveyances were stopped by 'road agents,' with cocked guns, compelling passengers to hold up their hands, lest they should grasp weapons, while their persons and vehicle were rifled. He who resisted was killed on the spot. An immigrant who had shot a grouse near the road, ran to pick it up; and found that it had fallen upon the corpse of one of these victims, lying in a sage-brush thicket. In a Virginia barber shop, revolvers were drawn, one man was shot dead and another wounded; but such affairs were so common that the barber did not even stop lathering his patron's face, nor did the patron leave his chair.

A STATE OF SUSPENSE.

After a hundred homicides, the Vigilantes organized, captured, tried, and executed twenty-four of the leading desperadoes; and banished many others. Two or three days before I visited Helena, the people awoke one morning to find a notorious reprobate in a state of suspense—hanging dead from a tree limb, and labeled: 'Murderer.' It was a sharp warning to the surviving cut-throats. The tree, near the heart of the city, has been used so frequently for this purpose that it is known as 'Tyburn.'

Every new State in its early history attracts thieves and murderers; and sooner or later, purges itself through the swift, terrible vengeance of Lynch law. But it was said that these Vigilantes had executed no man of whose guilt there was reasonable doubt; and they rendered life and property far safer than is usual in new gold regions.

'SPECIMENTS, MASS'R.'

In California, a miner gave a good illustration of the general sentiment of the frontier. When he was called up as juror in a murder case, the judge asked him the usual question:

'Have you any conscientious scruples about capital punishment?'

He responded:

'I have—*in all cases when it is not administered by a vigilance committee!*'

Montana suffers from the speculation mania—the financial measles which attack all infant States containing rich minerals. It has 'quartz on the brain.' Everybody has 'feet' for sale. In conversation, quiet gentlemen most unexpectedly produce bits of rock from their pockets, with the earnest remark:

'I have got the biggest thing in the Territory! Just look at that ore!'

A resident friend and his wife found the carpet-sack of an old negress who had long been their family servant, weighed down with a peck of fragments of granite.

'Why, Aunty,' he inquired, 'what are these?'

'Speciments, mass'r, speciments!' was her prompt reply.

The scenery of the whole region is exceedingly beautiful. Copper and iron are plentiful. Some coal, 'the portable climate of our civilization,' has been discovered. Agates, amethysts, and rubies are found, and I have seen a large collection of garnets, all picked up by a lady in her back yard.

The development of the next few years will be very rapid; and this little-known Territory will soon produce more of the precious metals than any State except California.

In all the social and material elements for a great and powerful Commonwealth, Montana is full of richness and of promise. Beautiful upon the mountains is this youngest and fairest of our national sisterhood, her arms heaped with shining gold, her hair dripping with morning dew.

Gold and silver, whether found in rock or in decomposed earth, work the miracles of our civilization. Palaces spring up in the wilderness, and cities among the mountain tops. The stream is imprisoned by the dam, and vexed with the wheel; fruitful farms are wrested from lonely valleys, and glowing treasures from rock-ribbed hills; newspapers and telegraphs bring in all the world for neighbors; the beaver must dive his quickest to avoid the plowing steamer; and buffalo and Indian run their fleetest to escape the gliding locomotive.

CHAPTER XL.

THE great Louisiana Purchase from Napoleon, was made by President Jefferson in 1803, for fifteen millions of dollars. It comprehended the present State of Louisiana, and the entire region west of the Mississippi, between the Spanish possessions on the south and British America on the north—more than half the present area of the United States.

Soon after this negotiation, in obedience to an act of Congress, Jefferson sent Lewis and Clark, captains in the United States army, to explore the vast, unknown region which his wisdom and sagacity had added to the young republic. The prime purpose of the expedition was to ascertain the possibility of a road across the continent; it was unconsciously the pioneer movement for a Pacific railway. They started from the then little French village of St. Louis, laboriously ascending the Missouri to its sources in the Rocky Mountains; crossed the range by a difficult pass; and reaching the head of the Columbia, followed it to the ocean. It was a daring journey, full of adventure and romance, over the untrodden continent, through hundreds of savage nations. It was an epic of exploration—a modern Argonautic pursuit of the Golden Fleece of the future. The little band were scouts and spies of a grand army for the conquest of a hemisphere—the army of civilization and freedom.

Twenty years ago, Lewis and Clark's report, in two large octavos, was eagerly read wherever the English language was spoken. The venerable volumes were found upon farm-house tables and mantels throughout the United States. Now the work is out of print.

The adventurous explorers journeyed along rivers in boats

propelled by sails, oars and tow-lines; and upon the land, both on horseback and on foot. They were the first white men to see the Great Falls of the Missouri, and the Gates of the Rocky Mountains; and to descend the Columbia, past all its whirlpools and rapids, to the broad, inhospitable mouth.

After the absence of more than two years, they once more reached St. Louis. The inhabitants who had long given them up as dead, deceived, at first sight, by their clothing of skins

GREAT FALLS OF MISSOURI RIVER, MONTANA.

and swarthy faces, supposed them Indians. Going out, they made the distance from the mouth of the Missouri to the mouth of the Columbia, four thousand one hundred and thirty-four miles. They returned by a nearer route, shortening it to three thousand five hundred and seventy-five.

Clark was a native of Kentucky, whose familiarity with Indian warfare from early boyhood, especially fitted him for this expedition. He acted as the military director, while Lewis devoted himself chiefly to scientific investigations.

After their return, Clark was successively brigadier-general, governor of Missouri Territory and superintendent of Indian affairs under President Monroe. He filled the last position with signal fidelity and success, until his death in St. Louis in 1838. The Indians uniformly named him 'Red Head.'

Lewis was a Virginian, who had been in the army, and afterward private secretary to President Jefferson. In 1809, serving as governor of Missouri Territory, he found that quiet life unendurable. At a wayside Tennessee inn, he died by his own hand, at the early age of thirty-five.

The patience and daring of these explorers, sent forth in obedience to the early national instinct which is now culminating in the trans-continental railway, excited the warm enthusiasm of their countrymen. Successive administrations recognized their services by retaining them in important public positions; and Congress made large grants of public land to each.

Simultaneously with the running of the first locomotive from the Atlantic to the Pacific, some fitting monument to their memory, reared by the American Government or people, should receive its crowning stone.

Their report describes the Great Falls of Missouri, two thousand five hundred miles above St. Louis, within the present limits of Montana, as 'a sublime spectacle, which since the creation has been lavishing its magnificence upon a desert unknown to civilization.' Lewis found the river three hundred yards wide, among precipitous cliffs, with the water falling eighty feet. On the north side the current was broken by projecting rocks and its spray flew up in vast snowy columns luminous with rainbows.

The stream in this vicinity is really a series of descents. In thirteen miles of cascades and rapids, the total fall is three hundred and eighty feet. The upper cataract, forty feet high, extending across the river like a slightly-bent bow, is picturesque and beautiful. Among the rapids at its base are many little falls, of from one to five yards, while the banks on either side form a deep narrow gorge, one thousand feet below the general level of the bare plains. These tremendous walls of yellow sandstone give peculiar grandeur and impressiveness to the wild, rugged scene.

The lower or Great Falls are best seen from a projecting point of rock. The thunder of the falling torrent, vailed in snowy foam, the bold banks, the dazzling rainbows, and the immense volume of water, will make the spot a favorite one for tourists in all coming time.

With regret I left Montana, her green valleys glad with streams and flowers, her rugged mountains somber with pines and firs. On the way back toward Salt Lake, at some stage stations we were feasted on wild geese and mountain trout, more toothsome

ROBBERY OF THE MONTANA COACH.

than the usual salt pork and beans. Once a traditional passenger, at a station breakfast, found nothing whatever upon the table except pork and mustard.

'Will you have some bacon?' queried the landlord.

'No,' replied the disgusted traveler; 'I never eat pork.'

'Then,' responded the complacent host, 'help yourself to the mustard!'

We passed through Port Neuf canyon, thirty miles long, where the mail coach, bringing gold dust from Montana, has been twice robbed. The last time, it was crowded with passengers all armed to the teeth, and keeping vigilant watch; for a suspicious, staring horseman, his face concealed by a slouching hat, had twice ridden past. The canyon is narrow, with high walls and shrubbery along the little brook which threads it.

In broad daylight, when all were riding with guns and revolvers cocked in their hands, seven men with blackened faces, abruptly rose up from the dense willows on each side, stopping the horses, and firing into the coach. The passengers returned the fire; but their courage was useless. In these stage robberies, persons are seldom able to defend themselves if they remain in the vehicle. By jumping out and scattering they often succeed in driving away the robbers. On this occasion one of the highwaymen was wounded but escaped; four passengers were killed—one, an old Kansas neighbor of mine, riddled with fifty bullets and buck-shots.

The robbers secured sixty thousand dollars in gold dust; climbed out of the canyon to the sand-hills, where waiting confederates guarded their horses; and made good their escape. None of them were ever caught.

Port Neuf creek is obstructed by multitudinous beaver-dams, only a few yards apart, with well-worn paths leading from them into the alder bushes. These unerring masons of the stream construct their dams in spring, just high enough for the coming season—instinctively knowing whether it will prove wet or dry. Sometimes they quite flood out the gulch miners above; and rebuild their dams every night, as often as the gold-seekers destroy them by day. They are so shy that the most skillful white hunters rarely get a glimpse of them. They cut down cottonwood trees fifteen inches in diameter. And it is affirmed that when a beaver is domesticated, if a bucket of water be upset on the floor, he will make a dam of sticks, blankets, cups, whatever he can reach,—in the sanguine hope of forming a pond to hide in!

At Bear River Junction, on the fifth morning, I took the left stroke of the Y for Idaho. Great Salt Lake stretched blue and shining at our left, near its west end, one hundred and forty miles from Salt Lake City. We were now in Idaho, barest and most desolate of all our Territories, with vast rolling wastes of lava, sand and sage-brush. But its lack in agriculture is more than counterbalanced by its richness in minerals. Here, as in Dante's Inferno, 'not green but brown the foliage.' Yet this nutritive bunch-grass, requiring no rain, keeps the stage-horses fat, and often subsists great herds driven hither to escape the drowths of California. Here is the world's pasturage. Hundreds of valleys await the tinkling sheep-bells; cattle shall browse upon a thousand hills.

Among these dreary uninhabited deserts we encountered few travelers and no settlers. The stage stations are built of lava

UTAH INDIANS, CAPTURED BY UNITED STATES TROOPS.

blocks, and their walls pierced with holes, for muskets and revolvers, in Indian warfare. Every man's house is literally his castle.

A few of the degraded Utahs still rove these forbidding tracts. They paint their bodies hideously; and with their long locks and gross faces look even more repulsive and brutal than the savages in general.

Our coach contains only two passengers. By night, with seats removed, we sleep upon a bed of hay in the bottom of the vehicle. We pass City of Rocks, a curious group of basaltic columns. Two rise sixty feet, the Gog and Magog of the desert.

Hill-sides are curiously mottled with pure snow, brown grass and dark evergreens; and ravines lined with kinnikinic, a shrub which Indians dry and smoke, both pure and mixed with tobacco.

Sixty miles east, and beyond our vision, is the great Camas prairie, thirty-five miles long by eight in width; rich, easy of irrigation from the mountains which inclose it, and threaded by the Mahlad river. This stream, after running more than a hundred miles, sinks into the earth like the waters of Damascus. The camas-plant, with clusters of pale blue flowers, leaf like a lily, and bulb like an onion, abounds beside our road. Indians dig the root with an iron hook, and subsist upon it during the winter.

I had heard much of the Shoshonee or Great Fall of the Snake; but was unable to find any white man who had seen it. It is only six miles from the stage-road, (two hundred and sixty-five miles from Salt Lake City; one hundred and eighty-five from Boise.) Hostile Indians had hitherto rendered visiting it unsafe; but the lieutenant in charge of a detachment of Oregon soldiers encamped at the station, undertook to conduct us.

Before daylight we started for the cataract, which Indians call *Pah-chu-lak-a*—gift of the Great Spirit. Probably our vehicle was the first that ever approached it. The tall sage-brush, crushed by our slow wheels, loaded the air with heavy perfume. Through the dim dawn we were guided by the everlasting pillar of cloud, rising from the troubled waters six miles away. Soon we heard faintly the eternal roar of the cataract.

And here we witnessed a mirage, quite as wonderful as the water-fall—a mirage as far surpassing any I had ever seen before in years of mountain and desert wandering, as the auroral splendors of northern night surpass the clouds of a summer day. The sun had not risen, and the morning horizon was dim amethyst. Suddenly there was born in the eastern sky an ocean of gold, glowing and blazing; then at its left, a sea of silver; and then, still further, a lake of steel—all broken by rich brown islands.

One of these celestial islands was symmetric and dark, recalling Fort Sumter; another was a black monitor anchored near it. The three bodies of water, bounded by purple shores, and occupying nearly one-quarter of the horizon, were as distinct and well-defined as a pine-tree, or a rock.

While we gazed in wonder, a horizontal shaft of blue, in fragments, but on a perfect level, slowly extended across them—a broken bridge with piers and arches, like the Bridge of Life in the immortal allegory of Addison.

Suddenly the sky warmed to saffron, as the great round face of the sun glowed between two sentinel mountains of purple, the Gateways of the Day. Then the heavenly vision which, constantly changing in form and color, we had viewed for nearly half an hour, disappeared like a vapor. Ah, could it have been perpetuated! But who can paint the mountains, the seas or the skies? And if Bierstadt could reproduce on canvas this miracle of the heavens, the art critics would say: 'It is utterly impossible—no living man ever looked upon such skies!' He who sees truly will no more place limits upon the wonders of the universe than upon the divine love which pervades and suffuses it. In nature, as in human life, nothing is impossible.

Still the river was invisible in its winding chasm, one thousand feet below the surface of the plain; but now at three miles we heard more clearly its thrilling roar, and saw the mist with its violet tinge of rainbow, which arises forever and ever, as if old Shoshonee were taking a vapor-bath or smoking his pipe.

At last we alighted on a broken floor of brown lava, descended the precipice for three hundred feet by a natural rock stairway, walked a few hundred yards across a terrace of grass, lava and cedars; and stood upon a second precipice.

Peering over the edge, five hundred feet beneath us we saw the river, after its terrific leap, peaceful as a mirror. Half a mile above, in full view, was the cataract. It is unequaled in the world, save by Niagara, of which it vividly reminded us. It is not all hight like Yosemite, nor all breadth and power like the Great Falls of the Missouri, nor all strength and volume like Niagara; but combines the three elements. Like most cataracts it has the horse-shoe form and the undying rainbow.

The torrent is less than at Niagara; and its crescent-summit appears less than a thousand feet wide. But the descent—two hundred feet—is one-third greater; while above the brink, solemn portals of lava rising for hundreds of feet on each bank, supply an element of grandeur which the monarch of cataracts altogether lacks. One of these lava columns is crowned with an eagle's nest. Below the fall, over the canyon side, shriveled cedars with roots like claws cling to the rock. Upon the withered branch of one perched a white-tailed magpie; while upon another, statuesque and motionless, was an enormous raven, black as jet.

SHOSHONEE, OR SNAKE RIVER, CATARACT, IDAHO.

Down the stream I could find no place where I dared attempt to descend the almost unbroken wall to the water's edge. But just below the brink I crept out to the edge of the projecting rock. Clinging to a hardy cedar, I saw the peaceful waters two hundred and fifty feet below me. Above, the surface of the water is broken into five channels by little islands. Thence I saw the river come gliding swift, clear and smooth to the dizzy edge; the long plunge; and the caldron, which boils beneath, under wafting clouds of spray. The fall itself is of purest white, interspersed with myriads of glittering glassy drops—a cataract of snow with an avalanche of jewels. Mocking and belittling all human splendor, Nature is here in her lace and pearls, her robe of diamonds and tiara of rainbow.

'The world, how far away it seemed, and God, how near!' Under the deafening roar, how the firm-set earth quailed and vibrated! How deep the chasm from which rose pearly mist, hiding forever from human eyes the secrets of its troubled heart! Long I lay upon the rock-shelf, gazing over the brink, riveted by the great white cataract, and the absorbing fascination of that profound, tempting gulf. How easy, by one leap, to leave behind all earthly cares and griefs—to solve the solemn mysteries of death—perchance to join the loved and lost, who wait us in the life beyond!

The river has several other picturesque falls within forty miles. Returning to the stage-road we continued our journey. At sunset came another mirage, in the west, where lakes of gold reflected mountains of cloud—'seas of mingled glass with fire.' When these faded, the actual mountains in the north were lapis lazuli; but the clouds beyond and above mirrored them as mountains of marble and sapphire.

In the dusk of the same evening, by a rope ferry, twenty miles below the Great Fall, we crossed the Snake, descending to the bottom of its deep chasm by precipitous roads. At the log station, half a mile from the river, we walked out by moonlight, to view a dark gorge, shut in by basaltic walls, three hundred feet high.

From one of these, fifty feet above the ground, gush twenty springs, varying in size from a man's arm to a flour-barrel. All lashed into silver spray they leap down jutting rocks, at whose base they merge into one. forming a stream a hundred feet wide. This wonderful spring, which has not even a name, is supposed to be the resurrection and new life of the Mahlad river, which died and was buried in the desert sixty miles away. To see it was a fit ending for an ever memorable day.

In nine days from Virginia Montana, my stage ride ended at Boise City. On the whole lonely road from Bear river we saw hardly a single team, nor any human habitation except stage stations. Indeed the most noticeable evidences of civilization we encountered were all lying together in the road: a whisky bottle, an old newspaper, and an empty match-box bearing a United States revenue stamp.

Boise, capital, commercial metropolis, and geographical center of Idaho, is a trading not a mining town, with about two thousand inhabitants. It is in the smooth valley of the Boise river—a valley fifty miles long by five or six in width, and with some agricultural capacity. The broad, level, treeless avenues, with their low, white, verandahed warehouses, log-cabins, neat cottages and ever-shifting panorama of wagons and coaches, Indians, miners, farmers and speculators remind one of a prairie town in Kansas or Iowa. It is overlooked by Fort Boise, which has a noble parade-ground, surrounded by tasteful buildings of sandstone; and is a singularly beautiful frontier post.

The capital was established here only after a violent conflict. The legislature, with the governor's approval, removed it from Lewiston, on the extreme western border of the Territory. The Lewistonians declared this illegal; armed and drilled for forcible resistance, and vowed they would never submit without bloodshed. Nevertheless, the law was carried out; and the threatening sovereigns finally acquiesced. As Webster ponderously suggested of Hayne's speech: 'It is not the first time in the history of human affairs, that the vigor and success of the war have not quite come up to the lofty and sounding phrase of the manifesto.'

Within a hundred miles of Boise are nearly all the present population and mining districts of Idaho:—1. The Boise Basin, of which Idaho City (containing five thousand people) thirty-five miles northeast, is chief town. The 'basin,' a deep, saucer-like tract among the mountains, twenty-five miles in diameter from rim to rim, contains some good ledges of gold-bearing quartz, and large, rich placer diggings. It has little farming land; but is timbered with noble pines. 2. Alturas county—chief town, Rocky Bar, ninety-five miles northeast. It embraces abundant pasturage and vegetable lands, including the Coamas prairies and the chief, almost the only, portions of Idaho giving farming promise. Here are few placers; but Rocky Bar, Red Warrior, Volcano, Yuba and other rich quartz districts. 3. Owhyee Region, seventy miles south; with very little farming land or placer gold, but the richest and most abundant lodes of gold and silver-bearing rock ever found in the United States.

EVIDENCES OF CIVILIZATION.

At the time of my visit, Idaho society was not attractive. Murders were frequent; for with a majority of industrious, law-abiding settlers, the Territory had also many late rebel soldiers and Missouri runaways; and the worst desperadoes from California, Nevada, Oregon and Montana. The legislature contained just one Union member; and during the war there was more disloyalty than in any northern community except Utah. Old Parson Strong of Hartford, the fierce political preacher in the days of Federalism, was accused of charging, from the pulpit, that all the democrats were horse-thieves. He replied:

'It is a slander; I never asserted any thing of the kind. But what I do say, and what I can prove, is, that all the horse-thieves are democrats.'

So in this community the Disunionists were not all desperadoes, but all the desperadoes were Disunionists.

Our new Territories in their early history show wonderful uniformity. At its first elections each invariably votes the democratic ticket. As time passes, each has its fevers of speculation, its wild inflations and paralyzing reactions, its bitter contests about locating the capital. Each elects some of its weakest and most corrupt men to office; and, sooner or later, is driven into purging itself of thieves and murderers through the application of Lynch law.

There are about fifty Indian tribes in Oregon, Washington and Idaho. No two speak precisely the same language; but a strange patois, known as the 'Chinook Jargon,' is comprehended by nearly all of them, and by most white settlers. As in all rudimentary

INTERIOR OF A QUARTZ MILL.

languages, the same word is either a noun or a verb, according to the context; as '*Ni-wa-wa*,'—'I speak,' or, 'My word.' Here are a few common terms of the Jargon, which frequently enters, as a sort of local slang, into general conversation:

Brave, *skookum tum-tum.*
Boots, *stick-shoes.*
Boil, *lip lip.*
Bag, *la sack.*
Bell, *ting-ting.*
Bow, *stick-musket.*
Cat, *puss.*
Cold, *cold.*
Come on, *hyar.*
Door, *la port.*
Day, *sun.*
Great, *hyas.*
Half, *sit-cum.*
Handkerchief, *hanker-chum.*

Iron, *chink-a-mim.*
Laugh, *he-he.*
Mind, *tum-tum.*
Sorry, *sick tum-tum.*
Window, *she-lock-um.*
Thank you, *mer-cie.*
One, *ict.*
Two, *moxt.*
Three, *clone.*
Four, *lock-et.*
Five, *quin-um.*
Six, *tah-hum.*
Seven, *sin-a-mox.*
Eight, *stoat-kin.*
Nine, *quoits.*
Ten, *tot-li-lum.*
Twenty, *moxt tot-li lum.*
Thirty, *clone-tot-li-lum.*
One hundred, *let tock-a-moo-nuck.*
One thousand, *tot-li-lum tock-a-moo-nuck.*

While in Idaho, imprisoned by the storms of early winter, I found much attraction and instruction in studying the quarrying and reduction of gold and silver ore. Conducted on a large scale, it is a peculiarly fascinating pursuit. The interior of a great steam mill with its heavy, complicated machinery turning out thousands of dollars in bullion daily, is full of interest.

First, the quartz is broken by sledge-hammers into fragments like apples. Next, it is shoveled into the feeders, where huge iron stamps, of from three hundred to eight hundred pounds weight, rising and falling sixty times a minute, thunder and clatter, making the building tremble, as they crush the rock to wet powder.

Quiet, silent workmen, with movements almost as mechanical as the stamps and wheels, run this pulp successively through settling-tanks, amalgamating-pans, agitators and separators—the refuse material passing away, and quicksilver collecting the precious metal into a mass of shining amalgam, soft as putty. This goes into the fire-retort, where it leaves the quicksilver behind; and finally into molds, whence it comes forth clear and pure, in bricks and bars of the precious metals.

Swift and simple appears the process which transforms dull worthless-looking rock into glowing gold or shining silver. Yet by what tedious toil, consummate skill and endless experimenting was this rare alchemy achieved; through what weary waiting and divine patience was this philosopher's stone discovered!

CHAPTER XLI.

FROM Boise I took a trip southward. Our road was over dreariest plains of sand and alkali, often too barren even for sage-brush. For leagues on every side swept the ashen, treeless desert, as sweeps the boundless sea. Thirty miles out we ferried the Snake, two hundred yards wide. A little steamer now plies upon it, from Salmon Falls, above our crossing, for one hundred and fifty miles down the stream. The stage stations are named with sardonic humor. One is called Forest Grove, because there is not a single tree within fifteen miles; another, Cold Spring, because not a drop of water exists in the vicinity.

A freighter of our company told us his experiences of a few days before. Just at dawn Indians attacked his camp. His party of six finally drove them off, but not until one had received a fatal bullet. The Snakes frequently kill travelers on leading thoroughfares. They are the most daring savages of our continent. More than once they have fought their own number of white men, without any special advantage of position—something unequaled in Indian warfare. They have even dashed into Fort Lyon, a Government post, and carried off horses and mules under the very eyes of the garrison.

Soon after dark we reached Owyhee. Its metropolis is a straggling strip of town far up among the mountains, at one end called Boonville, at the other Silver City, and in the middle Ruby City. We found Boonville, the pioneer settlement, consisting of a dozen deserted frame and log buildings, the gulch between them torn and gashed with ditches, where early miners used to work, with guns and revolvers lying on the bank beside them, in constant readiness for the Indians.

Two miles above is Ruby City, heart of the Owyhee district, and only six miles from the line of Oregon. It is a disorderly collection of buildings, on a wooded hill-side sloping down to Jordan creek. Hidden in the winding valley are many quartz mills—the cause, the support, the very life of the settlement.

The placers, once rich, are now little worked, though some hydraulic washing has been inaugurated; and in 1866 there were single miners who cleared twenty thousand dollars. Owyhee is so rich in quartz that she can afford to dispense with gulch mines.

Ruby lies near the bottom of a deep canyon. It is overlooked

RUBY CITY, OWYHEE DISTRICT, IDAHO.

by the summits of several mountains, from six hundred to two thousand feet above the town. Some are bare rock, gashed with gorges and pointed with turrets—the rest, greensward dotted with pines, and in fall and winter covered with snow.

War Eagle is king of all these peaks—its crest five thousand feet above the sea. It is the richest and most wonderful deposit of quartz yet discovered in the United States, even eclipsing the famed Comstock Lode.

Upon this mountain, only five miles in diameter at the base, more than one hundred lodes have been claimed, staked, and recorded; and the exceeding richness of many of them fairly demonstrated.

War Eagle mountain alone will doubtless add twenty millions of dollars to the treasure of the world. The large quartz mills are erected and owned chiefly by New York, Boston, and Providence companies. The oldest cost seventy thousand dollars; and during its first forty-five working days yielded ninety thousand dollars in bullion.

The lodes contain from two to seven parts (in value) gold to one of silver. Some of them yield incredibly. All are nearly perpendicular, and promise little opportunity for the litigation which was almost ruinous to Nevada. Most steadily increase downward in width, and in the proportion of silver to gold. Old miners hold the latter an indication of permanence, as silver mines are less prone to 'run out' than gold. I have seen no ore equal to this in plentifulness and richness.

All mining processes are imperfect; and machinery which extracts eighty per cent. of the precious metals does unusually well. Below these Owyhee mills, swarms of Chinamen find lucrative employment in washing and panning out the 'tailings' or crushed rock, after the mills have done their best and thrown it away. The ores are easy of reduction; a stamp will crush from one and a-half to three tons per day. In general they are softer than those of Nevada, though blasting is sometimes required to get out the quartz.

In Montana many new *grinding* processes have been introduced. Theoretically, on exhibition in New York, they work admirably; but practically, in the mines, they prove worthless. Throughout Idaho, Oregon, California, and Nevada, the old-fashioned stamps are almost exclusively used. They are simple and easy to put in repair; and have the law of gravitation to help them. They are also more durable—precisely as it wears the face of a sledge-hammer less to reduce rock by pounding, than by rubbing it to powder. Most of the Idaho machinery is from California. San Francisco, making quartz mills a specialty, is three or four years in advance of eastern cities in all improvements which are demonstrated successes. Beside, the quartz mill should be as near the foundry as possible, for 'shoes' and 'dies' wear out rapidly; and other new portions are often required at short notice, to supply breakages. The Chicago mills are cheaper and better than those of New York; but their foundries are too far away from Idaho. Chicago and St. Louis machinery is chiefly used in Colorado, Utah, and Montana.

Governor Caleb Lyon, in one of his messages, characterizes Idaho as 'a land of Italian summers and Syrian winters.' The summers may outshine Araby the Blest; but I think he should have said Siberian winters. My Owyhee visit was early in November. Every day brought its own separate storm; and most of the time snow enveloped the region. During the previous winter, it covered the ground from November twentieth to April first; but trappers and Indians declared that the severest season they had ever known.

The earliest gold discoveries in Idaho date back to the summer of 1862. These were placer mines; the first quartz lodes were found a year later. Hundreds of miles from civilization, in unknown mountains infested by fierce Indians, the early prospectors went steadily forward for many lonely months. After its richness was a demonstrated fact, the region labored under great disadvantages. A system of mining, new in many details, was to be learned; for quartz differs essentially in different sections. Labor and living commanded enormous prices. Supplies came up the Columbia, and then over the Blue Mountains of Oregon. Freights from San Francisco sometimes cost sixty-five cents a pound, in coin; and from Portland, fifty cents. The ordinary expense of sending bars of gold and silver to California and getting returns in coin was seven cents on every dollar!

During my stay, eggs were retailing at two dollars and-a-half a dozen; laborers receiving five dollars per day, and mechanics from six to eight, all in gold. Money loaned at from three to five per cent. a month.

In intervals of the storms, I glanced at a few of the rich Owyhee mines, in company with Messrs. George Collier Robbins, John Wasson, and other friends. In a biting wind which nearly swept us from the saddles, our horses climbed the corkscrew road which winds up War Eagle mountain. We found the crest covered with a foot of snow; two spots never lose their winter mantle through all the summer months. It afforded a superb view of scores of the lower hills, and the broad valley of the Snake. In that clear atmosphere we saw mountains hundreds of miles distant.

We threaded the tunnel of the Oro Fino mine, five hundred feet horizontally, to its terminus, where a perpendicular shaft lets in the daylight from one hundred and eighty feet above. Pine timbers, a foot in diameter, rib the roof, extending across from wall to wall, separated by strong upright posts. These quartz chambers often look frowning, but accidents are very rare; while in hydraulic and sluice mining, where there is no rock, banks of gravel often cave in and bury workmen. The Oro Fino walls are of granite, smooth and well defined, from two to seven feet apart. The ore is nearly white; some is as soft as wax, and streaked with slate. A mill eats but slowly into a rich, broad lode like this.

EXAMINING THE LEDGES ON WAR EAGLE MOUNTAIN.

We visited several other mines where the yield of the ore was reported to range from one hundred dollars per ton up to five, six, and even seven hundred. On the bleakest summit of War Eagle, the freezing wind stung our faces and stopped our breath. We saw stakes innumerable, marking the courses of lodes; and shafts, tunnels, and ditches without limit, for prospecting and developing mines. One Oregon company had spent a hundred thousand dollars in seeking to find here the continuation of a certain ledge of known richness; but had not succeeded.

Our last visit was to the Hays-and-Ray. At one of its tunnels, from ore so soft that it was easily cut with a knife, I picked sheets of native silver as large as a half-dollar. Higher up on the lode was pointed out Fort Baker, a log building fronted by breastworks, and its walls pierced for rifles.

Ye who listen with credulity to the whispers of fancy, and pursue with eagerness the phantoms of hope, who believe silver mining a pacific pursuit, and suppose quartz mills not subject to bombardment, attend to the history of Fort Baker and the 'Poorman war!' The Hays-and-Ray Lode, as claimed and staked, was sixteen hundred feet long. Other parties afterward claimed, for fourteen hundred feet, a lode which they called the Poorman, crossing the Hays-and-Ray at an acute angle, the two lines of stakes exactly representing the letter X. The Poorman party began to work their lode, not at either end, but at the very point of crossing the Hays-and-Ray; and there struck a 'pocket' or 'chimney' of ore of unprecedented richness—almost pure silver. Portions of it yielded sixty per cent. of bullion—a result never before equaled in mining history. The Poorman owners, it was alleged, took out two hundred and fifty thousand dollars in two weeks. They carried large quantities of the rock on the backs of mules, over the mountains, to be crushed in Portland.

FORT BAKER AND POORMAN MINE.

The Hays-and-Ray proprietors claimed that the adverse party were reducing *their* ore. The 'Poorman' not only denied this, but, with an armed force, drove off the Hays-and-Ray workmen from a portion of the ledge, and prepared for bloody warfare. And hence Fort Baker was erected.

The United States district court granted an injunction, restraining the Poorman party from taking out more ore, until both claimants could sink shafts, and trace their veins, and a jury decide which owned the disputed mineral. This just and equitable decision excited so much feeling, that threats of tarring and feathering the judge were even made by the friends of the discomfited claimants. But the belligerents finally compromised the matter and consolidated their interests. This was at least better than Nevada in early days, when in great quartz cases, one party and sometimes both, used to buy witnesses, jury, sheriff, prosecuting attorney and judge. The man in the play must have lived in a mining region before he learned the profound truth, that 'Honesty is the root of all evil, and money is the best policy.'

Mail coaches ply from Owyhee to Virginia Nevada, and three-fourths of the supplies for the Territory come by that route, hauled from the eastern terminus of the California Pacific railway. The completion of the railroad to a point due south of Owyhee, will bring the most important settlements of Idaho within three days of San Francisco. The intervening country, at some points, is very rugged. In Humboldt Pass, northern Nevada, the engineers of the Union Pacific road ran their line along almost perpendicular walls, hundreds of feet above the stream. For such surveying Blondin's facility on the tight rope would seem a more valuable preparation than any degree of accomplishment in mathematical science.

The first newspaper in our possessions on the Pacific coast, was published in Idaho, nearly fifty years ago, by Spaulding, a missionary among the Pierced-nose Indians. A log hut still marks his pioneer office; and beside it trees of his own planting flourish and bear fruit.

The crushing mills of Idaho contain between four and five hundred stamps. As in all our quartz regions, the larger portion of eastern capital invested has been squandered through incredible incompetency, recklessness and folly of management—through buying worthless mines at enormous figures, and spending immense sums in erecting mills, without first ascertaining whether the company had ore which would justify crushing. But enterprises conducted with the caution and good judgment requisite to success in any other legitimate business, have yielded large rewards. Quartz mining, growing year by year, will soon be one of our leading national interests; and no other pursuit offers larger inducements to the discriminating application of skill, industry and capital.

SURVEYING FOR PACIFIC RAILROAD, HUMBOLDT PASS, NEVADA.

Idaho, one of our very best mineral States, has little land attractive to the farmer. With irrigation the narrow valleys of the Boise, the Snake, and their few tributaries, produce good vegetables and small grain. Wheat, barley and oats yield from twenty-five to fifty bushels to the acre; and potatoes have produced two hundred and fifty bushels. But the country will never raise food for a large population. Its grazing capacity is excellent. Even these barren plains do not escape one pest of the frontier. Yearly, clouds of grasshoppers or 'black crickets,' covering the ground like a sable mantle, have swept the country in July and August, destroying the crops. The mountains are well timbered and abound in game. The population of the Territory is about twenty-five thousand. Though the winters are long and severe, the average temperature is milder than that of Illinois. The climate is exceedingly healthy.

Returning from Owyhee to Boise, I took the coach for Oregon. The second day, at Olds' ferry, we crossed Snake river into Oregon. Instantly it began to rain, and continued every day afterward until I left the State. In a deep, beautiful valley we dined at Miller's, who boasts scores of sheep, hundreds of cattle, and an immense barn. He sells fodder to winter travelers on this great thoroughfare, but never feeds it to his own stock. A ton of hay is worth more than an ox or a cow; so the poor animals must pick up their own subsistence or starve to death.

Near a little road-side grocery, supported by a post and flanked by an empty cask, stood a Noble Red Man. Indifferent to his tattered clothing, which afforded no protection from the sharp, wintry nights—with his long black locks flying in the wind—his whole soul was wrapped in a whisky bottle. He regarded it with a fixed stare, in which satisfaction at the quality of its contents and pensive regret at their diminishing quantity were ludicrously blended. Mr. Cooper died too early. I think one glimpse of *this* Aboriginal would have saved his pen much labor, and early American literature many Indian heroes.

Among these lonely hills, a few weeks earlier, the stage was robbed of sixteen thousand dollars in the hands of two Jewish merchants, taking money to San Francisco for themselves and their brethren, to avoid express charges. After this brilliant saving at the spigot to lose at the bung-hole, they began to transmit their bullion by the Wells-Fargo express, which assumes all risk of robberies. Its messengers travel thoroughly armed, and sometimes repel attacks with great gallantry. Only two nights before we passed, an unsuccessful attempt was made to rob the coach.

On the fourth morning, beyond Uniontown, we crossed the Grand Round prairie, thirty miles by thirteen, level as a floor and symmetrically inclosed by mountain walls. Its jet-black soil looks like Kansas or Iowa, producing excellent grass and wheat, but too cold for corn. It seems to be an old lake bed, and is submerged a part of the year. On one side is a hot sulphur spring, with a basin covering an acre. Lewis and Clark, half a century ago, noted the beauty and richness of this little valley.

THE NOBLE RED MAN.

Beyond, in deep, treacherous mud, which threatened to capsize us every five minutes, we began to ascend the Blue Mountains. They are fitly named; under white, gauzy clouds robing their snowy peaks, they are of deepest, richest blue.

Among the vehicular wrecks along our fathomless road, was a three-horse ambulance, loaded with apples, one fore-wheel so utterly crushed to fragments that it might have belonged to the original 'one-hoss shay.' On a log sat the driver eating an apple, and viewing the ruins with the utmost serenity.

'Rather heavy that;' ventured one of our passengers.

'Yes,' he replied, complacently, 'rather heavy on one wheel!'

In the deep mountains, whose grand sweeps revealed great expanses of yellow pines, our horses wallowed along, the coach rocking like a ship in a storm. After dark, our road was blocked by an emigrant, his horses hopelessly down in the mud, and his wife and three little children sitting forlorn upon a snow-bank, half-covered with fast-falling flakes. Two babies were crying, and the group formed a picture of utter dreariness and despair.

We rolled the horses three or four times over, down the hillside, till they again found their legs; and our driver hitched his own team to the stranded wagon and hauled it out of the quagmire. Then, taking the woman and children, we toiled slowly on in the darkness, passing several other emigrants despairingly mired. At last, blinking lights, through the deep, pine woods, indicated our approach to Meacham's, a large, cheery log station on the summit, where, with twenty passengers from the west, with a roaring fire, a wholesome supper, late newspapers and comfortable beds, we passed the night.

'HEAVY ON ONE WHEEL!'

At daylight we pressed on, in an open wagon. The roads had become impassable for coaches, and abounded in vehicles inextricably imbedded in mud. Emerging from the woods, we looked down upon the vast, bare, straw-colored valley of the Snake, dappled with sun and shade; and upon far, dim Walla Walla, the most populous town of Washington Territory. That evening (the fifth) we reached Umatilla, two hundred and ninety miles from Boise. In summer the trip is made in two days and-a-half.

Thence I took steamer down the beautiful Columbia, spending

one day at the pleasant town of Dalles, beside the boiling, whirling, surging river. From this point Bierstadt painted his Mount Hood. For nearly one hundred miles on the Columbia we see the noble mountain towering up grandly, with dark base and snowy scalp, though at the nearest point it is forty miles away. It is chiefest of a dozen isolated peaks rising from the backbone

MOUNT HOOD, OREGON, FROM DALLES OF COLUMBIA RIVER.

of the Cascade Range. Its hight is variously given at from fourteen thousand to seventeen thousand feet. It has been disturbed by several eruptions, simultaneously with earthquakes at San Francisco and other points down the coast.

At Portland, on the first of December, I found roses in full bloom in the open air. During my stay in the pleasant city, the steamer Pacific arrived, after a passage of six days from San Francisco. She had experienced some of the perils of winter navigation on this hostile coast. The weather was a continuous gale, and the ship crowded. She had no mate on board; and her pilot died during the trip. For three days and nights the passengers were shut in the cabin; no one could keep the deck save on hands and knees; and the master, Captain Burns, never left the wheel. Once he was compelled to turn and run before the storm for eighty miles. Being nearly out of coal, he could not go back to San Francisco; and the appalling bar at the mouth of the Columbia was so rough that he could only cross at imminent peril. Again and again he approached it; but the sea raged so madly that he dared not go on. At last, as children shut their eyes before plunging into cold water, he made a desperate attempt, and by good fortune succeeded in guiding the ship over in safety.

FLATHEAD INDIANS.

By the return trip of the Pacific I went down the river, past Astoria, past the second winter-encampment where daring old Lewis and Clark rested when half their wonderful journey was accomplished. In their notes, taken here, they report:

'The practice of flattening the head by artificial measures during infancy prevails here and among all the nations we have seen west of the Rocky Mountains; whereas to the east of that barrier the practice is perfectly unknown. This Columbus noted when he first landed in America. Soon after birth the child's head is placed between boards tightly strapped, and kept there ten or twelve months. The operation is so gradual as not to be attended with pain. The heads of children are not more than two inches thick about the upper edge of the forehead; and still thinner when first released from the bandage. The heads of adults are often a straight line from the nose to the top of the forehead.

The flowing of the great river to the sea has been sung by Mrs. Frances Fuller Victor, in a strain worthy of the inspiring theme:

The blue Columbia, sired by the eternal hills
  And wedded with the sea,
O'er golden sands, tithes from a thousand rills,
  Rolled in lone majesty—

Through deep ravine, through burning, barren plain,
  Through wild and rocky strait,
Through forest dark, and mountains rent in twain
  Toward the sunset gate.
While curious eyes, keen with the lust of gold,
  Caught not the informing gleam,
These mighty breakers age on age have rolled
  To meet this mighty stream;

Age after age these noble hills have kept,
  The same majestic lines;
Age after age the horizon's edge been swept
  By fringe of pointed pines.
Summers and winters circling came and went,
  Bringing no change of scene;
Unresting, and unhasting, and unspent,
  Dwelt Nature here serene,

Till God's own time to plant of Freedom's seed
  In this selected soil,
Denied forever unto blood and greed,
  But blest to honest toil.

* * * * * * *

Be mine the dreams prophetic, shadowing forth
  The things that yet shall be,
When through this gate the treasures of the North
  Flow outward to the sea.

Doubly pleasant seemed the kindly greetings and the cheerful comforts of San Francisco, after these long mountain wanderings. But our wild quartz regions are ever full of interest to the thoughtful visitor. Their early settlers have braved Indians and elements, endured hard fare, hard work, long banishment from civilization and from home. His spirit must be poor indeed, who can see in this nothing more than narrow greed for gold. With honorable ambition for pecuniary success, it blends that marvelous pioneer instinct which in thirty years has carried our freedom and our flag from the Mississippi to the Pacific—conquered half a continent for the future home of fifty millions of self-governed people, speaking the same language, obeying the same laws, acknowledging the same religion, of divine love and human brotherhood.

CHAPTER XLII.

On a December afternoon I left San Francisco by a little steamer which plies across the bay and winds up Petaluma creek or bayou —a channel crooked as a corkscrew, and often too narrow for a boat to turn around in, or for one to pass another.

Spending the night at Petaluma, the head of navigation, I strolled into the telegraph office for an evening chat with Dr. Lovejoy, the superintendent—a relative of Elijah P. Lovejoy, who was murdered by a mob at Alton Illinois in 1837, because he persisted in discussing slavery through his weekly religious newspaper. Now, when we go all over the world to find marble white enough for those who fell later, why have we no memorial of that young hero who gave the flower of his days, capacity of high order, and finally life itself, in defense of the right to speak and to print?

During our conversation, the operator, hearing a misdirected dispatch for me passing over the wires to Healdsburg, caught it on the wing, and transcribed it. The telegraph is a perpetual miracle. No familiarity however long, makes it prosaic. How rarely its confidences are violated! Yet daily the most important and delicate messages are sent for thousands of miles, where every operator on the line may hear them passing.

To what curious skill it trains the ear! An expert telegrapher stands in the middle of a room where twenty instruments are tapping out messages from as many different places, and easily reads by sound, any one of them, not in the least confused by the rest. Once, in a disagreement, the Cincinnati *Gazette* was cut off from the dispatches of the Associated Press. But still when important news came over the wires, the *Gazette* always obtained and printed it.

The association, chagrined at finding its excommunication harmless, was glad to make terms again with a newspaper which, denied the privilege of paying for its bulletins, succeeded in getting them without paying. The telegraph company believed that some treacherous employé had been stealing the dispatches. But the truth was, during summer, press news came late at night, when the city was very still. The telegraph office was in the upper story of

MADRONA TREE, HEALDSBURG, CALIFORNIA.

a high building on the south side of Third street. The *Gazette* employed a first class operator to stand on the north side. At that great distance, as the messages were spelled by the instrument, he heard them through the open windows, and transcribed them in his note-book under a street lamp!

How unmistakably individuality comes out, in this conversation through a system of the most delicate lines and the minutest dots! The Baltimore operator sitting at his table, reads by sound the messages always clicking to and fro between Washington and Philadelphia, New York and Boston. And after hearing half a dozen words of any dispatch, he can tell who is the sender, out of all the hundred employees with whose telegraph-writing he is familiar.

During one of John Morgan's raids into Indiana, he entered the telegraph office of an interior village; and with drawn revolver commanded the operator to ask a neighboring town on the Ohio river, whether any Federal gunboats were there. The young man could give no warning;—there was the six-shooter, and a rebel telegrapher who accompanied Morgan eyed him like a lynx. So he made the simple inquiry. But the operator at the river noticed the tremulousness and excitement in the sensitive metallic voice asking the question, and instantly surmised the cause. There *were* no gunboats within twenty miles; but he promptly replied:

'There are two at the landing; and from my window I see three more just coming around the bend!'

This was enough for Morgan. He sought some safer point for recrossing the river.

In Sacramento one evening, I sat beside an operator while the circuit was opened across the continent, for a little chatting between the offices along the line before saying 'Good night.' This message came from New York:

'Fire this moment broken out think on Chambers street near City Hall Park.'

While it was being spelled, my companion learned from the style of transmission who was the sender, and told me his name. Wonderful the invention through which, half across the world, men can talk familiarly, as we converse face to face! Far more wonderful the individuality which so reveals itself in the tapping of a little key, that we recognize it three thousand miles away!

The next morning I continued on by stage. The jet-black prairie soil, which the drivers call 'adobe,' is dotted with park-like groves of live-oak, and resembles portions of Texas. Low, flat and rich, abounding in pleasant shaded homes, it is excellent farming land, requiring no irrigation, and producing forty to sixty bushels of corn to the acre.

Most of the settlers are from prolific Missouri. Their neighbors of Yankee origin declare that they are 'shiftless;' that if one had to enter a field every day in the year, he would never make a gate or even a pair of bars, but only a gap in his hereditary Virginia fence.

In the afternoon we reached Healdsburg, an agreeable village, shaded with live-oaks and madronas, or mountain laurels. Here the live-oak attains perfection. I have seen no other tree so beautiful save the elm of the Connecticut valley. The madrona too, with its vivid green foliage, bright red stems and exquisite outline, is a marvel of grace and loveliness. One, in the principal street of the town, towering and spreading far above the highest buildings, is singularly picturesque and venerable. The boughs of all trees are richly festooned with great bunches of mistletoe.

From Healdsburg, Clark T. Foss, famous hereabout for good fare and uncomfortably-fast driving, took me eight miles to his station, where I spent the night. It occupies a little circular valley, and is the head of wagon navigation in winter. It has an immense barn, with great watering trough; and a long low snow-white cottage, with ample verandahs, which nestles among encircling hills of deep green, like a marble effigy in a niche of emerald. In summer it is crowded with visitors. Now it was deserted save by Foss and one hired man; but very pleasant was the evening before its blazing log fire, and the night in one of its inviting beds.

In the morning we started on horseback for the Geysers, twelve miles distant, through a nipping and eager air which made fingers tingle. We passed a single dwelling; hundreds of grazing sheep; and one immense doe with her long-legged fawn, galloping along the crests.

A few miles to our left were the snowy peaks of the Coast Range; and nearer, deep-down under our feet, the magnificent valley of Russian river, dotted with live-oak and redwood—a valley of rolling ridges, pleasant farm-houses with great barns, and broad, green meadows, their brooks and lakelets shining like mirrors.

After climbing for several miles, our path winds along a unique natural embankment, known as the Hog-back—a mountain summit, like a ridge-pole on a steep roof. Now the rains had cut and gashed it until, at some points, our horses could barely find a path; but, repaired in summer, it is just wide enough for carriage-wheels. On each side one looks down a precipitous bank fifteen hundred or two thousand feet. I think Foss's idea of paradise is to drive a coach-load of passengers, six-in-hand, twelve miles an hour, along some dizzy road like this. If the wheels happened to diverge ten inches from the track, the load would reach the bottom much in the condition of a bushel of apples after passing through a cider-mill.

ALONG THE HOG-BACK.

Timid visitors hold him in mortal terror. One lady, learning that he was to be her driver, jumped out of the vehicle, steadfastly refusing to ride behind such a reckless Jehu. But though he has conveyed hundreds of persons to and fro, he never met with a single accident.

Two miles from the Geysers we began to hear them roar like ocean steamers. The smoke is sometimes seen here; but this morning the atmosphere was not favorable. We were now fourteen hundred feet higher than Foss-station, and five thousand feet above the sea. From this point, our road abruptly pitches down into the sulphurous valley. In the remaining two miles, it descends sixteen hundred feet, with thirty-five sharp turns, often on the edge of precipitous banks. In August, Foss drove Messrs. Colfax, Bross and Bowles down this steep grade in ten minutes. At first it made them shiver; but growing accustomed to the break-neck pace, they enjoyed it keenly.

Turning a corner, I saw the column of smoke from Steamboat spring, rising fully three hundred feet from the ground. At this distance it sounds like a railway train in motion; but nearer it is a perfect imitation of a great boat blowing off her steam.

Down at the very foot of the valley, in sight of hundreds of steam-jets puffing up from the ground, we dismounted by the hotel, a pleasant, two-story-and-L white building, in summer filled with visitors, but now quite abandoned. In the season it accommodates six hundred guests. (Three dollars per day, or fifteen dollars per week, coin.)

Pluton river, twenty or thirty feet wide, and running westward, tumbles laughingly down the rocks, shaded by overhanging trees and vines. On its south bank we first visited the Iron spring, a little basin two or three feet square. The water, intensely irony to the taste, is covered with a yellowish-green scum and discolors every thing in the vicinity. With the late fall freshets the rustic log bridge spanning the river, had gone on a voyage of discovery; so we crossed the stream as best we might by jumping from rock to rock.

Then we were at the mouth of the Devil's canyon, which shuts in a little lateral creek running south and emptying into Pluton river. On this branch of the main stream are the principal Geysers. Two hundred yards up the creek we reached the bathhouses. The water, pure and cold at the head of the stream half a mile above, then heated by the springs, and afterward cooling by exposure to the air, is here just warm enough for pleasant ablution.

The steep walls of the narrow ravine rise from fifty to one hundred and fifty feet—bare, spongy, ashen, clayey soil, without the faintest sign of grass or shrub. Through this chasm rushes the curious stream. The narrow summer-path beside it was now washed away, compelling us to climb the slippery rocks, and sometimes to trust the seething, uncertain earth.

Soon we were among clouds of steam issuing from the soil at the water's edge, and thence extending far up the bank; the mud everywhere too hot for one to bear his hand in it. We visited the Grotto, where tree-trunks and branches extend across the creek, over wild, jagged rocks; and then a delicious little cascade which forms a natural cold shower-bath. Now we began to encounter hot *streams* bubbling up beside the creek, some clear and blue, others, within two foot of them, black; some very bitter, forming white incrustations of salt, and others depositing fine-fibred, exquisite flowers of sulphur, like delicate yellow or black moss. Hot, cold, and boiling springs are side by side, each with its own individual hue: blue, brown, black, red, green, yellow, pink or gray.

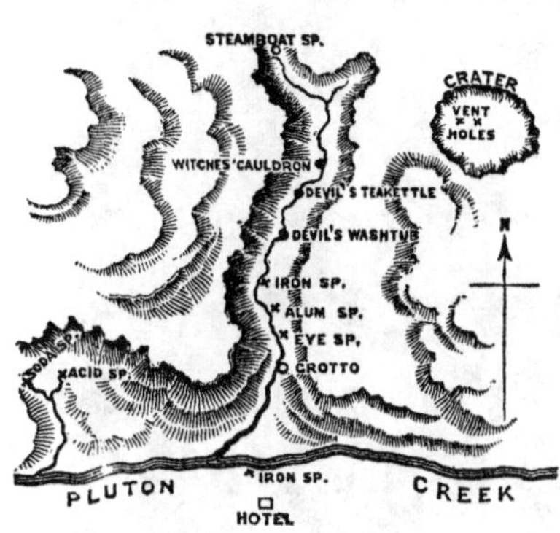

DIAGRAM OF DEVIL'S CANYON.

We passed the Devil's Wash-bowl, the Devil's Kitchen and other localities quite as infernal in sound heat and smell as in name. The jets of steam and the bubbling up of hot water are curious enough; but the boiling *within* hundreds of cavities under ground, dimly seen but clearly heard through their narrow mouths, is far more startling and impressive. The different springs emit many varieties of sound: the singing of a tea-kettle; the pulpy boiling of a huge tank of potatoes; the distant roar of a great quartz-crusher; the cob-cracking of a grist-mill; the sough of the wind; the murmur of the pine; the dash of the waves; all liquid, vibrating, tremulous tones.

The principal group is beside the creek for a quarter of a mile; but there are fully one thousand places where steam issues from the banks. At times the ground shakes so as to rattle crockery in the hotel, one-third of a mile away. The earth trembles and shudders as if in terror of going back to the first throbs of Chaos, of being again without form and void, and darkness upon the face of the deep.

The Witches' Caldron *was* seven feet deep, with circular walls two or three yards across; but the lower part of the rocky rim has broken away, leaving only a little seething pool of inky blackness, so hot that it will boil an egg. Several times we burned our fingers, and caught stifling blasts from the hot natural furnaces.

WITCHES' CALDRON, CALIFORNIA GEYSERS.

At the head of the canyon, fifty feet up a sharp hill, is Steamboat spring, greatest of all. It has no water, but consists entirely of steam. We climbed the bank and crept over brittle, yielding earth as near the mouth as we dared. Its aperture is as large as the body of a man. In the shifting wind, the enveloping, scorching, sulphurous steam is neither pleasant nor safe; but its constant roar and its great column, rising upright for hundreds of feet, are peculiarly impressive.

Recrossing the gorge, we ascended a high plateau, with a broken rim, called the Crater, and really suggesting the mouth of an extinct volcano. Here are the Vent Holes, two springs a few feet apart, which will boil an egg in a minute and-a-half; and from which steam escapes with great force. A stone as large as one's fist, dropped into either of them, bounds up three or four feet like an India-rubber ball. I confess a boyish desire to see two steam whistles inserted here, and listen to their shrill, unceasing, maddening screech. I know of no place where so much noise could be had for so little money.

Coming down, we passed one new hot spring which had broken out on the greensward within a few weeks; and saw another of recent birth where the bank was one hundred feet higher than at any of the rest. Even within a few yards of each other they vary greatly in altitude.

Other geysers abound for six miles along Pluton river; but I have named the largest and most interesting. In character their variety is very great; though soda, magnesia, alum, Epsom salts and various salts of iron predominate. They seem great safety valves and vent-holes of the globe; but actually are not volcanic. They are one of Nature's great laboratories, produced by the chemical action of acids in the earth.

When their discoverer first stumbled upon them, his sensations must have been worth experiencing. Indians, who regard them with wildest terror, cannot be induced to approach; and some white visitors never dare to enter the canyon. The smell of brimstone, hissing of steam, seething and throbbing of struggling waters, and the underground roaring and trembling, do seem peculiarly diabolical, and suggest the Inferno very thinly crusted over.

Travelers declare that these springs far surpass the famed geysers of Iceland. They are certainly one of the rarest features of a section where Nature delights to show the cunning of her hand. Of all the States which the great Pacific railway will open to the annual army of summer travelers—the seekers of health, of rest, and of pleasure, from our own and other lands—California will be most sought and enjoyed. No other region of equal area can boast half her natural beauties and wonders. The Yosemite, Sierras, Shasta, Big Trees, Geysers and glorious Lake Tahoe are among the first curiosities of the universe.

CHAPTER XLIII.

On the morning of December nineteenth I started homeward from San Francisco. Once, almost the entire population rushed to the wharf on the departure of a mail ship. 'Steamer day' is still a great event. Everybody spends the night before in writing letters; and for the last hour one or two thousand persons crowd the decks of the departing vessel. Some go to say 'Good-by,' some from curiosity, and some as a general tribute of remembrance to the old home, by the sea route six thousand miles away.

At eleven o'clock outsiders hasten ashore; the gong sounds; and with hundreds of fluttering handkerchiefs and pantomime kisses to receding faces on the wharf, the great steamer slowly rounds and passes out at the Golden Gate, on her voyage of thirty two hundred miles, from thirty-eight north latitude, to within seven degrees of the equator.

San Francisco harbor is not only one of the most beautiful, but one of the most defensible in the world. A notable feature of the region is seen from the Cliff House, on the shore four miles from the city. Here are scores of monstrous seals known as sea-lions, which sometimes weigh two thousand pounds. They disport on rocks near the land, their huge forms leaping and tumbling in awkward exuberance. Their eye bears a strange resemblance to that of a human being, and their barking is somewhat like that of a dog. It is made a penal offense to kill or injure them, as the Californians naturally desire to preserve so rare a curiosity at the very doors of their great city.

The ships of the Pacific Mail Company, running monthly from China and Japan to San Francisco, and tri-monthly from San Francisco to Panama and from Aspinwall to New York, include the finest vessels in the world. The largest are three hundred and sixty feet in length, of five thousand tons burden, and have cost about one million dollars each. Elegantly appointed, ably commanded, the perfection of system, they are at the head of our national marine and an honor to American enterprise.

Our steamer, one of the earlier and smaller ones, was the Sacramento, commanded by Captain J. M. Cavarly. She can carry one thousand people. Her upper deck, one-sixteenth of a mile long, affords a splendid promenade.

The great ocean is as calm to-day as when Ferdinand Magellan, after sailing for weeks without meeting a single adverse breeze, named it the Pacific. Vessels here can have more room, and require less strength, than on the stormy Atlantic. The sleeping apartments extend far over the water, upon supporting platforms. On either side the Sacramento has a row of three-berth state-rooms built entirely *outside her hull;* and still beyond them the guards, wide enough for sitting and promenading.

Her complement of men is about one hundred, all thoroughly drilled for duty. One day the long, shrill 'fire-blast' was sounded upon the steam whistle. Every man sprang to his post; and in four minutes eighteen streams of water were being thrown by steam. Once every voyage the crew is exercised in this fire-drill. Water-pipes ready for use, permeate all parts of the ship like great arteries; and with the alarm promptly given flames would be instantly extinguished.

The first-cabin passengers always embrace many cultivated, traveled and agreeable persons. Their average is said to be higher than upon any other route in the world. On the first day out, they are assigned places for meals; and nine-tenths are always disappointed at exclusion from the captain's table, the one especially desired. But they soon console themselves by cultivating each other, compelled by affinities and repulsions into groups and coteries. They breakfast at eight, lunch at one and dine at five.

The second-cabin passengers, whose state-rooms are not so good, eat from the same tables but at different hours. The steerage berths are comfortable and very tidy. Their inmates take their meals standing; but have a new bill-of-fare for every day in the week. All the compartments, steerage, cabins, engine rooms, kitchen, bakery, and butcher-shops, are clean as a drawing-room; plates bright; knives, forks and spoons shining; and every thing like clock-work.

The vessel is a great hotel in motion, with the disadvantage that it can send to market only once in two weeks. On the Pacific side cattle are carried along to supply the tables with beef. On the Atlantic, meats are brought from New York, packed in ice.

SEA-LIONS, SAN FRANCISCO BAY.

The vigilant captains inspect every corner of the vessel at least twice a day. They are justly proud of their ships. No commander can take his wife with him, even by paying her fare. On most steamships and many sailing vessels this rule is enforced, lest in fire or storm the master should neglect his passengers to save his family. On Sundays the service of the Episcopal church is performed in the first cabin.

We left San Francisco in weather so cold as to demand fires. Thousands of gulls flew around our ship and followed in her track, but fell off as we approached the tropics. The gull is found only in the north; the albatross only in the south. In air or upon water both are exquisitely graceful; but taken on board, they become utterly awkward; walk with difficulty; the deck soon blisters their feet; and the ship's motion makes them *seasick*—just as an old salt sometimes becomes nauseated in a little open boat upon smooth water. Sailors declare that both gull and albatross sleep with their heads under their wings while riding the waves of great storms; but, as the newspapers say, this 'needs confirmation.'

'We were seldom out of sight of the half transparent mountains for more than two or three hours. Our course was so easterly that watches required to be set forward fifteen minutes daily. As the weather warmed, we saw schools of young porpoises tumbling through the water, like rolling barrels; and frequently encountered the full-grown fish, twelve or fifteen feet long, lounging in the sea. The ship's approach stimulated them into wonderful activity, making them jump from the water, often twenty feet high, to fall, dashing up columns of spray visible at three or four miles. They are a reddish-brown, with dark spots and immense fins. Leaping through the air they assume a curious crescent form, and impart great animation to the quiet seas. Sometimes they are harpooned and eaten, being a favorite dish with old sailors. These declare that when one is wounded and its blood discolors the sea, all the rest stop and remain with him, even at the risk of their lives.

Great whales exhibited their brown backs, and threw up columns of water within a few yards of us. An ancient mariner assures me that on the north Pacific, he once saw a school of whales so large that the captain, who had unwittingly run his little steamer among them, was compelled to stop her for fear of breaking the wheels. I find many an old sailor in whom a good journalist was spoiled when he took to the sea. He at least makes his stories interesting, if he *is* sometimes 'indebted to his imagination for his facts, and to his memory for his jests.'

We passed the dull mountain of Cape Saint Lucas, with a white sandy beach rising half to the summit; and crossing the Gulf of California in a stiff breeze, threw a parting glance at the long peninsula of Lower California, which ought to belong to the United States. Then we were within the tropics, under the purple heavens of the south, where Christmas day was like New York in August. The ladies appeared at dinner in summer costumes; and our state-rooms were so hot as to render the least covering uncomfortable. Life on shipboard in these low latitudes is lazy and luxurious.

THE GOLDEN GATE, OUTLET OF SAN FRANCISCO BAY.

rious. Serious thought is too laborious; one requires no heavier literature than novels; spends long days in quiet whist, drowsy gossip, or weak flirtation; finds dressing for dinner, exhaustion; and sleeps twelve hours out of the twenty-four.

At dawn on the twenty-sixth, we were in the bay of Acapulco. As the entrance is narrow and dangerous, the Mail Company maintains a light on the southern point for one or two nights before each steamer is due. The imbecile Mexican authorities have no light-house whatever on the Pacific coast, and only a single one on the Atlantic—at San Juan d'Ulloa.

The Acapulco harbor, large enough for the navies of the world, is beautifully land-locked, chaparral mountains rising on all sides, from seven hundred to three thousand feet. Cocoa-palms with smooth stems and long green arms bending with fruit, grow on a strip of sand at the water's edge. Lying in the harbor were two French men-of-war, a Mexican coaster, a United States gunboat and naval store-ship, and a spare steamer of the Mail line. The sun blazed, the weak ripples pulsated, and the whole scene recalled Crabbe's drowsy lines:

'The ocean smiling to the fervid sun,
The waves that faintly fall and slowly run,
The ships at distance and the boats at hand.
And now they walk upon the seaside sand,
Counting their numbers, and what kind they be—
Ships softly sinking in the sleepy sea.'

A mile from shore our wheels stopped; and we were instantly surrounded by a small navy of natives in little boats, offering us green oranges and ripe limes. One skiff was *manned* by a gigantic negress, black as the ace of spades, with a stationary umbrella over her bare arms and head, apparently to protect her delicate complexion.

For a silver half-dollar a young ebony, whose wardrobe consisted of tattered straw hat and linen pantaloons, admitted me among a crowd of passengers whom he rowed ashore. He dragged the boat by hand up the bare sand of the beach; for Mexican enterprise is not equal to wharves. We landed at a little market protected by green bay trees from the fiery sun, and displaying on three or four rickety tables whisky, lemonade, sole-leather pies, limes, oranges, cocoa-nuts, and exquisite shell baskets. Most of our company were injudicious enough to eat fruit extravagantly, some seasoning it with unlimited whisky; and were rewarded a few hours later with the fevers and diarrheas they so richly deserved.

Three centuries ago Acapulco and Panama were the grand marts of Spanish commerce. Here Alvarado built his vessels to sail for Peru, twenty years after the conquest of Mexico; and annual caravans of loaded mules crossed the country to Vera Cruz, with the products of China, Japan, and the Spice islands. The town is wretchedly built, of thatched one-story adobe houses, shaded with palm trees. In peace times, during nights unlighted by the moon, the regulations require a lantern hung out from each door. About once in ten years, the city is shaken to pieces by an earthquake. One of these unwelcome visitors, ten days before our arrival, knocked down many dwellings and shattered the walls of the ancient cathedral. We looked into this rude place of worship, with stone floors, and crumbling ceilings adorned by cheap effigies and a single oil painting of the Virgin and the Savior; and glanced at the quaint steeple containing four or five rough bells from old Spain.

In its best estate Acapulco contains four thousand people; but now it was held by seven thousand Imperialists, (adherents of Maximilian) and only four hundred of the inhabitants remained. The garrison, French, Austrian and native troops, though aided by two French men-of-war, was not strong enough to dislodge Alvarez, the Republican, (President Jaurez) commander of the province, whose flag in full view flew defiant from a mountain top three miles in the rear. With good artillery he could have shelled them out of town, fort, and harbor in two hours.

It is always unsafe to predict how men will fight; but I think one regiment of Grant's veterans would disperse six times its number of the dusky soldiers we saw lounging about the barracks. It was a droll war. There was very little fighting except by guerrillas, who often robbed both sides with judicial impartiality. The Imperialists would capture two or three towns—the Republicans running away without resistance—and then issue a pronunciamento claiming the entire province, and threatening to hang everybody caught in arms against them; and vice versa. In the forty-three years since Mexico separated from Spain, she has had forty-one presidents and nearly as many revolutions. One resident American argued to me with great earnestness, that we ought to solve the problem by killing every native and making room for a race with some vigor and manhood!

Here, as in all Mexico, the civilization is that of three thousand years ago. The country illustrates Draper's sweeping theory, that no tropical climate ever produced a great man. Even those descendants of the daring old Spaniards, who have kept pure their

Castilian blood, never intermarrying with the natives, preserve nothing but their complexions, and are an imbecile and cowardly race. So in India the experience of a century has failed to produce a single person of genius or high talents born on the soil

A SCHOOL OF PORPOISES.

from European parentage; but there, several men of great power and ability have sprung from the lower classes of the native race. Acapulco does not contain a single wheeled vehicle. No wagon roads lead to the interior; and even in peace all supplies are brought in upon the backs of mules and donkeys.

We found Mr. Cole, the American consul, in a cool, airy adobe dwelling, with high walls, stone floor, and a garden in the rear, rich with oleander trees and other gorgeous growths. He was dressed all in white, and reposing at full length in a swinging hammock, prostrate with the prevailing fever. May and June are the hottest months, December the coolest. The town is warmer and unhealthier than Panama, six hundred miles further south.

Gladly we returned from this scorched and devastated city to our pleasant ship, which had been detained six hours for coaling. At length, with a supply of food for our hungry engines, we steamed out of the sleepy harbor into the ocean, so calm and smooth that our vessel often seemed as free from motion as a parlor-floor. Again and again, while reading in the captain's room on the upper-deck, I supposed we had stopped; but on looking out, found we were making eleven miles an hour. It is easily increased to fifteen; but ten or eleven knots is the most economical speed, requiring only half as much coal as fifteen, and causing far less wear and tear of machinery.

We crossed the Gulf of Tehuantepec, and skirting the low level shore of Guatemala, rich with foliage, saw dimly two huge volcanic mountains, smoking through their veil of cloud.

The North Star dipped lower and lower until it was only seven degrees above the horizon. We were unable to see its total disappearance because we did not go south of the equator, where the three Magellan clouds take its place in the northern sky to guide navigators on their pathless way. Every morning we gazed on the brilliant Southern Cross, only seen below twenty-two north latitude. Unlike most constellations, its form is suggestive of its name, four bright stars shaping a perfect cross. Great sea-green turtles appeared on our land side, and the shore foliage grew heavy, profuse and drooping.

The stars looked larger than in the north, perhaps from the deep blue of the sky and snowy whiteness of the cumulose clouds. As midnight approached the heavens were wonderful; it seemed almost a sin to turn away from gazing upon them and go to bed. O, these delicious tropical nights, with new vegetation on earth and new constellations in heaven—with luminous foamy track in the wake of our vessel, the soft vivid luxuriance of the shore, the perfumed air which makes physical existence an absolute luxury, and the Southern Cross blazing like a pillar of fire!

On the thirteenth day we met the Colorado, going north, crowded with passengers. The convexity of the earth hides the hull of a vessel nine miles away; but the beautiful steamer seemed to stand almost entirely out of the water, gliding by within a hundred yards, swarming with men and women shouting and waving hats and handkerchiefs, while flags lowered and guns fired.

To this day, the boom of the most Pacific cannon makes me instinctively and nervously glance about, to see where the shot will strike.

The heavy eyes of the fourteenth morning were wide open, when we approached Panama from the south. A long point of land compels vessels to go one hundred miles below before entering the great bay, surrounded by wooded hills. On our left appeared Toboga with two English steamers, which ply down the coast of South America, lying before it. Winding among high mountain islands, which stud the bay, we came in view of New Panama, while the old city, destroyed by earthquakes and buccaneers, was pointed out six miles distant. Three men-of-war—two English and one American—three ships of the Mail line, and one steamer of the Panama railway for plying up the coast, were lying in the harbor.

At ten o'clock—precisely the minute appointed at the beginning of our long voyage two weeks before—the Sacramento made fast to a buoy; for shallow water and wicked reefs forbid first-class steamers to approach within two miles of the shore. Three of us took passage in the captain's dispatch boat, protected by umbrellas from the broiling sun. We pulled two miles out of our course to avoid the sharp teeth of the long reef standing above water at that stage of tide. Here the Pacific rises and falls thirty feet; at Aspinwall, just across the narrow isthmus, the variation of the Atlantic is only as many inches.

Here close my journeyings on the Pacific, from snowy north to burning south, from Vancouver Island, within a thousand miles of the Arctic sea, down to a thousand miles within the tropics. Here is the beautiful bay studded with islands, fronting the quaint old city of a dead civilization. Here, three hundred and fifty years ago, armor-clad and sword in hand, Balboa waded into the Pacific, taking solemn possession of ocean *and all bordering lands* for the king of Castile and Leon, his heirs and assigns forever. Truly a magnificent domain, had there been no flaw in the title!

CHAPTER XLIV.

After our little boat was pulled up the beach by coal-black natives, we landed among tumble-down buildings. Climbing rickety stairs and passing under a crazy arch, we were in the narrow streets of Panama, shaded by tall dwellings of adobe and stucco. The population is six thousand.

As this was January first, a church holiday, the thoroughfares were thronged with gaily attired natives of every hue, from jet black to light buff. A few, boasting untainted Castilian blood, are as fair as the people of Louisiana and Mississippi; but chocolate is the prevailing tint of the mob. Interspersed were Frenchmen, Germans, Jews, English, and Americans, all in white linen from head to foot; and richly dressed Spanish ladies with dazzling eyes, and clear rich complexions tinctured with olive.

Women of the poorer classes (these low latitudes where bountiful Nature supplies absolute wants without labor, have *no* working classes) wore light linen lawns with immense frills about the neck, and exhibiting one entire shoulder and breast. The chariest maid of Panama is prodigal enough only when she unmasks her beauty, not merely to the moon, but to the blazing sun and entire populace. The whiteness of her drapery is in sharp contrast with her tawny skin. Some boys under twelve wear shirts, but most are entirely naked; while girls appear 'in the elegant costume of the Greek Slave.' They form striking couples for promenade—young ladies arrayed only in straw hats, and juvenile gentlemen in the same attire with hats omitted. The youthful republicans of New Grenada are incredibly callous to the prejudices of civilization, and flagrantly rebellious against 'the Paris milliner who dresses the world from her imperious boudoir.' If there be any Calvinism in dress, they are hopeless examples of total depravity.

The large, well-stocked trading houses sell goods cheaper than New York; for Panama is a free port, a paradise for smokers who love genuine Havanas, and for homeward-bound Yankees, who purchase for wives, daughters, and sweethearts, exquisite lawns of Irish linen which are said to last a hundred years. Price, thirty cents per yard, specie. Panama hats, which endure water and crushing like gutta percha, sell for from three to fifteen dollars.

There is a large American hotel, and a cathedral, seemingly a thousand years old. Many buildings are shattered by earthquakes and war. The 'old' city is reduced to a pile of ruins; and 'New' Panama, apparently about the oldest town in the world, is tending in the same direction. Crumbling walls surrounding the city, adobe ruins within, even roofs of tall buildings, and church towers, are profusely covered with growing vines and shrubs. Here Nature accumulates while men decay; here vegetation triumphs over masonry.

The ancient cathedral facing the plaza is a quaint, irregular pile of stone and stucco, with half-a-dozen medieval Spanish bells in one of its towers, and crumbling walls covered with mosses and vines. A tottering negro, in spectacles and gray hair, who looked old enough to be an Aztec king, and spoke only Castilian, invited us to enter. We passed in by a side door, through a cobbler's shop. The roof is supported by tall pillars, and the edifice will hold four thousand people. There is much silver-ware about the altar. Scores of marble grave-stones flat upon the ground, recite in mellow Spanish or sonorous Latin the virtues of departed cavaliers. Our cicerone pointed out one of the paintings as 'Saint Francisco,' another as 'Saint Sebastian,' a third as 'Mary and the Child;' and then, with polite beseeching, presented the contribution box. Just now no religious service was held, as the republican leader of the late revolution had driven away all the priests. Ordinarily, a revolution in a Spanish-American town attracts little more attention than a thunder shower in the United States.

At this coolest season of the year the blazing sun was fearful. A superannuated New York omnibus, drawn by two mules, rattled its bones through the streets, and a newsboy brought us the *Daily*

Star, printed in Spanish and English, damp from the press—two modern outcroppings in these ancient strata. One brawny negro, under a broad Panama hat, aired his English for our benefit:

'Shakspeare says: 'The white man rules the day and the black man rules the night;' but Gabriel says: 'The law rules the poor man, and the rich man rules the law.''

Gabriel, a sort of local Farquhar Tupper, seemed to be blowing his horn, after taking several horns too many; but drew one of the large and admiring audiences which usually attend that profound school of philosophy.

We obtained a glimpse of the great convent on the sea-shore, now closed by the revolution; and also of the huge dilapidated fort, half concealed under luxuriant vines and shrubs bearing gorgeous flowers. Then seeing a little steamer filled with our passengers, like a hive black with bees, moving to the shore, we hastened down the hot, narrow, winding streets to the railway station at the water's edge; and elbowed through the dense, panting crowd into the cars, which have cane seats, and wooden blinds instead of glass windows. The locomotive shrieked, and we moved out of the city, following endless curves, slowly winding around foot-hills and through jungles, toward the summit of that narrow neck of land which divides two unbounded seas.

The Panama railway, begun in 1848, was completed in seven years, costing one hundred and sixty thousand dollars per mile. Again and again its work was suspended; for the fever-breeding air poisoned all who breathed it. Natives, West Indians, Irish, French, Germans, Austrians, Coolies, and Chinese were successively employed as laborers, and to all it proved fatal. The forty-eight miles, ridged with graves, are said to have cost a man's life for every sleeper. Jamaica negroes and whites from our northern States bore the climate best, and finished the work. Think of men breathing fever, penetrating cane-brakes, wading swamps, fighting noxious insects, dodging boa-constrictors, cougars and crocodiles, and constantly braving death, for one or two dollars per day!

The road pays larger dividends than any other in the world. It charges twenty-five dollars in specie for a ride of forty-eight miles, and corresponding prices for freight. Seven-eighths of its passenger and two-fifths of its other receipts are from the California trade. This freight includes treasure; estimating it by the ton much the larger portion goes southward. The European and United States trade with the west coast of South America is very

ON THE ISTHMUS, BETWEEN PANAMA AND ASPINWALL.

heavy. British mail steamers ply from Valparaiso to Panama: and on the east side another line connects Aspinwall with Liverpool.

The sleepers are of lignumvitæ, the only timber which endures the ravages of climate and insects. The accompanying telegraph-poles are of cement, as no timber exposed to the air would last more than one year. Four miles apart are the local superintendents' houses, of uniform architecture; two stories, white, with green blinds, high ceilings, broad halls, deep balconies and piazza around the entire building, and separate kitchens in the rear. These frame dwellings, all made in New York, and sent out ready to be put together, look cool and inviting. Each superintendent is responsible for his four miles of road, which requires constant labor to keep it from being washed away by rains, or crumbled or covered by the irrepressible vegetation.

Beside the track are the dwellings of native workmen and villagers—little, steep-roofed cabins, thatched with tiles, grass or cane, with walls of sticks and plaster. They look dry and cool; but during the rainy season they must admit water like sieves, and their occupants become aquatic. The women were celebrating the day in clean frocks and bits of finery. All wear Panama hats like the men. Prolific Nature has blessed them with innumerable dusky babies. I have seen nothing like it save in Salt Lake streets and on Missouri prairies.

Here is the richest, densest vegetation in the world—an impenetrable tangle of mangoes, plantains, palms, oranges, bananas, limes, India rubber trees, and thousands of shrubs and parasites new to northern eyes. Here is primeval architecture—endless cloisters, colonnades, and bowers. Little vistas of greensward, fragments of water, hills and basaltic cliffs, are exceptional. As a whole, the isthmus is a vast jungle of trees, cane-brakes, and parasites, gay with gorgeous flowers and birds of brilliant plumage, rich with the cocoa-nut, and sometimes dazzling with the brightness of the orange.

Monkeys and parrots chatter on the branches; wild beasts hide in the dingles; insects swarm in the swamps; huge reptiles drag their slow lengths along the oozy soil, darkened by thick foliage which shuts out the light of the rich tropical heavens. From branches sixty feet high, vines hang down like ropes, mingling on the earth in mazes and labyrinths, and climbing and winding up the huge trunks. The old fact of nature and figure of rhetoric —the sustaining oak and clinging vine—man's strength and woman's tenderness—is reversed. The tree indeed supports the vine; but is smothered in the embrace of death. The trunks of some forest kings resemble huge pipes of lead, and even the stems of willows are in sections, with joints, like corn-stalks and sugar-cane.

Here are rarest combinations of color and form—wild palms with leaves eighteen inches long yet only a finger's width; immense groves of cultivated palms heavy with fruit; countless bananas upon which the natives subsist; pulpy stalks, with leaves, the thickness and texture of lily-pads, but sword-shaped, and ten or twelve feet in hight; birds of white, black and yellow; flowers of white, orange, crimson and scarlet, blazing out from the convolutions and tangles of greenness. All is profusion, luxury, gorgeousness. Every prospect pleases, and only man is vile.

Eleven miles from Panama we crossed the summit, through a natural gap three hundred feet above the ocean. From these mountains one can see both Atlantic and Pacific at once. For several miles we followed down the Chagres river, against whose muddy current natives used to pole up early California emigrants in canoes.

Aspinwall has an excellent harbor, enabling first-class steamers to come to the wharf without ferriage. On the chief street is a long row of wooden buildings, with projecting roofs or sheds, used as trading houses and eating and drinking saloons. The motley population of less than one thousand is composed of natives, Jamaica negroes, and Americans. Aspinwall owes its birth to the Panama railroad, and was surely born too soon—sent to this breathing world scarce half made up. Surrounded and intersected by stagnant pools—water unfit for drinking or cooking without distillation; air close and malarious; and population hybrid—it is the dreariest, wretchedest, most repulsive city of fact or fiction, not excepting Cairo Illinois, in the days of Martin Chuzzlewit.

The many-colored population was observing the holiday by clean clothing and a little more loafing than usual. The post-office was closed, but entering by a back door I found an amiable negro in charge, who spoke no English, but permitted me to ransack its dusty and disordered shelves for my file of waiting newspapers from home.

An hour after us arrived a second train, bringing only the

specie. Once admitted through the great gate and over the long wharf to the steamer New York, we could not leave the boat while the treasure was being transferred. Muscular, half-naked negroes received from freight cars the bare bricks of silver, bars of gold sewn in canvas, and boxes of coin, each taking a ticket describing his parcel, to deliver with it on the ship. Bending and perspiring under these precious burdens, the tawny workmen marched in constant procession between rows of men, illuminating wharf gangway and deck with lanterns. This novel spectacle lasted for two hours, convincing me that a million of dollars in

TRANSFERRING THE SPECIE AT ASPINWALL.

bullion is a good deal of money, and would be awkward to carry around. Afterward, while the heavy freight was coming on board, and the negroes pleasantly diverting themselves in smashing our trunks, we were permitted to go ashore to get limes for lemonades and claret punches, to soften the asperities of the trip.

At four the next morning the New York left Aspinwall wharf for her two-thousand-mile voyage, her passengers rested and invigorated by the isthmus trip, which breaks the monotony of the long sea-journey. She is a beautiful steamer, stanch, elegant and commodious, though smaller than those of the west side, which a single winter voyage on the Atlantic would strip to the hull. Her state-rooms are pleasant, each containing three berths and a sofa, with abundant drawers and shelves. A friend and myself occupied one. Another friend, his wife, five children and nurse, had three more, side by side; and in day-time we threw open the doors, converting the four rooms into a pleasant saloon.

The moment our wheels started, we felt the sharp contrast to the smooth Pacific, and the shining capacity of our steamer for rolling and pitching. It was difficult to decide which was hardest, to keep in bed through the night, dress in the morning, or eat during the day. The tables were a dreary expanse of empty seats, and our pretext of breakfasting very shallow and ridiculous. Huge waves drenched the upper deck with spray. It is wonderful how steamers ride them, with wheels now entirely submerged, and a moment after, lifted far out of the water.

For two days we staggered about or adhered to our sofas, battling the two difficulties of Artemus Ward—to keep inside of our state-rooms and outside of our dinners. The third was a little smoother; and wretched mortals began to creep out of their hiding-places, and appear at table. The women uniformly declared that they had not been seasick, but merely suffering from headache. Why is everybody ashamed of seasickness and innocent of its existence? Some thirty of our passengers were prostrated with Panama fever, often induced by the tropical voyage and crossing the isthmus. It is ordinarily prevented by taking two or three grains of quinine daily in the low latitudes.

Among the entertaining persons on board was a lady born near the Black sea, educated in Paris, conversant with most modern languages, and speaking English with just difficulty enough to make her chat piquant. With her husband, long in our public service, she has seen much of every quarter of the globe. Her comments upon American society were pungent.

'The Bostonians,' she said 'are very charming, very hospitable very cultivated; but they are *perfectly convicted* of their immense superiority to everybody else.'

She gave an amusing account of her three days' experience on this rolling vessel. Her beautiful hair, wonderfully fine and soft, is so long that when she stands upright, it sweeps the floor. Each morning she arranged it laboriously; but just as it was nearly finished a heavy lurch would fling her across the state-room, and down it came! After attempting again and again, she at last gave up in despair, sat down upon a trunk to enjoy 'a good cry,' and then returned to bed for the rest of the day.

However ill one feels, it is far better to partake of every meal, and, like Dr. Johnson, preserve the proud consciousness of 'a man

'ONLY A HEADACHE.'

who has endeavored well.' Iced champagne is the best remedy for this intense nausea. The sea is a relentless leveler, without the slightest regard for personal prejudices. One of our company, Congressional delegate from Arizona, was a member of the Maine legislature passing the original simon-pure, prohibitory law, of which he was an enthusiastic advocate. I now saw him upon a sofa for three days, pale as death, living upon champagne 'straight'—and he seemed to like it!

The third evening, on our left, we saw the dim mountains of Jamaica; and a few hours later, on our right, the little monitor-shaped island of Nevassa. The weather cooled, and the ship continued to roll, when we left behind the last of the Bahamas.

On the seventh day from Aspinwall, in the Carribean sea, the wind increased to a gale. Many declare that a storm does not equal one's imagination; that waves never run mountain-high. Actually I suppose they do not. Scientific measurements are said to prove that they seldom reach one hundred feet; yet standing on the hurricane deck, clutching a rope or iron rod for safety, we looked up at huge billows which gave the exact effect of tall mountains, far exceeding all my fancy had painted them. In beautiful, ever-changing colors they came rolling down upon us with great gulfs between, deep enough to hide a village church, steeple and all. Standing at the stern, we saw the bows of our gallant ship sometimes point up toward the sky, making the deck like a steep roof; and a moment after, dive down toward the bottom of the sea. It is a perpetual wonder to landsmen that a ship can ride such billows; but as long as they strike her bows or stern at a right-angle she breasts them easily, though a single broad-wise wave would be likely to swamp her. The New York behaved admirably under Captain Horner, an old and thorough seaman; but through that long rough night, it was difficult to keep in one's berth. Indeed, a new Jack and Gill in the bridal chamber fell down the steep hill of the careening floor, while all the mattresses came tumbling after.

At intervals in the darkness would come a tremendous lurch, straining the ship in every joint, and followed by crashing of glass and crockery. I had always longed to see a storm on shipboard; and here it was, to my heart's content. The anticipation was a good deal more agreeable than the reality. It was a memorable night—the only one in which I remember to have been kept awake solely from fear. By daylight it is appalling enough to watch vast waves upon which the ship seems the merest feather—to see every loose article flung across the cabin, and dishes from the tables scattered about like wheat from a sower's hand; but it is far more impressive for one to lie through the slow hours, wondering whether he will see the cheerful world again; remembering that a slight break of machinery would leave him at the mercy of the elements; that only a plank is between him and death.

The next morning we were laboring up the Gulf Stream, off Cape Lookout. We were able to make only three or four knots per hour—barely enough motion for steerage. Our forward bulkheads had been shaved off as with a razor; sheets of copper stripped from the hull; thirty feet of the upper deck broken off and floated away; four larboard closets carried overboard; and three-inch planks, thickly studded with spikes, torn up like paper. Old salts declared the weather as bad as ships ever live through; and after reaching port we learned that many vessels went down in the gale. At the thin breakfast tables, where dishes danced a Virginia reel, the passengers looked worn and haggard; but jested about the prospect with true national nonchalance. After lasting two days the gale abated.

Go outside in a storm, insure safety by clinging or being lashed to a safe object, and watch the wonderful seas. It makes one quite forget his terror to look out upon vast mountains of waves instantaneously changing in form, and in richness and variety of colors which no brush nor canvas can reproduce.

On the tenth evening from Aspinwall we saw Barnegat light off the New Jersey coast. The next morning our ship plowed the ice of New York harbor, among a hundred familiar scenes; and threw out her cable at the foot of Canal street, twenty-two days from San Francisco.

Ended were my eight months' wanderings, from the Missouri to the Pacific, and back to the Atlantic. I wish every American, before going abroad, might make the trans-continental journey. Without it he can have no creditable knowledge or intelligent appreciation of his own country. New York, New England, Pennsylvania, Ohio, the Atlantic slope—these are not wholly nor chiefly the United States. Let him view the great river, with its magnificent valley; the prairies which look up at the mountains; the mountains which look out on the sunset sea. They will give him home standards of comparison for every foreign scene; glimpses of our strongest national traits, both virtues and faults; suggestions of the vastness of our domain, our pageants of beauty and sublimity, our abounding resources and our great destiny.

CHAPTER XLV.

In September, 1866, a new line of sleeping-cars on all the routes radiating from Chicago, was paying forty thousand dollars per month to its chief owner—an old quartz miner from the Rocky Mountains. Thus he earned a frugal livelihood until Colorado mining should become an established success.

The cars each cost from twenty-eight thousand to forty thousand dollars, and are incomparably the finest in the world. A new improvement combines a sleeping, eating and saloon carriage. In its little apartments the passenger, by touching a bell-tassel, summons a waiter to serve him with coffee, oysters, chicken, or any thing else to be had at an ordinary restaurant.

I left Chicago upon a palatial sleeping-car, richly furnished, and running like a pair of skates upon even ice. The ample beds are as inviting as those of our best hotels. The masculine passenger undresses as at home, and sleeps soundly, unless on very bad terms with his conscience or his nerves.

Morning found us on a vast ocean of prairie, with great islands of corn rising from its depths, and white fleets of villages, neat clippers of country churches, and snowy schooners of farm-houses resting upon its bosom. The Illini Indians greeted old Father Marquette:

'How beautiful is the sun, O Frenchman, when thou comest among us!'

The scene is fair to-day; and no man can measure the richness of the Prairie State. The southern half is almost as level as a floor. I have personal prejudices in favor of regions where water will run one way or the other; but these endless sweeps, mellowed by laughing sunflower, rippling grass and tasseled corn, are the granary and garden of the world.

At Quincy a wheezy engine ferried us over the Mississippi;* and then the locomotive bore us across Missouri. Again, horizon-bounding prairies; thousands of cattle, white, black and spotted, grazing unfenced fields; forests more frequent and dense; streams more forbidding and muddy; log houses increasing; great farms inclosed wholly by heavy rails of black-walnut; white villages fewer and further between; at the bridges, empty log forts, with grass growing in their deserted camps, and flowers springing from their precious graves.

The railway left us at Atchison Kansas. In lieu of the Border Ruffian shanties of 1857, is now a well-built city of brick and stone, with heavy trade, two daily newspapers, and cars running sixty miles westward on a branch of the Union Pacific railroad.

Thence I took a little steamer down the Missouri. In 1858, Sumner, two miles below, had five hundred people. Now it has about twenty-five. All the buildings save five or six have been torn down and taken away. Young oaks and cottonwoods choke its deserted streets—to me peculiarly desolate, as it was my home for two years. Of its then residents, many have gone to the last, untroubled sleep; and the living are scattered all over the world.

We landed at Leavenworth, which looks more like a great city than any other point between St. Louis and San Francisco. It boasts three railway connections; three daily newspapers, printed in English, and two in German. It is lighted with gas; well built of brick; and has the air of a metropolis. As usual in this longitude, the citizens do not underrate its importance. There is enough of magnificent expectation to give point to the satire of a waggish resident, who insists that St. Louis and Chicago will be wood and water stations on the railways leading east; but admits that New York may exceed Leavenworth for several years to come!

St. Joseph, Leavenworth and Kansas City each started fair in the race. St. Joseph had age and a rich, well-settled surrounding country; Leavenworth, a military post and a fair prairie site; Kansas City, the lucrative New Mexican trade and a firm rock

---

* Indian: Great and long river.

landing on the river in front. But the two Missouri towns were Border Ruffian; and with the great war, the whirligig of time brought in his revenges. Their business went to Leavenworth, while Kansas troops swept Missouri with fire and sword. Now St. Joseph has eighteen thousand people; Leavenworth twenty-two thousand; Kansas City eleven thousand. Near by are Lawrence with eight thousand, Atchison, with six thousand, and Wyandotte with three thousand—all less than seventy miles apart, in a young, thinly-settled region. How they live is a mystery; yet each is

DELAWARE STREET, LEAVENWORTH, 1867.

busy, with great blocks going up, and its chief street a Broadway in miniature.

From Leavenworth I took railway to Topeka, fifty-eight miles. The road climbs ridges like saw-teeth; jolts one like corduroys, and rocks him like a rough cradle. It leads through the old Delaware reservation, not long open to settlement; but great cornfields and herds of cattle already appear. The remaining members of this and other Kansas tribes will soon be removed to the Indian Territory, or some other remote region. The whites want their lands—and have the power. Thirty-three miles out we reach the bank of the Kaw river, opposite Lawrence. Here North Lawrence has suddenly sprung up, with a population of fifteen hundred, and a weekly newspaper. Here we find the Kansas fork of the Union Pacific railway, pushing due west toward Denver. We follow it twenty-five miles up the Kansas valley, then debark and cross the river.

Topeka now contains twenty-five hundred inhabitants. At the chief street-crossing a tall liberty-pole is encircled by a log stockade, whose musket loop-holes stare down the avenues in four directions. It was built after Quantrell's wholesale massacre at Lawrence. Long may the flag stream above, with the rifles unneeded below! Brick and stone blocks are springing up like rows of young corn. Thus far the vertebræ are ill-defined; but the broad spinal street, whose jet-black loam is hard-baked in drowth and mushy in freshet, points northward, down a smooth prairie slope; then across a rich bottom, rank with vegetation, to the sluggish Kansas. The further bank is traversed by the great railroad, which brings mails and passengers from New York in three days. A State-house of dark magnesian limestone is begun; Lincoln college, under Presbyterian auspices, is in full operation; and the town has a most promising future.

Again I found a convention in session, as during my first visit. That was a 'Free State' assemblage, held in the open air; this, a 'Republican' gathering, within a hall, though upon the same spot. That was very bitter against James Buchanan; this equally so against Andrew Johnson. That was directed chiefly by Lane; this, held soon after his death, seemed a little bewildered at the absence of his aggressive, controlling will. I saw that the war had left great gaps among the Old Guard. Some present limped on crutches; some had empty sleeves and scarred faces; but there were scores of familiar countenances, including several attendants, and candidates too, at every convention since 1856! The Kansas politician is long-lived as the cedar of Lebanon and periodic as fever and ague.

This convention, after all these years of war, defeated a resolution to strike 'white' out of the State constitution, and substituted a recommendation submitting the suffrage question to a popular vote. Even Kansas, earliest to give the negro the musket, was reluctant to give him the ballot. Though placing within his grasp the first prizes of the university, she hesitated to open to his competition the highest honors of the State.

In Topeka I encountered Asa Hairgrove, a survivor of the Marais des Cygnes massacre of 1858, his face still scarred, a bullet still imbedded in his skull, his left hand still warped by the old charge of buckshot. Upon the admission of Kansas, he was elected State auditor. His father, William Hairgrove, had not yet lived to witness the death of all the criminals (see page 123.) But his neighbors chose him sheriff of Linn county; and six years after the butchery, with a military posse, he captured one of the murderers in Missouri; brought him back to Kansas; witnessed his trial and conviction by a civil court; and then hung him in the regular course of official duty! It was a curious example of retributive justice. During the war, several others of Hamilton's band fell fighting for the rebels.

Abandoning the locomotive for a horse and buggy, I left the capital with Thaddeus H. Walker. My own estates being chiefly in Spain, I find the sorrow of getting but small dividends tempered by the joy of paying no taxes. Not so with my friend Walker. Possessing one hundred and seven thousand acres in Kansas alone, he is probably the largest landholder in the Union. Six miles north of Topeka, we viewed the farm of a thousand acres where in 1858, before he was known to fame, or ever marched down to the sea, Sherman tilled the soil. A group of neighbors, discussing politics among their generous grain stacks, told us that unimproved lands were held at five to fifteen dollars per acre; and in one rare case a farm had sold for fifty dollars per acre.

We met a countless army of grasshoppers darkening the air like great flakes of snow. Our horse's feet crushed them by hundreds; everywhere they flew up so thick that he was reluctant to go on. They are about an inch and-a-quarter long, and look like our most familiar eastern grasshopper, but with more of the clipper build, and carrying more sail. They fly as high as one can fling a stone, and they can stay aloft like wild geese. What genius will achieve immortality by learning from them to construct a flying machine, as Sir Samuel Brown invented the suspension bridge from a spider-web across his path?

In a column one hundred and fifty miles wide and about one hundred deep, they mysteriously appeared near Fort Kearney, and were sweeping southwest. Some farmers burn the prairies before them. This confounds the troublesome visitors; like human armies, finding their supplies cut off, they make forced marches. They strip to skeletons shining cottonwood leaves. They devour every shred of tomatoes and onions. They gorge themselves upon cabbages, reckless of the great truth that cabbages are indigestible. They roll the springing wheat as a sweet morsel under their tongues. They feast upon tender leaves and milky kernels of softest green corn. Witnesses aver that in some places they eat ripe corn, cob and all! I did not hear of their consuming any fire-proof safes; and I am confident they never would have attacked the prisoners' rations at Castle Thunder or Salisbury. What produces them? Whence come they, and whither go?

AMONG THE GRASSHOPPERS.

We found the wild grasses six feet high, spangled with sunflower, golden-rod, and other blossoms of white and blue and royal purple. Plants brought here from eastern States abruptly change in form, shape of leaves and number of petals. Probably this greater elevation above the sea—at some points fourteen hundred feet—is the chief cause.

We spent the first night at Holton, Jackson county. The Border Ruffians of the first bogus legislature named the counties. Their Free State successors changed Calhoun to Jackson, Breckinridge to Linn, Wise to Chase, and were about transforming

Douglas to Lincoln, when the Little Giant became their advocate by opposing the Lecompton constitution. Atchison, Doniphan, Davis (from Jefferson Davis,) Marshall, Leavenworth, Coffey, Woodson and Johnson, all commemorating Pro-slavery leaders, are still retained.

We passed into Nemeha and Marshall, with many farms along the timbered creeks, but few on the high prairies. Here, seventy miles from the railway, though with the locomotive approaching by two lines, unimproved lands were held at two to five dollars per acre, and farms at eight to twenty-five dollars. Settlers have grown rich supplying emigrants, and freighters to Colorado and Utah. At Marysville, a large flouring mill, running night and day, supplies an extensive region. Until lately, Kansas farmers shipped their wheat to St. Louis, and bought flour from the same city; but with age comes wisdom. Marysville was long the outpost of civilization; now settlements extend a hundred miles westward.

We passed several thrifty villages, each with its weekly newspaper; and many excellent farms. Beside our road a threshing machine, run by eight horses and twelve men, was taking out of the straw four hundred bushels of wheat a day. Horse-rakes, mowers, planters, and quadruple 'stirring-plows' begin to abound. Machinery is increasing fourfold the efficiency of labor. This riding around the country on the spring seat of a mower or planter, is little like the old farming of New England! The great unsupplied need is the steam plow, but that will surely come.

We got lost on blind trails; feasted on wild plums; and gained scorched noses and tanned cheeks. At the week's end we again reached Topeka, whence I continued westward.

Manhattan, a busy town of one thousand people, at the junction of Kansas and Big Blue rivers, is within a few miles of the geographical center of the United States. On this remote frontier, beyond forty-nine fiftieths of our present population, is the hub of the continent, if not of the universe. Most business blocks and dwellings in the vicinity are of light magnesian limestone. The scarcity of lumber is a blessed thing for Kansas. It secures buildings of brick and stone, instead of log shanties and frame shells.

I encountered an old Boston and Colorado and Arkansas friend —a gentleman from everywhere—who had abandoned pioneering and soldiering for sheep-raising. He insisted that twenty thousand dollars capital and a few years of close attention to the business must insure an immense fortune.

The Agricultural college, a generous stone structure of three stories, overlooks Manhattan and a grand sweep of surrounding country. Tuition is free, the State supporting the institution. It is munificently endowed with ninety thousand acres of richest land. The regular course varies little from that of our older universities, though offering a liberal option in branches. One of the professors showed me a section of the backbone and vertebræ of *a whale*, lately found—the oldest inhabitant of Kansas yet heard from.

The college, like all other educational institutions sustained by the State, knows no distinction of race, color, or sex. Of the one hundred students, more than half are girls. They take the regular course; they will receive the regular degrees. Thus far they excel their masculine competitors even in composition, declamation and the higher mathematics. They have a debating club and learn parliamentary law. If women conduct our great charities, they must hold public meetings; if they hold public meetings, they must know the rules of deliberative bodies.

Under the laws of Kansas, women of eighteen and upward may vote on every question in district school-meetings, and are eligible to all offices in school-boards. In some sections they do not vote; in others they turn out en masse. Many, elected trustees and superintendents, serve with great zeal and practical wisdom. In several districts ladies have drawn plans, obtained proposals, let the contracts for new school-houses, and are the leading spirits. Nowhere did I hear a single complaint against the practical workings of the law.

All honor to young Kansas, color-bearer in the great army of progress! Is there any man who cannot see the common justice and common sense of giving mothers an authoritative voice in school matters? Beside, our civilization produces a large class of women to whom the traditional limits are cruelty, and the old formulas inapplicable. Many will always be without husbands or home duties. Many will always be denied God's best gift—the gift of children. And many, finding their little circle of possibilities barren, their lives empty and aimless, from mere energy and restlessness plunge into vanities and frivolities and—worse. The charities are blessed; of such is the kingdom of heaven. But not every woman, even of the best, can find her work in teaching a pauper school or sewing flannel for indigent contrabands. One may lack the offspring of Mrs. John Rogers and the opportunity of Florence Nightingale, without being at heart a Lady Teazle or a Becky Sharp. She may be fitted for some part in the great affairs and absorbing activities which make the lives of men worthy and satisfying, because purposeful and fruitful. Give her a chance—a fair field and no favor! Let old paths widen and new avenues unlock their rusted and creaking gates.

Next visiting Lawrence, I found the historic town—twice destroyed for its fidelity to freedom—so changed in six years that I was a stranger in a strange land. The stone fort of 1856 yet looks down from Mount Oread; but the circular mud forts have been leveled for remorseless 'improvements.' It was a great mistake. Real estate is plentiful, especially in wet weather. These old landmarks should have been preserved forever. I could recognize only three or four buildings.

Quantrell's raid in 1863, sacked and burned the town, left every business survivor bankrupt, and murdered one hundred and eighty unarmed and unresisting people. Yet the *Richmond Examiner* pronounced it 'justifiable and legitimate warfare.' It was the foulest deed of the great rebellion. One lady, whose aged husband had fallen to the ground, threw herself upon him and sought to shield him with her clothing and her encircling arms. when the pursuing murderer put her dress aside and blew out his brains. It is said that she has never smiled since that ghastly experience.

Massachusetts street, inclosed by brick blocks of two, three and four stories, has lengthened three-fold since 1860. During rain the black soil is just as muddy and sticky as when the pioneers, sitting upon barrels and boxes in a solitary tent, first welcomed Governor Reeder with the never-to-be-omitted speech-making.

From Mount Oread, the State universitv, of brick, painted in awkward imitation of stone, stares fixedly down upon the phœnix-like city and the green prairies that environ it. Lower, a huge windmill for grinding corn and wheat flaps its patient wings.

LAWRENCE KANSAS, AFTER THE QUANTRELL RAID.

Manufactories hum and clink among the dwellings. Lawrence has two daily newspapers, and a lucrative trade.

I visited Paola, county seat of Miami, fifteen miles from the Missouri line. A fort which did mount two guns survives the war. Through the rebellion, these people had to sleep upon their arms. Now and then raiders dashed in, sacked towns, robbed stores, and took prisoners. Still, the border counties of Wyandotte, Johnson, Miami, Linn and Bourbon, contain one-fourth the entire population of Kansas. Timber and water are more plentiful than in northern sections. The great salines are on the southern line. The immense coal-beds which underlie the State, and the deposits of marble and lead, crop out in the southeast corner, near Fort Scott, which already contains more than three thousand inhabitants, and is fourth town in the Commonwealth. In Miami, oil wells are being opened. The State geologist, in his survey of this county, found 'more than twenty places where petroleum flowed from rocks and soil in considerable abundance,' and 'numerous deposits in the solid form of asphaltum.'

Though Miami county is yet forty miles from the locomotive, unimproved lands command five to twelve dollars per acre. In Johnson county, adjoining, they are still higher. Near Spring Hill, a pleasant little prairie village, I found Mr. Sprague, who settled on this bare prairie nine years before, living in a white farm-house of two stories; with one barn of stone and another of lumber, luxuriant hedges of Osage orange, groves of locust and black walnut, young orchards, broad corn and wheat fields; and asking ten thousand dollars for his tract of one hundred and sixty acres. His is a type case. In riding five miles to the eastward, where in 1857 was no human habitation, I saw almost every quarter-section fenced, with dwellings of frame or stone, long hedges, young shade-trees and great expanses of grain.

A stage-coach carries the mail daily from Fort Scott to Kansas City, one hundred and twenty miles, for one cent per year. It is the lowest contract in the United States. The passenger business is heavy, and the proprietor means to keep off competition. By his line I passed through Westport Missouri, now dull and deserted, but once flourishing, and handsomely built. Hence issued Captain Henry Clay Pate of Border Ruffian memory to capture John Brown—and was himself taken, with all his men, by the old fighting saint. Pate afterward fell in the great war, leading a regiment of Virginia rebel cavalry.

Kansas City grows apace; but the dusky faces of the Santa Fe teamsters who first gave it life, are seen here no more forever. They now load their wagons at the railway terminus, two hundred miles westward.

The narrative of Lewis and Clark, picturing the first impressions of this region received by white visitors, is still pleasant reading to one familiar with the country. A negro servant who accompanied them was an unfailing source of wonder, and sometimes of terror, to the Indians. On the Missouri, an old chief told Captain Lewis that some foolish youths of his tribe had circulated reports of a man who was black; but he knew it must be a lie. When first confronted with the Ethiopian, the solemn brave thought the darkey must be painted. But finding that he could not, with wet finger, rub the color from his cheek, he went away bewildered and alarmed.

These pioneer explorers reported that the best land along the great river as between the mouth of the Osage and the mouth of the Platte. This undoubtedly embraces and borders upon the largest and best unbroken farming tract on the globe. Kansas has had only two injurious drowths in thirty years. With early planting and sowing, and deep plowing, she suffers no more from dry weather than New York or Massachusetts. Her soil is the very richest. There is not a swamp in the State. It is difficult to find ten acres of untillable ground. Coal underlies almost every county. Limestone and sandstone make excellent building material, and Osage orange admirable fences. Cottonwood, black walnut and maple grow large enough for sawing in five years from the seed.

A PAINTED DARKEY.

The average yield of corn is from forty to sixty bushels to the acre. With the best machinery, one man will plant, cultivate and gather fifty acres in a season. The hoe is never used. Weeds are kept down by plowing. Wheat yields from fifteen to forty bushels. Oats are easily raised and produce largely. In one instance one hundred and seven bushels of corn were gathered from an acre; in another, ninety bushels of oats. Hay is a natural crop, grass growing from five to ten feet high. It may be cut any time between the first of July and the middle of November. Hungarian and other cultivated grasses often produce three or four tons to the acre. The Chinese sugar-cane succeeds well.

Stock-raising is the most lucrative pursuit. In 1866, Kansas sold *more than a million dollars worth* of cattle to Illinois alone. Illinois is fenced in. She lacks grazing capacity, but winters the stock and then sends it to eastern markets. Grapes, cherries, apples, peaches, strawberries, gooseberries, currants, and blackberries thrive. As a fruit State, I think Kansas will have no equal in the Union, except California.

All vines and flowers grow luxuriantly. The sun never shone upon lovelier expanses. Nowhere else is Nature so kind. To build a road, the settler has nothing to do but drive over the prairie wherever he wants to go. To raise a grove, one need only plow the field, and trees spring up spontaneously. To open a farm, he simply breaks the soil and plants his corn upon the upturned sward. To inclose it, he puts in the Osage orange; for one or two seasons replants what the gophers destroy; and in four years he has a fence equal to a stone wall.

But in many sections the eye is pained by the absence of fruit and shade trees, and the lack of beauty in dwellings. Residences are plenty—*homes* few. The slovenly log houses, with jet-black bare soil all around them, and the stiff frame dwellings with naked walls and glittering white paint, all standing right beside the road after our detestable national fashion, have no single attractive feature. Beauty at first cost is as cheap as deformity, and a great deal more remunerative afterward. In a new country, settlers are poor. Meat and raiment, sheltering the head, keeping the wolf from the door, are first inexorable necessities. But these Kansas dwellings are plainer and uglier than those of Iowa, Wisconsin, or Minnesota.

Set them back a hundred feet or a hundred yards from the road. Then, though the home be only a cabin, have greensward not naked dirt about it; plant trees in front; open a flower-patch; throw a little stoop over the front door, or a bay-window into one end—any thing to break this square, dreary, coffin-like appearance. Let rose bushes smile under the window, and creepers cling to the eaves, and clematis fringe and entwine the doorway. Make a real home, be it never so homely, and let the boys and girls grow up under its mellowing and refining influence.

It seems only yesterday that Stephen A. Douglas introduced

his bill organizing Kansas and Nebraska; and we all began to ask:

'Where are they, and what Indians inhabit them?'

In 1853 there were not one hundred white settlers. There was absolutely no property except wild land. Kansas real estate and personal would not have sold under the hammer for one million dollars. Nothing was produced except a little corn and beef by missionaries and Indians.

Now, the value of property in the State, as assessed for taxation is fifty-five millions of dollars. And one encounters in full operation all the institutions of commerce, society, government, education and religion—school-houses on every prairie; homes dotting hill and valley; hamlets with neat churches, 'their taper fingers pointing to heaven;' great cities; generous universities; extensive manufactories; a net-work of railways; and these late lonely prairies teeming with the busy life of a quarter of a million of people. These be the victories of Peace, no less renowned than War.

CHAPTER XLVI.

From St. Joseph to Omaha I took the steamer Colorado. The little stern-wheel Ontario, which passed up the Missouri a week before us, loaded with railway iron, had snagged. An insurance agent came up on our boat to inspect her. He must have been satisfied that there was no fraud; for we found the wretched steamer with only one guard above water, lying half-overturned, and bayoneted through the heart. Workmen in skiffs were cutting her to pieces to save the iron.

Nebraska City, fronted by a sand-bar which compels boats to land below, has two thousand people. Once huge blocks were erected, and freighting for the plains made the town a miniature Babel. Now its glory has departed, drawn to Omaha by the all-potent locomotive. Plattsmouth is at the mouth of the shallow Platte, which stretches long arms into the very heart of the Rocky Mountains. The stream is as broad as the Mississippi, and looks large enough for the Great Eastern. But its actual depth can hardly average fourteen inches; and in dry weather it is barely navigable for shingles.

A bright ruddy boy of four years, who had been playing all over our cabin, was suddenly smitten with cholera, and died in a few hours. At midnight the engines stopped, a plank was put out, the rude coffin carried on shore; and in the deep woods, by flaring torches, the little fallen bud of life was given back to the kindly earth. The family were emigrants from Missouri to Iowa. After we started again, the agonizing shrieks of the poor mother disturbed every sleeper on board, though she had five other children with her—five other little mouths which her life slaves itself to fill. 'O human nature, human nature!'

Shallows and sand-banks forced us to land a mile below Omaha. The young city will have to compress the river by narrowing the banks, as St. Louis did the Mississippi. Omaha is not on the water's edge like Leavenworth and other Kansas towns; but

A PART OF OMAHA, IN 1867.

leads a sprawling existence back on a level and hill-side, with a broad strip of lowland intervening. Its area is immense; horizontally it is a great city.

From the boat I could not detect one feature of beauty, save the white capitol on a symmetric hill a mile away. But riding up to the summit, and looking back down upon the young metropolis, I saw the fairest town-site on the Missouri. This bird's-eye view takes in many shaded and beautiful dwellings upon neighboring hills; frame warehouses and brick blocks springing up like mushrooms; a level floor of prairie and corn-field which stretches for six miles up to Florence; broad, smooth, generous avenues pointing from the State-house down to the Missouri; the river itself; and beyond it, rich Iowa prairies extending back four miles to Council Bluffs. When Lewis and Clark penetrated this solitude, they found these bold hills upon the eastern bank the common conference ground of many tribes, and named them 'the Council Bluffs.'

That was but sixty years ago; yet this region was less known than Siberia. Now, in its early future, will rise a great city, heart of a dense population, on the grand highway of travel and traffic for the whole globe. And sixty years hence—what imagination so rich and wild as to paint *that* picture? The center of an empire stretching from north pole to equator; with every climate, every product, every industry; with more than a hundred millions of people, embodying democracy, illustrating Christianity; giving to each child, though the offspring of ignorance, poverty and vice, a fair start in the race of life, freedom from every burden, and the rich endowment of education and opportunity—recognizing in every man and woman, even those we name outcast and criminal, brothers and sisters of one great family, whom the same loving Father made, and the same Teacher died to redeem. That were a destiny worth the having!

From 1857 to 1864 Omaha had a hard struggle. But the great Pacific railroad infused wonderful vigor; and I found the little capital of Nebraska the liveliest city in the United States. The railway company had erected an immense brick car-house, engine-house, and machine shops; and five or six hundred buildings had gone up during the summer. One brick block cost a hundred thousand dollars. Streets were being graded, sidewalks thronged with returned gold-seekers, discharged soldiers, farmers selling produce, speculators, Indians, and other strange characters of border life. The population was eight thousand. Single grocery houses were doing a business of half a million dollars per year; and the pioneer merchants and bankers had accumulated fortunes. The railroad disbursed a quarter of a million dollars per month. Business lots commanded from two to five thousand dollars.

Here was George Francis Train, at the head of a great company called the Credit Foncier, organized for dealing in lands and stocks—for building cities along the railway from the Missouri to Salt Lake. This corporation had been clothed by the Nebraska legislature with nearly every power imaginable, save that of reconstructing the late rebel States. It was erecting neat cottages in Omaha and at other points west.

Mr. Train owned personally about five hundred acres in Omaha, which cost him only one hundred and seventy-five dollars per acre—a most promising investment. He is a noticeable, original American, who has crowded wonderful and varied experiences into his short life. An orphan boy employed to sweep the counting-room, he rose to the head of a great Boston shipping house; then established a branch in Liverpool; next organized and conducted a heavy commission business in Australia, and astonished his neighbors in that era of fabulous prices, with Brussels carpets and marble counters and a free champagne luncheon daily in his business office. Afterward he made the circuit of the world, wrote books of travel, fought British prejudice against street railways, occupying his leisure by fiery and audacious American war speeches to our island cousins, until he spent a fortune, and enjoyed the delights of a month in a British prison.

Thence he returned to America; lectured everywhere; and now he is trying to build a belt of cities across the continent. At least a magnificent project. Curiously combining keen sagacity with wild enthusiasm, a man who might have built the pyramids, or been confined in a straight jacket for eccentricities, according to the age he lived in, he observes dryly that since he began to make money, people no longer pronounce him crazy! He says Chicago and San Francisco have more 'men of brains' than any other cities in the world—'men who would know what to do in an earthquake, a fire, or a shipwreck'—a definition of brains worthy of Fosco. He drinks no spirits, uses no tobacco, talks on the stump like an embodied Niagara, composes songs to order by the hour as fast as he can sing them, like an Italian *improvisatore*, remembers every droll story from Joe Miller to Artemus Ward, is a born actor, is intensely in earnest, and has the most absolute and outspoken faith in himself and his future.

With the Government commissioners, who were present to accept a new twenty-miles of the line, I went out to the end of the Pacific railroad—then two hundred and forty miles west of Omaha. Making a short elbow to the south, at ten miles out the railway turns westward along the Platte valley. The embankments for the iron are seldom more than three or four feet high; and for a tangent of forty miles the road is as straight as the track of a rifle-ball. That is a good place for studying perspective. Eastern Nebraska is a capital farming country, though more sandy, and less rich than Kansas.

GEORGE FRANCIS TRAIN.

A hundred miles out, we passed Columbus, on the prairies. It promises to be a future railway focus. Mr. Train and his associates believe that it will be a great city, capital of Nebraska, and perhaps of the United States. Stranger things *have* happened. Two hundred miles out, at Kearney station, we spent the night in our passenger car, improvising beds, with boards, cushions and blankets, upon the backs of the seats. Having traveled to Fort Kearney seven times by wagon and coach, I found accomplishing it by rail in a few hours decidedly agreeable.

The next morning we started on. A few buffaloes had been killed here lately; and now we saw hundreds of antelopes from our train. Some came within two hundred yards, curious to scrutinize the iron monster screeching into their vast domain. While in motion we aimed hundreds of rifle-shots at them from the car windows. A single one, from General Merrill, took effect, and sent its beautiful victim limping into the sand-hills.

At the end of the track, on the smooth, well-built road, we found long sleeping and eating-cars for the workmen, who press forward so fast that only portable dwellings will serve them. All supplies come from the east. The sleepers are brought down the Missouri, from Iowa forests. About half are soft cottonwood;

BUILDING THE UNION PACIFIC RAILROAD IN NEBRASKA. PAGE 567.

but Burnetizing (infusing with zinc) is said to render them as durable as oak. Many of the timbers for bridges are of black walnut, often sixteen inches square. There are but two long bridges east of the Rocky Mountains—one of fifteen hundred feet across Loupe Fork; another of half-a-mile over the North Platte.

The charter permits only American iron. The rails are from Pennsylvania and New York. We found the workmen, with the regularity of machinery, dropping each rail in its place, spiking it down, and then seizing another. Behind them, the locomotive; before, the tie-layers; beyond these the graders; and still further, in mountain recesses, the engineers. It was Civilization pressing westward—the Conquest of Nature moving toward the Pacific.

Thomas C. Durant, vice-president and sole contractor of the road, has furnished the energy and most of the brains for carrying out this stupendous national enterprise. He has pushed the line westward with a rapidity never before equaled. It used to be thought a great feat to lay one mile of track per day; but here two miles and even two and-a-half have been laid daily for weeks. The head-quarters of the company are in New York. There Mr. Durant from his quiet office, directs by telegraph the labors of twelve thousand men—an army which it requires generalship to handle, particularly when its commander must be paymaster as well.

The Platte valley, from six to twenty miles wide, is incomparably the most favorable railway route in the world—almost a dead level from the Missouri up to the mountains. For five hundred miles the grade averages only seven feet to the mile.

When the range is reached, rolling mills will be erected for making rails, iron dug from the hills, and ties cut from the forests. Though the highest summit-crossing contemplated is more than eight thousand feet above sea-level, it is believed that no heavier grade than eighty feet to the mile will be required.

The company design building a branch to Denver. Their main line passes nearly one hundred miles north of that city. The chief Kansas fork, from Wyandotte up the Kaw and Smoky Hill, will join the main stem near Denver. It will probably make that connection about as soon as the California and Nebraska companies unite at Salt Lake. Of the two smaller Kansas forks the northern, from St. Joseph westward, will unite with the Platte valley line; and the southern, from Atchison, with the Smoky Hill. The Wyandotte and Atchison forks receive the same Congressional endowment as the Nebraska Union Pacific and the California Central Pacific—twelve hundred and eighty acres of land and sixteen thousand dollars in Government bonds for each

THOMAS C. DURANT. BUILDER OF UNION PACIFIC RAILROAD.

mile completed. Passing no hilly regions, they do not obtain the higher subsidies.

The uniform width established upon the trunk line and all its branches is four feet eight and-a-half inches. That corresponds with most eastern roads, and will give an unbroken gauge from San Francisco to New York, via Omaha and Chicago.

When the California builders have passed down the eastern side of the Sierras to find smooth sailing, the road from Omaha will strike the Rocky Mountains and hard work. But ample preparation is made for it. The summer of 1867 opens with twenty-five thousand men employed on the main stem of the Pacific Railway; *and the California and Nebraska companies expect their locomotives to meet in the vicinity of Salt Lake early in* 1870. Speed the day!

DISTANCES.

New York to Chicago,	979 miles.
Chicago to Omaha,	500 miles.
Omaha to Salt Lake City,	1,035 miles.
Salt Lake to Sacramento,	625 miles.
Sacramento to San Francisco,	80 miles.
New York to San Francisco,	3,219 miles.

HIGHTS ABOVE SEA LEVEL.

Omaha,	1,000 feet.
Crossing of North Platte,	2,790 feet.
Eastern base Rocky Mountains,	4,534 feet.
Highest summit-crossing Rocky Mountains,	8,230 feet.
Salt Lake City,	4,286 feet.
Summit-crossing of Sierras,	7,042 feet.
Sacramento, (on tide-water,)	00 feet.

Along the Platte are the old hunting-grounds of the Pawnee Loupes, whose horrible sacrifices of prisoners captured in war, to Venus their great star, are described by Lewis and Clark. The story of these old chroniclers, who saw the early and real romance of the continent, tempts me to borrow from it once more. Up the river, within the present limits of Dacotah,* they found ferocious brown bears, killing one whose foot measured eleven by seven and-a-half inches, exclusive of the claws. After a little experience in hunting them, Captain Lewis recorded in his journal: 'We had rather encounter two Indians than one brown bear!' A few days later, several soldiers wounded one of the brutes, when he suddenly turned upon them, undismayed by the pelting bullets. One ball broke his shoulder, but retarded him only for a moment. Giving the hunters no time to reload, he compelled them to throw away their guns, drove them pell-mell down a perpendicular bank of twenty feet into the river; and sprang after

* Original name of the Sioux nations, and signifying: 'Leagued' or 'allied.'

them. He had almost overtaken the hindmost, when a fatal bullet was lodged in his head. That was at least more exciting than the hunting of these days.

After I returned to Omaha, Destiny confronted me for three weeks in the form of malarial fever, with a daily six-hour paroxysm of neuralgia in the eye instead of the chill which ought to have accompanied it by all physiological proprieties. A protracted diet in darkened rooms, upon all the drowsy sirups of

BEAR HUNTING SIXTY YEARS AGO.

the East, taught me that the confessions of an opium-eater are more agreeable than his experiences.

The Herndon House, where I lodged, was a seat of war. The landlord's lease had expired, and the proprietor was trying to eject him. There was lively skirmishing all along the line. By night the owner would fling out the furniture and move in the effects of the new lessee. The next morning, host would put out this furniture and return his own. There was an incessant explosion of epithets and display of revolvers. The novelty (for a sick man) soon wore off; and I retreated to Council Bluffs, on the Iowa bank. Several railways will center here, and the town has a healthy trade. Growing trees shade its streets; and graceful homes nestle in little glens of the bluff which walls it in on the east.

'Iowa'—'the sleepy ones'—was the name of a branch of the Sioux Indians. The State is well watered, well timbered, rich in soil, and has already three-quarters of a million of people. From Council Bluffs I came eastward, the first sixty miles by stage, as a gap in the Chicago and Northwestern Railway was unfilled.

In the East, railroads are built for the towns; on the border they build the towns. Upon this Iowa line, locating the depots was left to two persons. They manifested an avarice for donations of lands and lots to themselves, unusual even in this longitude. If the owners of any village refused to comply, they could run the cars by, establish a station on the bare prairies beyond, and kill the town by establishing a new one. The chief owner of one flourishing hamlet assured me that he spent nineteen thousand dollars in buying every tract of land along the line for several miles, where by any possibility they could make a station and start a rival settlement. Then he gave them a liberal number of lots. So his town is a railroad point and he puts money in his purse.

He ought to succeed. Years ago he settled on the prairie be yond civilization, buying thirty thousand acres of wild land. When there were a hundred settlers and the county was organized, bids began to come in for the shire town, as that would make an important point wherever established. He offered to give the county forty acres in his prospective village; to build a brick court-house from his private means, and also a school-house, hotel, and store. Rivals hid their diminished heads; and his town became the county seat.

At midnight the train-boy awoke me with the information:

'We are crossing the Mississippi.'

Rising drowsily upon one elbow, I looked down from my window at the great river, as our train glided slowly over it. Soon we shall ride from New York to San Francisco in one week, without change of cars. Around the world by railway, with two ocean ferries!

CHAPTER XLVII.

AUTHORS and census-takers must be swift of foot to keep pace with progress beyond the Mississippi. Every twelvemonth it needs a new gazetteer and a revised map. The two years since this book went to press have witnessed so many changes that a few chapters are now added to bring it forward to the early summer of 1869.

Wyoming, twice as large as Pennsylvania, was formed in 1868 from portions of Dacotah, Montana, Utah, and Colorado. It probably averages six thousand feet above sea-level. It has enormous beds of rich coal, and promising veins of gold-bearing quartz. The barren-looking soil affords boundless pasturage, and may yet surprise the farmer by yielding bountifully of the root vegetables, the hardy fruits, and the small grains.

All the slender population thus far is along the Union Pacific Railway, an enterprise to which Wyoming owes its birth. The chief town is Cheyenne, where the Denver branch diverges. For several months it was the terminal station of the main line, and was infested by the thieves, gamblers, desperadoes, and prostitutes, who swarmed to each successive 'end town,' and gave it the name of 'Hell on Wheels.' Now and then a vigilance committee purified the atmosphere. It is related that when one notorious character was tried for stealing, and the evidence proved insufficient, the jurors returned this verdict: 'We find the prisoner not guilty, but if he is smart he will leave this town within twenty-four hours.' He glanced at the gallows from which two of his associates had been found dangling a few mornings before; and he did leave by the first train.

Though more than a mile above tide-water, Cheyenne is on the open, treeless prairie, with mountains only far away and dim-discovered. Thirty miles to the west, however, the track crosses Sherman's or Evans's Pass, eight thousand three hundred feet above the sea—the highest railway point in America, if not in the world. Even this is not the backbone of the Rocky Mountains, but only of the Black Hills, an eastern offshoot, whose summits do look almost black in the distance.

Colorado is growing steadily and healthily. It has seventy-five thousand head of cattle, and one hundred and fifty thousand of sheep; and the crops for 1868 were valued at six millions of dollars. Eighteen flouring mills are in operation. Thirty bushels of corn or wheat to the acre, forty of barley, and fifty of oats are average products. Exceptional yields are reported, of seventy-five bushels of wheat, two hundred and fifty of potatoes, and seventy of oats and barley; and one acre yielded three hundred and sixteen bushels of corn. Cabbages have been raised weighing sixty pounds, beets ten pounds, and onions two pounds. All this is very wonderful in a region which so lately had no white inhabitants, and was believed to be utterly sterile.

Female 'help' is scarce and correspondingly precious. In some mining districts, kitchen girls still attend the same balls with their mistresses, on terms of perfect equality. Even in Denver their services command from fifty to seventy-five dollars a month. But the scepter is departing from Hibernia; John Chinaman, with his willing hands, and his yellow, impassive face, will supersede Biddy the loud and intractable.

Summer travelers already throng to Colorado, to enjoy its delicious atmosphere and rare scenery. The four mountain parks, each more than a mile above the sea, and as large as Rhode Island or Massachusetts, are unmatched in the world. In the North Park, deer, antelopes, wolves, and bears are still plentiful. At the Middle Park Hot Springs, a stream five inches in diameter and with a temperature of one hundred and ten degrees Fahrenheit—as hot as the body can bear—tumbles over a bank a dozen feet high. It affords a delicious hot shower-bath, and a hot plunge in the pool below; and wonderful cures are attributed to its waters. The South Park is described on page 309. San Luis Park, the largest of all—partly in Colorado and partly in New

Mexico—holds a shining lake, framed in deep green sward, and fringed with graceful pines.

In the mountains and foot-hills, factories begin to spring up.

HANGING ROCK, ECHO CITY, UTAH—UNION PACIFIC RAILROAD.

How could it be otherwise where water-power, fuel, wool, and lumber abound, and the earth teems with gold, silver, copper, iron, and coal? Manufacturing, everywhere from Minnesota to California, is growing wonderfully. At a recent meeting of Northwestern woolen manufacturers in Chicago, almost three hundred factories were represented. The National Watch Company of Elgin, Illinois, is making a hundred and twenty-five watches a day, and not only selling more than half of them in the Eastern States, but actually filling large orders for India by the way of London. If the West can compete with the East in a manufacture so delicate, so complex, and so costly as that of watches, what possible branch is there in which it can not? And a few years hence, will the prairies and the mountains—dotted all over with factories—demand Protection as earnestly as they now demand Free Trade?

Utah, more remote than Colorado, is less known for its scenery. Like railways in general, the Pacific crosses the most uninteresting spots; but it could not dodge *all* the natural wonders. At Echo City it passes beside 'Hanging Rock,' a projecting mass of conglomerate a thousand feet high. Hard by, to the left, is 'Pulpit Rock,' or 'Brigham's Pulpit,' eighty feet high. Below winds a shining stream, and the whole forms a unique picture.

A Gentile, it is said, repeated to Brigham Young the common prediction, that the great thoroughfare would bring his people into close contact with the rest of the world, and thus destroy Mormonism. Brigham replied:

'Mine must be a d——d poor religion if it won't stand one railroad?'

Nevertheless all the leading railway towns are Gentile towns. They utterly defy Mormon authority and drive away Mormon officials, treating the Saints exactly as the Saints have always treated our Government, so far as they dared. As yet, therefore, it continues a very serious problem, whether Brigham's system will 'stand one railroad.'

The Big Canyon of the Colorado, illustrated on page 473, was lately the scene of a voyage, perhaps without parallel in authentic human history. Indians and trappers have always believed that no man could thread this stupendous gorge, hundreds of miles long, with its unknown cataracts and its frowning rock walls a mile high, and come out alive. But one has done it, and lives to tell the tale. In August, 1867, three Colorado gold-hunters were prospecting on Grand River, just above where it unites with Green River to form the Colorado. One morning while they were breakfasting, an Indian yell, accompanied by whistling bullets and singing arrows, suddenly saluted them. The Utes were upon them!

Baker, the captain of the party, fell, shot through the head. The two others, James White and George Strole, rushed down to the river. While the savages lingered, plundering their camp, securing their mules and scalping their dead comrade, White and Strole tied three or four cottonwood logs together with their lariat ropes, threw a little sack of flour on board, instantly pushed off upon the frail raft and floated down the river.

A MOST WONDERFUL VOYAGE.

They knew dimly of the great canyon, but fancied it so short that they could pass through it in two days. The first night, they tied their raft to a tree, supped on raw flour and water, as they had no matches, and slept upon the bank. All the second day they glided on, between low grassy shores. The current increased, and they passed over some rapids which swept their flour from the raft, and soaked and ruined the gunpowder in their revolvers. But they supped cheerily on wild mesquite beans, and again slept soundly upon the ground.

Before noon on the third day they had entered the vast gorge. Black towering walls shut out the sun, and compressed the river into narrow limits. The current grew swift, and ahead the roar of rapids was heard. White lashed himself to the logs, but Strole said:

'We can run this little fall without doing that. If we are tied we may get entangled with the logs and drown before we can free ourselves.'

The raft reached the edge, balanced upon it for a second, the two riders looking down with clinched lips and white cheeks, and then made the plunge. White was half torn from his lashings and nearly suffocated. Upon rising to the surface, he found himself clinging to one log, in an eddy. Twenty feet away Strole, probably bruised by a rock or log, was feebly buffeting the current. White shouted to him to be of good cheer; but before he could reach him Strole sank without a cry.

White crept upon an island and gave himself up to black despair. The loneliness of the grave beset him. To go back was impossible. To stay, was death from starvation. To go forward *might be* death from starvation, or from drowning, or from being mangled upon jutting rocks. Yet it involved a chance for life, and he finally rallied to try for it.

Again lashing his logs tightly together, he gathered for food all the mesquite beans he could find on the island. He wrote in his memorandum-book an account of his own condition and the loss of his companions and placed it carefully in his pocket, that his floating body might be identified and their fate explained if he should die before reaching the settlements.

Then he started on. His terrible journey lasted eleven days longer. He went over many rapids and cascades, from four to twenty-five feet high. He usually lashed himself to the raft on approaching a fall; and he had many hair-breadth scapes from drowning. The logs were often torn apart and the ropes cut by sharp rocks; but at the little island below each cascade he re-tied them as well as he could. On these islands too he slept, and sometimes found a few more mesquite beans.

Once, for two days he tasted nothing but the leather of a knife scabbard. Once a few wandering Indians gave him some mesquite bread. He would fain have killed and eaten the lizards on the sands, but he had grown too weak to catch even those sluggish reptiles. His hat, pantaloons, boots, and stockings were torn off by the rocks and waters. For hours he sat upon the logs under the broiling, vertical sun, until his legs were one mass of blisters. His strength failed until he could hardly hold up his head; and through long days he was half unconscious. Thus more dead than alive, on the twelfth evening he emerged from the canyon, and ate ravenously of the flesh of a dog, which he had induced some Indians to kill for him by the gift of his rusty revolver.

His whole journey lasted *fourteen days*, during seven of which he tasted no food whatever. Finally, he reached Callville, Nevada, the head of steamboat navigation on the Colorado. When his raft struck the shore he could not walk. His reason was almost gone, his frame emaciated, his half-naked body covered with loathsome sores, his cheeks hollow, his eyes wild and sunken, and his hair and beard as white as snow. The first person who saw this ghastly figure crawling along on the sand, exclaimed:

'My God! There is a man a hundred years old.'

Both his health and reason were finally restored. His unparalleled journey was over five hundred miles long. What a romance his adventures would make! Let Charles Reade or Victor Hugo take James White for a hero, and give us a new novel to hold children from play and old men from the chimney corner. But let the novelist for once pity and spare us, and not transform poor White into a walking cyclopedia of all knowledge, recorded and unrecorded, natural and supernatural, like Faria in 'The Count of Monte-Christo,' or Gilliat in 'The Toilers of the Sea,' or Robert Penfold in 'Foul Play.'

Montana grows apace. Half the quartz mills are idle; twenty per cent. perhaps from bad management, twenty per cent. from bad machinery, and ten per cent. from bad locations. One New York company, from a combination of all these causes, has spent half a million of dollars without realizing ten thousand. Still, in its yield of bullion Montana is exceeded only by California and Nevada. The most important quartz interests are in the hands of a young miner from Pennsylvania, who at fifteen did not know a letter of the alphabet, at twenty-one had made and lost a fortune in Nevada, and now, though under twenty-five, has dug out a second fortune in Montana. Flouring mills are becoming numerous, and the Territory is already producing wheat enough for home consumption. One forty-acre field in Prickly-Pear valley yielded fifty-seven and a half bushels to the acre. Helena, now the chief town, boasts seven thousand people, three daily newspapers, fine blocks of brick and stone, club-houses, a skating rink, agricultural fair-grounds, and many pleasant drives. Freight from New York to Helena, via Sioux City and Fort Benton, now costs but eleven cents a pound; expressage (overland) one dollar a pound; letter postage ninety cents a pound; passenger fare through, by railroad and stage, two hundred and sixty dollars, exclusive of meals.

Many hot springs gush from the mountains, some even ranging in temperature from one hundred and thirty to one hundred and sixty degrees Fahrenheit. Their water is often as pure as that of the purest cold springs. The population increases steadily. Several thousand Chinamen from California have already arrived, and Montana—alone, I believe, of all our mining States—has not a single law upon her statute books discriminating against them.

Idaho is prospering, particularly in the Owyhee region. The mines are gradually falling into the hands of experienced Western men. In the Flint district a party of old San Francisco miners, who have been millionaires and beggars half a dozen times apiece, have erected the largest gold and silver reduction works in the United States. The valleys are rapidly filling up with farmers.

Oregon is building railways, increasing steadily her lumber, gold, and wheat products, and developing her rich mines of iron and coal. The growth of Washington Territory is less rapid, but its future, perhaps, equally great.

California thrives in her manifold industries. The State is exporting eight millions of bushels of wheat annually—a large portion of it to China. Experience demonstrates that *we are to supply swarming Asia with breadstuffs.* Our deserts must be reclaimed; a Northern and a Southern railway must be opened from the Mississippi to the Pacific.

In the fall of 1868, San Francisco was disturbed by the severest earthquake ever yet felt in the United States. Four lives were lost; many buildings were shaken down, and the damage was estimated as high as five millions of dollars. At first the panic affected real estate, but it soon rallied. Experience will doubtless teach how to erect buildings that earthquakes can not demolish. At all events, no moving accidents are likely to check the metropolis of the Pacific slope. The outlet for half a continent—the great city on a coast-line which crosses seventy degrees of latitude—looking in upon all North America and out upon all Asia, San Francisco has perhaps the most commanding commercial position on the globe. Charles Wentworth Dilke, the English writer, conjectures that in time it may 'take rank as a second, if not a greater, London.'

The first shock of the recent earthquake occurred early in the morning. The ground pitched like a ship in a storm. In a few seconds panic-stricken, half-dressed people thronged the middle of the streets, to avoid the falling bricks and stones. Some ran for the water, and embarked in the first boats they could find. The shock lasted only a minute or two, but was followed by several others during the day. The inhabitants were thoroughly alarmed, and with good reason; but the newspapers told many droll stories even of this lugubrious occurrence. One related that a placid citizen, though implored by his wife to leave his bed, steadfastly refused, coolly declaring that there was no more danger in the house than out of doors. 'At last,' says the laconic narrator, 'as a final argument she told him that the streets were full of women in their night clothes. He rose with alacrity!'

SMITH'S CHOICE.

A Sacramentoan, in San Francisco on business, after 'assisting' at three shocks, telegraphed to his wife:

'11.40 A. M. I am all right with the exception of being badly scared. I have got enough earthquake to do me. *If she holds together until the boat leaves,* I will come home to-night!'

That has the genuine local flavor. The intense high-wrought life of the Pacific Coast has produced a peculiar humor, and several humorists of deserved note, as John Phenix, Charles H. Webb, Brett Hart, and Mark Twain. In extravagance and grotesqueness they represent fairly the Californian, who is an exaggerated Yankee—an American raised to a higher power. John Phenix, for example, prefaced his Astronomical Lectures:

'These lectures were prepared to be delivered before the Lowell Institute of Boston, Massachusetts; but owing to the unexpected circumstance of the author's receiving no invitation to appear before that institution, they were laid aside shortly after completion.'

And he thus hinted at the temperature of the hottest spot upon our entire continent:

'The planet Mercury * * * receives six and a half times as much heat from the sun as we do, from which we conclude that the climate must be very similar to that of Fort Yuma, on the Colorado River.'

Another unknown genius quite outdoes this. *He* relates that a soldier from Fort Yuma died and went to the Inferno; but the very first night had to come back and get his blanket!

One more story of the Pacific coast. In an interior town, as it runs, dwelt a wealthy miller, named Smith—one of the rigidly correct, the unco righteous. A favorite brand of his flour was known as 'Smith's Choice.' Among the Indians who frequented the little village was an old squaw, peculiarly filthy and hideous. One day she appeared in a bran new white blanket beside a waggish workman who was marking barrels. The stencil plate delighted her so, that he applied it to her back; and for the rest of the day she paraded the streets, boldly labeled 'Smith's Choice,' while the people shouted with laughter and indulged in pithy comments upon Smith's morals and his taste.

California literature, no less than California humor, begins to make a name for itself. Works of value, both originals and translations from the Chinese, are appearing from the San Francisco press, and commanding wide recognition. The *Overland Monthly*, too, in literary character, ranks second to none of our Eastern magazines, and in spirit and raciness it often excels them all. The Golden State is producing a new man, and, as the Nevada editor phrased it to a startled English tourist, he can certainly 'sling ink.'

CHAPTER XLVIII.

NEVADA, sterile as it looks, is not without farming attractions. In the scattered, narrow valleys, ranches multiply. In autumn the standing bunch-grass is cured by the frosts, and sustains cattle till the pods of the white sage—which grows upon millions of acres—crack open and release the seeds. Upon these seeds they fatten, and they prefer them to corn or oats.

Hot springs abound in the mountains, and are found at almost every station along the railway. Their healing power has gained high repute among persons who suffer from rheumatism or have been poisoned by mineral fumes from amalgamating-pans in the quartz mills.

On the great Comstock Lode the ore grows poorer as the miners descend. The United States Commissioner of Mining estimated the yield for 1868 as six millions of dollars less than that of 1867. Some mills are being removed to White Pine; others await the result of work in one central mine, where the owners have sunk a shaft fourteen hundred feet, and at that depth are 'drifting,' but thus far without finding the ore in satisfactory quantities. A terrible fire raged in several of the mines in the spring of 1869, consuming timbers and stagings, and suffocating a large number of workmen.

Just as the richest lode hitherto known begins to fail, a new silver region is creating the wildest excitement in our mining history. The memories of Washoe, Fraser River, and California in Forty-nine, all pale before it. Every man on the Pacific coast is talking of it; speculators and miners are thronging to it from every part of the country, in weary desert journeys of five hundred and a thousand miles. Hundreds of new mining companies based upon it are forming in California, Nevada, and the Mississippi valley; and even New Yorkers, who have been bled a dozen times over with quartz lancets, are fascinated by specimens of ore from the new region, and beginning to invest in 'the biggest thing yet!'

This is its history. In Nevada, a hundred and twenty miles east of south from Elko,—the nearest station on the Pacific Railroad—stands White Pine mountain. Its summit, covered with white-pine timber, is ten thousand feet above the sea, and the general altitude of the surrounding valleys fully eight thousand feet. Five miles to the east of it is Base Range, where silver ores are largely contaminated with base metals; and eleven miles further, Treasure Hill. These three mountains run north and south, and are each from six to twelve miles long.

'A few months before the period at which our story opens,' a party of miners had erected a mill, called the Monte-Christo, on the western slope of White Pine; and they were working there with indifferent success. Early one morning they discovered a familiar, impudent Indian thrusting his dirty fingers into their breakfast-pot of baked beans, and scooping the food by handfuls into his gaping mouth. With a few kicks and many curses, they sent him howling out of camp. He went, but he returned. Reappearing a few days later, he beckoned one of them aside, handed him a piece of odd-looking ore, and complacently sat down grunting:

'Um! May be pooty good!

It was almost pure silver. With dilating eyes the eager miner asked:

'Where did you get it, Jim—where?'

'Um!' muttered the now indifferent visitor. 'Me heap hungry! Me like um beans!'

No kicking out this time! Jim was treated to his fill of the best the camp afforded. Then he led the white man to Treasure Hill, and there, in September, 1867, the first mine, the Hidden Treasure, was located. The Eberhardt, the richest and most famous, was staked a few weeks later. The deposit of ore was an Aladdin's palace. Nothing like it had ever been known. One lad struck his pick into what looked like a mass of putty, but proved to be pure chloride of silver, worth twenty thousand dollars a ton. Some ore was so rich that when taken to a quartz mill it clogged the stamps until they could do nothing with it. The silver was found in 'pockets,' or masses like coal, not in quartz veins; and in a limestone instead of a granite formation.

The fortunate discoverers, working silently and shrewdly, kept the secret well for months, while they uncovered and extracted enormous sums. They induced a Captain Page to bring a ten-stamp mill from Austin. When it was set up on the new ground, it had cost Page about thirty thousand dollars. At first he began to burn bricks for furnaces, but a little experimenting proved that these ores required no roasting.

The mill started. The miners soon found that under their contract with Page, the ores were yielding him a profit of two hundred and thirty-five dollars a ton! After he had run the mill for seven days, they gladly bought it of him for ninety thousand dollars. Many more mills have since been set up in the district. The ores have assayed from one thousand to twenty thousand dollars per ton; and when crushed in large quantities, the *average* yields have ranged from three hundred to one thousand dollars.

'White Pine,' became the general name for the entire region. Ten thousand immigrants spent the winter of 1868–9 in it. Some had arrived on foot, some with teams, and some in the half-dozen coaches that started every morning from Austin, carrying twenty passengers apiece. Treasure City, Sherman, Hamilton, and other towns sprang up, swarming with people who dwelt in tents, in caves in the ground, in log huts, and in frame cabins.

Forest trees were abundant, but saw-mills scarce; lumber went up to five hundred dollars a thousand, and it became a common jest that one could carry away ten dollars' worth in his waistcoat pocket. Board commanded twenty dollars a week; laborers and mechanics, from five to ten dollars a day; and hay, three hundred dollars a ton. Three months before, building lots would not have brought fifty cents a dozen; now they sold at from five hundred to eight thousand dollars apiece. One plot of ground, purchased for forty-five hundred dollars, was disposed of twenty-two days later for twenty-five thousand. In silver claims the speculation was still wilder. Many an old miner, who reached the region without money enough to pay two weeks' board, soon had property which he could have sold for a hundred thousand dollars or more. And many another who carried in thousands with him, paid it all away in less than a week for claims as worthless as Sahara.

Before the richness of the region was known, a Nevada lawyer was offered two hundred feet in one mine for twenty-five dollars. He had risked thousands of dollars upon 'prospects' before, and invariably at a loss; and now, yielding to prudence for the first time in his life, he declined to purchase. Three months later he visited the district. A boy working in the mine he had refused *gave* him a piece of ore worth three hundred dollars; while the owner of the claim offered him five thousand dollars to spend a single week in arguing an injunction suit concerning it before one of the mining courts. He vowed that he would never be prudent again, however great the temptation.

A quiet visitor to the Eberhardt mine, after looking carefully through it, announced that he represented one of the wealthiest banks on the coast, and was authorized to purchase it. The owners, who had been poor men a few months before, replied:

'The Bank of California hasn't got money enough to buy this mine. But come around next fall, and we will buy the Bank of California!'

At the present rate it will not be many months before the region has a population of fifty thousand. There will be the usual preposterous inflation and reckless investments, and then the usual reaction, bringing things to their proper level. The lesson of quartz mining, like other lessons of life, can not be acquired by proxy; every generation must learn it for itself, every man for himself.

New Mexico begins to feel some mining excitements; yet with its inefficient Mexican population it makes little progress. During the summer of 1868, General William J. Palmer, of the Kansas Pacific Railroad, made an interesting survey through to the Pacific, along the thirty-fifth parallel. West of Albuquerque his party found the Zuni Indians, already described on pages 254 and 266. The group in our illustration was sketched by the artist of the expedition. The Zunis preserve the old Aztec faith pure and simple, and have not a single Catholic priest in their village. They raise fruit, corn, and sheep, in abundance, and under their sad faces, hide a fondness for barter and a shrewdness in it, quite unmatched among any other tribe. They sold grapes and mutton to the exploring party, but only at high prices and after hours of dickering. Education and a favorable geographical position would soon develop them into a great commercial people.

A GROUP OF ZUNI INDIANS.

Palmer saw one of their white Indians. He had red hair, blue eyes, and a complexion fair even for a white man. He showed none of that preternatural paleness of the eye, feebleness, and appearance of being a freak of nature, generally observed in Albinos; but seemed to be a strong, normal man. From generation to generation these white Zunians have white children—giving some color to a local tradition, that they sprang originally from a Welchman who lived for a while with the tribe. Why do not our scientific men study more this strange people, the traces of the Mound Builders of the Mississippi valley, and kindred subjects, which, treated intelligently and intelligibly, would have an absorbing popular interest?

One evening Palmer's company were led by an Indian trail down the side of a tremendous gorge, eight hundred feet deep. Two of the pack-mules, missing their foot-holds on the narrow shelf-path, tumbled off, and rolled to the bottom, bounding from rock to rock like foot-balls. One was killed; the other, despite his fall of three hundred feet, was not seriously hurt. The explorers named the chasm, Pack-mule Canyon.

The product of Nevada, Arizona, and New Mexico, shown below, is nearly all silver, that of Idaho one-third silver, and that of Colorado one-eighth silver; all the rest is gold. The estimates in the first column are by Rossiter W. Raymond, Commissioner of Mining; those in the second are my own, as given in the American Year Book for 1869:

OUR GOLD AND SILVER PRODUCT FOR 1868.

California	$22,000,000	....	$23,000,000
Nevada	14,000,000	....	18,000,000
Montana	15,000,000	....	13,000,000
Idaho	7,000,000	....	7,000,000
Washington and Oregon	4,000,000	....	6,000,000
Colorado and Wyoming	3,250,000	....	4,000,000
Arizona	500,000	....	250,000
New Mexico	250,000	....	250,000
Other sources	1,000,000	....	
Total	$67,000,000	....	$71,500,000

Some writers rate our product as high as one hundred and eight millions. Our great need is a National School of Mines. At present our own mining engineers are educated in Germany, not in America; and throughout our quartz regions the practical miners despise the geologists and mineralogists, and *vice versa*—often with good reason upon both sides. With a School of Mines right among the miners themselves, theories would be modified by practical experience, and the men with the picks and the men with the retorts would deserve and receive respect from each other. Our bullion yield would be enormously increased, and every year millions of dollars would be saved that are now wasted in fruitless mining.

Kansas advances with gigantic strides. Already she has ten daily and fifty weekly newspapers, over six hundred miles of completed railway, and a population of almost half a million. Thirteen years after her first settlement by whites, her values in three items alone were:

Farms and farming implements	$40,000,000
Live stock	40,000,000
Crops for 1867	35,000,000
Total	$115,000,000

These young States—how unexpectedly they spring up, how wonderfully they grow! To have seen personally something of the beginning of four—Kansas, Colorado, Montana, and Wyoming—makes one feel prematurely old, and wonder what the development of half a century will be.

Kansas City (Missouri) now bids fair to be a great metropolis. She has secured a bridge across the Missouri, and four or five new railway connections; and in modern towns the iron horse is mighty and must prevail.

The highest courts have practically decided that the steamboat is subordinate to the locomotive; that railway travel must be unimpeded, though at some expense to navigation. Already the 'Great Yellow River' is being bridged for railways at Kansas City, at St. Charles, Missouri, and at Omaha. The enormous works will cost from one to two millions of dollars apiece. The two farthest up the river are practically in the interest of wide-awake Chicago, securing to her a traffic which naturally belongs to St. Louis. St. Louis is rousing herself; but a good many slow coaches—relics of slaveholding influence and French origin—still retard her. There was point and wit in that visitor, who, being asked what the city most needed to promote its prosperity, replied, 'About thirty-five first-class funerals.'

Since 1865, Missouri has paid twenty-three millions of dollars principal and interest, upon her State debt. Since 1860, her assessed values—exclusive of slaves—have increased from two hundred and seventy millions of dollars to five hundred millions—a wonderful progress for eight years, four of them darkened by bloody and devastating war.

Fourteen hundred miles of railway are already in operation. The Southwest Road to the Lead Region, after twice reverting to the State, which had loaned the public credit largely for its construction, is now in the hands of Francis B. Hayes, Jacob Sleeper, Clinton B. Fisk, and a few other live capitalists, who, on depositing seventeen hundred thousand dollars as security that they meant business and would build the road, received a free gift of the hundred miles of railway already in operation, with its equipment, and its magnificent land grant of more than a million acres—worth enough to finish the entire line. They now have twenty-five hundred men working upon it and will, complete it within a few months. Ultimately it will be a chief eastern outlet for the Southern Pacific road.

The Indian Territory must soon open to white settlers. Three railways are already advancing toward it—the one just described; a second running south from Kansas City, via Olathe, Spring Hill, and Fort Scott; and a third leading south from Lawrence. Whenever immigration pours into this rich and beautiful region the Indians will readily merge into the white communities.

The history of the Cherokees has one very remarkable character. His Indian name was Sequoyah. He was born in northern Georgia in 1769—long before the tribe was removed beyond the Mississippi. His father was a wandering German peddler named Guest; his mother an untaught Cherokee woman, whom the peddler married and soon after abandoned. But she possessed great purity and vigor of character, and devoted her life to rearing her son. Neither he nor she could speak English, or even German.

Young Guest showed much mechanical aptitude. He became an expert blacksmith, having taught himself and made his own tools and bellows. He also learned the silversmith's art. Wishing to make a steel die for stamping silver ware, he got a white man to write his name. The stranger spelled it George *Guess*, and as Sequoyah did not learn English till several years later, the accidentally-appropriate surname, gained by a blunder, adhered to him through life, and in the biographical dictionaries.

The Cherokees had no written language. One day several, noticing a white prisoner in the act of reading a letter, raised the question whether the 'talking leaf' was a special gift from the Great Spirit, or a mere human invention. Sequoyah, though

SEQUOYAH (GEORGE GUEST), INVENTOR OF THE CHEROKEE ALPHABET.

scouting the suggestion that it was miraculous, grew interested in the subject. A lameness caused by a white-swelling kept him from active pursuits, and for three years he laboriously collected the words of the Cherokee language, and designated symbols to represent them, from birds, beasts, and trees. He had neither pens nor paper, but wrote upon bark with nails or sharp wire. At last the hopelessness of his task and a glimpse of the only practicable mode dawned upon him. He did not know a word of any language but his own. He had no help from the accumulated experience of other races and other men of genius. But, alone in the wilderness, this untutored half-breed discovered the great principle which it had taken accomplished nations many centuries to ascertain, and which other accomplished nations never ascertained—that arbitrary signs must stand not for ideas, but for sounds.

With the help of his wife, his own ear not being acute, he found the vowel sounds of the Cherokee language to be nine. These he multiplied by the consonant sounds. At first the resulting combinations or syllables numbered nearly two hundred, but he pruned them down to eighty-five. By this time an old English spelling-book had fallen into his hands. He adopted, at random, many of its letters, and invented new characters to fill out his list; and thus he formed a complete syllabic alphabet.

At first his fellows were utterly incredulous. But he had taught the system to his little daughter, and now he sent her away and wrote to her such messages as they dictated. When she easily read them, the stoutest braves were awe-stricken, and fancied that it must be necromancy. For a further test, he taught several of their young men his mysterious art. Then they confessed his triumph, gave him a great feast, and held him in high honor and veneration. They adopted the written language and have used it ever since. In their eyes, its most wonderful triumph was that it enabled them to send long messages back to the remnant of their tribe which still remained in Georgia. Really, Sequoyah's great achievement was his success in mastering the natural philosophy of his mother tongue. An Indian child who speaks English can not often learn to read it in less than a year, but will learn to read by Sequoyah's alphabet in a few days.

Once Sequoyah was a delegate from his tribe to Washington. There the portrait was painted from which our likeness is copied. He himself learned to paint portraits with success, and acquired some knowledge of perspective. Late in life he determined to write a philosophic work upon all the Indian languages, and to point out clearly their resemblances and differences. For this purpose he traveled among many tribes, taking copious notes. His only companion was a young Cherokee; the two journeyed together with an ox-cart, camping out whenever night overtook them. They visited many of the Plains Indians, and the Root Diggers of the Rocky Mountains; and were among the Pueblos of New Mexico, when, in August, 1843, Death overtook this modern Cadmus, this Admirable Crichton of the wilderness.

Every year the Cherokee Legislature appropriates three hundred dollars to the support of his widow—the only literary pension paid by any government upon our continent. During the Great Rebellion, one of his sons served with honor as a lieutenant under Colonel William A. Philips, of Kansas, who commanded the Union forces in the Indian Territory.

The population tables below include civilized Indians, but omit the wild tribes. Nearly all the figures are from official, or semi-official, sources.

STATE OR TERRITORY.	Population.		Area in acres.	Acres of public lands unsold, June 30, 1868.
	1860.	1869.		
Alaska	......	6,000	369,529,600	369,529,600
Arizona	......	10,000	72,906,240	68,855,890
Arkansas	435,450	500,000	33,406,720	11,574,430
California	379,994	600,000	120,947,840	104,538,420
Colorado	34,277	55,000	66,880,000	62,814,254
Dacotah	4,837	10,000	96,596,128	90,986,449
Idaho	......	25,000	55,228,160	52,150,806
Indian Territory	66,000	66,000	44,154,240	44,154,240
Iowa	674,913	1,000,000	35,228,800	2,902,528
Kansas	107,206	440,000	52,043,520	42,795,589
Minnesota	172,023	440,000	53,459,840	35,534,118
Missouri	1,182,012	1,500,000	41,824,000	1,483,715
Montana	......	38,875	92,016,640	86,904,569
Nebraska	28,841	100,000	48,636,800	41,624,126
Nevada	6,857	40,000	71,737,600	67,085,697
New Mexico	93,516	140,000	77,568,840	70,705,518
Oregon	52,465	100,000	60,975,360	52,518,014
Utah	40,273	120,000	54,065,043	48,976,310
Washington Territory	11,594	20,000	44,796,160	41,565,717
Wisconsin	775,881	1,000,000	34,511,360	9,258,627
Wyoming	......	20,000	62,645,068	59,164,787

Once it was proposed to name our country Alleghania, from the mountains which skirt its eastern border, but which were then its western frontier. Now, *fourteen hundred millions of acres* of our public lands remain unsold, though the tracts given and pledged to Pacific railways alone probably amount to a solid belt seventeen hundred miles long and forty miles wide. These magnificent and remunerative endowments are in keeping with our territorial area. They, and the national gift, the Homestead Act, kindled Walt Whitman—the most American and the most original of all our poets, in his apostrophe to the great republic:

'Dispensatress, that by a word givest a thousand miles—*that giv'st a million farms and missest nothing !*
Thou All-Acceptress!—thou Hospitable!—thou only art hospitable as God is hospitable."

Welcome to the continental railway! Farewell to the overland coach and to the log ranch, so lately the first-class hotel of the

FIRST-CLASS HOTEL ON THE PLAINS IN 1867.

Plains! They linger only in memory; they belong as really to the dead past as horse-hair wigs and three-cornered hats.

Exit Red Man! Enter Yellow Man! The United States already hold a hundred thousand Chinamen. Only three hundred of them live in New York, and they make execrable cigars and retail them in the streets. They do not wear their native costume, and they sedulously hide their long cues in their hats, for the Bad Boy of New York *will* throw stones at every bold Mongol who ventures forth in tunic and pig-tail. Only three or four have Chinese wives; but many have wedded Celtic women, and—insatiate Johnny!—more than one apiece at that. Sometimes the wives quarrel, but Johnny placidly permits them to fight it out in the yard. These unions produce bright, healthy children, who toddle about, prattling in Chinese to their fathers, and in Irish or English to their mothers.

On the Pacific coast the Celestials multiply. In California alone they number sixty thousand, and a single mail steamer from Hong Kong often brings a thousand of them. They begin to flow over into Colorado and Montana, and some even into East Tennessee, where they purpose to cultivate the tea plant. They will soon pour into every State upon the Atlantic slope. They will solve the great problem of 'help' that vexes the souls of American housekeepers, and in time they may throng into every other department of labor.

Hiram Walbridge, on receiving one day the card of an unwelcome visitor, sent word that he was engaged and could not see him for the present. The bore replied that he was in no haste, and could wait just as well as not.

'—— these men who can wait!' exclaimed the veteran politician, 'I'm afraid of them! Show him up at once.'

John Chinaman is a man that 'can wait.' He is patience embodied. And there are a great many of him! He constitutes two-thirds of the whole human race. His empire could send us as many immigrants as the total population of the United States, Great Britain, and France, and yet not spare us so large a percentage as Ireland has within the last ten years. Will this Coming Man—persistent, eager-eyed, stolid-faced—Americanize? The future has no question more vital to us; and the future alone can answer it.

The great railway which is attracting the Yellow Man hither displaces all the old landmarks. In lieu of the log hut with dirt roof, it gives us a first-class hotel of the most drearily modern pretensions and proportions—an enormous building with the iron pathway in front, and a huge windmill hard by to pump up water for the thirsty locomotive.

Many fascinating volumes might be written upon early explorations across our continent. The first and most remarkable was led by Cabeca de Vaca, a Spanish gentleman, with a few companions, sole survivors of the expedition of Narvaez, which had come to Florida with five ships and six hundred men. In the fall of 1528, after all their comrades had perished, De Vaca and

FIRST CLASS HOTEL ON THE PLAINS IN 1869.

his little party started westward from near the mouth of the Mississippi. They encountered terrible hardships, being often detained by hostile Indians, and once suffering so from hunger that they killed and ate one of their own number. They crossed what are now Louisiana, Texas, New Mexico, and Arizona, and finally, after *eight years* of wandering, four of the party, naked, wounded, and half dead, reached the Pacific in Lower California. Their wonderful story is found only in the rare records of old voyagers; what new Prescott, or Irving, or Motley will re-tell it for us?

Two hundred and thirty years later, Jonathan Carver of Connecticut, who as an officer in the King's service had taken part in all the wars by which the Canadas fell into the possession of

Great Britain, started westward from Boston. He journeyed slowly, via Albany, Lake Michigan, and Green Bay, to the 'Ouisconsin' river; and afterward to western Minnesota or Dacotah. Unable to go farther, he came back and visited London, where he sought aid from the British Government to prosecute his explorations through to the Pacific. But after long delay that was denied, and even his papers, which the authorities had taken, were not returned. From copies in his possession, however, he published in London, in 1778, an interesting account of his travels. His preface is full of prophecy and pathos. After urging the establishment of posts and settlements as likely to 'open communication between Hudson's Bay and the Pacific,' it continues:

'A settlement on the Pacific would not only disclose new sources of trade and promote many useful discoveries, but would open a passage for conveying intelligence to China and the English settlements in the East Indies, with greater expedition than a tedious voyage by the Cape of Good Hope or the Straits of Magellan will allow of. * * * That the completion of the scheme I have had the honor of first planning and attempting, will some time or other be effected, I make no doubt. * * * Whenever it is, and the execution of it is carried on with propriety, those who are so fortunate as to succeed will reap, exclusive of the national advantages that must ensue, *emoluments beyond their most sanguine expectations.* And whilst their spirits are elated by their success, *perhaps they may bestow some commendation and blessings on the person that first pointed out to them the way.* * * Mighty kingdoms will emerge from these wildernesses, and stately palaces and solemn temples with gilded spires supplant the Indian huts, whose only decorations are the barbarous trophies of their vanquished enemies.'

After Carver, came our Government expeditions—those of Pike and Long, for whom two noble mountains in Colorado are fitly named; that of Lewis and Clark, elsewhere described in these pages; that of Bonneville, in 1832, the first that ever crossed to the Pacific with wagons; and those of Fremont, who named Utah the 'Great Basin,' and who did more than any other one man to kindle interest in the western half of our continent, and to hasten its development.

CHAPTER XLIX.

THOSE remorseless levelers, the railroad and the telegraph, tread so closely upon the heels of the pioneer that new settlements have no longer the picturesque coloring, the strong local peculiarities of half a century ago. Each individual, each community grows more and more like all the rest. Perhaps when Alaska is cut up into half a dozen States, with gas, hot and cold water, and a private telegraph wire introduced into every dwelling, provincialisms will disappear altogether, and local nicknames become utterly obsolete.

As yet, a few remote localities retain the old features. Fort Benton, Montana, is one. The French trappers and traders of the American Fur Company have passed away, but many left Indian wives and half-breed children; and some whites of the present generation have also intermarried with Indians. The aboriginal women retain their ancient habit of Platonic kissing once every twelvemonth. On New Year's day they perambulate the settlement by twos, by tens, and by twenties, visiting each house and store, and kissing every white man they can find. The holiday closes with a 'squaw ball,' at which pies eaten from the fingers, and ice water drank from a tin dipper, constitute the refreshments.

In spite of all leveling influences, the man of the Far West will long retain his intensity, his hearty friendships, and his equally hearty enmities. Let us hope, too, that he will retain his quick perception of the ludicrous, his readiness to laugh at everybody's weak points, including his own. 'Gentlemen,' said a frontier candidate for Congress at the close of a public speech, 'these are my sentiments. They are the sentiments of an honest man, the principles of a consistent politician. But, gentlemen, if they don't suit you, they can be altered!"

Early Southern and Western nicknames will puzzle the antiquarian of the year of grace 2969. The North Carolinians were 'Tar-heels,' from the abundance of tar which their State produced; the people of Michigan, 'Wolverines,' from their prairie wolves; and those of Wisconsin, 'Badgers,' from the animal most common in their new settlements. 'Hoosier' has received two explanations. According to one, pioneer Indianians had huge frames, and were so formidable in fights that they became known as 'hushers;' and this, at first in jest, was transformed into 'Hoosiers.' The other relates that the name was applied to ridicule the common inquiry of the backwoodsman, when he heard a knock on his door at night, 'Who's yer?'

'Sucker' likewise has several theories of its origin. One is that every spring thousands of Illinoians went up the Mississippi by steamers, worked in the Galena lead mines through the summer, and returned home in the fall. Ascending and descending the river like fishes, they were called 'Suckers.' Another is, that as they were poor whites from Virginia and Kentucky, who had torn themselves away from the wealthy slave-owners, satirists predicted that they would perish like sprouts, or suckers, of the tobacco plant, stripped from the parent stem. Still a third relates that in crossing the dry prairies they used to carry a hollow reed, and when thirsty thrust it into holes in the ground made by crawfish in their descent to the water, and thus *suck* up the liquid. Let me suggest a fourth. The earliest

A YOUNG SUCKER.

white settlers of the Mississippi valley were Frenchmen, who adopted many Indian habits. They strapped their infants to boards like papooses. The mother, working in the fields, often left her baby alone in the cabin for hours; but, to alleviate his solitude, she gave him a huge piece of raw pork to suck, first tying it to his foot by a string, so that whenever he attempted to swallow it the natural impulse to kick would save him from choking. The custom is well authenticated. What more natural than that those who followed it should have been nicknamed 'Suckers?'

Who first suggested a Pacific Railway? In 1778, Jonathan Carver foreshadowed it, and he of all men was farthest ahead of the age in which he lived. In 1835 the Rev. Samuel Parker, in his journal of an overland trip across the continent, recorded his opinion that the mountains presented no insuperable obstacle to a railroad. In 1838, Lewis Gaylord Clark wrote in the *Knickerbocker:* 'The reader is now living who will make a railway trip across this vast continent.' In 1846, Asa Whitney began to urge his project upon State legislatures and popular gatherings, and he continued to agitate the subject for five years. He proposed to build a line from the Mississippi to Puget Sound (California was not yet settled by whites) if Congress would give him public lands to the width of thirty miles along the entire road. Later experience has shown that their proceeds would have been utterly insufficient. Yet Whitney did not fail on that account, but because he could excite no general interest in the subject.

In 1850, the first Pacific railroad bill was introduced into Congress by sturdy old Benton. It contemplated a railway only 'where practicable,' leaving gaps in the impassable mountains to be filled up by a wagon road. As yet even the Alleghanies were not crossed by any unbroken railway, but by a series of inclined planes, upon which the cars were drawn up and let down by stationary engines.

In 1853–4, by direction of Congress, nine routes were surveyed across the continent on various parallels between the British Possessions and Mexico. Among the young officers in charge of these explorations were McClellan, Pope, Saxton, Parke, and Whipple. Another, Lieutenant Gunnison, was murdered by the

Indians while in the performance of his duty. The surveys resulted in thirteen huge quarto volumes of reports, which are now curiosities of our historical literature. Being issued at Government expense, they were profusely illustrated with colored engravings of flowers, plants, reptiles, fishes, birds, mountain scenery, and other objects which had no intelligible bearing upon the ease or difficulty of building a railway. Under the supervision of Jefferson Davis, then Secretary of War, the results were summarised in the interest of the extreme Southern line, showing, with all the falseness of figures, that a road near the Gulf, along the thirty-second parallel, would cost only half as much as one further north, and that the route upon which our present line runs would be impracticable, on account of heavy grades and deep snows in the Sierras. Even up to 1864 the Canadians, and many of our own citizens, believed that a railway could not be built south of the British Possessions, unless it was carried far down toward Mexico.

In 1859, Congress indicated our natural and inevitable transcontinental system by authorizing the construction of three roads—a Northern, a Southern, and a Central. They were to receive no money endowment, but very liberal land grants. Before any active steps could be taken to build them, however, all such enterprises were extinguished for the time by our great war.

But what Government had failed to do, the steady course of emigration was accomplishing. The Mormon hegira from Illinois to Utah, the Mexican war, the California gold discoveries, the Kansas troubles, and the rush to Pike's Peak, had all carried settlements westward from the Mississippi, and railroads were following across Missouri and Iowa.

Simultaneously, too, civilization began to push eastward from the Pacific. In the Washoe country, now Nevada, was found abundant quartz rock, rich and sparkling with silver. A rush to Washoe followed, and a great State was founded. The travel and traffic grew so enormous that a turnpike was soon built from Placerville, California, over the seemingly insurmountable Sierras. The machinery and other freights passing over it in a single year paid tolls to the amount of three hundred thousand dollars (gold), and the cost of transporting them was estimated at thirteen millions, or more than twice their original value.

The absolute need of some cheaper and easier conveyance, revived the idea of a continental railway, always popular in California. But could the Sierras be crossed by the locomotive? And who would furnish twenty-five millions of dollars to build a road over them? Theodore D. Judah, a sanguine engineer of Sacramento, insisted that the project was practicable both topographically and pecuniarily. Neighbors laughed at him, but earnestness is always contagious. Through many a long winter evening he talked upon his favorite theme with a group who frequented the hardware store of Huntington & Hopkins, a firm of wealthy, but cautious and frugal merchants. In a country where everybody speculated, they had never invested a dollar in mining, but had adhered strictly to their legitimate business. One partner, with his family, lived in their store building, separated from their goods only by a board partition made from boxes brought around Cape Horn, all the way from Boston.

Huntington was the first convert. Soon, Hopkins, Crocker, a leading lawyer, and two or three of their neighbors, were also among the prophets. In the spring of 1860, these gentlemen subscribed fifty dollars apiece to enable Judah to devote the summer to a careful mountain survey. Other Californians had advocated a Pacific Railway; legislatures and public meetings had indorsed it; but this was the first money paid—the business germ of the greatest enterprise the world has ever seen.

In autumn Judah and his corps returned to Sacramento, ragged, jaded, and hungry; but with a report so favorable that fifteen hundred dollars more was promptly raised to support them through the next season. A second summer was spent in surveying, with equally encouraging results. Then Judah was dispatched to San Francisco to secure subscriptions for incorporating the company; but after a month of faithful canvassing he returned home without having obtained a dollar. A poor engineer had started the project; two plain hardware merchants had put it in business shape; and now, not rich San Francisco, but unpretending Sacramento was to make it a success. Even after the Central Pacific Company had been chartered by the California Legislature, only two San Franciscans subscribed for shares (fifteen thousand dollars, all told), and one of them was a woman!

The Company sent Judah to Washington, where he hung up his charts in the committee-rooms, explained that California was ready to take hold in earnest, and though civil war was raging, invoked the aid of the nation.

A few railway enthusiasts from New York and Massachusetts were already pressing the same request. At last the hour was propitious. Neither Congress nor the eastern public comprehended that our commerce and travel demanded such a road. Public opinion was not ripe for it as a business enterprise. But the conflict for the Union had already accustomed the North to such lavish outlay that the expense seemed less frightful than of yore. It had also developed some low mutterings about a Pacific Republic, and had shown that in case of a foreign war the isolated west coast would be our weak point. In the language of the hour, a continental railway was A Military Necessity; and as such, in July, 1862, one was chartered from the Missouri to the Pacific, with an endowment of unparalleled richness. (See page 461.)

Thomas C. Durant and a few other live spirits of the Union Pacific (the east end of the line), were full of faith in the enterprise; but old and 'safe' New York capitalists regarded it as chimerical, and the franchise as practically worthless. The charter could not have been sold in Wall Street for a million of dollars. But in 1864 Congress changed the Government lien to a second mortgage, enabling the company to issue fresh mortgage bonds of their own. Then the Union Pacific, after many struggles, made a beginning, and built:

In 1865,	40 miles.	In 1868,	425 miles.
" 1866,	265 "	" 1869,	105 "
" 1867,	245 "		——
		Total	1080 "

This was marvelously rapid work for a rough country, much of it destitute of wood, water, and supplies. For three hundred miles east of Salt Lake Valley the line averages nearly seven thousand feet above the sea. At this great elevation snows abound, but experience will teach how to overcome them.

Omaha and Council Bluffs, Siamese Twins of towns at the eastern terminus of the line, grow with its growth and strengthen with its strength. Omaha has twenty thousand people, and Council Bluffs ten thousand, with several diverging railways.

GOING TO CALIFORNIA IN 1867.

During construction, the 'terminal station,' moving forward with each advance of the track, was usually a place of five or six thousand inhabitants. Right upon the desert would spring up a crowded city, with enormous warehouses, daily newspapers, churches, banks, and gambling-saloons, and streets thronged with freight-teams starting westward. In a few weeks the scene would shift, and all this varied life disappear, leaving only a little station, with its water tank and forlorn dwellings.

In Wyoming, the line traverses the dreary Bitter Creek region. Here the alkali water is not only unfit to drink, but can not even be used in the engines, as it deposits a sediment choking and clogging up the boilers. Until some method of neutralizing its noxious qualities can be discovered, a water-train supplies tanks for one hundred and fiftymiles.

Indians have thrown one or two trains off the track, but in general have kept very clear of the locomotive. In Kansas, however, they have committed many outrages. Going to California in 1867, via the Kansas Pacific road, and thence by stage, through Denver and Salt Lake, was a hazardous undertaking. Near Fort Wallace, one day in June, a coach which carried five passengers, one soldier and a driver, had a running fight for five miles, with a hundred mounted Sioux and Cheyennes. The travelers made the best resistance they could with their rifles, and kept the savages at a little distance, while the driver put his horses to their utmost speed. Every man on board, except one, was killed or seriously wounded. An old frontier friend of mine, Charles H. Blake, happily escaped, though with a broken arm and a wound in the head. At last the vehicle, with its bleeding and dying inmates, reached the shelter of Big Timbers Station, and the savages sullenly retired without having taken a single scalp. The fight was probably one of the last, and certainly one of the most remarkable in the history of the Plains.

The Union Pacific road found for the first five hundred miles west from Omaha the easiest route ever followed; the Central, for a hundred and thirty east from Sacramento, one of the hardest. Before receiving any Government bonds the latter company must build and equip forty miles, which would carry the track far up the Sierras, and cost four millions of dollars. Money was worth two per cent. a month in California. The corporators put in their entire fortunes, and obtained help both from San Francisco and the State; but all was only a drop in the bucket. To surmount the range would cost millions upon millions more, and it seemed impossible to obtain the money either in the United States or in Europe, for a line that was to become one of the world's main arteries.

Huntington, the vice-president and financial manager, was in New York, vainly endeavoring to procure the necessary rolling stock and material. In casting about for help, he encountered

Fisk & Hatch, dealers in Government securities, who had done much to sustain the national credit through the darkest days of the war. 'Young men for action.' While older financiers shook their heads, these young bankers deliberately undertook to furnish the company with whatever money was needed, and as fast as it was needed. The amount proved to be from five to twenty millions of dollars per year; but they fulfilled their agreement. They went into the work in earnest, laboring with heavy capitalists in person; investing their own money in the company's bonds, which they put on the same basis with those of the Government; and calling to their aid Richard T. Colburn, an able and experienced journalist, who, with great skill and judgment, sent forth upon the wings of the press fact after fact, showing the greatness of the work and the value and safety of the security. At first money came in slowly, but it soon accumulated like a rolling snowball. The bonds were rapidly advanced in price to keep them from selling faster than funds were needed; and finally a party of European capitalists subscribed at one transaction for four or five millions of dollars' worth on condition that the loan should be closed.

After reaching the summit of the Sierras, the company pushed forward with wonderful vigor. There were no connecting roads from which to borrow rolling stock; and all their rails, locomotives, and other material had to be shipped sixteen thousand miles, around the Horn; yet, under these disadvantages, they built:

In 1863	20 miles	" 1867	46 miles
" 1864	25 "	" 1868	348 "
" 1865	25 "	" 1869	199 "
" 1866	35 "	Total	698 "

Upon the Sierras, where snow sometimes falls to the depth of thirty feet, twenty-two miles of snow-sheds protect the track. Once or twice portions have been swept away by avalanches, causing a few hours' detention, but in general they answer their purpose so well that eighteen miles more are to be added.

Of the seventeen hundred miles between Omaha and Sacramento, not one-third is really mountainous, but more than two-thirds were so counted, and received the higher Government endowments, thirty-two thousand or forty-eight thousand dollars per mile. Much of the Central Pacific traverses a flat country, yet not one mile received less than thirty-two thousand dollars. The Union Pacific obtained the highest figures per mile—forty-eight thousand dollars—for one hundred and fifty miles west of Cheyenne, as heavy mountain work, though the region is really one long, inclined plane—'as fine a country to build a railway through as lies on the face of the globe.'

Building and equipping the entire line probably cost on an average fifty thousand dollars per mile. The Government bonds issued averaged thirty thousand dollars per mile, and the companies' first mortgage bonds sold for nearly thirty thousand dollars more, leaving a cash profit of seventeen millions of dollars upon construction alone, in addition to the ownership of the road and its magnificent land grant. Carver was right; the builders, 'exclusive of the national advantages,' indeed reaped 'emoluments beyond their most sanguine expectations.' And they finished the road a year earlier than its friends expected.

One of its early results will be to secure us two additional lines—a Northern and a Southern. We need them to develop vast mining and farming regions now lying idle; to end, once for all, the Indian troubles; and to enable us to command that vast commerce of the East for which all the nations are striving. A French company after working ten years and expending a hundred millions of dollars, has completed a ship canal across the Isthmus of Suez, shortening by thousands of miles the old sea routes to Asia; the Emperor of Russia is building a railway across Siberia to the borders of China, and English capitalists are beginning one from the Mediterranean, via the valley of the Euphrates, the Persian coast, Upper India, and southern China, to the Pacific. The foreign commerce of China amounts to five hundred millions of dollars per annum. Hitherto, it has been chiefly in British hands. The resident English merchants still outnumber the Americans, but the latter are gaining steadily, and are much the more popular with the natives. China offers us a limitless field for the introduction of breadstuffs, railways, steamers, telegraph lines, machinery, Yankee notions, and manufactured goods. India and Japan, too, invite American enterprise. We have every advantage of position; but, to make the most of it, we must have two more trans-continental lines, and the sooner the better.

The main stem of the proposed Southern road starts westward from Memphis with forks to New Orleans and St. Louis. It traverses the thirty-fifth parallel, through the Indian Territory, New

GOING TO CALIFORNIA IN 1869.

Mexico, Arizona, and California, to San Francisco. It will afford a direct outlet from all our southern States to the Pacific, and give us in a few years a new belt of rich and populous commonwealths. The company now building the Southwest Road of Missouri has a land grant along this route, and may construct the line.

On the proposed Northern road, from Minnesota to Puget Sound, four States alone—Montana, Idaho, Washington, and Oregon—remote and inaccessible as they are, already furnish one-third of the entire gold and silver product of the United States. A railway will stimulate enormously the growth of our rich northern belt of States. It will make the distance between New York and China nearly a thousand miles shorter than by the Central route. Nor will it be seriously obstructed by snow, as there are no high mountain crossings. A company is chartered and has received a valuable land grant, but no money endowment. At an early day, and in the safest and most economical manner, the Government should secure the construction of both these lines.

The Atlantic is nearer to the Pacific than New York was to Boston fifty years ago. Going to California by our luxurious eating, sleeping, and drawing-room cars, is a wonder and a delight as contrasted with the old plains and mountain, or ocean and isthmus travel. At noon in New York it is nine A. M. in San Francisco. The line is so long that trains upon it are run by eight or ten different times. Ultimately we shall have a double set of hands upon all watches—one for local time, and one for general time—uniform all over the world.

ACROSS THE CONTINENT.

New York to Omaha....................................1479 miles.

UNION PACIFIC LINE.

		Miles.			*Miles.*
Omaha to	Summit Siding, NEBRASKA.	4	Omaha to	Overton, NEBRASKA	220
"	Papillion	12	"	Plum Creek	230
"	Elkhorn	28	"	Coyote	240
"	Valley	35	"	Willow Island	250
"	Fremont	46	"	Warren	260
"	North Bend	61	"	Brady Island	268
"	Shell Creek	75	"	McPherson	277
"	Columbus	91	"	North Platte	291
"	Jackson	99	"	O'Fallons	307
"	Silver Creek	109	"	Alkali	322
"	Clark	120	"	Roscoe	332
"	Lone Tree	131	"	Ogallala	341
"	Chapman	142	"	Big Spring	360
"	Grand Island	153	"	Julesburg	377
"	Pawnee	161	"	Lodge Pole	396
"	Wood River	172	"	Sidney	414
"	Gibbon	182	"	Potter	433
"	Kearney	191	"	Antelope	451
"	Stevenson	201	"	Bushnell	463
"	Elm Creek	211	"	Pine Bluff	473

	Miles.
Omaha to Egbert, Nebraska	484
" Hillsdale	496
" Archer	508
" Cheyenne, Wyoming	516
(Branch to Denver, 110 miles.)	
Omaha to Hazard	522
" Ottoe	528
" Granite Canyon	536
" Buford	542
" Sherman	549
" Red Butte	564
" Fort Sanders	571
" Laramie	572
" Wyoming	586
" Cooper's Lake	598
" Lookout	604
" Miser	615
" Rock Creek	622
" Como	637
" Medicine Bow	644
" Carbon	653
" Simpson	658
" Percy	665
" Dana	672
" St. Mary's	679
Omaha to Benton, Wyoming	694
" Rawlins	709
" Separation	721
" Creston	738
" Wash-a-kie	750
" Red Desert	759
" Table Rock	770
" Bitter Creek	783
" Black Buttes	792
" Point of Rocks	803
" Salt Wells	818
" Rock Springs	829
" Green River	844
" Bryan	858
" Granger, Utah	874
" Church Buttes	885
" Carter	901
" Bridger	912
" Piedmont	925
" Aspen	937
" Evanston	952
" Wasatch	963
" Echo City	986
" Ogden	1030
(Branch to Salt Lake City, 40 miles.)	

Omaha to Ogden ....1030 miles.

CENTRAL PACIFIC LINE.

	Miles.
Ogden to Brigham City, Utah	21
" Corinne (Bear River)	24
" Promontory City	53
" Monument Point	80
" Red Dome Pass	104
" Terrace Point	124
" North Point of Desert	136
" Passage Creek	158
" North Pass, Nevada	184
" Poquop Pass	202
" Independence Springs	207
" Humboldt Wells	222
" Deever	242
" Peko	258
" Osino	268
Ogden to Elko, Nevada	278
" Moleen	290
" Carlin	301
" Palisade	310
" Cluro	321
" Be-o-wa-we	329
" Shoshone	339
" Argenta	350
" Nebur	358
" Battle Mountain	367
" Stonehouse	381
" Iron Point	394
" Golconda	405
" Tule	416
" Winnemucca	422

	Miles.
Ogden to Rose Creek, NEVADA	432
" Raspberry Creek	443
" Mill City	450
" Humboldt	491
" Rye Patch	474
" Humboldt Bridge	491
" Browns	513
" Humboldt Lake	516
" White Plains	525
" Mirage	532
" Hot Springs	540
" Desert	550
" Two-mile Station	557
" Wadsworth	559
" Clarks	574
" Camp 37	586
" Reno	593
(Branch to Virginia City, 17 miles.)	
Ogden to Verdi	603
" Camp 24	619
" Boca, CALIFORNIA	620
" Truckee	628
Ogden to Summit, CALIFORNIA	642
" Cisco	656
" Emigrant Gap	664
" Blue Canyon	670
" China Ranch	672
" Shady Run	674
" Alta	679
" Dutch Flat	681
" Gold Run	683
" C. H. Mills	689
" Colfax	693
" N. E. Mills	699
" Clipper Gap	705
" Auburn	711
" Newcastle	716
" Rino	722
" Rocklin	726
" Junction	730
" Antelope	733
" Arcade	740
" Sacramento	748

Ogden to Sacramento.................................748 miles.
Sacramento to San Francisco...........................120 "

NEW YORK TO SAN FRANCISCO........3377 miles.

In naming stations many heroes of the great war have been fitly remembered. So have Fremont, Benton, Bridger, and Peter Ogden, the latter an old guide upon the Plains. But many more should have been commemorated—De Vaca, Carver, Lewis and Clark, Long, Pike, Bonneville, Gunnison, Whitney, Judah (who did not live to see his dream a reality), and the other pioneers and martyrs of the national highway.

Some sanguine writers believe that by running steamers and locomotives at their utmost speed, the entire time can be reduced to three weeks—ten days from Yokohama to San Francisco, four from there to New York, and seven from New York to London; but for the present we may be abundantly satisfied with nearly twice that time.

Upon these closing lines my pen lingers, and I listen for the voice of the future brakeman. Day after day, on the continental journey, he opens his door and shouts to sleepy passengers:

'Chicago. Change cars for New Orleans and Lake Superior.'

'Missouri River. Change cars for Saskatchewan, Kansas City, and Galveston.'

'Rocky Mountains. Change cars for Santa Fe, El Paso, Matamoras, City of Mexico, and all points on the Northern and Southern Pacific Railroads.'

'Great Salt Lake—twenty minutes for dinner. Change cars for Fort Benton, British Columbia, Big Canyon of the Colorado, White Pine, Panama, Lima, and Valparaiso.'

'Sierra Nevada. Change cars for Owyhee, Columbia River, Puget Sound, Sitka, and Kamschatka.'

'San Francisco. Passengers for New Zealand, Honolulu, Melbourne, Yokahama, Hong Kong, and all other points in Asia, Africa, and Europe will keep their seats till landed on the wharf of the daily line of the Pacific Mail Steamship Company. Baggage checked through to Pekin, Calcutta, Grand Cairo, Constantinople, St. Petersburg, Paris, and Liverpool!'

ALPHABETICAL INDEX.*

A.

B.

* For portraits, etc., see List of Illustrations, pages iii. viii.

N.

O.

P.